D0628218

The Gambia & Senegal

Andrew Burke
David Else

LONELY PLANET PUBLICATIONS
Melbourne • Oakland • London • Paris

THE GAMBIA & SENEGAL

St-Louis
Old colonial architecture, relaxed atmosphere and a major annual jazz festival

Parc National des Oiseaux du Djoudj
One of the most important wetland bird sanctuaries in the world

Dakar
Big, brash, exciting – urban Africa at its best

Île de Gorée
Early European settlement with Mediterranean feel and historical sites

Siné-Saloum Delta
Vast maze of mangrove creeks and forested islands

The Atlantic Coast Resorts
European-style beachside resorts just minutes away from bustling Serekunda

Abuko Nature Reserve
Gambia's flagship protected area; easy to reach and excellent for seeing birds and monkeys

Casamance
Lush inland delta, stunning coastline and charming people – Senegal's most beautiful region

Georgetown
Former colonial island settlement and a good base for exploring upcountry Gambia

ATLANTIC OCEAN

17° W
16° N
15° N
14° N
13° N

Senegal River

Rosso-Mauritanie
Rosso-Senegal
Dagana
Richard Toll
Podor
Treji
Guede
Ndioum
'New' Ndioum

Parc National des Oiseaux du Djoudj
Diama
Ross Béthio
Réserve de Faune du Ndiaël
Lac de Guier
Gnit

Maka
Réserve Sylvo-Pastorale de Sogobé
Réserve Sylvo-Pastorale des Six Forages

Makhana
St-Louis
Fass
Langue de Barbarie Peninsula
Parc National de la Langue de Barbarie
Gandiol
Maka Touré
Réserve Sylvo-Pastorale de Pal-Méringnène
Vallée du Ferlo
Réserve Sylvo-Pastorale de Khadar

Louga
Réserve Sylvo-Pastorale de Boulal
Réserve Sylvo-Pastorale de Louggéré-Lioli

Grande Côte
Réserve Sylvo-Pastorale de Déali
Linguère
Réserve Sylvo-Pastorale de Barédji-Dodji

Siné Kane
Kelle
Mekne
Mboro-sur-Mer
Réserve Sylvo-Pastorale de Khogne
Réserve Sylvo-Pastorale de Linde Sud

Tyllmakha
Darou Mousti
Réserve Sylvo-Pastorale d'Oldou Débokol

Pointe des Almadies
Kayar
Keur Moussa
Tivaouane
Baba Garage
Touba
Mbaké
Réserve Sylvo-Pastorale de Sab-Sabré

Malika
Rufisque
DAKAR
Thiès
Toubal Toul
Kbombole
Bambey
Diourbel
Réserve Sylvo-Pastorale de Doli

Toubab Dialo
Île de Gorée
Réserve de Bandia
Mbar
Réserve Sylvo-Pastorale du Siné-Saloum

Îles de la Madeleine
Saly-Portugal
Tiadiaye
Tataguine
Gossas
Forêt Classée de Mbégné

Mbour
Nianing
Fatick
Siné-Saloum Delta

Mbodiène
Joal-Fadiout
Foundiougne
Kaolack
Kaffrine
Forêt de Maka

Petite Côte
Ndangane
Saloum River
Passi
Trans-Gambian Hwy
Koumpentoum
Koungheul

Sokone
Maka-Gouye
Njau
Wassu Stone Circles
Kudang
Kuntaur
Georgetown (Janjang-bureh)

Toubakouta
SENEGAL
Saboya
Sotokoi
Wassu
River Gambia National Park
Pata
Bansang

Parc National du Delta du Saloum
Karang
Ginak Island
Amdallai
Barra
Jowara
Kerewan
Baobolong Wetland Reserve
Farafenni
Baro Kunda
Jappeni
Médina Yorofoula

BANJUL
Serekunda
Abuko Nature Reserve
Bakalarr
Jufureh
Mandaur
Kwinella
Soma
Sénoba
Forêt de Pata

THE GAMBIA
Faraba Banta
Kiang West National Park
Geneiri
Kalagi
SENEGAL

Brikama
Darsilami
Giboro
Bessi
Bintang
Somita
Bwiam
Bondali Jola

Gunjur
Seleti
Kandiadiou

Kartong
Forêts les Naparigs
Soungrougron
Forêt du Guimara

Abéné
Kafountine
Forêt de Sadiatia
Kolda

Bignona
Marsassoum
Forêt de Bari
Forêt du Balmadou

Tendouk
Forêt des Kalounayes
Forêt du Bondié
Sédhiou

Ziguinchor
Casamance River
Forêt de Bissine
Diattakounda

Île de Carabane
Oussouye
São Domingos
Cap Skiring

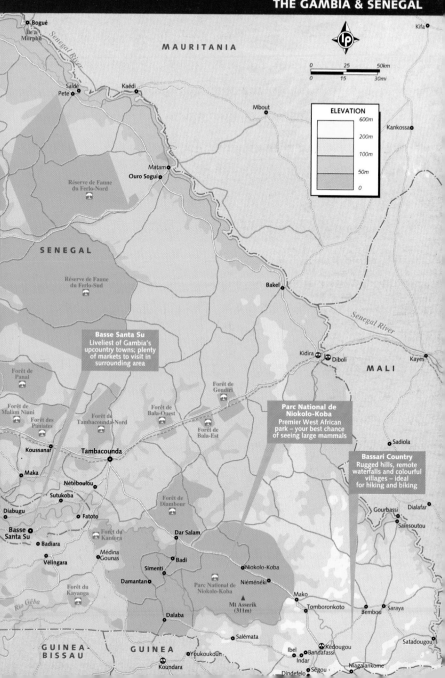

MAURITANIA

Kifa

Bogué
Île à
Morphil

Senegal River

Saldé
Pete

Kaédi

Mbout

Kankossa

Matam
Ouro Sogui

Réserve de Faune
du Ferlo-Nord

ELEVATION

600m
200m
100m
50m
0

SENEGAL

Réserve de Faune
du Ferlo-Sud

Bakel

Senegal River

Basse Santa Su
Liveliest of Gambia's
upcountry towns; plenty
of markets to visit in
surrounding area

Forêt de
Panal

Forêt de
Goudiri

Kidira   Diboli

Kayes

MALI

Forêt de
Malàm Niani

Forêt des
Paniates

Forêt de
Tambacounda-Nord

Forêt de
Bala-Ouest

Forêt de
Bala-Est

**Parc National de
Niokolo-Koba**
Premier West African
park – your best chance
of seeing large mammals

Sadiola

Koussanar

Tambacounda

Bassari Country
Rugged hills, remote
waterfalls and colourful
villages – ideal
for hiking and biking

Maka

Nétéboulou

Forêt de
Diambour

Gourbassi   Dialafar

Sainsoutou

Sutukoba

Diabugu

Fatoto

Basse
Santa Su

Badiara

Forêt du
Kanfora

Dar Salam

Médina
Gounas

Vélingara

Simenti   Badi

Niokolo-Koba

Forêt du
Kayanga

Damantan

Parc National de
Niokolo-Koba

Niéménéki

Mako

Rio Gêba

Dalaba

Mt Asserik
(311m)

Tomboronkoto

Bembou   Saraya

Satadougou

Salémata

GUINEA-
BISSAU

GUINEA

Youkoukdun

Ibel   Kédougou
Bandafassi

Indar

Niagalankome

Koundara

Dindefelo   Ségou

The Gambia & Senegal
2nd edition – September 2002
First published – January 1999

Published by
Lonely Planet Publications Pty Ltd ABN 36 005 607 983
90 Maribyrnong St, Footscray, Victoria 3011, Australia

Lonely Planet offices
Australia Locked Bag 1, Footscray, Victoria 3011
USA 150 Linden St, Oakland, CA 94607
UK 10a Spring Place, London NW5 3BH
France 1 rue du Dahomey, 75011 Paris

Photographs
Many of the images in this guide are available for licensing from
Lonely Planet Images.
W www.lonelyplanetimages.com

Front cover photograph
Man from St Louis, Senegal (Eric L Wheater)

Birds of Senegambia title page photograph
Glossy starling among flowering aloes (Mitch Reardon)

Music of Senegambia title page photograph
A band performs at the International Roots Festival, Gambia
(Ariadne van Zandbergen)

ISBN 1 74059 137 2

Printed through Colorcraft Ltd, Hong Kong
Printed in China

Although the authors and Lonely Planet try to make the information as accurate as possible, we accept no responsibility for any loss, injury or inconvenience sustained by anyone using this book.

Contents – Text

4 Contents – Text

LANGUAGE

GLOSSARY

INDEX

METRIC CONVERSION

Contents – Maps

The Authors

Andrew Burke

Andrew was raised in Sydney, Australia, and first set foot in Africa as an impressionable 19-year-old. The continent made quite an impression on him and during the next decade he returned several times. He also spent time as a journalist in Asia, the Middle East, North America and Europe. Andrew worked on newspapers including the *Australian Financial Review* in Sydney, and the *Financial Times* and *Independent on Sunday* in London, before embarking on a full-time career in travel writing. Andrew has also worked on Lonely Planet's *South Africa, Lesotho & Swaziland* and *West Africa* guides. He is based in Hong Kong.

David Else

After hitching through Europe for a couple of years, David Else kept heading south and first reached Africa in 1983. Since then, he has travelled, trekked, worked and written all over Africa, from Cairo to Cape Town, from Sudan to Senegal, via most of the bits in between. David has authored and coauthored many guidebooks for travellers, including Lonely Planet's regional guides to *West Africa* and *Southern Africa*, plus country guides on *Malawi* and *Gambia & Senegal*. He is also the author of *Trekking in East Africa*, and a longtime contributor to Lonely Planet's classic *Africa on a shoestring*.

FROM ANDREW

My thanks go to the countless people who informed, directed, transported, travelled, ate, drank or just chatted with me during my research in The Gambia and Senegal. But my first thank you goes to Anne Hyland in Hong Kong, a very special woman whose love and support endure great distances and extended separations and provide a steadying anchor in an often unpredictable existence. Thanks again for being there when I get home.

In Gambia, I'm especially grateful to Geri Mitchell and Maurice Phillips, whose hospitality, endless ideas, introductions and answers, and indefatigable energy for their adopted country were an inspiration; Ousainou Jagne of Timbooktoo in Fajara for imparting some of his encyclopedic knowledge of West African books and media to me; and Astrid Bojang for the fastest email replies in West Africa. Up river, thanks to Lawrence and James at Makasutu for living their dream and sharing it (and a lot of beer) with me; and Lamin Raul Bamba for expert guiding around Georgetown.

In Senegal, the great advice, lodgings and good company of Sonia Marcus, Anna Auster and Toubab the bunny were invaluable, and enjoyable, during repeated visits to Dakar.

Elsewhere, Peace Corps volunteers were invariably generous with their time and knowledge: a big thanks to Natalie Cash and Chubby, the wiliest dog in West Africa, for the lowdown on Kolda and the long ride to Dakar; Jamie Lovett for her help from remote Dar Salam; Randy Chester and Shannon Gordon in Tambacounda; Eduard Valor in St-Louis; Abigail, Betsy, Fred and particularly Vonnie Moler in Kedougou; good luck wherever you guys end up. In Casamance, thanks to the Chiche clan of Veronique and Philip in Ziguinchor and Pierre and Marie at Cap Skiring; and, on Île de Carabane, to Dennis Baker, Claire and Alphonse for news, views and an excellent meal.

Thanks too to overlanders Robert Hasse and Tim Urban; colleague Nick Ray; cyclist Holger Schulze; Nicole Fonck-Deruiseau in St-Louis; Ingemo Lindroos and Marcus Floman; Sarah Holtz in Dakar; 'chimp man' Michel Waller; Rassine Sy and family in Mbaké; and my wonderful family in Australia. At LP Melbourne the editors and cartographers were the height of professionalism during a difficult time; thanks to Julia, Pablo, Hilary and Kerryn, and to Kim and Vince – enjoy your new careers.

Finally, a big thank you to the people of The Gambia and Senegal – may you have even more to smile about in the future.

This Book

The first edition of this book was written by David Else. This second edition was thoroughly researched and revised by Andrew Burke.

FROM THE PUBLISHER

Julia Taylor and Kerryn Burgess coordinated the editing and proofing of this book, with assistance from Melanie Dankel, Evan Jones and Bethune Carmichael. Pablo Gastar coordinated the mapping and design. Amanda Sierp, James Ellis and Sarah Sloane assisted with mapping and Hunor Csutoros compiled the climate charts. Sarah Jolly drew the illustrations and Lonely Planet Images supplied the photographs. Margaret Jung designed the cover. Emma Koch organised the Language chapter. Senior Editor Kim Hutchins oversaw the project from start to finish, along with Senior Designer Vince Patton and, during layout, Project Manager Kieran Grogan. Kerryn Burgess, Tony Davidson and Ray Thomson assisted with artwork checking. Mark Germanchis provided Quark support. Special thanks to Graeme Counsel for contributing to the music section, John Graham for his expertise in West African arts, and David Andrew for his assistance with the bird section.

Acknowledgments

The photographs used on the Gambia and Senegal title pages were taken by Andrew Burke.

Thanks

Many thanks to the following travellers who used The Gambia & Senegal and wrote to us with helpful hints, useful advice and interesting anecdotes about travelling in Senegal and Gambia:

Heidi Albrecht, Nadine Allal, Dave Anderson, Gwen Becam, Jose Boehm, Filip Bogaert, Piero Boschi, Steve Brooks, Steve Bryant, Mary Buchalter, Christian Crolla, Silvia de Verga, Anna Dijkstra, Hamish Duncan, Matt Ebiner, Karen Espley, Jannie Faas, Lars Erik Forsberg, Marije Freeburg, Willem Van Haecke, Guy Hagan, Jennifer Hawkins, Jackie Heath, Shonah Hill, John Hindson, Lawana Holland, Sara Holtz, Tracy Jagger, Rozemarijn Jansen, Rogier Jaspers, Irma Jelsma, Wilza Kouwer, John Laidler, Joshua Taylor Barnes, Mark Leyland, Willem & Joany Lisman, Lisa Magnino, Seamus Martin, Phillip Mattle, Angus McCulloch, Markella Mikkelsen, Omelio Moreno, Anki Nilsson, Michael Padua, Brian Parkes, Nicola Parkes, Mary-Lou Penrith, Armand Pierro, Catherine Potter, Georgina Preston, Sara Richelson, Jacqueline Sawyer, Tom Schalken, Arjen Smith, Urs Steiger, Eduard Stomp, Janet Sullivan, Thijs Ter Avest, Bruce Toman, Carol Tompkins, Jaume Tort, Susan Towler, Lynne Trenell, Sylvia van der Oord, Chris Waters and Caroline Weston

Foreword

ABOUT LONELY PLANET GUIDEBOOKS

The story begins with a classic travel adventure: Tony and Maureen Wheeler's 1972 journey across Europe and Asia to Australia. There was no useful information about the overland trail then, so Tony and Maureen published the first Lonely Planet guidebook to meet a growing need.

From a kitchen table, Lonely Planet has grown to become the largest independent travel publisher in the world, with offices in Melbourne (Australia), Oakland (USA), London (UK) and Paris (France).

Today Lonely Planet guidebooks cover the globe. There is an ever-growing list of books and information in a variety of media. Some things haven't changed. The main aim is still to make it possible for adventurous travellers to get out there – to explore and better understand the world.

At Lonely Planet we believe travellers can make a positive contribution to the countries they visit – if they respect their host communities and spend their money wisely. Since 1986 a percentage of the income from each book has been donated to aid projects and human rights campaigns, and, more recently, to wildlife conservation.

> Although inclusion in a guidebook usually implies a recommendation we cannot list every good place. Exclusion does not necessarily imply criticism. In fact there are a number of reasons why we might exclude a place – sometimes it is simply inappropriate to encourage an influx of travellers.

UPDATES & READER FEEDBACK

Things change – prices go up, schedules change, good places go bad and bad places go bankrupt. Nothing stays the same. So, if you find things better or worse, recently opened or long-since closed, please tell us and help make the next edition even more accurate and useful.

Lonely Planet thoroughly updates each guidebook as often as possible – usually every two years, although for some destinations the gap can be longer. Between editions, up-to-date information is available in our free, quarterly *Planet Talk* newsletter and monthly email bulletin *Comet*. The *Scoop* section of our website covers news and current affairs relevant to travellers. Lastly, the *Thorn Tree* bulletin board and *Postcards* section carry unverified, but fascinating, reports from travellers.

Tell us about it! We genuinely value your feedback. A well-travelled team at Lonely Planet reads and acknowledges every email and letter we receive and ensures that every morsel of information finds its way to the relevant authors, editors and cartographers.

Everyone who writes to us will find their name listed in the next edition of the appropriate guidebook, and will receive the latest issue of *Comet* or *Planet Talk*. The very best contributions will be rewarded with a free guidebook.

We may edit, reproduce and incorporate your comments in Lonely Planet products such as guidebooks, websites and digital products, so let us know if you don't want your comments reproduced or your name acknowledged.

How to contact Lonely Planet:
Online: e talk2us@lonelyplanet.com.au, w www.lonelyplanet.com
Australia: Locked Bag 1, Footscray, Victoria 3011
UK: 10a Spring Place, London NW5 3BH
USA: 150 Linden St, Oakland, CA 94607

Introduction

Whatever it is that lights your fire – be it the rocking rhythms of Dakar or birdsong on the banks of the Gambia River – travelling in Gambia and Senegal provides a variety of experience seldom found anywhere else in West Africa. Big, buzzing cities contrast with villages virtually unchanged for centuries, and within these extremes is a plethora of people who will entertain, inform, inspire (and, yes, occasionally frustrate).

Most visitors arrive on relatively cheap, relatively short flights from Europe without even a hint of jet lag. Dakar, the capital of Senegal, and Banjul, its equivalent in Gambia, are in fact about as far removed as any two capitals on earth. The million-plus population of Dakar has created a thriving city that is bursting with vitality – a model for cities across the continent. The fast-paced nightlife and vibrant music scene are highlights, and a night listening to Senegalese star Youssou N'Dour playing in his nightclub is enough to get even the most leaden feet moving. At about one-twentieth

Dakar's size, Banjul is the smallest capital in Africa and is undoubtedly one of its most relaxed – time seems to move in slow motion hereabouts.

But the coast beyond the capitals is the biggest drawcard of both countries. In Senegal, an easy hour's trip north from Dakar could have you alone on the never-ending, windswept stretch of sand that is the Grand Côte. Head south and you will find a string of charming fishing villages lining the Petite Côte on either side of Saly-Portugal. Saly-Portugal, the antithesis of these villages, is a fully paid-up member of 'resort world', where your every whim can be catered for – all with a piña colada in hand and shaded by one of thousands of palm trees.

From Banjul, an overcrowded, torturously slow and quintessentially African ferry ride brings you, via Barra, to Ginak Island, a place so incredibly beautiful and home to such a stunning array of wildlife that local tour operators have renamed it

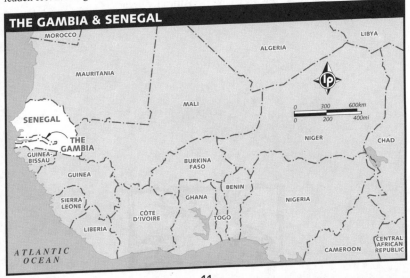

THE GAMBIA & SENEGAL

'Paradise Island'. Nearby are Jufureh, the *'Roots'* village, and James Island, two reminders of a wholly more sinister chapter in the history of West Africa – slavery. Together with Île de Gorée, off Dakar, these have become places of pilgrimage for blacks and of reflection for white visitors, and deserve to be visited by anyone seeking a better understanding of Africa, both past and present.

Of course, the colonial era was not just about slavery. The British in Gambia and the French in Senegal have left many influences, from cuisine to architecture, and, not least of all, language. Armed with English and even just a few words of French it's easy to engage the local people, and many travellers tell happy tales of marathon meals and tea-drinking sessions in local villages with the region's greatest assets – ordinary Gambians and Senegalese.

Away from cities and beaches Senegambia is home to several excellent national parks and nature reserves. Like so much else in West Africa, these parks bear little resemblance to the imaginings of most visitors. You won't see herds of wildebeests migrating across vast plains, and only Senegal's Parc National de Niokolo-Koba is anywhere near the scale of those more famous parks of East and Southern Africa. But small parks such as Senegal's Langue de Barbarie, Parc National des Oiseaux du Djoudj and Îles de la Madeleine, and Gambia's Abuko and Baobolong reserves, make the spotting of wildlife, particularly birds, much simpler. Indeed, Gambia is one of the best places on earth for spotting birds, more than 500 species of which have been spied there.

While mountaineers won't be rushing to Senegambia, for most this is more than made up for by the great river systems that punctuate both coast and country. The Gambia River is itself something of a natural wonder, with giant, saltwater mangroves reaching 150km upstream; and beyond here a cloak of dense gallery forest, straight out of a Tarzan movie, spills over the banks. Senegal's Siné-Saloum Delta and the lower reaches of the Casamance River are in fact an immense maze of mangroves and snaking creeks. Whether you're birdwatching, fishing or just looking, being paddled around these deltas in a pirogue is a must-do.

Wherever you are in Senegambia you're not too far from the comforts of home. And while this has seen the region described as 'Africa for beginners', it's still every bit as African as you dare to make it.

Facts about Senegambia

It's no surprise that The Gambia and Senegal are cohesive countries in many respects, or that the term Senegambia is often used when the region is discussed as a whole. Factors including landscape, climate, wildlife, people, religion, precolonial history and indigenous languages are common to both.

HISTORY
This section describes general history in the Senegambia region up until the late 19th century. While European influence has been felt in the region since the 14th century, it wasn't until just over 100 years ago that the modern countries of Senegal and Gambia were created. These colonial and postcolonial histories are covered separately in the history sections of the country chapters.

Prehistory & Early Societies
While Africa is considered the cradle of humankind, so far there is no evidence to suggest *Homo sapiens* inhabited the Senegambia region before about 350,000 years ago.

Flint weapons dating from about 100,000 years ago have been found in several places, most notably at Thiemassas on the coast south of Dakar, and Stone Age tools dating from about 2000 BC have been found in the sand dunes of Cape Point and Fajara in Gambia.

West Africa, according to scholars, skipped the Bronze Age and moved straight into the Iron Age, when populations began to grow and disperse across the region. The migration of communities was not a sudden mass movement, but by AD 500 towns and villages based on agriculture and the knowledge of iron were dotted across West Africa. Evidence of these early societies includes burial mounds, tombs, stone circles and shell mounds that can still be seen in Gambia and Senegal. (See the boxed text 'Shell Mounds' in the Facts about Senegal chapter.)

As the 1st millennium AD progressed, trade increased between the regions north and south of the Sahara. Goods transported across the desert included salt, gold, silver, ivory and slaves. Some settlements on the edge of the desert took advantage of the trade (eventually controlling it) and grew in size, wealth and power. Some became city-states, and a few developed into powerful confederations with hierarchical structures, in which society was divided into groups such as rulers, administrators, traders, artisans, soldiers, artists and commoners.

Kingdoms & Empires
The first major state to be established in the Senegambia region was the empire of Ghana. It was founded in the 5th century AD and flourished between the 8th and 11th centuries, covering much of what is now eastern Senegal and western Mali (it had no geographic connection with the present-day country of Ghana). Its power was based on the control of trans-Saharan trade, and Islam was introduced by traders from the north. The empire did not fully embrace the new religion, though, and was destroyed in the late 11th century by the Berbers of the Almoravid empire from Mauritania and Morocco.

At around the same time, the Tukrur empire was established by the Tukulor people in what is now southern Mauritania and northern Senegal. It also based its power on control of the trans-Saharan trade, and flourished during the 9th and 10th centuries, becoming an ally of the Almoravids in their battles against the Ghana empire.

In the middle of the 13th century, Sundiata Keita, leader of the Malinké people, founded the empire of Mali in the region east of the former Ghana empire. By the 14th century, the empire of Mali stretched from the Atlantic coast, encompassing the modern-day countries of Senegal and Gambia, all the way to today's Niger and Nigeria.

This vast empire controlled nearly all the trans-Saharan trade, and the rulers of Mali became incredibly wealthy. Contact with Arab states to the north led the rulers of Mali to embrace Islam with great enthusiasm. When Mansa Musa, the emperor of Mali, went on a pilgrimage to Mecca in the early 14th century, he took an entourage of 60,000 people. During this period the trans-Saharan trade reached its peak, and Mali's cities, most notably Timbuktu, became major centres of finance and culture.

Mali's influence began to wane in the mid-15th century, as it was eclipsed by the more powerful Songhaï empire. At around the same time, in the central region of today's Senegal, the Wolof people established the empire of Jolof (also called Djolof or Yollof). The Jolof spread north and west and dominated the Tukrur and Serer kingdoms. However, the empire eventually subdivided into a loose confederation of several separate kingdoms, including the Walo along the Senegal River and the Cayor north of the Cap Vert peninsula. Meanwhile, further south, the Serer people had migrated from south of the Gambia River to establish their own kingdoms of Siné and Saloum in the area between the river and the present-day towns of Thiès and Kaolack.

The Jolof empire's disintegration in the mid-16th century was largely due to the growing power of the coastal states, which found new trading possibilities following the arrival of Europeans in the area. The Siné and Saloum extended their influence and remained powerful until the 19th century, when they were defeated by French colonial forces.

Meanwhile, in northern Senegal, as the Mali empire broke up, the Tukrur empire was invaded in the early 16th century by the Fula people, under the leadership of Koli Tengala Ba. The new kingdom, Futa Toro, expanded over the next century along the Senegal River and southward into modern-day Guinea. Although the Fula people are found throughout West Africa (in other countries they are known variously as Fulani, Fulbe and Peul), and they began migrating across the region long before Futa Toro was established, many still regard Futa Toro as a cultural homeland.

At around the same time a group of Malinké people from the disintegrating Mali empire migrated into the valley of the Gambia River, although it's possible that ancestors of these people arrived as early as the 13th century. They brought Islam with them, and became known as the Mandinka. Some of the original inhabitants of the valley, the Diola (Jola), were absorbed, although others moved south to today's Casamance region of southern Senegal.

European Interest

Meanwhile, in Europe, interest in West Africa was growing. Much of the gold transported across the Sahara eventually reached the courts and treasuries of countries such as England, France, Spain and Portugal, and by the 14th century the financial stability of these European powers depended greatly on this supply. Along with the gold came hazy reports of the wealthy empires south of the Sahara, but at this time no European had ever visited the region (the metaphorical use of Timbuktu to describe faraway places possibly dates from this time).

In the early 15th century Prince Henry of Portugal (known as Henry the Navigator) encouraged explorers to sail down the coast of West Africa, hoping to bypass the Arab and Muslim domination of the trans-Saharan gold trade and reach the source by sea. In 1443, Portuguese ships reached the mouth of the Senegal River, and a year later they landed on the coast of Senegal at a peninsula they named Cabo Verde, or Green Cape. (It is now called Cap Vert, the site of Dakar, and is not to be confused with the Cape Verde islands, some 600km west in the Atlantic.) The Portuguese made contact with local chiefs on the mainland and established a trading station on Île de Gorée, a short distance off the coast.

In a series of later voyages, the Portuguese pushed increasingly further around the West African coast (which had then become known as Guinea). By 1500 they had established trading stations on the coast, and some distance upstream along the Senegal and Gambia Rivers, from where gold, slaves and other commodities were shipped back to Europe. It has been suggested that the Gambia River's name is derived from the Portuguese word *cambio*, meaning 'exchange', or in this context, 'trade'.

The Senegal and Gambia Rivers, along with the Saloum and Casamance Rivers, provided major routes into the interior of Africa, and become increasingly important strategically. Explorers such as the Scottish Mungo Park and the French René Caillé set forth in search of Timbuktu and its fabled riches along these waterways. As the years progressed, the French, English and Dutch fought with the Portuguese for control of these rivers and the resulting trade, which was predominantly in slaves.

The Slave Trade

By 1530 Portugal had established settlements in Brazil. Between 1575 and 1600, the establishment in Brazil of large commercial sugar estates led to a demand for labourers, so the Portuguese started to import slaves from West Africa – a development that was to have huge and serious repercussions throughout the continent.

Although slavery had existed in West Africa for many centuries, the Portuguese developed the trade on a massive scale. But by the 16th century other European powers became active in the trade. The French had been defying the Portuguese monopoly for some time and between 1500 and 1530 they captured hundreds of Portuguese vessels, not to mention the slaves. England joined the trade in the mid-16th century and in 1617 Dutch traders took over the settlement on Île de Gorée. The French established the Company of Senegal in 1633 and it was responsible, at least in part, for the French trade in slaves until 1791, when the company's privileges were revoked by the Constituent Assembly. In 1659 the French developed a trading station at St-Louis at the mouth of the Senegal River, and in 1677 finally secured Gorée.

By the 1650s Portugal had been largely ousted from the Senegambia coast. There was strong competition between traders, with frequent skirmishes over 'factories' (fortified slaving stations). Fort James, on an island near the mouth of the Gambia River, was controlled by Latvian, French and Dutch traders, plus several independent 'privateers' (pirates), and changed hands eight times in 60 years before finally being secured by the English. Nearby, on the northern bank of the Gambia River, the French built a factory at Albreda.

Through the 17th and 18th centuries, several European nations established plantations in the New World (including South America, the Caribbean, and the south of what became the USA). As well as sugar, other crops – most notably cotton and tobacco – were now being grown. The demand for workers in the plantations was great and the slave trade became increasingly lucrative.

In most cases the European traders encouraged African chiefs in the coastal areas to invade neighbouring tribes and take captives. These captives were brought to the factories and exchanged for European goods such as cloth and guns (the guns, in turn, allowed more slaves to be captured). The social and political change was profound in the kingdoms of Fouta Toro, Walo and Cayor, but the Siné were reluctant traders and the Diolas and Balants in Casamance actively opposed trade in humans.

A triangular trans-Atlantic trade route developed. The slaves were transported to the Americas; the raw materials they produced were transported to Europe; and finished goods were transported from Europe to Africa to once again be exchanged for slaves and keep the whole system moving. The demand for slaves was further maintained because the terrible conditions in the plantations meant that their life expectancy after arriving in the Americas was very low.

Between the 16th and 19th centuries, up to 20 million Africans were captured as slaves. Between a quarter and a half of this number died soon after capture, mostly during transportation. Accounts from the time describe hundreds of slaves packed so tightly between decks that they were forced to lie down. Only minimal food and water were provided, and the faeces or vomit from those above fell through the planking onto those lying below. Of the approximately 10 million slaves who actually reached the Americas, around 50% died within a few years.

These figures are hotly debated by historians, mainly because exact figures are impossible to gauge. But the debate sometimes obscures the main issue: whatever the actual numbers, the slave trade was undeniably cruel and inhuman, and its legacy in West Africa and many other parts of the world is still felt today.

The Rise of Islam

While the Europeans were active on the coast, events took a different course in the interior. For many centuries after its introduction to West Africa in the 10th century, Islam remained the religion only of the rulers and the wealthy. Generally, the commoners retained their traditional beliefs. It seems the elite were tolerant of this situation (to avoid alienating the populace) and skilfully combined aspects of Islam and indigenous religion in the administration of the state. This fusing of beliefs remains a feature of West African life today.

However, as the centuries ground on, Islam continued to expand, in particular a type of Islam called Sufism, which emphasised mystical and spiritual attributes. It also allowed for the influence of religious teachers called marabouts, many of whom were credited with having divine powers and the ability to communicate with Allah. While orthodox Islam is essentially more egalitarian and does not allow for intermediaries of this nature, historians have suggested that this master–follower relationship found favour in West Africa because it was similar to the hierarchical social structures already well established.

Following the decline of the old empires, a period of instability arose across much of the Sahel, partly because the balance of power had moved to the coastal states. It was also due to the rise in European influence and the corresponding rise in trade and slavery in the region, not to mention the introduction of guns. Islam filled the vacuum and the marabouts became particularly powerful. The Fula people, spread widely across the region, were strong adherents, and Islam eventually became the dominant religion of the Sahel.

In Senegal, the Wolof people had not embraced Islam and were supplying slaves from weaker tribes to the European traders. In the late 1670s the marabouts saw the Wolof as deserving targets for jihads – Islamic holy wars against nonbelievers. Jihads dominated the Senegambia region for more than two centuries, and forced the Wolof and the French into a series of alliances of convenience against the marabouts.

In the 1770s the Tukulor people entered the arena once again, as the descendants of Koli Tengala Ba were overthrown by a marabout called Suliman Bal. He turned Futa Toro into a base from which missionary soldiers could spread Islam across the Senegambia region. One of these soldiers was Omar Tall (also spelt Umar Taal), who in 1820 went on the haj to Mecca, where he was initiated into the Morocco-based Tijaniya brotherhood. By 1850 he had become leader of the brotherhood and created a vast Islamic empire based on the town of Segou in present-day Mali, which spread northeast to Timbuktu and west into Senegal. He was prevented from reaching the coast by the French, who were becoming increasingly well established in the region by this time.

European Expansion

While Omar Tall had been active inland, the Europeans had been busy on the coast. Throughout the 18th century, the French settlements on Gorée and at St-Louis grew considerably. As the Portuguese had done before them, French settlers intermarried with the local Wolof, and by the 1790s the majority of the towns' populations were of mixed race. In the early 19th century, egalitarian principles inspired by the French Revolution of 1789 meant these inhabitants were awarded French citizenship. Meanwhile, much of the mainland interior was controlled by the British, who did not integrate with the local populations with anything like the same enthusiasm.

In the early 19th century, events in Europe had major effects on the Senegambia region.

Britain imposed a ban on slavery in 1807, and while Napoleon officially abolished the trade in 1815, it wasn't until 1848 that it finally stopped. This was also the time of the Napoleonic Wars (which ended in 1815), so the slavery ban gave Britain a good excuse to attack the old enemy – French ships off the Senegambia coast were frequently chased and captured by the British navy. Slaves were freed and resettled on the mainland.

In 1816 Britain bought an island on the south side of the mouth of the Gambia River from a local chief (for two bottles of brandy, legend has it). The local name was Banjul Island, but the British built a fort there and renamed it Bathurst.

French power was still weakened by the Napoleonic Wars, so Britain formalised its sphere of control in Senegambia by declaring the Gambia River a British protectorate in 1820. The Gambia was administered from the colony of Sierra Leone, further along the West African coast, itself originally established as a haven for freed slaves in 1787.

In 1826 Fort Bullen was built on the northern bank, and in 1828 another fort was built about 200km upstream from the river mouth; this became Georgetown.

During this period the French introduced Catholic missions and, with the slave trade at an end, were forced to look for new sources of wealth. In 1829 the British planted groundnuts (peanuts) along the Gambia River, in the hope that exports of this crop would provide an income for the fledgling protectorate.

Meanwhile, the Royal Order of 1840 created administrative structures in France's West African colonies. A legal code was drawn up for towns, which became self-governing communes, with residents enjoying the same rights as their equals in France. Influence spread from St-Louis along the Senegal River and the governor, Baron Jacques Roger, tried by various means to establish settlements (most notably at Richard Toll, where the ruins of his chateau can still be seen) and groundnut plantations.

In the 1850s his successor, Louis Faidherbe, took a more direct approach by simply invading the lands of the Wolof (who until then had been uneasy French allies). He established large plantations and introduced forced labour. From the French point of view, this method was effective – he made the colonial administration self-financing within 10 years. To combat the forces of Omar Tall, who posed a threat from the north and east, Faidherbe established a chain of forts along the Senegal River (including Bakel, Matam, Podor and Kayes), many of which can still be seen today. Faidherbe also established a settlement on the peninsula opposite Île de Gorée, which was named after a local chief and became Dakar.

The Marabouts

Omar Tall's forces were finally defeated by the French in 1864, but his missionary zeal inspired followers to keep fighting jihads, which became known as the Marabout Wars, for another three decades. By this time, the Wolof had fervently embraced Islam and now fought fiercely against French expansionism. Notable battles included those between the French army and the Cayor Wolof, led by Lat Dior, when the French built a railway line between Dakar and St-Louis. The last significant Wolof battle was in 1889 at Yang-Yang (near present-day Linguère), where the army of Alboury Ndiaye was defeated by the French. Eventually, superior French firepower along with a divided marabout army allowed the French to gain control of most of Senegal and Mali.

At the same time, the British in Gambia experienced similar Marabout Wars, as local followers of Omar Tall attempted to overthrow their traditional Mandinka rulers. Some of the fiercest fighting took place in western Gambia, near the British outpost of Bathurst. The entry into the fray of the Fula from the north involved the British and French in some extremely touchy diplomatic incidents. The colonial powers finally decided to cooperate to overthrow the marabouts, although limited resistance by the tenacious Fodi Kabba continued into the early 1900s.

The final thorn in the French colonials' side was another marabout called Amadou

Bamba. By 1887 he had gained a large popular following, which eventually led to him being sent into exile until 1907. Today, Bamba remains an iconic figure, and the alliance between the brotherhood he founded and the government is still a feature of modern Senegalese politics. See the boxed text 'Bamba' in the West-Central Senegal chapter for more details.

Early Colonialism

By the mid-19th century, the French enclave of Dakar was becoming increasingly important as the gateway to the new and expanding territory of Afrique Occidentale Française (French West Africa). The British had protectorates on the Gambia River and elsewhere along the coast, notably at the ports of Freetown (Sierra Leone) and Lagos (Nigeria). Portugal was no longer a major force, but had retained some territory – today's Guinea-Bissau. There had been several military expeditions to the interior, but the main powers had very different approaches, with the French active mostly in the Sahel regions and the British penetrating the region from the coast in the south. Overall, however, there was still little in the way of formally claimed territory.

All this changed quite suddenly in the 1870s, when political and economic events in Europe increased competition among several nations, including France, Britain and the recently formed country of Germany. To a large extent the battle for European dominance was played out in Africa, marked by a rush of land-grabbing known as the Scramble for Africa.

The Scramble for Africa

The Scramble for Africa was triggered in 1879 by King Leopold of Belgium's claiming of the Congo (which later became Zaïre, and more recently was renamed Congo again). France responded by establishing territory in the neighbouring area, which became known as French Congo (now Congo) and Gabon. Meanwhile, the British were increasing their influence in East Africa, as part of a strategy to control the headwaters of the Nile. Germany's leader, Otto von Bismarck, also wanted 'a place in the sun' and claimed various parts of Africa, including territories that later became Togo and Cameroon.

All the European powers wanted to occupy their claimed territories as soon as possible, not for any value the colonies might hold in themselves, but simply to gain control and keep the others out. In 1883 Britain staked a claim to much of East Africa, and to territories in West Africa – such as Gambia, Sierra Leone, Gold Coast (modern-day Ghana) and Nigeria. Competition between France and Britain was particularly intense along the coast, with France slotting in its claims between the British possessions.

At the same time France laid claim to Afrique Occidentale Française – most of the Sahel belt, which stretched eastward from Senegal. France also claimed much of the Sahara, linking its possessions to North Africa (such as Algeria), which had become French territory earlier in the century.

The claims of the European powers were settled at the Berlin Conference of 1884–85, when most of Africa was split neatly into colonies. Belgium got the Congo, Germany kept Togoland and Cameroon and added what were to become Tanzania and Namibia, and Portugal kept Guinea-Bissau and Equatorial Guinea, plus territories in the south that would become the modern states of Mozambique and Angola. Britain got most of East and Southern Africa, plus its territories along the West African coast. France was awarded most of West and Central Africa – a vast area covering almost a third of the entire continent. This homogenous empire contrasted sharply with the other powers' territories scattered across Africa. It was to have a major effect on historical events over the next 100 years and is still important today.

It seems the European powers were happy with the results of the Berlin Conference. The map of Africa had been neatly divided and coloured in. What Africans thought of the conference remains unrecorded – they weren't invited to attend.

The colonial and postcolonial histories of Gambia and Senegal are continued in the history sections of the country chapters.

GEOGRAPHY

The Senegambia region lies within the Sahel, the semidesert or savanna region that forms a broad band across Africa between the Sahara desert to the north and the forested countries of the south. The landscape is largely flat, with the only hills being in Senegal's far southeastern corner and along the border with Mali. The Gambia has no hills at all.

The region's main geographical features include three major rivers, which all rise in the Fouta Djalon plateau, in the neighbouring country of Guinea. In the north is the Senegal River, forming the border with Mauritania. In the middle is the Gambia River, defining the borders of Gambia. In the south of Senegal is the Casamance River, which gives its name to the Casamance area.

More information about the geography of Gambia and Senegal is given in the geography sections of the relevant country chapters.

CLIMATE

This section gives an overview of Senegambia's climate and characteristics. For information on how climate affects travel, see When to Go under Planning in the Regional Facts for the Visitor chapter.

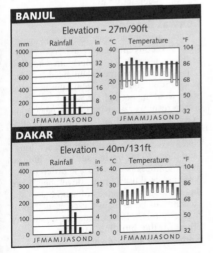

The Harmattan

The harmattan is a dry wind that blows from the north, usually from December to February. During this period the skies of most West African countries are grey from Sahara sand carried by the wind, and even when the wind stops blowing, skies remain hazy until the first rains fall. The effects are more noticeable away from the coast, and generally travel isn't too badly affected (although flights can sometimes be delayed as a result of poor visibility). Photographers can expect 'overcast' results, while people with contact lenses should be prepared for problems.

Temperatures

In Gambia, the coolest period is from December to mid-February, with average daytime maximums around 24°C (75°F). In October and November, and from mid-February to April, the average daytime maximums rise to 26°C (79°F), rising further through May and June to around 30°C (86°F) from July to September.

Senegal has a wider range. In Dakar average daytime maximums are around 24°C (75F) from January to March, and between 25°C and 27°C (77°F and 81°F) in April, May and December. From June to October they rise to around 30°C (86°F). In southern Senegal, though, temperature patterns are similar to those in Gambia. Temperatures along the coast are generally lower than these averages, while inland they are higher.

Rainfall & Humidity

Rainfall is a more significant factor than temperature in the climate of Gambia and Senegal. Generally the wet season is June to October, and the dry season is November to May, but the wet season is shorter (with lower total rainfall) in the north. The rainy period also gets shorter, and the amount of rainfall decreases, as you go inland. For example, in the far north of Senegal, the average annual rainfall is just 300mm, while in the far south it can top 1500mm. Dakar, about halfway down the country on the coast, gets around

Unpredictable Weather

In recent years the weather of Gambia and Senegal – and indeed the whole world – has become harder to predict. Scientists believe this is connected to the greenhouse effect and the overall rise in global temperatures, created by air pollution. All over Africa, rainfall levels have fallen since the early 1980s, and droughts in areas of low rainfall have become increasingly common. Pastoral people cannot rely on wells or seasonal oases that have supplied water for decades or even centuries. The wet seasons seem to start later and end earlier, although sometimes there are unexpected rainfalls during the normally dry season. These can be particularly disastrous, as they wash away soil that has been prepared for crops, or even wash away seeds that have already been planted.

600mm annually, while inland Tambacounda, at approximately the same latitude, normally gets half of this or less.

When high temperatures combine with rainfall, humidity becomes very uncomfortable. The most humid times in Gambia and Senegal are generally just before the wet period begins in June.

ECOLOGY & ENVIRONMENT

Ecological and environmental issues – including such worldwide problems as deforestation, sand and soil erosion, air and water degradation, urban encroachment, habitat and wildlife destruction, and the conservation of natural resources – are becoming increasingly important in Gambia and Senegal. However, most environmental and conservation issues are extremely complex and linked to wider economic, social and political considerations. On a local level, many conservationists argue that it is unreasonable to expect people with little money or food to worry about conservation, and that the key to conservation lies in reducing poverty and providing local people with a say in, and a tangible benefit from, conservation measures.

Maka Diama Dam

The Maka Diama Dam was built across the Senegal River estuary in the late 1980s. The dam's principal purpose was to stop salt water coming upstream (the Senegal River is tidal). This way, more land on the river bank could be irrigated for crop-growing, as rainfall in the area has always been insufficient or unreliable. While this may have been an admirable reason, crops now grown include groundnuts (peanuts), which quickly exhaust nutrients in the soil and involve a harvesting method that leads to erosion. (The boxed text 'Groundnuts' later in this chapter further discusses the environmental impact of this crop).

The Maka Diama Dam has created several other problems. Following the decrease in salinity, thick water weeds now cover the surface of many channels and creeks along this stretch of the main river. These cut out light and reduce oxygen levels, decreasing fish populations – a real disaster for local people who rely on fish for food or small-scale trade, and also for the many thousands of birds who feed in this area. On top of all this, the new areas of fresh water now harbour malarial mosquitoes and the snails that carry bilharzia, so local people have to deal with an increase in these diseases, which are both potentially fatal.

Coastal Erosion

Coastal erosion has gone from being an unsightly inconvenience to a very serious problem indeed, particularly in Gambia. Driven by the ever-increasing need for sand as a building material, illegal mining on the coast went unchecked for years.

The result is rather ironic; the very thing that made Gambia a tourist destination – the wide sandy beaches of the Atlantic coast – also poses the greatest long-term threat to the businesses upon which so many Gambians survive. In order to accommodate those hordes, developers have dug thousands of tonnes of sand out of the coastline to be used in the construction of roads, hotels, resorts and just about any other of the building sites you see on Kairaba Ave and elsewhere.

The problem has reached a climax in recent years, with some beaches around Cape St Mary and Kololi literally disappearing. What's left are ugly piles of sandbags, piled up steeply from the breakers to just outside the resorts. A US$20 million project aimed at rejuvenating the beaches was set to begin as this book went to press. The plan involves using Dutch technology to trap sand near the shore as it is washed in on the tide. However, it's not all good news; illegal sand mining continues apace.

The coast in Gambia is only short and yet sand is a needed commodity. Importing sand from Senegal sounds like a good idea, but it's a lot cheaper to just send a truck and a few guys down to the beach at night.

Overfishing

Overfishing off the coast of Senegambia is becoming a major environmental and economic issue. For many centuries local fishermen have harvested the seas off the Atlantic coast, but, until the middle of the 20th century, fishing was a sustainable industry. However, since this time, there has been a significant increase in demand (from a growing local population and to supply the increasingly important export market) and a big increase in the number of boats engaged in fishing.

Fish stocks near the coast have not kept up with the increased catches, so the boats have to go further out to sea to find new fishing areas. As these areas in turn become depleted, the fishermen have to go further still, sometimes spending many days at sea. The extra money the fishermen spend on petrol for their boats eats into their earnings from the catch, and the profit margins become ever slimmer. Each fisherman supports a family, and as their wages go down so poverty levels go up.

Unsustainable fishing methods further exacerbate the problem. Netting the fish in the traditional way is seen as too slow, so in some areas the fishermen also use dynamite, simply throwing the explosive into a shoal of fish and collecting the dead ones that float to the surface. Unfortunately, only about a quarter of the fish killed this way

can be 'caught' – the rest sink. In the area around Dakar, local fishermen were persuaded to stop using this method when a French scuba diver showed them video footage of the sea bed covered in dead fish.

Adding to the problem are large factory ships from Europe and east Asia that operate in the fishing grounds off the coast of Gambia and Senegal. These ships use large nets and highly efficient methods, landing catches far beyond the ability of local boats. Most of these factory ships have negotiated fishing rights with the governments of Gambia or Senegal and provide a vital source of income for the country. However, the frequency with which ships exceed their agreed quotas, or fish without any licence at all, is so great that the United Nations (UN) has entered the argument. But UN or no UN, for the local fishermen in their traditional boats making a living from the sea becomes increasingly precarious.

Deforestation

Away from the coast, deforestation is another major environmental issue faced by both Gambia and Senegal. Increased population growth, and a corresponding increase in the demand for farmland, means areas of natural forest and woodland are being cleared. On a larger scale, wooded areas are cleared to make room for cash crops, notably groundnuts. In Gambia, one of the major causes of deforestation is bushfires started by local farmers to promote new growth for livestock, to control pests such as the tsetse fly, and to flush out wild animals for hunting.

Whatever the reason, this clearing of natural woodland leads to soil erosion, and eventually the reduction of cultivable areas. More immediately, the loss of woodland also means reduced water catchment and a decrease in the availability of traditional building materials, foodstuffs and medicines. The destruction of wooded areas also leads to the loss of vital habitats for many of the region's bird and animal species.

In Gambia, this type of situation is being addressed by a long-term German-run project that aims to manage the remaining natural woodland. But the forest is not simply fenced off and local people forcibly kept out; instead it is utilised in a sustainable way for the benefit of local people. For example, dead wood can be used for timber, fruits and edible leaves can be collected, and grasses can be harvested for thatch. These products can be used by the local people or sold, but all the activities take place without destroying the forest itself. In this way the local people see the forest as a source of income or employment, both now and in the future, and have a real incentive to protect and manage it in a sustainable way.

Community-Based Conservation

Until recently, all over Africa local people have been excluded from national parks or other protected wildlife areas, because it was always assumed they damaged natural resources. Many conservationists now argue that indigenous communities should always be included in environmental planning and management. National parks and other protected areas are unlikely to succeed in the long term unless local people can obtain real benefits from them.

Put very simply, the argument goes like this: most protected areas contain wildlife

Groundnuts

Groundnuts are known by most visitors to Senegal or the Gambia as peanuts. In your travels around the region you'll find them – shelled, unshelled, roasted, boiled, plain, salted or sweet – for sale on every street corner, and groundnuts are the main ingredient of classic Senegambian meals such as *mafé* (a thick, brown groundnut sauce) and *domodah* (the same thing with meat or vegetables).

But domestic consumption is only a fraction of the total crop, and the economies of Senegal and Gambia are largely dependent on the cultivation of groundnuts. They grow like beans on low bushes, and can survive in relatively dry areas. The harvested nuts are shelled and crushed to make oil, which is exported to Europe for use in food manufacture.

Groundnuts were introduced into Senegal in the early 19th century, and large plantations were established along the Senegal River by the 1860s under the direction of governor Louis Faidherbe. By the early 20th century groundnuts had become a major cash crop in Senegambia, and this situation remained unchanged through the colonial period and the first decades of independence. In fact, favourable world prices for groundnuts in the 1960s and '70s bolstered the economies of the newly independent nations, particularly in the case of Gambia, which was not expected to survive as an independent state after the British withdrew.

By the end of the 1970s, groundnut prices had slumped and both Senegal and Gambia suffered from their reliance on the single cash crop. Problems were compounded in the 1980s when droughts severely reduced the harvest levels. Whereas Senegal was producing almost a million tonnes of groundnuts (representing about 50% of total export earnings) in the mid-1970s, by the mid-1980s this had fallen to about half that figure. During the same period, Gambia's crop fell from 130,000 tonnes to 50,000 tonnes.

Groundnuts remain the backbone of Senegambia's economy

Today in Senegal, the annual groundnut production is around 600,000 tonnes, which represents about 20% of export earnings (a result of a continued fall in value and because of diversification into other crops). Groundnut plantations cover about one million hectares (around 40% of the country's arable land) and the industry employs about a million people. The main groundnut-growing region or physical features that foreigners are willing to pay to come and see; if some of this money goes to the local people then they have an incentive to protect the areas and the animals; if there is no benefit, there is no incentive to conserve.

While schemes such as this allow local people to continue living in their traditional manner, they also mean income from the jobs that wildlife tourism creates: for rangers, for tour guides, and in the hotels, lodges and camps. Further spin-offs include the sale of crafts and curios – another way for local people to earn money directly from

tourists. Even in protected areas that are not of great interest to tourists, or that are difficult to reach, if local people gain some benefit (whether from employment or indirectly through wood harvesting, limited hunting etc) rather than being completely excluded, that essential incentive is still present.

In Senegal's Parc National de Niokolo-Koba, local men from the surrounding villages have been trained as guides to show tourists around, while in Parc National des Oiseaux du Djoudj various projects instigated by European conservation organisations ensure that park staff cooperate with

Groundnuts

is east of Dakar, around the towns of Diourbel, Touba and Kaolack (sometimes called the 'groundnut triangle'), which are centres of the powerful Muslim brotherhoods whose marabouts dominate much of Senegal's political and economic life (see the boxed text 'Marabouts & Brotherhoods' in the Facts about Senegal chapter). Gambia is even more reliant on groundnuts, which make up more than 80% of total exports but account for only 27% of foreign earnings.

Nuts are harvested after the rains, mainly from October through to January, but also up until June, and then transported to the crushing mills. The transport may be a horse and cart or riverboat, but as you travel around Senegal you will not fail to see the huge yellow lorries, perilously overloaded with sacks of groundnuts, trundling along the roads.

Although groundnuts contribute to the economy, the large plantations have a devastating effect on the environment. The crop absorbs nutrients from the soil, but replaces very little, and other parts of the crop (such as leaves and stems) are used as animal fodder, rather than ploughed back into the ground after harvest. When the crop is harvested, the whole plant – roots and all – is picked, leaving the loose, dry soil exposed and subject to erosion by wind, rain, or goats that come to feed on any discarded remnants. Particularly in areas with marginal rainfall, the soil is soon exhausted or simply blown away, and new plantations have to be established in other areas. The abandoned plantations are slow to recover and the erosion continues.

As new plantations are established, grassland, bush or other natural vegetation has to be cleared, which limits habitats for wildlife and cattle-grazing land for pastoral people. This has become a major issue in central Senegal, as groundnut farmers expand ever eastward into grazing reserves (réserves sylvo-pastorale) supposedly set aside for seminomadic people such as the Fula.

In 1991, the then president, Abdou Diouf, 'gave' part of a reserve called Mbegué to farmers from the Mouride brotherhood. New Internationalist magazine reported that subsequently, more than five million trees were cleared, the land was ploughed and groundnuts were planted, while 6000 Fula people and 100,000 cows were forced off the land. The following year, the Mouride leader urged his followers to support Diouf in the national elections.

Similar invasions have occurred elsewhere in Senegal. It's a classic example of conflict between farmers and nomads, but in this case the continuing quest for new groundnut plantations means the Fula are facing not just small-scale cultivators, but the combined power and strength of Senegal's political and religious establishment. Hopefully, the demise of the Diouf regime will bring actions like this to an end. Sadly, hope might not be enough.

local people in the surrounding villages. Even small things such as using park vehicles to transport water, which saves women walking long distances to collect it, helps to reduce the alienation many local people suffer when parks are established.

In Gambia, local people have been employed where possible at several national parks, and, at Kiang West, activities such as cattle grazing and (more controversially) rice cultivation are permitted in the park. At Kiang West and Niumi National Parks, community groups have been established to give the local people a voice in the park management structure – ideally so they can benefit from the sustainable use of natural resources within the park.

For information on tourism and its effect on the environment, along with guidelines for travellers who wish to minimise their negative impact on the environment, see Responsible Tourism in the Regional Facts for the Visitor chapter.

FLORA

Senegal and Gambia lie almost totally within the Sahel zone, where vegetation consists primarily of well-dispersed trees and low scrub. Only the better-watered southern Casamance region could be defined as woodland, while the vast networks of estuaries and mangroves also make a welcome change from typical Sahel landscapes – parts of northern Senegal come very close to being desert.

Trees characteristic of the Sahel include various flat-topped species of acacia, which usually have small thorny leaves. Other notable species include the baobab (see the boxed text) and the kapok, which is also known as the bombax tree or silk cotton tree. The kapok's most recognisable features are its yellowish bark, large pod-like fruit, and tall and narrow exposed roots, which form a natural maze around the base of the trunk. In Senegal this tree is called the fromager (from 'cheese' in French) because the wood in the trunk is so soft and light. It is used in some areas to make the floor of pirogues (traditional canoes) after being saturated, straightened and dried to

The Baobab Tree

Along with the flat-topped acacia, the baobab tree (Adansonia digitata) is an instantly recognisable symbol of Africa. Its thick, sturdy trunk and stunted rootlike branches are featured on countless postcards. Baobabs grow in most parts of Gambia and Senegal, and in many other areas of the continent, usually in savanna zones where rainfall is limited. Many cultures have their version of a story that involves the tree displeasing a deity who plucked it in anger and thrust it back into the ground upside down. Hence its rootlike branches.

However, despite the misdemeanours of its ancestor, today's baobab is held in high regard by local people. Its wizened appearance, combined with an ability to survive great droughts and live for many hundreds of years, means the baobab is often revered and believed to have magical powers. Very old trees develop cavities and these are sometimes used as a place to 'bury' a revered griot (traditional musician or minstrel who also acts as the historian for a village or tribe). Smaller holes are used by birds and animals.

The baobab has many practical uses too. The hollow trunk can hold rainwater, which may have percolated in from cracks higher up in the tree, and becomes a useful reservoir in times of drought. The tree's large pods (these are sometimes called 'monkey bread') contain seeds encased in a sherbetlike substance that can be eaten or made into a drink. The pods themselves are used to make cups or bowls (often for drinking palm wine). Any not suitable for this purpose are used as fuel; they burn slowly and are good for smoking fish. The leaves of the baobab can be eaten when chopped, boiled and made into a sauce. They can also be dried and ground into a paste to use as a poultice for skin infections and joint complaints. Even the flowers are used for decoration at ceremonies.

the required shape. (For more information on pirogue building, see the boxed text 'Soumbédioune' in the Dakar chapter.)

In Gambia and southern Senegal many villages are built around an ancient kapok or fromager tree because the trees are believed to have special significance, harbouring spirits who protect the inhabitants from bad luck. The men of the village use the tree as a *palava*, or meeting place; the exposed roots often make comfortable benches.

The palm is another common tree; species include the Doum palm, which grows to about 15m in height and produces an orange fruit called a drupe; the Senegal date palm, which grows to about 8m and produces small red berries; and the coconut palm, which can grow to 35m.

The dry, sparse landscape of the Sahel is interrupted by ribbons of dense gallery forest that occur along watercourses, most notably along the Gambia and Casamance Rivers. Gallery forest is quite similar to rainforest but is fed primarily by ground water, so many of the vines and epiphytes that are characteristic of rainforest are absent.

FAUNA

The birds of Senegambia are one of the region's main attractions, and are covered in the 'Birds of Senegambia' special section. By contrast, the mammals and other animals of the region are not a major feature for visitors, although several areas do exist where they can be seen.

Popular and easily recognised animal species in forested areas include baboons and three types of monkeys (vervet, patas and red colobus). Abuko Nature Reserve in Gambia is one of the best places to see these monkey species (see the Western Gambia chapter for details). Chimpanzee populations occur naturally in Senegal's Parc National de Niokolo-Koba, their northernmost outpost in Africa, and also inhabit the River Gambia National Park.

In the forest areas you also may see oribi and duikers (small members of the antelope family). In the drier grassland areas antelope species seen include cobs, roans, waterbucks and derby elands. The best place to

see these is in Niokolo-Koba; in most other parts of Senegal and Gambia they are rare or extinct. Other species found in this type of habitat include warthogs and bush pigs.

For the 'classic' African animals, such as elephants, lions and leopards, your best bet is once again Niokolo-Koba, although actually seeing any of these animals is unlikely. There are so few elephants remaining that the park has begun importing them in an effort to repopulate. They are extinct in Gambia. However, in Niokolo-Koba there is a chance of seeing hyenas and buffaloes, plus a few lonely hippos. Hippos have also been recorded on the Gambia River, and you might be lucky enough to see some if you travel by boat on its upper reaches. Other mammals occurring in creeks and lagoons include manatees (sea cows), although these are extinct in Gambia, and dolphins can sometimes be seen where large rivers enter the sea. Another river inhabitant in Senegambia is the crocodile, both the more common Nile species and the very rare dwarf crocodile.

Reptiles to watch for (but they shouldn't inspire bush paranoia) are snakes. Gambia and Senegal have their complement of both venomous and harmless snakes (including pythons, cobras and mambas), but most fear humans and you'll be lucky to even see one. One snake worth a special mention is the puff adder, which reaches about 1m in length and which, like all reptiles, enjoys sunning itself. Take care when hiking in bush areas, especially in the early morning when this snake is at its most lethargic. Other reptiles include lizards (such as the large monitor lizard), geckos and tortoises.

If you have an interest in fauna, a good regional field guide is recommended. See Books in the Regional Facts for the Visitor chapter for some suggestions.

GOVERNMENT & POLITICS

The Gambia and Senegal are two separate countries, with separate governments and political systems. A Senegambian Confederation did exist in the 1980s, with a view to eventual unification, but this broke down when Gambia resisted what would have been inevitable Senegalese dominance.

Following the military coup in Gambia in 1994 the new government was initially regarded with some apprehension by Senegal, but relations soon returned to relative normality. By 2001 the relationship was so harmonious that Gambia's President Yahya Jammeh was offering to help Senegal's new leader Abdoulaye Wade solve the long-running separatist issue in neighbouring Casamance. For travellers, all this cooperation means borders are usually relaxed and hassle-free, and transport connections run fairly smoothly.

More details are given under Government & Politics in the country chapters.

ECONOMY

The economies of Gambia and Senegal are dependent on agriculture, particularly peanuts (see the boxed text 'Groundnuts' earlier in this chapter). In Senegal in recent years, fishing has become a major part of the domestic and export markets. Money earned from tourism also forms a significant, although precarious, portion for both countries.

By any yardstick, Gambia and Senegal are among the poorest countries in the world. Their gross national product (GNP) figures show a bleak monetary situation, and even less financially biased standards, such as the UN's Human Development Index, do not paint a bright picture. The average Western citizen is up to 100 times better off than their Gambian or Senegalese counterpart.

The economic health of the region is not helped by the huge international loans both countries must service. The debt problem began in the 1970s when many countries were encouraged by commercial banks, Western governments and international bodies such as the World Bank and the International Monetary Fund (IMF) to arrange development loans. However, many loans were linked to the production of cash crops or minerals for export, or to sales of imported goods (such as armaments) from which the lending countries, rather than the recipient countries, would benefit. A lot of money was wasted and embezzled by senior political figures. Very little, if any, reached the ordinary people.

Meanwhile, the price for commodities (such as groundnuts) dropped, so these countries found it increasingly hard to meet their interest payments. This led to the 'debt crisis' of the 1980s, in which the Third World countries owed such large sums of money that when some began to default on their repayments, the entire global financial system was threatened with collapse. Such a situation would have hit every stock market, pension fund and savings account in the West, from New York to Alice Springs.

To avert a financial collapse, several Western governments bailed out the banks while the IMF introduced 'structural adjustment' and restrictions on spending by the debtor countries. In Gambia and Senegal, this may have controlled corruption and inefficiency to some extent, but for ordinary people things got worse: their wages went down, the price of food went up, and services such as education and health care were cut.

It has become increasingly obvious, and bitterly ironic, that although loans from the World Bank and other institutions are supposed to help, they actually siphon money from the poor countries to the richer countries. While the financial institutions of the West benefit, the vast majority of people in Gambia, Senegal and the rest of West Africa continue to suffer. Government corruption and inefficiency remain significant problems in the region, but the outstanding debts which absorb so much of the countries' GDP are also a major concern.

After years of campaigns by human rights and welfare organisations for Western banks and nations to write off the loans, a program of large-scale debt relief was started in 1996. Countries that fell into a group known as the 'heavily indebted poor countries (HIPC)' were told to reach a set of relatively achievable goals and they would be rewarded by having some of their debts cleared. Much of sub-Saharan Africa made it into the HIPC club, and by early 2001 a total of US$14.6 billion in debts had been forgiven. According to the World Bank, Gambia qualified for US$67 million in debt relief, or 27% of its net present total; Senegal US$452 million, or 19%.

With the money it saves on interest payments Senegal has promised to hire an extra 2000 teachers a year for the next few years. The World Bank and the IMF have promised to continue the debt-reduction programme, but there remains an argument that not nearly enough of Africa's extra spending power will filter down to the people who need it most.

On a personal scale, what can travellers in Gambia and Senegal do? The main thing is to be aware. Know that, while Africa has seen more than its fair share of corruption and mismanagement, many countries are in such deep debt holes because they followed instructions from the West. On a more immediate level, direct your spending as much as you possibly can in ways that bring direct benefits to the local people.

POPULATION & PEOPLE

Current estimates put Gambia's population at approximately 1.4 million, while Senegal's population is around 10.3 million.

Poverty in the region means a life expectancy of around 50 years. At 3%, birth rates are the highest on earth, but between 100 and 200 children in every 1000 die before the age of five. Unemployment is very high and literacy rates are very low, especially among women. The people have no money to buy food and can only grow cereal crops, so nutritional intakes are very low. As a result of this, a large proportion of the population – especially children – is susceptible to disease, for which there are very few medical services. It's a depressing scenario, and likely to get worse as the gap between Africa and the rest of the world continues to widen.

There are several ethnic groups in the region, but most are spread across the national boundaries. These include the following:

Wolof

The Wolof (spelt Ouolof in French) are widespread and dominant throughout the Senegambia region. In Senegal they live particularly in the central area to the north and east of Dakar, and along the coast. In Gambia they live mainly in the western areas of the country. Traditionally farmers and traders, the Wolof today control a great deal of commerce, especially in Senegal. The Wolof language is used as a common tongue in many parts of Senegal and Gambia, often instead of French or English, and some smaller groups complain about the ever-increasing 'Wolofisation' of their culture. The Wolof are almost exclusively Muslim.

Mandinka & Malinké

The Mandinka live largely in Gambia, and in parts of Senegal, especially to the north. The Mandinka are also called Mandingo, and are related to other Manding-speaking groups such as the Bambara of Mali, where they originated. They are thought to have migrated to the Senegambia region between the 13th and early 16th centuries, and to have brought Islam with them.

Traditionally engaged in farming and fishing, Mandinka people are Muslim, and they also have a strong musical tradition. Islamic feast days, such as Koraté at the end of Ramadan, and family celebrations, such as a wedding or circumcision, or even the arrival of a special guest, are often seen as very good reasons for some music and dancing.

The terms Mandinka and Malinké are often used interchangeably, but linguists regard Malinké as a separate language (also of the Manding group), although it shares many features with Mandinka. The Malinké people live mostly in eastern Senegal.

Fula

The Fula live across West Africa, as far east as Sudan and south into countries such as Ghana and Nigeria, although they look on the Futa Toro region in northern Senegal as their cultural homeland. The Fula are also called Fulani and Fulbe, and Peul or Peulh in Senegal. Their language is also known by these names, or as Fulfulde or Pulaar. A dialect called Fulakunda is spoken in southern and eastern Senegal.

The Fula are traditionally nomadic cattle herders, and the constant search for grazing land may go some way towards explaining their dispersal across the region. Wolof or people from other tribes who own cattle will often entrust them to Fula keepers. The Fula tend to have light skin, compared with most peoples of sub-Saharan Africa, and their own oral history says they have Caucasian origins. Other sources give them Semitic or Arab origin. Fula are mostly, but not exclusively, Muslim and their far-flung nature means they intermarry with other groups.

Tukulor

The Tukulor people (in Senegal this is spelt Toucouleur) are found predominantly in the Futa Toro region in northern Senegal, although their origins are vague, and their history and culture overlap with that of the Fula of Senegal. Some authorities say the Tukulor are Fula, or the outcome of inter-marrying between Fula and Wolof. Their language is classified as a dialect of Fula. One difference, however, is that the Tukulor embraced Islam much earlier than the Fula, in the 10th or 11th century when the religion was first carried south across the Sahara from Morocco. The Tukulor were known for their extreme religious zeal: they were responsible for converting many other groups, and for inspiring many of the anti-colonial jihads of the 19th century.

Serer

The Serer (also spelt Serere, and Sérèr in Senegal) are less widespread than any of the other groups mentioned above. They are concentrated in the Siné-Saloum region of Senegal, inland from there in central Senegal, and just across the border in northwest Gambia. They are thought to have migrated from southern Senegal in the 16th century (they seem to share common origins with the Diola) and in some areas they have inter-married with the Mandinka or Wolof people, or adopted their languages. In many cases the Serer have adopted Islam too, although there are pockets who are Christians.

Diola

The Diola live in the Casamance area in southern Senegal, and the area southwest of Gambia, where their name is spelt 'Jola'. They also live in various parts of northern Guinea-Bissau. Traditional Diola occupations include farming, fishing and palm-wine tapping.

The Diola do not have a strong oral tradition (that is, they do not have the equivalent of griots, who can keep traditions and history alive for centuries among other tribes) and their origins are obscure. It is thought they have probably lived in the area for many centuries, although their territory used to also cover the Gambia River and they were pushed south when the Mandinka migrated here between the 13th and 16th centuries. The Diola differ from their neighbours in other ways too: their society is segmented and flexible (not rigidly hierarchical like the Wolof's) and they have largely rejected Islam, preferring their own traditional beliefs or conversion to Christianity.

These strong differences have created a fierce sense of independence among the Diola, which is still strongly evidenced today, most notably by outbreaks of fighting between Casamance separatist rebels and the 'northern' army.

Serahuli

The Serahuli live in the eastern part of Senegal and groups can be found in the far eastern parts of Gambia. Exclusively Muslim, they are also known as Soninké or Soninke, and live in several other countries in the Sahel including Mali and Burkina Faso. (Soninke is also the Mandinka word for 'king', and the battles of the late 19th century between these traditional rulers and Islamic leaders were often called the Soninke-Marabout Wars.)

The origins of the Serahuli are unclear. They may have migrated to this area after the break-up of the ancient Songhaï empire in present-day Mali at the end of the 15th century. Or possibly they have been in the region for longer, and are the descendants of the original empire of Ghana.

Other Groups

Minor groups in Senegal include the Bassari and the Bédik, who live in the remote southeastern part of Senegal. The Lebu are another distinct group, living almost exclusively in the town of Yoff outside Dakar. In Gambia, the Aku people are similar to the Krio found in other parts of West Africa – for more information, see Population &

People in the Facts about The Gambia chapter. In both Gambia and Senegal, a significant number of Moors, from Mauritania, are involved mainly in small trade, and are famous as jewellery makers.

EDUCATION

Both Gambia and Senegal have state education systems following patterns established by their colonial powers (ie, with primary, secondary and tertiary stages), while Islamic schools run by the local mosques operate alongside the state-school system.

Primary education is theoretically available to all children, whereas only those who pass their exams go to secondary school. In reality, it's family income, rather than academic performance, that determines which children go to school and how far up the ladder they progress. Poor children may not be able to afford school fees or extra items such as uniforms and books (especially when they want to go beyond primary school). Children from poor families also may be kept away from school to work in the fields or to provide income from other employment.

These problems are compounded by a lack of government funds for education. Many schools have so many students that they operate two 'shifts', with one lot of children coming in the morning and another in the afternoon. Even so, classes may hold over 100 pupils, sitting three or four to a desk, and sharing books and pens. At the same time, teachers are grossly underpaid, many become understandably demoralised, and standards slip further.

However, it's not all doom and gloom. In Gambia the government is working to redress decades of neglect, indeed a policy of under-educating the populace, by building dozens of new schools. There are also proposals to offer free schooling to girls, who traditionally miss out in favour of their brothers.

Despite this, literacy rates in Gambia and Senegal are low. Official figures from 1998 show Senegal has a literacy rate of 35.5%, while Gambia is slightly higher at 37%.

ARTS

Music & Literature

Senegambia's richest artistic tradition is music. For many centuries musicians and praise singers called griots have kept alive the tales of families and clans, giving peoples such as the Wolof and Mandinka their strong sense of history and identity. Many griots sing accompanied by the kora – a kind of harp – and the Mandinka are particularly noted for their skill in crafting these instruments. More recently, musicians have tapped into the traditional sounds to produce a distinct West African style that is now enjoyed around the world, thanks to stars such as Youssou N'Dour. More details are given in the 'Music of Senegambia' special section.

The griots also formed the basis of Senegambia's contemporary literature, although with no written language, this was an oral tradition. Since the colonial era, and especially since independence, both Gambia and Senegal have produced a host of poets and novelists. These are discussed in more detail in the individual country chapters.

Architecture

The most tangible expression of the different cultural influences that have pervaded the Senegambia region over the centuries is their architecture. A string of African empires brought new ideas and styles, but, sadly, most of their building was done in wood and thatch; the hundreds of enigmatic stone circles north of the Gambia River are virtually the only structures surviving into the modern day.

In contrast, the European influence has been lasting. The Europeans' fancy for grand buildings and monuments, mastery of technology (such as the railway) and, on a more basic level, building materials of stone or brick mean that, as a visitor, you're likely to see a series of architectural styles dating back to the Portuguese era.

From a historical point of view, the islands of Gorée and St-Louis, and the Senegal River settlements of Richard Toll, Podor, Matam and Bakel, are virtual time capsules of 18th- and 19th-century French architecture. Many of the buildings have seen better days, but those on Gorée and St-Louis in particular are enjoying a tourism-driven renaissance. In St-Louis it's not unusual for a beautifully renovated building to stand imposingly beside a decrepit, weathered home that looks as if it hasn't seen a maintenance man for decades. The impact of Breton settlers on Île de Carabane at the remote mouth of the Casamance River is still plain to see in its large church and mission-cum-hotel. In Dakar more recent styles can be found, with several interesting examples of Art-Deco buildings located southwest of the city centre.

In Gambia, Banjul is home to wide avenues of grand homes once occupied by the colonial elite, while, nearby, stand small unpretentious Krio-style homes, some still occupied by the descendants of freed-slave families who moved to Banjul from Sierra Leone in the early 1800s. Fortifications were also important to the European colonists, and not far from Banjul you can see the remains of Fort James, a slaving station on James Island, and Fort Bullen in Barra, built to fight slavery.

But architecture in Gambia and Senegal is not just about the reminders of homes built by long-since-usurped colonists. While much of the construction since independence has been driven more by function and cost than by artistic values, a growing number of buildings have been designed and built by Africans for Africans. Many of these, such as Arch 22 and the international airport in Banjul, have been designed by internationally renowned Senegalese architect Pierre Goudiaby, and his success and recognition is inspiring more 'home-grown' design in both countries.

SOCIETY & CONDUCT

One of the highlights of travel in Gambia and Senegal is meeting the local people, so you'll get more from your visit by knowing something about how their society functions and how social customs work.

Social Structures

Senegal's main cultural group, the Wolof, have the most rigidly hierarchical system, but several other tribes in the region follow a similar pattern. At the top are traditional noble and warrior families, followed by the farmers and traders. Lower down the scale are the artisans – blacksmiths, leather workers, woodcarvers and weavers – arranged into castes according to occupation. Intermarriage between orders and between castes is usually forbidden.

Musicians are also a low caste, but at the same time highly respected. In song and poetry they recite oral tradition and maintain the histories of a particular family, village or clan, often going back for many centuries. This type of musician is called a griot, although this term is actually French in origin and probably a corruption of either the Wolof *gewel* or the Tukulor *gawlo*. The Mandinka word is *jali*.

At the bottom of the hierarchy were the slaves, originally taken in wars or bought from traders, but kept in this position for many generations. Although this status no longer officially exists, many descendants of former slaves still work as tenant farmers for descendants of their former masters.

However, modernity is finally eroding traditional hierarchies in Senegambia. Today, the government official who shows contempt for a rural chief may actually be a member of a lower caste who went to the city and acquired an education.

Social Events

Ceremonies are very important because they help reinforce social structures. Much of African life centres on social events, such as weddings, funerals and village festivals, and you may be lucky enough to get invited. Most events involve traditional music and dancing, but men and women may dance separately. If there's modern African music, the younger people may dance at the same time. Either way, if you want to join in, observe the protocol.

Weddings At weddings there is likely to be an official ceremony at the mayor's office followed by eating and dancing at someone's home. This is the culmination of a week of activities involving visits to relatives and the exchange of gifts. Among the Wolof, weddings are very important, and enjoyed with

Marriage

In Gambia and Senegal, along with many other parts of West Africa, marriage is an expensive affair. Gifts from the groom to the bride's family can easily cost several hundred dollars – this is not exactly peanuts in an area of the world where annual incomes of US$300 are typical. Many men can't afford to get married before their late 20s or 30s.

Despite the financial constraints, in traditional society, men who can afford more than one wife usually marry two, three or even four women (the Quran allows up to four). Visitors from monogamous backgrounds find this aspect of African society particularly fascinating. You will be told (by men) that women are not against the custom of multiple wives, and that the wives of one man become like sisters, helping each other with domestic and child-rearing duties. In reality, though, most first wives definitely don't like their husbands marrying again. On the other hand, there's not much the women can do, as leaving a marriage simply because their husband takes another wife would bring a lot of shame to the woman's own family. A particularly incisive account of the clash between modern and traditional values concerning polygamy is given in a book titled *So Long a Letter* by Miriama Ba.

great enthusiasm. Legal and religious ceremonies are performed early so the day can be spent celebrating. In a traditional wedding, the grandmother and the great aunts take the bride to the marriage chamber, lecture her and then summon the husband to consummate the marriage. Afterwards, the husband retires and the older women exhibit the bloodstained sheet to the guests; the bride is then smothered with gifts. (If you want to give a gift at any ceremony, a small amount of money is perfectly acceptable.)

Male Circumcision For Wolof men, the circumcision rite is an important step on the road to adulthood. Boys are circumcised shortly after reaching puberty. Before the operation the candidates are dressed like women, with shells and jewels in their long hair. Afterwards, still wearing their costumes, they stay in isolation, living in special huts until healed. Then there's a feast and they are given a magical potion that is believed to render their bodies immune to knife blows.

Female Circumcision Circumcision is culturally important for women in Gambia and Senegal, although the process of clitoral and labial removal is now less euphemistically termed female genital mutilation. In Senegambia, around 80% of girls and young women undergo this process, particularly in rural areas, where it forms part of the initia-

tion ceremonies or is perceived as an aspect of Islamic teaching. Apart from the pain caused at the time, these operations are carried out in basic conditions and frequently entail injuries that do not heal properly or lead to blood poisoning. Even the injuries that do heal can result in gynaecological problems, especially when women give birth, and obvious problems with sexual function. The psychological scars are harder to see and often harder to heal. While an increasing number of girls are being excised shortly after birth, many still undergo the crude operation at around age 10 to 12. There is little preparation and many are the stories of girls being told of a party being held in their honour, only to be led into the bush and 'circumcised' (always by an elderly woman) without anaesthetic. In Gambia, a local organisation called Gamcotrap is trying to discourage female genital mutilation and promote traditional health practices among women.

Festivals Village festivals *(fêtes)* may be held to honour dead ancestors or local traditional deities, or to celebrate the end of the harvest. Each festival is unique. Some include singing and dancing, while others favour parades, sports or wrestling matches. You may even see elaborate performances with masks or puppets used to tell stories.

Christian ceremonies are observed in Gambia and Senegal, particularly in the cities where a larger proportion of the population (although still a minority) is non-Muslim. At Christmas time in Banjul, St-Louis and Île de Gorée, crowds of people carry around large lanterns called *fanals*, which are brightly painted with intricate decorations or made in the shape of boats or houses. The tradition originated during French colonial times in St-Louis, although it may have been introduced by Portuguese settlers in the 15th century, when wealthy inhabitants going to midnight mass would be led by slaves carrying decorative lamps. Today, the people sing and chant as they parade their fanals around the streets, while onlookers donate a few coins to the group as a sign of appreciation.

Social Conduct

The best way to learn about a society's conduct is to watch the locals. The first thing to remember is not to worry because people in Gambia and Senegal are generally very easy-going towards foreigners. That said, public nudity, open displays of anger, open displays of affection (among people of the same or opposite sex), and vocal criticism of the government or country are frowned upon everywhere.

Greetings Great importance is placed on greetings. For example, Wolof or Mandinka people – particularly elders – greet one another with a ritual that lasts up to half a minute, starting with the traditional Islamic greetings, *'Salaam aleikum'* and *'Aleikum asalaam'* ('Peace be unto you', 'And peace be unto you'). This is followed by several more questions, such as 'How are you doing?', 'How is the family?', 'How is business?', 'How are the people of your compound?', 'Is your body in peace?'. The reply is usually *'Al humdul'allah'* ('Thanks be to God'). Even non-Muslim people use similar greetings, and go into all kinds of inquiries about relatives, health, work, the weather and so on. The answer is always that things are fine, even for people at death's door. In the cities, the traditional greetings sometimes give way to shorter versions in French or English, but they're never forgotten.

Although it's not necessary for foreigners to go through the whole routine, it's important to use greetings whenever possible. Even if you're doing something simple such as changing money, buying a train ticket or asking directions, it's appropriate to start with 'Good day, how are you? Can you help me please?' in French or English, as required. If you launch straight into business, you are likely to be met with a hostile or negative attitude.

In rural areas (and even in cities), if you can learn greetings in the local language, you will be an incredible hit. Even a few words make a big difference. (Some basic words and phrases are provided in the Language chapter at the back of this book.)

Thanks Gambian and Senegalese people are frequently very friendly towards foreigners and even after a few minutes of talking may offer you food or a bed for the night. You may want to repay such kindness, but it's not always possible to carry a range of gifts in your rucksack. Tobacco, tea and perfume are quite portable, and kola nuts are good (see the boxed text), but normally money is the easiest thing to give, and it's always appreciated. When deciding what to pay, consider what you would have paid for a similar meal or hotel room. Experiencing local hospitality will enhance your travelling; using it merely as a way to save money makes you a low-down parasite.

Kola Nuts

Kola nuts are yellow or purple, about half the size of a golf ball, and are sold everywhere in the streets and markets of West Africa. They are known for their mildly narcotic effects and make a good portable gift if you want to give people something in exchange for their kindness. They last longer if you keep them moist but go mouldy quite quickly if kept sealed in a plastic bag. Despite their popularity among locals, most foreigners find them too bitter to chew, and anyone looking for a 'high' is usually disappointed.

Shaking Hands The emphasis on greetings makes handshakes important. For men it is important to shake hands with other men when entering and leaving a gathering. Particularly in social settings you must go around the room, greet everyone and shake hands with the men, and maybe the older women, even if it takes a few minutes. Do the same when you leave. Use a soft handshake. A macho knuckle-cracker is rude, and even more inane than it is in the West.

Western women in a modern African situation find that the rules for men apply to them too. In a traditional situation, though, some Muslim men prefer not to shake hands with women, and local women usually do *not* shake hands with their male counterparts, so it might be considered odd if you do. However, most Western women in traditional situations generally find they hold the position of 'honorary man', and extraneous handshaking will not cause offence.

Deference In traditional societies, older people (especially men) are treated with deference. Professionals such as teachers and doctors (usually men) often receive similar treatment. Thus, when you're travelling and you meet people in authority such as immigration officers, police and village chiefs (you've guessed it – usually men), it is very important to be polite. Officials are normally courteous, but they can be awkward and unpleasant if provoked, and this is when manners, patience, a friendly smile and a little cooperation are essential. Undermining an official's authority or insulting an official's ego may only waste your time, tie you up in red tape and probably inspire a far closer scrutiny of future travellers.

At the other end of the spectrum, children rate very low on the social scale. They are expected to do as they're told without complaint. Unfortunately for half the region's population, the status of women is only slightly higher. For example, an African man on a bus might give his seat to an older man, but not normally to a woman – never mind that she is carrying a baby and luggage, and minding two toddlers. In traditional rural areas, women are expected to dress and behave modestly, especially in the presence of chiefs or other esteemed persons. Visitors should act the same way.

When visiting settlements, it is a good idea to ask to see the chief to announce yourself and ask for permission before setting up camp or wandering through a village. You will rarely be refused.

Another consideration is eye contact, which is usually avoided, especially between men and women in the Sahel. So if a local doesn't look you in the eye during a conversation, remember that they're being polite, not cold.

Eating Traditional-Style If you get invited to share a meal with a local family or group of friends there are a few customs to observe. Firstly, you'll probably sit or squat with your hosts on the floor in a circle around the food, which will be served in one or two large bowls – usually one with rice, and the other with a sauce of palm oil, peanuts, vegetables, fish or meat. It is sometimes considered polite to take off your shoes, so do this if your hosts do.

The food is normally eaten with the hands, and everybody washes their hands before eating, usually in a bowl that is passed around. Then you all just dig in. Take a handful of rice and part of the sauce, forming a ball in the palm of your hand, and eat. Taking a meal this way will seem odd the first time, and inevitably very messy, but the washbowl is passed around again afterwards. As an honoured guest you might be passed chunks of meat or other choice morsels by the head of the household. It's usually polite to finish eating while there's still food in the bowl to show you have had enough.

If all this sounds too daunting, you probably won't offend anybody by asking for a spoon. But however you eat, it is essential to use only the right hand, because traditionally the left hand is used for 'personal toiletries' such as wiping your bum. (Left-handed people should take special care, and consider sitting on their left hand in this kind of situation.) Should you accidentally pick up a morsel with your left hand, it's a social gaffe akin in Western culture to breaking wind among strangers. There'll be the same eyes-averted, embarrassed silence. The difference here is that no-one will be suppressing a snigger – and everyone will know it's you.

Dress Many people wear a traditional outfit commonly called a grand boubou. For men, this is an elaborate embroidered robelike gar-ment reaching the ground, with baggy trousers and shirt underneath. The women's boubou is similar, but may have more embroidery, and is often worn with a matching head-scarf. For more everyday wear, women wear a loose top and a length of colourful printed cotton cloth around the waist for a skirt. Because the designs are so distinctively

Islam

In the early 7th century, in the city of Mecca, the Prophet Mohammed called on the people to submit to the one true God (Allah). His teachings appealed to the poorer levels of society and angered the wealthy merchant class, and by AD 622 Mohammed and his followers were forced to flee to Medina. This migration, the Hejira, marks the start of the Islamic calendar year AH 1.

Mohammed died in 632 (AH 10) but within two decades most of Arabia had converted to Islam. Over the following centuries, Islam spread through North and West Africa, down the coast of East Africa, into several parts of southern and Eastern Europe and eastward across Southern Asia.

In the early part of the 2nd millennium, Islamic influence moved south across the Sahara to the countries now called Senegal and Mali, and from there spread throughout West Africa. In Senegal, Islam adapted to local social conditions by evolving several features that would not be recognised by purists in Cairo or Mecca. Most notable of these are the marabouts – holy men who act as a cross between intermediary, priest and adviser for local people. In Senegal they wield considerable political power. This is discussed in the boxed text 'Marabouts & Brotherhoods' in the Facts about Senegal chapter.

The Five Pillars of Islam

Islam is the Arabic word for 'submission' and underlies the duty of all Muslims to submit themselves to Allah. The five pillars of Islam are the basic tenets guiding Muslims in their daily lives:

Shahada (the profession of faith) 'There is no God but Allah, and Mohammed is his prophet' is the fundamental tenet of Islam.

Salat (prayer) Muslims must face Mecca and pray five times a day: at dawn, midday, mid-afternoon, sunset and nightfall.

Zakat (alms) Muslims must give a portion of their income to the poor and needy.

Sawm (fasting) Ramadan is the month of the Muslim calendar when all Muslims must abstain from eating, drinking, smoking and sex from dawn to dusk.

Haj (pilgrimage) It is the duty of every Muslim who is fit and can afford it to make the pilgrimage to Mecca at least once.

The Haj

All Muslims are supposed to make the haj, or pilgrimage to Mecca, at least once in their life if they have good health and the money for the journey. As the cost is typically several thousand dollars, for some this can involve a lifetime of savings, so it's not unusual for families to save up and send one member. Before the advent of air travel, the haj used to involve an overland journey of a year or more from West Africa, sometimes requiring stops on the way to earn money. Those who complete the pilgrimage receive the honorific title of *haji* for men, and *hajia* for women. If you meet someone with this prefix, you may appreciate the honour this bestows on them in the community.

African, it's surprising to learn that much of the better-quality cloth comes from Holland.

In general, people in Gambia and Senegal place great importance on appearance, and often dress in the best clothes they can. Thus it's not surprising that clothes often worn by foreigners (such as singlets and shorts or tight trousers) are often considered offensive, particularly in traditional areas. In Africa, the only people wearing shorts or tatty clothes are kids, labourers and the poor; no wonder some travellers get treated with contempt.

RELIGION

The religions of Senegambia fall into three main categories: Islam, Christianity and

---

Islam

Islamic Holidays

The most important Islamic holidays, when most commercial life in Gambia and Senegal comes to a stop, are:

Tabaski This is the most important celebration and usually a two-day public holiday (also called Eid al-Kebir). Muslims kill a ram to commemorate the moment when Abraham was about to sacrifice his son in obedience to God's command, only to have God substitute a ram at the last moment.

Eid al-Fitr Called Koraté locally, this is the second-major Islamic holiday, marking the end of Ramadan.

Eid al-Moulid This marks the birthday of the prophet Mohammed, celebrated almost three months after Tabaski.

Grand Magal Celebrated in Senegambia on the anniversary of the return from exile of the founder of the Mouride Islamic Brotherhood, Grand Magal takes place 48 days after the Islamic New Year and centres on the town of Touba.

Ramadan During the annual 30-day Muslim fast, adherents do not eat, drink, smoke or have sex from sunrise to sunset. (See also the boxed text 'Visits during Ramadan' in the Regional Facts for the Visitor chapter.)

Since the Islamic calendar is based on 12 lunar months, Islamic holidays always fall about 11 days earlier than in the previous year. The exact dates depend on what hour the moon is seen: for example, in 2001 Ramadan started a day later than expected after cloud cover prevented the moon being sighted. Many Muslims begin fasting when they see the moon, others follow the radio announcements of the religious leaders. Forthcoming dates for major Muslim events (clouds withstanding) are:

event	2002	2003	2004	2005
Ramadan begins	6 November	27 October	15 October	4 October
Eid al-Fitr	6 December	26 November	14 November	3 November
Islamic New Year	15 March	5 March	22 February	10 February
Tabaski	23 February	12 February	2 February	21 January
Eid al-Moulid	24 May	14 May	2 May	21 April

Tabaski Price-Hikes

Two weeks before Tabaski, sheep prices as much as double as every family is expected to provide one during the celebrations. Those who cannot afford a sheep are socially embarrassed, and most will do anything to scrape together the money. The slaughtered animal is divided into three equal portions, for the poor, for friends and for family.

traditional beliefs. In both Gambia and Senegal about 90% of the population is Muslim, mainly the Wolof, Tukulor, Lebu, Fula and Mandinka people. The Diola and the Serer favour Christianity, although many combine this with traditional beliefs. Many Muslims in Senegambia also combine their faith with traditional beliefs.

Traditional Religions

Before the arrival of Muslim and Christian evangelists, the people of West Africa practised their own traditional religions. Many in Senegambia converted to Islam or Christianity, but traditional religions have continued to have a strong presence in parts of the region.

There are hundreds of traditional religions in West Africa, and while there are no written scriptures, beliefs and traditions have long been handed down by word of mouth. For outsiders, these beliefs and traditions can be complex (and to the Western mind illogical or nonsensical). There are several factors common to these beliefs, although their descriptions here provide only an overview and are very simplified.

Almost all traditional religions are animist; that is, based on the attribution of life or consciousness to natural objects or phenomena. A certain tree, mountain, river or stone may be sacred, because it represents a spirit, or is home to a spirit, or simply *is* a spirit. Instead of 'spirit', some authorities use 'deity' or 'god.' The number of deities each religion accepts can vary, as can the phenomena that represent them.

Several traditional religions accept the existence of a supreme being or creator, although communication is possible only through the lesser deities or the intercession of ancestors. Thus, in many African religions ancestors play a particularly strong role. Their principal function is to protect the tribe or family and they may, on occasion, show their pleasure or displeasure at how things have been done. Displeasure may be shown in the form of bad weather, a bad harvest, or a member of the family becoming sick. Many traditional religions hold that the ancestors are the real owners of the land, and while it can be enjoyed and used during the lifetime of descendants, it cannot be sold.

Communication with ancestors or deities may take the form of prayer, offerings or sacrifice, possibly with the assistance of a holy man (or occasionally a holy woman). Requests may include good health, bountiful harvests and numerous children. Many village celebrations are held to ask for help from (or in honour of) ancestors and deities.

An important feature of traditional religions are 'totems' – objects (usually animals) that serve as emblems for a particular tribe or clan, usually connected with the original ancestor of that group. It is taboo for a member of the clan whose totem is, for example, a snake to harm any snake, because that would be harming the ancestor. Other totems include lions, crocodiles and certain birds.

Another important feature are 'fetishes'. These are sacred objects (or charms) and can take many forms. The most common charms found all over West Africa are small leather amulets – many containing a sacred object – worn around the neck, arm or waist. These are called grigri (pronounced gree-gree) and are used to ward off evil or to bring good luck. Interestingly, many Muslims in West Africa wear grigri, often with a small verse from the Quran inside.

Birds of Senegambia

Pelicans

Goliath heron

African jacana

Black-crowned crane

Hoopoe

ROB DRUMMOND

Pied barbet

JASON EDWARDS

Senegal parrot

ARIADNE VAN ZANDBERGEN

Carmine bee-eaters

ARIADNE VAN ZANDBERGEN

Red-billed firefinch

ROB DRUMMOND

Giant kingfisher

Ground hornbill

Bateleur eagle

African fish-eagle

The Gambia and Senegal are important sites for a diverse range of birds in West Africa. The region is at an ecological cross-roads between the rich fauna of equatorial Africa, the arid vastness of the Sahara, the bulk of continental Africa, and the Atlantic coast. This important transition zone, especially vital for migrating birds, supports a mosaic of habitats in which some 660 species of birds have been recorded.

Gambia's bird diversity reaches a concentration that seems out of proportion when compared with the country's tiny size – over 560 species have been recorded (just 80 fewer than in Senegal, which is almost 20 times larger) – and the country's unique shape makes many good bird-watching sites easily accessible. Senegambia's proximity to Western Europe further enhances the region's popularity as a bird-watching holiday destination, and Gambia in particular draws a great number of ornithologists every year.

BIRD HABITATS

Many birds are wide ranging, but the vast majority have feeding, breeding or other biological requirements that restrict them to a habitat or group of habitats. Of course, creatures as mobile as birds are not totally hemmed in by their preferred environment (in fact, the habitat of some, such as swallows and swifts, could perhaps best be described as 'air'), but a brief rundown of Senegambian bird habitats will be useful to travellers, who will notice the change in bird types as they move from area to area.

Cities, Towns & Villages

Since a city, town or village will be the first stop for nearly all visitors, it is worth mentioning a few birds that will be seen around human settlement. The grey-headed sparrow is the local representative of this cosmopolitan group; the red-billed firefinch frequents grain stores and village compounds; and swifts, swallows and martins nest under the eaves of buildings. Many travellers have their first introduction to Senegambian birds in a hotel garden. Look out for the gorgeous little cordon-bleu flitting among the vegetation; starlings and the brilliant yellow-crowned gonolek may be seen feeding on lawns; and weavers make their presence felt in noisy colonies. The piapiac, a long-tailed member of the crow family, can also be seen around towns.

Ocean Shore & Estuaries

The place where the land meets the sea is a rich habitat that attracts humans and animals alike to feast on creatures such as crustaceans and molluscs. Birds adapted to feeding in these habitats include waders, such as oyster-catchers and plovers, and the reef egret, which stalks fish and crabs.

The Gambia and Casamance Rivers both have extensive mangrove-lined estuaries. Historically they have been dismissed as 'swamps', but mangroves are now recognised as an important ecological resource. At low tide the fine mud floor is exposed and makes a rich feeding ground for migratory waders such as curlews, sandpipers, stints, godwits and plovers. Small birds such as sunbirds feed in the mangrove canopy and larger water birds, such as herons, ibises and spoonbills, may roost or nest among the larger stands.

Waterways

The major river systems of the Senegambia region – and the associated fringing forests, grasslands and swamps – support an astonishing variety of birds. Different groups of birds utilise waterways in different ways: some hunt along the shoreline or probe the soft mud at the water's edge; others stride on long legs into deeper water to seek prey. Some kingfishers dive from overhanging branches into the water, while warblers and flycatchers hunt insects in riverside vegetation. For the beginner and expert alike, freshwater habitats provide some of the best opportunities to view birds.

Low-lying areas may flood after the rains to create extensive ephemeral swamps, which are often superb for bird-watching. Egrets, herons and other wading birds stalk the shallows; the dainty African jacana walks across floating vegetation on its bizarre long splayed toes; and rails skulk in reed beds.

Savanna & Woodland

Large swaths of central and southeastern Senegal, plus adjoining parts of Gambia, are characterised by savanna vegetation dominated by a mixture of small trees. There can be rich pickings for bird-watchers in this habitat, from the perplexing cisticolas to huge birds of prey, plus weavers, finches, starlings, rollers and many more.

The southern part of the region once supported extensive woodland; most has now been cleared or modified by human activities, but patches of this woodland still remain in Parc National de Basse-Casamance and Abuko Nature Reserve. A number of rare birds, such as the African pied hornbill, the grey-headed bristlebill and the little greenbul, are found only in this habitat and manage to survive in these protected areas.

Arid Areas

The northern part of Senegal is sub-Saharan semidesert, a sparsely vegetated landscape that has been shaped by the low rainfall inherent in this area. This habitat is seldom visited by bird-watchers, but supports a few interesting species including wheatears, desert finches and migrants stopping on their way to or from the northern hemisphere.

THE BIRDS

The following is a group-by-group description of some of the diverse
birds a visitor will possibly see during a trip to Gambia or Senegal. This
is not a comprehensive list and readers are urged to refer to one of the
guides mentioned later in this section for further information.

Many birds have been left out: for example, a peculiarly African
group known as flufftails are so skulking as to be virtually invisible.

Sea Birds

Into this broad category can be lumped a number of bird families that
hunt over the open sea. They include the various petrels and shear-
waters, which usually live far out to sea and return to land only to
breed; the beautiful gannet, which feeds by plunging from a great
height after fish; and the fish-eating cormorants (shags), which also
make use of brackish and freshwater habitats.

Waterfowl

This large group includes the familiar ducks and geese, and as their col-
lective name suggests, they are found almost exclusively around
waterways. Waterfowl are strong flyers and can move vast distances
in response to rainfall. The increased availability of food after the rains
means they may be more easily seen at this time. In particular, the
large, black-and-white spur-winged goose is often abundant at such
times. Despite the significance of water as a habitat in Gambia, there
are comparatively few species of ducks and geese in the region.

Birds of Prey

Hawks, eagles, vultures and falcons fall under this heading and number
more than 50 species in the region. Their presence is almost ubiquitous and travellers will soon notice a few species, from soaring flocks
of scavenging vultures to the stately bateleur eagle watching for prey.
Several have specialised prey or habitat requirements; eg, the osprey
and striking African fish-eagle feed almost exclusively on fish.

Cranes

These graceful birds resemble storks and herons, but they are typically
grassland-dwelling birds. The one species found in the region – the
black-crowned crane – is eccentrically adorned with a colourful crest.

Long-Legged Wading Birds

Virtually any waterway will have its complement of herons, egrets,
storks, spoonbills and ibises. All have long legs and necks, and bills

adapted to specific feeding strategies: herons and egrets have dagger-like bills for spearing fish and frogs; spoonbills have peculiar, flattened bills that they swish from side to side to gather small water creatures; ibises have long bills, curved down to probe in soft earth or seize insects; and storks have large powerful beaks to snap up small animals and fish. Members of this group range in size from the tiny, secretive bittern to the enormous goliath heron, which stands 1.4m tall; and the ugly marabou stork, which feeds, along with vultures, on carrion. An unusual member of this group is the little hamerkop, which makes an enormous nest of twigs and grass.

Migratory Waders

Every year migrating shore birds leave their breeding grounds in the northern hemisphere and fly to their wintering grounds south of the Sahara. Generally nondescript in their winter plumage, these migratory 'waders' are an identification challenge for the keen bird-watcher. They're usually found near waterways, feeding along the shores on small creatures or probing intertidal mud for worms. The migrants include the long-distance champions, sandpipers and plovers; while residents include the boldly marked lapwings and the odd dikkops – lanky, cryptic, nocturnal species with weird wailing cries.

Pigeons & Doves

Familiar to city and country dwellers alike, members of this family are found all over the world and have managed to adapt to virtually every habitat. For example, the various turtledoves and the tiny Namaqua dove feed on the ground while the African green pigeon leads a nomadic life following the seasonal fruiting of trees. Two of the dove species, the cosmopolitan rock dove and the laughing dove, are common inhabitants of gardens and human settlements.

Turacos

These often beautifully coloured, medium-sized forest birds can be difficult to see because of their habit of remaining hidden in the canopy, but three species are common in the Senegambia region. The violet turaco is a stunning bird, although you may only be lucky enough to catch a tantalising view when it flies across a clearing, showing its vivid crimson wing patches.

Honeyguides

Honeyguides display one of the most remarkable behaviours of any bird. They actually seek out the help of mammals such as the ratel (honey badger), or even humans, and then 'guide' them to a beehive. Once it has attracted the attention of a 'helper', a honeyguide flies a short way ahead then waits to see if it is being followed. In this way it leads the helper to the hive (and its next meal), which the obliging creature breaks open and robs, while the honeyguide feeds on wax and bees' larvae and eggs.

Kingfishers

Colourful and active, the nine species of kingfishers found in Senegambia can be divided into two groups: those that typically dive into water after fish and tadpoles (and as a consequence are found along waterways); and those less dependent on water because they generally prey on lizards and large insects. Of the former, the giant kingfisher reaches 46cm in size and the jewel-like malachite and the pygmy kingfisher a mere 14cm. Of the not-so-colourful 'forest' kingfishers, the blue-breasted kingfisher is a boldly patterned example.

Barbets & Tinkerbirds

Barbets are closely related to woodpeckers but rather than drilling into bark after grubs, they have strong, broad bills adapted to eating fruit and a variety of insect prey. Most of the region's seven species are found in Senegal. Barbets are often brightly coloured and perch conspicuously; the tinkerbirds are noisy but tiny and sometimes difficult to see.

Bee-Eaters, Rollers & Hoopoe

One of the pleasures of bird-watching in Africa is that beautiful and spectacular species aren't always rare. The various bee-eaters are often brilliant and always watchable; eight members of this colourful family are found in Senegambia. Bee-eaters are commonly seen perched on fences and branches – sometimes in mixed flocks – from which they pursue flying insects, particularly, as their name suggests, bees and wasps. They may congregate in thousands; you won't quickly forget seeing a flock of stunning carmine bee-eaters.

The rollers are closely related to bee-eaters and most of the five species are common. Rollers are not as gaudy as bee-eaters, usually being decked out in blues and mauves; the Abyssinian roller sports two long tail feathers.

Mention should also be made of the hoopoe, a black-and-white bird with a salmon-pink head and neck and a prominent crest.

Owls

These nocturnal birds of prey have soft feathers (which make their flight inaudible) and exceptional hearing, and can turn their heads in a 180-degree arc to locate their prey. Owls have inspired fear and superstition in many cultures, but their elusiveness makes them eagerly sought by bird-watchers. There are 12 species in the region, ranging from the diminutive scops owl to the massive eagle owl, which measures up to 65cm in length. Their prey varies according to the species, from insects, mice and lizards among the smaller species to the roosting birds and small mammals favoured by others. Pel's fishing owl hunts along rivers and feeds exclusively on fish.

Hornbills

Hornbills are medium-sized birds found in forests and woodland. They all sport massive, down-curved bills. The African grey and red-billed hornbills are reasonably common; the extraordinary ground hornbill moves about in groups along the ground and stands nearly 1m high.

Nightjars

These small birds are another nocturnal group but are not related to owls, although their plumage is soft and their flight also silent. Nightjars roost on the ground by day, their subtle colouration making a perfect camouflage among the leaves and twigs. At dusk, they take flight and catch insects. Although they are not uncommon, you may be oblivious to their presence until one takes off near your feet. The identification of several species is difficult and often relies on their call, but when flushed during the day nightjars typically perch on a nearby horizontal branch, allowing a closer look. The incredible standard-winged nightjar is the region's most spectacular example, with two feathers unadorned except at the ends, making the bird seem to be flying flags to herald its flight.

Starlings

Africa is the stronghold of these gregarious and intelligent birds, and there are 11 species found in Senegambia. Several species of the so-called glossy starlings, including purple, long-tailed and blue-eared glossy starlings, may be seen in fast-flying, noisy flocks around the region; all are magnificent birds in iridescent blues and purples, although they may prove an identification challenge when they occur in mixed flocks. The yellow-billed oxpecker is another member of this family and can be seen clinging to livestock from which it prises parasitic ticks and insects.

Cisticolas

These drab little warblers are common and widespread, but sometimes difficult to see and even harder to identify. Many are so similar they are most easily separated by their calls, characteristics which have led to common names such as singing, croaking, siffling and zitting cisticolas. Many of the region's 12 species are typically found in long grass and riverside vegetation.

Finches, Weavers & Widows

This large group includes many small but colourful examples. They are readily seen in flocks along Gambian and Senegalese roads and wherever long grass is found in the region. All are seed eaters and while some, such as the various sparrows, are not spectacular, others develop showy courtship plumage and tail plumes of extraordinary size.

Weavers are usually yellow with varying amounts of black in the plumage and, as seed eaters, can become voracious pests of agriculture. The village weaver often forms big nesting colonies right in the centre of towns. The sparrows come typically in shades of brown and grey; widows are similar while not breeding, but males moult into black plumage with red or yellow highlights when courting. Whydahs, a type of weaver, develop striking tail plumes during courtship; the enormous tail of the exclamatory paradise whydah can be more than twice the bird's body length.

Swifts & Swallows

Although unrelated, these two groups are superficially similar and can be seen chasing flying insects just about anywhere. Both groups have long wings and streamlined bodies adapted to lives in the air; both fly with grace and agility after insects; and both are usually dark in colouration. Swallows, however, differ in one major aspect: they can perch on twigs, fences or even the ground while swifts have weak legs and rarely land except at the nest. In fact, swifts are so adapted to life in the air that some are even known to roost on the wing. There are many examples of the swallow family in Senegal and Gambia; two often seen around human habitation are the red-rumped and mosque swallows.

Sunbirds

Sunbirds are small, delicate nectar feeders with sharp down-curved bills. The males of most species are brilliantly iridescent while the females are drabber. Spectacular species include the pygmy sunbird, whose slender tail plumes almost double its 9cm length, the copper sunbird and the violet-backed sunbird.

WHERE TO LOOK FOR BIRDS IN SENEGAMBIA

Birds will be encountered virtually everywhere in your travels, although weather and temperature can affect bird activity. Both Gambia and Senegal have a number of reserves set up for the protection of wildlife and habitat, and these are good places to concentrate your birdwatching efforts, although some nonprotected areas can also be rewarding. Following is a brief rundown of popular sites; for more details see the relevant destinations in this book.

In Gambia, Abuko Nature Reserve is closest to Banjul and hosts a surprising diversity within its 105 hectares. Many forest species are easier to see here than in other parts of the country and observation hides have been set up. Tanji River Bird Reserve, on the west coast, protects a patchwork of habitat on the flyway for migrating birds. Although it covers only 612 hectares, more than 300 species have been recorded here. Kiang West National Park is one of the country's largest protected areas and a good spot to see a variety of wildlife, including birds. The adjacent Baobolong Wetland Reserve is also very rewarding. Other recommended areas include Niumi National Park, an extension of the Parc National du Delta du Saloum in neighbouring Senegal, and Bijilo Forest Park, which is easy to reach from the Atlantic coast resorts.

Senegal has six national parks, and several other areas set aside as reserves to protect wildlife. Near the mouth of the Senegal River in the north of the country is Parc National de la Langue de Barbarie and Parc National des Oiseaux du Djoudj – both are superb sites famous for flocks of pelicans and flamingoes, and Djoudj is a Unesco World Heritage site where some 400 bird species have been recorded. In the east, the magnificent Parc National de Niokolo-Koba protects more than 9000 sq km of savanna and associated habitats; about 350 bird species have been recorded and this is also the last stronghold of Senegal's large mammal populations. Near Dakar, the Îles de la Madeleine is an excellent spot for watching seabirds, while the beautiful Siné-Saloum Delta, an accessible area of coastal lagoons, mangroves, sandy islands and dry woodland, is also very rewarding.

TIPS FOR WATCHING BIRDS

A pair of binoculars will reveal the subtleties of form and plumage not usually detected by the naked eye. Be warned – once you've seen the shimmering iridescence of a glossy starling or the brash tones of a bee-eater through binoculars you may get hooked! Binoculars will also considerably aid identification and help you nut out the subtle – and vexing – differences occurring between species. They are also useful for spotting shy mammals in areas such as Parc National de Niokolo-Koba.

Basic binoculars can be purchased quite cheaply from duty-free outlets. If you like to keep baggage weight down, there are some very light and compact models available that will still help you get much more from your trip. If you get really serious about bird-watching you may want to invest in better-quality optics; expensive brands such as Leica, Zeiss and Swarovski should last a lifetime and offer unrivalled quality. You may also want to consider the purchase of a spotting scope; they can give you stunning views with a magnification usually at least twice that of binoculars. The drawback is their size (they must be mounted on a tripod for best results); on the other hand, a camera can be attached to some models and a scope then doubles as a telephoto lens.

To help you get the most out of bird-watching, bear the following in mind:

- Try to get an early start because most birds are generally active during the cooler hours of the day. This is particularly so in arid regions and during hot weather.
- Many species are quite approachable and will allow observation and photography if you approach slowly and avoid sudden movements or loud talk.
- Try to dress in drab clothing so as not to stand out. Birds are not usually too concerned about people in a vehicle or boat and stunning views can often be obtained from the roadside. Cruises on the rivers and through mangroves are rewarding and great fun.
- Water birds and waders respond to tidal movements. As tides go out, more food is available and larger flocks are attracted but the birds are spread out; as the tide comes in the birds may be 'pushed' closer to your observation position.
- Do not disturb birds unnecessarily and never handle eggs or young birds in a nest. Adults will readily desert a nest that has been visited, leaving their young to perish.
- Remember that weather and wind can adversely affect viewing conditions and you should not expect to see everything at your first attempt.

RESOURCES
Books

Gambia's popularity as a bird-watching destination has inspired a number of illustrated books and other publications. *A Field Guide to Birds of The Gambia & Senegal* by leading ornithologists Clive Barlow & Tim Wacher, with illustrations by award-winning artist Tony Disley, is undeniably the best. It lists over 660 species, illustrating 570, with colour plates, detailed descriptions and in-depth background information. This 400-page hardback is no featherweight, though, and costs UK£28 in Britain (US$42 in the US), but it's an essential purchase for any serious bird-watcher. It is also available in Gambia.

More portable is *Birds of The Gambia* by M Gore (UK£22) – an annotated checklist with extra information on habitat, distribution and vegetation, illustrated with photographs; it can be hard to find, though.

Another useful guide is *A Birdwatcher's Guide to the Gambia* by Rod Ward, a finely researched book concentrating on birding sites and likely sightings, rather than detailed species descriptions, with 28 maps.

A Field Guide to the Birds of West Africa by W Serle & GJ Morel is part of the long-running Collins field-guide series, with a broader ambit than is usual for this series.

For more detailed information – plus excellent illustrations – on all African birds, refer to the six-volume *Birds of Africa* by EK Urban, CH Fry & S Keith. The newest option is *Birds of Western Africa* by Nick Barrow & Ron Demey, a UK£55, 784-page monster that was released in 2002.

The Internet

Bird-watchers have found the Net an increasingly useful and efficient tool in recent years. While your computer is not actually going to spot the birds for you, the better sites often have lists of recent sightings, guides, tours and other useful information. Some of these include:

African Bird Club Set up by a charity aimed at conservation of bird habitats, this site has features on both Senegal and Gambia and regular bulletins and updates.
  W www.africanbirdclub.org
Gambia Birding This is an excellent site for bird-watchers with reports on what birds are where, how to find a guide, and links to birding tours.
  W www.gambiabirding.org
Gambia Hotspots The address looks unusual but this site is full of good links, photos and trip reports.
  W www.camacdonald.com/birding/africagambia.htm

Bird Guides

There are plenty of advantages in employing the services of a local guide – you can forget about maps and language barriers and expect to meet far more Gambians than you would on your own. In Gambia, local guides have formed a group called Habitat Africa. Organised by Solomon Jallow (W mobile 907694, e habitatafrica@hotmail.com), the group organises itineraries, transport and accommodation. Less formally, the bridge over Kotu Stream, near the Novotel in the Atlantic coast resort of Kotu, is a good bird-watching site and a traditional place to meet other birders and local guides looking for work.

Choose your guide with care – get personal recommendations if you can, and take him out for a few hours first to check his knowledge and approach. A fee of around D30 per hour, or D125 for a morning, is fair. Some guides offer week-long tours of the country for between D750 and D1500 per day, which includes a car and accommodation – but be warned that guides can overcharge wildly, or forget to mention that 'incidentals' (such as meals) are extra. Outright scams also happen. It's worth checking out the Bird Safari Camp's website (W www.bsc.gm/guides.htm) where several guides have been 're-viewed' and their contact details are listed. A couple even offer an online booking service.

Unfortunately there is no equivalent setup in Senegal, and visiting bird-watchers are pretty much on their own.

Regional Facts for the Visitor

This chapter covers information common to both Gambia and Senegal. For country-specific information, see the individual Facts for the Visitor chapters.

HIGHLIGHTS

In this part of Africa the atmosphere of the places, and the activities of their people, are often more interesting than tangible tourist 'sights'. You could tick off a city's official attractions (such as the mosque and museum) in half a day, but if you spend time strolling through the markets, sitting in pavement cafés to watch the world go by, or talking to the locals, you'll get much more out of your visit.

With that in mind, you could have a memorable trip in Gambia and Senegal without seeing any of the highlights mentioned at the beginning of each chapter. In fact, some travellers might avoid them, precisely *because* they are in this book! Still, some places (such as Île de Gorée) are unique and particularly fascinating, and worth making an effort to reach. If you don't like what we like, you can always go somewhere else – that's what travel is all about.

SUGGESTED ITINERARIES

Where to go depends on the time and money you have available, but the main factor affecting the number of places you can reach will be your form of transport. Although some people drive from Europe and tour Gambia and Senegal in their own vehicle, most travellers use buses and trains for their trip, and get to most places this way at a fairly low cost, albeit sometimes quite slowly. A hire car or organised tour cuts delays, but is much more pricey.

If time is limited, it's far better to concentrate on just one or two places rather than rushing around only skimming the surface.

One to Two Weeks

Cheap charter flights and quick flying times from Europe mean a visit of just one or two weeks is a very popular option. If you fly into Banjul, you could spend a few days on the Atlantic coast beaches with a few days touring upcountry Gambia, following the great river upstream to the old colonial outpost of Georgetown and the busy trading centre of Basse Santa Su. Or you could cross the border into Senegal, to explore the waterways of the Siné-Saloum Delta, or relax in Kafountine or the tranquil villages of Casamance.

If you fly into Dakar you could spend a day or two visiting the frenetic markets and peaceful Île de Gorée, before heading north to St-Louis and the nearby bird reserves, or south to the beaches of the Petite Côte and the Siné-Saloum Delta. One week isn't enough to do all this, but with two weeks you could combine some of these options into a fascinating holiday.

Three to Four Weeks

With three weeks the options expand further. You could fly into Dakar and do a circular tour, heading south to the Petite Côte, Siné-Saloum and Kaolack before going east to Tambacounda, then returning through Gambia, via Basse Santa Su and Georgetown, to Banjul (with maybe a visit to the coast) and then back to Dakar for the return flight. Of course, this circuit could be done by starting and ending at Banjul. Another option would be to do the eastward leg through Gambia and the westward leg through the beautiful Casamance region, to Ziguinchor and the beaches at Cap Skiring before returning north for your flight home. To do all this might be a rush in three weeks, but four should be enough.

Five Weeks to Three Months

With five or six weeks, or even two months, you could do the above route in a more relaxed manner, include excursions off the circuit to the great mosque at Touba, Parc National de Niokolo-Koba and the little-visited wilds of Bassari country in the far southeast. Or you might want to slow down for a while in one place to take advantage of the many cultural courses available in the tourist areas.

A grand tour of around three months could start in Dakar, head down the coast, through the deltas of Siné-Saloum, across the Gambia River to Banjul (an alternative start for this circuit), and onwards down the coast to Kafountine or deeper south to explore the backwaters and sandy tracks of Casamance, or relax on the beaches at Cap Skiring. From here, you could go inland, through the eastern part of Casamance, or along the Trans-Gambia Hwy to enter Gambia at Soma, where you can visit the famous weekly market at Farafenni, before going on to Georgetown and Basse Santa Su. From there head to Tambacounda in Senegal and visit the wilderness of Parc National de Niokolo-Koba and the culturally fascinating and scenically stunning Bassari country. Then go west to Kaolack and Thiès, with a branch north to Touba or St-Louis, or take the rarely travelled Senegal River route, skirting the country's northern border with Mauritania, passing through the former colonial outposts of Bakel, Matam and Podor to reach St-Louis from the north. From there return to Dakar to finish your trip.

PLANNING
When to Go

The best time to visit Gambia and Senegal is the period from November to February, when conditions are dry and relatively cool.

From December to February is also the local trading season, when the harvest is completed (assuming the rains have come when they were supposed to). Everybody is more relaxed, perhaps with a bit of extra money to spend, so the markets are noticeably busier at this time. From March to May, the weather is dry but hotter. From June to October is the wet season, which is usually considered not as good for travelling. However, some travellers prefer this time as there are fewer tourists, vegetation is greener and the rains usually last only a few hours a day, or fall at night. The periods just before and after the wet season can be uncomfortable, though: conditions are humid and there are no storms to clear the air.

The main problem during the wet season is getting around. Most major roads are tar or all-weather dirt, but minor roads can be turned to mud or virtually washed away. If you are in a 4WD, then you'll probably be OK, but on public transport you may have no hope of reaching some of the more remote spots. If you plan to do a lot of upcountry travel during the rains, you'll need patience, a sense of humour and a good book.

Most of the larger national parks and wildlife reserves are closed from June to November or December, as rain makes tracks impassable. However, if you are visiting just to take photographs, the wet season offers clearer air and allows better shots, whereas during the harmattan season the skies get very dusty (see the boxed text

Visits during Ramadan

The Islamic holy month of Ramadan affords a whole set of challenges for the traveller. During Ramadan, Muslims cannot eat, drink, smoke or have sex from dawn until dusk. And while most people do their best to remain friendly and even-tempered, the sacrifices do take their toll, especially at the end of the day.

Cooked food is harder to come by, and eating in public could earn you deathly looks. Public transport will stop more diligently at prayer times, and is guaranteed to stop at the nearest eatery when the sun sets. You'll find work slows almost to a stop as the day wears on and businesses that usually open into the evening close their doors nearer to 4.30pm. People will be less likely to engage you in conversation and could be downright rude. Don't take offence. While no-one expects non-Muslims to fast, some travellers try for a day or two to get a better idea of what the rest of the country is experiencing.

'The Harmattan' in the Facts about Senegambia chapter).

The final aspect to consider is the tourist season. Some coastal areas of Gambia and Senegal are packed with European sunbathers on package tours from December to March (and, to a lesser extent, in November and April) and a few places inland can also be quite busy. There are, however, many parts of Gambia and Senegal you can enjoy in glorious isolation – even at the height of the tourist season.

See the individual country chapters for information on festivals such as the St-Louis jazz festival in northern Senegal, and the International Roots Festival in Gambia. Lonely Planet's *Read This First: Africa* is also worth a look, particularly if your trip includes several countries.

What Kind of Trip

In both Gambia and Senegal, once you get away from the coast and the national parks, tourist facilities are limited. If you generally travel at the luxury end of the market, Gambia and Senegal have few top-class hotels outside the capitals, and offer very little in the way of exclusive wildlife lodges or tented camps as found in East or Southern Africa.

Independent travellers on tighter budgets are well catered for, although there are few of the backpacker lodges or cheap and cheerful safaris found elsewhere on the continent. However, most parts of the region can be reached by public transport (of variable quality) and in a lot of towns accommodation is available (similarly variable). Generally speaking, the cost of travel here is higher than in East or Southern Africa, and noticeably more than most parts of Asia, although it's cheaper than Europe.

Maps

Most maps of Senegal also show Gambia, but the level of detail on the smaller country is generally poor. Macmillan's *Traveller's Map of Gambia* (at a scale of 1:400,000) is by far the best – clear and easy to read, with most roads marked, plus tourist sights and places of interest – but can be hard to find. The most widely available map of Gambia is the 1:350,000 effort by Canadian group International Travel Maps. This is not bad, but there are several errors that can be frustrating. For Senegal, the locally produced *Carte du Senegal* (1:912,000) is the best and cheapest available and includes an excellent street map of Dakar, though its hard to find outside Senegal. Also good for country coverage is the *Senegal Carte Routière* (1:1,000,000) produced by the Institut Géographique National (IGN). Not as good, but more widely available internationally, is ITMB's *Senegal, Including Gambia* (1:800,000).

If your journey through Gambia and Senegal is part of wider travels in West Africa, the Michelin map *Africa – North & West* (sheet number 953, formerly number 153) is one of the few maps in the world to have achieved something like classic status. The detail is incredible, given the limitations of scale (1:4,000,000), and the map is regularly updated (check the date on the back cover to make sure you buy a recent version). You should expect a few discrepancies between the map and reality, particularly with regard to roads, as old tracks get upgraded and once-smooth highways become potholed disasters. However, no overland driver would be without this map. There's even a 153 Club (**W** www.manntaylor.com/153.html) for those people who have driven across the Sahara and around West Africa.

What to Bring

Temperatures are generally hot or warm (see Climate in the Facts about Senegambia chapter), so you won't need many clothes. The duration of your journey makes little difference to the amount of kit needed, so you should be able to keep things pretty light.

Clothes For day-to-day travel, all you need is a couple of pairs of trousers, or trousers and a skirt; two or three shirts; shorts; socks and underwear; and a pair of shoes plus sandals/flip-flops (thongs). A sunhat is essential, and a sweatshirt is useful from December to February for chilly dawn starts. Generally, military-style clothing or baggage is not appropriate because you may be taken for a soldier.

Second-Hand Clothes

The market stalls of Senegambia are loaded up with second-hand clothes, mostly collected by charities in Europe. You can also find factory overruns and items off-loaded by stores because they're out of fashion in the West. Most of these clothes are sold to commercial concerns that ship them to Africa in bulk. Traders then buy clothes by the bale and sell them individually in markets. The clothes are generally of good quality, selling for a fraction of what they'd cost new, so local people aren't having to fork out hard-earned money for fancy gear. But there's a downside: the second-hand imports have seriously hampered any chance of Africa's poorer countries establishing their own clothing industry. All over the region, tailors, who used to run up shirts and trousers from local material, are going out of business.

Anything you find yourself without can easily be bought along the way. In Banjul and Dakar or large towns, new clothes are priced comparably to or cheaper than those in Europe, and in many markets you can find decent second-hand clothes (see the boxed text).

It might be worth taking a smart shirt and pair of trousers or skirt to bring out for official occasions (such as visa applications) or if you're invited to somebody's house. If you visit during the rains, a waterproof jacket completes your outfit.

Equipment Absolute essentials include basic medical kit, mosquito net and repellent, water bottle, purifying solution, water filter, sunscreen (all covered under Health later in this chapter), a torch (flashlight) and spare batteries. A sheet liner will be useful in cheap hotels where bedding may be nonexistent or less than appealing.

Generally, it's not worth lugging around a tent and camping gear. There are few camping grounds in Gambia or Senegal (those that do exist cater mainly for travellers with their own vehicle), and, unless you've got your own set of wheels, there are very few opportunities for bush camping.

Optional items include camera and film, binoculars for wildlife- and bird-watching, universal washbasin plug and washing soap, small padlock to secure the contents of your pack from opportunistic thieves, travel alarm, pen knife, small calculator, length of cord for drying clothes or securing the mozzie net, sewing kit, paperbacks (books in English are difficult to find), and French–English phrasebook or dictionary.

Don't forget boring things such as a wash kit and towel (although some travellers class those as optional too).

Backpack Carrying all your gear in a backpack (rucksack) is the most practical option. When buying a backpack pay special attention to the strength of zips and straps. Many travellers favour 'travel packs', the type that turn into a normal-looking hold-all, and keep straps out of the way when it's being kicked about the world's airports and bus stations. The large, striped, woven-nylon bags found at markets all over the world are very useful for putting your whole pack inside before it's deposited onto the roof of your local transport. They're not completely waterproof but will keep most of the water and dust off your pack.

A smaller day-pack is useful and will probably be used far more often than your big pack, which spends most of its life on the floor of your room. However, in places where theft is a problem, a day-pack is a notice to all thieves saying 'all my valuables are in here', so don't be surprised if it attracts attention.

RESPONSIBLE TOURISM

Tourism itself is a major issue. A problem arises when destinations cannot cope with the number of tourists they attract, so that natural and social environments quickly become damaged.

Another environmental issue, particularly relevant for visitors to Africa, is the growth of so-called 'ecotourism'. Some travel companies claim to be practising 'ecotourism' just because they do things outdoors, but in reality activities such as desert-driving, hiking, camping, boating, wildlife-viewing and sightseeing trips to remote and fragile areas *can* be more environmentally or culturally harmful than a conventional holiday in a developed resort. Environmentalists point out that tourism relies on natural resources, such as healthy wildlife populations, clean rivers and rich cultural traditions, but quite often does little to maintain, sustain or restore them and may degrade them.

If you would like to support tour companies with a good environmental record, you have to look beyond the glossy brochures and vague 'ecofriendly' claims and ask what they are really doing to protect or support the environment – remember, that includes the local people, as well as animals and plants.

Visitors to Gambia, Senegal or any other part of the world are often asked by environmental organisations to spend as much of their holiday budget as possible in a way that ensures it stays within the 'host' country for the benefit of the local people. Gambia had a brief flirtation with the antithesis of this form of spreading the wealth when the government allowed operators to sell Caribbean-style 'all-inclusive' holidays. With these packages tourists pay for everything (flight, accommodation, food, drinks and activities) in their home country, and if they didn't buy any postcards or souvenirs then they didn't have to spend a single cent in Gambia. Thankfully these tours were banned before the local bars, restaurants, taxi drivers and anybody else trying to provide a similar service suffered too much.

Of course, the majority of visitors to Senegambia still come on self-catering or bed-and-breakfast deals, but they still contribute to local economies. Almost everything spent by independent travellers, backpackers and overland truck passengers goes to the local economy.

The effects of tourism are not just economic. It is important for visitors to behave in a manner that limits their impact on the natural environment and the local residents, human and animal. Some ideas are listed here. To be a responsible tourist you have to question some of your own actions and those of tour companies providing the services and facilities you use. You also have to look pretty closely at the actions of governments, both locally and internationally. Being a responsible tourist doesn't mean you have to get depressed and spoil your holiday. In fact, asking a few questions and getting a deeper insight can make your trip even more rewarding. The following guidelines may help:

- Support local enterprise by patronising locally owned hotels, restaurants, tour companies and shops, where possible.
- Don't buy items made from endangered species.
- Ask permission before photographing people. If they refuse, respect their wishes.
- Dress conservatively; cover your arms and legs (this applies to men and women). Women should wear a skirt well below the knees, or loose-fitting trousers, and cover the head and shoulders with a scarf.
- Women are not allowed to enter some mosques if prayers are in progress or if the imam (Islamic leader) is present.
- When you visit a mosque, take off your shoes.
- If you have hired a guide or taxi driver for the day, be aware that he'll want to say his prayers at the right times. When travelling, three times a day is allowed, so look out for the signs indicating he wants a few moments off, particularly around midday, late afternoon and sunset. Travellers on buses and bush taxis should be prepared for prayer stops at around the same time.
- Despite the Islamic proscription against alcohol, some Muslims may enjoy a drink. Even so, it's impolite to drink alcohol in their presence unless they show approval.

Membership of a British organisation called Tourism Concern costs UK£24 per year. For more information, check its website at W www.tourismconcern.org.uk. In the USA, the Rethinking Tourism Project (W www .rethinkingtourism.org) is similar.

You may also like to contact the locally based organisation called Gambia Tourism Concern (☎ 462057, fax 466180, W www .gambiatourismconcern.com), whose office is at Bakadaji Hotel (☎ 462307) in Kotu, near Banjul. Visitors are welcome.

VISAS & DOCUMENTS
Passport
A full passport is essential for entering both Gambia and Senegal. Some officials prefer passports that expire at least three months after your trip ends, so change yours if it's near the end of its life.

You could encounter trouble in Gambia or Senegal if your passport carries an Israeli stamp, although there is no official policy on this.

Visas
Depending on your nationality, you could need to buy a visa and have it stamped in your passport in order to enter one or both of Gambia and Senegal. If you do need a visa, or you're not sure, call the nearest Senegalese or Gambian embassy or consulate to find out. While you're talking to them, ask how long it takes to issue the visa, and whether you need to enter the country within a certain period. For details on who needs a visa and where to find one, see each country's Facts for the Visitor chapter. It's important to note that regulations change from time to time, so it's best to check at the relevant embassy, or on a website such as ⓦ www.lonelyplanet.com, before you arrive at the airport or border.

In addition to single-entry visas, some embassies also issue multiple-entry visas. This can be handy if you're flying into Senegal and then visiting Gambia before returning to Senegal for your return flight (or vice versa).

Visa Agencies It's distinctly possible, and in Gambia's case highly likely, that your attempts to get a visa will be frustrated by a lack of the relevant embassy. If so, or if you can't get to an embassy during their brief opening hours, you might want to use a visa agency. These companies can get any visa on your behalf, and several major flight agencies also offer this service.

Shop around because fees vary considerably, especially when the agency has to arrange to get the visa from another country. A final word of warning: Start the process early. Count on at least four weeks, though it will be less if you can download an application form from the Internet.

Visas at Borders & Airports At some borders, such as the Gambian border near Karang, you can get a visa on arrival. This works well if you are, for example, an EU citizen who doesn't need to pay. However, it can be rather bothersome if you come from a country whose nationals are seldom seen at the particular post. If possible, sort out your visa before you arrive.

At major airports, immigration staff will usually issue you with a visa on the spot (usually after some hassling and the payment of relevant fees). If you decide to take the risk and wait until you fly in, then make sure you look decent, have ample funds and have a good story as to why you couldn't get a visa (eg, there was no embassy in the country you've just flown in from). This scheme will probably not work if you're flying in from outside Africa because the airlines won't let you on the plane without a visa.

Travel Insurance
An insurance policy covering you for medical expenses and an emergency flight home is essential. Hospitals in Senegambia are not free, and the good ones are not cheap. Air ambulances and international medical evacuation (medivac) flights are frighteningly expensive, so you need to be fully covered.

Most travel insurance also covers your baggage in case of loss, and for other events such as cancellation or hijack. (It's important to read the small print, but some aspects they cover are enough to put you off flying!) It's possible to get medical travel insurance only; however, in our experience there is generally little difference in price for such policies covering Africa.

If your flight agent, insurance broker or credit-card company can't help you with a good policy, try a student travel service. It's preferable to get a policy from an insurance company that will directly pay any costs you incur, rather than reimburse you after you pay your bills.

Other Documents

It is essential to have a vaccination certificate to show you've been jabbed for yellow fever (see Health later in this chapter for details). Also useful will be your driver's licence and an international driving permit (if you intend hiring a car), and a student or young person's identity card (occasionally good for various discounts).

Copies

Photocopies of all your important documents, plus airline tickets and credit cards, will help speed up replacement if they are lost or stolen. Keep these records and a list of travellers cheque numbers separate from other valuables, and also leave copies with someone at home so they can be faxed to you in an emergency.

EMBASSIES & CONSULATES

For practical purposes, the term 'embassy' in this chapter encompasses consulates and high commissions as well as embassies. In some parts of Africa, countries are represented by an honorary consul (not a full-time diplomat, but usually an expatriate working in a local business or aid project who performs limited diplomatic duties on behalf of citizens). A list of embassies in the region, and Senegal's and Gambia's representatives abroad, is included in each country's Facts for the Visitor chapter.

MONEY

The unit of currency in Gambia is the dalasi (D), while Senegal uses the CFA franc. For detailed information on these currencies, see the country-specific Facts for the Visitor chapters.

In this chapter we have quoted prices in US dollars (US$) as these rates are likely to remain stable; however, local currencies may go up and down.

Exchanging Money

In Senegal and Gambia, major international currencies such as euros, US dollars and British pounds (in the form of cash or travellers cheques) can be changed in banks in the capital cities, major towns and tourist

---

Your Own Embassy

It's important to realise what your country's embassy can and can't do. Generally speaking, it won't be much help in emergencies if the trouble you're in is remotely your own fault. Remember that you are bound by the laws of the country you are in. Your embassy will not be sympathetic if you end up in jail after committing a crime locally, even if such actions are legal in your own country.

In genuine emergencies you might get some assistance, but only if other channels have been exhausted. For example, if you need to get home urgently, a free ticket is exceedingly unlikely – the embassy would expect you to have insurance. If you have all your money and documents stolen, it might assist with getting a new passport, but a loan for onward travel is out of the question. Embassies generally do not keep letters for travellers, and you can't expect them to have recent editions of home newspapers for your perusal.

On a more positive note, if you're travelling in remote or politically volatile areas, such as Casamance in Senegal, you might consider registering with your embassy so its staff know where you are. If you do this, make sure you tell them when you return or they could charge you for the cost of any search.

---

areas. In the cities, if you get stuck without money and the banks are closed, you can usually change money at hotel reception desks, although rates are often lousy or commissions high. Another option is to try asking discreetly at a shop selling imported items. Saying something like 'The banks are closed and I have US dollars – do you know anyone who can help me...?' is better than 'Do you want to change money?'

If you're heading to remote parts of these countries or to other parts of West Africa, euros might be a better bet than dollars or pounds, particularly in the CFA countries.

Cash & Travellers Cheques The best way to carry your money is as a mix of cash and travellers cheques. Cash is quicker to deal with and gets better rates, but cannot be replaced if they go missing. If your travellers cheques are lost or stolen, you can get a refund. Well-known brands of cheque are better to deal with as they're instantly recognised by bank staff.

Carrying some of your money in euros is recommended and you can easily buy them (in cash or travellers cheques) at any bank or major travel agent before you leave home. A mixture of high and low denomination notes

and cheques means you can change small amounts when necessary.

Because of counterfeiting, old US$100 notes and some other older notes are not accepted at places that don't have a light machine for checking watermarks.

ATMs Automated teller machines exist in Banjul, Dakar, tourist resorts and a few major towns in Senegal. Theoretically they accept credit and debit cards from banks with

New Currencies

By 2004 Gambia, Senegal and 13 other West African countries will share a single currency. Well, that's the plan anyway. You can expect the central bankers of Europe – who spent close to 10 years arguing, posturing and trying to meet various 'convergence criteria' before the euro finally hit the streets – to be at least a little sceptical as the Economic Community of West African States (Ecowas) tries to introduce two new currency unions in just four years.

Ecowas and its member states reason that a single currency, combined with common customs laws, common tariff levels and open borders, will help achieve regional economic integration and eventually prosperity in this, the poorest region on earth. The member states agreed to kick off this grand scheme by creating a West African Central Bank, to begin operating by September 2002. The launch of the two currencies will then follow.

First, in 2003, Gambia will join Nigeria, Ghana, Guinea, Liberia and Sierra Leone in introducing a currency known (until the naming competition is held) as the West Africa Second Monetary Zone (WAMZ). The launch depends on all the countries meeting the aforementioned convergence criteria, something only Gambia and Nigeria had managed by April 2002.

The second phase of the plan begins in 2004. Just as Gambians and the populations of five other countries are getting used to the WAMZ, they will be asked to go through the whole process again when their new currency merges with the CFA, which is used in Senegal plus seven other former French colonies in West Africa. The result: a currency that can be used in 14 of the 15 Ecowas states (so far no-one's mentioned the Cape Verde escudo).

So what does it mean for travellers? In the long term, not having to change and rechange your hard-earned as you travel through West Africa will be great, and will drastically reduce the chances of being ripped off every time you cross a border. In the short term, things aren't so positive. Ecowas has said the Gambian dalasi and the CFA, along with all the other local currencies, will have a fixed relationship with the new currency as well as with each other. All of the old national currencies will be phased out over time, and this is where it gets scary. During the transition periods everyone from market traders to bankers is likely to be confused. The rate of the dalasi will, in theory, continue to float against the US dollar, the euro and other hard currencies. But it will be fixed against the new regional currency, meaning you could buy dalasis on the street at a rate vastly different from (and better than) that being offered in the bank. At the same time the regional currency will be floating against the euro while the CFA is fixed, again leading to potentially big differences in official and black-market rates. Of course, the hard and fast plan for all this change has yet to be finalised. It's possible that the whole thing could be scrapped or thrown into the 'too hard' basket, but more likely are a series of delays as the creaking bureaucracy of West Africa attempts to absorb such an overwhelming change. Whatever the outcome, keep an ear out for the latest news before you leave home.

reciprocal agreements. Banks and card companies often use very fair exchange rates, which can make drawing money from the wall cheaper than changing travellers cheques. ATMs in Senegambia are by no means perfect, but we found them fairly reliable. Some banks only take Visa card; others also deal with MasterCard and the Cirrus, Maestro and Plus networks.

Credit & Debit Cards You can use credit cards (or charge cards) to pay for some items, but their use is usually limited to mid-range and top-end hotels and restaurants, car rental, air tickets and some tours. American Express (AmEx) and Visa are the most widely accepted.

You can also use a credit card to draw cash at banks in the capital cities and a growing number of other large towns or places used to handling tourists – but don't rely completely on your plastic, as computer breakdowns can leave you stranded.

Your card company will tell you which banks in Gambia and Senegal will accept your card. You'll also need to ask your bank or card company about charges, and arrange a way to pay card bills if you're travelling for more than a month or so, perhaps on the Internet. Debit cards can be used to draw cash and because there's no bill to pay off they are good for longer journeys.

International Transfers If you think your finances may need topping up while you're travelling, you could ask your bank about international bank-to-bank transfers. Even if you're lucky and your bank has links with a bank in your destination country, it can still be a complicated, time-consuming and expensive business, especially when you get outside Banjul and Dakar. Faster and a lot simpler than banks is Western Union Money Transfer, where all you need to do is phone someone with money, get them to send their cash and tell you the password, and bingo, the money's there.

Black Market You can sometimes get more local currency for your hard currency by using the so-called black market. In both

Bank Charges & Commissions

Generally, whenever you change money you have to pay something to the bank – that's how it makes its profit. The charge can be a flat fee (of around US$2), but sometimes it's a commission quoted as a percentage of the amount you change (usually between 1% and 2%). Sometimes you have to pay a charge in addition to a commission.

Alternatively there may be no charge or commission at all, but this doesn't necessarily mean it's a better deal, as the bank instead may make its money from the lower rate it offers you. For example, Bank A may give you CFA500 to the US dollar, and charge a commission of 2%. Over the street, Bank B may not charge any commission but only give you CFA480 per US dollar. Keep this in mind when looking around.

If you're dealing with CFA francs and euros, much of this is academic. The rate is fixed at 655:1 and all you need to compare between banks is the charge or commission.

Gambia and Senegal this is illegal and there's a fair chance you'll be scammed out of some of your money, or lose the lot in an outright robbery. In Senegal, the black market is hardly an issue because the CFA franc is fixed to the euro and you get the same rate wherever you change. You may be offered a few percent more than bank rates by shady-looking characters on the street, but it's likely to be a setup. If they offer more than 10%, you *know* it's a setup. Sleight-of-hand tricks are common; some dealers even work with corrupt police and can trap you in a setup where you may get 'arrested', scared to death and eventually lose all your money.

Sometimes unofficial moneychangers are the only option, though. For example, if you're travelling overland from Senegal to Gambia, you won't find a bank at the frontier, but moneychangers wait for customers at the border posts and ferry crossings, which are major transport bottlenecks. This is a fairly standard procedure and the moneychangers work quite openly under the eyes of police and custom officials. It's important to be alert though – count your money carefully and look for stunts such as notes folded in half.

In Gambia, you'll find moneychangers by the truckload around markets, banks and post offices. Dealing with these guys out in the open can be risky, but most of them are working for legitimate businessmen desperate for hard currency (see the boxed text 'Pockets Full of Money' in Gambia's Facts for the Visitor chapter).

Security

To keep your money and other valuables (such as passport and air ticket) safe from pickpockets, the best place is out of sight under a shirt or skirt or inside your trousers. Some travellers use a pouch or money belt that goes around their necks or waists, while others go for invisible pockets and other imaginative devices.

Costs

Travel costs in Gambia and Senegal are around 50% of what they are in Europe, Australasia and North America. Locally produced items (including food and beer) may be much cheaper, while imported items such as film might be twice what they cost in the West. Accommodation costs from about the equivalent of US$6 per night for a bed in a very basic local resthouse through to US$10 to US$15 for something a bit more comfortable. You'll pay US$25 to US$50 for mid-range hotels, and US$100 or US$200 for top-notch establishments. Couples can save on accommodation costs, as double rooms are normally about 25% to 50% more than for singles.

Food is very cheap if you eat from markets and road-side stalls (where it's often good) and shoestringers can survive on a few dollars a day. If you go to local restaurants, meals range from US$2 up to US$5, or US$8 in smarter places. In capital cities, several restaurants cater mainly for foreigners and serve international cuisine, which can easily cost US$30 for two at a restaurant, and more in a fancy hotel. More details are given under Accommodation and Food later in this chapter.

Transport options are equally varied. You can hitchhike for nothing (though you may be asked to pay) or go by chartered plane at a couple of dollars a minute. Renting a car can easily cost US$100 a day or more. Most people go by bush taxi, bus or train, and throughout Senegambia you can work on about US$1 to US$2 per 100km travelling this way.

You should take into account extra items such as visa fees, and national park entrance charges, plus the cost of organised tours or activities where you will need to hire local guides.

Taking all these aspects into account, shoestring travellers could get by on about US$12 per day. For a bit more comfort, US$15 to US$25 per day is a reasonable budget. With US$30 to US$50 per day at your disposal, you can stay in decent hotels, eat well and travel comfortably (whenever comfortable transport is available!).

Tipping

Tipping can be a problem in Senegal and Gambia (as in many other parts of Africa) because there are few clear rules. The situation is further complicated because tipping is related to the concept of *cadeaux*, a term used for tips, gifts and bribes (see Gifts & Tips under Dangers & Annoyances later in this chapter).

Tipping (as understood by Westerners) in Gambia and Senegal is only expected from the wealthy. This means well-to-do locals and nearly all foreign visitors. Anyone staying in an upmarket hotel is expected to tip porters and other staff, but there is not the same expectation from a backpacker in a cheap hotel.

Everyone is expected to tip around 10% at the better restaurants, but you'll find this is often included in the bill at restaurants and hotels in Senegal. At the other end of the scale are the more basic restaurants and eating-houses where no tipping is expected from anyone. There's a grey area between these two classes of restaurants, where tipping is rarely expected from locals, but may be expected of wealthy-looking foreigners.

In privately hired taxis, tipping is not the rule among locals, but drivers do expect well-heeled travellers to tip about 10%. In shared taxis tipping is almost unheard of.

Bargaining

In some African countries, bargaining over prices – often for market goods – is a way of life. People from the West are used to everything having a fixed price and often have difficulty with the idea of bargaining, whereas in Africa commodities are often considered worth whatever their seller can get for them. It really is no different to the concept of an auction and should be treated as one more aspect of travel in the region.

Basic Market Goods In markets selling basic items such as fruit and vegetables, some traders may raise their asking prices when they see you, a wealthy foreigner. If you pay this, whether out of ignorance or out of guilt about how much you have compared with the locals, you may be considered foolish, but you'll also be doing fellow travellers a disservice by creating the impression that all foreigners are willing to pay any price named! You may also harm the local economy: By paying high prices you put some items out of the locals' reach. And who can blame the sellers – why sell something to a local when a foreigner will pay twice as much?

That said, many sellers will quote you the same price that locals pay, particularly away from cities or tourist areas. You shouldn't expect everybody to charge high prices. Obviously it helps to know the price of things, and after a few days (when you'll inevitably pay over the odds a few times) you'll learn the standard prices for basic items. Remember though that prices can change depending on where you buy. For example, a soft drink in a city may be a third of the price you'll pay in a remote rural area, where additional transport costs have to be paid for. Conversely, fruit and vegetables are cheaper in the areas where they're grown.

Souvenirs At craft and curio stalls, where items are specifically for tourists, bargaining is very much expected. The vendor's aim is to identify the highest price you're willing to pay. Your aim is to find the price below which the vendor will not sell. People have all sorts of formulae for working out what this should be, but there are no hard-and-fast rules. Some vendors may initially ask a price two to ten times higher than they're prepared to accept. You decide what you want to pay or what others have told you they've paid; your first offer should be about half this. On hearing your offer, the vendor may laugh or feign outrage, while you plead abject poverty. The vendor's price then starts to drop from the original quote to a more realistic level. When it does, you begin making better offers until you arrive at a mutually agreeable price. And that's the crux – mutually agreeable. You hear travellers all the time moaning about how they were 'overcharged' by souvenir sellers. When things have no fixed price, nobody really gets overcharged. If you don't like the price, it's simple – don't pay it.

Some people prefer to conduct their bargaining in a stern manner, but the best results seem to come from a friendly and spirited exchange. There's no reason to lose your temper when bargaining. If the effort seems a waste of time, politely take your leave. Sometimes sellers will call you back if they think their stubbornness is counterproductive. Very few will pass up the chance of making a sale, however thin the profit.

If sellers won't come down to a price you feel is fair (or that you can afford), it means either that they really aren't making any profit, or that if you don't pay their prices, they know somebody else will. Remember the sellers are no more obliged to sell to you than you are to buy from them. You can go elsewhere or, if you really want the item, accept the price. This is the raw edge of capitalism!

Some tourists do not enjoy the prospect of bargaining, fearful of being overcharged or afraid of insulting the trader with an insultingly low offer. Note, though, that a few souvenir shops and stalls do offer items at a fixed price.

POST & COMMUNICATIONS

Post and telephone services are quite reliable in both Gambia and Senegal, but the service to and from towns and cities tends to be better than in rural areas. It definitely pays to make your calls or send your mail from the main centres. In both countries the postal services are relatively cheap, so if you're on a longer trip it could be worth holding off until you arrive before sending the next big instalment of your life back home. For postcards or any sort of stationery or packaging materials, the cheapest places are almost always located outside the post office. For details such as rates and prices, see Post & Communications in each country's Facts for the Visitor chapter.

Sending Mail
Letters sent from Dakar or Banjul take about a week to reach most parts of Europe, and eight to 15 days to reach North America or Australasia. Don't rely on this – sometimes it can take three times longer for a letter to arrive.

Receiving Mail
If you need to receive mail, you can use the poste restante service, where letters are sent to a post office (usually in a capital city) for you to collect. For details, see the country-specific Facts for the Visitor chapters.

To collect your mail, go to the main post office and show your passport. Letters sometimes take a few weeks to work through the system, so have them sent to a place where you're going to be for a while, or will be passing through more than once.

It's essential to write your name clearly in capital letters. If you can't find mail you're expecting, check under your other names. Ask people writing to use just your family name and initials. If your family name is common, it should be underlined with your given name written in lower case.

Telephone & Fax
Most cities and large towns have public telephone offices (either as part of the post office or privately run operations) where you can make international calls and send faxes. Connections between Senegambia and Europe/USA/Australasia have improved in recent years because international

calls now go by satellite. Calls between African countries, however, are sometimes relayed through Europe, in which case the reception is usually bad – *if* you can get a call through.

To phone Senegal or Gambia from another country, you need to dial your country's international access code (for example, ☎ 00 or ☎ 010), then the country code: ☎ 220 for Gambia, or ☎ 221 for Senegal. There are no area codes in Gambia or Senegal.

To phone overseas from either Gambia or Senegal, first dial the international access code (☎ 00 for both Gambia and Senegal), then the code of the country you want to reach, then the city code (omitting the first zero if applicable), and then, finally, the individual number.

Note that in Gambia's public Gamtel offices, and some other telephone centres in Gambia and Senegal, you might have to dial an extra zero before the number. Check with the office clerk before making your call just to make sure.

Mobile (Cell) Phones
Both Gambia and Senegal have steadily expanding GSM networks. There are a couple of options in each country, with cheap SIM cards available and prepaid cards coming in a variety of denominations. Note, however, that you don't have to get too far off the beaten track before your service disappears. See the individual Facts for the Visitor chapters for specifics.

Email & Internet Access
Access to the Internet is becoming increasingly easy and cheap in Gambia and Senegal; in Dakar and the tourist areas of the Atlantic coast in Gambia the service is world-class. See the individual Facts for the Visitor chapters for more details on Internet access.

Unless you're planning on staying in expensive hotels there's not much point in bringing your notebook or palmtop computer with you as you'll need to be very lucky indeed to find a phone jack. Even if there is a jack, at the time of writing none of the major ISPs had local dial-in numbers, meaning connecting to the Net could be both very slow and very expensive. If you do bring a computer, invest in a universal AC adaptor, a plug adaptor for each country you visit, and a reputable 'global' modem. Telephone sockets will probably be different too, so bring at least a US RJ-11 adaptor that works with your modem. For more information on travelling with a portable computer, see W www.teleadapt .com or W www.warrior.com.

If your Internet email account is hosted by a smaller ISP or your office or school network, your best option is to rely on cybercafés and other public access points to collect your mail. To do this, you'll need to carry three pieces of information: your incoming (POP or IMAP) mail server name, your account name and your password. Your ISP or network supervisor will be able to give you these. Armed with this information, you should be able to access your Internet mail account from any Internet-connected machine in the world, provided it runs some kind of email software (Netscape and Internet Explorer both have mail modules).

Of course, the easiest thing to do is get yourself a free eKno account (W www.ekno .lonelyplanet.com) and access it from any Internet café on earth. Saves on luggage too.

DIGITAL RESOURCES
The World Wide Web is a rich resource for travellers. You can research your trip, hunt down bargain air fares, book hotels, check on weather conditions or chat with locals and other travellers about the best places to visit (or avoid!).

A good place to begin your Internet explorations is the Lonely Planet website (W www.lonelyplanet.com). Here you'll find succinct summaries on travelling to most places on earth, postcards from other travellers, and the Thorn Tree bulletin board, where you can ask questions before you go or dispense advice when you get back. You can also find travel news and updates to many of our most popular guidebooks, and the sub-WWWay section links you to the most useful travel resources elsewhere on the web.

Other useful sites include:

All Africa.com Quite simply the most thorough news site on Africa, compiling the latest stories from a range of local sources.
W www.allafrica.com
Amnesty International Keep an eye on how the governments of Gambia and Senegal are dealing with human rights by going to this page and typing the country name.
W www.amnesty.org/search.html
BBC News Search If there has been a major incident in Casamance, or any other news, you'll read about it here.
W newssearch.bbc.co.uk
CIA World Factbook This site lists all those numbers and assessments from everyone's favourite 'intelligence' agency.
W www.cia.gov/cia/publications/factbook/

For more sites see the country-specific Facts for the Visitor chapters.

BOOKS
This section lists publications on Gambia and Senegal, and those on West Africa that include significant coverage of Gambia and Senegal.

Most books are published in different editions by different publishers in different countries. As a result, a book might be a hardcover rarity in one country while it's readily available in paperback in another. Fortunately, bookshops and libraries search by title or author, so these places should know the availability of the following recommendations.

We have only listed titles available in English; there are many more reference books and works of literature in French (mainly on Senegal).

Bookshops are listed in the Atlantic Coast Resorts & Serekunda and Dakar chapters, but there's not much in English to be found in Senegalese bookshops, although books in French are abundant. If you have an interest in Africa, specialist books are better bought at home.

Lonely Planet
If you're travelling through the region before or after Gambia and Senegal, Lonely Planet's *West Africa* covers 17 countries,

from Mauritania and Cape Verde to Nigeria and Cameroon. *Africa on a shoestring* is the budget guide to the whole continent.

To help with any language difficulties consider a copy of Lonely Planet's *French phrasebook*.

Mali Blues: Travelling to an African Beat by Lieve Joris is a collection of four stories set in Mali, Mauritania and Senegal. The gifted writer captures the rhythms of everyday life in the region and tells the uplifting and tragic stories of its people.

Field Guides

At some national parks in Gambia and Senegal, locally produced booklets detail local birds and other animals. If you have a deeper interest, a good regional field guide is recommended. Some bird guides are listed in the special section 'Birds of Senegambia'. For mammals, the classic volume for many years has been *Mammals of Africa*, but it could be hard to find. The *Kingdon Field Guide to African Mammals* by Jonathan Kingdon (1997) is highly regarded by naturalists. The author is a leading authority, and the book covers over 1000 species, discussing ecology, evolutionary relationships and conservation status as well as providing the usual notes on identification and distribution, with colour pictures and maps throughout.

Travel Manuals

There are a few good quality options here, particularly if you plan to explore the region by 4WD or motorbike.

Sahara Overland – A Route & Planning Guide by Chris Scott is a must-have for anyone contemplating a journey across the great sand. As well as where and when to go, how to maintain your truck/motorbike/bicycle, using a GPS, and camel riding in the dunes, the book also covers the history, geology, people and language of the Sahara. Of course there are also the all-important routes, 30 off-road itineraries in fact, including all those most commonly used and a whole lot of others. The book was published by Trailblazer in 2000 and can be 'upgraded' at Scott's website (W www.sahara-overland.com).

Africa by Road by Charlie Shackell & Illya Bracht is also recommended once you're across the desert. The book is full of helpful, no-nonsense advice on everything from paperwork and supplies to driving techniques, complemented by a complete country-by-country run-down.

The Adventure Motorbiking Handbook by Chris Scott was developed from the experienced author's earlier manual Desert Biking. It contains stacks of good information on the Sahara and West Africa, all combined with humour and personal insights. Look for the 4th edition, published in 2001.

Exploration, Travel & Experience

Travels in the Interior of Africa by Mungo Park is the classic, must-read account of expeditions through Gambia and Senegal to the Niger River in the late 18th and early 19th centuries.

Travels in West Africa by Mary Kingsley was written in the late 19th century and, despite the title, is mostly about Cameroon and Gabon. Nevertheless it captures the spirit of the age, as the author describes how she encountered wild places and wild people, all the while gathering fish specimens and facing every calamity with flamboyance, good humour and typical Victorian fortitude.

African Silence by Peter Matthiessen (1991) focuses on the author's journeys through parts of West Africa and Central Africa. The most compelling part of this deeply gripping, beautifully written book is his foray with other researchers to record elephant populations in the region; the numbers are smaller than feared.

Desert Travels by Chris Scott (1996) is a lighthearted and readable account of various journeys by motorbike in the Sahara and West Africa, as the author graduates from empty-tanked apprentice to expert dune-cruiser and desert connoisseur.

The Ends of the Earth by Robert Kaplan is not your usual kind of travel book. The author visits areas frequently seen as cultural, political and ecological disaster zones, including Iran, Central Asia and West Africa, analysing what he sees (Liberian refugee camps, the breakdown of society in Sierra Leone, the massive growth of urban poverty along the coastal strip from Lomé to Abidjan) in terms of the present and the future – about which he cannot help but be darkly pessimistic.

Novels

Novels, poetry and other works of literature by Gambian and Senegalese writers are discussed under Arts in the Facts about Gambia and Facts about Senegal.

Roots by Alex Haley was written in 1976. A mix of historical fact and imaginative fiction, it describes the black American author's search for his African origins. It is still probably the best-known work inspired by events in Gambia, and was hugely influential among black Americans throughout the 1970s and '80s, although most of the events described in this book take place in the USA.

The Music in My Head by Mark Hudson is engaging and darkly amusing, describing the power, influence and everyday realities of modern African music set in a mythical city that is instantly recognisable as Dakar. The oppressive urban atmosphere is perfectly captured, and extra twists include a Nabokov-style unreliable narrator.

Anthologies & Criticism

Traveller's Literary Companion – Africa, edited by Oona Strathern, contains over 250 wonderful prose and poetry extracts from all over Africa, with an introduction to the literature of each country, plus a list of literary landmarks – real features that appear in novels written about the country. Ideal to read before you go or to carry on your trip.

The Companion to African Literatures, edited by Douglas Killam & Ruth Rowe, is for people with a scholarly bent. It is a comprehensive guide to writers, publications, literary genres, influences and connections throughout African continent.

For further guidance, we recommend you try *Reading the African Novel* by Simon Gikandi; *Journeys through the French African Novel* by Mildred Mortimer; and *Essays on African Writing*, edited by Abdulrazak Gumah.

History

A Political History of Gambia by A Hughes & D Perfect covers the period in Gambian history from 1816 to 1992.

Ethnic Groups of the Senegambia by Patience Sonko-Godwin describes in some detail the histories of the main peoples of Gambia and Senegal, going back wherever possible to the period of the great Sahel empires or earlier. This small paperback is available locally.

To understand the history of Gambia and Senegal in the wider context, we recommend you start with *A History of Africa* by JD Fage, and *A Short History of Africa* by Fage & Roland, comprehensive and concise paperbacks covering the whole continent.

West Africa Since 1800 by Webster & Boahen (1980) provides good in-depth treatment of the region in recent times.

African Civilization Revisited: From Antiquity to Modern Times (1990); *The African Genius: An Introduction to African Social & Cultural History* (1990); *Africa in History* (1994); *Modern Africa* (1994); *A History of West Africa 1000–1800* (with FK Bush & JFA Ajayi, 1992); *Pre-colonial West Africa* (1998); and *West Africa before the Colonial Era* (1998) are just some of the books by Basil Davidson, a leading and influential writer on African history. The British newspaper the *Guardian* said Davidson's 'committed, left-wing approach to writing history opened up the stuffy, chauvinist world of British professional historians and reached a popular audience far beyond academia'.

Politics, Economics & Development

Texts to help you understand the complex geopolitical and economic picture in Africa include *The Africans* by David Lamb (1984), a portrait of early 1980s Africa, rich in political and social detail. The author travelled widely, revelling in midnight flights to witness little-known coups in obscure countries, but some critics suggest this gung-ho approach prevented an in-depth understanding.

Africa: Dispatches from a Fragile Continent by Blaine Harden (1993) provides provocative and pessimistic reading on several topics, including the failure of African political leadership (the 'big man' syndrome), although the author believes positive African values still endure and make the continent a joy.

Masters of Illusion – The World Bank and the Poverty of Nations by Catherine Caufield (1996) discusses the global development lending agency's influence on poor countries around the world. The book's observations (that the social and environmental effects of projects are inadequately analysed) are shocking, while the conclusions (that, despite loans totalling billions of US dollars, the people of the Third World are worse off now than before) calls the whole institution seriously into question.

Reference Books

Africa by Phyllis Martin and Patrick O'Meara (1995) is affordable, and the nearest you'll get to a pocket library on all matters African. It has scholarly but accessible essays on a wide range of subjects including history, religion, colonialism, sociology, art, music, popular culture, law, literature, politics, economics and the development crisis.

New African Yearbook (published yearly by IC Publications) gives a good political and economic rundown of every country in Africa.

Sub-Saharan African Travel Resource Guide by Louis Taussig has an extensive, critically reviewed list of all guidebooks, maps, travelogues and specialist manuals to the region, plus information on travel magazines, bookshops, publishers, libraries, tourist organisations, special-interest societies and conservation projects. Volume 1 covers East and West Africa; volume 2 covers Central and Southern Africa.

Dictionaries & Phrasebooks

The *French phrasebook* from Lonely Planet is an excellent guide to the language, with a comprehensive two-way dictionary and guidance on grammar and pronunciation. It has easy-to-use sections covering just about every travel situation, including greetings, small talk, accommodation, getting around and health.

French Dictionary from Collins (in the Gem series) is also useful, and a good size.

NEWSPAPERS & MAGAZINES

Newspapers published in Gambia and Senegal are discussed in each country's Facts for the Visitor chapter. Magazines – mostly monthly – in English covering the region include:

African Business (IC Publications) Economic reports, finance and company news

Africa Today (Afro Media) Good political and economic news, plus business, sport and tourism

Focus on Africa (BBC) Excellent news stories, accessible reports and a concise run down of recent political events

New African (IC Publications) A reputation for accurate and balanced reporting, with a mix of politics, financial and economic analysis. Has features on social and cultural affairs, sport, art, health and recreation

West Africa (West Africa Publishing) A long-standing and respected weekly; focuses on political and economic news

Of these, *Focus on Africa* is the easiest to find in Gambia and Senegal. In Western countries, some titles are stocked in larger mainstream newspaper shops; others can only be tracked down at specialist suppliers or libraries. There are many more periodicals produced in French. The most widely available is *Jeune Afrique*, a popular weekly magazine covering regional and world events.

PHOTOGRAPHY & VIDEO
Film & Accessories

Film is relatively expensive in Gambia and Senegal because it has to be imported. Outside the major cities only standard print film is available; indeed, in Gambia slide film is almost impossible to find no matter where you are. Even if the expiry date has not yet been reached, the film may have been damaged by heat. It's best to bring all you need with you.

The sunlight is frequently strong, so most people find 100 ASA perfectly adequate, with possibly 200 ASA or 400 ASA for long-lens shots. Useful photographic accessories might include a small flash, a cable or remote shutter release, filters and a cleaning kit. Also remember to take spare batteries.

The old x-ray machines at some airports may not be safe for film. Even newer film-safe models can affect high-speed film (1000 ASA plus), especially if the film goes through several checks, so use a protective lead bag. Alternatively, carry film in your pocket and have it checked manually by officials.

Books with advice that could improve your travel snaps include Lonely Planet's *Travel Photography: A Guide to Taking Better Pictures* by Richard I'Anson, and National Geographic's excellent *Photography Field Guide* by Peter K Burian & Robert Caputo.

Technical Tips

Timing The best times to take photographs on sunny days are the first two hours after sunrise and the last two before sunset. This takes advantage of the colour-enhancing rays cast by a low sun. A polarising filter can help to cut out glare, which is especially useful during hazy periods before the rainy season.

Exposure When photographing animals or people, take light readings on the subject and not the brilliant African background or your shots will turn out underexposed.

Camera Care Heat and humidity can take a toll on your camera, but the biggest danger is the all-pervading dust that accompanies almost every trip out of town. If you don't take precautions, grit will soon find its way into lenses and camera bodies. Try to find a camera bag that closes with a zip or some other form of seal – the traditional top-opening shoulder bags are pretty hopeless at keeping dust out. Another suggestion is to carry snap-lock or zip-lock bags to put lenses into when they're not in use. The worst time of year for dust is during the harmattan – see Climate in the Facts about Senegambia chapter.

Restrictions

Generally, you should avoid taking pictures of bridges, dams, airports, military equipment, government buildings and *anything* that could be considered strategic. You may be arrested or have your film and camera confiscated.

Some local people are not happy if you take pictures of their place of worship or a natural feature with traditional religious significance. Respect these views.

Photographing People

Like people everywhere, some Africans enjoy being photographed, while others do not. They may be superstitious about your camera or suspicious of your motives. To some people in poor areas, a foreigner with a camera is – understandably – seen as a chance to make money. If you want a picture, you have to pay. Other locals maintain their pride and never want to be photographed, money or not.

Some tourists go for discreet shots with long lenses. Others ask permission first. If you get 'no' for an answer, accept it. Just snapping away is rude. Some local people may agree to be photographed if you give them a picture for themselves. If you don't carry a Polaroid camera, take their address and make it clear that you'll post the photo. Your promise will be taken seriously. Never say you'll send a photo unless you intend to. Alternatively, just be honest and say that so many people ask you for photos that it's impossible to send one to everyone.

Photographing Animals

To score excellent wildlife shots, a long lens helps, although you'll need a tripod for anything over 200mm. If your subject is nothing but a speck in the distance, resist wasting film but keep the camera ready.

Video

A video camera, if properly used, can give a fascinating record of your holiday. As well as the obvious things – sunsets, spectacular views – remember to record some of the ordinary everyday details of life in the country.

One good rule to follow is to film in long takes, and don't move the camera around too much. Otherwise, your video could well make your viewers seasick! If your camera has a stabiliser, you can use it to obtain good footage while travelling on various means of transport, even on bumpy roads. Video cameras often have sensitive microphones, which can be a problem if there is a lot of ambient noise.

While travelling, you can recharge batteries in hotels as you go along, so take the necessary charger, plugs and transformer.

You should follow the guidelines outlined under Photographing People (earlier) regarding people's sensitivities; many locals find video cameras even more annoying and offensive than still cameras. Always ask permission first. And remember, you're on holiday – don't let the video take over your life.

TIME

Gambia and Senegal are at GMT/UTC, which for most European visitors means there is no or very little time difference. The time is the same all year; neither country has daylight savings. When it's noon in Gambia or Senegal, it's 7am in New York, noon in London, 1pm in Paris and 10pm in Sydney.

ELECTRICITY

The electricity supply in both Gambia and Senegal is 220V. Plugs in Senegal usually have two round pins, as are those in France and continental Europe. This plug type is also used in Gambia, but you'll also find plugs with three square pins, as used in Britain.

WEIGHTS & MEASURES

The metric system is used in both Gambia and Senegal. To convert between metric and imperial units refer to the conversion chart on the inside back cover of this book.

LAUNDRY

Throughout Gambia and Senegal, finding someone to wash your clothes is fairly simple. The top-end and mid-range hotels charge per item. At cheaper hotels, a staff member will do the job, or find you somebody else who can. The charge is usually per item, but cheaper than at the big hotels, and often negotiable.

TOILETS

There are two main types of toilet in Africa: the Western style, with a bowl and seat; and the African or Eastern style, which is a hole in the floor, over which you squat. Standards for both vary tremendously, from pristine to unusable. Some travellers complain that African toilets are difficult to use, or that you have to remove half your clothing to use them. This is not so, and it only takes a small degree of practice to master a comfortable squatting technique.

In rural areas squat toilets are built over a deep hole in the ground. These are called 'long drops', and the crap just decomposes naturally, as long as the hole isn't filled with too much other rubbish (such as paper or synthetic materials, including tampons, which should be disposed of separately).

In remote wilderness areas, there may be no toilets at all, and you have to find a quiet bush or rock to relieve yourself behind.

Some Western toilets are not plumbed in, but just balanced over a long drop, and sometimes seats are constructed to assist those who can't squat. The lack of running water usually makes such cross-cultural mechanisms a disaster. A noncontact squat loo is better than a filthy box to hover over any day.

HEALTH

Travel health depends on your predeparture preparations, your daily health care while travelling and how you handle any medical problem that does develop. While the potential dangers can seem quite frightening, in reality few travellers experience anything more than an upset stomach.

Predeparture Planning

Immunisations Plan ahead for getting your vaccinations: Some of them require more than one injection, while some vaccinations should not be given together. Note that some vaccinations should not be given during pregnancy or to people with allergies – discuss with your doctor.

It is recommended you seek medical advice at least six weeks before travel. Be aware that there is often a greater risk of disease with children and during pregnancy.

Discuss your requirements with your doctor, but vaccinations you should consider for a trip to Gambia or Senegal are listed here (for more details about the diseases themselves, see the individual disease entries later in this chapter). Carry proof of your vaccinations on an international health certificate, especially for yellow fever, as this is sometimes needed to enter some countries.

Diphtheria & Tetanus Vaccinations for these two diseases are usually combined and are recommended for everyone. After an initial course of three injections (usually given in childhood), boosters are necessary every 10 years.

Hepatitis A Vaccine for Hepatitis A (eg, Avaxim, Havrix 1440 or VAQTA) provides long-term immunity (possibly more than 10 years) after an initial injection and a booster at six to 12 months. Alternatively, an injection of gamma globulin can provide short-term protection against hepatitis A – two to six months, depending on the dose given. It is not a vaccine, but a ready-made antibody collected from blood donations. It is reasonably effective and, unlike the vaccine, it is protective immediately, but because it is a blood product, there are concerns about its long-term safety. Hepatitis A vaccine is also available in a combined form, Twinrix, with hepatitis B vaccine. Three injections over a six-month period are required; the first two provide substantial protection against hepatitis A.

Hepatitis B Travellers who should consider vaccination against hepatitis B include those visiting countries where there are high levels of hepatitis B infection, where blood transfusions may not be adequately screened or where sexual contact or needle sharing is a possibility. Vaccination involves three injections, with a booster at 12 months. More rapid courses are available if necessary.

Meningococcal Meningitis Vaccination is recommended, especially during the dry season from November to June. A single injection gives good protection against the major epidemic forms of the disease for three years. Protection may be less effective in children under two years.

Polio This is still prevalent in Senegambia, so everyone should keep up to date with this vaccination, which is normally given in childhood. A booster every 10 years maintains immunity.

Rabies Vaccination should be considered by those who will spend a month or longer in a country where rabies is common, especially if they are cycling, handling animals, caving or travelling to remote areas, and for children (who may not report a bite). Pretravel rabies vaccination involves having three injections over 21 to 28 days. If someone who has been vaccinated is bitten or scratched by an animal, they will require two booster injections of vaccine; those not vaccinated require more.

Tuberculosis The risk of TB to travellers is usually very low, except for those living with or closely associated with local people. Vaccination against TB (BCG) is recommended for children and young adults living in these areas for three months or more.

Typhoid Vaccination against typhoid may be required if you are travelling for more than a couple of weeks. It is available either as an injection or as capsules to be taken orally.

Yellow Fever A yellow fever vaccine is now the only vaccine that is a legal requirement for entry into Gambia and Senegal, usually only enforced when coming from an infected area. At the time of research, yellow fever was still affecting small numbers in Senegal. For immunisation you may have to go to a special yellow fever vaccination centre.

Malaria Medication Antimalarial drugs do not prevent you from being infected but kill the malaria parasites during a stage in their development and significantly reduce your risk of becoming very ill or dying. Expert advice on medication should be sought, as there are many factors to consider, including the area to be visited, the risk of exposure to malaria-carrying mosquitoes, the side effects of medication, your medical history and whether you are a child or an adult or pregnant. Travellers to isolated areas in high-risk countries may like to carry a treatment dose of medication for use if symptoms occur. See Malaria later in this section for more details.

Health Insurance Make sure that you have adequate health insurance. See Travel Insurance under Visas & Documents earlier in this chapter for details.

Travel Health Guides Lonely Planet's *Healthy Travel Africa* is a handy pocket size and packed with useful information on pretrip planning, emergency first aid, immunisation and disease information and what to do if you get sick on the road. *Travel with Children* from Lonely Planet also includes advice on travel health for younger children.

For those planning on being away for a while or working abroad (as a Peace Corps worker, for example), *Where There Is No Doctor* by David Werner is a very detailed guide ideal for self-diagnosing almost anything.

Medical Kit Check List

Following is a list of items you should consider including in your medical kit – consult your pharmacist for brands available in your country.

☐ **Aspirin or paracetamol (acetaminophen in the USA)** – for pain or fever

☐ **Antihistamine** – for allergies, eg, hay fever; to ease the itch from insect bites or stings; and to prevent motion sickness

☐ **Cold and flu tablets, throat lozenges and nasal decongestant**

☐ **Multivitamins** – consider for long trips, when dietary vitamin intake may be inadequate

☐ **Antibiotics** – consider including these if you're travelling well off the beaten track; see your doctor, as they must be prescribed, and carry the prescription with you

☐ **Loperamide or diphenoxylate** – known as 'blockers' for diarrhoea

☐ **Prochlorperazine or metaclopramide** – for nausea and vomiting

☐ **Rehydration mixture** – to prevent dehydration, which may occur, for example, during bouts of diarrhoea; particularly important when travelling with children

☐ **Insect repellent, sunscreen, lip balm and eye drops**

☐ **Calamine lotion, sting relief spray or aloe vera** – to ease irritation from sunburn and insect bites or stings

☐ **Antifungal cream or powder** – for fungal skin infections and thrush

☐ **Antiseptic (such as povidone-iodine)** – for cuts and grazes

☐ **Bandages, Band-Aids (plasters) and other wound dressings**

☐ **Water purification tablets or iodine**

☐ **Scissors, tweezers and a thermometer** – note that mercury thermometers are prohibited by airlines

☐ **Sterile kit** – in case you need injections in a country with medical hygiene problems; discuss with your doctor

There are also a number of excellent travel health sites on the Internet. From the Lonely Planet home page there are links to a range of sites (W www.lonelyplanet.com/weblinks). Also good is the World Health Organization's (WHO) travel site (W www.who.int/ith).

Other Preparations If you wear glasses take a spare pair and your prescription. If you require a particular medication take an adequate supply, as it may not be available locally. Take part of the packaging showing the generic name rather than the brand, which will make getting replacements easier, but be sure to remove or black out the price you paid at home, or you could encounter a sudden dose of hyperinflation. It's a good idea to have a legible prescription or letter from your doctor to show that you legally use the medication to avoid any problems.

Basic Rules

Food There is an old colonial adage that says: 'If you can cook it, boil it or peel it you can eat it...otherwise forget it'. Vegetables and fruit should be washed with purified water or peeled where possible. Beware of ice cream sold on the streets of Banjul or Dakar or anywhere it might have been melted and refrozen. Seafood is generally some of the safest food available in Senegal and Gambia, but shellfish such as mussels, oysters and clams should be treated with caution, while undercooked meat, particularly in the form of mince, should be avoided. If a place looks clean and well run and the vendor also looks clean and healthy, then the food is probably safe. In general, places that are packed with travellers or locals will be fine, while empty restaurants are questionable. The food in busy restaurants is cooked and eaten quite quickly with little standing around, and is probably not reheated.

Water The number one rule is *be careful of the water* and especially of ice. If you don't know for certain that the water is safe, assume the worst. Having said that, we travelled throughout Senegal and Gambia and in most towns the tap water was OK to drink. However, people respond differently, and

Nutrition

If your diet is poor or limited in variety, if you're travelling hard and fast and therefore missing meals or if you simply lose your appetite and find you can't eat, you can soon start to lose weight and place your health at risk.

Make sure your diet is well balanced. Cooked eggs, beans and nuts are all safe ways to get protein. Fruit you can peel (bananas, oranges or mandarins, for example) is usually safe and a good source of vitamins. Melons can harbour bacteria in their flesh and are best avoided. Try to eat plenty of grains (including rice) and bread. Remember that although food is generally safer if it is cooked well, overcooked food loses much of its nutritional value. If your diet isn't well balanced or if your food intake is insufficient, it's a good idea to take vitamin and iron pills.

In hot climates make sure you drink enough – don't rely on feeling thirsty to indicate when you should drink. Not needing to urinate or voiding small amounts of very dark yellow urine is a danger sign. Always carry a water bottle with you on long trips. Excessive sweating can lead to loss of salt and therefore muscle cramping. Salt tablets are not a good idea as a preventative, but in places where salt is not used much, adding salt to food can help.

water that's fine for some might spark a marathon session on the throne for others – you'll soon know where you stand (or sit).

Bottled water and soft drinks are generally fine and are widely available, although in some places bottles may be refilled with tap water – check the seals. Take care with fruit juice, particularly if water may have been added. Milk should be treated with suspicion as it is often unpasteurised, though boiled milk is fine if it is kept hygienically. Tea or coffee should also be OK, since the water should have been boiled.

The simplest way to purify water is to boil it thoroughly. Alternatively, you could buy a water filter for a long trip. There are two main kinds of filter. Total filters take out all parasites, bacteria and viruses and make water safe to drink. They are often expensive, but they can be more cost effective than buying lots of bottled water. Simple filters (which can even be a nylon mesh bag) take out dirt and larger foreign bodies from the water so that chemical solutions work much more effectively; if water is dirty, chemical solutions may not work at all. It's very important when buying a filter to read the specifications, so that you know exactly what it removes from the water and what it doesn't. Simple filtering will not remove all dangerous organisms, so if you cannot boil water it should be treated chemically. Chlorine tablets will kill many pathogens, but not some parasites such as giardia and amoebic cysts. Iodine is more effective in purifying water and is available in tablet form. Follow the directions carefully and remember that too much iodine can be harmful.

Medical Problems & Treatment

Self-diagnosis and treatment can be risky, so you should always seek medical help. An embassy, consulate or expensive hotel can usually recommend a local doctor or clinic. Although we do give drug dosages in this section, they are for emergency use only.

Everyday Health

Normal body temperature is up to 37°C (98.6°F); more than 2°C (4°F) higher indicates a high fever. The normal adult pulse rate is 60 to 100 per minute (children 80 to 100, babies 100 to 140). As a general rule the pulse increases about 20 beats per minute for each 1°C (2°F) rise in fever.

Respiration (breathing) rate is also an indicator of illness. Count the number of breaths per minute: Between 12 and 20 is normal for adults and older children (up to 30 for younger children, 40 for babies). People with a high fever or serious respiratory illness breathe more quickly than normal. More than 40 shallow breaths a minute may indicate pneumonia.

Correct diagnosis is vital. In this section we have used the generic names for medications – check with a pharmacist for brands available locally.

Note that antibiotics should ideally be administered only under medical supervision. Take only the recommended dose at the prescribed intervals and use the whole course, even if the illness seems to be cured earlier. Stop immediately if there are any serious reactions and don't use the antibiotic at all if you are unsure that you have the correct one. Some people are allergic to commonly prescribed antibiotics such as penicillin; carry this information (eg, on a bracelet) when travelling.

Environmental Hazards

Heat Exhaustion Dehydration and salt deficiency can cause heat exhaustion. Take time to acclimatise to high temperatures, drink sufficient liquids and do not do anything too physically demanding.

Salt deficiency is characterised by fatigue, lethargy, headaches, giddiness and muscle cramps; salt tablets may help, but adding extra salt to your food is better.

Anhidrotic heat exhaustion is a rare form of heat exhaustion that is caused by an inability to sweat. It tends to affect people who have been in a hot climate for some time, rather than newcomers. It can progress to heatstroke. Treatment involves removal to a cooler climate.

Heatstroke This serious, occasionally fatal, condition can occur if the body's heat-regulating mechanism breaks down and the body temperature rises to dangerous levels. Long, continuous periods of exposure to high temperatures and insufficient fluids can leave you vulnerable to heatstroke.

The symptoms are feeling unwell, not sweating very much (or at all) and a high body temperature (39°C to 41°C or 102°F to 106°F). Where sweating has ceased, the skin becomes flushed and red. Severe, throbbing headaches and lack of coordination will also occur, and the sufferer may be confused or aggressive. Eventually the victim will become delirious or convulse. Hospitalisation

is essential, but in the interim get victims out of the sun, remove their clothing, cover them with a wet sheet or towel and then fan continually. Give fluids if they are conscious.

Motion Sickness Eating lightly before and during a trip will reduce the chances of motion sickness. If you are prone to motion sickness try to find a place that minimises movement – near the wing on aircraft, close to midships on boats, near the centre on buses. Fresh air usually helps; reading and cigarette smoke don't. Commercial motion-sickness preparations, which can cause drowsiness, have to be taken before the trip commences. Ginger (available in capsule form) and peppermint (including mint-flavoured sweets) are natural preventatives.

Sunburn In the tropics, in the desert or at high altitude you can get sunburnt surprisingly quickly, even through cloud. Use a sunscreen, a hat, and a barrier cream for your nose and lips. Calamine lotion or a commercial after-sun preparation are good for mild sunburn. Protect your eyes with good quality sunglasses.

Infectious Diseases

Bilharzia Also known as schistosomiasis, this disease is common in Gambia and Senegal. It is transmitted by minute worms that infect certain varieties of freshwater snails found in rivers, streams, lakes and particularly behind dams. The worms multiply and are eventually discharged into the water.

The worm enters through the skin and attaches itself to your intestines or bladder. The first symptom may be a general feeling of being unwell, or a tingling and sometimes a light rash around the area where it entered. Weeks later a high fever may develop. Once the disease is established, abdominal pain and blood in the urine are other signs. The infection often causes no symptoms until the disease is well established (several months to years after exposure) and damage to internal organs irreversible.

Avoiding swimming or bathing in fresh water where bilharzia is present is the main method of preventing the disease. Even deep water can be infected. If you do get wet, dry off quickly and dry your clothes as well.

A blood test is the best way to diagnose the disease, but the test will not show positive for some weeks after exposure.

Diarrhoea Simple things such as a change of water, food or climate can all cause a mild bout of diarrhoea, and many people experience a few rushed toilet trips soon after arriving in Africa. If there are no other symptoms then don't worry, this is just your body dealing with the change – it doesn't mean you've got dysentery!

Dehydration is the main danger with any diarrhoea, particularly in children or the elderly as dehydration can occur quite quickly. Under all circumstances *fluid replacement* is the most important thing to remember. Weak black tea with a little sugar, soda water, or flat soft drinks diluted 50% with clean water are all good. With severe diarrhoea, a rehydrating solution is preferable to replace minerals and salts lost. Commercially available oral rehydration salts (ORS) are very useful; add them to boiled or bottled water. In an emergency you can make up a solution of six teaspoons of sugar and half a teaspoon of salt to a litre of boiled or bottled water. You need to drink at least the same volume of fluid that you are losing in bowel movements and vomiting. Urine is the best guide to the adequacy of replacement – if you have small amounts of concentrated urine, you need to drink more. Keep drinking small amounts often. Stick to a bland, fat-free diet as you recover.

Gut-paralysing drugs such as loperamide (Imodium) or diphenoxylate (Lomotil) can be used to bring relief from the symptoms, although they do not actually cure the problem. Only use these drugs if you do not have access to toilets, eg, if you *must* travel. Note that these drugs are not recommended for children under 12 years.

In certain situations antibiotics may be required: diarrhoea with blood or mucus (dysentery), any diarrhoea with fever, profuse watery diarrhoea, persistent diarrhoea not improving after 48 hours and severe diarrhoea. These suggest a more serious cause of diarrhoea and, in these situations, gut-paralysing drugs should be avoided.

In these situations, a stool test may be necessary to diagnose what bug is causing your diarrhoea, so you should seek medical help urgently. Where this is not possible the recommended drugs for bacterial diarrhoea (the most likely cause of severe diarrhoea in travellers) are norfloxacin 400mg twice daily for three days or ciprofloxacin 500mg twice daily for five days. These are not recommended for children or pregnant women. The drug of choice for children would be co-trimoxazole with dosage dependent on weight. A five-day course is given. Ampicillin or amoxycillin may be given in pregnancy, but medical care is necessary.

Two other causes of persistent diarrhoea in travellers are giardiasis and amoebic dysentery.

Giardiasis is caused by a common parasite, *Giardia lamblia*. Symptoms include stomach cramps, nausea, a bloated stomach, watery, foul-smelling diarrhoea and frequent gas. Giardiasis can appear several weeks after you have been exposed to the parasite. The symptoms may disappear for a few days and then return; this can go on for several weeks.

Amoebic dysentery, caused by the protozoan *Entamoeba histolytica*, is characterised by a gradual onset of low-grade diarrhoea, often with blood and mucus. Cramping abdominal pain and vomiting are less likely than in other types of diarrhoea, and fever may not be present. It will persist until treated and can recur and cause other health problems.

You should seek medical advice if you think you have giardiasis or amoebic dysentery, but where this is not possible, tinidazole (Fasigyn) or metronidazole (Flagyl) are the recommended drugs. Treatment is a 2g single dose of tinidazole or 250mg of metronidazole three times daily for five to 10 days.

Fungal Infections These occur more commonly in hot weather and are usually found on the scalp, between the toes (athlete's foot) or fingers, in the groin and on the body (ringworm). You get ringworm (which is a fungal infection, not a worm) from infected animals or other people. Moisture encourages these infections.

To prevent fungal infections wear loose, comfortable clothes, avoid artificial fibres, wash frequently and dry yourself carefully. If you do get an infection, wash the infected area at least daily with a disinfectant or medicated soap and water, and rinse and dry well. Apply an antifungal cream or powder such as tolnaftate. Try to expose the infected area to air or sunlight as much as possible. Wash all towels and underwear in hot water, change them often and let them dry in the sun.

Hepatitis This is a general term for inflammation of the liver. It is a common disease worldwide. There are several different viruses that cause hepatitis, and they differ in the way they are transmitted. The symptoms are similar in all forms of the illness, and include fever, chills, headache, fatigue, feelings of weakness and aches and pains, followed by loss of appetite, nausea, vomiting, abdominal pain, dark urine, light-coloured faeces, jaundiced (yellow) skin and yellowing of the whites of the eyes. People who have had hepatitis should avoid alcohol for some time after the illness, as the liver needs time to recover.

Hepatitis A is transmitted by contaminated food and drinking water. You should seek medical advice, but there is not much you can do apart from resting, drinking lots of fluids, eating lightly and avoiding fatty foods. **Hepatitis E** is transmitted in the same way as hepatitis A; it can be particularly serious in pregnant women.

There are almost 300 million chronic carriers of **hepatitis B** in the world. It is spread through contact with infected blood, blood products or body fluids; for example, through sexual contact, unsterilised needles and blood transfusions, or through contact with blood via small breaks in the skin. Other risk situations include shaving, tattooing or body piercing with contaminated equipment. The symptoms of hepatitis B may be more severe than those of type A and the disease can lead to long-term problems such as chronic liver damage, liver cancer or a long-term carrier state. Hepatitis C and D are

spread in the same way as hepatitis B and can also lead to long-term complications.

There are vaccines against hepatitis A and B, but there are currently no vaccines against the other types of hepatitis.

HIV & AIDS Infection with the human immunodeficiency virus (HIV) may lead to acquired immune deficiency syndrome (AIDS), which is a fatal disease. HIV is a growing problem in Gambia and Senegal, though as yet nowhere near as widespread as in East and Southern Africa. Any exposure to blood, blood products or body fluids may put the individual at risk. The disease is often transmitted through sexual contact or dirty needles – vaccinations, acupuncture, tattooing and body piercing are potentially as dangerous as intravenous drug use. HIV/AIDS can also be spread through infected blood transfusions; some developing countries cannot afford to screen blood used for transfusions. If you do need an injection, ask to see the syringe unwrapped in front of you, or take a needle and syringe pack with you.

There are two types of HIV, and both are fairly common in West Africa. Unfortunately, many HIV tests do not test for both variations. What this means is that unprotected sex with someone who has tested negative for the virus might not be as safe as it sounds. Fear of HIV infection should never discourage treatment for serious conditions.

Meningococcal Meningitis This is a serious disease that attacks the brain and can be fatal. There are recurring epidemics in various parts of the world, including the interior regions of Gambia and Senegal.

A fever, severe headache, sensitivity to light and neck stiffness that prevents forward bending of the head are the first symptoms. There may also be purple patches on the skin. Death can occur within a few hours, so urgent medical treatment is required.

Treatment is large doses of penicillin given intravenously, or chloramphenicol injections.

Sexually Transmitted Diseases (STD) HIV/AIDS and hepatitis B can be transmitted through sexual contact – see the relevant sections earlier for more details. Other STDs include gonorrhoea, herpes and syphilis. Sores, blisters or rashes around the genitals and discharges or pain when urinating are common symptoms. With STDs such as the wart virus or chlamydia (both common in Gambia and Senegal), symptoms may be less marked or not observed at all, especially in women. Chlamydia infection can cause infertility in men and women before any symptoms have been noticed. Syphilis symptoms eventually disappear completely but the disease continues and can cause severe problems in later years. While abstaining from sexual contact is the only 100% effective prevention, using condoms is also effective. Gonorrhoea and syphilis are treated with antibiotics. The different STDs each require specific antibiotics.

Typhoid This is a dangerous gut infection caused by contaminated water and food. While it's seldom seen in Gambia and Senegal, if you suspect you have typhoid seek medical help immediately.

In its early stages sufferers may feel they have a bad cold or flu on the way, as early symptoms are a headache, body aches and a fever that rises a little each day until it is around 40°C (104°F) or more. The victim's pulse is often slow relative to the degree of fever present – unlike a normal fever where the pulse increases. There may also be vomiting, abdominal pain, diarrhoea or constipation.

In the second week the high fever and slow pulse continue and a few pink spots may appear on the body; trembling, delirium, weakness, weight loss and dehydration may occur. Complications such as pneumonia, perforated bowel or meningitis may occur.

Insect-Borne Diseases

Filariasis, leishmaniasis, sleeping sickness, typhus and yellow fever are all insect-borne diseases, but they do not pose a great risk to travellers. For more information on them see Less Common Diseases at the end of this health section.

Malaria This serious and potentially fatal disease is spread by mosquito bites. Nowhere in Gambia and Senegal is completely free of malaria so it's extremely important to avoid mosquito bites and to take tablets to prevent this disease. Symptoms range from fever, chills and sweating, headache, diarrhoea and abdominal pains to a vague feeling of ill-health. Seek medical help immediately if malaria is suspected. Without treatment malaria can rapidly become more serious and can be fatal.

If medical care is not available, malaria tablets can be used for treatment. You need to use a malaria tablet different from the one you were taking when you contracted malaria. The standard treatment dose of mefloquine (Larium) is two 250mg tablets and a further two six hours later. For Fansidar, it's a single dose of three tablets. If you were previously taking mefloquine and cannot obtain Fansidar, then other alternatives are Malarone (atovaquone-proguanil; four tablets once daily for three days), halofantrine (three doses of two 250mg tablets every six hours) or quinine sulphate (600mg every six hours). There is a greater risk of side effects with these dosages than in normal use if used with mefloquine, so medical advice is preferable. Be aware also that halofantrine is no longer recommended by the WHO as emergency standby treatment, because of side effects, and should only be used if no other drugs are available.

Travellers are advised to prevent mosquito bites at all times. The main messages are:

- Wear light-coloured clothing.
- Wear long trousers and long-sleeved shirts.
- Use mosquito repellents containing the compound DEET on exposed areas (prolonged overuse of DEET may be harmful, especially to children, but using it is preferable to being bitten by disease-transmitting mosquitoes).
- Avoid perfume and aftershave.
- Use a mosquito net impregnated with mosquito repellent (permethrin) – it may be worth taking your own.
- Impregnating your clothes with permethrin effectively deters mosquitoes and other insects.

Take Your Drugs

Make no mistake: malaria is a killer and it kills with sobering regularity in Gambia and Senegal. Malaria is the biggest single cause of death in both countries and thousands in Senegambia die of the disease every year. But it's not only Africans who are dying. Some long-term expats and short-term package tourists are also among the more than one million who succumb to the *Plasmodium falciparum* parasite each year in Africa. Many more have their holidays, plus some, turned into a nightmare, usually because they haven't bothered to take the recommended prophylactics, or haven't taken them as prescribed.

Nowhere in the two countries is completely free of malaria, not even Dakar or Banjul, so even if you're only visiting for a week on the beach you should be taking an antimalarial prophylactic. There is much debate about which anti-malarial drug to take. The WHO recommends mefloquine (aka Lariam) for both Gambia and Senegal, though the side effects can be quite literally mind-altering for a small percentage of users. If the high cost of antimalarials in Europe, the USA or Australia is a concern, consider getting enough to cover your first week (remembering that you will need to start taking them before you arrive) and buying generic versions of the drug for a fraction of the cost once you arrive. Mefloquine, doxycycline and several other drugs are readily available in most cities and major towns.

While malaria deaths are steadily rising, the news is not all bad. Doctors from London working with the Medical Research Council in Fajara, Gambia, are reported to have made encouraging advances in the search for a malaria vaccine. Progress is slow, with trials and refinements continuing as funding allows, but researchers are genuinely excited by recent breakthroughs.

In the meantime, if you're experiencing flu symptoms, or any kind of fever at all, head straight for a clinic to have a blood test. This is a fast, cheap and painless procedure that might save your life. Recommended clinics are listed in the Dakar chapter for Senegal, and the Atlantic Coast Resorts & Serekunda chapter for Gambia.

Dengue Fever This viral disease is transmitted by mosquitoes and is fast becoming one of the top public-health problems in the tropical world. The disease has been reported in small numbers in both Gambia and Senegal. The *Aedes aegypti* mosquito, which transmits the dengue virus, is most active during the day (unlike the malaria-carrying mosquito), and is found mainly in urban areas, in and around human dwellings. Symptoms of dengue fever include a sudden onset of high fever, headache, joint and muscle pains (hence its old name, 'breakbone fever') and nausea and vomiting. A rash of small red spots sometimes appears three to four days after the onset of fever. In the early phase of illness, dengue may be mistaken for other infectious diseases, including malaria and influenza. Minor bleeding such as nose bleeds may occur in the course of the illness, but this does not necessarily mean that you have progressed to the potentially fatal dengue haemorrhagic fever (DHF). This is a severe illness, characterised by heavy bleeding, which is thought to be a result of secondary infection due to a different strain (there are four major strains) and usually affects residents of the country rather than travellers. Recovery even from simple dengue fever may be prolonged, with tiredness lasting for several weeks.

There is no vaccine against and no specific treatment for dengue. Aspirin should be avoided, as it increases the risk of haemorrhaging. The best prevention is to avoid mosquito bites – see Malaria earlier.

Bedbugs These are a particular problem in the budget-accommodation places of Gambia and Senegal. These evil little bastards live in various places, but are found particularly in dirty mattresses and bedding, and are evidenced by spots of blood on bed-clothes or on the wall. Bedbugs leave itchy bites in neat rows, often along a line where your body touched the mattress. They won't kill you, but bites often itch for days, making sleep difficult. Calamine lotion or a sting relief spray may help, but your best bet is to just find another hotel.

Ticks You should always check all over your body if you have been walking through a potentially tick-infested area as ticks can cause skin infections and other, more serious diseases. If you find a tick attached, press down around its head with tweezers, grab the head and gently pull upwards. Avoid pulling the rear of the body as this may squeeze the tick's gut contents through the attached mouth parts into the skin, increasing the risk of infection and disease. Smearing chemicals on the tick will not make it let go and is not recommended.

Women's Health
Gynaecological Problems Antibiotic use, synthetic underwear, sweating and contraceptive pills can lead to fungal vaginal infections, especially when travelling in hot climates. Fungal infections are characterised by a rash, itch and discharge and can be treated with a vinegar or lemon-juice douche, or with yogurt. Nystatin, miconazole or clotrimazole pessaries or vaginal cream are the usual treatment. Maintaining good personal hygiene and wearing loose-fitting clothes and cotton underwear may help prevent these infections.

Sexually transmitted diseases are a major cause of vaginal problems. Symptoms include a smelly discharge, painful intercourse and sometimes a burning sensation when urinating. Medical attention should be sought and sexual partners must also be treated. For more details see Sexually Transmitted Diseases earlier. Besides abstinence, the best thing is to practise safe sex.

Pregnancy It is not advisable to travel to some places while pregnant as some vaccinations normally used to prevent serious diseases (eg, yellow fever) are not advisable during pregnancy. In addition, some diseases are much more serious for the mother during pregnancy (eg, malaria) and may increase the risk of a stillborn child.

Beating River Blindness

It's not often you hear good news about a disease, especially where that disease is in West Africa. Which makes the near-total elimination of onchocerciasis, more commonly known as river blindness, in the region all the more remarkable.

Onchocerciasis causes blindness, skin lesions, disfigurement and almost unbearable itching and, according to WHO figures, some 1.5 million people were once afflicted with the disease across West Africa. It is caused by a parasitic worm, Onchocerca volvulus, which grows from a parasite introduced into humans by the bite of a blackfly. Over its 14-year life span, the adult worm produces millions of microscopic parasites that spread through the body causing the disease.

The program to wipe out onchocerciasis dates back to the mid-1970s, when French scientists reasoned that if blackflies could be controlled for at least 14 years – the time an adult worm lives in the human body – then the parasite colony in humans would die out. The World Bank funded a huge program to spray chemicals into river valleys where blackfly larvae developed in fast-flowing water. To complement the spraying, pharmaceutical company Merck donated 65 million doses of the drug Ivermectin, to be administered once a year to people living in the affected areas.

The results are startling. The World Bank claims there are only one or two remaining pockets of the disease within 11 West African nations. A partnership including Merck, a variety of non-governmental organisations, the World Bank, the WHO and the UN Development Program now aims to rid Central, East and Southern Africa of river blindness by 2010.

Most miscarriages occur during the first three months of pregnancy. Miscarriage is not uncommon and occasionally leads to severe bleeding. The last three months of pregnancy should be spent within reasonable distance of good medical care. A baby born as early as 24 weeks stands a chance of survival, but only in a good modern hospital. Pregnant women should avoid medication, although vaccinations and malarial prophylactics should be taken where needed.

Less Common Diseases

The following diseases pose a small risk to travellers, and so are only mentioned in passing. Seek medical advice if you think you may have any of these diseases.

Cholera This is the worst of the watery diarrhoeas and medical help should be sought. Outbreaks of cholera are generally widely reported, so you can usually avoid such problem areas. *Fluid replacement is the most vital treatment* – the risk of dehydration is severe as you may lose up to 20L a day. If there is a delay in getting to hospital, then begin taking tetracycline. The adult dose is 250mg four times daily. It is not recommended for children under nine years or for pregnant women. Tetracycline may help shorten the illness, but adequate fluids are required to save lives.

Filariasis This is a mosquito-transmitted parasitic infection found in many parts of Africa, including Gambia and Senegal. Possible symptoms include fever, pain and swelling of the lymph glands; inflammation of lymph drainage areas; swelling of a limb or the scrotum; skin rashes; and blindness. Treatment is available to eliminate the parasites from the body, but some of the damage already caused may not be reversible. Medical advice should be obtained promptly if the infection is suspected.

Leishmaniasis This is a group of parasitic diseases transmitted by sandflies, which are found in many parts of the Middle East, Africa, India, Central and South America and the Mediterranean. Cutaneous leishmaniasis affects the skin tissue causing ulceration and disfigurement, and visceral leishmaniasis affects the internal organs. Seek medical advice, as laboratory testing is required for diagnosis and correct treatment. Avoiding sandfly bites is the best precaution. Bites are usually painless, itchy and yet another reason to cover up and apply repellent.

Rabies This fatal viral infection is found in many countries. Many animals can be infected (such as dogs, cats, bats and monkeys) and it is their saliva that is infectious. Any bite, scratch or even lick from an animal should be cleaned immediately and thoroughly. Scrub with soap and running water, and then apply alcohol or iodine solution. Seek medical help promptly to receive a course of injections to prevent the onset of symptoms and death.

Sleeping Sickness In parts of tropical Africa tsetse flies can carry trypanosomiasis, or sleeping sickness; however, it is seldom seen in Gambia and Senegal. The tsetse fly is about twice the size of a housefly and recognisable by the scissorlike way it folds its wings when at rest. Only a small proportion of tsetse flies carry the disease, but it is a serious disease . No protection is available except avoiding the tsetse fly bites. The flies are attracted to large moving objects such as safari buses, to perfume and aftershave and particularly to the colours purple and dark blue (avoid dark-blue hire cars). Swelling at the site of the bite, five or more days later, is the first sign of infection; this is followed within two to three weeks by fever.

Tetanus This disease is caused by a germ that lives in soil and in the faeces of horses and other animals. It enters the body via breaks in the skin. The first symptom may be discomfort in swallowing, or stiffening of the jaw and neck; this is followed by painful convulsions of the jaw and whole body. The disease can be fatal. It can be prevented by vaccination.

Tuberculosis (TB) This bacterial infection is usually transmitted from person to person by coughing but may be transmitted through consumption of unpasteurised milk. Milk that has been boiled is safe to drink, and the souring of milk to make yogurt or cheese also kills the bacilli. TB is quite a problem in parts of Gambia, though travellers are usually not at great risk as close household contact with the infected person is usually required before the disease is passed on.

Typhus This disease is spread by ticks, mites or lice. It begins with fever, chills, headache and muscle pains followed a few days later by a body rash. There is often a large painful sore at the site of the bite and nearby lymph nodes are swollen and painful. Typhus can be treated under medical supervision. Seek local advice on areas where ticks pose a danger and always check your skin carefully for ticks after walking in areas that may harbour ticks, such as tropical forests. An insect repellent can help, and walkers in tick-infested areas should consider having their boots and trousers impregnated with benzyl benzoate and dibutylphthalate.

Yellow Fever This viral disease is endemic in many African and South American countries and is transmitted by mosquitoes. The initial symptoms are fever, headache, abdominal pain and vomiting. Seek medical care urgently and drink lots of fluids.

WOMEN TRAVELLERS

Generally speaking, most women travellers (alone or with other women) in Gambia and Senegal will not encounter problems such as harassment from men any more than they might in other parts of the world. Many women travellers report that the region is relatively safe and unthreatening, compared with North Africa, South America and a few Western countries, and that friendliness and generosity are met far more often than hostility.

There are some parts of this region where mugging is a possibility, and as elsewhere, women (particularly lone women) are generally seen as easy targets, so it pays to be careful in these areas. Such 'danger zones' are listed in the relevant sections of the country chapters. See also Dangers & Annoyances later in this chapter.

When it comes to evening entertainment, West Africa is definitely a conservative, male-dominated society and women travellers may come up against a few glass walls and ceilings. Cultural conventions dictate that women usually don't go to bars without a male companion – however distasteful it may be to Westerners – and trying to buck the system could lead to trouble.

Because of these conventions, it can be hard to meet and talk with local women in Gambia and Senegal. It may require being invited into a home, but because many women have received little or no education, language barriers can be a problem. However, this is changing to some extent because a number of girls go to school while boys are sent away to work. This means many of the staff in tourist offices, government departments and so on are educated, young to middle-aged women, and their workplaces present opportunities to try striking up a conversation. In rural areas, a good starting point might be women teachers at a local school, or staff at a health centre.

When you're actually travelling, the best advice on what can and can't be undertaken safely will come from local women. Unfortunately, many white expats are likely to be appalled at the idea of a lone female traveller and will do their best to discourage you with horrendous stories, which are often of dubious accuracy. Although both Gambia and Senegal are considerably safer than some other parts of the world, hitching alone is not recommended. If you decide to thumb it, you should refuse a lift if the driver is drunk or the car full of men (often the case with military vehicles). Use your common sense and things should go well.

Sexual Harassment

Despite sexual harassment being less of a problem for women travellers in Gambia and Senegal than in some other parts of the world, it is something women, particularly lone women, occasionally have to deal with. Unwanted interest is always unpleasant, but it's well worth remembering that although you may encounter a lewd border official, or an admirer who won't go away, physical harm or rape is very unlikely.

Part of the reason for the interest shown in you arises from the fact that local women rarely travel long distances alone, and a single foreign female is a very unusual sight. Another reason is that, thanks to imported television and Hollywood films, Western women are frequently viewed as being 'loose'. What you wear may greatly influence how you're treated. African women dress conservatively, in traditional or Western clothes, so when a visitor wears something significantly different, she will draw attention. In the minds of some men this peculiar dressing will be seen as provocative. In general, look at what other women are wearing and follow suit. Keep most of your legs covered, at least below the knee, with trousers, a skirt or culottes. Many women travellers also report that covering their hair, especially long hair, and even more so with long blonde hair, helps keep unwanted attention at bay. If you're alone in an uneasy situation, act 'prudishly'. Stick your nose in a book. Or invent an imaginary husband who will be arriving shortly either in the country or at that particular spot. If you are travelling with a male companion, one of the best ways to avoid unwanted interest is to introduce him as your husband.

Tampons

Tampons (usually imported from Europe) are available at supermarkets and pharmacies in large towns such as Dakar and Banjul. In tourist areas (eg, the Atlantic coast resorts in Gambia), they are also available at large hotels. In Senegal, a tampon is usually called a *tampon hygiénique*, but might also be called a *tampon periodique* or *serviette hygiénique*. By simply asking for a tampon you'll be requesting a stamp, as in a passport stamp, which just won't suffice.

GAY & LESBIAN TRAVELLERS

Most people in both Gambia and Senegal, especially the older generation, are conservative in their attitudes towards gays and lesbians, and gay sexual relationships are both a cultural taboo and very rare among locals. Strictly speaking, being gay or lesbian is illegal in Senegal. Some parts of the predominantly Muslim community are actively antigay – some villagers have prevented gays being buried in the village cemetery. Most Senegalese, though, have a fairly 'live and let live' attitude. Flirting from Westerners is more often met with embarrassment and flattery than with anger. There have even been reports of male travellers being propositioned by Senegalese men.

Among the expat community, which is pretty much confined to the Atlantic coast resorts in Gambia, and Dakar and the tourist areas in Senegal, there is a percentage who are gay (as in any Western community), but there are no established regular meeting places or 'scene', so it is usually quite difficult for visitors to make contact. In most places in Senegambia, any open displays of affection are generally frowned upon, whatever your orientation.

DISABLED TRAVELLERS

People who don't walk will find it hard travelling around Gambia and Senegal. Even though there are more disabled people per head of population here than in the West, wheelchair facilities are virtually nonexistent. In the capitals, a few official buildings are constructed with ramps and lifts – but not many, and probably not the ones you want to visit. On the other hand, the tourist facilities in Gambia and Senegal make travel in these countries more straightforward than in some other parts of West Africa. For example, many smarter hotels are on only one or two levels, so access is fairly easy, and where there are more levels, there's usually a lift. For getting around the country, especially in Gambia where distances are short, hiring a car with a driver for the day (or longer) is a feasible and relatively inexpensive option (see Gambia's Getting Around chapter for more details).

SENIOR TRAVELLERS

West Africa is generally regarded as not ideal for senior travellers (on the assumption they want to rough it less than the younger folk) because good hotels and other facilities are limited, and travel by public transport can be hard. Gambia and Senegal, however, are exceptions to this general rule, as both have large hotels and resort areas catering mainly for tourists of any age who fly in from Europe for all-inclusive package tours. This makes them ideal for people who prefer to hold on to home comforts while also seeing something of another continent and culture. In fact, both countries (Gambia particularly) are excellent stepping stones between Europe and Africa, and both see plenty of senior travellers. Facilities include coach and taxi tours, car hire (with or without driver) and good medical services. We met several retired people roaming around the more remote parts of Gambia and Senegal having the time of their lives. It's more about attitudes and expectations than dates of birth.

TRAVEL WITH CHILDREN

In Gambia and Senegal, most of the larger hotels in the resorts on the coast cater for package tourists, many of whom come as families. If interest in the beach or the pool fades, many hotels also arrange games, events and other attractions for children, plus child-minding in the evening.

Some other places, not necessarily expensive, have family rooms with three or four beds for only slightly more than the price of a double. Alternatively, arranging an extra bed or mattress so children can share a standard adult double room will generally not be a problem.

Apart from this, there are few children-oriented facilities available in the region. In nontourist hotels there are no discounts for children – a bed's a bed, whoever sleeps in it. Likewise, on public transport if you want a seat it has to be paid for. Most local kids go for free on buses and bush taxis, but spend the journey on their parent's lap.

Attractions that appeal to adults (markets, mosques, mud-brick architecture, endless desert wilderness) do not have such a hold over children. Distances between 'sights' can be long, especially on public transport, so parents need to have a good supply of distractions to hand. ('Let's count how many David Beckham shirts we can see in this village…')

On the positive side, travelling with children allows you to see life through their eyes – you'd be amazed how many scrawny chickens you never notice. It's also likely to make interaction with the local population easier and more rewarding. Turn up with young kids and the initial surprise will soon turn to delight, with everyone wanting to help.

Lonely Planet's *Travel with Children* provides more detailed advice, and ideas for games on the bus.

DANGERS & ANNOYANCES

On a world scale Gambia and Senegal are fairly safe places to visit. Outside Dakar violent crime is almost unheard of; even in Dakar, relatively few people report being robbed, and only a tiny percentage of those suffer any actual physical harm. The following advice is well worth reading, though, and especially in Dakar it's important to be on guard. But whatever you do, don't treat everyone you meet as a potential assailant – only downtown Johannesburg deserves that level of caution.

Mugging

Not surprisingly, the danger of robbery is much more prevalent in cities and larger towns than in rural or wilderness areas. But even towns can differ; there's more of a danger in those frequented by wealthy foreigners than in places off the usual tourist track.

By far the most dangerous place in Senegambia is Dakar, where many people have bags snatched and pockets picked, occasionally violently (see the Dakar chapter for more details). In the resorts near Banjul attacks are rare but not unknown; tourists have on occasion been pushed to the ground and had bags or cameras stolen, but they haven't been knifed or otherwise seriously injured (see the Atlantic Coast Resorts & Serekunda chapter). In both capital cities, it's very rare to hear of thieves carrying guns.

More details of specific danger zones that travellers should be aware of are given in the country chapters.

Precautions

Taking some simple precautions will hopefully ensure your journey to Senegambia is trouble-free. Remember that many thousands of travellers enjoy trips without any problems whatsoever, usually because they were careful. Most of the precautions that we have suggested below are particularly relevant to cities, although some of them might apply in towns and other places too.

• Don't make yourself a target. It's good to carry around as little as possible; leave your day-pack in your hotel room. Leave your camera and personal stereo behind too. Even passports, travellers cheques and credit cards can be left behind at the hotel. If you're worried about theft from the hotel, ask the manager to put your valuables in a safe or a security box (if they have one). If you're travelling in rural Gambia or Casamance you'll need to keep your passport handy as there are regular military checkpoints. But elsewhere try carrying around a photocopy or some other less-valuable ID instead.

• Don't display your money and other symbols of wealth. Don't wear jewellery or watches, however cheap they actually are, unless you're prepared to lose them. Use a separate wallet for day-to-day purchases, and keep the bulk of your cash out of sight, hidden in a pouch under loose-fitting clothing. Travellers who keep everything in a colourful bag clearly visible around their waist, or (even worse) over their shoulder, or who have wallets bulging through trouser

Scams

The hustlers of Dakar and Banjul, and some other places frequented by tourists (for example St-Louis and Ziguinchor), have perfected a dazzling array of scams and con-tricks. Some are imaginative and amusing; others are serious and cause for concern. Their aim is always to get some (or all) of your money.

The Visitors Book

In both Gambia and Senegal, the 'visitors book' has become one of the most popular and definitely the most effective means of extracting cash from tourists. There are several variations, but this is a classic of the genre. You're in the market, carrying your camera, when a man approaches telling you he has a newborn child. Could you please, if it's no problem at all, come to his compound and take a photo of him and the child. It's not far away, it won't take long, and it would mean the world to him and his sick wife. When you get to the compound you meet his sick 'wife' but the baby is nowhere to be seen. Dad explains that his child is also unwell and has been taken back to the hospital, but seeing as you're here would you like a Coke – it's free! 'It is our duty to be hospitable,' he says. 'We have lots of tourists here, and we never take money for a drink.' As there is no baby around you have had your suspicions for a while – but you feel too rude to walk out while they bombard you with a string of questions about your country. When you get up to leave, the 'visitors book' appears, listing the names of dozens of other Western tourists who've allegedly donated money to the family to help pay for rice – D500 being the average 'donation'. When it gets to this stage few are able to escape. Your only chance is to leave as soon as you see the baby is not there, or better, to say at the outset that you don't want to give money.

Sock Sellers

A youth approaches you in the street with a couple of pairs of socks for sale. Even though you make it clear you don't want them he follows you for several minutes – checking you out. Then his buddy approaches you from the other side and he also tries to persuade you to buy the socks. He bends down and starts playing with your trousers and shoes, supposedly to show you how well the socks would go with what you're wearing. You are irritated and distracted, and while you bend down to fend him off, whoosh, the other guy comes in from the other side and goes straight for the wallet in your pocket.

pockets are just asking for trouble. You might just as well wear a sign saying 'rob me'.

• Don't stroll or amble – never look as though you're lost (even if you are), and try not to look like a tourist! Remember to walk purposefully and confidently. If you need to keep your bearings, tear out the map you need from this guidebook, or photocopy it, and use that instead as your reference. If you need to consult the map, step into a shop or some other place where your disorientation is not so obvious.

• Don't walk in the backstreets, or even on some of the main streets, at night. Take a taxi. A dollar or two for the fare might save you a lot of trouble.

A final suggestion is to hire a local to accompany you when walking around a risky area in a town or city. It's usually not too difficult to find someone – ask at your hotel reception – who wouldn't mind earning a few dollars for the task of guiding you safely around the streets.

Begging

In most of Africa there is no government welfare for the unemployed, sick, disabled, homeless, or old. If such people have no family to help, they are forced to beg, and you will undoubtedly encounter this during your trip. The extended family support system is very effective, however, and there are remarkably few beggars considering West

---

Scams

The solution? Be firm, walk purposefully, stay cool, and don't be distracted. And don't carry your wallet in your back pocket.

Remember Me?

A popular trick in the tourist areas is for local lads to approach you in the street and say 'Hello, it's me, from the hotel, don't you recognise me?' You're not sure. You don't really remember him, but you don't want to seem rude either. So you stop for a chat. Can he walk with you for a while? Sure. Nice day. A few more pleasantries. Then comes the crunch: how about a visit to his brother's souvenir shop? Or do you wanna buy some grass? Need a taxi? A tour? By this time you're hooked, and you probably end up buying or arranging something. A variation involves the con-artist pretending to be a hotel employee or 'son of the owner' out to get supplies for the bar or restaurant. There's been a mix-up at the shop. Can you lend him some money? You can take it off the hotel bill later. He'll know your name and room number, and even give you a receipt. But, surprise surprise, back at the hotel they've never heard of him, and the money is never seen again.

The way to avoid the trap is to be polite but firm: you don't remember anyone, and you'd like to be alone. You could ask 'which hotel' after the first greeting, but the guy may really work there, or at least have noticed you coming out, and then perfectly calls your bluff.

A Nice Welcome

You may be invited to stay in someone's house, in exchange for a meal and drinks, but your new friend's appetite for food and beer may make this deal more expensive than staying at a hotel. More seriously, while you are entertaining, someone will be at the house of your 'friend' going through your bag. This scam is only likely in tourist areas – we heard about it in St-Louis – but remember in remote or rural areas you'll come across genuine hospitality.

Police & Thieves

If you buy grass or other drugs from a dealer, don't be surprised if he's in cahoots with the local police who then come to your hotel or stop you in the street and find you 'in possession'. Large bribes will be required to avoid arrest or imprisonment. The solution is very easy – do not buy grass from total strangers.

Reality Check

Lest you get too paranoid, remember this. Considering the wealth of most tourists and the unimaginable poverty of most locals, the incidence of robbery or theft in most of Senegambia is incredibly low. Even a shoe-string traveller's daily budget of about US$12 a day is more than most Gambians make in a month. When you sit in a bus station sipping a soft drink that costs half a US dollar, look around you. You'll see an old man selling fans carefully woven from palm leaves for about half this price, or a teenage youth trying to earn that amount by offering to clean your shoes. It reminds you with a jolt that the vast majority of local people are decent and hard-working and want from you only respect and the chance to make an honest living.

Africa is the poorest area on earth. Because helping the needy is part of traditional African culture, and one of the pillars of Islam by which Muslims reach paradise, you will see even poor people giving to beggars. If you want to give, even a very small coin is appreciated. If you don't have any change, just say 'next time' or something similar.

Gifts & Tips

One great annoyance for visitors to Africa is local people (not beggars) asking for gifts. 'Do you have something for me?' ('Donnez-moi un cadeau') becomes familiar everywhere you go, usually from young children, but also from youths and even adults. Part of this expectation comes from a belief that anyone God has been good to should be willing to spread some wealth around. Because non-African foreigners are thought to be rich (which, relatively speaking, they are), generosity is generally expected. The usual gift asked for is, of course, money, but people may request your hat, shoes, camera or bicycle, all within a couple of minutes of meeting you. In this kind of situation you are not really expected to give anything. It's a 'worth a try' situation, and your polite refusal will rarely offend.

The situation changes when the gift is given in return for service, in which case it becomes more like a tip. The situation is further confused in Senegal where the word 'cadeau' is used for both tip and gift. There are no hard-and-fast rules when deciding whether to give. If somebody simply points you the way to the bus station that would not be a significant service, whereas helping you for 10 minutes to find a hotel probably would be. When deciding how much to give, think how much a bottle of Coke or beer costs. Giving your helper enough 'to have a drink' is usually sufficient. If you're not prepared to offer a tip, don't ask for significant favours. Of course, some people will help you out of kindness and will not expect anything. However, in tourist areas you'll encounter locals who make a living by talking to foreigners, then providing 'friendly' services (from information and postcards to hard drugs and sex) for money. Other Africans tend to scorn these hustlers. Avoid them unless you really need something and do not mind paying.

Bribery

A gift or tip becomes a completely different matter when you *have* to pay to get something done. In this case it's effectively a bribe (still called 'cadeau' in Senegal, and often a 'dash' in Gambia).

Bribery is a way of life throughout Africa. Gambians and Senegalese, while by no means the worst offenders, are no exception. Put simply, poorly paid officials are using 'rich' tourists to top up their salaries. For example, at an airport or border, a customs official may go through your belongings then ask: 'Don't you have something extra?' This implies that if you don't give them a small gift the search could go on for hours.

Travellers have different ways of dealing with this kind of situation. The best method is to feign ignorance and simply bluff your way through. If this doesn't work, state clearly you are not going to give them anything. Occasionally the requests by the officer may become threats, such as denying entrance into the country. This is usually just a bluff, although it can last several minutes. It is essential to remain polite. You might ask to see a senior officer, but you should never return the threats. Give the official you're dealing with plenty of room to back down and save face. In virtually all cases, you'll soon be allowed to continue.

If your documents are not all in order, you're more vulnerable, but keep an ear out for the totally fictitious regulations that are invented simply to create a bribe situation.

Sometimes you have to play the system. For example, if officials are slow in processing a visa request, offering a small dash or cadeau may be your only option. But tread very carefully here. Never simply offer to pay. Wait to see whether the official hints for something extra. Ask whether any 'special fee' is required to speed up the process.

LEGAL MATTERS

While marijuana is widely available in both Gambia and Senegal, its use is illegal in both countries. If you're caught in possession you could face up to two years in an African jail; a less-than-attractive proposition. However, unless you're caught by an unusually straight cop, or are carrying a particularly large quantity of the drug, it's more likely you'll be 'persuaded' to buy your way out of trouble, which usually results in a very one-sided bargaining session. Either way, you are in deep shit if you get caught.

ACTIVITIES
Cycling

Cycling can be an excellent way to tour around Gambia and Senegal. For more information, see Activities in each country's Facts for the Visitor chapter. See also the Getting Around Senegambia chapter later in this book.

Fishing

Deep-sea sport fishing can be arranged in Dakar, and in the hotel resorts near Banjul, where you can also arrange more relaxed outings in the surrounding creeks and rivers. More details are given in the country chapters. Depending on the season, ocean catches include barracuda, tuna, sailfish, blue marlin, swordfish, sea bass and wahoo.

Football

Football (soccer) is Africa's most popular participation and spectator sport. If you want to play, the universities and municipal stadiums are by far the best places to find a good-quality game, but outside every town in Africa is a patch of ground where informal matches are played most evenings (in coastal areas the beach is used). The ball may be more suitable for tennis, and the goal area a couple of sticks (not necessarily opposite each other). While you may have to deal with puddles, ditches and the odd goat or donkey wandering across the pitch, the game itself is taken very seriously. Play is fast and furious, with the ball played low. Foreigners are usually warmly welcomed, and joining in a game is one of the best ways to meet the locals. If you bring along your own ball you'll be the hit of the day.

Swimming & Water Sports

In Senegambia's tourist areas, most major hotels have pools that nonguests are able to use for a fee. Otherwise, you have a long coastline with several beaches to choose from, although large waves, steep shelves and a heavy undertow can make some of them dangerous. It is sensible to always seek local advice before attempting to swim in the ocean.

In tourist areas, such as Gambia's Atlantic coast resorts and Senegal's Petite Côte, you can hire sailboards, or arrange water-skiing as well as several other motor-assisted sports. Dakar is also a base for diving and kayaking. For more details on arranging water sports refer to the country chapters.

COURSES

There are several places in Gambia and Senegal where you can learn how to play local instruments, especially drums, or study traditional dance. Other options are courses in local storytelling techniques, arts and crafts, batik-making and cookery. In Gambia, several hotels near Banjul offer courses, and some local workshops offer lessons by the hour or day. More details are provided under Courses in the Atlantic Coast Resorts & Serekunda chapter. In Senegal, places to learn drumming near Dakar include Malika and Île de Gorée. There are also many places in and around Kafountine and St-Louis. See the relevant chapters for details.

ACCOMMODATION

Gambia and Senegal both have a wide range of places to stay, from international-class hotels in the capitals, through to comfortable mid-range establishments, and down to the most basic lodging houses out in the sticks or the rough end of town. Generally, quality reflects price. Top-end hotels have clean, well-appointed rooms with air-conditioning, and private bathrooms with hot showers and toilets that work all the time. In the middle range, rooms have a private bathroom, but there may not always be hot water, and there will probably be fans instead of air-con. In the budget range, hotel rooms are not always clean (they are sometimes downright filthy), bathrooms are usually shared and are often in an appalling state, and the only source of fresh air may be a hole in the window.

Many hotels, particularly the cheap ones, double as brothels. But even the more classy establishments can serve this purpose – the standard of the room reflects only the wealth of the clients.

In any class of hotel, bargaining on the price is always a possibility, especially during the low season. For the management a full room is always better than an empty one so if rates are beyond your reach, it's worth asking for a discount.

In Gambia's Atlantic coast resort area, you'll find everything from simple guesthouses to luxury hotels. But in the 'upcountry' provinces your choice is limited to a few smart lodges, a small number of simple places designed for tourists, a few cheap and very basic hotels usually frequented by locals, and the occasional government resthouse that also caters for the public.

Most towns in Senegal have a *campement*. This could be loosely translated as 'hostel', 'inn' or 'lodge', or even 'motel', but it is not a camping ground. Traditionally, campements offered simple accommodation, less elaborate than hotels. However, while some campements remain cheap and simple, others are very good quality with prices on a par with mid-range hotels. You'll find the occasional auberge and gîte too – this is also something like a 'hostel', 'inn' or 'lodge', again with a wide range of quality. A *maison de passage* (or *casse de passage*) tends to always be on the basic side, often near markets or bus stations; it provides a bed for travellers and little else, and a good number of your fellow guests will be renting by the hour.

Most hotels catering to tourists have high- and low-season rates. High-season rates (November to April) are quoted throughout this book. Low-season rates are about 25% to 50% cheaper, and you can get rooms for even less if you're prepared to negotiate, although some hotels close completely in the low season. If breakfast is included it's usually on a par with the standard of accommodation: a full buffet in more expensive places; coffee and bread further down the scale.

Some hotels charge by the room, so whether you are alone or with somebody makes no difference to the price (apart from the tourist tax in Senegal). Some other hotels allow couples to share a single.

Electricity is frequently cut off at night (although most large hotels have a generator), so it's always a good idea to have a torch and some candles.

There are not many camping grounds in Gambia and Senegal, and those that do exist cater mainly for overlanders in their own vehicle. However, some hotels and campements allow camping, or provide an area where tents can be pitched. Grassy sites are very rare – you often have to force pegs through hard-packed gravel.

Tourist Tax

Apart from the CRI campements in Casamance, all accommodation places in Senegal charge a tourist tax of CFA600 per person. Sometimes this is included in the price, sometimes it isn't. You have to ask. Throughout this book, wherever possible we have included tourist tax in the price.

FOOD

By West African standards Senegambia is a veritable culinary paradise. Local food tends to be of a high standard and is complemented, particularly in cities and larger towns, by a wide range of international cuisines at good prices.

Eating African food need not mean eating poorly – Gambia and Senegal have some wonderfully tasty dishes. Even travellers with sensitive stomachs can usually get away with eating traditional African food, if they ease themselves gently into the change of diet. In any kind of restaurant, you might get a bit of stomach trouble if plates or cutlery aren't clean, but that can happen anywhere, and it doesn't happen often.

In West Africa, food is generally prepared and cooked in the open, and a lot is sold outside too, at markets or road-side stalls. Nevertheless, local-style food is usually safer than Western-style food because it's cooked much longer (sometimes all day) and the ingredients are invariably fresh. On the other hand, food in a smarter restaurant may have been lingering in a refrigerator – power cuts notwithstanding – for days.

For vegetarians, West Africa can be a challenge. It's not that you can't find food without meat – it's what most poor people eat. Rather, in a region where meat is the most sought-after of foods the concept of vegetarianism is misunderstood (see the boxed text 'You Don't Want Meat?' in the Atlantic Coast Resorts & Serekunda chapter).

Note, however, that even if you order a dish with 'no meat' you might still get a nasty surprise. Chicken is usually not regarded as 'real' meat, and even the simplest (and seemingly most innocuous) vegetable sauce may have a small bit of meat or animal fat added. It's nothing sinister, it just 'tastes better with meat' you'll be told.

Street Food

A feature of West African travel is the availability of cheap 'street food', ideal if you're on the move, or if you prefer to eat little and often. Street food rarely involves plates or knives – it's served on a stick, or wrapped in paper or in a plastic bag.

On street corners and around bus stations, especially in the morning and particularly in Senegal, you'll see small booths selling pieces of bread cut from fresh baguettes, with fillings of butter, chocolate spread, mayonnaise or sardines. The price depends on the size of the piece of bread you want, and the type of filling. It's quite usual to ask for a CFA100 chunk, with CFA75 worth of mayonnaise, giving you a sandwich for CFA175. Among the region's finest institutions are the coffee stalls, where clients sit on small benches around a table, and drink glasses of Nescafé mixed with sweetened condensed milk, served with French-style bread, butter or mayonnaise, all for around CFA300 or D6. Some also offer tea (made with a tea bag), or even Milo, and a more enterprising café stand might fry up eggs or serve sardines. Sometimes the tea or coffee is made with a weak solution of local herbs called *kinkilaba*, which turns the water brown, and gives the drink a slightly 'woody', although not unpleasant, taste. Another popular variation is spicy coffee, known as *café Touba* or *café saf*.

Also in the mornings, women with large brown bowls covered in a wicker lid sell a local yogurt called *sow* (Wolof) or *kossam* (Pulaar), which is often mixed with pounded millet (*cheri* or *latcheri*) and sugar to make *chacori*. This sells for about CFA150 a portion. A variation is *fanday* (Wolof) or *monaye* (Pulaar) where the millet is boiled before being mixed with the yogurt to make more of a porridge.

At night the women sell pounded millet mixed with a leaf sauce called *haako/mboom* for CFA200 to CFA300 per portion. Beans – especially the black-eyed variety *(niebe)* – are another common street-food ingredient, either pounded into a paste and deep fried, or mashed and served in a sandwich. Either way these are commonly eaten at breakfast, but can be found at other times of day. There is also *cheri bassi*, which is black-eyed beans, millet and groundnuts pounded together.

In the evening you can buy brochettes – beef, sheep or goat meat cut small, skewered and grilled over a fire – for around D3 or CFA150 per stick. Or you can buy larger lumps of roasted meat sold by guys who walk around pushing a tin oven on wheels. Another hot option is deep-fried chips of cassava. Grilled or roasted meat, usually mixed with onions and some spices, is sold in a shack called a *dibieterie* in Senegal and an *afra* in Gambia (basically an oven with a few walls around). You can eat here on the spot (a rough bench might be provided) or take away. It's usual to ask for an amount according to how much money you want to spend. For example, in Senegal, CFA1000's worth (about D30 in Gambia) will feed one or two people. If it's not enough you can always ask for another CFA500 lump. The term afra is used for the meat-grilling process, and for the place where it's done. Thus an afra can be a simple take-away, or a smart restaurant where the process might otherwise be called charcoal grilling or barbecuing.

Another popular standby found in the larger towns and cities are Lebanese-style *chawarmas*, which are very similar to doner kebabs – thin slices of lamb or chicken grilled on a spit, served with salad (optional) in pita bread with a sauce made from chickpeas. These cost about D15 or CFA800.

For snacking, you can also buy groundnuts everywhere – shelled, unshelled, boiled, roasted, salted or sugared. You can also find *beignets* (donuts) in some areas.

Meals

West African food typically consists of a staple food served with a sauce, and it's the great variety of ingredients that make it interesting. Senegal is particularly known for having some of the finest cuisine in West Africa, and many of the classics can be found at very reasonable prices in local-style restaurants, as well as in the posh places. African dishes can be simple or complex according to the skill of the cook, the availability of ingredients and the budget of the customer.

Some travellers have been lucky enough to stay with local people, and a great way to repay their hospitality is to pay for a special meal for the whole family. This way you'll also be able to see how meals are put together. For the full picture, visit the market with the lady of the house (it's always the women who do the cooking in domestic situations) and see the ingredients being bought.

Rice is the common staple everywhere in Gambia and Senegal. Millet, which is also common, has to be pounded into flour before it can be cooked. In most rural areas this is done by hand with a large wooden mortar and pestle, sometimes for several hours. In some places, an entrepreneur or aid scheme will set up a mechanical mill to do this, although many people cannot afford the extra cost of this service. The millet flour is steamed and then moistened with water until it thickens into a stiff 'porridge' that can be eaten with the fingers.

Groundnuts are grown almost everywhere in Gambia and Senegal, so a thick brown groundnut sauce called *mafé* in Senegal and *mafay* in Gambia is very common. *Domodah* is another version, usually with something else like meat or vegetables mixed with the nuts. Sometimes, deep-orange palm oil is also added.

Tiéboudienne (spelt in various ways, eg, thieboudjenne or thieboudjen, but pronounced chey-bou-jen) is the national dish of Senegal and consists of rice baked in a thick sauce of fish and vegetables. It comes in two varieties: *thieb khonkhe* (pronounced cheb-honk), with tomato paste; and *thieb wekh*, without. In Gambia it's called *benechin*. Also popular is *yassa poulet*, which is grilled chicken marinated in an onion and lemon sauce. Variations on the theme, and depending on location, are *yassa poisson* (the same thing, but with fish) and *yassa viande* (meat), or sometimes simply *yassa* – what it's actually made of is a bit of a lucky dip. Another favourite, and equally variable, is *yollof rice* (*riz yollof* in Senegal and often called *thieb yape*), which is vegetables or meat or both, cooked in a sauce of oil and tomatoes.

All the above dishes are usually served with rice. *Bassi-salété* ('couscous' on some restaurant menus) is millet covered with vegetables and meat; it is frequently served for the evening meal, as well as on special occasions. In Gambia you might also find *plasas* (meat or fish cooked with vegetable leaves in palm oil) and served with *fufu* (mashed cassava). Cassava leaves may also

Le Menu

In Senegal's smarter restaurants, the *menu du jour* (often shortened to *le menu*) is the meal of the day – usually a starter, a main course and a desert – at a special price. If you want to see the menu (ie, the list of meals available), ask for *le carte* instead. This may include the *plat du jour* (the dish of the day), usually at a special price too.

be used for cooking. Other common vegetables include onions, tomatoes, potatoes (*pomme de terre* in French), sweet potatoes (*patate*), okra *(gombo)* and green beans (*haricot verte)*. Look out for *jaxatu* (pronounced ja-kah-too). It's like a green or yellow tomato, but extremely bitter.

For flavouring, chilli peppers are often used. Stock cubes and sachets of flavouring are ubiquitous across a region where Maggi is the most common trade name.

Where to Eat

The best place to eat – if you're lucky enough to be invited – is somebody's house. Most days, though, you'll probably be heading for a restaurant. The smallest, simplest local-style eating house is called a *chop shop* in Gambia and a *gargotte* in Senegal. Many appear nameless, but can usually be identified by coloured plastic strips hanging in their doorways. Prices for a plate of rice and sauce are sometimes as low as D5 or CFA300, with slightly more elaborate meals (ie, those with a small bit of meat or fish thrown in) a bit more. Most chop houses only have one or two types of meals available each day. It's usual to ask what they have (*'Qu'est ce que vous avez pour manger?'* in Senegal).

When frequenting small restaurants, it's important to go for the right food at the right time of day. For example, in Senegal tiéboudienne is only made and served at lunch time, and millet dishes only in the evening. In Gambia, rice and sauce from stalls may only be sold in the morning, not at lunch time. Dibieteries and afras are open only in the evening.

In slightly smarter places, your choice may also include 'international' meals such as fried chicken or fish, served with chips (french fries) in Gambia and *frites* in Senegal. Mid-range restaurants cater mainly to well-off locals and foreigners and they may only serve international dishes. These meals are usually relatively expensive, particularly if some of the ingredients are flown in from Europe.

In many places 'fast food' is available. The term refers less to the time it takes to serve the food than to the type of meal served – pizzas, burgers, hot dogs, and Lebanese pita-bread sandwiches.

Fruit

The availability of fruit depends on the season, but you'll find oranges, mandarins, grapefruit (often with green skin despite being ready to eat), bananas (many different colours and sizes), guavas and mangoes. In the cities and larger towns you'll find fruit imported from other West African countries, such as apples and pineapples. Interestingly, although papaya (pawpaw) trees grow all over the region, they are regarded almost as a weed, and the fruit is often left to fall to the ground and be eaten by goats.

DRINKS
Nonalcoholic Drinks

International and local brands of soft drink are sold virtually everywhere in the region. A tiny shop in a remote village may sell little food, but the chances are it'll have a few dusty bottles of Coke for sale. (Coke is called 'Coca' in Senegal). Bottled mineral water is available in cities, tourist areas and all but the smallest towns.

As with beers, prices for soft drinks vary from dirt cheap at a road-side stall to extortionate at posh restaurants. As a guide, the price of a soft drink is usually about half the price of a beer at the same place.

Home-made soft drinks include ginger 'beer' and *bisap* (a purple mixture made from water and hibiscus leaves). These drinks are usually sold in plastic bags by children on the street. Although they are refreshing, the water may not be clean, so unless you're blessed with a cast-iron stomach they're best avoided.

Tea comes in two sorts: the type recognised in Britain and other Western countries and made with a tea bag (its local name is 'Lipton tea' even if the brand is actually something else); and local tea (often called *attaya*), made with green leaves (often imported from China) and served with loads of sugar in small glasses. Mint is sometimes added, or the tea may be made from mint leaves alone. If you're invited into someone's house you'll almost certainly be offered *attaya*. Be warned, though, that when you accept the first glass you're buying into an hour-long ritual in which the tea is brewed three times; each brew produces a different (usually sweeter) taste. Rejecting subsequent glasses can cause offence. Coffee is almost exclusively instant Nescafé, although *where* you drink it will determine the flavour. At the coffee stalls mentioned under Street Food in the Food section earlier in this chapter, it's mixed with sweetened condensed milk. At the smarter restaurants it comes as a cup of warm water, with a Nescafé sachet in the saucer – you add milk and sugar as required.

Alcoholic Drinks

You can often find imported beers from Europe and America, but both Gambia and Senegal brew their own brands. In Gambia, it's JulBrew, which is usually served in 280mL bottles, but also available as a draught beer in smarter bars and hotels. Prices for a bottle start at about D10 in the simplest watering hole, and range up to around D25 in posh restaurants. In Senegal, Gazelle comes in 630mL bottles and costs between CFA500 and CFA900. Flag is a stronger, more upmarket brew. A 330mL

Collecting Palm Wine

As you travel along the backroads of Gambia and southern Senegal, you'll almost certainly see men collecting 'palm wine'. This alcoholic liquid is the sap of the oil palm tree, which comes out of the tree already fermented, and is a highly prized commodity – especially in areas where beer or wine in bottles and cans is unaffordable. Each collector climbs his own trees, using a loop of rope (called a *kandab* in Diola) that fits like a large belt around man and tree, holding him close to the trunk. Just below the point where the palm fonds sprout from the tree, the collector punches a hole through the bark into the soft sap. The liquid drips slowly through a funnel (traditionally made from leaves, although these days it's usually a piece of plastic), and is collected in any handy container (once a natural gourd or calabash, today more likely to be a plastic bottle). After a few hours, the collector comes back, the bottle is full and the wine – sweet, thick and white, usually with a few insects swimming around in it – is ready to drink. At this stage, it's stronger than beer although not as strong as 'real' wine. But sometimes yeast or sugar is added, and the brew allowed to ferment overnight or for a few more days. This makes it come closer in strength to your average Chardonnay (although lacking the refined flavour), and sometimes even stronger – with a real kick.

Palm wine is collected by punching a hole into the tree just under the sprouting palm fronds

bottle costs CFA500 in a cheap place, and up to CFA1500 or more in posh bars and hotels (where they wouldn't dream of offering Gazelle). Flag is also available in 650ml bottles and on draught.

A traditional 'beer' made from millet-rough looks brown and gritty and is common, but the region's most popular home-made brew is palm wine.

SPECTATOR SPORTS

Football (soccer) is very popular in Gambia and Senegal, just as it is all over Africa. Games can be played at any time, but evenings and weekends during the cool dry season are the most popular.

Every town and large village has a football pitch, and matches against teams from neighbouring towns draw large crowds, with people standing four or five deep around the touchline, and young boys hanging from surrounding trees to get a better view. Matches of this nature are very rarely advertised, so you will need to ask around for information.

Larger towns and cities have stadiums where matches take place, most notably the Independence Stadium in Bakau near Banjul, and the Stadium Senghor on the northern side of Dakar. Games against sides from neighbouring countries are advertised and draw massive crowds. Football in Senegal has improved markedly in recent years, culminating in the national team going to the 2002 World Cup in Japan and Korea (see the boxed text.)

A more traditional sport is wrestling. Traditional wrestling (*les luttes* in French, *boreh, buray or beauré* in Wolof and other local languages) is a very popular spectator sport in Gambia and Senegal, and usually attracts great crowds of locals and tourists. It's a fascinating experience and always lots of fun.

The preliminaries can be just as entertaining as the actual fights: Wrestlers enter the arena in full costume, a loincloth in bright patterned materials arranged with a tail falling behind, and their bodies and arms smothered in leather grigri (charms), before slowly strutting around the ring.

World Cup Runneth Over

It wasn't supposed to happen like this. Senegal, a nation whose footballing history included forgetting to enter the 1990 World Cup qualifiers, had used the opening game of the 2002 World Cup in Japan and Korea to manufacture what has been described as 'the greatest football upset ever' by beating defending champions France 1–0. The irony was everywhere: the Lions of Teranga, as the Senegal football team is known, was made up almost exclusively of France-based players expertly marshalled by Bruno Metsu, a Michael Bolton lookalike Frenchman who calls Dakar home.

In Dakar, supporters who had simply hoped the team would not be embarrassed went mad. Jubilant hordes massed outside the Presidential Palace and even President Wade was seen kicking a ball around before venturing into the throng.

The victory over France was just the beginning of Senegal's excellent World Cup adventure. Players such as El Hadji Diouf, Pape Bouba Diop, Ferdinand Coly, Khalilou Fadiga and Salif Diao became underdog heroes to much of the world as the Lions went on to draw 1–1 with Denmark before a nail-biting 3–3 draw with Uruguay took them to the second round.

Two thrilling goals from Henri Camara, the latter an extra time golden goal, saw Senegal beat Sweden 2–1 and become only the second African team in World Cup history (Cameroon was first in 1990) to reach the quarter finals. However, it was there the dream ended when Turkey scored their own golden goal winner.

They always perform with an eye to the audience. True champions are showered with gifts from their admirers and some may even be preceded by griots beating drums.

Every section of town has its heroes. Between matches there's a cacophony of sounds – drums, flutes, whistles and girls chanting like cheerleaders. There are usually many matches, as each lasts only a few minutes until one contestant forces the other to the ground (technically one knee touching the ground ends the match). As many as four matches may be going on at any one time. And during the fight anything goes: biting, kicking, punching. No fancy hand-locks, technical throws, or points. Just get him down.

Matches can be held any time of year, but reach a peak in November and December.

The most popular places to see matches are in Dakar in Senegal, and in Serekunda in Gambia.

SHOPPING

Keen shoppers can spend many hours browsing in the shops, stalls and markets of

---

Playing the Market

The markets in Gambia and Senegal are large, vibrant, colourful and always fascinating, and well worth a visit even if you don't want to buy anything.

There are two main sorts of market. The first is where local people come to buy and sell everyday things such as fruit, vegetables, clothes and farm tools. In larger places, you'll see stalls selling radios, cassette players and other electrical goods, imported shoes, hard-ware and second-hand car parts. The second type of market is aimed more at tourists, where art and craft items (such as those outlined under Shopping in this chapter) are sold; these places are often called the 'craft market', or the 'village artisenal' in Senegal. In some places the locals' main market and the tourist-oriented craft market are in the same place, and these can be the most interesting to visit.

The largest markets are in the capitals and

Visiting the market is a great way to connect with the locals and pick up some mementos

large towns such as Banjul, Serekunda, Dakar and Kaolack, but the markets in smaller places are also well worth a visit. In rural areas, near the borders of Gambia and southern Senegal, many villages hold a weekly market called a *lumo*. Some of these are major events, attracting traders and customers from the surrounding area, and from as far away as Mauritania, Mali, Guinea and Guinea-Bissau.

Most travellers love to visit markets, but dealing with overeager, sometimes desperate, traders can be annoying, to put it mildly. Keeping a smile on your face when they grab you by the arm and not-so-gently pull you over to their stall 'just to see' *('pour voir seulement')* can be tough. The import-ant thing to remember is that if you don't like something, you do not have to buy it. 'I don't like it' is a perfectly legitimate reason not to buy; you don't need to assume the guilt of the developed world on your shoulders and fork over more money just because you've got more than the vendor. Just walk on and the traders will soon back off.

Markets in smaller towns are nowhere near as confronting, but if you're heading into one of the big sprawling city markets (such as those in Serekunda or Dakar) for the first time, you might want to go early when the stalls are just opening and the vendors are still in low gear. It's cooler then, as well.

In a few markets, the hassle can verge on danger, as pickpockets work the crowds, and gangs of youths posing as merchants can surround tourists and snatch bags and cameras. For information on precautions to take, see Dangers & Annoyances earlier in this chapter.

Gambia and Senegal. Wherever there are tourists, you will find stalls full of wooden carvings of variable quality, the same designs endlessly repeated. It is easy to be disdainful of hastily made 'airport art', but if you look hard you may well find something that catches your eye. Many wooden carvings are stained brown or black, and shoe polish seems to be the dye of choice.

Alongside the carvings will probably be a large selection of jewellery, usually brightly coloured, painted and polished glass beads made into necklaces and earrings. For finer pieces, seek out the Mauritanian silversmiths who have a tradition of creating delicate, silver filigree jewellery. You'll find them near Marché Sandaga in Dakar.

Every market in Senegambia has a very wide selection of fabrics. The colours are vibrant (watch out when you wash them) and the designs, whether tie-dyed or printed, are dramatic. Many people choose a length of fabric and then have it made into clothing by a local tailor, often basing the pattern on something they already own. You will find a row of tailors in most markets who can run something up in a day or two at a reasonable rate. Alternatively, you can buy ready-made clothing. Brightly coloured baggy trousers and shirts are popular. These are cheap and likely to fall apart at a moment's notice! On the coastal strip in Gambia a number of shops sell better quality traditional-style clothing.

For lovers of West African music, there is an enormous supply of locally produced CDs and cassettes, usually sold in markets or by merchants on the street. International artists such as Youssou N'Dour frequently produce albums for the local market that never reach Europe. You take your chances on quality, with prices around US$2 per tape and US$6 for the CD.

Many people come to this region to learn drumming. Traditional *djembé* drums are widely available at tourist markets, especially along the coast. They make fine souvenirs, even if you never master a good drumming technique. Admittedly they are not very portable. As usual, quality is highly variable and will be reflected in the price. Koras are less easy to find but it may well be worth going to Keur Moussa Monastery near Dakar, where the Benedictine monks are famous for making these instruments.

More portable, and found everywhere, are the paintings created by local artists on pieces of cloth. Batiks are churned out in their hundreds, but you may have to search to find something of quality.

Genuine collectors of African art are likely to be more interested in the wooden sculptures, particularly masks, headdresses and stools, that have found their way from all over West and Central Africa to the galleries of Dakar, and to a few stalls in the markets of Banjul and Brikama in Gambia. Some of the dusty pieces are genuine, which raises questions about whether travellers should encourage the people of Africa to sell off the best parts of their cultural inheritance, while others are replicas made specifically for sale. At some market stalls you may see ivory for sale. While it's not illegal to buy ivory within Gambia or Senegal, it *is* illegal to export it in any quantity, so if you carry it home to Europe (or wherever) and it's discovered in your luggage you face arrest, fines or imprisonment. By buying ivory, you'll also be supporting the poaching of elephants.

Getting There & Away

This chapter gives you information about reaching Gambia and Senegal from Europe, North America and Australasia, and about leaving the region after your travels. Details on getting to Gambia and Senegal from other parts of Africa can be found in the country-specific Getting There & Away chapters later in this book.

An overview of travel within Gambia and Senegal is given in the Getting Around Senegambia chapter, and more specifics are given in the country chapters.

AIR

The demise or transformation of several European airlines has not been good news for travellers to Gambia and Senegal. There are far fewer scheduled services and while these have been replaced to a certain extent by cheaper charter flights, these often only operate during the high season from November to April. At the time of writing you could fly to Dakar (capital of Senegal) and Banjul (capital of Gambia) from a number of cities in Europe and Africa, or, for the very brave, on a weekly flight from the USA. If you're coming from anywhere else you'll need to pass through Europe. Charter flights are increasingly popular. Those to Gambia come mostly from Britain, Holland and Scandinavia, while Senegal sees flights from France and Belgium.

Buying Tickets

World aviation has never been so competitive, making air travel better value than ever. But you have to research the options carefully to make sure you get the best deal, and the Internet is an increasingly useful way to do this.

Generally, there is nothing to be gained in buying a ticket direct from the airline, especially on airline websites. Discounted tickets are released to selected travel agents and specialist discount agencies, and these are usually the cheapest deals going. Start looking as early as possible: some cheap

tickets must be bought months in advance, and some popular flights sell out early. Fares are normally determined by the quality of the airline, the popularity of the route, the duration of the journey, the length of any stopovers, the departure and arrival times, and any restrictions on the ticket.

Not all scheduled flights are direct. For example, if you fly from London or Frankfurt to Dakar on Air France, you have to stop over (change planes) at its 'hub' in Paris. Flights where you have to change planes are usually cheaper than direct flights.

Charter flights are generally cheaper than scheduled flights, and are usually direct too, so they're well worth considering. In fact, most of the tourists arriving in Gambia, and a significant proportion of those arriving in Senegal, come on charter flights. Some charter flights come as part of a package including accommodation or other services you may not want, but an increasing number of charter companies sell flights with nothing attached, and these are often very good deals.

If you're using the Internet you'll find many travel agencies have websites, or can only be found on the web, which can make the Internet a quick and easy way to compare prices. Online ticket sales work well if you are doing a simple one-way or return trip on specified dates. However, online superfast fare generators are no substitute for a travel agent who knows all about special deals, has strategies for avoiding layovers and can offer advice on everything from which airline has the best vegetarian food to the best travel insurance to bundle with your ticket. With the exception of European discount airlines like Easyjet and Ryanair, most ordinary airlines rarely advertise their cheapest fares online. This is especially true for flights to Dakar.

You'll probably find the cheapest flights are advertised by obscure 'bucket shops'. Many such firms are honest, but there are a few rogues who will take your money and disappear. If you feel suspicious, pay only a small deposit. Once you have your ticket, ring the airline to confirm you are actually booked onto the flight before paying the balance. If the agent insists on cash in advance, go elsewhere.

You may decide to opt for a more reliable service by paying more than the rock-bottom fare. You can go to a better-known travel chain (such as STA Travel, which has offices worldwide, Campus Travel in the UK, Council Travel in the USA, or Travel CUTS in Canada) or to an independent agent, where your money is also safe if they are 'bonded'. Once you have your ticket, keep a note of the booking reference, flight codes, dates, times and other details. The easiest thing to do is make photocopies – carry one with you and leave another at home. If your ticket is lost or stolen, this will help you get a replacement.

It's sensible to buy travel insurance as early as possible. If you get it the week before you fly, you may find, for example, that you're not covered for delays to your flight caused by industrial action (see Travel Insurance under Visas & Documents in the Regional Facts for the Visitor chapter).

Several airlines offer 'youth' or 'student' tickets, with discounts for people under 26 (sometimes 23) or in full-time education. If you're eligible, make a point of asking the travel agent if any student fares are available – they might 'forget' to tell you. Regulations vary, but you'll need to prove your age or student status.

Travellers with Special Needs

If they're warned early enough, and then reminded when you confirm and check in, airlines can often make special arrangements for travellers, such as wheelchair assistance at airports or vegetarian meals on the flight. International airports and airlines in Europe, North America and Australasia are usually pretty helpful and fully equipped to deal with most disabilities. However, airports in both Gambia and Senegal are not. Toilets on local airlines may also present a problem; if in doubt speak with the airline at an early stage.

Children under two years travel for 10% of the standard fare (or free on some airlines) as long as they don't occupy a seat. They don't get a baggage allowance. 'Skycots', baby food and nappies should be provided by the airline if requested in advance. Children aged between two and 12 can usually occupy a seat for half to two-thirds of the full fare, and do get a baggage allowance. The disability-friendly website W www.allgohere.com has an airline directory that provides information on the facilities offered by various airlines.

UK & Continental Europe

The number of airlines operating between Europe and Banjul or Dakar has fallen in recent years to the point where Gambia is served almost exclusively by charter operators. This is fine during the tourist season, but can be a problem in the quieter months.

The only scheduled airline to fly regularly to Banjul from Europe is SN Brussels Airlines, the reincarnated Sabena, with five flights a week via Dakar. A return flight from Brussels to Dakar starts at about €550, to Banjul is €600, while flights from London to either start at UK£480.

Air Travel Glossary

Alliances Many of the world's leading airlines are now intimately involved with each other, sharing everything from reservations systems and check-in to aircraft and frequent-flyer schemes. Opponents say that alliances restrict competition. Whatever the arguments, there is no doubt that big alliances are the way of the future.

Courier Fares Businesses often need to send urgent documents or freight securely and quickly. Courier companies hire people to accompany the package through customs and, in return, offer a discount ticket which is sometimes a bargain. However, you may have to surrender all your baggage allowance and take only carry-on luggage.

Fares Airlines traditionally offer 1st class (coded F), business class (coded J) and economy class (coded Y) tickets. These days there are so many promotional and discounted fares available that few passengers pay full fare.

Lost Tickets If you lose your airline ticket, an airline will usually treat it like a travellers cheque and, after inquiries, issue you with another one. Legally, however, an airline is entitled to treat it like cash and if you lose it then it's gone forever. Take very good care of your tickets.

Onward Tickets An entry requirement for many countries is that you have a ticket out of the country. If you're unsure of your next move, the easiest solution is to buy the cheapest onward ticket to a neighbouring country or a ticket from a reliable airline which can later be refunded if you do not use it.

Open-Jaw Tickets These are return tickets where you fly out to one place but return from another. If available, this can save you backtracking to your arrival point.

Overbooking Since every flight has some passengers who fail to show up, airlines often book more passengers than they have seats. Usually excess passengers make up for the no-shows, but occasionally somebody gets 'bumped' onto the next available flight. Guess who it is most likely to be? The passengers who check in late. If you do get 'bumped', you are normally offered some form of compensation.

Reconfirmation Some airlines require you to reconfirm your flight at least 72 hours prior to departure. Check your travel documents to see if this is the case

Restrictions Discounted tickets often have various restrictions on them – such as needing to be paid for in advance and incurring a penalty to be altered or cancelled. Others are restrictions on the minimum and maximum period you must be away.

Round-the-World Tickets RTW tickets give you a limited period (usually a year) in which to circumnavigate the globe. You can go anywhere the carrying airlines go, as long as you don't backtrack. The number of stopovers or total number of separate flights is decided before you set off and they usually cost a bit more than a basic return flight.

Ticketless Travel Airlines are gradually waking up to the realisation that paper tickets are unnecessary encumbrances. On simple one-way or return trips, reservations details can be held on computer and the passenger merely shows ID to claim their seat.

Transferred Tickets Airline tickets cannot be transferred from one person to another. Travellers sometimes try to sell the return half of their ticket, but officials can ask you to prove that you are the person named on the ticket. On an international flight, tickets are compared with passports.

Charter flights are available from holiday operators or travel agents. Although these cater mainly for package tourists, independent travellers can get 'flight-only' deals, and some agents offer special deals which include accommodation for only a little extra. Even if you don't stay in the hotel all the time, the airport transfers and a first- or last-night bed can be very useful. Last-minute stand-bys can drop to UK£320 or less – ideal if your dates are flexible. In the UK, the best place to find last-minute deals is Teletext (W www.teletext.co.uk), where some amazing deals are available if you're *very* flexible.

The leading British charter operator is The Gambia Experience (see Organised Tours later in this chapter for details) with one- or two-week flight-only deals from UK£335 return. Flights depart from Gatwick, Manchester and Bristol. There's plenty of competition in the tourist season, with Thomson Holidays, Airtours, Cosmos, First Choice, JMC, Panorama and Unijet all organising regular tours and flights. Gambia is also a popular package destination elsewhere in Europe . To check what's on offer in the Netherlands and Germany start with Sunair and Olympia; in Belgium Xeniar Tours and Sunsnacks; and from Scandinavia try Scandinavian Leisure Group (DLG).

From Gambia back to Europe you can go with SN Brussels for the prices mentioned above, or use a charter company. The Gambia Experience (office outside the Kairaba Hotel in Kololi) has charter tickets from UK£335 (and sometimes less), making this one of the cheapest places in West Africa to fly home from.

Airlines from Europe serving Senegal include Air France, Alitalia, Iberia, TAP (Air Portugal), Aeroflot and SN Brussels. Air France's daily flights between Paris and Dakar are €449/928 one way/return, though better deals can sometimes be found. Alitalia flies twice or four times a week, depending on the season, between Milan and Dakar from about €500 return, while Iberia flies from Madrid and TAP Air Portugal has several flights a week from Lisbon, also starting at about €500 return. Fares on scheduled flights from London, via Europe,

to Dakar start at about UK£450 rising by another UK£75 in the high season (October to May). There are plenty of charter flights to Senegal with French and Belgian package-tour companies, all of them a lot cheaper than the scheduled flights. An example is Anyway.com, which has packages including flights, accommodation and some meals from about €350 for up to two weeks – even if you don't stay at their hotel and don't eat the free food, this is still excellent value.

In Senegal, the best agency for charter flights is Nouvelles Frontières in Dakar (see Information in the Dakar chapter), with singles to Paris from around €380.

The UK In Britain, London a good place to buy your ticket, although these days specialist agents outside the capital are just as cheap and can be easier to deal with. Advertisements for many travel agencies appear in the travel pages of the weekend broadsheet newspapers, in *Time Out,* the *Evening Standard* and in the free magazine TNT.

For students or travellers under 26 years, STA Travel (☎ 020-7361 6262, W www .statravel.co.uk), which has an office at 86 Old Brompton Rd, London SW7, and branches across the country, is a popular travel agency in the UK. It sells tickets to all travellers, but caters especially to young people and students. A bit more upmarket, but also good, is the Africa Travel Centre (☎ 020-7387 1211, W www.africatravel .co.uk) at 21 Leigh St, London WC1H 9QX.

France One recommended agency is OTU Voyages (☎ 0 820 817 817, 01-44 41 38 50, W www.otu.fr), 39 ave Georges-Bernanos, 75005 Paris, with branches nationwide. It offers special deals to students and young people. Other recommendations include Voyageurs du Monde (☎ 01-42 86 16 00, W www.vdm.com), 55 rue Ste-Anne, 75002 Paris; Nouvelles Frontières (☎ 08 25 00 08 25, 01-45 68 70 00, W www.nouvelles -frontieres.fr), 87 blvd de Grenelle, 75015 Paris, with branches across the country; and Anyway.com (☎ 0825 84 84 83, W www .anyway.com). These three agencies all specialise in charter flights.

Belgium Joker Toerisme (☎ 02-502 19 37, ℮ brussels@joker.be), Blvd Lemonnier 37, 1000 Bruxelles, is the place where a lot of budget travellers begin their research. It is affiliated with the Via-Via travellers café in Yoff. Other options include Nouvelles Frontières (☎ 02-547 44 44, ⓦ www.nouvelles-frontieres.be), Blvd Lemonnier 2, 1000 Bruxelles.

Germany Recommended agencies include STA Travel (☎ 030-311 0950), Goethest-trasse 73, 10625 Berlin, which also has branches in most of the major cities across the country.

Italy Recommended travel agents include CTS Viaggi (☎ 06-462 0431), 16 Via Genova, Rome, a student and youth specialist with branches in major cities, and Passagi (☎ 06-474 0923), Stazione Termini FS, Galleria Di Tesla, Rome.

The Netherlands Recommended agencies include Budget Air (☎ 020-627 1251, ⓦ www.nbbs.nl) at 34 Rokin, Amsterdam. Another agency, Holland International (☎ 070-307 6307), has offices in most cities.

Spain Recommended agencies include Barcelo Viajes (☎ 91-559 1819), Princesa 3,

Overland Through the Western Sahara

There are three main routes across the Sahara leading to West Africa: the Route de Hoggar (through Algeria and Niger); the Route de Tanezrouft (through Algeria and Mali); and the Atlantic Route through the Western Sahara (through Morocco and Mauritania). With the decade-long fundamentalist insurgency in Algeria seemingly finished, regular traffic ran in both directions along the Route de Hoggar in 2001 for the first time since the late 1980s. However, news of the peace and love in Algeria has apparently not reached the smugglers (or bandits, depending who you talk to) who are still taking advantage of whomever they can along the northern Mali section of the once-popular Tanezrouft route. Thus, at the time of writing the Atlantic Route is still the most popular for tourists. It's also the most direct overland route to Senegal. It would be almost criminal negligence to travel in the Sahara without first checking the excellent, up-to-date and entertaining website put together by desert specialist Chris Scott at ⓦ www.sahara-overland.com, where you can also buy his books. Other decent websites include that of the 153 Club (named after the old Michelin map of North West Africa) at ⓦ www.manntaylor.com/153.html; the thorough ⓦ www.sahara-info.ch (in German); the French Sahariens site ⓦ jmt.ch-hyeres.fr; and ⓦ www.sahara.it (in Italian).

The Atlantic Route – Southbound

Travel through Morocco is pretty straightforward (see Lonely Planet's *Morocco* guide). About 500km south of Agadir you enter the disputed territory of Western Sahara, but the road continues along the coast all the way to Dakhla.

Dakhla has some cheap hotels and a decent camping ground (which also has some rooms to rent) where all the overlanders stay, and this is the very best place to find other vehicles to team up and travel with. If you are hitching, drivers taking second-hand cars from Europe (especially from France and Germany) to sell in West Africa may occasionally offer lifts, but you would be expected to share fuel and paperwork costs. Hitchers are not allowed in Mauritanian vehicles, and there have been occasional scams where hitchers with local drivers are abandoned in the desert unless they pay a large 'fee'.

For years a twice-weekly convoy headed south from Dakhla, but as of 2002 this is no more. All immigration and customs facilities have moved south to the border at Fort Guergarrat, from where you cross into Mauritania and the last 100km to Nouâdhibou. It's important to take supplies for at least two days on this leg, and for inexperienced or 2WD drivers to go in a group in case someone

28008 Madrid, which has branches in major cities. Nouvelles Frontières (☎ 91-547 42 00, W www.tuiviages.com) has an office at Plaza de España 18, 28008 Madrid, plus branches in major cities.

North America

Since the demise of Air Afrique, the only direct flight between North America and this part of West Africa is Ghana Airways' weekly service from Washington to Accra via Dakar and Banjul. Many travellers have reported problems with service, so if you fly this route, factor in extra time for delays and setbacks.

This means all but the bravest of Americans and Canadians must fly via Europe. Most flights between North America and this part of West Africa are on European airlines, via Europe, in which case it may be cheaper to fly to London or Paris and buy a discounted ticket onwards from there.

Citizens of Canada will also probably find the best deals travelling via Europe, especially London (although there are some very cheap flights from Montreal to Paris). Contact some of the travel agents listed in the Britain section earlier.

Discount travel agents in the USA and Canada are known as consolidators. San

---

Overland Through the Western Sahara

gets stuck. The route is clearly marked and no matter how bad the road gets, do not stray – twisted wrecks are proof of how near landmines can be.

From Nouâdhibou, most vehicles go south down the coast to Nouakchott, through the Banc d'Arguin National Park (including a 160km stretch along the beach at low tide, with soft sand on one side and waves breaking over your windscreen on the other). Some cars, and most bikes and hitchers, go east on the iron-ore train to Choûm and then take the route via Atar and Akjout to Nouakchott. The train heads east from Nouâdhibou to Choum on Monday and returns on Saturday, and you'll need to be at either end the day before to guarantee a space. From Nouakchott to Rosso, the southern border, is a straightforward run on a good tar road. Rosso is a hustlers' paradise, but for those with their own vehicle there is a less bothersome way into Senegal. Turn right (west) along a sandy track just as you enter Rosso and follow the Senegal River for 97km to Maka Diama. There are border posts on both sides of the river and crossing will cost you CFA5000/10,000 in winter/summer, landing you just a short drive to the comforts and cold beer of St-Louis. Remember to stock a few packets of cigarettes before you set off as they are the best 'bribe' – cheap and usually enough to keep the official happy.

The Atlantic Route – Northbound

It is now legal to travel north through Mauritania along this route, but because so much of the southbound traffic is on a one-way journey to the vehicle purgatory that is West Africa, going north without your own transport can be pretty tough. It's probably best to try and arrange your transport before you leave Nouakchott. If you can't find anything, an increasingly popular (and more adventurous) alternative is to head to Choum via Atar on whatever transport you can find, and take the iron-ore train to Nouâdhibou.

From Nouâdhibou you need some form of transport to go north, and this can be hard to find. Your best bets are the camping grounds. If you have your own vehicle, head north and have your passport stamped at the small post, then drive on to Fort Guergarrat to complete the border formalities for Morocco. Despite all this being far easier than it once was, it's still advisable to wait in Nouâdhibou for other vehicles to form a mini convoy for the trip to Dakhla. It's also worth noting that inexperienced drivers will probably need a guide to get between Nouâdhibou and Nouakchott, which will likely cost about €150 for five vehicles.

Francisco is the ticket consolidator capital of America, although some good deals can be found in Los Angeles, New York and other big cities. Agencies also tend to advertise in the travel sections of big newspapers, such as those in the *New York Times*, *Los Angeles Times*, *Chicago Tribune* and *San Francisco Examiner*.

North America's largest student travel organisations, Council Travel (☎ 800-226 8624, W www.counciltravel.com), and STA Travel (☎ 800-777 0112, W www.statravel.com) have offices throughout the USA.

In Canada, consolidators tend to sell tickets for about 10% more than those sold in the USA. Travel CUTS (☎ 800-667-2887, W www.travelcuts.com) is Canada's national student travel agency and has offices in most major cities.

Some of the companies listed under Organised Tours later in this chapter also sell flights.

Australasia

There are not many route options from Australia and New Zealand to Gambia and Senegal. Most people fly via Europe or, occasionally, East Africa, using several different airlines. The cheapest way of getting to/from Gambia and Senegal is usually on a round-the-world (RTW) ticket, which sells for around A$3000; you'll probably have to look hard to find one routing through West Africa.

In Australia and New Zealand, inexpensive deals are available mainly from STA Travel, which has branches in all capital cities and on most university campuses. In Australia phone ☎ 1300 360 960 for the latest fares, and ☎ 131 776 for details of your nearest STA office. Another option is Flight Centre (☎ 131 600, W www.flightcentre.com.au). In New Zealand phone STA on ☎ 0800 100 677 or check W www.statravel.co.nz. For more options check the ads in travel magazines and weekend newspapers.

Africa

If your journey in Gambia and Senegal is part of a longer trip through Africa, you may need to leave the region by air, either because time is short or simply because land routes are too difficult. One section frequently hopped is Western Sahara (because it can be tricky for travellers without vehicles) by flying from Dakar to the Moroccan city of Casablanca. The usual one-way fare between Dakar and Casablanca on Royal Air Maroc is US$530, and youth tickets are US$370. For travellers heading towards East or Southern Africa, good luck! Despite the obvious geographical advantages, flying from Dakar or Banjul to these parts of Africa regularly takes longer and costs more than going via Europe. Flights are often delayed and layovers in 'interesting' airports can be interminable. If you are travelling long-haul in Africa, make sure you look on it as an adventure, and give yourself plenty of time, for the sake of your mental health. From Dakar or Banjul there are no direct flights to East Africa or Southern Africa. Expensive, multi-airline tickets to places such as Nairobi (Kenya), Harare (Zimbabwe) and Johannesburg (South Africa) are available. These go via at least one other West African capital, usually Lagos (Nigeria), Accra (Ghana) or Abidjan (Côte d'Ivoire). You can reach most other West African capitals from Dakar; details are in the country Getting There & Away chapters.

LAND
Border Crossings

Any overland journey to Gambia goes through Senegal, as the latter country surrounds its tiny neighbour (except for the coast). Senegal shares borders with four other West African countries. To the north is Mauritania, with the main border point at Rosso, where a ferry crosses the Senegal River (although there are several other crossing points along the river).

To the east is Mali, and most travellers go between here and Senegal by train, but improved roads in this area mean a bush-taxi option is becoming increasingly popular. Either way, the main crossing point is between Kidira (Senegal) and Diboli (Mali).

The busiest route to Guinea is via Koundara and Labé, but some transport also goes to Labé via Kedougou (in the far southeast of Senegal) and the small town of Mali (usually called Mali-ville, to distinguish it from the country of the same name).

South of Senegal is Guinea-Bissau, and the main border crossing is at São Domingos, between Ziguinchor and Ingore, although there are also some smaller, quieter crossings further east. For more details on all of these crossings see the Senegal and Gambia Getting There & Away chapters.

If you're travelling independently overland to Senegal – whether hitching, cycling, driving your own car or going by public transport – the usual approach is from the north, across the Sahara.

Driving Your Own Vehicle

Driving your own car or motorbike to Senegal (and then presumably around other parts of West Africa, and possibly onwards to Central, Eastern or Southern Africa) requires plenty of research and planning, and is a subject far beyond the scope of this book. See Books in the Regional Facts for the Visitor chapter for manuals covering matters such as vehicles, spares, equipment, *carnets de passage* (effectively passports for the vehicle acting as a temporary waiver of import duty), insurance paperwork, recommended routes (and current conditions), driving techniques, maintenance, repairs, navigation, survival, useful organisations, magazines and websites. However, these manuals are usually pretty thin on practical information about places to eat and sleep (mainly because most overlanders camp) and general background information about the country (such as history and economy). So in this book we leave the practical vehicle information to the experts and hope drivers and passengers find us invaluable for everything else!

Shipping a Vehicle

If you want to travel around Senegambia using your own car or motorbike, but don't fancy the Sahara crossing, another option is to ship your vehicle. The usual way of doing this is to load your car or motocycle on board at a port in Europe and take it off again at either Dakar or Banjul.

Costs range from US$500 to US$1000 depending on the size of the vehicle and the final destination. However, apart from cost your biggest problem is likely to be security. Many drivers report theft of items from the inside and outside (such as lights and mirrors) of their car. Vehicles are usually left unlocked during the crossing and when in storage at the destination port – so chain or lock all equipment into fixed boxes inside the vehicle.

Getting a vehicle out of a port is frequently a nightmare, requiring visits to several different offices where stamps must be obtained and mysterious fees paid at every turn. Consider using an official handling agent or an unofficial 'fixer' to take you through this process.

We heard of one biker who avoided these pitfalls when sending his bike 'air mail' from Dakar to Paris using Air France Cargo (☎ 820 07 43) for what seems like a pretty good price. He went to the Air France Cargo office at Léopold Sédar Senghor International Airport, at Yoff; filled out forms with the assistance of a local 'transiter' (recommended by Air France); loaded his bike (about 200kg) onto a bike stand; and took photos of it for security; all in less than a day for just over US$500. From the UK, Allied Pickfords (☎ 020-8219 8000, 0800-289 229, W www.allied-pickfords.co.uk) is not the cheapest, but has been recommended.

SEA

The days of working for your passage on commercial boats have long gone, although a few lucky travellers do manage to hitch rides on private yachts sailing from Spain, Morocco or the Canary Islands to Senegal, Gambia and beyond.

Another nautical option available is taking a cabin on a freighter. Several cargo ships run from European ports, such as London-Tilbury, Bordeaux, Hamburg or Rotterdam, to various West African ports (including Dakar) with comfortable officer-style cabins available to the public. There are few, if any, options from the USA.

A typical voyage from Europe to Dakar takes about eight days, and costs vary according to the quality of the ship. Don't take this option if you want to save money – single fares from Europe to Dakar are around US$1500 to US$1800 per person in a double cabin.

For more information see *Travel by Cargo Ship*, a handy book written by Hugo Verlomme, or contact a specialist agent such as:

Associated Oceanic Agencies Ltd (☎ 020-7930 5683, fax 7839 1961) 103 Jermyn St, London SW1Y 6EE UK

Freighter World Cruises (☎ 626 449 3106 or toll-free 1-800 531 7774, fax 449 9573, W www.freighterworld.com) 180 South Lake Ave, No 335-1, Pasadena CA 91101 USA (publishers of *Freighter Space Advisory*). Excellent website with listings of freighter trips worldwide, including to Dakar and Banjul.

Maris Freighter Cruises (☎ 1-800 996 2747 or 203 222 1500) 215 Main St, Westport, CT USA

Strand Voyages (☎ 020-7836 6363, fax 7497 0078, e voyages@strandtravel.com.au) Charing Cross Shopping Concourse, Strand, London WC2N 4HZ UK

ORGANISED TOURS

Two main sorts of tour are available: overland tours and inclusive tours. On an overland tour, passengers usually travel on a truck with a driver and guide. Some go all the way from Europe to West Africa, visiting several countries, while others are shorter with flights at either end. On an inclusive tour you fly to your destination and spend one to three weeks, usually in a single country.

In North America and Australasia many overland and inclusive tour companies are represented by specialist travel agencies, and the best place to start hunting for details are the advertisements in travel magazines and weekend papers, or on the Web.

Overland Tours

For people with time to spare, especially if lone travel does not appeal, these trips are ideal. You travel in an 'overland truck' with about 15 to 28 people, a couple of drivers/leaders, plus tents and other equipment. Most hassles (such as border crossings) are taken care of by the leader.

Disadvantages include a fairly fixed itinerary and not being able to choose your travelling companions.

Most, but not all, overland companies are based in the UK. They change their tours regularly, depending on what's popular or possible. For links to overland companies around the world, their routes, prices, timetables and contact details, check out W www.go-overland.com/comm/directory. At the time of writing most trans-Africa routes bypassed Senegal and Gambia. However, there are a couple of companies operating shorter trips which take in Senegal. These include Guerba (☎ 788-570 8828, e limosaholidays@ compuserve.com, W www.guerba.co.uk) and Nomadic Expeditions (☎ 870-220 1718, W www.nomadic.co.uk), which are both based in Britain. The Swiss-based Adventure Fantasy Tours (☎ 91-976 0777, W www.overlandtravel.com) also offers trips taking in Senegal.

Inclusive Tours

You can reach Gambia and Senegal from your home country on a tour that includes flight, transport, accommodation, food, excursions, a local guide and so on. These inclusive tours are usually two to three weeks long, and ideal if you lack the time or inclination for overland trucks.

The number of tour companies operating in West Africa is much smaller than in East or Southern Africa, but there's still a fair selection, mostly based in Britain, France and the USA. Some overland companies also do shorter inclusive tours.

The following list will provide some idea of the range of companies available. In Britain, try:

Drumdance (☎/fax 01524-64616) 11 Bank Rd, Lancaster LA1 2DG. This organisation offers all kinds of trips including cultural, musical and special-interest tours for independently minded travellers.

The Gambia Experience (☎ 023-8073 0888, fax 8073 1122, W www.gambia.co.uk) Kingfisher House, Rownhams Lane, North Baddesley, Hampshire SO52 9LP. This is a leading operator of package holidays to Gambia, with some options in Senegal, plus an interesting selection of specialist birding, fishing and cultural tours; it also sells good-value charter flights.

Guerba (☎ 788-570 8828, e limosaholidays@compuserve.com, W www.guerba.co.uk) Limosa. This company offers a range of tours.

Holidays (☎ 01263-578143, fax 579251) Suffield House, Northrepps, Norfolk NR7 0LZ. Specialist birding trips, including tours to Gambia are offered by this company.

Wildwings (☎ 0117-984 8040, fax 961 0200, W www.wildwings.co.uk) International House, Bank Rd, Bristol BS15 2LX. Here you will find birding and wildlife specialists offering expeditions and tours worldwide, including to Senegal and Gambia.

In France, some good places to start include:

Esprit d'Aventure et Terres d'Aventure (☎ 01 53 73 77 73, W www.terdav.com) 6 rue Saint-Victor, 75005 Paris. Various adventurous trips in West Africa and the Sahara region, including Senegal and Mauritania, are offered.

Explorator (☎ 01 53 45 85 85, W www.explo.com) 16 rue de la Banque, 75002 Paris. This company's destinations include the Sahara region, Mauritania, Senegal, Gambia and Mali.

Nouvelles Frontières (☎ 01 41 41 58 58, W www.nouvelles-frontieres.fr) 87 blvd de Grenelle, 75015 Paris. Branch in Paris plus numerous other branches in France and French-speaking countries. Wide range of mainstream holidays and adventurous tours in Senegal, all over West Africa, and beyond are found here.

Voyageurs en Afrique (☎ 01 42 86 16 60) 55 rue Sainte-Anne, 75002 Paris. Tours in Senegal, plus hotel bookings and car rentals are on offer at Voyageurs.

In the USA, you could start with:

Adventure Center (☎ 510-654 1879 or 1-800 228 8747, W www.adventure-center.com) 1311 63rd St, Emeryville, CA 94608

Born Free Safaris (☎ 1-800 472 3274 or 818-981 7185, fax 753 1466, W www.bornfreesafaris.com) 12504 Riverside Dr, North Hollywood, CA 91607

Turtle Tours (☎ 888-299 1439, 480-488 3688, W www.turtletours.com) Box 1147, Carefree, AZ 85377

Wilderness Travel (☎ 1-800 368 2794, 510-558 2488, fax 510-558 2489, W www.wildernesstravel.com) 1102 Ninth St, Berkeley, CA 94710

In Canada, start with the following:

Adventures Abroad (☎ 604-303 1099, 1-800 655 3998, W www.adventures-abroad.com) Vancouver. This company has an online list of offices worldwide.

Adventure Centre (☎ 416-922 7584, 1-800 267 3347, W www.theadventurecentre.com) 25 Bellair St, Toronto, Ontario M5R 3L3. Offers tours with several operators and has a good website that is worth checking out.

Getting Around Senegambia

This chapter briefly outlines the various ways of travelling around Gambia and Senegal. For specific details, see the Gambia and Senegal Getting There & Away and Getting Around chapters.

AIR

Flights around the Senegambia region are limited to daily services between Banjul and Dakar on the regional airlines Air Senegal International and Gambia International Airlines. There are no domestic flights within Gambia. Within Senegal, Air Senegal International flies daily between Dakar and Ziguinchor, and less frequently to Cap Skiring and Tambacounda. It's hardly worth flying between the capitals, but the flights to Ziguinchor and Cap Skiring are reasonably cheap and make sense if you're in a hurry, or don't fancy a less than comfortable 12 hours in a bush taxi.

BUS & BUSH TAXI

The most common forms of public transport in Gambia and Senegal are bus (*car* in French) and bush taxi *(taxi-brousse)*. Buses and bush taxis are almost always located at the garage (bus and bush-taxi station), known in Senegal as the *gare routière*.

Travel by bus and bush taxi generally costs between US$1 and US$2 per 100km, although fares depend on the quality of the vehicle and the quality of the route. On all bush taxis and some buses you have to pay extra for baggage – see the boxed text 'Luggage Fees'.

Bus

The long-distance bus (sometimes called 'big bus' in Gambia, and usually called the *car mouride* or *grand car* in Senegal to distinguish it from all smaller forms of the species) varies considerably in size and services. On the main routes buses are often good quality, with a reliable service and fixed departure times (arrival times may be more fluid). Seats can often be reserved a

day or two in advance, and in Senegal this is recommended.

Bush Taxi

'Bush taxi' is the generic term for all public transport smaller than a big bus. In effect, bush taxis are small buses that leave once they are full. They might take half an hour to fill, or several days.

The best time for catching bush taxis is usually from 6.30am to 8.30am, although departures are sometimes determined by market days, when, if you're in a market town, you'll find a wide choice of transport leaving in the late afternoon. Tickets (or scraps of paper) may be issued – but not always. Early customers can choose where they want to sit. Latecomers get no choice and are assigned the least comfortable seats.

Touts at the *Gare Routière*

At most *gares routière* (bus or bush-taxi stations, also known as garages), bush taxis leave on a fill-up-and-go basis, but problems can arise when you get more than one vehicle covering the same route. As soon as you arrive you'll almost certainly be approached by a tout (one of the local terms is *coti-man*) trying to persuade you to take 'his' car. These guys are not actually drivers, but they earn a commission by finding passengers and will tell you anything to get you on board. Some common lines include 'This one is very fast', 'This minibus is going soon' and 'This bus is a good cheap price'. Another trick involves putting your baggage on the roof rack as a 'deposit' against you taking another car. These guys can be pretty full-on and are none too popular with either visitors or locals, whom they also pester mercilessly. In short, you shouldn't need a 'guide' or any help to negotiate the gare routière. Just say the name of your destination often enough and you'll soon be in the right place, haggling over luggage space.

There are five main types of bush taxi. From fastest to slowest they are: Peugeot taxi, minibus (15 to 20 seats), Mercedes bus (about 35 seats), pick-up and *cars rapide* (small blue and yellow buses seating about 20 people), which, far from being '*rapide*', are in fact the slowest of the lot.

Peugeot Taxis Peugeot 504s are used all over Gambia and Senegal and are referred to by various names, including Peugeot taxi, *sept-place*, *cinq-cent-quatre* and *brake*. Occasionally you will find other makes and models (some old bush taxis may be 503s, and there are many new 505s on the road these days); we have used the term Peugeot taxi throughout this book.

The quality varies. Some drivers are safe and considerate, others verge on insanity. Some cars are quite new and well maintained with comfortable seats. Others are very old, reduced to nothing more than chassis, body and engine; there's more weld than original metal, tyres are bald, most upholstery is missing, while little extras like windows, door handles and even exhaust pipes have long since disappeared.

With three rows of seats, Peugeot taxis are built to take the driver plus seven passengers (hence the name *sept-place*). On the main routes in Gambia and Senegal, this limit is observed. But as you get into more remote areas it's often flagrantly flouted: you might be jammed in with at least a dozen adults, plus children and bags, with more luggage and a couple of extra passengers riding on the roof. The fact that these cars do hundreds of thousands of kilometres on some of the worst roads in the world is a credit to the manufacturer and the ingenuity of local mechanics.

If a Peugeot taxi looks as though it might get uncomfortably full, you can buy two seats for yourself – it's simply double the price. Two travellers might buy three seats between them. By the same token, if you want to charter the whole car, take the price of one seat and multiply it by the number of available seats, then add some more for the equivalent of seven people's luggage.

If a group of passengers has been waiting a long time, and there are only two or three

Luggage Fees

Wherever you travel by bush taxi there is always an extra fee for luggage, which varies according to the size of the baggage. The baggage charge is partly because bush-taxi fares are fixed by the government and may not reflect true costs. So the only way the driver can earn a bit extra is to charge for luggage. Local people accept this, so travellers should too, unless of course the amount is beyond reason.

The fee for a medium-sized backpack is usually around 10% of the fare, though you'll usually have to bargain hard to get away for less than 20%. Fares tend to rise with the size of the luggage, or if the item is likely to dirty the vehicle. Indeed it's not uncommon, especially around the Islamic holiday of Tabaski, to be sitting under several bleating and pissing sheep lashed to the roof with old rope. If this is you, keep your windows wound firmly UP!

If you think you're being overcharged, stand your ground politely and the price will soon fall.

seats to fill, they may club together and pay for these. If you do this, don't expect to pay less just because you're saving the driver the time and hassle of looking for other passengers – time is not money in Africa. If you do pick up someone along the way, however, the fare they pay goes to the passengers who bought the seats, not to the driver.

Minibus Many routes are served by minibuses *(minicars)*, which usually seat about 15 to 20 passengers. Typically about 25% cheaper than the Peugeot taxis, they can be slower (which usually means safer) and less comfortable than cars. Borders or roadblocks can take longer to negotiate because there are more passengers to search.

Mercedes Bus On short city trips or longer journeys, the boxy white Mercedes bus is almost always the slowest, cheapest and most common form of transport. Mercedes buses are known by a variety of different names, including, in Senegal, *petit* *car*, Alham, and N'Diaga N'Diaye (pronounced njagga-njaye). These buses have no timetable, and usually go when full or when the driver feels like it. They travel anywhere and, seemingly, everywhere to drop or collect passengers, and it's not unusual for one of these buses to take twice as long as a Peugeot taxi for the same journey. Breakdowns are common. It sounds grim, but these buses are very social (particularly in remote areas) and if you're not in a rush can be a great place to meet the locals.

Pick-Up Covered pick-ups (called *bâchés* in Senegal), with wooden seats down the sides, are sometimes the only kind of bush taxi available, particularly in remote areas. They may officially take around 16 passengers, but are invariably stuffed with people, baggage, and a few live chickens, and your feet may be higher than your waist from resting on a sack of millet. Up on the roof go more bags, bunches of bananas, extra passengers and goats (also live). Pick-up rides are often very slow, and police checks interminable as drivers or passengers frequently lack vital papers. The ride is

guaranteed to be unpleasant unless you adopt an African attitude, which means each time your head hits the roof as the vehicle descends into yet another big pothole, a roar of laughter rings forth. There's nothing like African humour to change an otherwise miserable trip into a tolerable, even enjoyable experience.

TRUCK & HITCHING

The further you venture into rural areas, the more dramatically the frequency of buses or bush taxis drops – sometimes to nothing. The only way around this is to ride on local trucks, in the same way as the locals. A 'fare' is payable to the driver – so in cases like this the line between hitching and public transport is blurred – but if it's the only way to get around you've got no choice anyway. Usually you'll be riding on top of the cargo; it may be cotton or rice in sacks, which are quite comfortable, but it might be logs or oil drums, which aren't.

Hitching in the Western sense (because you don't want to get the bus, or more specifically because you don't want to pay) is also possible, but may take a very long

Waiting time for ferries across the Gambia River, such as here at Bambatenda, can literally be days

Slow Down or I'll Vomit!

By African standards the driving in Senegal and Gambia is quite good, with most drivers taking their responsibility quite seriously. There are even occasions when a bush-taxi driver needs to be asked to apply himself to the accelerator. But then there's always the odd madman who thinks nothing of thrashing his rusted conveyance over innumerable potholes at hair-raising speeds, overtaking on blind corners and racing through villages to be as close to the front of the queue as possible for the return journey. Life-threatening or not, few people complain, usually because drivers take no notice. If you are feeling so unsafe that moments of your life you'd really rather not remember are starting to flash before your eyes, say you are feeling sick. The thought of a vomit-lined vehicle will scare most drivers far more than the prospect of a head-on collision with a peanut truck.

time. Most people with space in their car are likely to want a payment – usually on a par with what a bus costs. The most common vehicles for lifts of this sort are nearly new white Toyota Land Cruisers driven by locals working for government bodies, international agencies or aid organisations.

Remember though, as in any other part of the world, hitching is never entirely safe, and we don't recommend it. Travellers who decide to hitch should understand that they are taking a small but potentially serious risk. If you're planning to travel this way, take advice from other hitchers (locals or travellers) first. Hitching in pairs is obviously safer.

TRAIN

There is no train service in Gambia, while in Senegal there's only one line operating – between Dakar and Bamako (in neighbouring Mali). Details about this service are in Senegal's Getting There & Away chapter.

CAR & MOTORCYCLE

Some general points about driving your own vehicle to and around the region are covered

under Land in the regional Getting There & Away chapter. The other option for getting around is to rent a car or motorbike. A major consideration when driving is road conditions. Some dirt roads can be used all year while others are impassable in the rains. Some tar roads are perfect, while others become so badly potholed that a dirt road would be much better. Conditions change from year to year, so the best way to keep up-to-date is by talking to other drivers.

Rental

Renting a car in Gambia or Senegal is invariably expensive. By the time you've added up the cost of the car, the distance travelled, insurance and tax, you can easily end up paying over US$1000 per week. You will also need a credit card to pay the large deposit. For those still interested, there are car-rental agencies in the capitals and main tourist areas. In Senegal all the international names (Hertz, Avis, Budget etc) are represented, and there are also smaller independent operators. Hertz is the only big name in Gambia – and there are few independent operators.

Taking a rental car across a border is usually forbidden, although the rules about going between Gambia and Senegal are less stringent. Driving from northern Senegal to southern Senegal will almost always take you through Gambia anyway, so most Senegalese companies accept this.

Warning

If you have never driven in a developing country before, hiring a car or motorbike in Gambia or Senegal is not something to be taken lightly. Road conditions outside the capitals are often bad, and dangers (apart from the potholes) include people and animals moving unexpectedly into your path. Smaller roads are not tarred, so you need to be comfortable about driving on dirt. There are very few signposts, so you should be able to read a map. And in the event of trouble some basic mechanical knowledge, at the very least being able to change a wheel, is useful.

Several rental companies can provide a chauffeur at very little extra cost – sometimes it's cheaper because you pay less for insurance.

Scooters can be hired in Gambia in the tourist area of the Atlantic coast (see the Atlantic Coast Resorts & Serekunda chapter).

TAXI

Before you rent a car, consider hiring a taxi by the day. It will probably cost you less (anywhere from about US$20 to US$50 per day) and if you suffer a breakdown it'll be the driver's problem, not yours – which is especially useful if you're in Senegal and you don't speak French. You can hire a city taxi or a bush taxi. In Gambia, there are special 'tourist taxis' particularly for this purpose. Whichever way you go, make sure it's mechanically sound before agreeing to anything.

If you hire a city taxi, the price you pay will have to be worth the driver taking it out of public service for the day. If you want a deal including petrol, the driver will reduce the speed to a slow trot and complain incessantly every time you take even the most minor detour. A fixed daily rate for the car only (you pay petrol direct) is easier, but finding a car with a working petrol gauge may be tricky. If you allow for 10km per litre on reasonable roads (more on bad roads) you should be OK.

BICYCLE

Cycling is a cheap, convenient, healthy, environmentally sound and fun way to travel, and gives you a deeper insight into Senegambia, as you often stay in small towns and villages, interact with the local people, and eat African food more frequently. In general, the remoter the areas you visit, the more serious the conditions, but the better the experience.

If you've never cycled in Africa before, Gambia and parts of Senegal provide an ideal starting point. We've heard from many travellers, particularly British, who take bikes on the cheap charter flights to Banjul and enjoy a couple of weeks cycling in the sun. The landscape is flat and the distances between major points of interest are not so large.

A mountain bike or fat-tyred urban hybrid is most suitable to the dirt-and-sand roads and tracks. However, some tracks are so sandy that no tyre is ever thick enough, and you will have to push, but these are best avoided. Generally speaking, away from urban areas the main tar routes are relatively quiet and don't get too much traffic.

When you do encounter traffic however, drivers are more cause for alarm than any road surface. Cyclists are regarded as second-class citizens in Africa, so make sure you know what's coming behind you and be prepared to take evasive action onto the verge, as locals are often forced to do. A small helmet-mounted rear-view mirror is worth considering.

The best time to bike is the cool period from mid-November to the end of February. Even so, you'll need to carry at least four litres of water. If you get hot, tired, or

Bringing a Bike to West Africa

If you come to Senegambia with your bike on the plane, you can dismantle it and put the pieces in a large bag or box, but it's much easier simply to wheel your bike to the check-in desk, where it should be treated as a piece of baggage (some airlines don't even include it in the weight). This way the baggage handlers see a bike and are unlikely to pile suitcases on top of it. Some travellers say that if your bike doesn't stand up to airline baggage handlers it won't last long in Africa anyway, but that's a matter of opinion. If you do go for the nondismantle approach, you'll probably still have to remove the pedals, deflate the tyres and turn the handlebars sideways. Unfortunately, some airlines have started charging extra for bicycles, even if the bicycle and luggage is within the weight limit, because they're of nonstandard dimensions. In this case you'll have to partly dismantle the bike and pack it. Check all this with the airline well in advance, preferably before you pay for your ticket.

simply want to cut out the boring bits, bikes can easily be carried on buses and bush taxis. If you're camping near settlements in rural areas, ask the village headman each night where you can pitch. Even if you don't have a tent, he'll find you a place to stay.

It's important to carry sufficient spares, and have a good working knowledge of bike repair and maintenance – punctures will be frequent. Take at least four spare inner tubes, some tyre patching material and a spare tyre. Consider the number of tube patches you might need, triple it, and pack those too.

Anyone considering doing some serious cycling in Senegambia should contact their national cycling association. For example, in Britain the Cyclists' Touring Club (☎ 087-0873 0060, e cycling@ctc.org.uk, w www .ctc.org.uk) provides members with route details and information for many parts of the world. In the USA, the International Bicycle Fund (☎/fax 206-767 0848, w www.ibike .org/bikeafrica), a low-budget, socially conscious organisation, organises tours, provides information and has an excellent website with information on cycling in West Africa, a huge range of links and a list of cyclist-friendly airlines.

If you don't have a bike of your own, there are several places (notably tourist areas such as the coastal resort areas in Gambia or the Casamance region) where bicycles can be hired. Your choice may range from a new, lightweight mountain bike (*velo tous terrains* or *VTT* in French) to an ancient steel, single-gear sit-up-and-beg roadster. Costs range from US$1 to US$10 per day. Otherwise, local people in villages and towns are often willing to rent their bikes for the day to travellers; ask at your hotel or track down a bicycle repair man (every town market has one).

BOAT

It is possible to travel along the coast between Gambia and Senegal on a *pirogue* (canoe), but these trips can be dangerous. The three major rivers in the region – the Senegal, the Gambia and particularly the Casamance – can also be navigated, although there are no scheduled services. When it's operating, the *Joola* ferry runs between Dakar and Ziguinchor via Carabane, but don't plan your trip around this ferry trip, as there's a good chance it won't be running when you arrive. More details are given in the country Getting There & Away and Getting Around chapters.

LOCAL TRANSPORT
City Bus

There is a well-developed city bus network in Dakar. Alongside the big buses, minibuses also connect the city centre and suburbs. In most other towns and cities, it's minibuses only.

Shared Taxi

Many cities have shared taxis, which will stop and pick up more passengers even if they

Pont Faidherbe, named after an early governor of Senegal, links the mainland to St-Louis

already have somebody inside. Some run on fixed routes, and are effectively a small bus, only quicker and more comfortable. Others go wherever the first passenger wants to go, and other people are picked up if they're going in the same direction. These prospective passengers normally shout the name of the suburb they're heading for as the taxi goes past. Once you've got the hang of this system it's a good way to get around cities. It's quick, safe and quite cheap. It's always worth checking the fare before you get in the car though, as it is not always fixed, and meters don't usually apply to shared trips. If you're the first person in the taxi, make it clear that you're expecting the driver to pick up others and that you don't want *deplacement* (chartering or having the vehicle all to yourself).

Private Hire Taxi

Only in Dakar do taxis have meters *(compteurs)*. For all other places in Gambia and Senegal, either bargaining is required or you'll be given the legally fixed rate, which is not negotiable (such as for the ride from Dakar or Banjul airport into town). Typical fares are given in the country chapters. The price always includes luggage, unless you have a particularly bulky item.

ORGANISED TOURS

In Gambia and Senegal local tour companies are usually located in the capital cities, and offer excursions for groups or individuals, from one day to one week. On most tours, the larger the group, the lower the cost per person.

Facts about The Gambia

HISTORY

Senegambian history up to the end of the 19th century is covered in the Facts about Senegambia chapter. The boundaries of Gambia and Senegal as they exist today were ratified at the Berlin Conference of 1885–86, which settled claims made by European powers following the Scramble for Africa.

The Colonial Period

Although Gambia was a British protectorate from 1820 and became a full British colony in 1886, the decision-makers in London didn't really want this sliver of land surrounded by French territory. Attempts were made to exchange Gambia for land elsewhere – a common practice among the colonial powers of the time – but no matter how much the British talked up the qualities of the territory, no-one was interested. Thus Britain was lumbered with Gambia, and the little colony was almost forgotten as events in India and other parts of Africa dominated British colonial policy in the first half of the

20th century. Little wealth came out of Gambia and as a result very little 'development' was attempted – administration was limited to a few British district commissioners and the local chiefs they appointed.

In the 1950s, Gambia's groundnut plantations were improved as a way to increase export earnings and a few other agricultural schemes were set up. There was little else in the way of services, and by the early 1960s Gambia had fewer than 50 primary schools, and only a handful of doctors. While the rest of West Africa was gaining independence, this option seemed unlikely for Gambia. There was hardly any local political infrastructure and Britain was against the move – mainly because it believed an independent Gambia could not survive economically. The county's economy was still based on groundnuts, and there were very few other sources of income. A federation with Senegal, which had just gained independence from France, was considered but came to nothing.

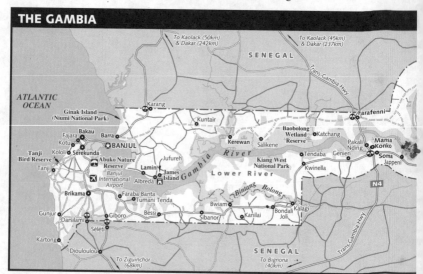

THE GAMBIA

Around this time, David Jawara, a Mandinka from the upcountry provinces, founded the People's Progressive Party (PPP). The few small parties that had existed before this were either Banjul-based, dominated by the Wolof or Aku ethnic groups, or tended to be Christian in outlook. The PPP was the first party to attract mass support from rural Mandinka Muslims – the overwhelming majority of people in Gambia. To prepare for at least partial self-government, a Gambian parliament – the House of Representatives – was instituted, and elections were held in 1962. These were easily won by Jawara's PPP.

Independence

In 1965 Gambia became independent, with Jawara as prime minister, although Britain's Queen Elizabeth II remained as titular head of state. Without any official explanation, Gambia was renamed The Gambia. More understandably however, Bathurst was renamed Banjul.

Although the tiny nation appeared to have no viable economic future, two events occurred that enabled it to survive and even prosper. For a decade after independence,

the world price for groundnuts increased significantly, raising the country's gross national product (GNP) almost threefold. The second event had an even more resounding effect – Gambia became a tourist destination. In 1966 the number of tourists visiting Gambia was recorded as 300. By the end of the 1960s, this number had risen to several thousand, initially mostly from Sweden, and then in greater numbers from Britain. By 1976 the number of tourists visiting Gambia topped 25,000 per year.

Economic growth translated into political confidence. In 1970, Gambia became a fully independent republic. Prime Minister Jawara became president and changed his name from David to Dawda. Opposition parties were tolerated, and there was a relatively free press. At the same time, the Gambian tradition of political lethargy continued unchanged. The PPP was deeply conservative and Jawara's opponents accused his government of benign neglect and financial corruption, claiming that the president, ministers and other PPP politicians retained power through a complex web of largess and patronage, rather than through any genuine level of public support.

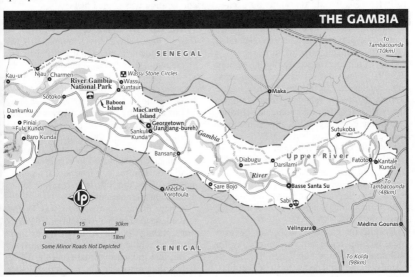

The 1980s

The first major sign of discontent over the PPP's grip on the country came in 1980 when a group of disaffected soldiers staged a coup. Calling on the mutual defence pact between Senegal and Gambia, Jawara asked the Senegalese government to oust them, which it did. There was another coup attempt the following year, while Jawara was in London, once again defeated with help from Senegalese troops (a contingent of British soldiers also assisted). Acknowledging this debt, Jawara announced that Gambian and Senegalese armed forces would be fully integrated. In 1982 the Senegambian Confederation came into effect, under which Senegal agreed to provide military protection for Gambia (in other words for Jawara), while Gambia made some noncommittal noises about an eventual Senegambian country.

The confederation, however, lacked popular support. The Gambian Mandinka who formed the PPP's power base saw it as a Wolof takeover, which it was. Smuggling was another problem: high customs duties in Senegal made some imported goods there more expensive, while prices for groundnuts in the two countries varied. Periodically tensions flared. At a football match in Banjul, rioting provoked the Senegalese ambassador to call in Senegalese troops to protect the players. The Gambia responded by asking Senegal to recall him.

Tourist numbers rose steadily throughout the 1980s, and tourism became an increasingly vital source of foreign currency for the country. However, relatively few Gambians saw any benefit from the tourists' contribution to the economy. While tourist numbers rose, groundnut prices had been falling since the late 1970s (the government had made no significant attempts to encourage diversification) and most ordinary Gambians began to feel increasingly worse off. The discontent led to increased support for various opposition groups, most notably the Movement for Justice in Africa (MOJA).

Despite increasing evidence of government incompetence and corruption, Jawara still enjoyed a large popular following, especially in the rural areas (most of Gambia), and won the elections of 1982 and 1987. Opposition parties, including the National Convention Party and the Gambia People's Party, gathered support but were never a real threat to the PPP. (MOJA by this time had been banned, and its leaders arrested or went underground.)

At the end of the 1980s the tide began to turn. There was increasing dissatisfaction in rural areas as groundnut prices continued to fall, and agricultural subsidies and spending on public services were cut as part of an International Monetary Fund (IMF) restructure. Reports of malnutrition and starvation were not uncommon in remote areas, but the government made few attempts to alleviate this situation, and was seen by many Gambians as being too far removed from the everyday problems they faced.

In the political arena, there were another couple of coup attempts, allegedly with support from Senegalese opposition figures, and in 1989 the Senegambian Confederation was dissolved. Both Gambia and Senegal imposed severe border restrictions, and tensions ran high well into 1990. After a year, relations between the countries improved again, and a treaty of friendship and cooperation was signed in 1991.

Time Up for Jawara

Despite their many obvious failures, in April 1992 President Jawara and the PPP were re-elected for a sixth term. To the outside world Jawara appeared to remain popular. It came as a surprise, therefore, when on 22 July 1994 a protest by soldiers over late salaries and treatment by Nigerian officers (during Ecomog peacekeeping duties in Liberia and Sierra Leone) turned into a coup d'etat. The coup leader was Yahya Jammeh, a young lieutenant who appeared in public wearing regulation combat fatigues and dark sunglasses, which did little to endear him to the international community.

A new military government was hastily formed, headed by the Armed Forces Provisional Ruling Council (AFPRC). It was composed of senior military officers, most of whom had trained in Britain and the USA, and civilian ministers who had served under the previous government. Ex-president Jawara managed to reach a US warship, which happened to be in Banjul harbour, and was finally granted asylum in Senegal.

Jammeh initially promised that the AFPRC would be back in the barracks within a few months, but in October 1994 he announced he would stay in power at least until 1998. Although this may not have come as a complete surprise to international observers familiar with the machinations of African politics, aid donors such as the European Union (including Britain), the USA and the World Bank were displeased by what they saw as a blatant disregard for democracy and threatened to cut their support.

But Jammeh was unrepentant. Although still only 29 years old and completely inexperienced, he remained firmly at the helm. An indication of his leadership style came after the independent *Daily Observer* newspaper ran a story suggesting the cut in overseas aid would be bad for the country. The editor was arrested and eventually deported, and the paper was temporarily closed down.

The political turbulence hit Gambia's tourist trade hard. Advice from the British Foreign Office caused many tourists from Britain (about 50% of the total number of visitors) to cancel reservations, and several major tour companies halted flights to Gambia. The advice was regarded by most people in the tourism industry as a political move, a warning to the new rulers of Gambia that their major source of income, and thus their very survival, still depended on the say-so of Britain and the West. Whatever the reasons, tourist numbers in the 1994–95 season dropped by around 65% to less than 40,000.

In 1995 Jammeh pragmatically switched tack and announced elections would be held the following year. In March 1995, the British Foreign Office advised tourists that Gambia was safe again, with the proviso the political situation was still uncertain, and tourism picked up.

Jammeh Takes Charge

Jammeh and the AFPRC remained in control, and a new constitution, ushering in the Second Republic, was introduced. This was accepted by the Gambian people in a national election held, after some delay, in September 1996, confirming the Gambian people's desire for a return to civilian rule.

At the same time, elections were held for the post of president. Political parties were permitted for the first time since the coup and there were four candidates, each from a different party. One of these parties was the AFPRC (now neatly renamed the Alliance for Patriotic Reorientation and Construction), and its candidate was none other than Yahya Jammeh. He was the clear winner, with 56% of the vote, completing his smooth transition from minor army officer to head of state in just over two years.

In January 1997 the AFPRC also dominated the election for the national assembly, consolidating President Jammeh's hold on power. His opponents claimed the election and the constitution were manipulated to disadvantage the fledgling opposition parties, and Amnesty International criticised moves to ban three opposition parties and the content of the new constitution.

Despite these claims, and other complaints from within the country and abroad, President Jammeh remained popular with the Gambian people. Most saw him as a fresh new force, keen to sweep away the lethargy and corruption of the old days. To consolidate this support, Jammeh announced a series of impressive schemes to rebuild the country's infrastructure and economy. A new airport was constructed and a national television station opened. New clinics and schools were promised for the upcountry provinces.

But in the Gambian parliament, opposition members continued to question the new president's rule. Funds originally destined for development projects were allegedly moved into private overseas bank accounts. The *New African* magazine reported in November 1997 that a Swiss prosecutor had seized an account in the name of one of the president's close advisers. The article also alleged that a multimillion-dollar loan from Taiwan never arrived in Gambia, but was diverted directly to an account in New York. Politicians attempting to discuss this issue in parliament were prevented from doing so by the Speaker, even though the Gambian government indignantly denied having done anything wrong.

Human rights was another issue. The new government released several opposition members who had been imprisoned after the July 1994 coup, however the United Democratic Party later claimed some of its members had been arrested and detained.

This sort of low-level intimidation of political opponents and media organisations that dared to criticise has become a hallmark of Jammeh's rule. So too has the ever-increasing wealth of the man. Since he came to power Jammeh has acquired a series of properties and businesses including the Kairaba Hotel at Kololi and the high-class Sindola game reserve, making him one of the richest, as well as the most powerful, men in Gambia.

While Jammeh quietly built his own fortune – in true African-leader style – he also launched an ambitious building programme with schools, clinics and roads the priority. Soon Jammeh was boasting of building more schools in five years than Jawara had in almost 30. Happily, stability returned to Gambia and tourist numbers rose almost to the highs experienced back in the early 90s.

In April 2001 a student demonstration protesting the untimely death of a colleague, ended with 14 people being shot dead in battles with police. Despite this, and a damning condemnation of the country's human rights record by Amnesty International, many ordinary people had grown to regard Jammeh as a force for good. The rest of the world was waiting for a second election as a test of his commitment to democracy before embracing the former military man wholeheartedly.

In October 2001 Jammeh won his second five-year term as president, taking 53% of the vote against second-place Ousainou Darboe's 33%. International observers proclaimed the elections to be free and fair, but Darboe's United Democratic Party claimed the result was rigged, saying 50,000 people were registered to vote despite being ineligible because they were not Gambians.

The UDP claim the vast majority of these ineligible voters had cast their ballot for Jammeh.

In response the UDP boycotted parliamentary elections held in January 2002. The result was that Jammeh's APRC (having jettisoned the 'F') won comfortably, with more than two thirds of seats not even contested. While the international community was generally satisfied with the presidential election, Jammeh's rounding up of several opposition figures in the weeks following the parliamentary poll raised new doubts about his commitment to democracy.

Fair or not, the elections confirmed Jammeh's position and Gambia is expected to remain stable and peaceful at least until 2006, when the next presidential elections are due.

GEOGRAPHY

The Gambia's shape and position epitomise the absurdity of the national boundaries carved by the European colonial powers at the end of the 20th century. About 300km long, but averaging only 35km wide, Gambia has an area of 11,295 sq km and, except for about 80km of coastline, is entirely surrounded by Senegal. In real terms this means Gambia is half the size of Wales, or less than twice the size of Delaware, and is the smallest country in Africa.

The country's territory, and its very existence, is determined by the Gambia River which flows into the Atlantic Ocean, dividing Gambia's coastline into northern and southern sections. Banjul, the capital, is on the southern side of the mouth of the Gambia River. On the opposite bank is the small town of Barra and 25km upstream is the village of Jufureh, made famous by *Roots* author Alex Haley (see the boxed text 'The Roots Debate' in the Western Gambia chapter).

West of Banjul are the holiday resorts of Bakau, Fajara, Kotu and Kololi, the centre of Gambia's tourist industry. Nearby is the town of Serekunda, which is a hub of commercial activity. Further up the river are many more villages, but the only towns of any size are Farafenni, Georgetown and Basse Santa Su.

Current estimates put Gambia's population at about 1.4 million, while Senegal's is around 10.3 million. There are several ethnic groups in the region spread across national boundaries.

ERIC L WHEATER

ARIADNE VAN ZANDBERGEN

ANDREW BURKE

ERIC L WHEATER

Headgear serves as both protection from the sun and colourful adornment. In a region where 90% of the people are Islamic, it also has religious significance.

Cannon Ball Run

The boundaries of Gambia largely follow the course of the Gambia River so that, from about 50km upstream, every meander of the river is echoed by a precise twist or turn in the borders running parallel less than 20km to the north and south. Local legend tells that the border was established by a British gunship sailing up the river and firing cannon balls as far as possible onto each bank. The points where the balls fell were then joined up to become the border. This may not be strictly true, but Gambia was initially established as a Protectorate, and in the 19th century protection could be most easily administered by gunship.

The Gambia has no hills or mountains, or any other major topographical features. In fact, the country is so flat, that the Gambia River drops less than 10m in around 450km between the far eastern border of the country near Fatoto and the mouth of the river at Banjul.

FLORA & FAUNA

Away from the river, Gambia's position in the southern Sahel means natural vegetation consists mostly of dry grassland or open savanna woodland. See Flora & Fauna in the Facts about Senegambia chapter and the special colour section 'Birds of Senegambia'.

National Parks & Reserves

The Gambia has six national parks and reserves, covering 3.7% of the national land area, plus several forest parks. The national parks and reserves are administered by the Department of Parks and Wildlife Management and have been set aside (gazetted) to protect representative samples of main habitat types and their associated fauna.

The forest parks have been established to preserve existing forest or provide renewable timber stocks – with the exception of Bijilo Forest Park, which is primarily a nature reserve.

All the parks and reserves listed here are open to the public (except River Gambia National Park) and between them provide a good cross-section of the different types of habitat in the country. The Department of Parks and Wildlife Management has done an admirable job so far to protect a variety of natural habitats, and hopes to open more protected areas, bringing the national coverage up to about 5%. New protected areas to look for include mid-river islands in the freshwater-saline transition zone and freshwater swamps on the upper river in the east of the country.

Abuko Nature Reserve is Gambia's oldest protected area. It covers 105 hectares in western Gambia near the holiday resorts on the Atlantic coast and is visited regularly by tourists. The reserve protects a large tract of gallery forest, and is particularly noted for its bird and monkey populations.

Baobolong Wetland Reserve is on the northern bank of the Gambia River in central Gambia, opposite Kiang West. Its 22,000 hectares stretch inland almost to the Senegal border. It is most easily reached from Tendaba, on the southern bank. This wetland was designated as Gambia's first Ramsar site (the convention on wetlands of international importance).

Kiang West National Park is on the southern bank of the Gambia River in central Gambia. Its 11,000 hectares are dominated by dry woodland vegetation, with areas of mangrove and mud flat. It is most easily reached from Tendaba.

River Gambia National Park is more commonly known as Baboon Islands. It is a 580-hectare park covering five mid-river islands near Georgetown in eastern Gambia. It was established mainly as a rehabilitation sanctuary for chimpanzees. Visitors are not permitted on the islands.

Niumi National Park is in the northwest of Gambia, contiguous with the Parc National du Delta du Saloum in neighbouring Senegal, and incorporates the coastal island of Ginak. It covers 5000 hectares and features dry woodland, sand dunes, mangroves, salt marshes and lagoons.

Tanji River Bird Reserve is on the coast, south of the Atlantic coast resorts area in western Gambia. Its 612 hectares include dunes, lagoons, mangroves, dry woodland and coastal scrub, plus a section of the Tanji River and the offshore Bijol Islands.

Bijilo Forest Park is one of several forest parks in Gambia, but it is unusual in that it is not conserved for its potential as a renewable timber source, but is primarily a nature reserve. It covers 51 hectares and is near the resort of Kololi. It is easy to reach from the other Atlantic coast resorts.

Tanbi Wetland Complex is expected to eventually become a national park. It covers around 6000 hectares and incorporates the coastal strip and mangrove swamp from Banjul to Cape Point and south along the river to Lamin and Mandinari Point. It is currently designated as a Ramsar site.

GOVERNMENT & POLITICS
Following the coup of 1994, Gambia temporarily became a military dictatorship under the Armed Forces Provisional Ruling Council (AFPRC). Elections for president in late 1996 and for members of the national assembly in January 1997 returned the country, officially at least, to democratic civilian rule. The government is based on the British parliamentary system, which was introduced in colonial times, maintained by President Jawara and has been largely retained by the constitution of the Second Republic, adopted in 1996.

The 1996 and 1997 elections were contested by representatives from four main political parties, and five parties contested the presidential elections of 2001. The dominant party is the APRC, which has now been renamed the Alliance for Patriotic Reorientation and Construction. With the main opposition party, the United Democratic Party, boycotting parliamentary elections in January 2002, the APRC won 45 of the 48 elected seats in the national assembly. The Peoples Democratic Organisation for Independence and Socialism won two seats, while the National Reconciliation Party won one. Five more members of the assembly, including the Speaker, were appointed directly by the president. The national assembly includes three female members.

Elections are to be held every five years by universal adult suffrage. The next elections are due in 2006.

ECONOMY
The Gambia's economy is dominated by exports of the country's major cash crop – groundnuts (peanuts; see the boxed text 'Groundnuts' in the Facts about Senegambia chapter.) The value of this crop on the world market has fallen since the 1970s, and Gambia has had a negative balance of trade for every year since 1975. During the 1980s, in an attempt to combat this downward slide, the IMF granted loans to Gambia on the condition the government-controlled groundnut trade was opened to private traders. The Gambia found the loans hard to repay, as harvests were hit by several droughts during this period, but the conditions were kept.

In the early 1990s the IMF-supported Economic Recovery Programme was deemed a success and was replaced with the Programme for Sustained Recovery. Opponents of IMF policies see the reclassifications as merely cosmetic, and point out that any benefits are not felt by most ordinary Gambians. The country's total foreign debt stands at around US$330 million after the World Bank, the IMF and other international creditors agreed to relieve Gambia of US$91 million of its obligation. Gambia qualified for this relief after it was classified as a highly indebted poor country – not an international club Gambians are proud to be a member of. To put all this in perspective, the

Personal Economics

The Gambia's gross national income (GNI) is about US$330 per capita, less than what many visitors to the country would earn in a week. But to put a personal perspective on The Gambia's economy, here is a small selection of average monthly salaries. A waiter may earn D450 (around US$25 per month), while teachers and police officers officially earn about D1000 (US$57), and a senior civil servant's official monthly salary might be D7500 (US$430).

UNDP's 2000 Human Development Index ranked Gambia 161st out of 174 countries.

Relief or not, interest still needs to be paid on the remaining debt and uses up a major portion of any export earnings. And as long as the balance of trade figure remains negative it's unlikely the loans will ever be paid off. Recent attempts at diversification in the economy have met with only limited success. Agriculture, fisheries and forestry have actually grown as a percentage of GDP, making it one of the few countries on earth so devoid of industry. Groundnuts still account for some 70% of the GNP, and world prices remain unfavourable.

The Gambia's other main economic activity is tourism. The number of visitors from Europe (mainly Britain, Germany and Scandinavia) grew considerably during the 1980s. Tourist numbers peaked in the 1988–89 season, with more than 110,000 visitors, but the figure dropped dramatically in 1994 following the July coup. Visitor numbers have been steady at about 90,000 in recent years.

Despite its high profile, tourism only accounts for between 15% and 20% of Gambia's total GNP. One of the reasons for this is that a large number of tourists are on package tours paid for in their home countries, so relatively little revenue remains in Gambia. Yet the government continues to spend a significant portion of its capital-development budget on tourist-related projects, thus diverting funds from sectors directly benefiting Gambians, such as agriculture.

Less than 20,000 local people are employed in the tourist industry, mostly in low-earning or insecure jobs, which only last for the six-month tourist season. However, because many wage earners support a large extended family, it is estimated that five to 10 times this figure is actually dependent on the money tourism provides.

POPULATION & PEOPLE

Gambia's population is around 1.4 million, with 45% of that total less than 14 years old. This total is growing by 3.1% a year, and the population density of around 115 people per square kilometre is one of the highest in Africa.

The major ethnic group is the Mandinka (also called Mandingo), who comprise about 42% of the total population. Other large groups include the Fula (about 18%) and the Wolof (about 16%). Minor groups include the Serer and Jola. A small but significant group are the Aku who live only in Gambia, and mainly in the Banjul area. Other minorities, mainly from Lebanon and Western Europe, account for less than 1%.

Among ethnic groups intermarriage is not uncommon. The common denominator is religion – over 90% of Gambians are Muslim.

The Aku

The Aku are a small but significant group, mostly descendants of freed slaves brought to Gambia in the early 19th century when the British established a protectorate here. Some came from plantations in the Americas, while others were released from slave ships leaving West Africa. Many also came from Sierra Leone, where a similar group of freed slaves became the Krio people. The Aku language – a mix of 18th-century English and various indigenous tongues – is also similar to the Krio and 'pidgin' spoken in other former British West African colonies.

Today there are still strong links between the Aku and Krio (sometimes the terms are used interchangeably) with many families having members in both countries. During the recent civil wars in Sierra Leone and Liberia, many Krio refugees came to Banjul and settled.

The Aku are mostly Christian and generally have names of British origin, such as Johnson or Thompson. Traditional Krio houses have steep tin roofs, gable windows and clapboard walls, a design thought to have originated in the southern states of the USA. They can still be seen on the old part of Banjul.

In colonial times many were Aku people were employed in the civil service. The distinction between the former civil servants and other locals has its legacy in attitudes that prevail today.

ARTS

An overview of the Senegambian arts scene is given under Arts in the Facts about Senegambia chapter, and further discussed in the special section 'Music of Senegambia'. More information on fabrics and other crafts are given in the Shopping sections throughout Gambia's chapters.

Literature

Along with many countries of the Sahel, Gambia's literary tradition is based upon the family histories and epic poems told over the centuries by the griots (traditional musicians or minstrels). More details on griots are given in the special section 'Music of Senegambia'.)

In more recent times, especially since independence, a number of contemporary writers have emerged, although compared to many other West African countries, Gambia does not have a major literary output, and relatively little is available. That the works of Gambia's best-known novelist, William Conton, date from the 1960s is indicative of this.

William Conton was born in Banjul, although his family came from Sierra Leone (many Sierra Leoneans settled in Gambia during colonial times), and his writing reflects this influence. His 1960s classic, *The African*, is a semi-autobiographical tale of an African student in Britain, who experiences confusion and unhappiness there. He returns to his homeland where he gets involved in nationalist politics and finally becomes president, still suffering from pangs of alienation and self-doubt. Published at a time when many former colonies were gaining independence, this book was an influential bestseller in many parts of Africa.

Lenrie Peters is another Gambian writer with a Sierra Leonean heritage. His best-known novel, *The Second Round*, which was also published in the 1960s, is a semi-autobiographical work about an African doctor who lives overseas and has trouble readjusting to local ways when he returns home. Peters' poetry collections include *Satellites*, *Katchikali* and *Selected Poetry*, in which the same themes of alienation and dealing with change frequently appear. His precise and economic style has been fittingly described as 'surgical'.

Whereas Conton and Peters have their roots in the colonial era, author Ebou Dibba is seen as part of the new Gambian generation, even though his first and best-known novel *Chaff on the Wind* (1986) is set in the pre-independence period. This book follows the fortunes of two rural boys (one keen and studious, the other looking only for a good time) who come to work in the capital city, both eventually suffering at the hands of fate, despite their attempts to control their own destinies. Dibba's second novel, *Fafa*, describes the lives of two women in a riverside village, and once again pessimism and fatalism are the central themes. His most recent work is *Alhaji*.

Another new generation writer is Tijan Salleh, primarily known as a poet – his main collection is *Kora Land*, published in 1989 – although he has also written essays and short stories. His style has been described as blunt, abrasive, radical and confrontational. Common themes include the debunking of political hypocrisy and despair at the corruption and poverty endemic in African society.

Gambia's Own Alphabet

It's got a way to go before it rivals the Latin, Cyrillic or Chinese scripts, but as of 2001 Gambia has its own alphabet. The 28-letter Soni alphabet was created by a Gambian businessman to complement the Soninke language, spoken by only a tiny fraction of the population. Kaa Bully Nimaga said he planned to start a school where Gambian children could learn the language – which he says is the only language that is truly Gambian – for nothing. Nimaga described the new alphabet as a gift from God, and said he had realised a childhood dream by inventing something useful. But in an age where languages are dying faster than they're appearing, its usefulness is dubious. For a closer look, check out the outside wall of LK Fast Food in Serekunda, where the alphabet is on display.

Facts for the Visitor

For general visitor information pertaining to the whole Senegambian region, see the Regional Facts for the Visitor chapter.

SUGGESTED ITINERARIES
The Gambia's compact size and easy transport system make it ideal for a one- or two-week visit, either tied in with charter flights from Europe or as part of a longer trip. The small and dusty capital, Banjul, has little in the way of 'sights', but you should allow a few days to visit places nearby, such as the Bijilo Forest Park, Abuko Nature Reserve, Serekunda market and Jufureh (the 'Roots' village), or take a boat ride through the mangroves of Oyster Creek to Makasutu. Allow extra days if you simply want to lie on the beach at one of the Atlantic coast resorts.

From Banjul your first stop might be Farafenni, which hosts a big market every Sunday. Wildlife fans should try and stop at Tendaba, a base for visiting both Kiang West National Park and Baobolong Wetland Reserve (two to three days). Further upcountry is peaceful Georgetown, from where you can reach the Wassu Stone Circles or the River Gambia National Park, and the lively trading centre of Basse Santa Su, always worth visiting for a day or two, from where you can return to Banjul, or head east into Senegal.

MAPS
Supermarkets and hotels in the Atlantic coast resorts stock the colourful and tourist-orientated *The Gambia: The Map, the Land, the People* (D60), a cartoon-style production that will get you around if you can't find anything else. For more details about available maps, see Maps in the Regional Facts for the Visitor chapter.

TOURIST OFFICES
The Gambia is represented in Britain by the Gambia National Tourist Office (☎ 020-7376 0093, ⓔ enquiries@gambiatourism.info,

ⓦ www.gambiatourism.info) based at the Gambian high commission. This office has a decent website, responds promptly to calls, faxes and emails and will send a useful colour brochure anywhere in the world. The newly formed Gambia Tourist Authority plans to open information booths in the coastal resorts.

VISAS
General information about visas and how to get them is given in the Regional Facts for the Visitor chapter.

Visas are not needed by nationals of Commonwealth countries, Belgium, Germany, Italy, Luxembourg, the Netherlands, Spain or Scandinavian countries for stays of up to 90 days. For those needing one, visas are normally valid for one month and are issued in two to three days for the equivalent of about US$45; you'll need two photos. You can find out whether you need a visa by emailing ⓔ enquiries@gambiatourism.info. An application form can be printed out from ⓦ www.gambia.com, though if you're applying by snail mail in the US allow at least two weeks for the process.

It's best to get a visa before you arrive, but if you can't, don't sweat. You can usually get one at the border if you are coming from southern or eastern Senegal (but this is not guaranteed). If you're arriving at Banjul international airport, you'll be comforted by the official government brochure for tourists which states that tourists and others travelling on last-minute bookings will be allowed entry but will have to submit their passport to the Department of Immigration in Banjul within 48 hours to be issued a proper visa.

If this is you, take yourself to the Immigration Office (☎ 228611) on OAU Blvd in Banjul between 8am and 4pm and 30 minutes later you'll be legal.

Your visa can be extended at the same office for D250. It's a painless exercise that takes about five minutes.

EMBASSIES & CONSULATES
Gambian Embassies & Consulates

The few West African countries with Gambian embassies, high commissions or consulates include Senegal (see the Senegal Facts for the Visitor chapter), Guinea-Bissau, Nigeria and Sierra Leone. Elsewhere, Gambian embassies and consulates include the following:

Belgium (☎ 02-640 1049) 126 ave Franklin-Roosevelt, Brussels 1050
France (☎ 01 42 94 09 30) 117, rue Saint-Lazare, 75008 Paris
Germany (☎ 030-892 31 21, fax 891 14 01) Kurfurstendamm 103, Berlin
Guinea-Bissau (☎ 251099) Avenida de 14 Novembro, Bissau, 1km northwest of Mercado de Bandim
Nigeria (☎ 01-682 192) 162 Awolowo Rd, Ikoyi, Lagos
Sierra Leone (☎ 225191) 6 Wilberforce St, Freetown
UK (☎ 020-7937 6316) 57 Kensington Court, London W8 5DH
USA (☎ 202-785 1399, e gamembdc@gambia .com) Suite 1000, 1155 15th St NW, Washington, DC 20005

The Gambia is also represented in Austria, Canada, Italy, Japan, the Netherlands, Norway, Spain and Switzerland. For a complete list of Gambian embassies and consulates, see W www.ifc.org/abn/cic/gambia/english /embassies.htm.

Embassies & Consulates in Gambia

The following list includes embassies of some 'home' countries, and of neighbouring countries for which you might have to get a visa. Most are open 9am to 1pm and 2pm to 4pm Monday to Friday. Opening times different from these appear in the list. It's always best to go at the beginning of the morning session, as lunch hours can be very flexible. Note that for every visa application you need to provide between one and four (usually two) passport photos.

Some embassies and consulates are in Banjul, and others are scattered along the Atlantic coast. For details of embassies in Gambia not listed here, check in the phone book (most Gamtel offices have one).

Guinea (☎ 226862, mobile 909964) Top floor, 78A Daniel Goddard St, Banjul. The embassy is open 9am to 4pm Monday to Thursday, 9am to 1.30pm and 2.30pm to 4pm Friday and sometimes Saturday (but call and ask for Mr Bah first). A visa costs CFA20,000, FF200 or US$40 and if you arrive early you can collect it the same day.
Guinea-Bissau (☎ 494854) Atlantic Rd, Bakau, above Distripharm. Visas cost D120/150 for 30/60 days at this embassy, open 8am to 3pm Monday to Friday, and take between 30 minutes and a day to issue.
Mali (☎ 226942) VM Company Ltd, Cherno Adama Bah St, Banjul. The consul here cannot issue tourist visas. There is an embassy in Dakar, or you can get a 72-hour transit visa at the border or at the airport.
Mauritania (☎ 461086) Just off Badala Park Way, Kololi. This is the best place in West Africa to get a Mauritanian visa. One-month visas cost D300 and are issued the same day; the office is open 8am to 4pm Monday to Friday.
Senegal (☎ 373752, fax 373 750) One block west of Kairaba Ave, behind the mosque. Visas are cheaper here than in Europe, but for some reason you can only apply on Monday and Wednesday (the office is open 8am to 2pm and 2.30pm to 5pm Monday to Thursday; to 4pm on Friday). One month costs D57, three months multi-entry is D132; they're issued in 48 hours.
Sierra Leone (☎ 228206) 67 Daniel Goddard St, Banjul. The high commission issues single-entry visas in 48 hours for US$45. You can apply 8.30am to 4.30pm Monday to Thursday, 8.30am to 1.30pm Friday.
UK (☎ 495133/4, fax 496134) 48 Atlantic Rd, Fajara, opposite the Medical Research Council. The embassy is open 8am to 3pm Monday to Thursday, 8am to 1pm Friday.
USA (☎ 392856/8, 391971, fax 392475) Kairaba Ave, Fajara.

Several European countries have honorary consuls in Gambia, including Belgium (at the Kairaba Hotel, Kololi), Sweden and Norway (above the Point Restaurant, Saitmatty Rd, Bakau). These people have limited diplomatic powers, and are mainly there to assist holiday makers who run into difficulties. Germany and Denmark also have consuls – often an expatriate connected with the tour industry, who can change from year to year. If you need either of these consuls, you can get information about them from one of the holiday reps working for the German and Scandinavian tour companies, usually contactable through the larger hotels.

CUSTOMS

There are no restrictions on the import of local or foreign currencies, or on the export of foreign currency, but you cannot export more than D100, not that you'd want to. The usual limits apply to alcohol (1L of spirits, 1L of wine) and tobacco (200 cigarettes).

MONEY

For general information on money matters, see the Regional Facts for the Visitor chapter.

Currency

The Gambia's unit of currency is the dalasi (pronounced da-la-see). This is abbreviated to D or d, and is written before or after the numbers. Throughout this book, we have put it before, eg D200. The dalasi is not fixed and floats against other international currencies, although locals will tell you it's been drowning for years.

The dalasi is divided into 100 bututs, and there are coins for five, 10, 25 and 50 bututs, although apart from the 50 these are rarely seen. Notes in circulation are D5,

---

The Disappearing Dalasi

If all goes according to plan the dalasi will be phased out and replaced during the lifetime of this book – the latest details available when we went to press are in the boxed text 'New Currencies' in the Regional Facts for the Visitor chapter. It's expected there will be a considerable period of crossover between the dalasi and its two replacements. But until more solid plans are announced our best advice is to remember that the US dollar was worth D17.50 when we researched this guide, and if dalasi (or any new currency) prices are different from those quoted here, their dollar price should remain about the same. Carrying a small calculator could be a good idea.

D10, D25, D50 and D100. There is also a D1 coin.

If you come to Gambia from Senegal, or you're travelling between northern and southern Senegal on the Trans-Gambia Hwy, many items can be paid for in CFA, the currency of Senegal and much of West Africa.

Exchange Rates

The value of the dalasi has steadily eroded during the past few years and expectations are that this will continue. Generally costs have risen at the same rate as the value of the dalasi has fallen, so some simple arithmetic will soon tell you whether you're paying over the odds or not. At the time of writing, exchange rates were:

country	unit		dalasi
Australia	A$1	=	D9.00
Canada	C$1	=	D10.50
euro zone	€1	=	D15.00
New Zealand	NZ$1	=	D7.80
UK	UK£1	=	D25.00
USA	US$1	=	D17.50
West African CFA zone	CFA1000	=	D23.00

Exchanging Money

Cash & Travellers Cheques Gambia's main banks are Standard Chartered, Trust Bank and IBC (formerly BICIS) and each has branches in Banjul, Serekunda and the Atlantic coast resorts. You can change cash and travellers cheques in these banks, and there are also money-changing bureaus and plenty of black-market traders who operate in these areas (see the boxed text 'Pockets Full of Money'). Trust Bank charges a D25 fee for cashing travellers cheques, while IBC has no charge at all but its rates might be slightly lower. See the boxed text 'Bank Charges & Commissions' in the Regional Facts for the Visitor chapter.

Upcountry, banks are harder to find. Only Brikama, Farafenni and Basse have branches, though Georgetown and Soma are expecting to join that club. There's a branch of Trust Bank at the airport, but no ATM. If it's closed, the police will help you find an unofficial but tolerated money-

THE GAMBIA

changer (but they don't deal in travellers cheques).

In and around Banjul, changing cash or travellers cheques is fairly quick and straightforward. Generally the money-changing bureaus give a slightly better rate for cash, and a slightly worse rate for travellers cheques, but as rates and commissions can vary, it might be worth shopping around.

ATMs & Credit Cards ATMs have begun to appear at Standard Chartered branches and a couple of petrol stations around the Atlantic coast. They are generally well stocked with crisp new D100 notes, but seem to dispense them only to Visa cardholders. Despite the prominent stickers on the machines, we met several very unhappy travellers whose money was still 'earning interest' in their Plus, Cirrus, Maestro or Switch accounts, untouchable in Gambia. If you can't find an ATM, you can use your Visa, MasterCard or Eurocard to draw cash at any bank branch for a flat charge of D100. (Your home bank may apply its own charges as well.)

Pockets Full of Money

In Banjul near the Albert Market and at West-field Junction in Serekunda you'll see young men with pockets jammed full with wads of dalasis, holding calculators and loitering with intent. There are plenty of these black market dealers and each is carrying the equivalent of about six months average wage. With their exchange rates about 5% better than the banks they are in effect making a net loss on most transactions, so how on earth can they afford to carry so much cash? The answer is that the money belongs to desperate Lebanese businessmen who, because no-one outside Gambia will even look at dalasis, are prepared to make a loss on current rates just so they can get enough hard currency to pay for the next shipment of imports. For the traveller the black market is usually a quick and easy way to change money, but there's always a risk of being short-changed or robbed, so caution is essential.

POST & COMMUNICATIONS
Post
The postal service out of Gambia is reliable; most cards and letters arrive at their destinations in not much more than a week. Letters to Britain and Europe cost D5, to North America D7 and to Australasia D10. A 2kg package will cost D200 to the UK or continental Europe, D270 to North America, and D365 to Australasia.

The best place for poste restante is the main post office in Banjul; mail should be addressed as follows:

```
Your name
Poste Restante
General Post Office
Banjul
Gambia
```

Telephone
Public telephone and fax offices are run by Gamtel (the state telephone company) and are open evenings and weekends. They run a good service. You'll also find privately owned 'telecentres' in most towns.

Calls within Gambia cost around D8 for three minutes; international calls outside Africa cost about D50 per minute at peak time (7am to 6pm). Calls are cheaper by about 33% between 11pm and 7am. Rates are also cheaper at weekends, when a call to Europe comes down to about D30 per minute. You can buy phonecards at Gamtel offices but you'll be lucky to find a card-phone that works.

Making reverse charge (collect) calls is also possible, but the easiest thing is to get the number of the Gamtel office where you are, make a quick call to whoever you want to speak to and get them to phone you back. This seems to be the normal procedure and it's cheaper for your caller.

For directory assistance dial ☎ 151. For the international operator dial ☎ 100.

Fax
All Gamtel offices have public machines for receiving faxes. Many smaller hotels and tour companies use the service of their nearest Gamtel office to receive faxes, or

'borrow' the fax number of a neighbouring hotel or business. Mark all faxes you send clearly for the intended recipient. Never assume it will go directly to their desk.

Mobile Phones

Two GSM phone networks operate in Gambia. You can buy SIM cards for the government-run Gamcel (D500) from all Gamtel offices, and for Africell (D450) from agents in Serekunda or Banjul. Prepaid calling cards cost D50, D100, D150 and, for Gamcel, D300.

Email & Internet Access

Internet cafés are common in Banjul and on the Atlantic coast, and a couple of upcountry towns have also been wired into the Internet age. There are three operators whose signs can be seen fairly frequently: CyberWorld, Quantumnet (W www.qanet.gm) and Gamtel. All charge about D30 an hour as a base rate. The service is generally reasonably fast, with newish terminals and extras like microphones and cameras standard. However, frequent power cuts have the potential to ruin your whole day (we met one man who seemed on the verge of violence saying his 'whole week' had been lost by an ill-timed outage) so it's wise to ask whether the café has a back-up generator, or at the very least a surge protector, before logging on.

Away from the coast and all the cashed-up tourists, Net access is harder to find, slower and more expensive, though you can expect this to change soon.

DIGITAL RESOURCES

You wouldn't describe Gambia as a powerhouse of Internet creativity, but if you're looking for predeparture tips there are a few sites worth a visit.

The Gambia Birding Group This is an excellent site for bird-watchers with reports on what birds are where, how to find a guide, and links to birding tours.
  W www.gambiabirding.org
The Gambia National Tourist Office This is a good site with general information and links to hotels and tour operators.
  W www.gambiatourism.info

Gambia Tourist Support UK-focused, this site has links to gap year and working holiday information.
  W website.lineone.net/~gambiagts/homep.html
International Roots Festival This is the official site which lists the festival programme.
  W www.rootsfestival.gm
Momodou Camara's site In English and Danish, Momodou offers a thorough insider's view of his home country. There's lots of cultural information plus links to news organisations and businesses.
  W home3.inet.tele.dk/mcamara/index.html

BOOKS

Books about the whole Senegambian region and field guides are listed under Books in the Regional Facts for the Visitor chapter. See also Arts in the Facts about The Gambia chapter for a discussion of novels and poetry by Gambian writers.

An Overview of Protected Areas in The Gambia, produced by the Department of Parks and Wildlife, is bland-looking but useful. It has a short introduction to each national park and wildlife reserve in Gambia, with details on vegetation, birds and other animals. Also good is *Sites & Monuments of The Gambia* produced by the National Council for Arts and Culture and available at the National Museum in Banjul.

NEWSPAPERS & MAGAZINES

There are several pamphlet-thin newspapers published in Banjul and distributed mainly in the west of the country. The best-edited is *The Gambia Daily*, which is nominally independent but closely aligned with the government. Once a vocal critic of the government, *The Daily Observer* is now about as ferocious as a baby seal. This might have something to do with it being bought by close friends of the president. The slightly 'subversive' *Forroyah* appears three times a week, while *The Point* is moving slowly into antigovernment mode but still keeps opinion to a minimum. The twice-weekly *News & Report* is an independent run by a veteran local journalist, while *The Independent*, which appears Monday and Friday, is probably the most provocative of all the local papers, with an attitude that places its future in peril.

Day-old British papers can be found around the coastal resorts, especially during the high season. Timbooktoo, on Kairaba Ave, has a good range, with magazines such as *Time* and *Newsweek* also available. The US embassy is the best place to start looking for American papers.

Perhaps the most interesting magazine for tourists is *Concern*, produced locally by Gambia Tourism Concern (W www.gamb iatourismconcern.com), with interesting and pertinent features by Gambian and non-Gambian writers. When all goes well it is printed quarterly, available in some hotels and also sold by beach boys as part of a scheme to enable them to earn money without having to hassle visitors.

RADIO & TV

When you consider that in 2000 Gambia was estimated to be home to just 5000 televisions, while more than 200,000 people owned radios, you start to understand the importance of the humble transistor. Radio stations include the government-run and rather staid Radio Gambia (648MW or 91.4FM), and Radio Syd (909MW), which broadcasts in Swedish and German as well as English. FM stations include Sud FM (92.1FM) and West Coast Radio (95.3FM), with a heavy music weighting. The mainly music Radio 1 FM (102.1FM) and Citizen FM (105.7FM), have both been repeatedly harassed by the government for their aggressive reporting. Citizen FM has been closed for most of the past four years after being labeled 'antigovernment' in 1998, while Radio 1 FM was severely damaged in an arson attack in 2000. When it's allowed to broadcast, Citizen FM relays the BBC World Service. In the meantime you can hear the Beeb on shortwave frequencies 15400 and 17830.

The Gambia's only TV station is the government-run GTV.

PHOTOGRAPHY

In Gambia, no permit is required for photography, and in most parts of the country you'll have no problem with a camera (providing, of course, you observe the usual rules of politeness). Note, however, that you should avoid taking photos of military installations, airports, ferries, harbours and government buildings, as it could get you into trouble. See Photography in the Regional Facts for the Visitor chapter for more general information.

ELECTRICITY

In theory, Banjul and the major towns have electricity all day, but power cuts are increasingly and annoyingly common (daily in some parts), usually in the evenings. Most hotels have generators to overcome this problem, although if you're staying in budget accommodation you should have a torch or candles handy. In upcountry towns electricity is usually only provided from about 6pm to midnight.

HEALTH

You absolutely need to take precautions against malaria, and you will need a yellow fever vaccination certificate if you're coming from a yellow fever infected area. For more information on these and other health-related matters, see Health in the Regional Facts for the Visitor chapter earlier in this book.

The country's main government-run hospital is in Banjul, but there is a better selection of private clinics and doctors in the area around the Atlantic coast resorts. If you're upcountry, there are hospitals in Bansang and Farafenni. See the individual place entries for more details.

DANGERS & ANNOYANCES

The main danger you may encounter in Gambia is the possibility of being robbed in Banjul or in the resorts on the Atlantic coast, although the chances of this are relatively low. Annoyances include street traders and hustlers, known as 'bumsters', mostly in the main tourist areas.

It's worth noting that Gambia's police don't enjoy an overly friendly relationship with the country's students, or anyone else inclined to public protest. Indeed, being part of a protest gives you an all-too-real chance of being shot, so it's probably best to avoid public demonstrations.

For more details on the kinds of problems you may face, see Dangers & Annoyances in the Atlantic Coast Resorts & Serekunda chapter.

Dangers & Annoyances in the Regional Facts for the Visitor chapter provides useful information on the different types of scams you may encounter while travelling in the region, as well as giving advice on taking sensible precautions.

EMERGENCIES

For the police dial ☎ 17. For the fire brigade or an ambulance dial ☎ 18.

LEGAL MATTERS

A combination of tourism and urban deprivation around Banjul and the tourist resorts means some drugs are cheap and readily available (a handful of grass can go for as little as D25), but despite what you may hear, no drug is legal in Gambia. If you're a smoker, be careful: Some dealers are in cahoots with the police. Several tourists have been arrested (either by real policemen or by impostors – it doesn't really matter) and forced to pay large bribes to avoid arrest and jail.

BUSINESS HOURS

Business hours for government offices are 8am to 3pm or 4pm Monday to Thursday, and 8am to 12.30pm Friday and Saturday. Shops and businesses usually open 8.30am to noon and 2.30pm to 5.30pm Monday to Thursday and 8am to noon Friday and Saturday. Bank opening hours vary depending on where you are, and are listed under the individual place entries.

PUBLIC HOLIDAYS & SPECIAL EVENTS

Annual holidays in Gambia include the following:

New Year's Day 1 January
Independence Day 18 February
Good Friday March/April
Easter Monday March/April
Workers' Day 1 May
Anniversary of the Second Republic 22 July
Christmas 25 December

The Muslim holidays of Eid al-Fitr (end of Ramadan), Tabaski, Islamic New Year and Mohammed's Birthday are also public holidays; these are determined by the lunar calendar and occur on different dates each year (for more details, see the boxed text 'Islam' in the Facts about Senegambia chapter).

International Roots Festival

The Roots homecoming festival is held in the Gambia for one week every two years. The festival is aimed primarily at Americans and Europeans of African descent but is open to all visitors. It includes displays of Gambian music, dance, art and craft, plus excursions to cultural sites (including, of course, the village of Jufureh), and more serious seminars and educational workshops.

Venues for events and exhibitions include the National Museum and Arch 22 in Banjul, the museum at Jufureh, and the Alliance Française on Kairaba Ave near Serekunda. For further details see the website **w** www.roots festival.gm.

Getting There & Away

Details on getting to Gambia from Europe, North America and Australasia are given in the regional Getting There & Away chapter. This chapter covers travel between Gambia and Senegal, and between Gambia and some other West African countries.

AIR

Schedules and prices change frequently, so for more precise information contact an airline or travel agent. See Getting There & Away in the Banjul and Atlantic Coast Resorts & Serekunda chapters for details.

Airports & Airlines

The Gambia's main airport is Banjul International Airport at Yundum, about 20km from the city centre, and about 15km from the Atlantic coast resorts. There is no airport bus – see To/From the Airport under Getting Around in the Banjul chapter.

The only airline serving Gambia from Europe is SN Brussels Airlines, the reincarnated Sabena. Most visitors come on charter flights as these are cheaper and usually direct. The leading charter holiday operator is The Gambia Experience – see Organised Tours in the regional Getting There & Away chapter for details.

The main airlines flying between Gambia and Senegal are Gambia International Airlines and Air Senegal International, although few travellers fly between Gambia and Senegal, as land connections are good.

Departure Tax

An airport tax of D180 is usually included in your ticket price. If it is not included, the tax is levied at the airport and can be paid in local currency or other hard currencies.

Senegal

The only flights between Gambia and Senegal are the services between Banjul and Dakar on Gambia Airlines International and Air Senegal International. Tickets cost D1104/1604 one way/return, and the ser-

---

vice operates once daily, except on Wednesday and Friday, when there are two flights.

Other West African Countries

It's almost impossible to keep track of who's flying where in West Africa. Chances are half the airlines here will be closed or have stopped operating by the time you are reading, so it's best to start your inquiries at a travel agency. The following will provide you with a rough idea of what might be available at the time you travel.

Gambia International Airlines flies to Conakry via Freetown once a week. Ghana Airways flies twice weekly to Conakry for D1311, Abidjan (Côte d'Ivoire) for D5039 and Accra (Ghana) for D5825. Air Guinée has weekly flights between Banjul and Conakry via Labé in northern Guinea – perfect for reaching the Fouta Djalon. Bellview Airlines is a Nigerian company that has twice-weekly flights to Lagos via Freetown for US$274 one way. From Lagos, flights connect to destinations including Nairobi and Mumbai.

If you're heading for Morocco, it's better to go overland to Dakar and fly from there (see Getting There & Away in the Senegal chapter for more details).

LAND

The Gambia is completely surrounded by Senegal (except for the coast), which you can reach by travelling north towards Dakar, south towards Ziguinchor or east towards Tambacounda. Almost all journeys by public transport involve changing transport at the border.

Bus & Bush Taxi

To/From Dakar From Banjul north to Dakar, you first have to take the ferry across the mouth of the Gambia River to Barra (for more details about the ferry, see Getting There & Away in the Banjul chapter). On the Barra side there's plenty of transport to the border at Karang and the occasional bus straight through to Dakar. From Karang you can get to and from other destinations in northern and central Senegal. Options include the state-owned Gambia Public Transport Corporation (GPTC) bus, which parks at the end of the pier. The express version departs at 9am (D100 or CFA5000, five to six hours) but you'll have to be quick off the ferry to get a seat. A second bus leaves between 10am and noon on a fill-up-and-go basis (D80 or CFA4000, seven to eight hours). This bus also stops at Kaolack (D40 or CFA2000, two hours).

The area outside the Barra ferry terminal is full of hustlers and touts. It's a dirty, noisy, crowded place where it's easy to get hot, confused and angry. Don't let the hustlers wind you up. Stay calm and keep an eye on your pockets and gear. Unless the rules have changed again (if in doubt ask a fellow traveller, not a tout), you'll probably have to get yourself to Karang in a bush taxi (D6) or a yellow taxi (D35 for the whole vehicle). Once you've completed the immigration formalities, take a minibus to the Senegalese side for D2 or CFA100, where you'll need to greet the Senegalese customs folk. From Karang to Dakar you can take a Peugeot taxi (CFA4500 or D90, about five to six hours), a minibus (CFA3000 or D60, seven to eight hours) or a Mercedes bus (CFA2500 or D50,

nine hours). A Peugeot taxi to Kaolack is CFA2000 or D40. For more details on the different forms of transport, see the regional Getting There & Away chapter.

Most drivers accept dalasi, but prefer to charge fares in CFA. There's no bank in Barra or Karang, so you should change dalasi into CFA in Banjul before starting this journey. Alternatively, there are plenty of moneychangers at the ferry terminals, and at the border.

If you're coming from Dakar and think you might miss the last ferry across to Banjul (it leaves at 7pm), accommodation in Barra is limited to a couple of sleazy hotels. You'd be better off staying in Kaolack or Toubacouta and getting the ferry from Barra to Banjul next morning.

To/From Ziguinchor & Kafountine To get to Ziguinchor you must take a bush taxi from the Serekunda garage to the Gambian border at Giboro (D25). From here it's about 3km to the Senegalese border post at Séléti, where a bush taxi to Ziguinchor is D40 or CFA2000. You can also get to Giboro from Brikama.

If you're heading for Kafountine, you could get yourself to Diouloulou via Giboro, then change for Kafountine. Easier, but with a greater risk of encountering men with guns (see the boxed text 'To Go or Not to Go?' in the Casamance chapter), is to take a minibus from Brikama direct to Kafountine via a series of sandy back roads (D30, 90 minutes).

With a new road running from the coastal resorts south to Kartong it might become easier to cross into Casamance via the Allahein River; however, at the time of research this was still a route plagued by problems. See Kartong in the Western Gambia chapter for details.

To/From Tambacounda From Basse Santa Su bush taxis go through Sabi to Vélingara (D20 or CFA1000, about 30 minutes). The bush taxis leave when they fill up, which can mean several hours of waiting, but one taxi usually leaves at 7am (full or not). This is one of the few borders where you don't have to change vehicles, making the trip pretty straightforward. Your transport arrives in Vélingara at a small garage on the western side of town. Vehicles for Tambacounda go from another garage on the northern side of town, and *caleshes* (horse-drawn taxis) shuttle between the two for CFA250 per person. Vélingara to Tambacounda is CFA1500 by Peugeot taxi, CFA1100 by minibus.

The hassle from youths eager to get you on 'their' vehicle is out of all proportion to the amount of traffic leaving from this sleepy garage. If you want to know how many people are already on the bush taxi, ignore the touts and speak to the ticket man who resides in a small, thatched shelter on the edge of the taxi park.

Car

If you're driving between Banjul and Dakar there are two routes. The most direct is via the Barra ferry, Karang (the border) and Kaolack (Senegal). The road is tar all the way but in a terrible state between Karang and Kaolack, though this was being rebuilt at the time of research. Once you've crossed on the ferry, the drive takes a minimum of five hours, possibly a lot longer. The second option between Banjul and Dakar is longer but more interesting: drive east from Banjul to Soma, across the Gambia River by ferry to Farafenni, and then north on the Trans-Gambia Hwy to Kaolack and Dakar. The route is tar all the way, but this fact is nothing to be celebrated – the potholes between Brikama and Soma, and from Farafenni to Kaolack, mean most vehicles spend much of the journey beside the road, not on it.

Between Banjul and Ziguinchor, the road is tar and in fair condition most of the way. Driving time is about three hours.

SEA

There is nothing in the way of public transport by sea to/from Gambia, although you could try asking around at the harbour for information about freighters headed north to Europe and east along the West African coast.

Some travellers take one of the sea-going pirogues (canoes) that are used by local people, but these don't run to a set timetable and are notoriously unsafe. Options include sailing between Banjul and Ziguinchor (Senegal), but the most commonly used route is between Banjul and Djifer in the Siné-Saloum Delta. For more details about this route, see the Petite Côte & Siné-Saloum Delta chapter.

Getting Around

This chapter covers specific aspects of getting around in Gambia. For more general information about travel in the Senegambia region, see the Getting Around Senegambia chapter.

BUS & BUSH TAXI

There are two main routes though Gambia: the potholed dirt road along the northern bank of the river, and the potholed tar road along the southern bank. The northern road has been described as 'dire' and often gets washed away in the rainy season. Few people use it by choice.

The southern route is well served by bush taxis and Gambia Public Transport Corporation (GPTC) buses. These run several times daily between Banjul and Basse Santa Su (360km by road) and fares are cheap – crossing the country by ordinary GPTC bus costs D75, or D85 on the express. For more details on these buses, see Getting There & Away in the Banjul chapter.

Bush taxis on the southern route go from Serekunda, but usually only as far as Soma (about halfway up the country), where you must change vehicles for onward travel. Bush-taxi fares are about the same as the ordinary bus fares.

Transport along the northern route is limited mostly to basic bush taxis. To reach the northern route from Banjul, take the ferry to Barra and find a vehicle there, or go first along the southern route then cross the river upstream between Soma and Farafenni, or at Georgetown, Bansang or Basse Santa Su.

Other public transport routes are from Serekunda and Brikama to points on the southern coast (see the Western Gambia chapter for more details) and north or south across the border into Senegal.

CAR & MOTORCYCLE

It's possible to hire a car or motorbike in Gambia's resort areas (see Car & Motorcycle under Getting Around in the Atlantic Coast Resorts & Serekunda chapter), but before doing this read the boxed text 'Warning' under Car & Motorcycle in the Getting Around Senegambia chapter. If you want to hire a car with a driver, you should consider using a taxi – see Organised Tours later in this chapter.

Despite the British heritage, traffic in Gambia drives on the right, in line with Senegal and most other countries in West Africa. Petrol in Gambia costs D9.75 per litre, and diesel (which is called *gasoil* locally) costs D7.75.

BICYCLE

Hiring a bicycle for a few days or a week is a great way to get around the country. See Bicycle in the Getting Around Senegambia chapter for more information.

BOAT

In colonial times and the early years of independence, public passenger boats and barges carrying groundnuts used to chug up and down the Gambia River between Banjul and Georgetown. Today, there is very little river traffic between towns, mainly because road transport is cheaper and quicker. This is a great shame as the Gambia River is the heart and lifeblood of the country, and often cannot be seen when you're travelling by bus. However, a few tour companies run private excursions along the river – see Organised Tours later in this chapter.

The only regular passenger boat is operated by River Gambia Excursions (☎ 497603, fax 495526, ⓔ mosa@qanet.gm) and runs between Tendaba and Georgetown. The two-day trip starting from Georgetown can only be taken as part of the 14-day Senegambia tour operated by British company Explore Worldwide (☎ 01252- 760000, fax 760001, ⓦ www.exploreworldwide.com). However, the return journey usually leaves every second Thursday and is really the best way to see the river, particularly as you go further east. The trip with all meals costs D1200. Depending on the season, the boat could also be running from Basse to Georgetown once every two weeks – call or email for details.

A high-speed river boat between Banjul and Georgetown was due to begin service at the time of publication. The trip will take three hours each way but won't come cheap. Call Pleasuresports (☎/fax 462125, mobile ☎ 962125) for details.

LOCAL TRANSPORT

There are two sorts of taxi in Gambia. 'Town taxis' are painted yellow with green stripes. These are far and away the fastest, easiest and cheapest means of getting around the Atlantic coast resorts. They operate as shared taxis, with people getting in and out as they like along set routes, and fares are usually just a few dalasis and are not negotiable. Town taxis can also be hired in a more traditional manner (where you are the only passenger/s): this is called a 'town trip'. The cost will be very negotiable, and generally cheaper than the same trip in a tourist taxi.

'Tourist taxis', painted green with a white diamond on the door, are specifically for tourists and can go anywhere in the country. Tourist taxis can be found at ranks near large hotels, and drivers offer rides to all the places of interest in Gambia. A list of rates is on display outside most hotels and at the airport, though like all tariffs they are negotiable.

ORGANISED TOURS

Nearly all places of interest in Gambia can be reached by public transport, but taking an organised tour can be a good way to get around the country if time is short or money is not a primary concern. Tours can last from a few hours to several days, but before joining any tour you should check whether the price is all-inclusive; otherwise, you may have to pay for extras.

There are several large companies based in the Atlantic coast resort area that run organised tours. Most cater specifically for groups of tourists at the big hotels, but many of the excursions are open to independent travellers, too.

Large hotels usually have an in-house tour company or tour desk where trips can be arranged. In smaller hotels, tours can usually be arranged through the reception desk. Hotels act as agents for a small number of local tour operators. This is not a problem, but it does explain why the coach you're in stops to pick up other passengers at several other hotels before the tour starts.

Your other option is to go to the local tour operator direct. Some of the larger outfits are unused to dealing with individual clients, and prefer to have groups arranged for them by hotels and holiday reps, but others are happy to take anyone. The larger local tour operators tend to charge the same rates as their agents (to undercut might lose them business in the future) but several of the smaller tour companies offer keener prices than the big boys. Some of the smaller companies have offices in the main resort areas, or have their own reps who patrol the beach or hotel bars looking for business.

Large Tour Companies

To give an idea of prices, the following are some sample per-person rates quoted in UK pounds by major tour companies at the large beach-front hotels. Because so many tourists come from the UK, and the dalasi is so liable to devaluation, most big operators only quote in pounds.

Abuko Nature Reserve Half-day tours cost UK£20.

'Birds & Breakfast Tour' This half-day tour to Lamin Lodge includes a boat ride and costs UK£24.

'Champagne & Caviar' A luxury boat cruise for a full day costs UK£30.

Fishing in the Creeks This tour costs UK£24 per day.

Georgetown or Tendaba Camp This two-day tour includes overnight accommodation and costs UK£75.

'Jeep Safari' or 'Bush and Beach Tour' To the south coast for a full day costs UK£30.

Makasutu & Brikama A full-day tour by bus and boat costs UK£30.

'Roots Tour' to Jufureh, Albreda and James Island This full-day boat tour includes lunch and costs UK£30. (For details on Alex Haley's *Roots*, see Jufureh & Albreda in the Western Gambia chapter.)

Sport Fishing in the Ocean A day's fishing will cost you UK£70 for two people.

'Sunset' or 'Romantic River Cruise' UK£26.

If you want to go direct to one of the more mainstream tour companies, Discovery Tours (☎ 495551, fax 496662, W www.discovery tours.gm), Gambia Tours (☎ 462601/2, fax 462603. W www.gambiatours.gm) and West African Tours (☎ 495258, fax 496118, W www.westafricantours.com) are reckoned to be among the best, with prices similar to those above. If you want an idea of what they offer check out their websites, all of which are pretty good and have email links.

Small Tour Companies

The following smaller tour companies can be approached directly. This is a very small selection, but gives you an idea of prices and options. Most are more than happy to take credit cards or currencies apart from the dalasi.

Abaraka Jeep Safari (☎ 465847, fax 465544) Abaraka has an office above the Standard Chartered Bank in Kololi. These guys offer trips in Land Rovers to most of the destinations mentioned above, plus day trips to Makasutu (D450), dolphin spotting (D400), or overnight trips to Tendaba (D1050).

Gambia Sport Fishing (☎ 495683, mobile 908577, ☎/fax in UK 01509-569963, W www .gambiafishing.com) These guys have a good reputation and offer beach- and river-fishing excursions. Some sample trips include inshore or creek fishing for UK£45 per person; beach fishing for UK£35 per person; or a four-day upriver freshwater-fishing trip for UK£290 per person including accommodation. Costs for all trips are based on a minimum of three anglers per boat and include transport to and from Denton Bridge, bait, tackle, soft drinks, an experienced skipper and fuel, but not lunch.

Pleasuresports Ltd (☎ 462125, mobile 962125, e psg@qanet.gm) This company specialises in boat tours aimed at groups, but independent travellers are welcome to book direct, which works out cheaper, too. For example, a 'Roots' tour costs D300 if you make your own way to the port, as the price the hotel groups pay includes transfers. Pleasuresports also runs dolphin-watching trips and has plans for a fast boat to Georgetown.

Tropical Tours (☎ 460536, fax 460546, e trop icaltour@gamtel.gm) A German-Gambian business (English and French also spoken) based at the entrance to the Kairaba Hotel in Kololi. Its tours include 'Roots' by boat (D690), a southern-coast beach safari (D625) and a day trip to Kafountine (D650). Trips to Georgetown and Tendaba are also available, plus a five-day safari to Parc National de Niokolo-Koba in Senegal for D8500 per person with bed and breakfast (for two people), less for each extra person up to a maximum of five. Special-interest trips can be arranged, including birding, brewing, beekeeping, nature walks, traditional medicine and visits to a local marabout (Muslim holy man) – either for interest or for a serious consultation. The management is also very happy to provide information for independent travellers – even if you buy nothing more than a couple of postcards.

Smaller operators are difficult to list, as companies seem to come and go with alarming regularity. It's not unusual to see a minibus or 4WD with a company name painted on the door carefully (or not so carefully) obscuring the name of last year's owner, and sometimes even the one before that.

Independent Operators Tours around Gambia can also be arranged through various individuals who have set up their own small independent tour operations. Two recommended operators are as follows:

Mr Musa Bah (mobile ☎ 914630) has a car for hire (he is the driver). We've heard good reports from travellers who've taken day trips or longer tours upcountry. You can pay petrol yourself, or Mr Bah will do you an all-inclusive price. Either way, there is a little room for negotiation. To Tendaba Camp costs around D800 including petrol, or D450 without petrol.

Mr Saiko Demba (the manager of the Leybato Guesthouse in Fajara) has a car and minibus (both with driver) available. He charges per vehicle, not per person, so it's obviously cheaper if you get a group together. Some sample rates include: Brikama, Gunjur and Lamin Lodge for D700; Georgetown for D1200; and Tendaba for D900. Clients pay for their own food and accommodation. Tours to Parc National de Niokolo-Koba in Senegal, or even to Guinea-Bissau, for anything between four and seven days, are also available.

Two other private guides who come most highly recommended are Wally M Faal (☎ 372103, e wallyfaal@yahoo.com) and Akassa (☎ 908453), who is described as a 'lovely rasta man'. For details of how to

THE GAMBIA

find good independent bird-watching guides see the 'Birds of Senegambia' special section.

Taxi Tours

Most tours by taxi are for a day, but you can easily go for longer if you want. Rates for the driver's board and food must be negotiated separately, although at some upcountry lodges (eg, Tendaba Camp) drivers get free accommodation anyway. It's worth arranging longer trips at least a day in advance.

Prices are fixed, but you should check with the driver whether they include entrance fees to places of interest, ferry charges (if you're going across the river) and any unofficial 'taxes' imposed by the police. It's also very important to check that the driver's licence and insurance are up-to-date, and that the vehicle you hire is in good condition. Another thing to check is the driver himself – most are professional, informative and considerate, but there are a few funky wide boys who speak with mock-American accents and think their job is to get from A to B as quickly as possible, before leaving you stranded for hours at a line of tacky souvenir stands.

We've heard from several travellers who have taken tours by taxi and had a marvellous time. The driver's local insights have added considerably to the tour, and non-scheduled visits to the far-flung family in country compounds can turn out to be the best part of it. But if you're not prepared for a few rough edges, then stick to the air-conditioned coach.

Below are some sample prices for tours in a four-seater taxi from Bakau, Fajara, Kotu and Kololi. Eight seaters and 4WDs cost about 20% more.

destination	price (D)
Abuko	200
Basse Santa Su	2500
Brikama	280
Cap Skiring	2000
Dakar	2500
Georgetown	1700
Lamin Lodge	270
Lamin Lodge & Abuko	300
Southern Gambia	900
Tendaba	1100
Ziguinchor	1500

The 'bumsters' who lurk around the hotels in the resort areas will offer to arrange tours for you, but be warned – we've heard plenty of stories about cars breaking down, drivers having no money to buy petrol, unforeseen extra charges, and even things being stolen. See Dangers & Annoyances in the Atlantic Coast Resorts & Serekunda chapter for more details.

Banjul

pop 50,000

Banjul is one of the smallest, and perhaps the most unlikely, capital cities in Africa. People aren't flocking to Banjul, no new buildings are going up and there are few traffic jams. Wander around the sleepy streets of this island and the shadow of neglect haunts many of the crumbling buildings.

Despite all this Banjul is well worth a visit. The bustling markets, dusty museum, faded history and lethargic disposition combine to make Banjul a truly African urban experience, all just 30 minutes from the plush resorts of the Atlantic coast. Many tourists come solely for Gambia's beaches and never even bother to take the half-hour trip into the capital – don't make the same mistake.

ORIENTATION

Banjul was founded in 1816 and many of its streets were duly named after the English heroes of the Battle of Waterloo. Not any more. In one sweeping move recently the name of nearly every street in the city was changed – they're now named after the heroes of Gambia's independence.

The upshot of this is a large dose of confusion. While the new names have brought a full set of street signs to the capital for the first time in years, few locals seem to be reading them. Indeed, most businesses and even a few government bodies still use the old names in their addresses. We've included a list of some of the streets and their old names, but if you're still stuck, look for the addresses painted on the front of shops and businesses.

Banjul is small enough to walk around without too much trouble. The centre is July 22 Square, a dusty public park, from where several main streets run south, including Russell St, which leads past the bustling Albert Market into Liberation St. West of the October 17 Roundabout is the old part of Banjul – a maze of narrow streets and ramshackle houses where few

Highlights

- Soak up the history in the backstreets of Banjul, the most understated capital in Africa
- Find everything from spices to souvenirs in the colourful, chaotic Albert Market
- Check out what's changed in the city with a look at the dusty photos in the National Museum of The Gambia

tourists ever venture, which is a good reason to go.

July 22 Dr runs west from July 22 Square, becoming the main road out of Banjul. On the edge of the city it goes under the vast structure of Arch 22 and turns into a dual carriageway which, after about 3km, crosses Oyster Creek on Denton Bridge to reach the mainland proper. Remember, though, that only the president is allowed to drive under Arch 22 – all others must go around.

After another 2km the road splits: The right fork goes to Bakau, Fajara and the other Atlantic coast resorts; straight on goes to Serekunda, the airport, and everywhere else along the southern bank of the Gambia River.

INFORMATION
Money

Banks in Banjul city include Standard Chartered Bank and Trust Bank, both on Ecowas Ave, and IBC (formerly BICIS) at the corner of Liberation St and Davidson Carrol St. Standard Chartered has an ATM that takes Visa cards and Trust Bank is the Western Union Money Transfer agent. All banks in Banjul city are open 8am to 1.30pm Monday to Thursday, 8am to around 11am Friday.

Black-market moneychangers can be found near July 22 Square, opposite the entrance to the Albert Market and at the Barra ferry terminal. Several shopkeepers along Liberation St and near the ferry terminal will also change money – these are better places to conduct this kind of business than on the street.

Post & Communications

The main post office (GPO) is on Russell St, near Albert Market. It is open 8am to 4pm Monday to Saturday. You can buy postcards, paper or envelopes from the hawkers outside. Next door is the Gamtel public telephone office, where the staff are inimical but making a call is straightforward enough. It's open 8am to 11.30pm every day.

You can get online at either Quantumnet or Gamtel, both on Nelson Mandela St.

Travel Agencies

The most efficient agencies in Banjul seem to be the Banjul Travel Agency (☎ 228813, e bta@qanet.gm) on Ecowas Ave, and Olympic Travel (☎ 223370/1, fax 223372, e olympictravel@gamtel.gm) on Nelson Mandela St. If these can't help you, there are more at the north end of Ecowas Ave, while others are listed in the Atlantic Coast Resorts & Serekunda chapter.

Medical Services

The Royal Victoria Hospital (☎ 228223) on July 22 Dr was renovated in 1993. However, its quality still lags behind that of the private establishments on the Atlantic coast, which are better for illnesses, minor injuries and malaria tests (see the Atlantic Coast Resorts & Serekunda chapter for details).

Street Name Changes

Some streets in Banjul have been renamed, although many old name signs remain and the new signs are often hard to find. To add to the confusion, most old names are still commonly used by locals.

old name	new name
Bund Rd	Kankujeri Rd
Clarkson St	Rene Blain St
Cotton St	Cherno Adamah Bah St
Dobson St	Ma Cumba Jallow St
Grant St	Rev William Cole St
Hagan St	Daniel Goddard St
Hill St	Imam Lamin Bah St
Hope St	Jallow Jallow St
Independence Dr	July 22 Dr
Liberation St	Wellington St
MacCarthy Square	July 22 Square
Marina Pde	Muammar al Gadhafi Ave
Orange St	Tafsir Ebou Samba St
Picton St	Davidson Carrol St
Wellington St	Liberation St

Across the road is the Banjul Pharmacy (☎ 227470), which is open 9am to 8.30pm.

Dangers & Annoyances

While violent crime is rare in Banjul, pickpockets are rife. Their favourite hunting ground is the human sardine tin otherwise known as the Barra ferry, but you can be sure they'll be artfully investigating the contents of your pockets at the ferry terminal and in Albert Market, where tourists are seen as the easiest of targets.

At night the streets of Banjul centre are pitch black, making them dangerous – not so much because of thieves (so few tourists come here at night that there's little for them to prey on) but because of the maze of open drains and sewers that cross the town.

THINGS TO SEE

Banjul feels more like a very large village than a national capital, and this dusty, sleepy

BANJUL

To Oyster Creek,
Denton Bridge, Palm
Grove Hotel (3km),
Bakau (7km),
Serekunda (15km) &
Banjul International
Airport (30km)

ATLANTIC
OCEAN

Muammar al Gadhafi Ave

July 22 Dr

Tafsir Demba Ndow St

Ousman Jeng St

Antouman Faal St

Dawur Caye St

Tafsir Wally Joof St

Samba Njimeh Wanie St

Ousman Njie Keen

Mosque Rd

Pierre Njie Tce

Amie Sarr St

Jack Chow St

Jallow Jallow St

Master Fowlis

Rebecca Savage

J R Forster

Sagarr Jobe St

Alhassan Ndure St

Jeremiah Allen St

Alpha Tapsiru St

Rev William Cole St

Mann Mberry Njie St

Hannah Forster St

Rene Blain St

Abdou Wally Mbye St

Marma Bah St

Freedom
Lane

October 17
Roundabout

Davidson Carrol St

Serign Sillah St

Ma Cumba Jallow St

Daniel Goddard St

OAU Blvd

Imam Lamin Bah St

Ecowas Ave

Tafsir Ebou Samba St

Tafsir Balla
Joof St

Kankujeri Rd

Cherno Adama Bah St

Brown St

Tanbi Wetland
Complex

Wallace Cole Rd

This Area
Strictly
Out of Bounds

Main Entrance
to Albert Market

Craft
Market

Albert
Market

July 22
Square

Nelson Mandela St

Liberation St

Russell St

To
Jufureh
& James
Island

To Barra

Gambia
River

0   200   400m
0   200   400yd

PLACES TO STAY
3 Atlantic Hotel
4 Princess Diana Hotel
6 Carlton Hotel
21 Duma Guesthouse
30 Abbey Guesthouse
47 Ferry Guesthouse
49 Apollo Hotel

PLACES TO EAT
5 Michel's
26 Café Central
27 Mandela Alles
   Klar Fast Food
35 Ali Baba Snack Bar
43 Jummy T Restaurant
44 St Raphael's

OTHER
1 The Unknown
  Soldier Monument
2 Arch 22
7 King Fahad Mosque
8 Gamtel Office
9 Royal Victoria Hospital
10 Petrol Station
11 State House
12 National Museum
   of the Gambia
13 Banjul Pharmacy
14 Minibuses to Bakau
15 The Quadrangle
   (Government Offices)

16 St Mary's Anglican
   Cathedral
17 Boats (on Beach)
18 Fountain
19 Post Office;
   Gamtel Office
20 War Memorial
22 Minibuses to Serekunda
23 Guinean Consulate
24 Trust Bank
25 Queen Nightclub

28 Quantumnet
29 Happy Bar
31 Gamtel Office
32 West Coast Airlines
33 Olympic Travel
34 Ghana Airways
36 Air Senegal International
37 Gambia International
   Airlines
38 Standard Chartered Bank
39 Police Station

40 Air Guinée
41 Banjul Travel Agency
42 IBC Bank
45 Sierra Leonean
   High Commission
46 Immigration Office
48 Pirogues to Barra
50 Ferries to Barra
51 Mariam Ceesay
   Bar & Restaurant
52 GPTC Bus Station

atmosphere has a quaint kind of charm. If you've come to Gambia to experience Africa, rather than a slice of Europe laid down on a tropical beach, a day or two here is far preferable to the nearby Atlantic coast resorts. But to best experience Gambia's rural delights spend time upcountry or on the southern coast.

The vibrant heart of Banjul city is Albert Market on Russell St – for details see Shopping later in this chapter. Nearby, on July 22 Square, look out for the **War Memorial** and the **fountain** 'erected by public subscription' to commemorate the coronation of King George VI of Britain in 1937. The fountain is a dry and dusty affair these days, but fear not, you can quench your thirst at the surrounding drinks bar. You get the feeling the worthy colonials who funded this monument would be turning in their graves.

The **National Museum of The Gambia** *(July 22 Dr; admission D15; open 8am-4pm Mon-Thur, 8am-1pm Fri & Sat)* has some dog-eared and dated exhibits, but the explanations are generally good, especially in the musical instruments section. Upstairs there is a dusty but fascinating display of photos, maps and text about archaeology, African peoples and the colonial period, all of which make this worth an hour or so.

Arch 22 *(Independence Dr; admission D10; open 9am-11pm)* is a gateway built to celebrate the military coup of 22 July 1994. At 35m high, it's by far the tallest building in Gambia. The balcony is open to the public, and provides excellent views over the city and coast. On the western side is an enormous statue of a soldier carrying a child in his arms, presumably symbolising the small Gambian nation safe and secure in the arms of the military. While Senegalese architect Pierre Goudiaby's design is indeed grand, the engineering of the arch might have been less than inspired. Some claim the arch's concrete structure is unsound, and some critics have even suggested the whole thing might come crashing down. This seems unlikely (and the claims might well be politically motivated), but at close inspection the arch does seem to have aged very poorly during its short life.

Although there's little more in the way of major sights, it's interesting to walk in the streets of the old town. Ma Cumba Jallow St is a wide avenue lined with a few old colonial buildings and traditional Krio-style clapboard houses, many of which still belong to families who came here from Sierra Leone, some as long ago as the 1820s. (See also the boxed text 'The Aku' in the Facts about The Gambia chapter.)

PIROGUE TRIPS
Pirogues are local wooden boats, long and thin, usually with an outboard motor at the back. They are anywhere between 3m and 10m long (some sea-going models are even larger) and mostly used by local men for fishing, but a few do a service carrying tourists on the quiet waterways of Oyster Creek, the main waterway separating Banjul island and the mainland.

Oyster Creek and its minor tributaries (creeks and rivers are all called *bolongs* locally) are a popular destination for birdwatching, fishing or just lazy afternoons messing about in boats. The dense mangroves are particularly interesting. Many people come on a trip organised through their hotel, but you can do things informally at Denton Bridge, which crosses Oyster Creek some 4km from the city centre.

To reach Denton Bridge by public transport, take any minibus running between Banjul and Bakau or Serekunda and ask the driver to let you off at the bridge. The main 'port' (a patch of mud with a few boats tied up) is on the mainland side of the creek. Ask around here for a boatman willing to take you out on the water. If you go in a motorised canoe, the price will be quite stiff (around D150 per hour for the boat, but a lot depends on how much petrol you use). A trip in a hand-paddled canoe will be cheaper, but you won't go so far – for birdwatchers this may not be such a problem. If you've got time, it's better to arrange things the day before.

You can also hire a pirogue to take you upriver to Jufureh and James Island. See Jufureh & Albreda in the Western Gambia chapter for details.

TANBI WETLAND COMPLEX

If you like watching birds but don't fancy the pirogue, Kankujeri Rd might be more your scene. The stretch of mangrove either side is known as the Tanbi Wetland Complex and is so popular with bird-watchers there is talk of it becoming a protected reserve, though our sources in the planning department suggest this will only happen if the government can't persuade anyone to pay for the right to develop it.

PLACES TO STAY

Not many tourists stay in Banjul city, preferring instead the beach and comforts of the Atlantic coast. However, if you want a more African environment you're more likely to find it here. None of the budget options take credit cards.

PLACES TO STAY – BUDGET

Ferry Guesthouse (☎ 222028, 28 Liberation St) Bed on the veranda D70, singles/doubles D130/190, rooms with air-con D290. Possibly the best budget place in town is this three-storey place with big, airy rooms overlooking the hubbub of Liberation St and the Barra ferry terminal. There's no breakfast but it's easy enough to find food at the stalls opposite. Entry is via a short lane leading to a stairwell at the rear of the building. Even if you don't stay, the balcony is a great people-watching perch.

Duma Guesthouse (☎ 228381, 1 Jallow Jallow St) Singles D100, doubles with bathroom D200. In the heart of old Banjul, where tourists rarely go, this is another friendly place. The rooms are clean and have fans although electricity is erratic. Food can usually be ordered; otherwise there's a good, cheap *chop shop* (small, simple, local-style eating house) nearby. There's no sign so look for the two-storey yellow building.

Abbey Guesthouse (☎ 225228, 38 Rev William Cole St) Rooms D80-150. Also in old Banjul, this building used to be the German consulate and has a great balcony, but the rooms, which sleep one to three people, are not so great. However, the shared bathrooms are fine, the food is good and cheap,

and the manager is friendly and honest – the sign out the front advertises 'modest accommodation'.

Apollo Hotel (☎ 228184, Tafsir Ebou Samba St) Singles/doubles with fan D150/200, with air-con D300/360. This hotel was probably stylish once, but it's plain and soulless now. Rooms have bathrooms and are reasonably clean. Couples can share a single.

Princess Diana Hotel (Kantora Hotel; ☎ 228715, July 22 Dr) Singles/doubles with fan & breakfast D165/225, doubles with air-con D275. Since the former owner (he was the Di fan) left town this place has gone downhill, but remains a decent option with clean rooms.

Carlton Hotel (☎ 228670, fax 227214, 25 July 22 Dr) Singles/doubles D165/250, with air-con D315/400. The Carlton is near the Princess Di Hotel, but the staff are less than accommodating.

PLACES TO STAY – TOP END

Atlantic Hotel (☎ 228601, fax 227861, e atlantic@corinthia.com, w www.corinthia .com, Muammar al Gadhafi Ave) Singles/doubles with air-con D950/1200. This is central Banjul's only upmarket hotel. It's a vast affair with numerous bars, restaurants and leisure facilities peopled mainly by British package tourists and government types. There's a smelly beach, and bird-watchers will enjoy the miniforest that has been created by ornithologist Clive Barlow, who is a regular guest. An evening buffet in the restaurant here is D250, a small beer costs D20 and credit cards are accepted.

Palm Grove Hotel (☎ 201620, fax 201621, e palmgrove@gamtel.gm, w www .gambia-palmgrovehotel.co.uk) Singles/doubles D460/750, suites D750/1000. About 3km out of Banjul toward Serekunda, the Palm Grove is smaller, more personal, more stylish and better value than the Atlantic. It has a decent swimming beach and all the usual activities and watersports you'd expect at a resort. The management prides itself on having flexible prices, especially during the low season when bargains can be had. The room rates include breakfast.

THE GAMBIA

PLACES TO EAT

The shift from Banjul to the coast has taken with it most of Banjul's decent eateries. Only a couple of the remaining places could reasonably be described as restaurants, most of the rest being fast-food joints. If you're self-catering you'll have to shop in Albert Market as there are no supermarkets.

Cafés & Fast Food

Banjul has several cheap stalls and chop shops where plates of rice and sauce start at about D6. Worth trying are the *food stalls* in Albert Market and around the Barra ferry terminal, which are open all day (closed evenings) – some cater mainly for locals while others are more for tourists (with prices to match). Breakfast at the ferry terminal, skewered meat on fresh bread rolls with sweet coffee, is highly recommended.

Ali Baba Snack Bar (☎ 224055, Nelson Mandela St) Open 9am-5pm. More than just a kebab shop, this place is an institution with a deserved reputation for the best *chawarmas* (sliced, grilled meat and salad in pita bread; D15) and felafel sandwiches in the country. A whole roast chicken will cost you D70.

Other options in this area include the *Mandela Alles Klar Fast Food (☎ 223455, Ecowas Ave)*, around the corner from the Ali Baba, though some people have complained about the freshness of the food. The tiny *Café Central* opposite is open from 7am to 6pm and serves tasty sandwiches (D25 to D30) and beer (D9).

Jummy T Restaurant (☎ 222627, 7 Ma Cumba Jallow St) Open 9am-10pm. This place, farther south, is where to head if you're looking to eat African dishes like cow feet, *fufu* (mashed cassava) or comparatively boring *domodah* (the usual stew with groundnut sauce), all D10.

Restaurants

Michel's (☎ 223108, 29 July 22 Dr) Open 8am-11pm. Bucking the trend of closures, this new multi-cuisine restaurant is the classiest place in town. The food and the prices will impress, with dishes ranging from breakfast croissants (D8), through

prawn sandwiches and chicken curry (both D25), to fish and steak dishes (D50 to D95). The paella (D60) and giant tiger prawns (D95) are both great value.

Princess Diana Hotel (☎ 228715) Dishes around D40. Near Michel's in location, but not necessarily quality, the restaurant here does edible food, although it's limited to chicken/fish with rice or chips.

St Raphael's (☎ 226324, 17 Davidson Carrol St) Open 9am-midnight Mon-Sat. Once a snack bar, this place has graduated to restaurant status but has forgotten to hike the prices. The large menu includes spicy seafood in foil (D20), pepper steak (D40) and spaghetti (D35), but a few items are often unavailable. Still, it's the pick of the bunch for lunch.

ENTERTAINMENT
Bars

Banjul city used to have a good selection of local bars, but most of them have closed.

Mariam Ceesay Bar & Restaurant (☎ 226912) Open 10am-7.30pm. Mariam Ceesay's, next to the ferry terminal, is one of the few places you can reliably get a beer (D10). It's popular with fishermen, wharfies and ferry workers.

Happy Bar (Rev William Cole St) Open 11am-late. The owner of this bar in old Banjul says, 'if you are not happy, you can't come in'. It's a tiny joint with a 'beer garden' out back and a suitably cheery crew of local regulars. As well as the cheapest beer in town it serves Gambian and Ghanaian food. Check it out.

For an evening drink, your other choices are the *Atlantic Hotel*, the *Palm Grove Hotel* and *Michel's*.

Nightclubs

Queen Nightclub (Rene Blain St) Admission from D10. If you want a night out moving to an African beat, this is the only regularly operating option in the capital. This is a pretty raw scene and it could be quite intimidating for women on their own; if possible, take a Gambian friend along. It opens late and gets busy even later – after midnight.

SHOPPING

In Banjul, the best place to go shopping is *Albert Market*. If you enter via the main entrance you will pass stalls selling clothes, shoes, household and electrical wares and just about everything else you can imagine. Keep going and you'll reach the myriad colours and flavours of the fruit and vegetable market. Beyond here you'll find stalls catering mainly for tourists, usually called the *Craft Market*. The sort of things you can buy here are discussed in greater detail under Shopping in the Regional Facts for the Visitor chapter.

Another way to reach the Craft Market is via the road that circles behind the market (where coaches from the big hotels come). If you want to avoid the market rush hour come early in the morning or late in the afternoon.

Give yourself a good couple of hours to wander around Albert Market, long enough to see everything but not feel rushed into buying things you don't want at a price you didn't want to pay. There are several drinks stalls and chop shops in the market if you need a break for refreshment.

Kerewan Sound (Russell St), near the main entrance of Albert Market (ask when you're under the arch), seems to be the best place for cassettes of African music. Upstairs is the *Camara Jua* recording shop. At *Lann Sarr's shop*, close to Kerewan Sound, you can buy tapes, videos and equipment.

GETTING THERE & AWAY
Air

For details of international flights to Banjul from Europe, North America and Australasia see the regional Getting There & Away chapter. For information on flights between Banjul and the rest of West Africa, refer to the Gambia Getting There & Away chapter.

To confirm reservations on a flight you've already booked, it's easiest to deal directly with airline offices. SN Brussels Airlines (☎ 496301/2, Ⓦ www.brussels-airlines .com) has an office at 97 Kairaba Ave in Fajara, and a few other airlines maintain offices in Banjul centre, including the following:

Air Guinée (☎ 223296, mobile 903935) 72 OAU Blvd
Air Senegal International (☎ 472095) Ecowas Ave
Gambia International Airlines (☎ 223703/4, fax 223700, Ⓔ gia-marketing@gamtel.gm) 78 Daniel Goddard St
Ghana Airways (☎ 228245) Corner Ecowas Ave and Nelson Mandela St
West Coast Airlines (☎ 201954, fax 201956) 7 Nelson Mandela St

Bus

The state-owned Gambia Public Transport Corporation (GPTC) runs buses several times a day between Banjul and Basse Santa Su (normally shortened to Basse), via several towns south of the river. The buses leave from a wide piece of road that GPTC likes to call a bus station on Cherno Adama Bah St, near the port.

Ordinary buses leave at 6.45am, 7.30am, 9am, 10am and 1pm. The fare from Banjul is D37.50 to Soma, D62.50 to Georgetown and D75 to Basse, and the journey time to Basse is around seven hours.

The express bus leaves at 8am, costs D10 more to each destination, and takes five to six hours to reach Basse (on a good day). Ask about the special express bus (the supersonic version stopping only at Serekunda, Brikama, Soma and Bansang), which might have resumed service by the time you arrive.

Reservations are not possible for any service, but demand is high, especially for the express. The best way to be sure of a seat is to catch the bus from the depot at Jimpex Rd, in the suburb of Kanifeng just outside Serekunda. The buses leave from here half an hour before their time of departure from the Cherno Adama Bah St station. You pay an extra D2 to get on here, but it gives you a much better chance of getting a seat, and it's easier if you're staying in Serekunda or on the Atlantic coast.

Bush Taxi

Minibuses and Mercedes buses to Brikama and upcountry towns, and to places in southern Senegal, all go from the Serekunda garage. For details, see the Gambia Getting There & Away and Getting Around chapters.

Boat

Ferries run between Banjul (the terminal is on Liberation St) and Barra (on the northern bank of the river). There are two rusty, dirty, seemingly unseaworthy tubs that chug slowly back and forth during the daylight hours. They are supposed to run about every one to two hours, officially from 7am until 7pm, but there are frequent delays and often one ferry is out of action. The trip should take about 30 minutes but usually takes about an hour – longer if the tide is strong. For the latest information, call the ferry office (☎ 228205).

The ferries take vehicles, but car space is limited as two trucks fill about half the deck. It's not unusual for cars and 4WDs to wait hours for a place, and trucks regularly wait days! There are no limits on foot passengers – everybody just piles on. Upstairs on each side of the ferry are some seating areas. The fare is D5 per person and you buy your ticket before going through to the waiting room.

Remember that you're more likely to have your pockets picked during these couple of hours than at any other time in Gambia.

If the ferry isn't running, or you're in a hurry, large pirogues cross between Banjul and Barra from the beach next to the ferry terminal on either side of the river. The fare is from D5 to D7 per person, depending on demand and the time of day (check with the 'captain' before you board). Be warned, though, that these pirogues are almost always dangerously overloaded and during an evening trip in February 2002 dozens of people were drowned when one broke up and sank.

Fares rise sharply after dark (as does the risk) and negotiating passage at this time will be the acid test of your bargaining skills.

GETTING AROUND
To/From the Airport

A green 'tourist taxi' from Banjul International Airport to Serekunda costs D120. To anywhere on Kairaba Ave it is D150. To Banjul or the Atlantic coast resorts (Bakau, Fajara, Kotu and Kololi) the trip costs D150. Most taxi drivers will quote you the official rate, painted on a board at the taxi rank, so bargaining is usually not required. Fares are the same in either direction.

However, there is a cheaper way. Fend off the tourist-taxi drivers (no mean feat) and walk straight ahead out of the terminal. Beyond the initial row of cars is a secondary car park and you'll probably find a few yellow taxis parked here. These drivers are not allowed into or even near the terminal, but they are allowed to carry you if you seek them out. With a bit of bargaining a trip to Banjul will cost D120 and Serekunda or anywhere on the coast no more than D100.

There is no airport bus but minibuses run along the main road between Brikama and Serekunda, passing the airport turn-off. It's a 3km walk between the airport and the turn-off, but you may be lucky and get a lift.

Minibus & Shared Taxi

Minibuses run between Banjul, Serekunda and the other coastal towns, while shared taxis run between Serekunda, Fajara and

---

International Harmony

Relations between Gambia and Senegal are variable, and a few years ago, when things were at a low ebb, the Banjul-Barra ferry happened to be crossing the Gambia River in particularly windy weather. The ferry started to pitch and roll, waves crashed over the low vehicle deck, and the ship began to sink. The situation was critical so the captain decided that radical action was required: The cargo of cars and lorries was the main source of the problem and something was going to have to be jettisoned. Fortunately, one of the largest trucks was standing near the ramp within easy reach of the water. Even more fortunately, it was a Senegalese truck, and a band of Gambian passengers needed very little persuasion to push it swiftly overboard.

Bakau. Both shared taxis and minibuses serve the route between Serekunda, Kotu and Kololi.

From Banjul, minibuses to Bakau (D4) leave from the stand opposite the Shell station on July 22 Dr. If you're going to Fajara, take a minibus to Bakau and either walk from there or take an onward shared taxi to Serekunda and hop off in Fajara. Vehicles from Banjul to Serekunda (D4) and Brikama (D9) leave from a road-side corner opposite July 22 Square. To these fares add a further D1 for baggage.

See also Getting Around in the Atlantic Coast Resorts & Serekinda chapter.

Private Taxi

In a taxi to yourself (known as a 'town trip'), a short ride across Banjul city centre will cost about D25, and negotiation is required. From Banjul it costs about D70 to Bakau, D80 to Serekunda, D90 to Fajara, and D100 or more to Kotu and Kololi. Check the price with the driver before getting in.

A taxi by the hour within city limits should cost around D80. Hiring a taxi for the day starts at D450, although for a tour out of the city most drivers charge by the destination.

Private taxis are plentiful during the day but difficult to find at night in Banjul. The best place to find one is at the Atlantic Hotel.

Atlantic Coast Resorts & Serekunda

THE GAMBIA

Just half an hour from Banjul, the Atlantic coast resorts of Bakau, Fajara, Kotu and Kololi are the heart of Gambia's tourist industry. Along this 10km strip of beach is a line of about 20 hotels. Back from the beach are more hotels, with restaurants, bars, nightclubs, souvenir stalls and all the other paraphernalia of tourism.

Despite the relative urbanisation, most of the Atlantic coast is calm and low-key compared with many other sun-and-sand resorts around the world. Fields, lagoons and palm groves stand between the concrete, and most buildings are no more than a couple of storeys high. And despite the influx of European holiday-makers, the area hasn't completely lost the feel of Africa, particularly in and around the old town of Bakau, a lively concentration of clapboard and corrugated iron rarely penetrated by tourists. In Fajara, and down the coast to Kololi, the buildings are more widely spaced; between hotels you'll see several embassies and many smart residences belonging to expats and well-to-do Gambians.

The strip of beach between Fajara Golf Club and Kotu Stream has lots of hotels, with shops, restaurants and a taxi rank wedged in between. This is a busy area, full of tourists, cars, guides, hustlers and bumsters, making Bakau and Fajara seem relaxed by comparison.

Kololi, which is referred to by most Gambians as 'Senegambia' after the hotel of the same name, is Gambia's greatest monument to tourism. In addition to several hotels, there's a taxi rank, banks, exchange bureaus, car-hire depot, several shops, bars, cafés and restaurants, dry cleaners, tour agencies, a casino, telephone office and Internet bureaus – you won't have to look far to find pork pies or sauerkraut here. Naturally, the crowds of tourists attract crowds of hustlers.

Highlights

- Enjoy the sun, sea and life's luxuries in the coastal resorts, all for a fraction of the price of home

- Negotiate your way around noisy, busy and unrelenting Serekunda, Gambia's largest town

- Get close up to the crocodiles at Kachikaly; Charley might even let you pat him

- Gibber with the monkeys or just sit and watch the birds at Bijilo Forest Park ·

In complete contrast, Serekunda is 100% Gambian. Once a small village (the name means 'the home of the Sere family'), Serekunda has become the largest town in Gambia, absorbing the overspill from Banjul and attracting people from the rural areas who come in search of work. It is the hub of the country's transport network and a stroll around the town or the bustling, thriving market is recommended for a real taste of in-your-face urban West Africa.

140

ORIENTATION

The main road in from Gambia's upcountry towns passes by Banjul International Airport and reaches the busy town of Serekunda. After passing through the suburbs of Serekunda, this road divides: straight ahead is the dual carriageway for about 14km to Banjul; and to the left is Kairaba Ave, which leads to Bakau, Fajara, Kotu and Kololi.

In Bakau and Fajara, the main drag is Atlantic Rd, which runs parallel to the coast, linking Kairaba Ave and Old Cape Rd. Just south of Atlantic Rd, and running parallel to it, is Garba Jahumpa Rd (formerly New Town Rd). Badala Park Way branches off Kairaba Ave at the Fajara end and leads to the hotel/beach areas of Kotu and Kololi, and onto the airport and the south coast. An extension of Badala Park Way now sees it cross Kairaba Ave at the country's first set of traffic lights and link with Saitmatty Rd, thus avoiding the bottleneck of Westfield Junction at Serekunda.

INFORMATION

The newly formed Gambia Tourist Authority plans to open information booths in the coastal resorts. In the meantime most visitors seek advice from their hotel. Alternatively, Tropical Tours & Souvenirs (☎ 460536), outside Kairaba Hotel, offers good advice without being too pushy.

Money

The main banks have branches in both Bakau and Serekunda. Standard Chartered Bank is also in Kololi. Banks open in the morning (usually from 8.30am or 9am to noon or 2pm), as well as in the afternoon from 4pm to 6pm, and for a few hours on Saturday morning (Trust Bank) or afternoon. The Standard Chartered Bank in Serekunda is open 9am to 3pm Monday to Thursday, 9am to noon Friday and Saturday.

Several supermarkets on Kairaba Ave and in Bakau also operate exchange bureaus (St Mary's Food & Wine is safe but rates are crappy) and there are a few other independent offices around that do slightly better deals.

ATMs have finally reached Gambia and Standard Chartered Bank have machines at Bakau, Kololi and at the Shell petrol station on Kairaba Ave. They accept Visa cards and, allegedly, cards in the Plus network.

If all else fails, or you fancy yourself as a wheeler dealer, you can usually change cash with the hordes of black market traders at Westfield Junction, you'll know them by their calculators and bulging pockets. See the boxed text 'Pockets Full of Money' in Gambia's Facts for the Visitor chapter.

Post & Communications

The main post office is just off Kairaba Ave, about halfway between Fajara and Serekunda. There are Gamtel offices in Bakau, Kololi and Serekunda, and private telecentres are everywhere, but especially in Serekunda and just off Kairaba Ave in Fajara.

There are more than a dozen cybercafés along this well-touristed part of the coast. Kairaba Ave is a favourite, with Quantumnet, Gamtel and CyberWorld here, all with fast connections and all for about D30 an hour. You can also get online in Kololi, Bakau and Serekunda.

Travel Agencies

Most agents are on Kairaba Ave between Serekunda and Fajara. They tend to represent specific airlines and operators so you might have to try a couple to get the best deal. A good starting point is Olympic Travel (☎ 497204), which is just off Kairaba Ave on Garba Jahumpa Rd. Afri-Swiss Travels (☎ 371762/4, fax 371766) has also had good reports.

The Kombos

The four Atlantic coast resorts of Bakau, Fajara, Kotu and Kololi, along with Serekunda and the other suburbs of Sukuta, Kanifeng, Faji Kunda and Dippa Kunda are sometimes known collectively as The Kombos. This is because the area around Banjul is divided into several local administrative districts called Kombo North, Kombo South, Kombo Central and Kombo St Mary.

THE GAMBIA

ATLANTIC COAST RESORTS & SEREKUNDA

PLACES TO STAY
2   Cape Point Hotel;
    911 Nightclub
8   Bakau Guesthouse
9   Sambou's
11 Romana Hotel;
    Buddies; Kumba's Bar
13 Jabo Guest House
16 Crocs Guesthouse
24 Ngala Lodge
28 Leybato
35 Francisco's Hotel
    & Restaurant
36 Fajara Hotel
37 Fajara Guesthouse
39 Safari Garden Hotel;
    Flavours Restaurant
43 Friendship Hotel
44 Bungalow Beach Hotel;
    Kombo Beach Novotel
45 Bakotu Hotel
55 Kanifeng YMCA Hostel
58 Badala Park Hotel;
    Reggae Yard
62 Palma Rima Hotel
65 Bunkoyo Hotel
67 Bakadaji Hotel
    & Restaurant
85 Douniya Hotel
88 Kololi Inn & Tavern
89 Senegambia Hotel;
    AB Rent-a-Car
91 Balmoral Apartments
92 Keneba Hotel
95 Kairaba Hotel;
    Tropical Tours
    & Souvenirs
104 Praia Motel
115 Coconut Residence
116 Green Line Motel

PLACES TO EAT
4   Baobab Sunshine Bar;
    Calypso Restaurant
14 The Clay Oven
17 Buggerland
29 Wheels
30 Weezo's
31 The Butcher's Shop
38 Eddie's Bar & Restaurant
40 Gambia Etten
41 The Sailor;
    Paradise Beach Bar;
    Fajara Watersports Centre
42 Golden Bamboo
50 MacFadi's; La Parisienne
51 Afra Kairaba
53 Le Palais du Chocolat
59 Solomon's Beach Bar
61 Luigi's Italian Restaurant
68 Come Inn
71 LK Fast Food
72 Safe Way Afra King
75 Sen Fast Food
87 Village Gallery & Restaurant
93 Al Amir
96 Dolphin Bar & Restaurant;
    Coco Beach
98 Scala Restaurant
101 C&B Grill
113 Amsterdam Café

OTHER
1   Botanical Gardens
3   St Mary's Food
    & Wine
5   Fawlty Towers
6   One For The Road Bar
7   Catholic Church
10 Minibuses to Banjul
    & Serekunda
12 Lacondula International Pub
15 Gena Bes Batik Factory
18 The Bulldog
19 IBC Bank
20 Guinea-Bissau Embassy
21 Standard Chartered
    Bank (ATM)
22 Trust Bank; Gamtel Office;
    Green Taxis
23 Police Station
25 British Embassy
26 Medical Research Council
27 African Living Art Centre
32 Olympic Travel
33 Quantumnet; Timbooktoo
34 Jackpot Palace
46 ATM; Shell Petrol Station
47 CyberWorld
48 Harry's Supermarket
49 St Mary's Food & Wine
52 US Embassy
54 Afri-Swiss Travels
56 Mosque
57 Senegalese Embassy
60 Churchill's
63 Jobort Laboratories
64 Water Tower

66 Salz Bar
69 Post Office
70 Jimpex Rd GPTC Bus Depot
73 Alliance Franco-Gambienne
74 Malak Chemist
76 Castle Petrol Station
77 Shared Taxis to
    Fajara & Bakau
78 Standard Chartered Bank
79 Gamtel Internet Office
80 Maroun's
81 Quantumnet
82 Westfield Clinic
83 Jokor Nightclub
84 Minibuses to Banjul
86 Mrs Musu Kebba
    Drammeh Batik Factory
90 Spy Bar
94 Standard Chartered Bank (ATM);
    Abaraka Jeep Safari; Gamtel Office
97 The Pub
99 Waaw Nightclub
100 Mauritanian Consulate
102 IBC Bank; Shell Petrol Station
103 Trust Bank
105 Serekunda Bus & Taxi Station
106 Minibuses to Banjul
107 Gamtel Office
108 Bobby's Choice
109 Police Station
110 Asiamarie Cinema
111 Arena Babou Fatty
112 Hertz; Bakoteh Elf Station
114 Bijilo Forest Park Headquarters
117 Lana's Bar
118 Petrol Station

ATLANTIC
OCEAN

Kotu Point

Koloh Point

Kololi

Badala Park Way

Kololi Rd

Bijilo Forest
Park

To Baobab Lodge (300m),
Tanji (8km), Airport (18km),
& Kartong (38km)

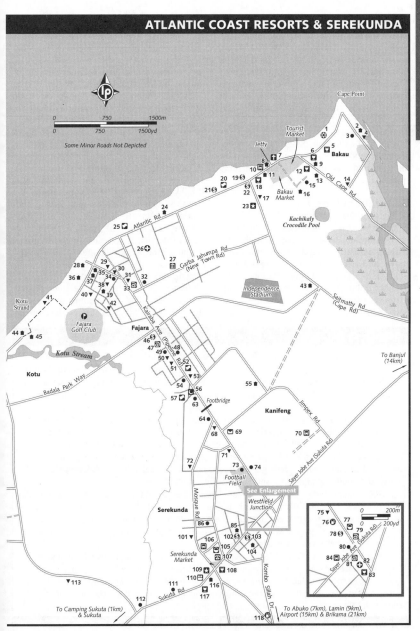

ATLANTIC COAST RESORTS & SEREKUNDA

0   750   1500m
0   750   1500yd

Some Minor Roads Not Depicted

Cape Point

Tourist Market

Jetty

Bakau

Old Cape Rd

Bakau Market

Kachikaly Crocodile Pool

Atlantic Rd

Garba Jahumpa Rd (New Town Rd)

Kotu Strand

Fajara Golf Club

Kotu Stream

Independence Stadium

Saltmatty Rd (Cape Rd)

Kotu

Badala Park Way

Fajara

Kairaba Ave (Pipeline)

To Banjul (14km)

Footbridge

Kanifeng

Jimpex Rd

Football Field

See Enlargement

Westfield Junction

Serekunda

Mosque Rd

Serekunda Market

Sayer Jobe Ave (Sukuta Rd)

Kombo Silah Dr

To Abuko (7km), Lamin (9km), Airport (15km) & Brikama (21km)

To Camping Sukuta (1km) & Sukuta

Sukuta Rd

0   200m
0   200yd

Sayer Jobe Ave (Sukuta Rd)

Bookshops

One of the best English-language bookshops in the region is Timbooktoo (☎ 494345/6), on the corner of Kairaba Ave and Garba Jahumpa Rd, which has a good range of African fiction and non-fiction, mainstream fiction, travel guides (including Lonely Planet), maps and local and international press. It's open 10am to 7pm Monday to Thursday, 10am to 1pm and 3pm to 7pm Friday, and 10am to 8pm Saturday. A smaller branch should have opened at the airport by the time you read this. Most supermarkets stock magazines and postcards.

Cultural Centres

At the southern end of Kairaba Ave is the Alliance Franco-Gambienne (☎ 375418). It runs language courses (in French and Wolof), as well as regular concerts, films, shows and exhibitions, including some in English. You can even play pétanque.

Other cultural events in the area are advertised at the centre. It's open 9.30am to 5pm Monday to Friday.

Medical Services

If you have a potentially serious illness head for the British-run clinic at the Medical Research Council (MRC; ☎ 495446) off Atlantic Rd in Fajara. Other options include the Westfield Clinic (☎ 398448) at Westfield Junction in Serekunda, or, if you want to be tested for malaria, head for Jobort Laboratories (☎ 375694), where a slide will cost D30 to D50 and take about 30 minutes. If you are involved in an accident you may well be taken to the Royal Victoria Hospital in Banjul.

A well-stocked and central pharmacy is Malak Chemist (☎ 376087) on Kairaba Ave at the Serekunda end. It's open 9am to midnight Monday to Saturday, 4pm to 1am Sunday. For more information about medical problems, see Health in the Regional Facts for the Visitor chapter.

Dangers & Annoyances

Petty thefts and muggings are always a possibility but incidents are minimal. There are few hotspots, although be vigilant on the

Bumsters & OTGs

Many visitors complain about local 'bumsters' or 'beach boys' who loiter in the resort areas and offer tourists everything from postcards to drugs and sex. High unemployment and no welfare system in Gambia means that for many young men hustling or providing sexual favours to tourists is their only way to make money. As well as selling, bumsters can earn commissions from tour companies and restaurants.

Most bumsters are very pushy and can be a real pain in the ass. If you don't want their services it's best to be polite but firm in declining their offers. If you get an angry response, just ignore it, and feel safe in the knowledge that violence against tourists is almost unheard of. However, some visitors take a different tack, hiring a bumster as a guide, either to show them around or just to keep other hustlers away. This can be a good idea, and now has the potential (see following) to also be a way to support responsible tourism.

In 2001, with bumsters being blamed for huge numbers of visitors deciding not to return, the local Association of Small Scale Enterprises in Tourism (Asset) selected 66 bumsters and, in a six-week training camp, taught them how to better deal with tourists. Hotel managers, restaurateurs, and other industry representatives explained how one could go from being an annoying 'bumster' to a more respectable (and more acceptable) guide.

The result is a team of Official Tourist Guides (OTGs). The OTGs wear grey uniforms and can be found in an open shelter outside Senegambia Hotel at Kololi, or on the beaches. They charge set rates: D50/80 for a half/full day. Most importantly, while still keen to win your business, they will not walk kilometres along the beach bothering you until you break. So, if you choose to hire a guide, choose an OTG.

ANDREW BURKE

ANDREW BURKE

ARIADNE VAN ZANDBERGEN

Interesting sites in Senegambia include the mysterious stone circles at Wassu, Gambia (top); Senegalese mud houses, called *cases à impluvium,* which kept up to 40 villagers and their cattle safe during wartime (middle); and Jufureh, Gambia (bottom), reputedly the home village of Kunta Kinte of *Roots* fame

European colonisation of Senegal was presided over by people like Governor Faidherbe (top left) and led to the creation of grand buildings such as this house in St-Louis (top right), Dakar's train station (middle), and the Fort d'Estrées on Île de Gorée (bottom), which now houses the IFAN Historical Museum path around Fajara golf course between Fajara and Kotu.

One of the major annoyances in this area is the constant hustling of tourists by 'bumsters'. See the boxed text 'Bumsters & OTGs' for more information.

THINGS TO SEE

In Bakau, deep in the village is **Kachikaly Crocodile Pool** *(admission D10; open 9am-6pm)*, a sacred site for the local people, who traditionally come here to pray, as the crocodiles represent the power of fertility. Success rates are apparently high (many children in this area are called Kachikaly) and the 80 fully grown crocodiles and 'countless' smaller ones remain protected and easily seen. The pool is a popular tourist spot, but it's also probably the nearest you'll get to a crocodile anywhere in Africa without having your leg chewed off. Some of the crocs float in the slimy pool, while others bask on the bank, undisturbed by the crowds. The largest crocodile is known as Charley (quite possibly not a traditional name) and seems resigned to tourists touching his scales or popping camera flashes in his eyes.

Also in Bakau, at the northeastern end of Atlantic Rd, the **Botanical Gardens** are worth a look. They were established during colonial times and are looking a little dilapidated now, although it's still a peaceful shady place and good for spotting birds. Not far away, a road turns north off Atlantic Rd and leads down to the jetty, where fishing boats come and go while thousands of fish dry in the sun. Morning and late afternoon are the best times.

Bijilo Forest Park *(admission D20 per day, weekly season ticket D60; open 8am-6pm)* is a small wildlife reserve on the coast, just a short walk from Kololi. It's a beautiful place to visit, and should be supported, as it helps prevent more hotel development down the coast. A well-maintained series of trails of different lengths leads through the lush and shady vegetation, and you'll easily see monkeys and numerous birds.

The monkeys are habituated to humans, mainly because visitors feed them. Birds are more easily spotted on the coast side. The dunes near the beach are covered in grass and low bush, with tall stands of palm just behind. Further back, away from the dunes, the trees are large and dense and covered in creepers. Many trees are labelled, and you can buy a small booklet (D15) that tells you a little about their natural history, traditional uses and so on.

On weekdays there is sometimes a guide available to show you around.

ACTIVITIES

The **beaches** are relatively safe for swimming, as there's little undertow. However, drownings still occur every year, so check conditions locally before plunging in (see the boxed text). The beaches in Bakau are OK, but those in Fajara and Kotu are better. The beaches at Kololi had been badly eroded at the time of research, see Coastal Erosion under Ecology & Environment in the Facts about Senegambia chapter.

If the Atlantic doesn't appeal, all the major hotels have **swimming pools**. If your hotel doesn't have them, **sailboards** and other equipment can be rented on the beach

Beachwatch

When eight children drowned off Fajara beach in 1999, exactly a year after six others had drowned on the same stretch of beach, English retirees Paul and Val Brooker were so shocked they started Beachwatch. Today 10 trained lifesavers patrol the beach between Leybato and the hotels at Kotu, and in three years no-one has drowned on their watch.

You'll know the lifesavers by their distinctive blue and yellow uniforms. They patrol every day of the year and operate a system of flags indicating the swimming conditions. There are also plans for outreach programs to train local people, both on the coast and up-river, in water safety. However all this good work doesn't come for free (it costs about D600 a month to employ a lifesaver), so donations are gratefully received. If you'd like to contribute it's best to give direct to Val or Paul, who can usually be found at the Paradise Beach Bar.

from the **Fajara Watersports Centre** (☎ *912002*).

For microlight rides, contact **Maddox Microlights** *(☎ 374259, Banjul)*, or book through any large hotel or tour company.

Fajara Golf Club *(☎ 495456)* is the country's main golf course, where an 18-hole round with clubs, balls and caddy is about D275. Smooth grass is hard to grow here, so the holes are surrounded by well-maintained 'browns', not greens! The club also has a pool and courts for tennis, squash and badminton. Temporary membership is available by the day (about D100) or week (D400).

COURSES

The **Gena Bes Batik Factory** (see Shopping later in this chapter) runs traditional batik-making courses. For a group of five people it costs about D400 each for the day, with all materials provided. Smaller groups can also do this course, but it costs more.

Several of the hotels and guesthouses in this area run courses in traditional dance, singing and drumming.

African Living Art Centre

So you've seen 1000 wooden carvings, countless masks and a variety of other stuff that's impossible to classify, but have no clue about what it all means. You might like to head to the African Living Art Centre (☎ 495131), where Suelle Nachif runs classes (by appointment only) in the appreciation of African art. Suelle is something of an artist himself and one of his greatest works is this centre at the Fajara end of Garba Jahumpa Rd. The centre is part gallery, part café, part orchid garden, part home and (wait for it ladies) the best full-service salon in West Africa. Admittedly, this last function seems hard to credit in Gambia, but before returning to his birthplace in 1995 Suelle had spent most of the previous two decades cutting and styling for Vidal Sassoon in London and Elizabeth Arden in New York. Even if you don't want to know more about African art and don't need a cut, the centre is a great place to just relax with a coffee in the garden.

ORGANISED TOURS

Organised excursions in the immediate area usually take in Bijilo Forest Park and Kachikaly Crocodile Pool at Bakau, or they go to Banjul city for a visit to Albert Market and the museum. It's unlikely that independent travellers would want to take an organised tour to any of these places, as they are very easy to reach by taxi, public transport or hired bicycle. But if you do want something organised, trips to these nearby spots and to places further afield can be arranged with the tour companies listed under Organised Tours in Gambia's Getting Around chapter, or any hotel.

Another popular option is a tour by motor yacht through the mangroves of Oyster Creek between Banjul and the mainland, recommended especially for those who otherwise won't get a chance to travel up the Gambia River. The scenery along the way is wonderful, and you may spot a monkey or two, as well as numerous birds, such as herons, hawks and kingfishers. Most cruises go from Denton Bridge and cost about D550 each. (For a do-it-yourself version, see Pirogue Trips in the Banjul chapter.)

PLACES TO STAY

You'll find everything from plush resorts to grotty dives on the Atlantic coast. Competition is so intense that if you're here out of the peak season you'll almost always be able to negotiate a better deal.

The list here is not exhaustive, but gives a good cross-section of options, especially for independent travellers. All rooms have bathrooms unless otherwise specified.

PLACES TO STAY – BUDGET
Bakau & Fajara

Crocs Guesthouse *(☎ 496654)* Singles/doubles D150/200. Near Kachikaly Crocodile Pool, deep in the maze that is Bakau village, this is the place to be if you want to stay in a typical urban Gambian environment. The management is friendly and there are four large, self-catering rooms at no-frills prices. A local boy will direct you there for D5.

Bakau Guesthouse *(☎ 497460, mobile 921854, Atlantic Rd)* Singles/doubles

D180/250. The huge, clean, airy rooms with fan and fridge overlooking Bakau market or the beach make this guesthouse good value. It also has a kitchen for self-catering and discounts for long stays. However, it was being extended when we visited and you can expect prices to rise.

Friendship Hotel (☎ 495830, fax 497344, e ifh@qanet.gm) Singles/doubles with fan D195/225, with air-con D250/300. Next to Independence Stadium, this hotel was built at the same time as the stadium as a gift from China. The spotless rooms with hot water, TV and mosquito net are a steal. Guests can also use the pool, tennis court and gym. The downsides are the location and the overly inquisitive staff.

Romana Hotel (☎ 495127, e modou barry@hotmail.com, Atlantic Rd) Rooms D200. Near the market, this hotel has big, clean rooms, but some beds are twins that can't be joined.

Jabo Guest House (☎ 494906, fax 494905, 9 Old Cape Rd) Doubles D150. Popular for long stays, this place has five comfortable rooms in a quiet location.

Kanifeng YMCA Hostel (☎ 392647) Singles/doubles D70/105. Southeast of Fajara, this is a good budget option that has simple but clean rooms for men and women. Breakfast is D10 and other dishes include *fufu* (mashed cassava) with okra and rice (D10) and sandwiches (D5). It's also a training centre and is often full, so phone first. Bathrooms are shared.

Kololi

Kololi Inn & Tavern (☎ 463410, fax 460486) Singles/doubles D150/200. About 1.5km from the beach, this inn has a very African feel, with brightly decorated rooms in thatched bungalows, all in a shady compound. Breakfast is included and there's a small bar-restaurant, and a kitchen for guests.

Keneba Hotel (☎ 460093) Rooms per person D175. In the same area as Kololi Inn, this friendly place has had good reviews from shoestring travellers but prices have gone up recently. The small double bungalows include breakfast in the price. There's

a calm, shady if slightly tatty garden, bar and restaurant. You can get here on a minibus from Serekunda heading for Kololi; get off at the junction by the Spy Bar.

Serekunda

Green Line Motel (☎ 394015, Sayer Jobe Ave) Singles/doubles D200/300. This place is an old favourite, but God knows why. The rooms are hot, noisy and the air-con and water supply are failing. Perhaps they're designed for the more short-term guest. Look for the blue sign.

Praia Motel (☎ 394887, mobile 900902, Mame Jout St) Rooms D200, air-con D50 more. A few minutes' walk off Sayer Jobe Ave, these simple but clean rooms in a very local part of Serekunda are worth your consideration. Amiable manager, Mr Ceesay, is full of advice and serves cheap beer too.

Douniya Hotel (☎ 370741/2, mobile 902638) Singles/doubles with fan D120/220, with air-con D180/280. Just off the north side of Sayer Jobe Ave, this place is cheap, if a little lacking in soul. The room rates include breakfast.

Camping Sukuta (☎ 917786, fax 460023, e campingsukuta@yahoo.de, Sukuta) Camp sites per person D40, plus D10 per vehicle, singles/doubles D95/145, with bathroom about D70 extra. This quiet place in Sukuta southwest of Serekunda, on the main road south towards Gunjur, has long been a favourite with overlanders but now offers comfortable rooms as well. Everything here, from the restaurant-bar and self-catering kitchen to the small store selling canned rations and red wine in Tetra paks, is clean and organised with true German efficiency by the friendly owners Joe and Claudia. These guys have spent a long time on the road (evidenced by signs to Sukuta in the middle of nowhere in Mauritania) and know about routes, spares and where to buy and sell vehicles. Guests (and guests only) can also hire cars and 4WDs at bargain rates. From Serekunda, take any minibus towards Brufut or Gunjur (D3), and get off near the junction where the roads to Gunjur and Brufut divide. Walk toward Brufut and follow the signs.

PLACES TO STAY – MID-RANGE

Several of the hotels in this range are small, owner-managed, and more used to dealing with individual travellers than the larger top-end establishments (although many also cater for groups). All rooms have their own bathroom and most hotels accept credit cards.

Bakau

Sambou's (☎ 495237, Old Cape Rd) Singles/doubles D200/350. Better known as a restaurant, Sambou's also has a few straightforward rooms. Don't stay here if you want an early night though – they're a bit too near the bar and restaurant.

Cape Point Hotel (☎ 495005, fax 495375) Doubles with fan/air-con D500/600, apartments D700. At the east end of Atlantic Rd, this place has attractive gardens, a small pool and plenty of package tourists. The apartments have two double rooms and kitchen.

Fajara

Leybato (☎ 497186, fax 497562, e ley bato47@hotmail.com) Bungalows D350-400, with kitchen D450. This small Gambian guesthouse and restaurant overlooks the beach and the Atlantic from one of the best locations anywhere on the coast. All the rooms are a bit different and single rates are not available, although the friendly manager says all prices are negotiable, especially for stays of more than one night. A pair of masseuses also work here full time. Leybato is reached along a small dirt track off Atlantic Rd, opposite the end of Kairaba Ave.

Fajara Guesthouse (☎ 496122, fax 495292) Rooms D300-400. Close to Leybato, in the streets of Fajara just east of the beach, this small and quiet place was being renovated when we visited. (This place is not to be confused with the top-end Fajara Hotel nearby.)

Safari Garden Hotel (☎ 495887, fax 497841, e geri@qanet.gm) Singles/doubles/triples D350/500/650. A couple of blocks back from the beach, and the same from Kairaba Ave, this small British-Gambian enterprise is excellent value and should be the first place in the mid-range bracket you call. The helpful management has put a strong emphasis on staff teamwork and as a result the Garden has become a favourite in this area as much for its friendly and efficient atmosphere as for its stylish rooms, lush garden and sparkling swimming pool. Rates include buffet breakfast and discounts are available in the low season. An extra bed is D150. Other meals are available in Flavours, the courtyard restaurant. In every way, highly recommended.

Francisco's Hotel & Restaurant (☎/fax 495332, Atlantic Rd) Singles/doubles D550/680. Just back from the beach, this is another small, well-run place where comfortable air-con rooms with TV and fridge come with a full English breakfast. Good value.

Kotu & Kololi

Badala Park Hotel (☎ 460400/1, fax 460402) Singles/doubles D400/500. If you don't mind mixing with package tourists and want a resort-style stay, this place is pretty good value. The fan rooms are clean and comfortable, and the pool and bar are crowded all day.

Bakadaji Hotel & Restaurant (☎/fax 462307, e bakadajikn@hotmail.com, Badala Park Way) Singles/doubles with breakfast D300/450, bungalows D650. This remarkably good-value hotel is towards the southern end of Badala Park Way. It has self-catering bungalows (with two double rooms, lounge and kitchen) and rooms without kitchens for two or three people. These are set in extensive grounds, complete with access to the beach and a flock of sheep to keep the grass short.

Bunkoyo Hotel (☎/fax 463199, e bunk oyo@gamtel.gm) Singles/doubles with fan D350/500, with air-con D510/660. Near Bakadaji Hotel, this is more upmarket, but still small and homely, with comfortable rooms and breakfast for D50.

Balmoral Apartments (☎ 461079, mobile 903634, w www.balmoral-apartments.com) Self-catering apartments D450. East off Badala Park Way, this small British-run place with a pool is fair value.

Baobab Lodge (☎/fax 461270, e lnbn@ qanet.gm) Apartment singles/doubles with breakfast D450/550, with air-con D100 extra. About 2km south of Senegambia, these apartments are really very nice, with TV, fridge and even an oven. The Gambian management is young, friendly and well organised. Excellent value.

PLACES TO STAY – TOP END

The top-end hotels along the beach, and in the area just behind it, deal mainly with groups. They vary considerably in size, style and cost, although prices can be very flexible (see the boxed text). All rooms have air-con and bathroom, and most include breakfast. Nearly all hotels are on the beach and have a pool. Most accept credit cards.

Fajara

Fajara Hotel (☎ 495605, fax 495339, Atlantic Rd) Singles/doubles D650/750. One of the oldest hotels on the coast, this huge place has all the facilities of a resort (pool, expensive bars and restaurants, tennis courts) but all the green-roofed buildings make it look more like an army barracks by the sea. Rooms come with breakfast and a buffet dinner is D200.

Ngala Lodge (☎ 497429, W www.ngala lodge.com, Atlantic Rd) Junior/luxury suites US$150/250. This large house overlooking the sea is completely different in size and ambience from Fajara Hotel. One word sums this place up: style. The Dutch owners have decorated each room with a combination of traditional African materials and fascinating modern sculptures. Guests include tourists, business travellers and temporary embassy staff. But style doesn't come cheap. Each double suite comes with breakfast, and the three-storey penthouse has a glass dome above the bed to allow for very relaxed star-gazing. The restaurant is similarly select.

Kotu

Several hotels are packed into the strip of beach between Fajara golf course and Kotu Stream and tend to attract young people on package holidays. Three include:

Bungalow Beach Hotel (BB Hotel, ☎ 465288, fax 466180, e bbhotel@qanet .gm) Self-contained singles/doubles D700/900, with air-con D810/1010. Despite the name, this place consists of dozens of apartments in two-storey long-houses.

Bakotu Hotel (☎ 465555, fax 465959) Singles/doubles including breakfast D720/960. Smaller than the BB, the bungalows here are around a pool in a pleasant garden.

Kombo Beach Novotel (☎ 465466, fax 465490, e kombo@gamtel.gm) Singles/doubles D1000/1200. A favourite with sexy

Hotel Rates & Discounts

Most large hotels in Gambia cater primarily for visitors on package holidays and are not used to dealing with individual tourists. While researching for this book, we found several hotels so completely geared for groups that reception clerks did not even know the 'rack rate' (the standard individual room price).

We have quoted high-season rack rates here as it gives an indication of standard, and allows one hotel to be compared against another. But if you're an independent traveller and you want to stay at one of these big hotels, with a bit of forward planning it's unlikely you'll actually have to pay the full whack. Most big hotels offer vast discounts to groups (some places were charging the big tour operators less than 20% of their advertised per-person rates) and are happy to make reductions to individuals if they have spare rooms. Discounts are only normally possible, however, if you make a reservation in advance, either through a travel agent or direct to the hotel.

We've heard from some travellers who fancied a bit of luxury after a hard trip around Senegal and Mali. Their bush taxi dropped them in Serekunda, where they went to a public phone office, and simply rang around a selection of top-end hotels asking what discounts were available, finally finding something that charged half the advertised rate.

THE GAMBIA

young Europeans on group tours, facilities here include a swimming pool, clinic and nightclub, and hired help to encourage the punters around the pool.

Kololi

Palma Rima Hotel (☎ 463380, fax 463382) Rooms per person D800/1000. Off Badala Park Way at the Kotu end of Kololi, this place is looking a bit tired and well overpriced. Facilities include tennis, squash, a good pool and a nightclub.

Kairaba Hotel (☎ 462940, fax 492947, W www.kairabahotel.com) Singles/doubles D1840/2240. The Kairaba claims to be the best hotel in Gambia and isn't far wrong. Facilities include four restaurants, three bars, health studio and observatory, which is open to nonguests for D25.

Senegambia Hotel (☎ 462718/9, fax 461839, W www.senegambiahotel.com) Singles/doubles with fan D900/1060, with air-con D1100/1360. Next door to the Kairaba, age has wearied the Senegambia a little, but you won't be uncomfortable and might be more relaxed staying here than at its neighbour. Breakfast is included.

For the above three hotels, you'd be daft to pay the full rates: see the boxed text 'Hotel Rates & Discounts' earlier for advice on how not to.

Other top-end hotels in this area include the opulent and utterly exclusive *Coconut Residence (☎ 463377, fax 461835, e co conut@qanet.gm, Badala Park Way)* a few hundred metres south of the Senegambia strip. There are 24 large, luxuriously appointed rooms (though some are significantly more luxurious than others), three very inviting swimming pools and gardens with mature palms and other trees brought here from the Caribbean. Rooms start at US$140 and get up to US$350 – a night, that is. But then again, this is the sort of place where if you need to ask the price, you probably can't afford it. The excellent restaurant is open to nonguests.

PLACES TO EAT

Mass tourism has made the area around the Atlantic coast resorts one of the best places to eat in West Africa. There is no shortage

of cuisines, many of them jammed onto the Senegambia strip at Kololi. But for quality and individuality Fajara and Bakau are better bets. Of course, there's no shortage of local food either – Serekunda and, to a lesser extent, Bakau, are the places to go if you came to Africa with the idea that you might like to eat some African food. These are also the places to find cheaper food.

It's worth remembering that when you walk into any restaurant, be it European or African, there's a good chance you'll be handed a menu with dishes from the four corners of the globe. The logic is that if you cater to every taste, everyone will be happy. Unfortunately it means, especially in the Senegambia strip at Kololi, that you end up with lots of restaurants serving similar food, little of it worth writing home about.

All the upmarket hotels have their own restaurants which, along with several other stand-alone restaurants, tend to have at least one all-you-can-eat buffet a week – usually D100 to D150. Some travellers, seemingly unconcerned about the half-life of a raw prawn, have been known to leave the restaurant with full stomachs and full day packs.

Bakau

At the taxi ranks and in the market there's usually *stalls* where a couple of women cook up rice and sauce, which goes for about D7 a plate, and other stalls selling fruit, nuts and other snacks. Otherwise, good cheap food can be found at the following two places:

Buggerland (☎ 497697, 52 Saitmatty Rd) Meals D30-50. Open 11am-midnight. We suspect the signwriter had imbibed one-too-many Julbrews before he started work for this tiny burger joint. Meals are slow coming but good, with, err...buggers (D25), pepper steak or fish and chips (both D35) the pick.

Kumba's Bar (☎ 496123, Atlantic Rd) Open 10am-2am. Near the GSC Supermarket, the charming Kumba serves a plate of afra or half a chicken for D40.

Buddies (☎ 495501, Atlantic Rd) Meals D40-90. Open 9am-2am. Near the market, this place does a good mix of Gambian and

European dishes as well as afra. There's also a good all-day breakfast (D40).

Sambou's (☎ *495237, Old Cape Rd*) Snacks from D35. Sambou's has a varied menu that includes a few Gambian dishes. It serves snacks and light meals, while large pepper steaks are D135 and small beers are D13.

Calypso Restaurant (☎ *496292*) Meals D50-100. Open 10am-10pm. On the beach at Cape Point, this place has terrific views, a relaxed atmosphere and serves seafood, Gambian dishes and a most impressive range of Hungarian food – try the chicken *kotkoda* (D85).

Baobab Sunshine Bar Dishes D25-40. Open until 8pm. Well worth checking out, this friendly, local-style bar is about 50m south along the beach from Calypso Restaurant. It does great-value meals such as fish and chips, shrimp sandwiches, and Gambian dishes.

The Clay Oven (☎ *496600*) Mains D90-120, side dishes D40-60. Open 7pm-11pm. Just off Old Cape Rd, this stylish place does excellent Indian food, so good in fact that it's been described as the best in West Africa. Seating is both indoor and out and the service attentive without being overbearing. We enjoyed the *chingri shashlick* (D50) and *karami gosht* (D105).

For self-catering options, visit *St Mary's Food & Wine* (*Cape Point Rd*).

Fajara

Golden Bamboo (☎ *494213*) Meals D40-70. Open 5pm-11pm. Hidden away in the backstreets of Fajara, this place does good, cheap Western-style Chinese food. The noodle dishes (D30) and pork ribs wrapped in paper (D55) aren't bad.

Eddie's Bar & Restaurant (*Off Kairaba Ave*) Dishes D25-35. Open 8am-2am. This local favourite offers afra and other good Gambian dishes, as well as European fare, in a relaxed setting. Guests at the nearby top-end hotels have been known to sneak down here for a taste of genuine Gambian cooking.

Flavours Dishes D30-80. Open from 8am-midnight. Situated in the colourful courtyard of the Safari Garden Hotel (see

Places to Stay – Mid-Range), this restaurant serves some of the most imaginative dishes in Gambia and will appeal to carnivores and vegetarians alike. The menu changes weekly but a typical selection could include shrimps in garlic and coconut (D70) or a crepe filled with ratatouille and cheese sauce. Dining here allows you use of the pool and there's a BBQ on Fridays for D75.

Gambia Etten (☎ *496754, mobile 924205*) Meals D70-200. Open 8am-midnight. About 50m from Safari Garden, this quiet, romantic restaurant in a garden setting gets good reports from locals. It's renowned for big pepper steaks (D85) and lobster thermidor (D190) and service is good.

Francisco's Hotel & Restaurant (☎ *495332, Cnr Atlantic Rd & Kairaba Ave*) Grills D75-130. Open until midnight daily. Francisco's has a stylish garden setting, quiet music, good atmosphere and grills (served on wooden platters), or a big mixed seafood platter for D130.

Leybato (☎ *497186*) Dishes around D60. The food here isn't the best in town but it's hard to argue with the setting – overlooking the Atlantic Ocean. Sunset here, even if you just stop for a drink, shouldn't be missed. If you do eat, you'll find seafood, pizza and grilled chicken and steak.

Ngala Lodge (☎ *497672, Atlantic Rd*) Open Mon-Sat 11.30am-3pm & 7.30pm-11pm. It doesn't get much better than Ngala Lodge, where Belgian chef Peter specialises in wonderful fish dishes while JoJo keeps everything in a state of calm under the swaying palm trees looking down on the ocean. A three-course meal with drinks will set you back D300 to D500 per person. A jazz band plays every Friday.

Kairaba Ave offers many more choices. The best thing to do is stroll down during the day and check out your options, but here's a few names to get you started:

Afra Kairaba Meals D40. This small and unpretentious eatery serves takeaway grilled meat in the evenings.

Weezo's (☎ *496918, 132 Kairaba Ave*) Mains around D130-150. Open 11am-3.30pm & 7pm-3am. This very classy place morphs with the clock: it's a fusion-flavoured café for lunch, with excellent food ranging from sandwiches (D40) to exotic steak (D120); a smart Mexican cantina for dinner; and a lively, trendy cocktail bar after 11pm. A wide range of tapas (D50 to D70) is available all night.

MacFadi's (☎ 390412, 61 Kairaba Ave) The burgers at this local variation of a fast-food joint, are actually quite good (D25). There's also fish and chips (D40), chicken kebab (D25) and pizza (from D55).

Le Palais du Chocolat (☎ 395397, 19 Kairaba Ave) This is a café-patisserie that does good coffee and English breakfast (D50), great ice cream and imported chocolate. Enough to answer any calorie craving.

La Parisienne (☎ 372565) Open 8am-midnight. Opposite the US embassy, this French-style café is frequented by embassy staff and other expats.

The Butcher's Shop (☎ 495069) Dishes D25-65. Open 10am-6pm. At the north end of Kairaba Ave, this place is primarily a delicatessen with a mix of European and locally made hams, salamis, cheeses, quiches and cakes. There's also a small café that serves sandwiches, salads, light lunches (a

Kairaba Avenue

Kairaba Ave is one of the busiest streets in the resort area, lined with several places to eat, plus many shops, offices, travel agents and other businesses. But despite its settled appearance this road was originally a service track for the pipeline laid in the late 1970s to carry water from the Fajara pumping station to the expanding town of Serekunda. When the pipeline was finished the track became a handy short cut between Serekunda and Fajara, and became known as Pipeline Rd. Over the next few years, a few houses and shops were built along the road. Then somebody with influence persuaded the government to put down tar and even more establishments grew up. By the late 1980s, Pipeline Rd became one of the best places in Gambia to open a retail business. Now Pipeline Rd has been renamed Kairaba Ave and the rents here are the highest in the country.

baguette with a platter of cold meats and cheeses is D45) and more substantial meals.

The biggest supermarkets are found about halfway along Kairaba Ave and *Harry's (☎ 397444)* is probably the pick as it has the best hours (9am to 10pm Monday to Saturday). There's a branch of *St Mary's Food & Wine* here too, open from about 9am to 7.30pm Monday to Saturday and 10am to 1.30pm Sunday.

Kotu

Most restaurants in Kotu are unremarkable, but at the northern end of the resort are some notable exceptions.

The Sailor (☎ 4605210) Meals D30-100. Open 9am-midnight. Readers recommend this as one of the best beach bars on the coast. Burgers, pizzas and very fresh fish are all available – the grilled fillet of barracuda in garlic and lime sauce (D90) is rather good.

Paradise Beach Bar (☎ 466624) Dishes D20-60. Just a few metres along the beach from The Sailor, this place is more laid back and offers sandwiches (D25), grills (D45 to D60) and Gambian dishes (D55). The Sunday barbecue (D100, 8pm) is popular.

Kololi

There are plenty of generic tourist restaurants in Kololi, but these are ones worthy of mention:

Dolphin Bar & Restaurant (☎ 460929) Meals D40-110. Open 9am-11pm. Through the arch near the entrance to Kairaba Hotel, the Dolphin's new management have given the place a more relaxed atmosphere. All the favourite Euro-dishes are served here, as well as Gambian specialities, and draft Julbrew at D25 a pint.

Al Amir (☎ 460860, Senegambia Rd) Meals D110. On the Senegambia strip, this Lebanese place has been recommended by readers. The mezza (D45) is said to be delicious and the mains not bad either. There's a D125 buffet on Fridays.

Scala Restaurant (☎ 460813) Meals from D110. If you are looking for a night out in your best holiday clothes, this place on the Senegambia strip is for you. The

European food gets regular compliments, but don't forget to go to the bank first.

Coco Beach (☎ *461983*) Mains about D100. Open 9am-11pm. The classiest of the seaside restaurants, this place is on the beach just south of Kairaba Hotel and has an international menu with a touch of African infused. There's a decent wine list, a barbeque buffet on Monday (D150), Chinese buffet on Wednesday (D125) and Saturday is West African night. If you're going to splash out, this is a good choice.

Solomon's Beach Bar (☎ *460716*) Meals D40-80. Open 10am-midnight. At the northern end of Kololi beach, this place is famous for its seafood grill and chips (D50) – try it.

Bakadaji Hotel & Restaurant (☎ *462307, Badala Park Way*) Mains around D75, buffets D100. This place does very good African and European food. Thursday- and Saturday-night buffets are great value and include traditional entertainment.

Luigi's Italian Restaurant (☎ *460280*) Dishes about D85, small/medium/large pizzas D65/95/130. Near Palma Rima Hotel, a road leads down to the beach and passes Luigi's. It does good pasta dishes and serves house wine for D100 per litre.

Amsterdam Café (☎ *461805*) Starters D20. Open 5pm-2am. On the road to Serekunda, this friendly and lively place is off the tour-group radar and thus is a great venue for meeting Gambians. It's good value too, Amsterdam special fish is D50 or grilled barracuda D40. And beer is just D10!

Village Gallery & Restaurant (☎ *460369,* ℮ *bahs@qanet.gm*) Meals D50-100. Open 10am-midnight. Surrounded by a gallery displaying a diverse range of works from Gambian and West African artists, it seems appropriate there is a certain element of art to the food too. The smoked catfish on toast (D25) is a good way to start and the special steak (D80) is not bad either. The accompanying chips are some of the best in the country. Excellent Gambian dishes cost just D50, a variety of vegetarian dishes are D40 to D50 and the Saturday-night Gambian buffet is value at D100. This place can be hard to find and is best reached by a taxi (D15 to D20).

You Don't Want Meat?

The gulf between culinary cultures is perhaps best illustrated by a conversation between a British restaurant owner in Gambia and her head chef. Asked why diners (almost always Western) were repeatedly being told the kitchen did not have the ingredients for vegetarian dishes, even though it did, the chef angrily replied: 'These people can afford to eat meat, why shouldn't they eat meat!' The idea that people would choose to eat vegetarian dishes for any reason other than lack of money – and actually enjoy them – is quite simply foreign to most West Africans.

There's a branch of **St Mary's Food & Wine** here, located on the Senegambia strip, which will take care of any self-catering needs. It's open 9am to 7.30pm Monday to Saturday and 10am to 1.30pm Sunday.

Serekunda

There are several cheap *eating houses* around the market and taxi station entrance, and several others scattered through the streets of Serekunda. Heading up Kairaba Ave from Westfield Junction you'll find **Sen Fast Food** (☎ *372792*), a longtime preference of shoestringers with omelettes (D20) and chawarmas (D15) standard fare. Further along is the similar **LK Fast Food** (☎ *375858*), which does a mean fish and chips (D20). Both open from 9am to midnight. Past LK is the **Come Inn** (☎ *391464*), a German-style garden restaurant that serves bar snacks from D20 and tasty mains (such as shrimp in garlic-and-cream sauce) for about D70.

On Mosque Rd is **Safe Way Afra King** (☎ *391360*), open 5pm to midnight, which serves afra, sandwiches, fufu, 'cowfoot' and other African dishes, all for less than D25. Further along is the **C&B Grill** ☎ *375906*) with similar fare at slightly higher prices.

Maroun's (*Westfield Junction*) Open 9am-7.30pm Mon-Sat, 10am-1.30pm Sun. This local supermarket is the place to go for the basics, such as local and imported food, toiletries etc.

ENTERTAINMENT
Bars
Many of the restaurants and hotels listed previously have bars, some large and formulaic, others more personal and a few in breathtaking locations. The bars mentioned below are generally smaller and more intimate affairs more likely to have local patrons than purely package tourists.

Bakau & Fajara The shanty-like *Lacondula International Pub (☎ 495945, 21 Old Cape Rd)* is open 4pm to 2am, plays reggae music and is worth investigating if you're up for a Gambian pub experience, or just want cheap beer.

One For The Road Bar (Atlantic Rd) Near Lacondula, this is a breezy place with just two tables, a fridge and owner/barman Sajo.

Fawlty Towers (☎ 495252), a couple of doors further north, is a lively place where African beats rule late at night.

South along Atlantic Rd is *Kumba's Bar (☎ 496123)*, a local favourite where beer is D12 and decent food can be had; and *Buddies (☎ 495501)*, where local bands play every night during the tourist season and pints of Julbrew cost D22. Both these places are open from 9am to 2am. Also on

Atlantic Rd near the market is *The Bulldog (mobile ☎ 916119)* where, during the tourist season, bands play on Wednesday, Friday and Saturday, with DJs on other nights.

Most bars in Fajara are attached to hotels or restaurants. *Leybato* has fine sea views. After 11pm *Weezos* gets busy and is a lot of fun, and the nearby *Wheels (☎ 496553)* has a beer-garden-style backyard that becomes a well-frequented pick-up joint as the night progresses. Wheels also serves good afra and is open 6am to 4am.

Kotu & Kololi The liveliest strip in the country is probably Senegambia Rd, where tourists, and to a lesser extent locals, have an impressive choice of drinking establishments. *The Dolphin* at Kairaba Hotel is popular and several street-side bars and restaurants are also available, though you'll constantly be fending off touts. *The Pub* has an upstairs terrace from where you can watch *other* people being hassled.

At the small and local *Salz Bar (☎ 460434)*, near Palma Rima Hotel, laid-back Sal manages to open by 9pm for the regulars most nights, and earlier for big football matches (on the big screen). Nearer the beach is *Churchill's*, the closest thing to an English pub in Gambia.

Overlooking the sea, *The Sailor* and *Paradise Beach Bar* at Kotu, and *Solomon's*

Palm Wine

For a cheap drink, local style, you could head for the palm-wine sellers who work in a large stand of palm trees between Kotu Creek and Fajara golf course. Their selling area is in the bush off Badala Park Way, but is best reached via the southwesternmost street of Fajara. There's no sign, and it can be hard to find – if you can't, ask a local for guidance, or take a taxi. However you get there, remember that this stuff can pack a punch – and the odd dud batch can knock you out cold! Also, as we heard from Mark Leyland, be ready for a classic con:

'As you're buying your palm wine, men invite you to visit "Grandfather", the original wine-tapper, now a Muslim priest *(marabout)* and patriarch of the biggest local family. If you agree, you're led to a compound nearby. Grandfather, apparently, is busy at prayer, but sends a message of welcome. You're offered Coke, then "holy water". If, as I did, you manage to deflect these, the crunch comes in the form of the "visitor's book", a sheet of paper with columns for name, country etc, plus the key one for the amount you're going to donate to Grandfather's charitable work with local orphans. Previous "visitors" from all over Europe have supposedly given, on average, D500, and of course you're expected to follow suit.'

Beach Bar at Kololi are all excellent spots for an afternoon ale.

Serekunda Here you'll find bars with a more local feel. *Lana's Bar (☎ 395424)* is a small affair on a corner of Sukuta Rd and is ideal for refreshments during the day. Opposite the market, *Bobby's Choice (☎ 901638)* affords a perfect view of the surrounding bustle.

Nightclubs
Generally speaking, Friday and Saturday are the liveliest nights in the clubs. Some places cater for a mixed crowd of locals and visitors, while others are aimed specifically at tourists and expats, and tend to be European in style and more expensive.

Most of the large hotels have nightclubs. Other places include the *911 Nightclub* near Cape Point Hotel in Bakau, frequented by locals and tourists. The *Reggae Yard*, next to Badala Park Hotel in Kotu, is smarter and sees a lot of Europeans. In Kololi there are a few more choices: the *Waaw Nightclub* was about the hottest spot in town when we passed; and the enormous *Spy Bar (☎ 463 211)*, which has live bands and discos featuring techno, pop, hip hop and rap music plus a lively mix of tourists and locals.

In Serekunda the *Joker's Nightclub*, on the south side of Westfield Junction, is the most popular place for Gambians, and it sometimes has live music.

Casinos
Kololi Casino (☎ 460226) Open from 9pm. Near Senegambia Hotel, this casino is reckoned by most to be the best in the country. The casino offers roulette, poker, blackjack and jackpot machines (from 4pm), plus a bar and coffee shop. Attached is La Valbonne Italian Restaurant.

Slot-machine fans can find relief at *Jackpot Palace* on Kairaba Ave, or a host of places in Serekunda.

SPECTATOR SPORTS
Football
The Gambia's main stadium is Independence Stadium in Bakau, and this is the site for major football matches and other sporting events, which are advertised locally on posters. Major matches are impossible to miss, as seemingly the entire population of Gambia heads for the stadium, many dressed in national colours or carrying flags. The atmosphere at times like this is electric, and it's well worth going along just for this, even if you don't actually see the match.

Traditional Wrestling
Another spectator sport popular with locals and visitors is traditional wrestling (see also Spectator Sports in the Regional Facts for the Visitor chapter). This occasionally takes place at Independence Stadium in Bakau but it's more interesting, and much more fun, to see the matches at one of several smaller 'arenas' (open patches of ground) in Serekunda. These include *Arena Babou Fatty*, off Sukuta Rd, west of Green Line Motel, and at *Arena Tuti Fall Jammeh*, also on the west side of town, a couple of hundred metres south of Sukuta Rd – ask around outside Lana's Bar.

Matches take place in the late afternoon, usually on Sunday (less frequently in the dry season, and not during Ramadan). The entrance fee is usually about D15 for tourists. There's normally a crowd of 300 to 400 spectators, including a couple of coach-loads of tourists from the large hotels.

To see a wrestling session you can arrange a tour through a large hotel; the cost is about D250. Taxis do this trip for a bit less, including waiting time. Or you can get to Serekunda by shared taxi for about D5, and follow the crowds to whichever arena is the venue that day.

SHOPPING
Bakau Market sells fruit and vegetables, but also has several stalls selling carvings, traditional cloth and other souvenirs (see Shopping in the Regional Facts for the Visitor chapter for more details on what to buy). There is a string of similar stalls nearby along Atlantic Rd. Opposite the Gamtel office is a particularly hassle-free shop selling batiks and brightly coloured clothing of good quality, which is also reasonably

priced. The ***Baba Samba Shop***, near the market, is a smart place with fixed prices, and craftwork of mixed quality that comes from Gambia and several other African countries. Ask for directions at the market.

Original and good-quality batik paintings are hard to come by. Try one of the ***stalls*** at the far eastern (Cape Point) end of Atlantic Road, or the ***Gena Bes Batik Factory***, open 9am to 6pm Monday to Friday, 9am to 5pm Sunday, near Cinema Kachikaly in Bakau. Gena Bes means 'new arrival' in the local language, and at this shop a good selection of batiks and tie-dyed cloth sells for around D65 per metre. If you can't find it, get a local boy to show you or ask for Queen Amie. Several readers have written to recommend a ***batik factory*** (☎ 392258) deep in the back streets of Serekunda, run by a lady called Mrs Musu Kebba Drammeh. It's difficult to find on foot, unless you take a guide, but all the taxi drivers know her place.

If you're looking for music, the best selection is in Banjul centre (see Shopping in the Banjul chapter), but in Bakau a place well worth a browse is the ***Bakau Sound Shop***, on the small street leading down towards the Kachikaly Crocodile Pool, and there are several stores upstairs at the Serekunda market.

Needless to say, there are souvenir stalls inside many of the big hotels, and craft markets selling the same kind of stuff at Kotu and Kololi.

GETTING THERE & AWAY

The various ways to reach upcountry destinations or other countries by air and bus are covered in the Banjul chapter.

Bush taxis depart from the Bus & Taxi Station in Serekunda, which is the main transport hub for the whole country. Minibuses and Mercedes buses also go to upcountry towns on the south of the river. Serekunda to Soma is D35, and to Farafenni it's D45. If you're heading for the south coast you can get bush taxis to Brufut (D4), Tanji (D5) and Sanyang (D6). A direct bush taxi to Gunjur is D9 via Brikama (D5), though the opening of the new coastal highway should mean direct transport all the way to Kartong. Vehicles for Brikama leave from Westfield Junction.

New Roads

When this book was being researched, the smooth, sealed and long-overdue Coastal Hwy was nearing completion. The road links Kololi and Serekunda with Kartong on the Senegal border, running through or near all the coastal towns in between. Add this to the already completed highway linking the airport and Kololi and all of a sudden coastal Gambia is just an easy drive away.

You can expect public transport to have started direct services along the coast by the time you read this – meaning no more roundabout journeys to Gunjur via Brikama. Badala Park Way was also being upgraded and extended to link it with Saitmatty Rd, meaning people going from Kololi to Banjul will be able to avoid the nightmarish traffic jams at Westfield Junction. For all this we can thank Kuwait, which has funded much of the coastal roads project. Maybe if the Kuwaiti benefactors take a leisurely Sunday drive from Brikama to Georgetown they'll find some more highway money.

Bush taxis (mainly Peugeots) go from Serekunda to Kafountine and Ziguinchor in southern Senegal via the border at Séléti. See Gambia's Getting There & Away chapter for more details.

GETTING AROUND

See also Getting Around in the Banjul chapter for details on private taxis and shared taxis operating between the Atlantic coast resorts and Banjul city centre.

To/From the Airport

A green tourist taxi from Banjul international airport to Serekunda is D100, and to any Atlantic coast resort is D150. Yellow taxis cost about a third less in either direction, depending completely upon your powers of negotiation.

There isn't any public transport to the airport, but minibuses between Brikama and Serekunda can drop you at the turn-off 3km from the airport.

Shared Taxi

From Bakau, at the junction of Saitmatty and Atlantic Rds, you can get shared taxis and minibuses to Banjul city centre or Serekunda. From Fajara, some shared taxis go from near the junction of Kairaba Ave and Atlantic Rd, but you usually have to walk to the junction of Garba Jahumpa Rd and Kairaba Ave, where you can pick up one coming from Bakau.

From Serekunda, you can get shared taxis to Bakau from outside the Gamtel office at the southern end of Kairaba Ave (Westfield Junction). For Fajara, it's usually necessary to be dropped at the Garba Jahumpa Rd junction on Kairaba Ave. There are no shared taxis between Fajara and Kotu or Kololi. You have to wait at the junction of Kairaba Ave and Badala Park Way, and flag down the occasional taxi or just hope for a lift.

From the Serekunda bush-taxi station there are minibuses or shared taxis to Kololi (the drivers call the taxi park in Kololi 'Senegambia'). They leave from near the northwest corner of the market (ask anyone) and mostly go via the junction near Badala Park Hotel (where you can get off and walk to Kotu), but sometimes go via the junction near Palma Rima Hotel. From Kololi taxi park, minibuses run to Serekunda.

In Serekunda, minibuses to Banjul city, or shared taxis up Kairaba Ave to Fajara and Bakau go from near Westfield Junction.

If you want to go directly from Kololi or Kotu to Fajara, there's no regular minibus service along Badala Park Way, so you'll have to walk or wait for a taxi to come by.

The following are some shared-taxi fares:

from	to	fare
Bakau	Fajara	D2
Serekunda	Abuko	D3
Serekunda	Brikama	D5
Serekunda	Fajara/Bakau	D2

Private Taxi

In the Atlantic coast resorts there are literally hundreds of green 'tourist taxis'. These taxis do not usually cruise for business (petrol is too expensive for the drivers), although, if you flag down an empty taxi in the street it will of course stop. In Bakau, the green-taxi rank is near the corner of Atlantic Rd and Saitmatty Rd; in Fajara, a few taxis lurk outside Fajara Hotel; in Kotu, the rank is near Bungalow Beach Hotel; and in Kololi, there are ranks outside Palma Rima Hotel and near Senegambia Hotel.

The taxis do not have meters, but fixed prices are set by the drivers' syndicates and are usually advertised on a board or on leaflets in each car. Some sample one-way 'town trip' taxi fares from Bakau include: Kololi D120, the airport D180, Banjul city centre D100/150 one way/return. For longer trips outside Banjul and the Atlantic coast area, see Organised Tours in Gambia's Getting Around chapter.

Of course, you don't have to use a 'tourist taxi', it's usually significantly cheaper to take a yellow 'shared taxi' and negotiate the fare yourself. As a guide, work out how much the driver would make with a car full or share passengers, then add about 20%. For example, Bakau to Serekunda should cost you about D10, to Kololi about D25.

Car & Motorcycle

Outside Senegambia Hotel in Kololi, AB Rent-a-Car (☎ 460926) is your best option for self-drive car rental. Most cars are no more than a few years old, and rates for their smallest car (Fiat Uno) start at D400 per day, dropping to D350 per day for seven days. A larger car (Peugeot 309) is D50 more per day. A Suzuki jeep is D550 for one day or D470 per day for seven days. To all these prices you have to add between D100 and D150 for full insurance, and another 10% tax. The deposit of D10,000 and the rental can be paid by credit card. Half-day rates are also available. Drivers must be aged 23 or over.

Hertz have an office at Bakoteh Elf Station (☎ 390041) and at the airport (☎/fax 473156), but their rates are higher. There are also a few local one-man-and-his-car operations that advertise in hotels, shops and supermarkets in the resorts. These certainly offer cheaper rates, but tend to come and go pretty quickly, so names are not worth listing. Unless you are an expert mechanic, beware – some vehicles can be ropey in the extreme (see Organised Tours in Gambia's Getting Around chapter for details on hiring cars with drivers).

Scooters can be hired from a number of hotels and small operators, but the 'asking' rates are usually ridiculous (we were told D1500 a day!), so be ready to bargain – hard.

Bicycle

Mountain bikes and traditional roadsters (of varying quality) can be hired from several hotels in Bakau, Kotu and Kololi, or from private outfits nearby. Prices seem to be standardised: D20 per hour, D80 for a half-day and D100 for a full day. Bargain hunters can negotiate these rates down by at least half.

Western Gambia

This chapter covers Gambia's coastal areas (apart from those areas already described in the Banjul and Atlantic Coast & Serekunda chapters) and several places inland such as the nature reserve at Abuko and the 'Roots' village of Jufureh. Most of these places are easily visited as day trips – either as an independent traveller or on an organised tour.

South Coast

Gambia's western border is the coast, which is only around 50km in length as the crow flies, but over 80km if all the bays and promontories are included. South of Banjul and the coastal resorts the south coast proper begins, continuing all the way to the border at Allahein. Only about 30km long, this stretch of the coast has long been over-looked by travellers because of the diabol-ical state of the roads. But the completion of coastal highways from Serekunda and Kololi to Kartong is set to end this blissful seclusion. Most of the coastal towns now have at least one accommodation option, meaning a visit here doesn't need to be rushed – you can wander through traditional fishing villages or enjoy the huge beaches long after the day-trippers have retreated to their hotels.

BRUFUT BEACH

Brufut Beach is less eroded and more at-tractive than many of its northern neighbours. About 17km from Serekunda and a little nearer to Kololi, the coastal highway has made it an easy and increasingly popu-lar destination for day-trippers. You can get here by bush taxi from Serekunda, either direct or via Brufut Town (the last 3km costs D1 in a bush taxi). This is a busy working beach, where fishing boats come in and out according to the tide, and their catch is sold, still twitching on the sand, to dealers from Serekunda. Most of the fish-ing is done by Ghanaians who live in

Highlights

- Motor up the Gambia River to Fort James and Jufureh, the 'Roots' village
- Walk across Ginak Island to the pristine Atlantic beaches of Niumi National Park, a good place for seeing turtles and dolphins
- See monkeys, crocodiles and hundreds of varieties of birds on a short walk at Abuko Nature Reserve
- Learn of the medicinal properties of some of the local flora at the Tanji Village Museum
- Soak up the atmosphere at Makasutu, one of the most beautiful and peaceful places in Gambia

nearby Ghana Town, their pirogues identi-fied by the coloured flags in their bows. About 50m back from the sea is ***Brufut Beach Bar*** (☎ 906331), which serves meals for about D50 to D60 and drinks and snacks for D25. If you have to wait a little while for your food, and this means miss-ing the last taxi home, the management has rooms with bathroom for about D150 per person.

TANJI RIVER BIRD RESERVE

About 5km south of Brufut Beach is the small village of Tanji. The area in-between these two points is called Karinti by locals, and is the site of the Tanji River Bird Reserve *(adult/child D31.50/D15.75)*. An area of dunes, lagoons, dry woodland and coastal scrub, the reserve also incorporates the mangrove creeks and estuary of the Tanji River, and the offshore Bijol Island with its surrounding reefs and islets.

The wide range of habitats here attracts an excellent selection of birds, including indigenous species and European migrants; more than 300 species have been recorded. Although waders and waterbirds are the most prolific species, there are also 34 raptor species. Other animals include the vervet, patas and red colobus monkeys; hyenas; porcupines; and the occasional bushbuck. The reserve, Bijol Island in particular, is also an important green turtle breeding area. To get to Bijol Island, known locally as Kajonyi, there are twice-weekly boat trips between October and March. Boats take only five people and fill on a first-come first-on-board basis, each seat costing D200. To book, call park manager Amadou Camara on ☎ mobile 919219.

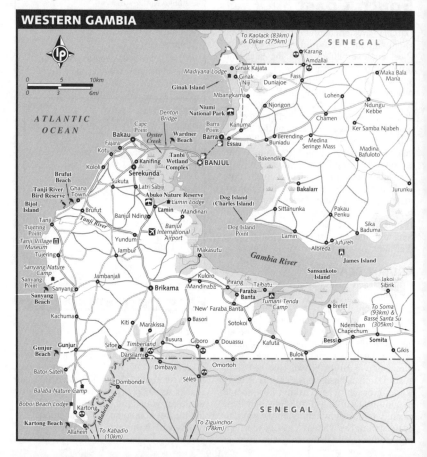

If you're already at Brufut Beach, it's easy enough to walk 2km along the road to the reserve office, signposted on the right (western) side of the road, where you pay your entry fee. Otherwise, stay in the bush taxi from Serekunda and go directly to the office.

TANJI

About 3km south of the reserve office, the road crosses a small bridge to reach the village of Tanji. You can walk through the reserve or along the beach to get to this point. Just south of the bridge is *Nyanya's Safari Lodge* (☎ 394759), which has a few huts for D200 or D250 with bathroom, and serves lunch by the beach, often to tour groups. Opposite Nyanya's is **Pepe's Camel Safaris** (☎ 461083, mobile 994041), from where you can rent a well-groomed dromedary for an unusually comfortable ride along the beach.

About a 15-minute walk inland is the far superior *Paradise Inn Lodge* (☎ 414013, mobile 912559, e paradiseinnlodge@ gamtel.gm), a peaceful place well situated for visits to the bird reserve and other points along the Tanji River. Simple, comfortable rooms with two or four beds in thatched bungalows set in a tropical garden are D260, including breakfast. There are a range of activities available, including jeep trips (D600 per day), boat trips (D90 an hour) and mountain-biking, plus workshops for people interested in dancing, drumming, batik-making or African cooking. Guides will show you around the area, including the local school, for D75 a day, and the lodge's meal of the day is also D75.

At the south end of Tanji Beach are a few local restaurants, with plates of food from D5, including *Merel & Els*, which is just a few tables under a tree. Fresh fish is available, but it's best you order well in advance. The *Suu Berry Beach Bar* at Tujereng Point, about 3km south of Tanji village down a dirt track from the main road, has long been a favourite of expats and bird-watchers, but was closed for renovation when we passed through. Ask in Tanji before heading there.

SANYANG BEACH

The small town of Sanyang is about 20km south of Serekunda. About 4km west is

Tanji Village Museum

On the southern side of Tanji, about 2km from the centre, is the fascinating Tanji Village Museum (☎ 371007, e tanje@dds.nl; admission D25; open 9am-5pm). It was planned, developed and built largely due to the vision of Abdulaye Bayo, who worked for 20 years at the National Museum in Banjul before establishing this museum at Tanji, free of government bureaucracy. Environmental education is part of Gambia's school curriculum so many students come here, but it's also very popular with tourists.

The museum is actually more like an African village. Mud and thatch huts of various designs (according to styles developed by Gambia's different ethnic groups) are spread over a large area and contain displays of traditional artefacts and furniture, with explanations about their use and significance. For example, huts for older men, senior wives and young sons all have different shapes and styles. In the main building there are four displays in a more traditional museum format. In the vegetation section there are local plants with names in Latin, English, Wolof, Mandinka, Serer and Jola. The display of traditional insect repellents might get you thinking about alternatives to DEET. There is a comprehensive collection of traditional instruments which, unlike most museums, are all available to be played. As wear and tear takes its toll on the drums, koras, balafons and simbingo, a small donation is appreciated.

A nature trail winds around the compound and there is an artisan area with woodcarvers, blacksmiths, weavers and others in action. A restaurant sells food and drinks, and there are regular music and dance performances. Mr Bayo has also built a few very simple huts at the back of the museum where visitors can stay, in traditional style of course, for D125 per person, including breakfast.

Sanyang Beach, one of the cleaner beaches on this stretch and a popular destination for day-trippers. Like so many villages on the coast, Sanyang Beach boasts an active fishing fleet and its share of beach bars. Where the road meets the beach you'll find the **Kolokoloto Fish Restaurant**, open 9am to 6pm, where fresh fish and chips is D45 and fish fillets in banana leaves are D70. This place has badly underutilised its location, but goes some way to compensate by selling beer for D12. Further north along the sand is the much larger **Osprey Beach Bar** (☎ 417011), which barbecues whatever fish comes out of the pirogue on the day as well as serving chicken and chips (D70) or lobster (D250), and puts an interesting spin on the local cuisine by serving *benechin Provençale* (a tomato-based version of the traditional rice dish).

During the tourist season, especially around lunch time, this place can be less than idyllic when visitors from the resorts arrive en masse. If you're looking for peace and quiet you might want to head elsewhere.

About 1km inland from the beach is **Sanyang Nature Camp** (☎ 497186, fax 497562), a secluded operation run by the people from Leybato in Fajara. This place will appeal especially to bird-watchers or to anyone who doesn't want to do too much. Comfortable bungalows are spread around a leafy setting and cost D150 per person, with breakfast. The only drawback is the inconsistent water supply.

GUNJUR & GUNJUR BEACH

Gunjur is a small town, about 30km south of Serekunda and about 20km (by road via Sifoe) southwest of Brikama – a long way in feel, if not in actual distance, from the touristy areas near Banjul. On the road from Brikama the scenery changes from green farmland to sandy palm groves and grassy dunes. The road crosses creeks and lagoons, and monkeys can often be seen. It's not all jungle paradise, though, as the road passes through the village of Sifoe, where about 500 refugees live in a camp established for people escaping the fighting in the Casamance region of neighbouring Senegal.

In Gunjur there's a *market*, plus a few shops and a small bar-restaurant. It's more interesting, however, to head west to Gunjur Beach, which is about a 3km walk or a D2 local bush-taxi ride.

At Gunjur Beach there's a lot of activity: boats going in and out, nets being mended and fish being gutted. This is a place to sit quietly and just watch what's going on. If you want to sunbathe, it's best to go along the beach, away from the boats, to get a bit of seclusion and avoid upsetting the locals.

Places to Stay & Eat

About 500m south of the fishing village, and clearly signposted from the road, is the **Gunjur Beach Motel** (☎ 486065, fax 486066). Nicely decorated bungalows have bathroom, netting on the windows and some solar power and cost singles/doubles/triples/quads D170/270/370/470, including a hearty breakfast. Camp sites are D25 per person and D15 per tent, plus D15 per car. The restaurant offers fresh fish dishes from D55, *rösti* (a potato, onion and bacon dish traditionally eaten with fondue) for D60, spaghetti for D55, steaks for D90 and a fondue for D140. Beers are D15. The Swiss manager is a wine specialist, so the list is elaborate, with bottles priced from D150 to D350; unfortunately he has plans to sell and it would probably be a bit much to expect him to leave his vintage cellar behind. Fishing trips can be arranged and a one-way transfer to/from the airport is D200, plus D20 per person.

Cheap food is available in the village. One of the better options is the intriguingly titled **Cardiff South Wales Restaurant**, a basic hang-out for local fishermen, where you can get simple meals for about D10.

The **Balaba Nature Camp** (☎ mobile 919012, fax 486026, W www.tribes.co.uk) is about 5km south of Gunjur Beach along the coast road and 2km in from the coast. This ultra-laid-back camp is set amid dense savanna woodland and prides itself on running as sustainable and environmentally friendly an operation as possible. Activities include courses in drumming, kora playing and African dancing, bird-watching excursions, boat trips and basket weaving. Basic huts with open-air bathrooms and full board cost D165 per person. Look for the yellow sign pointing left off the Kartong Hwy and follow the track.

Getting There & Away
The new coastal road should make it simple to get to Gunjur Beach from Serekunda; ask around at the Serekunda garage. When we passed through, services had not yet begun, so it was still easiest to come in a bush taxi from Brikama (D8), then take a local bush taxi the last 2km to the beach (D2).

KARTONG
Kartong is about 10km south of Gunjur, just north of the border with Senegal. Not much English is spoken in this town, which is made up of a main street with a few small shops, a bar and the market, shaded by a giant tree.

A few kilometres from the village is **Kartong Beach,** used mainly by local fishermen. To get to the beach follow the road south, past the army, police and customs posts, to a fork in the road (2km from the village); keep right and pass through grassy dunes for about 1km to reach the beach. You can swim and sunbathe here, but skimpy clothing in view of the villagers is considered bad form. If you head north up the beach a small way, it's easy enough to find seclusion.

If you go left at the fork, the road meets the Allahein River (also spelt Halahan) marking the border. There's a small harbour here, plus the Kartong Fishing Centre (where fish are sold to wholesalers from Serekunda) and a small ferry that crosses between the Gambian and Senegalese sides of the river.

If you're interested in **bird-watching trips** on foot, Morgan's Grocery (see Places to Stay & Eat) can arrange them for a cost of D100 for a small group, plus D100 per person if a boat is required. This is also a good place to seek directions to the **Kartong Crocodile Pool**. Boboi Beach Lodge (see Places to Stay & Eat) can also arrange bird-watching trips, as well as other activities including horse riding on the beach, mountain biking, boogie-boarding, fishing, boat trips on the Allahein River, and art and music workshops.

Kartong is home to the only legal sand mine in Gambia and the dozens of newly dug holes around this area are fast becoming favourites with birders as they fill with water. There are similar sites north of Kartong, nearer to Boboi Beach Lodge, where laterite was excavated for the new road. Any of these can be easily reached from the road and don't require a guide.

Places to Stay & Eat
Along a dirt road leading west as you enter town is the village-run *Folonko Resthouse* with rooms at D75 per person. There are two rooms available and the friendly manager will cook up local meals for about D50 if you order in advance. Otherwise, you can use the kitchen. There's an outside toilet and shower, and a water tank filled by a windpump. If there's no wind you get a bucket from the well! The resthouse is on a small hill and the veranda overlooks grassy dunes stretching for about 1.5km to the beach. The view is spoilt only by the lorries which come here to fill up with sand for building sites in Banjul and Serekunda.

While the Folonko is near to town, you'd be stupid not to stay at the *Boboi Beach Lodge (fax 486026,* W *www.gambia-adven ture.com)*, on the coast about 2km to the north. With its beautiful beach setting and great food, this ecolodge is one of Gambia's gems. Large tents cost D50 per person, share bungalows D75 and double bungalows D175; management encourages you to haggle – it's more African this way.

For eating, *Morgan's Grocery* is your best bet in town. About 300m west of the village along a sandy track, Morgan's is a shop, bar and restaurant that stands all alone atop a sandy hill from where it's an easy walk to the crocodile pool or Folonko Resthouse. Dishes start at about D20 for simple meals like fish and rice, while beers are D15. The boss, Lamin Morgan Jabang, is always keen to help, and can provide more elaborate dishes to order.

Otherwise, Boboi Beach Lodge serves excellent African dishes, using organically grown ingredients, for about D50, and the chef will prepare Western dishes on demand.

Getting There & Away

Most of the tour companies listed under Organised Tours in Gambia's Getting Around chapter arrange day trips to Kartong for around D400, including lunch.

It used to take independent travellers hours to get from Serekunda to Kartong, meaning few people bothered. This should have changed by the time you read this, with regular bush taxis expected to run between Serekunda garage and Kartong. If masochism is your bag, the old route goes from Brikama to Gunjur (D8) from where a local bush taxi to Kartong is D3.

On the map, Kartong seems like the perfect launch pad for a trip to Casamance, but with no regular transport, no border post and a 10km hike on the Senegal side, this is just an illusion. The police post at the south end of Kartong village is supposed to be able to stamp your passport, but several readers say

Kartong Crocodile Pool

On the edge of Kartong, about 300m southwest of the village along a dirt track, is a small green pool, covered in weeds and water plants, which is home to several crocodiles. For the local people these animals are sacred, and there are similar pools in several other villages, including the well-visited Kachikaly in Bakau. The pool in Kartong is smaller and much quieter and more interesting than Kachikaly, and still sees a steady stream of Senegalese and Gambians who come to bathe in its sacred waters.

It is commonly believed that crocodiles can intercede between the living and the dead, so people come to ask for help – maybe for assistance in growing crops or in finding a job, but mainly for the successful procreation of children. Be warned, though, that you won't see anywhere near the number of crocodiles here as you would at Kachikaly, as several have moved on and now lurk in the newer sand-mining pools. Finding the pool can be difficult, so it's easiest to ask one of the local boys for directions – the pool is known locally as *bambo folonko* (crocodile pool) – you'll probably get a guided tour for a couple of dalasis.

this just doesn't happen, leaving you with some potentially difficult questions to answer in Senegal. If you can get that all-important stamp in Kartong, you can cross the Allahein River border at Kartong Fishing Centre on a small ferry for D2. On the other side, motorised traffic heading south is almost nonexistent, so you'll have to walk about 10km to reach Kabadio, a village on the road between Kafountine and Diouloulou. Once you get to Abéné or Kafountine, you can arrange to have your passport stamped at Séléti without even going there, see the Casamance chapter for details.

The more adventurous might find fishing pirogues going from Kartong straight to Kafountine, and there's even supposed to be a weekly boat between Kartong and Guinea-Bissau.

North Bank

Gambia's north coast is even smaller than its south coast, stretching all of 10km from Barra at the mouth of the Gambia River to the island of Ginak, which marks the border with Senegal. Upriver from Barra are the historical sites of Albreda and James Island, and the world-famous '*Roots*' village of Jufureh.

BARRA

The town of Barra lies on the northern bank of the Gambia River, opposite Banjul, and ferries regularly chug between the two (see Getting There & Away in the Banjul chapter). Most travellers pass through Barra as quickly as they can, taking transport to/from Senegal, and those with an historical interest may want to have a look at **Fort Bullen** *(open 9am-5pm; admission D15)*. Built by the British in the 1820s and 1830s to complement the fort in Bathurst (now Banjul) and to control slave shipping on the Gambia River, the fort was abandoned in the 1870s, but was rearmed briefly during WWII before falling into disuse again. It was renovated in 1996 as part of the Roots Homecoming Festival (see the boxed text 'International Roots Festival' in Gambia's Facts for the Visitor chapter) and is open to visitors. The large, rectangular fort has low round bastions at each corner, and you can walk along the battlements overlooking the river mouth. An informative leaflet on the fort's history is available from Banjul's National Museum.

GINAK ISLAND (NIUMI NATIONAL PARK)

Niumi National Park incorporates a large part of the mainland plus the long narrow island of Ginak (also spelt Jinak), which is separated from the mainland by a narrow creek, and is contiguous with the Parc National du Delta du Saloum in neighbouring Senegal.

A dead-straight border dating from colonial times runs through the island, and its northern section is in Senegalese territory. There are three main villages on the island. The two in Gambia are Ginak Kajata and Ginak Niji, and the one in Senegal is Djinakh Diatako, but the locals are all of the same Mandinka-speaking Serer clan, and ignore the international boundary. This doesn't seem to matter as very few government officials from other countries ever venture onto Ginak. The islanders themselves are fiercely independent and the island has a reputation among other Gambians for harbouring various spirits.

The island has a good range of habitats in a very small area (beach, mud flats, salt marsh, dunes, mangrove swamps, lagoons, grassland and dry woodland), and is very good for bird-watching – especially waders and water birds, but many other species can be seen, including birds of prey. Dolphins are often spotted from the shore, and turtles nest on the beach. The park protects small populations of manatees, crocodiles, clawless otters, hyenas, bushbucks and duikers, plus various monkey species. Tales of leopards occasionally wandering in from the Fathala Forest over the border might be a touch tall.

Places to Stay

Madiyana Lodge (☎ 494088, mobile 920201, fax 495950) Singles/doubles D420/700. On the western side of the island, close to the beach, this place was privately built in close cooperation with the local people and the national park authorities. Quite simply, it's in one of the most beautiful settings anywhere on the whole Gambian coast. The price includes breakfast and dinner.

Accommodation is in stylish brick bungalows, each with private bathroom, lounge and a shady veranda overlooking the sea. There's also a breezy bar-restaurant serving excellent food. You can visit the lodge just for the day on a tour, which costs about D800 per person. This includes a transfer from your hotel, a boat ride across the mouth of the Gambia River from Banjul to Ginak Island (and return), lunch and a tour by boat around the island. If you take this tour and also stay the night, half board (dinner, bed and breakfast) costs D1600 per person.

Not as well located, but a fair bit cheaper, is *Coconut Lodge (☎ 461152, mobile 996905)*, between the villages of Niji and Kajata. This place is about 20 minutes' walk from the beach, and has basic accommodation and, according to one reader, good food.

Getting There & Away

The easiest way to reach Ginak Island is by organised tour. Many large hotels and tour companies along the Atlantic coast offer trips here, although some dub it 'Paradise Island', 'Coconut Island' or 'Treasure Island', just in case Ginak doesn't sound tropical enough. Mercifully, no-one has yet branded it 'Fantasy Island'. The main booking agent for Madiyana is Tropical Tours (see Organised Tours in Gambia's Getting Around chapter), or you could try phoning the lodge direct.

To get there by public transport, cross from Banjul to Barra on the ferry and then take a bush taxi to Ginak Niji. The fare is D15, but there's only one or two trips a day, so you'll probably have to hire a yellow taxi to take you there, which will cost D80. In either kind of taxi, or in your own car, you take the main road north for a few kilometres to the village of Kanuma, then turn left and follow the sandy track northwest to reach the lagoon opposite the village of Ginak Niji. A place in a dugout canoe across to the island costs D3, and from the village it's a 20-minute walk directly west across the island to reach the lodge. If you need a guide, ask any small

THE GAMBIA

boy in the village to show you the way (the fee should be around D5).

JUFUREH & ALBREDA

Jufureh (formerly spelt Juffure, and today also spelt Juffereh) is a small village on the northern bank of the Gambia River about 25km upstream from Barra. It became world famous in the 1970s following the publication of *Roots*, in which African-American writer Alex Haley describes how Kunta Kinte, his ancestor, was captured here and taken as a slave to America some 200 years ago. Today Jufureh is still a tourist trap, as it's easily reached from Banjul, although it's not as busy as it was in the 1980s when Haley's book was still fresh.

Jufureh itself is nothing out of the ordinary – like hundreds of other villages along the Gambia River – but when the daily groups of tourists arrive things leap into action. Women pound millet at strategic points, babies are produced to be admired and filmed, the artisans in the (better-than-average) craft market crank into gear, and an old lady called Binde Kinte (a descendant of Alex Haley's own forebear) makes a guest appearance at her compound. Photos are displayed of Alex Haley and Binde (Haley paid to have the village connected to the water and electricity supplies), and of the griot who first told Haley the story of his family. There's even a photo of Kunta Kinte, but on closer inspection it turns out to be an actor who played him. Tourists give money to take photos of the photos.

Albreda village is very close to Jufureh (a 500m walk) and usually visited at the same time. It's a peaceful place, with huts and houses between baobabs, palms and silk-cotton trees. The main thing to see here is the ruined 'factory' (fortified slaving station) originally built by French traders in the late 17th century. It's on the river's edge near the quay where the tour boats land. Nearby is a large British **cannon** dating from the same period.

Between Jufureh and Albreda is a small **museum** (☎ 710276; admission D25; open 10am-5pm, Mon-Sat) with a simple but striking exhibition tracing the history of

The *Roots* Debate

Alex Haley based his research for his novel *Roots* on recollections of elder relatives who knew their African forebear's name was Kinte and that he'd been captured by slavers while chopping wood for a drum outside his village. This later tied in with a story Haley was told by a griot at Jufureh.

Critics have pointed out (quite reasonably) that the story is flawed in many areas. Kinte is a common clan name throughout West Africa, and the griot's story of Kunta Kinte's capture would hardly have been unique. Also, as the slave stations of Albreda and James Island had been very close to Jufureh for some decades, it's unlikely that a villager from here would have been taken by surprise in this way. While the story of Alex Haley's ancestor is almost certainly true, it's exceedingly unlikely that he actually came from Jufureh. Despite the inconsistencies, Haley seemed happy to believe he was descended from the Kintes of Jufureh, and the myth remains largely intact.

Detractors may delight in exposing fabrication, but there is a danger that the debate on the accuracy of Haley's story may obscure a much more serious, and undeniable, fact: the slave trade was immoral and inhuman, and had a devastating effect on Africa. Millions of men and women were captured by European traders, or by other Africans paid by Europeans, and taken to plantations in the Americas. Many historians also hold that their labour, and the slave trade itself, was fundamental to the economic development of Europe and the USA in the 18th and 19th centuries, an assertion that was being tested in court in the USA when this book went to print.

slavery on the Gambia River. One of the many quotations displayed around the walls includes the following from an unnamed 18th-century slaver operating from Albreda or nearby James Island:

The Negroes are so willful and loth to leave their own country that they have often leaped out of the canoes, boat and ship, and kept under water till they were drowned, to avoid being taken.

Places to Stay & Eat

Behind the museum in Albreda is the *Home at Last Motel* which has cheap and clean singles/doubles for D80/D100, and food if you order far enough in advance. The *Jufureh Resthouse* (☎ 398439 ask for Amadou, mobile 907065) is more lively, with drumming lessons for just D50, if you call ahead. Facilities here are a bit run-down, but it's hard to argue with the prices (singles/doubles for D25/50, full board for D125).

On the square are the *Rising Sun Restaurant*, which is home to freelance 'guides' and uninspiring meals for D40 to D60, and *Mary's Restaurant*, where larger-than-life Mary Sawyer serves very hearty traditional meals for D25.

Getting There & Away

The usual (and easiest) way to visit Jufureh and Albreda is by tourist boat (see Organised Tours in Gambia's Getting There & Away chapter). Alternatively, take the ferry across to Barra, dodge the touts who try to get you into a private taxi and find a shared taxi to Jufureh, which costs D15. There are only a few vehicles per day on this route, so if you want to do the trip in a day, you'll have to catch the first ferry. But if you're making the effort to come all this way, you should consider staying overnight; both Jufureh and Albreda are at their best in the evening, when the tourist groups have left.

If you're flush for cash or can get a group together, try hiring a pirogue from behind the Albert Market in Banjul to take in Jufureh, Albreda and James Island before returning to Banjul. If you bargain well with the 'agent' on the beach in Banjul you'll get a 10-seater pirogue for six hours for D1100, including petrol. Don't forget your hat and sunscreen.

JAMES ISLAND

James Island is in the middle of the Gambia River, about 2km south of Jufureh and Albreda. On the island are the remains of **Fort James**, built in the 1650s and the site of numerous skirmishes in the following centuries. The fort was held variously by British, French and Dutch traders and a couple of privateers (pirates) during this

time, and was completely destroyed at least three times (twice by the French, and once by accident when a gunpowder store exploded). It was used as a slave collection point by British traders until slaving was outlawed, and was finally abandoned in 1829 when the British built a new fort at Bathurst on Banjul Island.

Today, the ruins of the fort are quite extensive, although the only intact room is a food store, which is often called the slave dungeon because it sounds more interesting. The island is rapidly being eroded, and at some points the water is lapping around the battlements. Only the sturdy baobab trees seem to be holding the island together. An excellent illustrated leaflet on the fort is available from the museum in Albreda for D15.

Most people take in James Island as part of a boat trip from Banjul to Jufureh, but you might be able to arrange a pirogue to take you over from Albreda, especially if you stay overnight in the village.

Lamin, Abuko, Brikama & Darsilami

Lamin is a village on the main road southeast of Serekunda, near Banjul International Airport. It's unremarkable in itself, but has two popular attractions nearby: Abuko Nature Reserve and Lamin Lodge. A few kilometres further south is Brikama, the first 'upcountry' town reached on the route to the interior. And if you're heading to Casamance the border town of Darsilami makes a peaceful stop.

LAMIN LODGE

Lamin is a very popular male name in Gambia (in Mandinka society it means simply 'first-born son') and this village is one of many with the name. About 3km east of Lamin village is *Lamin Lodge* (☎ 497603, mobile 900231, fax 495526, e gamriv@ gamtel.gm), a unique restaurant built on stilts overlooking a mangrove creek. The lodge is open from 7am to 8pm and is a favourite with groups on their 'birds-and-breakfast' trip – the surrounding swamps and rice fields are great for bird-watching or strolling around.

The restaurant is built entirely of wood; it's like a cross between a ship and a log cabin. The upstairs 'watchtower' has excellent views. The whole place creaks in high winds, and any coins you drop go straight through gaps in the floor into the water.

Snacks include oysters from the surrounding mangroves for D30, a larger meal of Gambian-style fish and rice (D55), shrimps (D60) and the 'elephant ear' (D70). The fish buffet has to be ordered in advance, as does the special breakfast (D60).

You can hire small motorboats (D250 per hour) or go out in a canoe with a paddler for D100 an hour. A motorboat ride to Banjul costs D300, and to Denton Bridge, on the main road west of Banjul city centre, it's D350.

Lunch times are often busy in the tourist season, so you might consider coming here in the late afternoon for a gentle boat ride through the mangroves followed by a beer at sunset in the lodge.

Getting There & Away

Lamin Lodge can be reached from the Atlantic coast resorts by private taxi (D150/D270 one way/return), or combine Lamin Lodge with time at Abuko for D300. Alternatively, from Banjul or Serekunda you can take any minibus towards Brikama, get off in Lamin village and then follow the dirt road for about 3km to the lodge. Look for the small sign. A good day trip is to combine visits to Lamin Lodge and Abuko Nature Reserve, going out by road and returning by boat.

ABUKO NATURE RESERVE

Size matters in the world of African national parks and nature reserves. The best parks are usually vast affairs with grand 'game' and fleets of 4WDs (and even planes) to chauffer visitors around. With a reputation as one of the best places to view plant and animal life anywhere in West Africa, it's remarkable that this nature reserve (☎ 472888, e wildlife@gamtel.gm; open 8am-7pm daily; admission D31.50) has no roads and that you can walk from one end to the other in less than an hour.

Abuko covers an area of just 105 hectares, less than one-8000th the size of Senegal's main national park, Niokolo-Koba. But within the high wire fences that surround Abuko are myriad species of flora and fauna. The Lamin Stream runs through part of the reserve and is integral in attracting many of the more than 250 bird species regularly seen in the reserve, making Abuko one of the best places in West Africa for bird-watching.

Birds to excite most twitchers include collared sunbirds, green hylia, African goshawks, oriole warblers and yellowbills. Although green turacos, white-spotted flufftails, ahanta francolins and western bluebills are all at the northern edge of their distribution, this is still among the best places in Gambia to see them.

The reserve is also famous for three monkey types: green or vervet monkeys, endangered western red colobus monkeys, and patas monkeys, or red patas monkeys.

It also hosts about 20 Nile crocodiles. Unlike those found in the various sacred pools (such as Kachikaly at Bakau), the crocodiles of Abuko are completely wild. There is no artificial feeding – they survive on whatever birds, fish, turtles, mammals and smaller creatures they're quick enough to get their teeth around. Take care, though, these guys are not used to being patted like Charley and co at Kachikaly.

Among the 52 mammal species calling Abuko home are bushbucks, duikers, porcupines, bushbabies and ground squirrels. Among the 37 species of reptiles are an impressive array of snakes that include pythons, puff adders, green mambas and forest cobras. They can sometimes be seen sunning themselves on the paths, but usually make for the undergrowth at the slightest approach – since the park's establishment, no visitor has been bitten by a snake.

Assuming that the mamba you've spied does decamp into the bush, it could be sliding off underneath any one of more than 115 species of plants, many of which are labelled.

At the far end of Abuko is a small animal orphanage. Most of the animals staying here will be returned to the wild when ready, but there are also a few permanent residents including hyenas, lions and various monkeys.

Information
To avoid the heat, most people come here for a couple of hours in the mid-morning or mid-afternoon. Birders go in the early morning or late afternoon when the birds are more active, and this is undoubtedly the best time if you're a keen spotter – the gate opens at 6.30am for bird-watchers. Most of the hides face west, which is another good reason to come in the morning; in the evening you're looking into the sun. If you come in the evening it's best to walk straight to the animal pens at the end of the reserve then come back slowly with the sun behind you.

The quietest time to visit is the middle of the day. Although it's quite hot, the vegetation provides plenty of shade, and this is a very good time to enjoy being in the forest. To follow the longest trails takes about two hours, but there are a couple of shorter options indicated on the map at the main entrance gate.

A thin book about the reserve can be bought at the ticket office for D35. There is also information (and a great deck for viewing the main pool) at the education centre inside the entrance to the park, but while this opens at 8am it's not unusual for it to be deserted by 3.30pm.

Places to Stay & Eat
Most people come to Abuko as part of a day trip. But if you're really keen you might chose to stay at *African Zoo Rest & Lodge* (☎ 473414) opposite the reserve's entrance. Basic but quite clean rooms with shared

Reflecting on Legends

Abuko has a long and entertaining history steeped in the lore of local legends.

Lamin Stream was originally a source of water for nearby villages and for generations the home of several crocodiles. It is seen locally as representing good spirits, with power to intercede with ancestors and improve men's and women's fertility.

Its history as a protected area began around 1915 when the stream was tapped by a British colonial official to supply the growing settlement of Banjul. Local legend has it that the villagers were unhappy with this turn of events, mainly because they believed that, along with the crocodiles, a malevolent spirit or 'dragon' lived in one of the largest pools and would become angry at the intrusion. When a watchman guarding the early waterworks inexplicably died, their worst fears were confirmed.

The colonial official acted fast, and asked his superiors to send from London a large mirror, which he set up by the side of the pool. The story goes that the dragon came out of the pool, saw

According to Gambian legend, dragons were malevolent spirits

its reflection and was scared off, never to be seen again. The colonials got their water supply, and the locals could now safely use the stream for traditional ceremonies. It seems everyone was happy. Except the dragon.

As a water source Abuko received some protection, but it wasn't until 1968 that Eddie Brewer, an active conservationist and then director of Gambia's Wildlife Conservation Department, was able to convince the government to set aside part of the area as a nature reserve. A further area of savanna forest – the bird extension at the far end of the reserve – was added in 1978.

THE GAMBIA

bathroom cost D150/200 with breakfast, and the restaurant serves *afra* (grilled meat with onions and spices). Opposite is *Mado's Bar & Grill House*, which also serves afra and other cheap local dishes.

Getting There & Away

A private taxi to Abuko from the Atlantic coast resorts costs about D220, including two hours of waiting time. Alternatively, take a minibus from Serekunda towards Brikama (D3). The reserve entrance is on the right (west) of the main road (you pass the exit about 200m before reaching the entrance).

BRIKAMA

Brikama is Gambia's third-largest settlement, and the first proper 'upcountry' town you reach going inland from Banjul and the coast. The main road bypasses the town, so you could pass it without even noticing. If you're going to/from the south coast or Ziguinchor in Senegal by bush taxi, you might have to change here.

The main reason visitors come to Brikama is the famous **Craft Market** (also known as Woodcarvers' Market) at the edge of town on the right as you come in from Banjul or Serekunda. It's a very popular stopping-off point for tourist groups from the large hotels, and while it does have a few guys bashing out souvenir-quality carvings, most of the stalls just sell items that have been made elsewhere. What's more, there are far too many stalls (all selling the same kind of stuff) and far too many eager salesmen. In short – a lot of tat and a lot of hassle.

Trust Bank has a branch near the town centre and the neighbouring Gamtel office has the town's only Internet bureau.

Places to Stay & Eat

There are only two places to stay, and luxurious they definitely are not. More restaurant than hotel, *Domor Deema* (☎ 903302) is on Mosque Rd about 300m from the taxi park. The four basic rooms are D100 each, and the chatty manageress serves food all day – about D20 for a plate of *benechin* (rice baked in a thick sauce of

fish and vegetables) or *domodah* (meat or vegetables with groundnut sauce).

The other option is a private *guesthouse* belonging to AFET (a local organisation) and intended for their staff. However, tourists are also welcome and pay D100 per night. To make arrangements, go first to the AFET office (☎ 484611) near the hospital. The organisation's president, a Mr Gassama, is friendly and can help with local information.

For eating, you could try the *Red Cross Restaurant* (☎ 484471), open 8am to midnight, and next door, funnily enough, to the Red Cross office. A mix of West African dishes are D15 each.

A good place to seek respite from the constant greetings of 'hello boss man' in the craft market is the *Bantang Bantaba* (☎ 484853), open December to May. On your right as you head out on the new Sanyang Rd, this peaceful place is part of the Methodist mission and serves excellent sandwiches for D15 to 25. It also sells a range of top-notch jams, mustards and a famous hot sauce, all made from produce grown on site.

Getting There & Away

Brikama is easily reached by public transport, as minibuses go up and down the main road between Banjul and Brikama, via Serekunda, about once every ten minutes during the day. See the Banjul and Atlantic Coast Resorts & Serekunda chapters for fares.

Onwards from Brikama, you can reach Gunjur and change for Kartong. If you're heading upcountry, the GPTC buses all stop in Brikama, but are often full, so you'll probably have to get a minibus as far as Soma (D35) and change there. From Brikama you can also get transport to Ziguinchor and Kafountine in Senegal (see Gambia's Getting There & Away chapter for details).

DARSILAMI

The tiny border village of Darsilami sees only the occasional tourist en route to Kafountine in Casamance. Apart from the small border post (usually a man sitting on a chair) there is really not much here. But at the edge of the village a Dutch-Gambian couple have built *Timberland* (☎ 484704, *fax 484100,* [e] *wioster@hotmail.com),* a traditional thatched roundhouse where the focus is on African living. There's a squat toilet, basic washing facilities and, unless otherwise requested, African food. A bed is D75, breakfast is D30, lunch D45 and dinner D60. The phone numbers listed are for Darsilami's telecentre, so be sure to ask clearly for Willemina or Tabo. From mid-May to early November Willemina can be contacted in the Netherlands on ☎ 20-623 06 49.

MAKASUTU

Makasutu means 'sacred forest' in Mandinka and after ten years of effort by a couple of wandering souls from Britain it has developed into one of the most complete, and popular, ecotourism sites in Gambia. Not far outside Brikama, the ***Makasutu Culture Forest*** (☎ *483335,* [e] *makasutu@hotmail.com*) occupies about 1000 hectares of land along Mandina Bolong. A day in the forest costs D320 and includes a large lunch, a demonstration of traditional dancing, a mangrove tour by pirogue, and guided walks through a range of habitats, including a palm forest where you can watch palm wine being tapped, and then taste the nectar. Even if you're not interested in wildlife it's worth a trip just to admire the stunning 'fusion' architecture and original artworks. Most people come on a tour arranged through one of the ground operators, but if you're making your own way to Brikama, then either take a yellow taxi for about D50, or ask a bush taxi to drop you at Tuti Falls Rd (D2) and walk the last 3km. In line with Makasutu's policy of subtlety and harmony with the environment, there are no signs pointing to the forest, but you'll know you're on the right track if, coming from Brikama, you turn left on a road that is sealed for the first few hundred metres (it leads to the president's ex-wife's compound).

For those with money to spend it is possible to stay at Makasutu. While founders James (who has visited almost 200 countries) and Lawrence originally planned to open a place aimed at backpackers, the accommodation they have created is rather more luxurious than your average budget lodgings. The stunning site was designed by Lawrence, an architect, and is hidden away in the mangroves at the far end of the forest. Building had almost finished when we visited and is expected to include five luxurious floating rooms, a bar, an intimate dining area, a riverside terrace and *bantaba* (communal meeting point) spread around the grand centrepiece – a pool with a central bar and decorated with Turkish mosaics. Rates weren't available, but you can safely assume you'll pay for what you get. For details contact Makasutu direct or the Safari Garden Hotel in Fajara (see the Atlantic Coast Resorts & Serekunda chapter).

TUMANI TENDA CAMP

The ***Tumani Tenda camp*** (☎ *mobile 903662,* [e] *tumanitenda@hotmail.com*) is another ecotourism venture situated about an hour from the coast on a *bolong* (creek) near the Gambia River. It's owned and operated by the residents of the neighbouring Taibatu village, who use the profits to fund community projects within the village. There are five traditional-style huts, each maintained by a different family from the village, where you can stay for D100 per person including breakfast. Other meals are D30. This is basic living, but for a taste of village life in a great location it's hard to beat.

Take a bush taxi from Brikama (D7) and ask to be dropped off at the turn-off to Taibatu (look for the sign). From here it's a 2.5km walk.

Central & Eastern Gambia

As you head east from Brikama, past the turn-offs to Makasutu and Tumani Tenda, you slowly enter the real and remote 'upcountry Gambia'. The main road becomes surprisingly quiet as it winds through crop fields, rice paddies, palm groves and patches of natural forest. Every 10km or so there's a junction where a dirt track leads north towards the Gambia River, which is never far away, but always frustratingly out of view. There are a few villages along the road; some no more than a couple of huts, some a bit bigger with facilities such as shops, clinic, Gamtel office and maybe even a petrol station.

The road is surfaced in too few places – large sections are so badly potholed that all but the big GPTC buses eschew the road and seek smoother passage on the dirt beside. And this is the main vehicle artery for the country! Traffic is limited to a few private cars and tour buses, plus bush taxis that veer alarmingly in vain attempts to avoid the potholes. This general lack of traffic is good news for cyclists, several of whom have reported this route to be fun, rewarding and fairly safe.

Places in this section are described west to east.

Central Gambia

BINTANG BOLONG

Bintang Bolong is a large, meandering tributary of the Gambia River that rises in Senegal and joins the river about 50km upstream from Banjul. (In the Mandinka language, *bolong* means river, but when used among English speakers the term has come to mean a stream or creek.) Bintang Bolong is tidal and its banks are lined with mangroves.

Bintang Bolong Lodge (☎ *488055, fax 488058*) Huts D150 per person. About 10km upstream from the Gambia River and 3km off the main road at Bintang village, this stunningly located lodge was once popular with tourists from the coast, but has experienced a

Highlights

- Take a pirogue from Tendaba to the labyrinth of mangroves in the Baobalong Wetland Reserve

- Follow in the footsteps of history old and new at Georgetown (Jangjang-bureh), where relics of African and European cultures tell very different stories

- Shop at a market or drink palm wine with the boys in Basse Santa Su, the liveliest of Gambia's upcountry towns

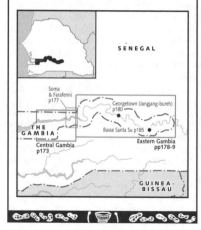

steep fall from grace in recent years. Two thatch-and-reed cottages are still in good order, but the rest are steadily sinking into the mud and make a sorry site. The pool looked like a crocodile-and-mosquito breeding ground when we passed. However, there is a pleasant restaurant, built among the mangroves, which sells decent food and cold beer, and you can hire pirogues for D150 an hour.

Getting There & Away

If you're driving from Banjul follow the main road east through the village of Somita, and at Killy turn left (north) along the dirt road to reach Bintang village and the lodge.

By public transport, if you can't get dropped off at Killy, go to Sibanor (about 3km beyond Killy) from where a bush taxi goes about three times a day to Bintang via Killy.

BWIAM

Bwiam is a small village on the main road about 20km after Killy village. Some maps mark a feature called the Iron Pot and give it 'place of interest' status but, unless you have your own wheels and a penchant for small and obscure traditional monuments, a visit here is not worth the bother. The pot, a semispherical metal object, sticks about half a metre out of the ground and local people claim it is impossible to move, although nobody seems to know its significance. If you're determined, it's about 2km off the main road, near the school.

Much more interesting is **St Joseph's Family Farm Centre** (*☎/fax 489050*), a project that helps local people increase food security, with an emphasis on adapting and improving existing agricultural practices so they incur no expense and the environment is not degraded. The centre tries to encourage use of pesticides produced from existing plants (rather than chemical imports) and offers advice on food preservation so supplies last long after harvest. Much of their work is with local women, as they are the main subsistence farmers in the Gambia. Visitors are welcome.

KANILAI

Kanilai is a small village near the Senegalese border, notable mainly because it is the home-town of President Jammeh. For this reason it is also the location of **Sindola Safari Lodge** (*☎ 483415/6, fax 483413, e kairaba@gamtel.gm*), the latest enterprise of President Jammeh, who also controls the Kairaba Hotel. Sindola is a luxury lodge aimed at attracting guests for a couple of nights away from the Atlantic coast resorts. Facilities include a pool, tennis court

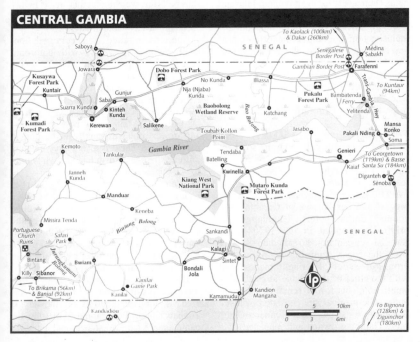

CENTRAL GAMBIA

Elephants in Gambia?

Visitors to West Africa have long bemoaned the lack of the big and exciting mammals found in the east and south of the continent – their days of moaning may soon be over. The **safari park**, a huge area between Bintang Bolong in the north and Jurungkumani Bolong (and a large electric fence) in the south, is set to bring big game several flying hours closer to Europe, and Europeans. The park's owners, believed to be associates of President Jammeh, plan to stock it with elephants, rhinos, big cats and a range of antelopes. The animals are currently cooling their heels in Kanilai Game Park pending the completion of the park. These include zebras, kudus, elands, impalas, wildebeests and blesboks – none of which are native to West Africa. Nevertheless it will certainly be exciting to see elephants, once Gambia's national animal, back in the country for the first time since being hunted out in 1913.

and a classy restaurant. Accommodation is in 40 very well-equipped huts, with singles/doubles at US$40/53 for a standard hut, and US$73/80 for a suite, with rates lower during summer. Sindola has been designed with the new safari park (see the boxed text 'Elephants in Gambia') in mind. Until the safari park is finished a range of animals is being kept at **Kanilai Game Park** adjoining Sindola. There are walking, mountain-bike and viewing trails through the park.

To get there, you could take an all-inclusive tour from the Kairaba Hotel, or if you only want to go for the day a taxi tour should cost you about D500. On public transport, take a bush taxi from Brikama (D30) and get off at the police checkpoint where the highway and the road to Kanilai meet. Kanilai is 6km further south.

TENDABA

Tendaba is a small village on the southern bank of the Gambia River, 165km upstream from Banjul. The village is dominated by *Tendaba Camp* (☎ 541024, fax 541030, ℮ tendaba@qanet.gm), one of the biggest and best known of Gambia's up-country tourist hotels. The camp was originally founded in the 1970s by a Swedish sea captain who sailed up the river from the coast, returning regularly with groups of visitors. He finally made a deal with the chief of the village to establish a small hotel here, and remains a regular guest. The original site consisted of just a few basic huts, but today Tendaba Camp (now Gambian owned and managed) is a

large place catering for at least 150 people, with bungalows closely packed together in the grounds. There's also a restaurant, swimming pool and a pleasant bar on a jetty overlooking the river – ideal for a sunset drink, before the mossies arrive.

Tendaba's attraction is its excellent position as a base for visiting Kiang West National Park and the Baobolong Wetland Reserve. Bird-watching in this area is highly recommended, and most birding groups will spend at least a couple of days here.

There is a range of accommodation: small bungalows without/with bathroom cost D150/165 per person, and VIP rooms with TV cost D180. The best VIP rooms (which also have small verandas) are on the river's edge. In the *restaurant*, an early buffet breakfast is D50 and snacks are from D20 to D40. Main meals cost about D60 and are very good, especially the bushpig in pepper sauce. There is also a large evening buffet, where each dish has its own waiter, for D100.

From Tendaba an excursion by 4WD to Kiang West costs D100 per person (with a minimum of six people). Boat rides around the creeks of the Baobolong Wetland Reserve are the same price (with a minimum of four). On tours, you get a guide, but they are not especially well trained, so keen birders should not expect too much.

If you don't want to take a vehicle trip, there are lots of options for walking in this area. A good destination for the day is Toubab Kollon Point about 7km from the camp (see Kiang West National Park for details). Otherwise, keep an eye out for 'Tendaba Airport', a mud flat marked by a wooden bench that's about as far from the vast concrete halls of Heathrow as you can imagine. But it obviously has a caretaker with ambition, or a good sense of humour – the sign standing above the rickety wooden bench reads 'Tendaba: Terminal 3'.

On some evenings, dance shows are arranged, but this is not the usual professional troupe in traditional costume that you might see in the coastal hotels. Instead, the camp invites people from the nearby village, then provides a fire and some drummers, and maybe some refreshments. There's no timetable and no programme, just people having a good time in their own way. You'll see some women taking it in turn to dance wildly, while others with babies on their backs move around more gently. Kids lark around on the edge of the circle, while old men just sit watching or chewing the cud. It may be quite a short 'show', but if the atmosphere is right they can go on for hours, long after most tourists have gone to bed.

Getting There & Away

Most people come to Tendaba Camp as part of a tour. Two-day excursions from one of the Atlantic coast hotels cost from D900 to D1200 per person, including transport, accommodation, food and side trips.

Another option is to come by green tourist taxi (about D800 to D1000 for the car, carrying up to four people) and pay for your own room, food and day trips directly to the camp (for more details on taxis see Organised Tours in Gambia's Getting Around chapter).

For independent travellers on public transport, take a bus or bush taxi from Banjul or Serekunda along the main road towards Soma. Get off at the village of Kwinella, from where the camp (signposted) is 5km north along the dirt road. There are no regular minibuses, but Saja Touray, the camp manager, promises to collect anyone from Kwinella for free. If he doesn't show up, you will probably have to thumb a lift or walk. We heard from some travellers who were offered a donkey and cart by an enterprising local. The cart carried their packs, while they enjoyed the walk.

KIANG WEST NATIONAL PARK

South of the river, and to the west of Tendaba Camp, Kiang West National Park is one of the largest protected areas in Gambia, and boasts its largest and most diverse animal population. Habitats include mangrove creeks and mud flats (the river is still tidal this far upstream), plus large areas of dry woodland and grassland. A major natural feature is an escarpment, which runs parallel to the river bank. We're not talking Rift Valley here, but even 20m is significant in a country as flat as Gambia, and from this high point you can look over the narrow plain between the escarpment foot and the river itself. Animals are often seen here, especially at the three water holes.

Mammals most frequently observed include baboons, colobus monkeys, warthogs, marsh mongooses and bushbucks. An antelope that you may see is the roan – a large and horse-like animal (hence the name) that migrates into the area from Casamance. Making very rare appearances are sitatungas, a larger relative of the bushbuck. They are aquatic and adept at swimming and moving through river vegetation on their wide hooves.

Other rarely sighted species include hyenas, leopards, manatees, dolphins and crocodiles. Birds are also plentiful, with more than 300 species recorded, including 21 raptors (the most impressive are martial eagles and bateleurs), and some rarer birds such as brown-necked parrots – the guides usually know the best places to see them.

A popular place for viewing is **Toubab Kollon Point**, a river promontory to the northeast of the park. Behind the point, the escarpment runs close to the river bank, and 2km west is a viewing hide overlooking a water hole, which attracts a good range of animals, especially in the dry season – November to January are the best months to visit, but wear pants to avoid being bitten by tsetse flies. Entry is D31.50, although this is included in the price of tours from Tendaba.

BAOBOLONG WETLAND RESERVE

A tributary of the Gambia River, Bao Bolong rises in Senegal and enters the main river on the northern side, upstream from Tendaba. It contains several other bolongs, as well as mangroves and salt marshes, which together with the surrounding dry savanna woodland and grassland make this a reserve of international importance. Baobolong (also spelt Baobolon) is a Ramsar (the international wetlands convention) site.

The mangroves in this area are some of the largest in the region, growing over 20m high in places and becoming a virtual forest. Birds are a major attraction for visitors and this is a good place to see rare Pel's fishing owls, white-backed night herons and mouse-brown sunbirds. The reserve also protects various aquatic mammal species, such as manatees, clawless otters and sitatungas.

The best way to experience this wonderful maze of islands and waterways is by boat, which is most easily arranged at Tendaba Camp (see Tendaba earlier in this chapter).

SOMA & MANSA KONKO

Soma is a junction town where the main road crosses the Trans-Gambia Hwy, and where you change transport if you're head-ing upcountry by bush taxi. Soma is a dusty, flyblown place, with the main street full of trucks and rubbish, and nothing in the way of attractions. The border is only a few kilometres to the south, and the Gambian customs and immigration post is on the eastern edge of town. About 10km north of Soma is Yelitenda, where you catch the ferry across the Gambia River to Bambatenda, and then continue to Farafenni.

Near Soma is Mansa Konko, originally an important local chief's capital (the name means 'king's hill'), and then an administrative centre during the colonial era. Today it's a sleepy ghost town with a few reminders of the glory days, such as the district commissioner's residence and the crumbling colonial villa, which now houses a team of Cuban doctors (old capitalist colonialists would be turning in their graves).

Places to Stay & Eat

If you get stuck in Soma, the lively *Moses Motel* (☎ *531462*) on the north side of the main junction is the best option. Rooms without/with bathroom are D60/100 per person.

On the road north to Farafenni you go through a town called Pakali Nding, which is home to what looks like a bungalow farm but is actually the *Trans Gambia Motel*

Baobolong Wetland Reserve is a great place to spot a rare bird or two, but don't forget to bring a quality pair of binoculars

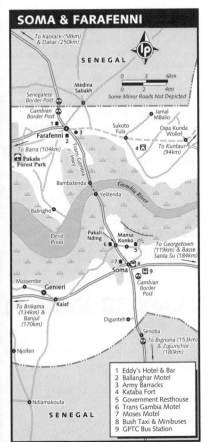

SOMA & FARAFENNI

To Kaolack (58km)
& Dakar (250km)

SENEGAL

Médina
Sabakh

Senegalese
Border Post

Gambian
Border Post

Farafenni

To Barra (104km)

Pakala
Forest Park

0   3   6km
0   2   4mi
Some Minor Roads Not Depicted

Jamal
MBallo

Sukoto
Fula

Dipa Kunda
Wollof

To Kuntaur
(94km)

Trans-Gambia Hwy

Bambatenda

Yelitenda

Gambia River

Balingho

Devil
Point

Pakali
Nding

Mansa
Konko

To Georgetown
(119km) & Basse
Santa Su (184km)

Soma

Gambian
Border
Post

Massembe

Genieri

Kaiaf

To Brikama
(134km) &
Banjul
(170km)

Diganteh

Sénoba

To Bignona (153km)
& Ziguinchor
(180km)

Njolfen

Ndiamakouta

SENEGAL

1 Eddy's Hotel & Bar
2 Ballanghar Motel
3 Army Barracks
4 Kataba Fort
5 Government Resthouse
6 Trans Gambia Motel
7 Moses Motel
8 Bush Taxi & Minibuses
9 GPTC Bus Station

(☎ 531402). Sparkling-clean rooms are great value at D30 per person or D100 for a room with bathroom. At the motel there's a good chance you'll end up eating with the owner's family, otherwise you'll probably have to head to Soma, where basic bars and chop stalls abound around the taxi park.

In Mansa Konko itself the *Government Resthouse* is 2.5km from the main road and officially for government staff only, but you can stay in the clean singles/doubles for D100/150. Just up the road is the old district commissioner's residence. This is the highest point for several miles around, with

some fine views over the Gambia River valley, and is also where to go if there's no-one around at the resthouse.

Getting There & Away
Buses between Banjul or Serekunda and Basse Santa Su (see Getting There & Away in the Banjul chapter for details) usually stop for about half an hour at the GPTC compound at the east end of Soma, where you can stretch your legs, buy a snack, or marvel at the large flock of scabby vultures that survive off the detritus discarded by passengers.

Most minibuses and bush taxis from Serekunda terminate at the bush-taxi park in the centre of Soma (the fare is D35) or go onto Farafenni (D40). Transport to Georgetown (D30) and Basse Santa Su (D35) leaves from the taxi park in Soma's town centre. If you're heading south, you can also get bush taxis from the border to Bignona and Ziguinchor in southern Senegal. If you're heading north from Soma, take a local bush taxi to the Gambia River ferry at Yelitenda (D3), go across as a foot passenger (D3), and take one of the vehicles waiting on the northern bank at Bambatenda to Farafenni (D3), where you can find transport to Kaolack or Dakar.

The ferry operates between 9am and 9pm, usually every half-hour, though you could wait a lot longer. If you're on foot, pirogues run much more often, charge D2 and leave when full. A whole pirogue should cost about D30. If you're driving, the ferry costs D50 for a normal car and D65 for a 4WD. You'll probably have to wait a while for a place on the ferry, but it's not as bad as the Banjul to Barra ferry. For truck drivers the waits can be interminable – a Senegalese driver at the front of the queue told us he'd been waiting for four days.

FARAFENNI
Farafenni is on the Trans-Gambia Hwy north of the Gambia River. It's a busy little town, and much more pleasant than Soma. The main *lumo* (weekly market) is on Sunday, when people come from surrounding villages, and merchants come from as far as Mauritania and Guinea to sell their wares.

THE GAMBIA

This is a good place to sample upcountry life, although it feels more like Senegal than Gambia: CFA is used more than the dalasi, and more French than English is spoken. If you're low on cash visit the Trust Bank; it's the only bank for many miles. The border with Senegal is only 2km to the north and is open from 7am to midnight.

Places to Stay & Eat

Eddy's Hotel & Bar (☎ 735225) Singles/doubles with bathroom D150/200. This place has been a popular travellers' meeting point for many years. You can eat chicken and chips or *benechin* (rice in a thick sauce of meat and vegetables) for D35 to D45 in the shady garden courtyard while the apparently carefree Eddy shoots (unsuccessfully) at small birds with an air gun. Self-contained rooms come with either double beds or two beds; air-conditioning is an extra D50. There's also safe parking, cold beer and a disco at weekends.

Ballanghar Motel (☎ 735431) Singles/doubles D80/125. Just north of the barracks and two blocks back from the main road, this quiet place has simple but good-value rooms with bathroom. For cheap food, there are several *chop houses* on the main street heading south from the junction. *Sunu Yai (☎ 735597)*, open 8am to midnight, is one such, with palm-oil stew and bean stew for D25, plus a variety of more mundane and tardy 'fast food'.

Getting There & Away

If you're heading for Banjul, direct minibuses from Farafenni go to Serekunda most mornings for D40. If you're heading south or anywhere upcountry on the southern bank, you have to go to Soma and change. If you're heading for Dakar there are bush taxis for CFA3000; some go from Farafenni itself, but most go from the Senegal side of the border. A minibus between Farafenni and the Senegal border post is D3.

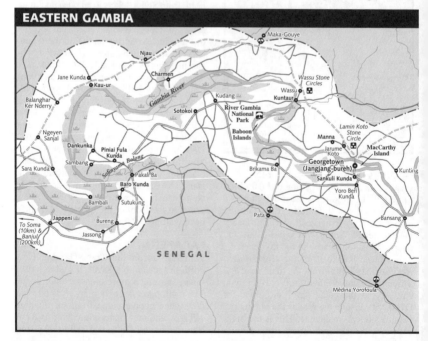

EASTERN GAMBIA

Eastern Gambia

Beyond Farafenni is the Gambia River's transition zone where it changes from saline to fresh water. The character of the river is also different: the tidal change is less noticeable, the mangroves thin out and thick forest grows down to the water's edge. Another major characteristic is the islands; the most famous being Baboon Island, which is part of the River Gambia National Park. As you head up the river there are several colonial-era towns. Georgetown and Basse Santa Su are both well worth visiting, as are the Wassu Stone Circles, enigmatic relics of an entirely different era.

GEORGETOWN (JANGJANG-BUREH)

Under the British, Georgetown was a busy administrative centre and trading hub full of grand buildings. Today it's got a new (or should that be old?) name, a host of crumbling monuments to history and the sort of sluggish atmosphere that discourages all but the most necessary work – the perfect place to relax for a couple of days.

Located on the northern edge of Mac-Carthy Island in the Gambia River, about 300km by road from Banjul, the traditional and now officially reintroduced name for the town and island is Jangjang-bureh, but most people still call it Georgetown. The island is 10km long and 2.5km wide, covered with fields of rice and groundnuts, and has ferry links to both river banks. There are no banks and only one available Internet-linked computer.

While in Georgetown you'll undoubtedly be approached by local youths offering their services as guides. These guys are more polite than their counterparts on the coast, though no less persistent, but you'd need to be very directionally challenged indeed to get lost around here, so a guide is not really necessary. A few young men also tout for

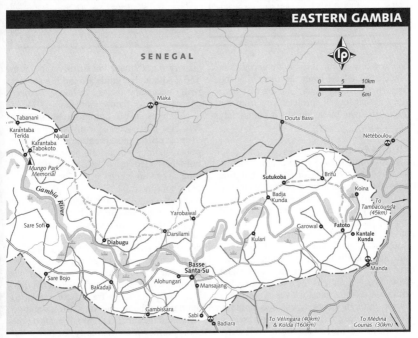

EASTERN GAMBIA

SENEGAL

Maka

Tabanani
Karantaba
Tenda   Njallal
    Karantaba
    Tabokoto

Mungo Park
Memorial

Gambia River

Sare Sofi

Diabugu

Sare Bojo

Bakadaji

Gambissara

Douta Bassi

Nétéboulou

Sutukoba   Brifu

Badja   Koina
Kunda   To
              Tambacounda
Yarobawal   (45km)

Darsilami   Garowal   Fatoto
          Kulari   Kantale
                          Kunda

Basse
Santa-Su   Manda

Alohungari   Mansajang

Sabi   To Vélingara (40km)   To Médina
Badiara   & Kolda (160km)   Gounas (30km)

0   5   10km
0   3   6mi

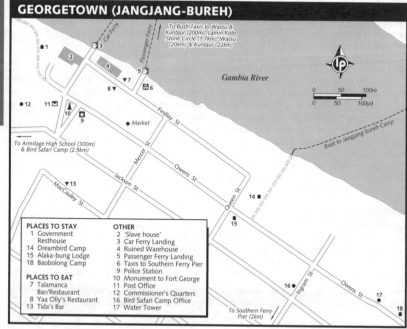

GEORGETOWN (JANGJANG-BUREH)

Gambia River

To Bush Taxis to Wassu & Kuntaur (200m), Lamin Koto Stone Circle (1.7km), Wassu (20km) & Kuntaur (22km)

To Armitage High School (300m) & Bird Safari Camp (2.5km)

• Market

Findlay St
Mercer St
Owens St
Jackson St
MacCauley St
Queen St
Ingram St

Boat to Jangjang-bureh Camp

To Southern Ferry Pier (2km)

PLACES TO STAY	OTHER
1 Government Resthouse	2 'Slave house'
14 Dreambird Camp	3 Car Ferry Landing
15 Alaka-bung Lodge	4 Ruined Warehouse
18 Baobolong Camp	5 Passenger Ferry Landing
	6 Taxis to Southern Ferry Pier
PLACES TO EAT	9 Police Station
7 Talamanca Bar/Restaurant	10 Monument to Fort George
8 Yaa Olly's Restaurant	11 Post Office
13 Tida's Bar	12 Commissioner's Quarters
	16 Bird Safari Camp Office
	17 Water Tower

business around the ferry, which crosses to MacCarthy Island from the main road on the southern river bank, and part of their story is that they'll 'protect' you from the guides in town, but again this is completely unnecessary.

Things to See

It's only going to take you a couple of hours to wander around Georgetown, but this hides the fact that there is probably more to see here and in the surrounding area than in almost any other town in Gambia. Most of the 'sights' have a historical bent, with two of the most interesting being crumbling warehouses situated on the waterfront either side of the northern ferry landing. Imaginative local youths refer to the more intact downriver building as the **slave house**, but although records show slaves were transported through Georgetown, it is unlikely these structures were in any way used in this trade as they were built well after

slavery was abolished in British colonies in 1807. Although a guide around town is not really necessary, the 'slave house' is more entertaining for their commentary (D1).

Nearby is the old **Commissioner's Quarters**, now inhabited by the district governor; the **post office**; and a **monument** outside the police station, which tells how the British built Fort George in 1823 after the local king asked for their protection against a neighbouring tribe. There are plans for a museum on this last site. West of town is the colonial **Armitage High School**.

Another place to visit is the **stone circle** of Lamin Koto. Only 1.5km away from the north bank ferry ramp, it's worth a look, especially if you don't make it to the larger circles at Wassu. The circle is on the right (northeast) side of the road, under a big tree. The passenger ferry from Georgetown to the northern bank runs on a fill-up-and-go basis, and the fare is D2. Small boats do the same journey more regularly for D1.

Places to Stay

Apart from those at the Government Rest-house, all these rooms (even the tents) come with bathroom.

Government Resthouse Rooms D80 per person. Off the main street, the three rooms here are comfortable and, like many of these government places, have the stuffed-chair atmosphere of your grandmother's lounge. The clean shared bathrooms often have hot water. The caretaker can arrange for someone to cook you a meal.

Alaka-bung Lodge (☎ 676123, e alaka bung@qanet.gm, Owens St) Twin bungalows D80 per person. Renovated and expanded, Alaka-bung is Georgetown's hippest and cheapest option. There are few package tourists here, but plenty of local drinkers and the only email access in town.

Baobolong Camp (☎ 676133/51, Owens St) Rooms D100 per person. At the eastern end of town, this camp is set in lush gardens near the river and run by enthusiastic local bird-watchers Lawrence and Augustine. It's a comfortable place and attracts a lot of groups. Breakfast is D50 and meals cost D50 to D80 for the buffet.

Bird Safari Camp (☎ 676108, fax 674004, e bsc@gamtel.gm, w www.bsc .gm) Singles/doubles in either rooms or luxury tents D275/475, camping D75. About 1.5km west of town, this secluded and peaceful camp has good-quality rooms and luxury tents. The price includes breakfast. It's probably the best in the area and is popular with bird-watchers – with a resident or-nithologist, private hides and guided walks and boat trips on offer. There's also a swimming pool and a generator – which means constant power.

Jangjang-bureh Camp (☎/fax 676182, 497603, e mosa@qanet.gm, w www.gre .gm) Rooms D110 per person. On the north side of the river, this is an eclectic collection of rustic bungalows set in a maze-like garden. Lighting is by oil lamps, and a drink at the bar overlooking the river is a fine way to spend the evening. A large buffet breakfast is D55, and good meals around D30 to D80. Motorboat trips (for up to six people) cost D150 per hour.

To reach Jangjang-bureh Camp, go to *Dreambird Camp*, from where a transfer boat – free to guests and diners – shuttles between the two. Dreambird has a few rooms at D75 per person.

Places to Eat & Drink

Few options exist outside the camps and lodges, especially after dark. There are a couple of cheap *eating houses* around the market, and near the ferry is *Talamanca Bar/Restaurant*, a low-key place run by a keen young local who claims to be open 24/7 and can arrange snacks like jacket potatoes (D15) or more substantial fare (D50). Sadly, it was out of beer when we passed. Near the taxi garage is *Yaa Olly's Restaurant*, which serves local food for about D10 from 8am to 5pm.

Beer should be available at *Tida's Bar*, a bar in a traditional compound run by the local school headmistress and reached through an unmarked green gate on the southwest side of town. If not, Alaka-bung is your best bet.

Tours & Day Trips

Possibilities for day trips from Georgetown include the Mungo Park Memorial at Karantaba Tenda, the River Gambia National Park (RGNP), and the Wassu Stone Circles.

All the places to stay in Georgetown organise boat tours, bird-watching and other day trips. Alaka-bung offers boat trips to see hippopotamuses (D500 per boat) as well as bird-watching trips (D50 per hour) and day trips to the Wassu Stone Circles and RGNP by road and river (D750 for a maximum of four people).

Bird Safari Camp has guided bird walks (D200 per person), three-hour boat trips to the RGNP (D750 per boat), or circumnavigations of MacCarthy Island by boat for the same price. It also rents bikes.

Baobolong Camp sees plenty of bird-watching parties and independents can join these groups for D210, including lunch. Baobolong Camp also has trips to RGNP (D1500 per boat up to 10 passengers), bird walks in the surrounding area (including at night, if you're keen to see owls) for D75, and plans for tiger fishing trips.

Another option is Jangjang-bureh Camp, where you can hire a small motorboat with driver, which takes about six people, for D175 per hour or D800 per day. A trip round the island is D450, and to the RGNP it's D1000 for the boat. Trips to the stone circles at Wassu, by river or land, also can be arranged. If you want to paddle your own canoe, kayaks can be hired for D50 per hour or D250 per day.

Getting There & Away

MacCarthy Island is reached by ferry from either the southern or northern bank of the river. The main road between Banjul and Basse Santa Su does not go directly past the southern ferry ramp, but most buses and bush taxis turn off to drop or pick up passengers here. Crossing on the ferry costs D15 for cars, D20 for 4WDs and D2 for passengers. On the far side pick-ups take people across the island to Georgetown for D3.

Near the south bank ferry ramp, have a quick look at the memorial erected to the memory of a Chinese agricultural adviser who introduced rice-growing to this area.

When leaving Georgetown, take a local pick-up to the southern ferry, and cross over to the southern bank. You may find a direct minibus to Basse Santa Su for D18. Alternatively, take a local minibus or bush taxi to Bansang (D5) and change here for transport to Basse Santa Su (D13). If you're heading west, go to Bansang or just to the main road. From there you can get to Soma, then change for Banjul and other destinations.

WASSU STONE CIRCLES

The area between the Gambia River and the Saloum River in southern Senegal is noted for its concentration of stone circles; the group at Wassu, 20km by road northwest of Georgetown, and about 2km north of Kuntaur, is a particularly good example.

There are several circles each consisting of between 10 and 24 reddish-brown and massive stones, standing 1m to 2.5m high and weighing several tonnes. Most of the stone circles in the region date from the period AD 500 to AD 1000, before the Mandinka people migrated to this area. Excavations have unearthed human bones and artefacts at the centre of many circles, indicating that they were burial sites, although dating techniques indicate that bodies may have been buried some time after the circles were constructed. Despite this archaeological excavation, little is known about the people who built these structures. Theories suggest these earlier people were farmers because all the sites are near rivers, but some are buried with spears suggesting they were hunters.

The entrance fee is D15. The caretaker will show you to a small but well-presented museum with exhibits discussing the possible origins of the circles. It has to be said they're not a major attraction for everyone. Go if you want to see evidence of ancient African cultures, but not if you're expecting Stonehenge.

Getting There & Away

The stone circles are about 500m before the village of Wassu, coming from Georgetown. Wassu can be reached from Farafenni, but the only regular bus seems to go on Sunday to tie in with Farafenni's Sunday lumo, and the beginning of Wassu's lumo on Monday.

Most people come from Georgetown. A bush taxi to Wassu waits most mornings at the north bank ferry ramp, but this only goes when full (which can take several hours), and even if you reached Wassu in reasonable time there might be nothing coming back. The fare is D9, so you could consider buying several seats, which might persuade the driver to get moving. To avoid these hassles we strongly advise visiting Wassu on a Monday, the day of Wassu's particularly colourful lumo.

Other options include arranging a tour with a camp in Georgetown, or hiring a bush taxi for the whole round trip; this will cost around D300. Cycling is possible, but the dirt road is a horrible nightmare and until it's fixed (by 2004, fingers crossed) this would be a rather masochistic 40km round trip.

RIVER GAMBIA NATIONAL PARK

South of Kuntaur, five islands in the Gambia River are protected as a national park.

The islands are known as Baboon Islands and the park is often referred to by this name. This is the site of a privately funded project that takes chimpanzees captured from illegal traders and rehabilitates them to live in the wilds. Boat trips are available in the area, but visitors are not allowed to land or get close to the islands. This is partly because it interferes with the rehabilitation process, but mainly because the chimps (there are more than 60) are nervous about humans getting too close, and while females and young ones may be docile enough, the males can be very quick to attack. Having lost their fear of people, they are more aggressive than 'wild' chimps. As they are several times stronger than humans, they're capable of awesome deeds when riled by a potential threat. If they are not able to get at the object of their frustration, they will often vent their spleen on the females and youngsters of their own troop.

Because of the dense cloak of gallery forest on the banks of the island, it is unusual to see chimp, and getting in close might result in your boat being boarded by a bristling alpha male. This has happened – forcing people in the boat to rapidly abandon ship!

If you visit the area, it's best to go with the aim of having a good day out on this beautiful stretch of river. You'll quite likely see baboons and monkeys, and possibly crocs and hippos too, plus an excellent selection of birds. And if you do happen to see any chimps – while keeping a responsible distance – it will be a bonus.

Getting There & Away

You can take a boat tour all the way from Georgetown; several places to stay have boats for hire at D800 to D1000 per day. Alternatively, you can go to Kuntaur by road and hire a boat there. Several people provide the service; the going rate is about D250 for a three- or four-hour trip, after some bargaining.

Boats are only permitted on the main channel between the islands and the east bank of the mainland, and are not allowed to approach the islands nearer than midstream. Boatmen often try to please their passengers by getting closer, but this should be positively discouraged.

MUNGO PARK MEMORIAL

Historians interested in exploration may want to head for Karantaba Tenda, about 20km east of Georgetown. Near this village, on the river bank, is the memorial pillar marking the spot where the Scottish explorer Mungo Park set off into the interior to trace the course of the Niger River.

A bush taxi comes here most mornings from the north-bank ferry ramp opposite Georgetown, but if your time is limited, hiring the whole car may be the only certain way of getting there and back in a day. Expect to pay around D250. The pillar is outside the village, but local boys will guide you there for a small fee. Another option is to go by boat. You can hire one for the day from places in Georgetown from about D1000.

BANSANG

Bansang is a large town on the main eastwest road and is home to Gambia's biggest up-country hospital. Unless you're very unwell or a keen bird-watcher, you'll have no reason to stop for long in Bansang. Bird-watchers come because they are almost guaranteed to see the spectacular red-throated bee-eater, which nests in a nearby quarry.

Hippos

The best time to see hippos is at low tide, when the shallower water cannot hide them so well. If you see a hippo, it's best to admire it from afar. These giants of the river are notoriously cantankerous creatures. Forget lions, leopards and snakes, hippos are responsible for more deaths in Africa than any other animal. It might seem obvious, but don't be tempted to throw fruit or stones at them so they come up for a better view. In 2000 a local boy did just that and the consequences were terrible. The irate hippo charged into the boat and sank it. Seven people drowned. So think before you antagonise a hippo.

Mungo Park

By the end of the 18th century, the incentive for exploring the interior of West Africa had switched from being commercial to 'scientific' (and evangelical – to convert 'heathens' to Christianity). Scientific exploration was based around solving two main puzzles: the position of Timbuktu (the mysterious 'city of gold') and the route of the Niger River. Although the Niger's existence was well known, its source and mouth, and even its direction of flow, were a mystery.

In 1795, the London-based Association for Promoting the Discovery of the Interior Parts of Africa sent a young Scotsman called Mungo Park to the Gambia River, which he followed upstream by boat, sailing between British trading stations. He based himself near present-day Georgetown, where he learnt several local languages, and then set off across the plains, with just two servants and three donkeys. He took a north-east direction, crossing the Senegal River, getting captured and escaping, and eventually reached the Niger at Segou, confirming that it flowed in a northerly direction. After more adventures and incredible hardships, he eventually managed to return to the Gambia River and to Britain where he wrote *Travels in the Interior of Africa*.

In 1801 Park returned to the Gambia River and again set out for the Niger. This time he took a larger support crew, although most of the men were actually army deserters and completely unprepared for the rigours of the expedition. By the time they reached the Niger River, many had already died, and even more perished as they took a boat downstream, either from disease or attacks by local people on the bank. Park and the few remaining members of his party all died under attack at the Bussa Rapids, in the east of present-day Nigeria.

BASSE SANTA SU

Commonly called Basse, this is Gambia's easternmost town, a traditional trading centre and by far the liveliest of the up-country settlements. It is also the last major ferry-crossing point on the Gambia River, and is a transport hub for the surrounding area. The most interesting sections of the town are the waterfront and the market. The latter is especially active on Thursday when the streets of the town centre are lined with shops and stalls. The whole place gets busy each evening when drink stalls open and grilled-meat shacks get fired up.

Both Trust Bank and Standard Chartered have branches in Basse that can change travellers cheques and advance money to Visa cardholders. Otherwise there are plenty of moneychangers lurking about the market and garage. The enterprising Nigerian owner of the Ultimate Barbing Salon also has Basse's single Internet-able computer, which he cranks up in the evenings, power permitting.

Things to See & Do

Down by the waterfront, an old colonial warehouse dating from 1906 has been converted into a cultural centre and café called **Traditions** (☎ *668533*, [e] *ann@ qanet.com; open 9am-6pm)*. After the building was gutted by fire in 1999, Traditions' exhibition of high-quality cloth and pottery, for show and sale, has been restored and still makes a refreshing change from the tat sold on the coast. Particularly attractive are the wall-hangings, clothes and mats hand made from locally grown cotton. Instead of being bleached white these retain their natural colour – rich shades of yellow, gold and light brown – or are turned into striking hangings using indigo from Guinea and a traditional Fula tie-dying process. If you want to learn about weaving cloth or making pots, some hands-on experience can be arranged if you organise it in advance. Otherwise Ann, the owner, is an expert on the crafts of the area and can answer all your questions.

Between June and February, the veranda at Traditions is also one of the best places in Gambia to see the Egyptian plover, a rare species, known locally as the crocodile bird. This small wader might be missed when standing quietly on the river bank, but it is

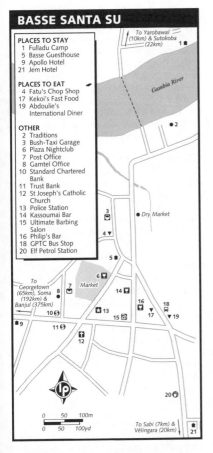

BASSE SANTA SU

PLACES TO STAY
1 Fulladu Camp
5 Basse Guesthouse
9 Apollo Hotel
21 Jem Hotel

PLACES TO EAT
4 Fatu's Chop Shop
17 Kekoi's Fast Food
19 Abdoulie's
   International Diner

OTHER
2 Traditions
3 Bush-Taxi Garage
6 Plaza Nightclub
7 Post Office
8 Gamtel Office
10 Standard Chartered
   Bank
11 Trust Bank
12 St Joseph's Catholic
   Church
13 Police Station
14 Kassoumai Bar
15 Ultimate Barbing
   Salon
16 Philip's Bar
18 GPTC Bus Stop
20 Elf Petrol Station

To Yarobawal
(10km) & Sutokoba
(22km)

Gambia River

Dry Market

To
Georgetown
(65km), Soma
(192km) &
Banjul (375km)

Market

To Sabi (7km) &
Vélingara (20km)

0   50   100m
0   50   100yd

instantly recognised in flight by its swept-back wings and beautiful black-and-white markings. Several other birds can also be seen in the area. Traditions has a boat for hire if you want go along the river, and can also put you in touch with bird guides.

Boat rides to see the birds (with a faint chance of seeing hippos and crocodiles too) can also be arranged with local boatmen on the waterfront, but rates are negotiable. Expect to pay about D100 an hour for a motor boat (although a lot depends on how much of this time the engine is actually running) or less for a paddled canoe.

Places to Stay

Basse is not blessed with a selection of fine hotels.

Apollo Hotel (☎ 668659) Rooms D75. On the main street, this place is as basic as it gets and a step or two down from spotless.

Basse Guesthouse Rooms D60. Probably the pick of the budget range and overlooking the central square, this place is friendly enough and a good spot for people-watching.

Jem Hotel (☎ 668356) Singles/doubles with bathroom D150/300. About 500m southeast of the town centre this place is better than the Basse, but still a bit run down compared with Fulladu. Some travellers have found the obsequious behaviour of the manager rather disconcerting. The hotel has a restaurant where breakfast costs from D20 to D35, and evening meals D60. It should have a new name by the time you arrive.

Fulladu Camp (☎ 668743, mobile 917007) Rooms D165 per person. On the north bank of the Gambia River, about 100m east of the ferry landing, this sprawling camp is undoubtedly the best place to stay in Basse. Clean, comfortable bungalows are complemented by probably the best kitchen in Basse. Meals include beef goulash (D65), pasta dishes for D55 and sandwiches and omelettes for D20 to D30. Fulladu has a pool, several monkeys (kept in cages) and a boat that runs guests across the river for free. River trips can be organised for D100 per person.

Places to Eat

There are several *tea shacks* in and around the bush-taxi park, and a couple of stalls selling coffee and bread, or cheap bowls of rice and sauce. A popular spot is *Fatu's Chop Shop*, where big bowls of *benechin* and *domodah* (groundnut sauce on meat or vegetables) are excellent and cost just D6. Along the main road, especially to the west of the market, several *roast-meat stalls* open at night.

In town, cheap restaurants include *Abdoulie's International Diner*, open 7am to midnight, and *Kekoi's Fast Food*, open evenings, both of which are local hang-outs with unpretentious meals from D5 to D20.

It's worth eating at *Traditions* (see Things To See & Do) for the views alone. Tables are

Lumos around Basse

Several of Basse's surrounding villages have a weekly market (called a *lumo*) – all on a different day of the week. For example, at Lamwe, near Fatoto, the lumo is on Saturday; at Sabi, on the road towards Vélingara, it's Sunday; at Sarengai on the north bank, it's Monday; and at Gambissara, southwest of Basse, it's Wednesday. Traders and shoppers come from other parts of Gambia, across the border from Senegal, and from as far as Mali, Guinea and Guinea-Bissau. Bush taxis from Basse run to wherever the lumo is that day, and visiting the market is always a lively and interesting day out.

on a balcony overlooking the river, and clients include local volunteers and aid workers, well-to-do locals and the few tourists who make it this far upcountry. Sandwiches, soups and omelettes cost from D15 to D25. The café usually shuts at 6pm unless dinner has been booked for later. Campers can pitch tents in the yard for D50 for two people.

Entertainment

Beers are available at the *Fulladu Camp* and the *Jem Hotel* (see Places to Stay), and the *Kassoumai Bar*, which only seems to get active late at weekends. For a more local feel head to *Philip's Bar* (☎ 918617), open from 5.30pm to 4.30am, where you can sit around the open compound with the animated owner (Phil), and drink Julbrews for D12. That is unless he persuades you to imbibe some of his palm wine or the house speciality *ogorogoro*, which is apparently a more potent member of the palm wine family and one for which Phil has a liking.

With a few ogorogoros under your belt you should head to the *Plaza Nightclub*, open from 8pm to 1am, which was the hippest place in town when we passed. There is an inside dance area and a beer-garden-style courtyard where you can listen to a range of African sounds, reggae, and occasional drum and no bass shows. Entry ranges from D5 to D25 and beer is D12.

Getting There & Away

GPTC buses between Banjul and Basse (D70) leave throughout the day (see Getting There & Away in the Banjul chapter). From Basse, ordinary buses leave from the main road (not the bush-taxi garage) at 7am, 9am and 1pm; and the express bus leaves at 8am.

Bush taxis and minibuses go to the eastern outpost of Fatoto (D10, 40 minutes); the ferry ramp for Georgetown (D18, one hour); Soma (D35, four hours); and Serekunda (D70, eight hours).

The ferry to the Gambia River's northern bank takes one car at a time, officially on demand, although if the ferry's on the opposite bank prepare for a wait. The charge for a car is D30, and passengers D1. There are also smaller boats taking passengers across; the fare is D2.

If you're heading for Senegal, you can go by bush taxi to Tambacounda via Vélingara (see Gambia's Getting There & Away chapter). If your horizons are even further afield a Peugeot taxi goes more or less daily (passengers depending) to Labé in northern Guinea. The fare is CFA15,000 and the trip takes around 24 hours (or longer if there are delays at roadblocks).

Facts about Senegal

HISTORY

A comprehensive history of the Senegambia region up until the end of the 19th century is given under History in the Facts about Senegambia chapter. This section continues on with Senegal's history from the late 19th century up to the present day.

The Colonial Period

At the Berlin Conference of 1884–85, following the Scramble for Africa, the continent was divided between powerful European countries. While Britain (with Germany and Portugal) got most of East and Southern Africa, the greater part of West Africa was allocated to France and became the territory of Afrique Occidentale Française – French West Africa.

Even before this time, from 1848, the four largest towns (Dakar, Gorée, St-Louis and Rufisque) had been seen as part of France, with delegates sent along to the French national assembly in Paris, although the delegates from these towns were white or mixed-race rather than African. In 1887 Africans from these four towns were also granted limited French citizenship, and became *citoyens* (citizens). However, most of the 14 million other French West Africans remained *sujets* (subjects). Only those needed in the colonial administration received secondary education in Dakar, which by this time had become the capital of French West Africa. St-Louis remained the capital of Senegal-Mauritania.

In 1914, Blaise Diagne was the first black delegate to go to the French national assembly. That same year, the first political party in West Africa was established, but it became fashionable for politically conscious Senegalese to join French parties. In the 1930s, many joined the increasingly powerful Socialists and Communists. A notable figure at this time was Lamine Guéye, mayor of St-Louis, who formed strong links with the French Socialist government. In the same period, several Senegalese intellectuals went to France to study. One was Léopold Senghor who, after his studies (where Georges Pompidou was a classmate), became the first African secondary-school teacher in France. During this period, he began writing poems, and founded *Présence Africaine*, a magazine promoting the values of African culture.

After WWII, France continued to regard its overseas possessions (including Senegal, Mali and Côte d'Ivoire) as territories that were part of the mother country, rather than mere colonies. Delegates were still sent to the national assembly in Paris, but each territory was also granted its own assembly. Senghor returned from France and was elected to the new assembly. He was initially seen as an unlikely political candidate: as well as being young, Catholic and a member of the minority Serer tribe, he spoke little Wolof, was married to a white French woman and was somewhat aloof from his people – but he was remarkably astute, and went on to become Senegal's most influential politician of the 20th century.

Senghor played on his own sujet status and was seen as a man of the people. He introduced social reforms such as the abolition of forced labour, and improvements in education. In 1948 he founded the Bloc Democratic Senegalese. Meanwhile, the marabouts (Islamic leaders; see the boxed text 'Marabouts & Brotherhoods' later in this chapter) had become increasingly involved in politics, and through the 1950s Senghor made several deals with leading figures. He allowed them partial autonomy and control of the lucrative groundnut economy in return for their public support, which ensured safe votes from their followers in the rural areas.

Towards Independence

In the 1950s, the potential independence of France's African colonies became a major issue. Senghor was in favour of independence, but promoted the idea of a strong federal union of all French territories in Africa, to prevent them from being 'balkanised'

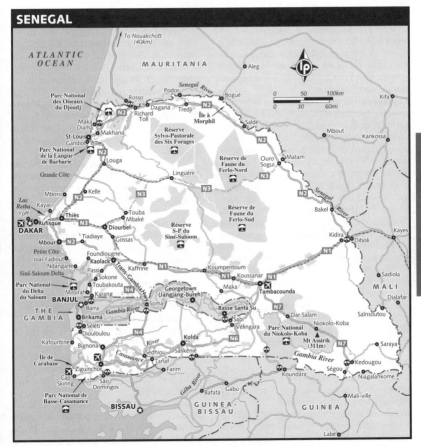

SENEGAL

ATLANTIC OCEAN

MAURITANIA

To Nouakchott (40km)

Parc National des Oiseaux du Djoudj

Rosso
Podor
Senegal River
Bogué
Aleg
Kifa

Dagana
Richard Toll
Tredji
Île à Morphil
Saldé

Maka Diama
Makhana

St-Louis
Gandiol

Réserve Sylvo-Pastorale des Six Forages
Mbout
Kankossa

Parc National de la Langue de Barbarie

Louga
Ouro Sogui
Matam

Réserve de Faune du Ferlo-Nord

Grande Côte
Linguère

Mboro
Kelle

Lac Retba
Yoff
Kayar
Thiès
Touba
Mbaké
Réserve de Faune du Ferlo-Sud
Bakel
Senegal River

DAKAR
Rufisque
Diourbel
Réserve S-P du Siné-Saloum

Mbour
Tiadiaye
Gossas
Kidira
Diboli
Kayes

Petite Côte
Joal-Fadiout
Foundiougne
Kaolack
Koumpentoum

Ndangane
Passi
Kaffrine
Koussanar
Sadiola

Siné-Saloum Delta
Sokone
Maka
Tambacounda
MALI

Parc National du Delta du Saloum
Toubakouta
Georgetown (Janjang-bureh)
Dialafar

BANJUL
Missirah
Karang
Soma
Basse Santa Su
Dar Salam

THE GAMBIA
Barra
Gambia River
Sabi
Vélingara
Parc National du Niokolo-Koba
Niokolo-Koba
Saïnsoutou

Brikama
Séléti
Kolda
Mt Assirik (311m)
Saraya

Kafountine
Diouloulou
Bignona
River
Sédhiou
Salikénié
Kédougou

Île de Carabane
Casamance
Tanaf
Gambia River
Ségou
Niagalankome

Ziguinchor
São Domingos
Farim
Koundara

Cap Skiring
Géba River
Bafatá
Gabú
Mali-ville

Parc National de Basse-Casamance
BISSAU
GUINEA-BISSAU
GUINEA

Labé

0 50 100km
0 30 60mi

SENEGAL

– divided, weak and still dependent on their former ruler. His rival was Côte d'Ivoire's leader, Houphouët-Boigny, who wanted French West Africa divided, fearing that within a federal union the richer territories (such as Côte d'Ivoire) would have to subsidise the poorer ones.

In the late 1950s, Senghor gained support from French Soudan (present-day Mali), Upper Volta (present-day Burkina Faso) and Dahomey (present-day Benin) to form a single union, the Mali Federation. But in 1958, General Charles de Gaulle came to power in France and offered the overseas

territories a stark choice – complete independence and a total break from France, or limited self-government within a union still controlled by France.

Independence

Upper Volta and Dahomey withdrew from the Mali Federation under pressure from both France and Côte d'Ivoire, but in 1959 the Mali Federation (now consisting of just Senegal and Mali) continued to demand complete independence, not as individual countries, but as an independent union. De Gaulle realised he stood to lose more than he might gain, and suddenly switched tack. On 20 June 1960, Senegal and Mali became completely independent, while remaining within the French union. But two months later, the Senegal-Mali union broke up. Houphouët-Boigny had won the day; French West Africa had become nine separate republics.

Senghor became the first president of Senegal, but the early independent years did not always run smoothly. In 1968, in the wake of protests in France and amid mounting economic difficulties at home, students rioted at the University of Dakar. Senghor sent in troops, but the national trade union supported the students and called for a general strike. Even with a show of force supported by French troops stationed in Senegal, Senghor had to make concessions to the union and the students.

The 1970s were less turbulent: Senghor held on to his position and remained a popular figure while his party, now renamed the Parti Socialiste (PS), consolidated its hold in government. In 1980, after 20 years as president, he did what no other African head of state had done before – voluntarily stepped down. His hand-picked successor, Prime Minister Abdou Diouf, took over.

The Diouf Era

Soon after gaining the presidency, Diouf was asked to help Dawda Jawara, the president of Gambia, who had been ousted in a coup. Diouf sent in Senegalese troops and, after a considerable amount of bloodshed, Jawara was restored. This cooperation became formalised when the Senegambia Confederation was established later the same year.

In 1983 Diouf's PS won national elections with over 83% of the vote. Two years later his major opponent, Abdoulaye Wade, moved to try and unite the various opposition parties. Diouf was clearly worried and banned the organisation on the grounds that it violated election law.

In 1988 Wade contested the presidency, but when violence erupted during the campaign Wade was arrested and charged with intent to subvert the government. Diouf won the election with 73% of the vote against Wade's 26%, but rumours of rigging were

rampant. Wade was given a one-year suspended sentence and left for France.

By this time the Senegambia Confederation was in trouble and, in 1989, it was dissolved completely. But while Diouf was contending with this break-up and calls for political reform, he had two other major problems to deal with: one was a dispute with Mauritania (see the boxed text 'The Mauritanian Crisis'), and the other was a campaign against separatists in the southern region of Casamance.

There had been periodic calls for independence in Casamance for many years, but they came to a head in 1989, when rebels from the Mouvement des Forces Démocratique de la Casamance (MFDC) started attacking government installations (see the Casamance chapter for further details). Quite apart from the effect the fighting had on the local people, it also hit Senegal's money-spinning tourist industry as visitors stayed away and tour companies suspended their operations.

Abdoulaye Wade returned from political exile in 1990, which brought huge crowds out onto the streets chanting *sopi* ('change' in Wolof). In an attempt at appeasement, in March 1991 the national assembly approved the participation of a number of opposition parties in the government and Wade was made minister of state, but with little real effect.

Wade resigned his position to stand against Diouf in the presidential election of February 1993. Diouf won with an absolute majority of 58% (against Wade's 32%) and was thus elected for a third term. Parliamentary elections were held three months later and while Wade's Parti Démocratique Sénégalais (PDS) and other opposition parties improved their performance, Diouf's PS still won over two-thirds of the seats. This led to violent protests in many parts of the country, particularly in Casamance where anti-Diouf feeling still ran high. Large numbers of troops were once again sent into the region. After long negotiations another cease-fire was declared in June 1993 and further talks saw full peace return to Casamance.

However, although Casamance was quiet again, sporadic outbreaks of antigovernment protest continued in other parts of the country. In August 1993, the government introduced a number of unpopular austerity measures and, following a series of violent demonstrations in Dakar, Wade was arrested again. A major devaluation of the CFA franc in early 1994 didn't improve the situation.

Wade went on trial in March 1994, accused of conspiracy, following the Dakar demonstrations, and on charges related to the murder of a state official. The following May, the charges were dismissed and Wade was released. French officials persuaded President Diouf to again include Wade, and some other opposition figures, in the government. But despite the political manoeuvring, Diouf and the PS held firmly onto power.

The Mauritanian Crisis

In 1989, two Senegalese peasants were killed by Mauritanian border guards in a clash over grazing rights. In Senegal, people reacted by looting Mauritanian-owned shops in Dakar, and killing several people. Mauritanians retaliated in their country by deporting thousands of Senegalese. Hundreds were killed in the process, and the Senegalese retaliated by deporting Mauritanians. Large-scale airlifts by humanitarian organisations helped to get the Mauritanians out of Senegal and the Senegalese out of Mauritania, but not before horrendous atrocities were committed on both sides.

The problem is complex and stems from the time when the Maurs (who are of Arab or Caucasian origin) would raid villages of black Africans and take away slaves. The resentment remains deeply entrenched, and is not helped by the Mauritanian government, which took until 1980 to outlaw slavery. Today there are an estimated 100,000 black slaves in Mauritania.

Following the outbreaks of violence, the borders between Senegal and Mauritania were closed, and diplomatic relations were broken off for two years. They were resumed in April 1992, and ambassadors were exchanged a few months later. Today, you can once again travel overland between these two countries.

Sopi – Change

The PS won the 1998 parliamentary elections in another landslide and were again accused of rigging the result. But it was evident that the opposition was gaining momentum and a growing number of the electorate were dissatisfied. Nor could electoral success prevent more rebels, soldiers and, more frequently, civilians being killed in Casamance. The pressure on Diouf was mounting, but a change in the constitution had extended the president's term to seven years, and Wade had to wait until 2000 to challenge Diouf once more.

By the time voting began in February 2000 tensions were running high in Senegal. Wade's sopi campaign had captured the imagination of the nation, but violent encounters between government and opposition supporters threatened to give the government an excuse to postpone the poll. The threat was averted and for the first time the president did not win the all-important 50% of the vote needed to be automatically re-elected, gaining just 41%. The poll went to a runoff between Diouf and the second-placed candidate, Wade, who had won 31% of the vote in the first round. Other opposition candidates soon pledged their support for Wade and, when the dust settled on the second round, Wade had won an historic victory, securing 58% while Diouf could again only muster 41%.

If Senegal and the rest of the world was stunned by the electoral defeat of an African incumbent of such long standing, even more unusual was Diouf's acceptance of the result and the peaceful transfer of power. The people of Senegal were rightly proud of this affirmation of the strength of democracy in their country and, in January 2001, more than 90% voted for a new constitution allowing the formation of opposition parties, giving enhanced status to the prime minister and reducing the president's term of office from seven years to five.

After his election Wade had appointed another longtime Diouf opponent, Moustapha Niasse, as prime minister, but it didn't take long for divisions to emerge between the two men and, in March 2001, Niasse was sacked. His replacement was a judge and, significantly in such a male-dominated society, a woman – Madior Boye.

Despite the disharmony at the top, Wade's Sopi coalition, an alliance of 40 parties, won 89 of the 120 seats in the April 2001 parliamentary elections. After dominating parliament since 1960, the PS came third with just 10 seats.

After such a monumental shift in the balance of power, change has been disappointingly slow. Many Wade supporters are already showing signs of discontent, and allegations of corruption are surfacing. Some are saying Wade's coalition has too much power, and that Senegal is again, in effect, a one-party state. All this sounds a little extreme, but it's safe to say that the people's appetite for change has yet to be sated.

GEOGRAPHY

Senegal is the westernmost country on the African continent, with an area of just under 200,000 sq km, similar in size to South Dakota in the USA; the Australian state of Victoria; and England and Scotland combined. Senegal is largely flat, with a natural vegetation of dry savanna woodland. It lies at a latitude between 12° and 17° north of the equator, at the western edge of the Sahel. The country's western border, some 600km in length, is marked by the shore of the Atlantic Ocean. About halfway down the coast, the large Cap Vert peninsula juts out west into the ocean. At the end of this peninsula is Dakar, with its surrounding suburbs and satellite towns, one of the largest cities in West Africa.

To the north of the Cap Vert peninsula, the coast faces northwest and is known as the Grande Côte (Great Coast), stretching unbroken almost to Senegal's border with Mauritania. South of the peninsula, the Petite Côte (Small Coast) faces southwest, making the weather conditions more agreeable for tourism, and this area is among the most popular for visitors.

Senegal's other important geographical features include three major rivers, which all flow east to west from the Fouta Djalon highlands in neighbouring Guinea to the Atlantic Ocean. In the north the Senegal River forms

Shell Mounds

Ancient mounds of shells occur all along the Atlantic coast between the mouth of the Senegal River and Guinea-Bissau. In essence, they are middens (rubbish dumps) created by people who inhabited this area about 1000 years ago and seem to have eaten a lot of shellfish. The mounds consist almost entirely of shell, but pieces of broken pottery, ash and other debris have also been found.

Most shell mounds are in mangrove swamps, but there are a few completely artificial shell islands, most notably Dioran Boumak on the Saloum River just north of Toubakouta. Dioran Boumak measures 400m by 300m by 12m, and is thought to have been created deliberately between AD 730 and 1370 and used as a burial site. There are more than 120 graves in the island, in three burial mounds. The bodies were buried at different times, but were all laid out in similar positions, with straight legs and arms folded over the face. They wore jewellery, and weapons and pottery were buried with them.

In some sites there is evidence of Stone Age occupation below the mounds, and there is a tem-poral correlation between these sites and the stone circles around the Gambia River. However, despite extensive excavation, scientists remain uncertain whether any of the current ethnic groups in Senegambia are descended from these Late Stone Age shell people. Researchers have tried to establish links by studying the patterns on pottery and weapons, but with little conclusive result. There is a possible link between the Diola people of the Casamance and the early shell-mound people of the same area.

Despite their archaeological importance, shell mounds in Senegal and Gambia attract little interest and even less in the way of official protection. Many are in relatively remote areas and remain untouched, but the shells are sometimes used instead of gravel in the construction industry, and are quarried when the need arises. A large shell mound near Denton Bridge in Banjul was virtually destroyed this way, with the shells used to build a road.

the border with Mauritania. St-Louis, the old capital, is at this river's mouth. In southeastern Senegal, the Gambia River flows through Parc National de Niokolo-Koba before entering the country of Gambia itself. In the far south is the Casamance River, which gives its name to the surrounding Casamance area, a fertile zone of forest and farmland. Senegal's most beautiful beaches are also here, around Cap Skiring. Another major river is the Saloum, which enters the ocean via a large delta to the south of the Petite Côte.

FLORA & FAUNA
National Parks & Reserves

Senegal has six national parks, and several other areas where natural habitats are protected. The main parks visited by tourists are Parc National de Niokolo-Koba, the country's largest park, in southeast Senegal, with a wide range of habitat types and large numbers of birds and mammals; Parc National du Delta du Saloum, an area of coastal lagoons, mangroves, sandy islands and a section of dry woodland in the coastal area just north of Guinea; Îles de la Madeleine, a couple of small islands near Dakar; Parc National des Oiseaux du Djoudj and Parc National de la Langue de Barbarie, near St-Louis in northern Senegal, both especially noted for their birdlife. The Parc National Basse-Casamance, an area of forest and mangrove in the Casamance region, has been closed for years because of rebel activity.

Other protected areas include the Ferlo wildlife reserves in the northcentral part of

SENEGAL

Mangroves

As you travel around the coast of Senegal you will find plenty of examples of mangroves. It is a tropical evergreen plant that grows on tidal mud flats and inlets all along the coast of West Africa. It plays a vital role for both the local populations and wildlife and has a fascinating reproductive system, perfectly adapted to its watery environment. It is one of very few plants that thrive in salt water, and this allows rapid colonisation of areas where no other plant would have a chance. In Senegal, the best place to see mangroves is the Siné-Saloum Delta, although they also grow in other river estuaries, and if you travel in Gambia, you will find them a long way upstream in the Gambia River.

Two types of mangrove can be seen and easily identified. The red mangrove (of which there are three species, although to the untrained eye they all look the same) is most prominent. It's easy to recognise by its leathery leaves and dense tangle of stilt-like buttress roots. The seeds germinate in the fruit while still hanging on the tree, growing a long stem called a 'radical'. When the fruit drops, the radical lodges in the mud and becomes a ready-made root for the new seedling.

The white mangrove is less common and is found mainly on ground that is only covered by particularly high tides. It does not have stilt roots. Its most recognisable characteristic is the breathing roots, with circular pores, that grow out of the mud from the base of the tree.

Mangrove trees catch silt, vegetation and other floating debris in their root systems. The mangrove's own falling leaves are added to the pile. As this mire becomes waterlogged and consolidated, it forms an ideal breeding ground for young mangroves. In this way, the mangrove actually creates new land. As the stands expand on the seaward side, the older growth on the landward side gradually gets further from the water. Eventually they die, leaving behind a rich soil perfect for cultivation.

Mangrove forests are a common sight along Senegal's waterways

The mangrove has many other uses. Oysters and shellfish cling to the roots as the tide comes in. When the tide retreats, they are left exposed and are easily gathered by local people. Mangroves are also fertile fishing grounds, as fish like the darkness and the hiding places between the roots.

Senegal, the Réserve de Bandia near the Petite Côte, and the Biosphere Reserve at Samba Dia on the northern fringe of the Siné-Saloum Delta.

GOVERNMENT & POLITICS

Senegal is a republic, with the president and 120 members of the national assembly elected every five years by universal adult suffrage. The political system is a multiparty democracy; Senegal was the first genuinely multiparty democracy in West Africa. A coalition called Sopi (Change) is currently in power, led by President Abdoulaye Wade's Parti Démocratique Sénégalais (PDS).

The Sopi coalition holds 89 seats, while there are several opposition parties, the main ones being the Alliance of Forces of Progress (AFP), with 11 seats, and the Parti Socialiste (PS), which ruled for 40 years until 2001, with just 10. Like the PS before it, President Wade and Sopi maintain an unofficial but essential alliance with the marabout leaders of Senegal's Islamic brotherhoods (see the boxed text).

In terms of political stability, Senegal has done extremely well since independence. Although the country's human rights record is by no means unblemished, the press has a great deal of freedom and Senegal is still one of the least politically repressive countries of the former French colonies.

ECONOMY

Senegal's economy is based on agriculture, which employs 70% of the working population for just 19% of the GNP, a reflection of the gross inefficiency that plagues the sector. Many of those people work in the production of groundnuts (see the boxed text 'Groundnuts' in the Facts about Senegambia chapter). Some diversification has been achieved, notably into cotton and rice, but production of subsistence crops, such as millet, is declining and Senegal now imports about 35% of its food requirements. Fishing is a major activity on the coast and fish, and fish products, account for a huge 27% of all foreign exchange earnings (US$2.8 billion).

Marabouts & Brotherhoods

An understanding of Senegal's marabouts and the power of the Islamic brotherhoods (confréries) is fundamental to an understanding of Senegal itself. The subject involves religion, politics, economy, God and the State, and is remarkably complex.

Whereas orthodox Islam holds that every believer is directly in touch with Allah, the traditionally hierarchical societies of North and West Africa found it more natural to have religious leaders ascribed with divine power providing a link between God and the common populace. These intermediaries became known as marabouts, and many are venerated by their disciples (talibés) as saints. The concept of brotherhoods – groups who followed the teachings of a particular marabout – was imported from Morocco. The leader of a brotherhood was known as a cheik, or khalif, and these terms are still used today.

The earliest brotherhood established south of the Sahara (in the 16th century) was the Qadiriya, which encouraged charity and humility and attracted followers throughout the northern Sahel. It spread through Senegal in the 19th and 20th centuries. Today, most Qadiriya followers are Mandinkas, both in southern Senegal and in Gambia.

The Moroccan-based Tijaniya brotherhood was introduced to Senegal by Omar Tall in the mid-19th century, and remains powerful today, with large and important mosques in the towns of Tivaouane and Kaolack. Later in the 19th century, a smaller brotherhood called the Layen broke away from the Qadiriya under a marabout called Saidi Limamou Laye, who is believed to be a reincarnation of the Prophet Mohammed. Most Layen are Lebu people, who inhabit the town of Yoff outside Dakar.

The Mouridiya was founded by a marabout called Amadou Bamba in the late 19th century (see the boxed text 'Bamba' in the West-Central Senegal chapter) and is now the largest brotherhood,

Despite being the most industrially advanced of the countries that once formed French West Africa, Senegal still suffers from high urban unemployment and poverty. The economy enjoyed an enviable rate of growth during the '90s, averaging about 5% a year, but much of the wealth disappeared into the pockets of the political elite.

As with many other developing countries, foreign debt remains a huge problem. Despite receiving debt relief to the tune of almost US$1 billion in recent years, Senegal still owes US$3.5 billion, give or take a few CFA francs, to commercial banks and international bodies such as the World Bank. As Senegal becomes eligible for a variety of debt-relief initiatives this total is expected to fall significantly. In the meantime, debt continues to absorb a large portion of the country's export earnings and, while trade figures remain negative, the loans cannot be cleared, and the interest bills still need to be paid. While he is a long-time supporter of the free market, President Wade has indicated he is unhappy with World Bank programmes and plans to appeal to private investors for capital improvements, using the country's proximity to Europe and political and economic stability as the main lure. However, when it comes to struggling African nations, 'My Way' has never been a favoured tune of the international financial institutions. And while Senegal's achievement in becoming the first West African nation to be given a credit rating by the Standard & Poors agency is significant, the slightest hint of failure will see the big-money loans dry up and the credit rating plummet.

Tourism is an increasingly important part of Senegal's economy, accounting for about 15% of total earnings, although activity is restricted mainly to the coastal regions. According to the government, in 1999 just over 500,000 tourists visited Senegal. Most were package tourists from France, with others coming from Germany and Scandinavia.

Marabouts & Brotherhoods

with over two million followers. One of Bamba's followers was Ibra Fall, who took readily to hard work but found prayer and study difficult. With Bamba's blessing he founded the Baye Fall sect for whom labour became religious observance. His followers called him Lamp Fall, and Bamba excused them from prayer and fasting during Ramadan so long as they worked hard – yet another Senegalese spin on conventional Islam.

Today, you'll see images of Lamp Fall and Bamba painted on walls and buses all over Senegal, and the Baye Fall disciples, with their dreadlocks, patchwork robes and begging bowls, are a constant reminder that Mouridism continues to thrive. Bamba's return to Senegal in 1907, after being exiled by the French, is celebrated by the annual Magal pilgrimage to Touba, and it's significant that this, rather than any other Islamic holiday, is the major Mouride event.

The alliance between the brotherhoods and the government continues to be a major feature of Senegalese life. The Parti Socialiste (PS) has relied on marabout backing – especially from the khalif of the Mourides, who has about a quarter of the population hanging on to his every word – for at least 40 years. To keep the brotherhoods sweet, the government publicly reinforced the marabouts' power and, behind the scenes, allowed them a completely free hand in the all-important groundnut harvest.

But when Abdou Diouf lost the support of the khalif in 2000, he also lost power. Soon after his electoral success, new president Abdoulaye Wade publicly thanked the Mourides for their support, and then announced Senegal's new international airport would be built outside Touba, the spiritual home of the Mourides – a mere 194km from Dakar. Thankfully, sense prevailed and the plan was scrapped.

SENEGAL

POPULATION & PEOPLE

The population of Senegal was estimated at 10.3 million in mid-2001, 45% of whom was under 15 years old. Small families are not popular, with the average woman having five children. The dominant ethnic group is the Wolof (about 43% of the population), who live mostly in the central area, north and east of Dakar, and along the coast. The Serer (15%) also live in the central regions, while the Fula (23%), also called Fulani, Fulbe and Peul, live throughout northern and eastern Senegal. Other groups include the Tukulor (also spelt Toucouleur), inhabiting the north; the Mandinka, in the areas bordering Gambia; the Malinké in the northeast; and the Diola (also called Jola), who live mainly in the Casamance. Minority groups include the Bassari and Bédik, who live in the remote southeastern part of Senegal, and the Lebu, who live almost exclusively in the town of Yoff outside Dakar.

Most Senegalese speak Wolof and about 90% are Muslim. Further homogeneity derives

Bukut: A Diola Masking Tradition

Although the traditional use of wooden masks is almost unknown in the Senegambia region, several tribal groups utilise masks and costumes manufactured from plant fibre in their initiation ceremonies. The Diola people, who live in the Casamance region of Senegal and the southwestern parts of Gambia (where their name is spelt Jola), have a long history of the use of such masks in a male initiation ceremony called the Bukut.

The Bukut takes place every 20 to 25 years and involves the gaining of knowledge and social status by the current generation of young Diola men. Preparations for the Bukut start months in advance as the celebrations entail huge feasts involving the sacrifice of many cattle. It is during these preparations that mothers compose songs that are sung by the initiated during a ritual involving the passing of cloth called Buyeet. Each youth has his own song, which will not be sung again publicly until his death.

Distinctive woven-cane masks called Ejumbi, which have tubular eyes and are surmounted by a pair of massive cattle horns, are worn by the initiates when they return from the sacred forest. Not all initiates wear these masks, but those who do are considered to possess special powers of clairvoyance.

Other types of mask include the Fulundim, a cloth mask decorated with mirrors, beads, buttons and cowries, and the Gatombol, an abstract costume of plant material.

The masks are created by the initiates with the help of tribal elders and have retained their traditional form, although their construction can now incorporate the use of enamel paint and plastic fringing.

The Bukut represents Diola identity and is still considered a very important event. It has survived and adapted to Christianity and Islam.

Woven cane masks such as the Ejumbi are an integral part of initiation ceremonies for the Diola people

John Graham

Travelling 'light' in Senegal

from the *cousinage*, or 'joking cousins', relationship that exists between different ethnic groups or clans, which allows very jocular and personal conversations even among strangers, and symbolises a deeper level of support against outsiders.

ARTS

Although Senegal has many writers (producing novels, poetry and drama), much is written in French (or indigenous languages). Comparatively little is translated into English or other languages, so many of Senegal's writers remain unknown outside the country.

Of those who have been translated into English, Sembène Ousmane is probably Senegal's most famous writer. His classic *God's Bits of Wood* (published in 1970) is said to be the most widely acclaimed book by any Senegalese author. Through the struggles of strikers on the Dakar-Bamako train line in the late 1940s, it describes the emergence of a grassroots political consciousness in pre-independence Africa. His other books include *Black Docker*, based on his experiences in the French port of

Marseilles in the 1950s, and *Xala*, an attack on the privileged elites of Dakar.

Sembéne Ousmane is also a well-known film-maker, and is regarded by many people as one of the most influential cinema figures in West Africa. The ideas expressed in *Xala* were also portrayed in a film of the same name.

Senegal's most influential writer is Léopold Senghor. Studying in France during the 1930s, he coined the term 'negritude', which emphasised black-African ideas and culture, countering the colonial policy of 'assimilation'. Naturally, these beliefs influenced Senghor's own political thought, and he went on to become a most prominent nationalist, eventually becoming president of his country at independence.

A more recent Senegalese writer is Mariama Bâ, whose short but incisive novel *So Long a Letter* was first published in 1980 and won international acclaim as well as the Noma Award for publishing in Africa. The common theme of ungainly transition between traditional and modern society is explored by a woman narrator whose much-loved husband suddenly takes a young friend of their schoolgirl daughter as a second wife. Her second novel, *The Scarlet Song*, is about the marriage between a Senegalese man and a French woman.

Another woman writer is Aminata Sow-Fall. Her 1986 novel *The Beggars' Strike* is an ironic story highlighting the striking differences between the rich and poor, and questions the power of the political elite – these are popular themes in modern Senegalese literature.

Other common themes include the move from traditional rural roots to modern urban societies, and these are discussed in the landmark 1930s novel *Karim*, by Ousmane Socé, one of the earliest Senegalese writers to have his work published (although an English translation of this is very difficult to find), and in *The Wound* by Malick Fall, which has been published in English by Longman (1973).

Books by non-Senegalese are listed under Books in the Facts about Senegambia chapter. The music of Senegal (both traditional and pop) is described in the 'Music of Senegambia' special section.

Facts for the Visitor

To help prepare for your trip to Senegal, see Highlights and also Planning in the Regional Facts for the Visitor chapter.

VISAS
General details about visas are given in the Regional Facts for the Visitor chapter.

Senegalese Visas
Visas are not needed by citizens of the European Union (as it stands at the time of writing), Canada, Norway, South Africa, Japan, Israel, USA and several other (mainly African) countries. Tourist visas for one to three months cost about US$15 to US$20. Australians and New Zealanders definitely *do* need a visa, despite what some Senegalese embassies (most notably the one in Bamako, Mali) have advised.

EMBASSIES & CONSULATES
Senegalese Embassies & Consulates
Outside of West Africa, Senegalese embassies include:

Belgium (☎ 02-673 00 97) 196 Av Franklin-Roosevelt, Brussels 1050
Canada (☎ 613-238 6392, fax 238 2695) 57 Marlborough Ave, Ottawa ON K1N
France (☎ 01 44 05 38 69) 22 Rue Hamelin, 75016 Paris
Germany (☎ 0228-21 80 08) Argelanderstrasse 3, 53115 Bonn
Japan (☎ 03-3464 8451, fax 3464 8452) 1-3-4 Aobadai, Meguro-ku Tokyo 153
Morocco (☎ 07-754171) 17 Rue Cadi Amadi, Rabat
UK (☎ 020-7938 4048) 39 Marloes Rd, London W8 6LA
USA (☎ 202-234 0540) 2112 Wyoming Ave NW, Washington, DC 20008

In West Africa, Senegal has embassies in Banjul (see Gambia's Facts for the Visitor chapter), Abidjan (Côte d'Ivoire), Freetown (Sierra Leone), Lagos (Nigeria), Niamey (Niger) and Praia (Cape Verde) as well as the following:

Guinea (☎ 46 29 30) Corniche Sud, Coléah, Conakry. Open 9am to 12.30pm and 1.30pm to 5pm Monday to Friday. One-month single-entry visas cost GF6000, require four photos and are ready within 24 hours.
Guinea-Bissau (☎ 212944) Southwest of Praça dos Heróis Nacionais, Bissau. Open 8am to 5pm Monday to Friday. One-month multiple-entry visas cost CFA3000, require four photos and are issued in two days.
Mali (☎ 218273/4, fax 211780) South of the centre, off Av de l'Yser, Rue 287 Hippodrome, Bamako. Open 7.30am to 1pm and 1.30pm to 4pm Monday to Friday. One-/three-month visas (CFA3000/7000) are issued in 24 hours or less.
Mauritania (☎ 525 72 90) Av de l'Ambassade du Sénégal, Nouakchott. One-/two-month visas cost UM1015/2030, require two photos and 24 hours to issue.

Senegal is also represented by embassies, consuls or honorary consuls in Addis Ababa, Algiers, Berne, Brasilia, Cairo, Geneva, Libreville, New Delhi, New York, Rome, Stockholm, Tunis, Yaoundé, Bordeaux, Lyon, Marseilles, Toronto, Vancouver, Vienna and Zürich.

Embassies & Consulates in Senegal
The following is a list of some embassies, consulates and diplomatic missions in Senegal. You usually need to provide between one and four passport photos when applying for a visa for a neighbouring country.

Many embassies are in or near central Dakar, but there is a steady movement of the diplomatic corps toward the Point E and Mermoz areas, about 5km northwest of the centre. If you need to find an embassy that is not listed here, check the phone book, one of the listings magazines, or W www .ausenegal.com/practique_en/ambassad.htm

Belgium (☎ 821 40 27) Route de la Corniche-Est
Canada (☎ 823 92 90) Immeuble Sorano, 4th floor, 45–47 Blvd de la République

SENEGAL

France (☎ 839 51 00) 1 Rue Assane Ndoye, near the Novotel
Germany (☎ 823 25 19) 20 Av Pasteur
Italy (☎ 822 00 76) Rue El H, Seydou Nourou Tall
Morocco (☎ 824 6927) Av Cheikh Anta Diop, Mermoz, near the Total petrol station where all the *cars rapide* wait
Netherlands (☎ 823 94 83) 37 Rue Kléber
Spain (☎ 821 11 78) 41 Rue Amadou A Ndoye
Switzerland (☎ 823 58 48) Rue René Niaye
UK (☎ 823 73 92) 20 Rue du Dr Guillet, one block north of Hôpital Le Dantec
USA (☎ 823 34 96, 823 34 24) Av Jean XXIII

Embassies and consulates of other West African countries in Dakar include:

Burkina Faso (☎ 827 9509/8) Lot 1, Liberty VI Extension. Open 8am to 3pm Monday to Friday. Visas cost CFA13000, take two days and require three photos.
Cape Verde (☎ 821 3936) 3 Blvd el Haji Djily Mbaye. Open 8.30am to 3pm Monday to Friday. Visas cost CFA21,200 and take 24 hours.
Côte d'Ivoire (☎ 821 34 73) 4th floor, 2 Av Albert Sarraut. Open 9am to 12.30pm and 3pm to 5pm Monday to Friday. Visas for one month cost CFA70,000 (CFA27,000 for US citizens) and take two days to issue.
Gambia (☎ 821 72 30, 821 44 76) 11 Rue de Thiong. Open 9am to 3pm Monday to Thursday and 9am to 1pm Friday. Visas cost CFA15,000 and there is same-day service or within 24 hours.
Guinea (☎ 824 86 06) Rue 7, Point E, directly opposite Ker Jaraaf. Open 9.30am to 2pm Monday to Friday. Visas cost CFA20,000 and are issued in 24 hours.
Guinea-Bissau (☎ 824 59 22) Rue 6, Point E, near the Guinean embassy. Open 8am to 12.30pm Monday to Friday. Visas cost CFA10,000 for one month and are issued the same day, if you arrive before noon. Don't join the queue in front of the embassy; go around the back to the consul's office. There is also an efficient consulate in Ziguinchor (see the Casamance chapter for details).
Mali (☎ 894 69 50/9) 23 Route de la Corniche Ouest, Fann. Open 8am to 11am Monday to Friday. Visas cost CFA7500 and take 48 hours.
Mauritania (*consulate*; ☎ 822 62 38) Rue 37, Kolobane, around the side of the embassy, opposite the post office near the Independence Monument. Open 8am to 2pm Monday to Friday. Visas cost CFA6000 to CFA9000, depending on nationality, and are issued on the spot. A *note verbal* (letter of introduction) from your own embassy may be required. Americans might find this consulate less than welcoming.
Togo Visas are issued by the French Consulate for CFA40,000 in one day. You will need a letter from your embassy.

CUSTOMS

There are no limits on foreign currency that tourists are allowed to bring into Senegal, although CFA200,000 is the maximum amount of local currency foreigners may export. Duty must be paid on some electrical and electronic items, such as computers and VCRs.

MONEY

See also Money in the Regional Facts for the Visitor chapter.

Currency

The currency of Senegal is the West African CFA franc, called the 'franc CFA' in French (pronounced franc see-eff-ahh, and also called 'seefa' by English-speaking travellers). CFA stands for Communauté Financière Africaine. It is also the official currency of Benin, Burkina Faso, Côte d'Ivoire, Guinea-Bissau, Mali, Niger and Togo.

There are 100 centimes in one CFA franc and they come in 5, 10, 25 and 50 denominations. There are coins for CFA5, CFA10, CFA50, CFA100 and CFA250 and there are notes for CFA500, CFA1000, CFA5000 and CFA10,000.

Note that Senegal's currency is due to change in 2004. See the boxed text 'New Currencies' in the Regional Facts for the Visitor chapter for details.

Exchange Rates

The CFA franc is pegged to the euro at 655.957:1, so the rate of exchange against other hard currencies (US dollar, UK pound etc) is determined by how the euro moves against them. CFA francs can also be used (or easily exchanged for local currency) in some nearby countries that have their own currency, including Gambia, Guinea and Ghana.

Exchange rates since 1994 have been fairly stable, but dealing with cash in West Africa looks like being pretty interesting during the next few years; things could change – a lot. At the time of going to press exchange rates were:

country	unit		CFA
Australia	A$1	=	CFA392
Canada	C$1	=	CFA453
euro zone	€1	=	CFA656
New Zealand	NZ$1	=	CFA331
UK	UK£1	=	CFA1030
USA	US$1	=	CFA700
Gambia	D1	=	CFA38

Exchanging Money

Banks where you can change cash and travellers cheques in Senegal include Citibank; Compagnie Bancaire de l'Afrique Occidentale (CBAO); Banque Internationale pour le Commerce et l'Industrie Sénégalaise (BICIS), which is affiliated with and accepts cheques from BNP in France; and Société Générale des Banques du Sénégal (SGBS). There are branches in all main towns and at Dakar airport. If the airport branch is closed, you can change money at the airport bookshop, where commissions are lower.

There are plenty of ATMs in Dakar and a couple in Kaolack, St-Louis, Saly and Ziguinchor. SGBS and CBAO ATMs take Visa and MasterCard, but BICIS accepts only Visa cards. You can sometimes get a cash advance on your credit card, although some readers say this is more trouble than it's worth. In Dakar, the best place for a non-ATM credit card advance is the SGBS branch at the south end of Place de l'Indépendance.

Cashing travellers cheques in any major currency is easy in Dakar and St-Louis, but can be a protracted nightmare elsewhere. Western Union Money Transfer signs seem to be breeding in Senegal, but the official agent for Western Union is CBAO.

POST & COMMUNICATIONS
Post

Senegal's postal service is relatively good, and items sent to or from the country generally arrive. Sending a 10g letter to France/ Europe/North America/Australasia costs CFA370/390/425/535, while a 2kg parcel costs CFA9600/10,600/12,100/20,100.

If you need to receive mail, you can use the post restante service. Letters should be addressed in this form:

Your name
Poste Restante
PTT
Dakar
Senegal

The country's main poste restante in Dakar should be avoided unless you're desperate.

Telephone & Fax

There's a telecommunications revolution occurring in Senegal, with use of traditional and mobile (cell) phones soaring. *Télécentres* provide a convenient and efficient service; alternatively, the government-operated Sonatel has four offices in Dakar and one in St-Louis, open from 9am to 11.30pm daily. Call prices have fallen recently but still aren't cheap. Local calls work out at about CFA50 per minute, but this rises sharply if the call is long distance or to a mobile phone number. International calls and faxes from either Sonatel or télécentres cost about the same at CFA600 per minute to Europe and CFA800 per minute to the USA, with a 20% reduction after 8pm and at weekends. Not surprisingly, rates to Australia are rather a bit higher.

Linking your mobile phone into one of the two local GSM phone networks is easy. SIM

Télécentres

Thousands of privately owned *télécentres* have popped up across the country – they are apparently the closest thing to a guaranteed earner you can get here. All but the most remote of communities will have a télécentre of sorts. Some are very smart offices with air-conditioning and mood music, others are just a tiny booth in the corner of a shop or bar where the mercury hovers at about 40°C. All télécentres have a *compteur* (meter) showing the number of units you've used. The per-unit price ranges between CFA60 and CFA100 and is advertised outside, but it's a good idea to check the per-minute rates for international calls.

SENEGAL

cards for either the Hello or Alize networks cost CFA25,000, with prepaid cards selling for CFA5000, CFA10,000 or CFA50,000. Coverage is constantly improving, but the further you are away from the coast, or a big town, the more likely you are to be without any service. This is not quite as bad as it sounds: Senegal is so flat that you need to be a long way from a tower before you lose touch.

Email & Internet Access
The number of Internet bureaus in Dakar, with kids laying waste to foreign worlds and youths using chat sites, is proof that the cyber age has arrived in Senegal. There are bureaus in Dakar and most major towns, the general rule being that further away from Dakar the town, the slower and more expensive the service will be. In Dakar, Internet phone and video facilities are common. An hour online will usually cost from CFA500 to CFA1000.

DIGITAL RESOURCES
While most websites about Senegal are in French, there are a few that have English options. If not, you could use Google (W www.google.com) to translate the site for you.

Au-Senegal Tourist Probably the best, most useful and most regularly updated site specifically for use by tourists.
W www.au-senegal.com

BBC News If there has been a major incident, for example, in Casamance, read about it here. Just type 'Casamance' into the search box for the full archive.
W newssearch.bbc.co.uk

St Louis city Not all the links are in English, but details of transport, accommodation and cultural events usually are.
W www.saintlouisdusenegal.com/english

Senerap.com Some stories are in French, but you don't need to be a linguist to download MP3s of Dakar's latest rap and hip-hop hits.
W www.senerap.com

Stanford Site Guide Put together by Stanford University, this page has links to hundreds of websites about Senegal, both in French and English. If it's out there, you will probably find it here.
W www.sul.stanford.edu/depts/ssrg/africa/sene.html

BOOKS
General books about Senegal, many of which also cover Gambia, are listed under Books in the Regional Facts for the Visitor chapter. Novels and poetry by Senegalese writers are discussed under Arts in the Facts about Senegal chapter.

NEWSPAPERS & MAGAZINES
Most newspapers and magazines are published in French, with a few in Wolof or other indigenous languages. There were 11 newspapers being published in Dakar at the time of research, though this number tends to fluctuate. The biggest seller is *Le Soleil*, which is nominally independent but has close links to the government. Other publications come out weekly or erratically, and are usually linked to other political parties. Imported papers, plus international or regional publications such as *Time*, the *Economist*, the BBC's *Focus on Africa* and *West Africa* magazine, are sometimes available in bookshops, supermarkets or major hotels in Dakar.

RADIO & TV
The government radio stations broadcast in French, Wolof and other local languages. Government TV is all in French. Independent radio stations, also French-language, include Dakar FM and the lively Sud-FM. Independent TV is dominated by Canal + Horizons and French satellite stations, although some large hotels have sets tuned into CNN or BBC World. In Dakar it's possible to hear a BBC World Service relay on FM105.6.

PHOTOGRAPHY & VIDEO
In Senegal, no photography permit is required. You can photograph most things – even the colourfully clad guards outside the Presidential Palace – providing, of course, the usual rules of politeness are observed, although snapping military installations, airports or government buildings could still get you into trouble. For more general information and advice, see Photography & Video in the Regional Facts for the Visitor chapter.

HEALTH
Malaria is a killer and exists year-round throughout the country. It is essential that you take appropriate precautions, especially if you're heading out of Dakar. For more information on other health matters, see Health in the Regional Facts for the Visitor chapter.

Water in Senegal's main cities and towns is generally clean and OK to drink, and even in some of the more remote places we had no trouble. Bottled water is also available in all but the smallest towns.

In Dakar, you'll find the country's main hospitals as well as many private clinics and doctors. Around the country, most large towns have hospitals, doctors and clinics; if you need to find any of these, ask at an upmarket hotel.

DANGERS & ANNOYANCES
There are two main dangers you may encounter: the possibility of civil unrest in Casamance (see the boxed text 'To Go or Not to Go?' in the Casamance chapter) and the possibility of being robbed in Dakar (see Dangers & Annoyances in the Dakar chapter).

Annoyances include persistent street traders and hustlers, mostly in Dakar but to a lesser extent in St-Louis and Ziguinchor.

EMERGENCIES
In an emergency, contact the police on ☎ 17, the fire department on ☎ 18, and the SOS Doctor (Medicin) can be contacted on ☎ 821 32 13, although this service may only be available in Dakar.

BUSINESS HOURS
Businesses and government offices are open from 8am to noon and 2.30pm to 6pm Monday to Friday, and 8am to noon on Saturday. Most banks are open from 8.30am to 11.30am or noon, and 2.30pm to 4.30pm Monday to Friday. Some banks also open until 11am on Saturday mornings. The bank at Léopold Sédar Senghor International Airport is open until midnight.

PUBLIC HOLIDAYS & SPECIAL EVENTS
Both Christian and Islamic events are celebrated. Islamic feasts are set according to the Islamic calendar – see the boxed text 'Islam' in the Facts about Senegambia chapter for more information, including dates. Other holidays include:

New Year's Day 1 January
Independence Day 4 April
Easter Monday March/April
Whit Sunday/Pentecost 7th Sunday after Easter
Whit Monday Day after Whit Sunday
Ascension 40th day after Easter
Workers Day 1 May
Assumption August 15
Christmas Day 25 December

Other annual festivals include the Grand Magal pilgrimage and celebration, held in Touba 48 days after the Islamic New Year to celebrate the return from exile of the founder of the Mouride Islamic brotherhood; and the Paris-Dakar Rally, which ends at Lac Retba in the middle of January.

SENEGAL

Getting There & Away

Details on travelling between Senegal and Europe, North America or Australasia are given in the regional Getting There & Away chapter. This chapter covers travel between Senegal and neighbouring countries (including Gambia).

AIR

This section covers flight possibilities and provides an idea of fares only. Schedules and prices change frequently, so if you need more precise information contact the airline or a travel agent. All the airlines have offices in Dakar and these are listed in the Dakar chapter. There is no departure tax payable upon exiting Senegal.

The Gambia

Within the region, Air Senegal International does the short hop from Dakar to Banjul five times a week for CFA48,000 one way, with Gambia International Airlines operating the other days for the same price.

Other West African Countries

Dakar is linked to most other capital cities in West Africa, but the number of airlines and the number of flights have both dropped in recent years.

Ghana Airways flies from Dakar to Accra via Banjul on Sunday and Wednesday for CFA280,000/338,600 one way/return. Air Mali flies to Bamako on Monday and Friday for CFA83,800/154,800. TACV Cabo Verde Airlines flies three times a week to Praia for CFA115,000/145,500. On Tuesday Air Guinée flies to Conakry via Banjul and Labe for about US$125/165.

Morocco

Many travellers fly from Dakar to Casablanca (Morocco) to avoid the difficult overland section through Mauritania and Western Sahara. Royal Air Maroc has two flights a week, with one-way fares costing US$530. You could pick up a youth ticket from the same airline for US$370.

LAND
Bus & Bush Taxi

Senegal completely surrounds Gambia, and there are several places to cross the border. For details on the various forms of bus and bush taxi found in Senegal see the Getting Around chapter later in this book.

Gambia This section outlines your options for crossing the border. More details are in Gambia's Getting There & Away chapter.

The main crossing point between northern Senegal and Gambia is at Karang, a short drive north of Barra. From Dakar there are buses (CFA3000 to CFA3500, six to nine hours) to Barra (from where you get the ferry across the Gambia River to Banjul), or Peugeot bush taxis (CFA4500, six hours) to the border at Karang.

From the Casamance region of southern Senegal, bush taxis (Peugeots or minibuses) run regularly between Ziguinchor and the border town of Séléti (CFA2000, 1½ hours), where you change for Serekunda (CFA1000, one hour), and between Kafountine and Brikama (CFA1200, 1½ hours). Between Dakar and Ziguinchor the Trans-Gambia Hwy swings inland from Kaolack and crosses Gambia via the towns of Farafenni and Soma, and a ferry across the Gambia River.

It's also possible to travel between Tambacounda in eastern Senegal and Basse Santa Su in Gambia via the border at Sabi and Vélingara.

Guinea Nearly all traffic between Senegal and Guinea goes to/from Labé, a large town in northwestern Guinea. The busiest route is via Koundara, but some transport also goes via Kedougou (in the far southeast of Senegal) and the small town of Mali (usually called Mali-ville, to distinguish it from the country of the same name). If you're leaving Senegal, the best place to pick up transport is Tambacounda, from where, most days, a battered bush taxi goes to Koundara via Medina Gounas and Sambaïlo (where you may have to change). This rough, slow trip costs around CFA8000.

Guinea-Bissau Bush taxis run several times daily between Ziguinchor and Bissau (CFA4000, 147km) via São Domingos (the border) and Ingore. The road is in fairly good condition, but the ferries on the stretch between Ingore and Bissau can make the trip take anything from four to eight hours. Occasionally the São Domingos border closes unexpectedly, apparently on the whim of the guards, but this doesn't usually last too long. Other options are to go from Tanaf to Farim or from Tambacounda via Vélingara to Gabú.

Mali Travellers have traditionally taken the train most, if not all of the way from Dakar to Bamako. But a brand new highway, probably the best in the country, now links Tambacounda and the border at Kidira, making the bush-taxi option much more attractive. From Tambacounda to Kidira (three hours, 184km) a Peugeot bush taxi costs CFA4000, a minibus CFA2700 and the large express bus CFA2300. In Kidira, you cross the road bridge to Diboli, from where bush taxis go to Kayes for CFA2500. From Kayes, most continue by train, which travel to Bamako on most days.

Mauritania The main border point is at Rosso, where a ferry crosses the Senegal River. You can go direct to Rosso from Dakar in a Peugeot bush taxi (CFA4600, six hours, 384km), but most travellers stop off at St-Louis, from where a Peugeot to Rosso (two hours, 106km) is CFA1540. You cross the river on the large ferry, which is free for passengers, or by pirogue (canoe) for CFA650. From the Mauritanian immigration post it's 500m to the *gare routière* (bus and bush-taxi station), from where bush taxis go to Nouakchott.

Train

In theory, trains run between Dakar and Bamako twice a week in each direction and the trip takes about 35 hours. In practice, this is crap – one train is often out of action; the trip usually takes 40 hours or longer; the train has lots of thieves; and it's not unusual to find broken tracks and derailments on the Malian side. In spite, or because of these hardships, this trip will be one of the most memorable of your life, particularly the Malian leg.

From Dakar, you can also get on or off at Tambacounda (eastern Senegal) or Kayes (western Mali), but between Kayes and Bamako the train is your only real option. Seats are numbered, although for 2nd class you should get to the train two hours before

---

Trains between Senegal & Mali

The *Mistral International* (Senegalese) train departs Dakar at 10am on Wednesday. Tickets are sold from 8am to noon and 1pm to 5pm on Monday and Tuesday. The *Express International* (Malian) train departs Dakar at 10am on Saturday. Tickets are sold from 8am to noon and 1pm to 5pm on Friday. Times and fares for the *Express International* from Dakar are shown in the following table. Times for the *Mistral International* are the same and fares are about 15% more expensive, but it's oh so worth it. Trains leave from Bamako for Dakar at 9.15am Wednesday and Saturday.

destination	arrival time	1st class (CFA)	2nd class (CFA)	sleeper (CFA)
Thiès	11.30	6685	4900	n/a
Tambacounda	19.05	12,330	9035	n/a
Kidira	23.23	17,050	12,495	n/a
Kayes	03.55*	19,800	14,515	33,320
Bamako	15.20*	34,250	25,100	51,390

* Denotes the day after departure

Cars & Motorbikes on the Train

It's possible to put a car on the train between Dakar and Bamako, but the costs can be so high and the hassle so great that most people prefer to drive, at least as far as Kayes. However, if you're on a motorbike and have had enough of eating dirt, it's a different matter. The road to Kayes is easy enough, so it's best to ride there and then load the bike onto a train, any train, for the last leg to Bamako. The official fares for motorbikes and rider come to about CFA12,000. To that you add another CFA8000 or so to cover 'incidentals' such as lifting and, well, loading. In Bamako there will be no shortage of muscle ready to unload the bikes for a couple of thousand CFA francs.

departure. The 1st-class seats are large and comfortable, while 2nd class is more crowded, though perfectly adequate and more fun. Sleepers (couchettes) are basic but adequate. You can get cheap food at stations along the way, and the *Mistral International* (Senegalese) train has a restaurant car. In fact, the *Mistral International* (which departs Dakar on Wednesday) is superior in almost every way to its Malian counterpart (Saturday), and train veterans strongly recommend holding out for the *Mistral*. (For details on the timetable and fares, see the boxed text 'Trains between Senegal & Mali'.)

If there are no seats available at the station, look out for touts on the platform selling unused tickets. Another option is go to Tambacounda from Dakar by road and buy your train ticket there, although usually only 1st-class tickets are available.

At each border post you will have to take a short hike to the immigration office. Foreigners sometimes have their passport taken by an immigration inspector on the train, but you still have to collect it yourself by getting off the train at the border post. Nobody tells you this, so if your passport is taken, ask where and when you have to go to get it back.

Theft can be a problem on this train. It's no overstatement to say the Artful Dodger would be out of his depth, and it wouldn't surprise if Fagin himself was a regular train traveller. All you can do is be prepared: Be sure to carry a torch; if you leave your seat, especially at night, ask a fellow passenger to watch your gear; and expect to become a target when the lights go out (often in the train and the station) as the train pulls into Kayes and Bamako. Good luck!

Car & Motorcycle

It's possible to drive your vehicle between Senegal and any neighbouring country, although conditions vary. For entering Gambia, see Gambia's Getting There & Away chapter.

Going to Mali, the route from Tambacounda to Kayes is straightforward, but the onward route beside the railway is bad as far as Kita. The European Union has promised an upgrade, but at present the best way is to go down to Diamou and then to Bafoulabe, from where a detour via Manatali takes you along decent dirt roads to Bamako.

Heading for Mauritania, *avoid* the main crossing point at Rosso. Several readers wrote to us with stories of harassment, extortion and frustration – and it's better than it used to be! If you're in a 2WD, arrive early and have as little as possible on show. If guards ask for a bribe, offer cigarettes. If they want more, just say no. If you're coming into Senegal, the ferry costs CFA2000 for a car and CFA3000 for a 4WD or truck.

To avoid all this go via the Maka Diama barrage, 97km southwest of Rosso and just north of St-Louis, although the track between the barrage and the main road on the Mauritanian side is soft sand. The crossing here costs CFA5000/10,000 in winter/summer, and there is a theoretical maximum weight for vehicles of 2.8 tonnes. Drivers also occasionally cross the Senegal River at several ferries east of Rosso.

SEA

Pirogues go between Senegal's Siné-Saloum Delta and Banjul (Gambia) – for details see Djifer in the Petite Côte & Siné-Saloum Delta chapter.

Getting Around

This section covers specific aspects of getting around Senegal. For more general information about travel in Senegambia, see the Getting Around Senegambia chapter.

AIR

Air Senegal International has daily flights from Dakar to Ziguinchor for CFA44,000 one way. These go all the way to Cap Skiring twice a week for CFA59,500/110,500 one way/return. There's one flight a week to Tambacounda for CFA64,500 one way, though it's hardly worth it.

For plane charter, your best bet is Senegalair Avion Taxis (☎ 821 34 25) in Dakar, which flies to Simenti in Parc National du Niokolo-Koba, or anywhere else you'd like to go.

EXPRESS BUS & BUSH TAXI

The many and varied modes of public transport in Senegal can lead to some confusion. To minimise this we've grouped them into the two types: express buses and bush taxis *(taxis brousse)*.

Express buses are large 50- to 60-seat buses that you're probably used to seeing on suburban routes in cities the world over. Those in Senegal are not exactly luxurious, but apart from the Peugeot bush taxis they're generally the quickest way from A to B, and among the cheapest. They go by several names – you might encounter *grand car* or even *trés grand car* – but the most common (and best understood) name is *car mouride*, acknowledging that all these are owned and operated by the leaders of the powerful Mouride brotherhood. The name on the side of the bus will be Transport Alzhar, being the company name, but, again, few people refer to them by this name. To minimise confusion with all these different names, we've referred to them throughout the Senegal chapter simply as 'express buses'.

Bush taxis are more complicated. This group includes several different vehicle types, most of which look as if they've done a million miles (though you'll *never* see a working odometer), leave when full and stop regularly (the bigger the conveyance, the more often it stops). The fastest is the Peugeot, which is most often known locally as a *sept-place* (there are seven seats for seven passengers) but might also be called (confusingly) a *taxi brousse*. Peugeot taxis are usually comfortable, safe, and as fast as private vehicles once they're on their way.

Next quickest, but still slow, is the minibus, typically a Nissan Urvan seating about 20 people and known as a *petit car*.

Even slower are the ubiquitous white Mercedes buses that usually carry about 35 people and seem to stop every 200 metres. These can take twice as long as a Peugeot taxi but, thank God for small mercies, everyone gets a seat. In Dakar these are often called N'Diaga N'Diaye (pronounced *njagga-njaye*), but elsewhere this might not be understood. It's safer to ask for an Alham (shortened from Alhamdoulilahi, which means 'Thanks to God' and appears on the front of every such vehicle), or if this doesn't work a *grand car*, a term that seems to be interchangeable with the bigger express buses. In this section we've called them Alhams.

Finally there are the misleadingly named *cars rapide*, ancient French minibuses, usually painted orange and blue, which are battered, slow, crowded but generally very social. It's unlikely you'll find these on long-distance routes as they usually stick to towns and cities.

All public-transport fares are fixed by the government. To give an idea, some Peugeot bush taxi prices from Dakar include: Kaolack (CFA2200, three to four hours); St-Louis (CFA3100, four to five hours); Ziguinchor (CFA6500, nine to 10 hours). Minibuses are typically about 20% to 25% cheaper than Peugeot taxis, and Alhams about 30% to 35% cheaper.

TRAIN

Many visitors take the express train that runs between Dakar and Bamako (Mali), but very few use this line to travel by train around Senegal itself, although you could use it between, say, Dakar and Tambacounda. For details see Senegal's Getting There & Away section. Senegal's only commuter trains run between Dakar and Thiès (CFA600) via Rufisque (CFA300) from Monday to Saturday. Ironically, the railway lines the French fought so hard to build to link Dakar with St-Louis, Mbaké and Linguère are seldom used.

CAR & MOTORCYCLE

Most car-rental companies are based in Dakar; for rates, conditions, and company addresses see Getting Around in the Dakar chapter. There are also options for hiring cars in St-Louis. Petrol costs about CFA450 per litre, diesel *(gasoil)* about CFA350.

BOAT

The MS *Joola* is a large ferry that is supposed to run between Dakar and Ziguinchor via Île de Carabane. Sadly, it seems to spend much of its time anchored in Dakar. Promises of its return were issued regularly but at the time of research it had failed to materialise. If it does sail again, you can expect the trip to take about 20 hours. We were told the *Joola* would operate to its old timetable, departing Dakar on Tuesday and Friday, Ziguinchor at Thursday and Sunday.

One-way fares from Dakar are the same to Île de Carabane or Ziguinchor: CFA3500 in economy class; CFA6000 in 2nd class; CFA12,000 in a cabin with four beds; CFA15,000 in a cabin with two beds; and CFA18,000 in a one-bed cabin. There are seats in economy class but no guaranteed places, while 2nd class has reservable reclining seats. Ziguinchor to Carabane is CFA1500.

The *Joola* could well be pensioned off and replaced by a newer and faster boat. To check the latest, call Sentram in Dakar (☎ 821 5852) or Ziguinchor (☎ 852 5443).

ORGANISED TOURS

Most places of interest in Senegal can be reached by public transport or car, but if you're short of time you could get around the country on an organised tour. A small selection of operators based in and around Dakar is included here. For tours in northern Senegal, see also St-Louis in the Northern Senegal chapter, and for trips to Parc National du Niokolo-Koba see the Tambacounda section in the Eastern Senegal chapter. Most tours require six or eight people; however, options for two or four people exist.

Inter Tourisme (☎ 822 45 29) 3 Av Allées Delmas. Friendly and cheap, Inter Tourisme offers one-day trips to Lac Retba for CFA20,000 per person, two-day trips to Siné-Saloum for CFA85,000 each for two people and five-day trips to Parc National du Niokolo-Koba and Bassari country for CFA200,000 per person (minimum of six).

Motor Dakar (☎ mobile 646 86 83, in Spain 696-480 444, W www.motordakar.com) If you've got a few spare euros and fancy a taste of the Paris-Dakar Rally, this is for you. Multilingual former Internet entrepreneur Charly runs trips on Honda XR600 bikes, ranging from one-day desert riding classes (€225) to week-long raids up the coast (€1800). Motorbike, equipment, 4WD support, food and accommodation are included.

Nouvelles Frontières (☎ 823 34 34, fax 822 28 17) 3 Blvd de la République. The local office of the French international tour operator offers a wide range of excursions and helps with hotel reservations.

Safari-Evasion (☎ 849 52 52) 12 Av Albert Sarraut. Safari-Evasion mainly arranges flights, but has a few tours to popular destinations, including four-day trips to St-Louis for CFA135,000 per person, and day trips to Lac Retba and Joal-Fadiout for about CFA25,000 per person.

Musicians in Senegambia traditionally come from the griot class. Their instruments include the *balafon*, a wooden xylophone (top); the *djembe*, a very popular drum made of wood and goat skin (bottom left); and a variety of other drums, some less traditional (bottom right).

Music is everywhere in Gambia and Senegal: loud and full of bass from the market cassette stalls; pure and sweet from a singer's mouth; scratchy and distorted on a bush-taxi radio; in the background at restaurants; and in your face at nightclubs. For many travellers the haunting rhythms and melodies of West African music become the most memorable aspect of a visit to the region.

African music can be divided into two basic categories: traditional music and pop music. The main difference is that traditional music is predominantly rural, while pop is largely an urban phenomenon. But African pop draws inspiration from the styles and rhythms of traditional music, so there's no firm line between the two.

TRADITIONAL MUSIC

Traditional music is at the heart of West African cultures, but it is difficult for foreigners to appreciate. To the uninitiated it may sound random or simply monotonous. However, with careful listening you can pick out the structure of the song. If you're listening to a drum ensemble, try to focus on the sound (or rhythm) being produced by just one of the drums – you'll then begin to notice how it fits in with the other drum beats, and the whole pattern will become clearer. African music is typically polyrhythmic (it has many rhythms) and polyphonic (many

Right: Women's groups have their own distinctive type of traditional music

melodies), which allows the listener to identify certain melodies or rhythms and concentrate on them, which is exactly what dancers do.

While membership of a pop group is essentially open to anyone, the same cannot be said of traditional music. In much of West Africa (including Gambia and Senegal, plus neighbouring countries such as Mali), music has long been the province of one social group – the griots. The term 'griot' is of French origin and the most synonymous English terms are minstrel, musician or praise singer. While griot is useful as a generality, the local terms are more appropriate – *jali* in Mandinka, *gewel* in Wolof or *gawlo* in Fula.

Many West African societies (including the Wolof, Mandinka and Fula people of the Senegambian region) were, and still are, highly stratified with the nobility at the top and the descendants of slaves at the bottom. The artisan classes – such as blacksmiths, weavers and leatherworkers – form a class above the descendants of slaves. Griots are in the artisan class, but despite their low social rank, they fulfil many important social functions. Historically, griots had a close relationship with the royal courts, where they acted as translators and diplomats, yet it is perhaps their role as historians that is most revealing.

In West Africa, the spoken word is the means by which the younger generation has traditionally learned about the history of their society. The griots' role in this is crucial as they are the keepers of their culture's history; a history they reveal through narratives or songs. For example, all griots know about the epic of Sundiata, which describes the exploits of the warrior who founded the empire of Mali in the 13th century AD. This song is well known throughout West Africa and is just one of a large repertoire of narratives that deal with a variety of issues. Other narratives include love songs, anticolonial songs and praise songs to famous warriors.

Griots are also genealogists, and at weddings, naming ceremonies or other important events are called upon to recount the names and deeds of the host's ancestors. Like blacksmiths and other artisans, they are thought to possess spiritual powers, and this, coupled with their intimate knowledge of the past, leads some people to fear them.

Traditional music also serves a social purpose. Each social occasion has its own type of music, and in addition, there are different kinds of music for women's groups, hunters, warriors etc.

Another feature of traditional music is its instrumentation. Unlike the pop groups with electric guitars, traditional musicians use only instruments they make with local materials, such as gourds, leather, cow horns and shells.

Traditional Instruments

Drums The *tama* drum of the Wolof has gained much attention through its use in the pop music style known as *mbalax*, popularised by Senegal's Youssou N'Dour. The tama is a small single-faced drum with strips of leather affixed to the skin and base. Squeezing the drum under

the musician's arm changes the tension of the surface of the drum's skin and, therefore, the drum's pitch. This variable pitch quality gives rise to the name 'talking drum', and good players can obtain a wide range of notes.

Other Wolof drums include the *sabar*, shaped like a tall, thin hour-glass and played while the musician stands; and the *mblatt* and the *gorong*. Seeing these drums in an ensemble performance is a real treat, and dancing to the rhythms is hard to resist. The *djembe* is probably the most popular of all African drums, and has an appeal that has reached beyond Africa and deep into Europe. A trawl of the Internet reveals dozens of sites dedicated to this shorter drum, shaped like a medieval chalice and usually covered with goat hide. Djembes are for sale, and lessons are available, throughout Senegal and Gambia. The djembe is almost always played while sitting down.

Stringed Instruments The variety of stringed instruments ranges from the Mandinka single-stringed *moolo* (plucked lute) and the *riti riti* (bowed fiddle) to the 21-stringed kora. The kora is the pre-eminent instrument of the griots, and is arguably one of the most sophisticated instruments in sub-Saharan Africa. Essentially it's a cross between a harp and a lute, with its strings divided into two rows – one of 11 strings, the other of 10. These are supported over a long neck (made of rosewood) by an ornately carved wooden bridge with a notch for each string. The neck pierces a large hemispherical gourd covered with cowhide. Studs fasten the hide to the gourd and many koras feature stud patterns, sometimes showing the player's name. The instrument sits almost vertically in the lap of the seated player who plucks the two rows of strings with the thumb and index finger of each hand. Kora players are often very highly skilled musicians who start learning their craft in early childhood. If you're able to attend a traditional Mandinka or Wolof ceremony, such as a naming day or a wedding, the chances are a kora player will be there to provide the music and ceremony. Urban performances are difficult to come by, although in tourist areas such as Gambia's Atlantic coast, kora players entertain at hotels and restaurants – look out for Bajaly Suso who often plays here.

Above right: The pitch of the *tama* drum changes according to the pressure applied when the drum is squeezed under the arm

For kora music performed in the traditional style, look for the excellent recordings by Jali Nyama Suso, a Gambian, who wrote his country's national anthem. He appears on a double-set entitled *A Search for the Roots of the Blues* as well as *Songs from Gambia* and a self-titled release through FMP Records in Berlin. In a different style is the kora music of Lamine Konté, a Casamançais, whose best work appears on *The Kora of Senegal*, volumes one and two.

Another important instrument of the griots is the *xalam* (a Wolof word pronounced khalam). It is known by a variety of names including *konting* in Mandinka and *hoddu* in Fula, and has from three to five strings that are plucked. Interestingly, this instrument is regarded by musicologists as the ancestor of the banjo. Some xalam epic narratives performed by griots include Bowdi, Duga Koro and Jaro.

Wind Instruments The most notable wind instrument is the flute. Fulani shepherds are reputed to play the most beautiful flute music; their instrument is simply a length of reed. You'll also see flutes made from millet stalks, bamboo and gourds. Other wind instruments include trumpets made from gourds, metal, shells or wood. These are found all over West Africa, taking a slightly different form in each area. If you're looking for something a little unusual to collect but light and inexpensive, flutes are a good buy.

Xylophones The *balafon* is a type of wooden xylophone that usually has between 15 and 19 rectangular keys made out of hardwood. These are normally suspended over a row of gourds, which amplify the sound. The player (sometimes two) is usually seated and strikes the keys with two wooden mallets. Balafon is the name given to the instrument played by griots – other types of xylophones have different names depending on the particular language group in the region. Some epic narratives performed by griots on the balafon include Almami Samari Tour, Kala Jula and Lambang.

POP MUSIC

The development of the pop music scene in Senegal and Gambia has been greatly influenced by Cuban music, which was popular in the region in the 1960s. At that time it was not unusual for local bands to sing in Spanish, even though they didn't know what the words meant. Cuban groups such as Orchestra Aragon were very popular, and you can still buy their cassettes today. The influence of Cuban music extends all the way from the first bands at independence to the recent recordings of Youssou N'Dour and Africando. Today, you can still go to any bar and put on some salsa music and watch the place begin to jump!

Orchestras In the 1970s, the pop music scene in Senegal (and to a lesser extent Gambia, Mali and Guinea) was dominated by large bands or 'orchestras'. The most famous of these, Orchestra Baobab, re-formed in 2001 and re-released their classic early '80s album *Pirate's Choice* to mark the occasion. Five of their CDs are available internationally, and at least eight of their cassettes can be purchased locally.

The father of modern Senegalese music is Ibra Kass, who formed an orchestra called the Star Band de Dakar to play at his nightclub, the Miami, in the early 1960s. In the line-up were Pape Seck and Labah Sosseh on vocals. Kass is now dead but his music has enjoyed a revival. Other great ensembles were Canari de Kaolack, the Royal Band, and Etoile de Dakar, the last of which shot Youssou N'Dour (see the boxed text) to stardom. Etoile de Dakar's first cassette, *Xalis*, with El Haji Faye on vocals, is excellent.

In Gambia, the music of the band Guelwar fused modern jazz with rock and Cuban rhythms. In Senegal, an excellent six-volume series of CDs entitled *The Dakar Sound* contains material that traces the development of the modern Senegalese style.

Salsa Showing direct Cuban influences are the popular bands Africando and Le Super Cayor de Dakar. Africando was fronted by three vocalists – Pape Seck, Medoune Diallo and Nicholas Menheim. Pape Seck was one of Senegal's most respected singers, famous for his gravelly voice, and his death in 1995 was a great loss. Recent releases from Africando include the two-CD set *Africando Live*, and the very popular *Mandali*. A good cassette of Le Super Cayor's is *Sopent*.

Mbalax An exciting development in Senegalese music was the incorporation of traditional drums and rhythms with Latin sounds. The Wolof tama drum is used in a lead role, driving the music forward and highlighting the skills of the player through long passages of improvisation. It's excellent music to dance to. The leading exponent of this

Youssou N'Dour

Youssou N'Dour began his singing career at an early age, taking inspiration from his mother, who was a *gawlo* (griot). He first performed at traditional ceremonies and it didn't take long before the extraordinary beauty of his voice found him with a regular spot at the Miami, Dakar's most famous nightclub of the '70s. In 1979 N'Dour formed his own band, Etoile de Dakar, and *Xalis*, their first release, was a huge hit. The band's fusion of traditional Wolof rhythms via the *tama* drum with a funky Latin-based sound (a fusion known as *mbalax*) proved irresistible and launched N'Dour into superstardom. Etoile de Dakar and the subsequent formation Super Etoile have released dozens of CDs and cassettes, many of which are available in Senegambia. On the international stage N'Dour has collaborated with other singers, notably Neneh Cherry (on the superb '7 Seconds') and Peter Gabriel. N'Dour's style of mbalax continues to be the trendsetter in Senegal, where he remains the undisputed king.

style is Youssou N'Dour, who began his career with Etoile de Dakar. N'Dour has now become a major international star with many CD releases and international tours. Some of his best recordings are *Wommat* and *Set*, and more recently *Joko* and *Ba Tay*. Other performers of the mbalax style include Thione Seck and Le Super Cayor.

Other Styles & Musicians The band Toure, Kunda (meaning 'Toure, Family') was founded by four brothers in Casamance and blends mbalax and Ghanaian 'highlife' with other musical styles to create a unique sound. They toured internationally years before many other West African bands. Some of their best recordings are *Paris-Ziguinchor Live* and *Natalia*.

The group Xalam, which developed a unique style combining African music with jazz and rhythm and blues, was one of the first West African bands to gain recognition in Europe, though they disbanded after the death in 1989 of their lead singer.

Baaba Maal (see the boxed text) and Mansour Seck fuse the music of the Fouta Toro region, the cultural homeland of the Fula people along the Senegal River in the north of the country, with Western rock and folk. Their critically acclaimed releases include *Djam Leeli* and *Nouvelle Génération*. A few more names to look out for when you're browsing the cassette racks are Super Diamono, Ismael Lô and Étoile 2000.

Pop stars from Gambia are outnumbered by those from Senegal, but the smaller country has a few famous names. Jaliba Kuyateh hails from Brikama and incorporates the kora with Western instrumentation. He has at least three cassettes available, including a two-volume release from 1995, *Jaliba Kuyateh & the Kumarehs*. Other Gambian musicians include Ifang Bondi, Abdel Kabirr and Bubacar Jammeh.

Baaba Maal

Baaba Maal hails from the Fouta Toro region of Senegal, which borders Mauritania and Mali. Sources of inspiration for his music are the traditional Fula songs of this area, especially the kora music, and his popularisation of them has led to a greater interest in Fula music in general – no mean feat in a country where the *mbalax* and salsa styles dominate. His music incorporates elements from reggae and jazz, and is characterised by tight, interlocking drum rhythms. Traditional instruments such as the *balafon* (a type of xylophone) are used on all of his recordings and are backed up by electric guitar. Although not a griot by birth, Maal sees himself as a commentator on all facets of life in Senegal. His lyrics frequently address the difficulties and aspirations of youth, as well as political issues. He sees music as a way of building greater understanding between people and as having an educative role. His first recording, *Djam Leeli* (made with his 'mentor', the griot Mansour Seck), is recommended, as are his superb *Firin' in Fouta* and the more recent *Missing You*.

RESOURCES

A good introduction to African music can be found in *Africa Never Stands Still*, a boxed set of three CDs with a 48-page booklet. For a fix of pure West African sounds try *The Music in My Head*, a compilation CD with tracks by Jaliba Kuyateh, Youssou N'Dour, Etoile de Dakar and the cream of the region's singers and bands, from the raw 'golden age' of the 1970s to the sophisticated '90s. There's also a five-CD series that focuses on music from Gambia and Senegal called *Sénégal Flash*.

Recommended books include *The Da Capo Guide to Contemporary African Music* (published in the UK as *Stern's Guide to Contemporary African Music*) by Ronnie Graham, although it has been out of print since the early 1990s. *African Rock* (also titled *African All Stars: The Pop Music of a Continent*) by Chris Stapleton & Chris May is a good introduction to the pop scene, as are *West African Pop Roots* by John Collins and *Africa Oh Yeah* by Graeme Ewens.

The Roots of the Blues by Samuel Charters describes the author's journey to West Africa in search of traditional music. Other good books on traditional music include *African Music – A People's Art* by Francis Bebey; and *The Music of Africa* by JH Kwabena Nketia.

The UK magazine *FRoots* (W www.frootsmag.com) is a good source for the latest news and interviews. Other good websites include Roots World (W www.rootsworld.com), and African Music Encyclopedia (W www.africanmusic.org), which has background information on a vast array of African musicians. Scholarly journals include *African Music* and *The Journal of Modern African Studies*.

Music Shops

UK, USA & Australia Specialist world-music stores in Britain include Stern's (☎ 020-7387 5550, fax 7388 2756), 74 Warren St, London W1P 5PA, which also runs an excellent website and online store at W www.sternsmusicshop.com.

In the USA, Stern's (☎ 212-964 5455, fax 964 5955) has a store at 71 Warren St, New York, NY 10007, and another good source of African music is Africassette Music (☎ 313-881 4108, fax 881 0260, W www.africasette.com), PO Box 24941, Detroit, MI 48224. Africassette operates a mail order and online sales business, but it's not a patch on Stern's.

In Australia, contact Blue Moon (☎ 03-9415 1157, fax 9415 1220) at 54 Johnston St, Fitzroy, Victoria 3065.

Gambia & Senegal Every town market has a small cassette shop, and in many places young men sell cassettes or CDs on the streets. Original cassettes cost from US$2 to US$3, CDs US$10 to US$12. Watch out for poorly recorded or pirated cassettes, though.

Graeme Counsel, Alex Newton, David Else & Andrew Burke

Dakar

Some people say Dakar does not represent the 'real' Africa, but they're wrong. This city is the big, crowded, dirty, raw, chaotic, ambitious, in-your-face and utterly exciting face of the 'dark' continent, and for a glimpse of African urban future, look no further than Dakar. This *is* as real as it gets. The cosmopolitan atmosphere, temperate climate, rocking range of bars and nightclubs, fascinating mix of African, French colonial and modern architecture and culture, and especially the range and quality of restaurants, make it well worth making Dakar's acquaintance.

The central area is easily explored on foot, and a variety of city buses run frequently to the suburbs. Also within reach are several good beaches, traditional fishing communities and some fascinating islands of historical and ecological interest.

Of course, Dakar won't be everyone's cup of tea. The noise, fumes and crowds can be bad, but what's most likely to wind you up is the unwanted attention you'll get from pestering traders, and the risk of theft. For advice on coping with these notorious hustlers and muggers, see Dangers & Annoyances later in this chapter. If your courage fails, it's easy enough to spend time in parts of the city that tourists, and consequently the bad guys, don't frequent.

ORIENTATION

Dakar is on the Cap Vert peninsula, which has two main points: the northern tip is Pointe des Almadies, and just to the east of here are the beaches of N'Gor and Yoff (described in the Cap Vert Peninsula chapter); the southern tip is Cap Manuel, and Dakar city centre begins just north of it.

Dakar's heart is the Place de l'Indépendance, from which Av Léopold Senghor (formerly Av Roume and usually shortened to Av Senghor) heads south in the direction of the Palais Présidentiel and the Hôpital Principal. Av Pompidou (still known to most as Av Ponty) heads west with the city's

Highlights

- Watch the sun go down over Soumbédioune as hundreds of fishermen return from the sea

- Embrace a case of consumer euphoria in the Marché Sandaga, where if you can't find it, you don't need it

- Understand the origins of West African art and culture through the displays at the IFAN Museum

- Eat, drink and dance your way through the best choice of restaurants, bars and nightclubs in West Africa

largest market, Marché Sandaga, at its western end. A good selection of shops, hotels, restaurants, cafés, bars, nightclubs and hustlers are in and around this central area.

Leading from the eastern side of Place de l'Indépendance is Av Albert Sarraut, a major shopping street with another market, Marché Kermel, near its eastern end. The eastern edge of the city is marked by the ocean, and the Route de la Corniche-Est (Petite Corniche) which winds above the cliffs and small beaches, linking the main port to the north and Cap Manuel.

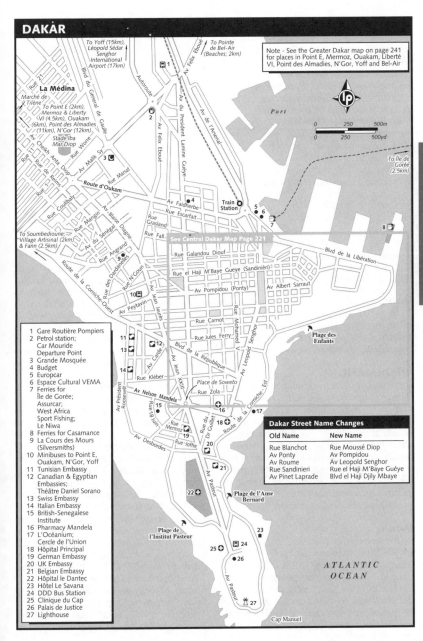

DAKAR

To Yoff (15km),
Léopold Sédar
Senghor
International
Airport (17km)

To Pointe
de Bel-Air
(Beaches; 2km)

Note - See the Greater Dakar map on page 241
for places in Point E, Mermoz, Ouakam, Liberté
VI, Point des Almadies, N'Gor, Yoff and Bel-Air

La Médina

Marché de
Tilène

To Point E (2km),
Mermoz & Liberty
VI (4.5km), Ouakam
(6km), Point des Almadies
(11km), N'Gor (12km)

Stade Iba
Mar Diop

Port

To Île de
Gorée
(2.5km)

Rue 21

Blvd du Général de Gaulle

Av du Président Lamine Guèye

Av Felix Eboué

Autoroute

Av du President Lamine Guèye

Av Felix Eboué

Av de l'Arsenal

Av Felix Eboué

Rue 11

Cheikh Anta Diop

Rue de Reims

Rue 1

Av Malik Sy

Rue Worre

Rue Marsat

Route d'Ouakam

Rue Mangin

Av Blaise Diagne

Av du Sénégal

Rue Coulibaly

Rue Angrand

Rue N'Goun

Rue des Dardanelles

Route de la Corniche-Ouest

Av Peytavin

Av Jean Jaurès

Av Faidherbe

Rue Escarfait

Rue Grasland

Rue Fall

Train
Station

Rue Galandou Diouf

Rue el Haji M'Baye Gueye (Sandinièri)

Av Pompidou (Ponty)

Av Albert Sarraut

Blvd de la Libération

To Soumbedioune;
Village Artisinal (2km)
& Fann (2.5km)

Rue Carnot

Rue Jules Ferry

Rue Mohamed V

Av Léopold Senghor

Plage des
Enfants

Rue Carde

Blvd de la République

Av Jean XXIII

Rue Kléber

Av Président Roosevelt

Av Nelson Mandela

Place de Soweto

Rue Zola

Rue du Dr Guillet

Route de la Corniche-Est

Rue Mermoz

Rue 18 Juin

Av Desbordes

Rue-Joffre

Av Pasteur

Plage de l'Anse
Bernard

Plage de
l'Institut Pasteur

Av Pasteur

ATLANTIC
OCEAN

Cap Manuel

0 ——— 250 ——— 500m
0 ——— 250 ——— 500yd

SENEGAL

See Central Dakar Map Page 221

1 Gare Routière Pompiers
2 Petrol station;
   Car Mouride
   Departure Point
3 Grande Mosquée
4 Budget
5 Europcar
6 Espace Cultural VEMA
7 Ferries for
   Île de Gorée;
   Assurcar;
   West Africa
   Sport Fishing;
   Le Niwa
8 Ferries for Casamance
9 La Cours des Mours
   (Silversmiths)
10 Minibuses to Point E,
   Ouakam, N'Gor, Yoff
11 Tunisian Embassy
12 Canadian & Egyptian
   Embassies;
   Théâtre Daniel Sorano
13 Swiss Embassy
14 Italian Embassy
15 British-Senegalese
   Institute
16 Pharmacy Mandela
17 L'Océanium;
   Cercle de l'Union
18 Hôpital Principal
19 German Embassy
20 UK Embassy
21 Belgian Embassy
22 Hôpital le Dantec
23 Hôtel Le Savana
24 DDD Bus Station
25 Clinique du Cap
26 Palais de Justice
27 Lighthouse

Dakar Street Name Changes

Old Name	New Name
Rue Blanchot	Rue Moussé Diop
Av Ponty	Av Pompidou
Av Roume	Av Leopold Senghor
Rue Sandinieri	Rue el Haji M'Baye Guéye
Av Pinet Laprade	Blvd el Haji Djily Mbaye

West of here are Place de Soweto, the IFAN Museum, the Assemblée Nationale and many embassies. From Place de Soweto you can head north along Av du President Lamine Guéye, eventually reaching the Gare Routière Pompiers and the main autoroute (motorway/freeway) out of the city, which ends at Patte d'Oie.

Av Blaise Diagne heads northwest from the centre, passing near the Grande Mosquée and La Médina, to become Av Cheikh Anta Diop (also known as Route d'Ouakam). This road runs between Fann, with Dakar's main university and chic Point E, with a range of trendy restaurants and bars, before reaching Mermoz, Ouakam, and finally Pointe des Almadies and N'Gor. The Route de la Corniche-Ouest (Grande Corniche) runs along the Atlantic Ocean roughly parallel to Av Cheikh Anta Diop; here you'll see joggers and the city's finest homes and embassy residences.

Maps

By far the best map of the city is on the back of the locally produced *Carte du Sénégal*, which is also a good map of the country. It's available in bookshops for about CFA3500.

INFORMATION

For details of events, consult one of the free listings magazines, including *Dakar Tam Tam* and *l'Avis*. These are available in hotels, restaurants and travel agencies and include phone numbers for these places plus a full list of embassies and hospitals – a shorter list of embassies are given in Senegal's Facts for the Visitor chapter. For passport photos, there are several places in central Dakar, including the camera shops on the Place de l'Indépendance.

Money

On the west side of Place de l'Indépendance are BICIS, CBAO and Citibank, which all change money, while SGBS is at the southern end. CBAO has the quickest service, and BICIS is the next best. Exchange rates and commissions vary between banks and for cash or travellers cheques (see the boxed text 'Bank Charges & Commissions' under

Dakar Bank Opening Times

bank	days	opening hours
BICIS	Mon-Thur	7.45am to 12.15pm
		1.40pm to 3.45pm
	Fri	7.45am to 1pm
		2.40pm to 3.45pm
CBAO	Mon-Fri	7.45am to 3.45pm
	Sat	9am to 11pm
Citibank	Mon-Thur	8.30am to 2.30pm
	Fri	8am to 1pm
		2.30pm to 3.30pm

Money in the Regional Facts for the Visitor chapter.) Except Citibank, which won't even deal with Citibank credit cards, all of these banks have ATMs with guards outside 24 hours.

If the banks are closed, some travel agencies may change cash (and take a small commission). There's also an exchange bureau inside the nearby Hôtel de l'Indépendance. If all else fails you can find a black market currency trader by just standing still for about 30 seconds outside one of these banks. These guys are notorious for short-changing, or just plain theft, so don't hand over your cash until you've carefully counted theirs.

For money transfers Western Union is in the CBAO Pompidou Branch, but the office is on Rue du Docteur Thèze, just off Av Pompidou, and is open from 7.30am to 5.30pm Monday to Saturday.

Post & Telephone

The main post office is on Blvd el Haji Djily Mbaye, near Marché Kermel. Its opening hours are 7am to 7pm weekdays, 8am to 5pm Saturday, closed Sunday. This is where you'll find the poste restante, but readers report this service is unreliable, holds letters for only 30 days and charges CFA250 per letter. There's a smaller post office at the eastern end of Av Pompidou that seems to run more smoothly. DHL (☎ 823 13 94) is at 2 Av Albert Sarraut and opens from 8am to 6.30pm Monday to Thursday, 8am to 7pm Friday, 8am to midday Saturday.

For phone calls, Sonatel has an office on Blvd de la République (open from 7am to

11pm Monday to Saturday), and there are dozens of *télécentres*, mostly with similar rates. See Post & Communications in Senegal's Facts for the Visitor chapter.

Email & Internet Access

There are a stack of cybercafés in Dakar, most of which offer a reasonably good service for between CFA500 and CFA1000 an hour. The fastest connection (for the highest price) is found at GSM Cybercafé (☎ 823 73 26, Av Pompidou), which is open from 8am to midnight daily. Just around the corner is NTIC (☎ 823 09 80, 77 Rue Gomis*)*, where a terminal is only CFA500 an hour and is available 24 hours every day. Another option is Cyber-Business Centre (☎ 823 32 23, Av Léopold Senghor), which opens from 8am to midnight daily and has English-speaking staff. An hour will cost CFA1000.

Several Internet bureaus line Av Cheikh Anta Diop in Point E and Mermoz, while nearby is CyberEspace (Rue D), which has a good service for CFA500 an hour between 9.30am and midnight daily.

Travel Agencies

For reconfirming flights, most airlines have offices in central Dakar (listed under Getting There & Away later in this chapter). If you're looking for a ticket, using a travel agency saves a lot of shopping around. The agencies' fares are standardised, and usually the same as the airline (or cheaper), although special deals are sometimes available, particularly to/from Paris.

Agencies include Senegal Tours (☎ 839 99 00, fax 823 26 44), 5 Place de l'Indépendance, which is also the American Express agent; SDV Voyages (☎ 839 00 81, e dkrs dvagv@sdvsen.net), 51 Av Albert Sarraut, which is the Diners Club agent; M'boup Voyages (☎ 821 81 63, e mboup@tele complus.sn), Place de l'Indépendance, where some staff speak English; and Planete Tours Voyages (☎ 823 74 23), under the Hôtel de l'Indépendance. Nouvelles Frontièrs (☎ 823 34 34, fax 822 28 17), 3 Blvd de la République, sometimes has cheap seats to Paris on charter flights.

Bookshops

Librairie Clairafrique, at the northwest corner of Place de l'Indépendance, and Librairie aux Quatres Vents (☎ 821 80 83), Rue Félix Faure, have a wide range of books and magazines (although very little in English) and also sell maps. Both are open from 8.45am to 12.30pm and 3pm to 6.45pm Monday to Saturday. The second-hand bookstalls in the streets around the Marché Sandaga are also a good bet.

Universities

The city's main campus is the University of Dakar, now renamed Université de Cheikh Anta Diop, in the suburb of Fann, to the northwest of the city centre.

Cultural Centres

The lively Centre Culturel Français (Alliance Franco-Sénégalaise; ☎ 823 03 20, e ccf@sentoo.sn) occupying a whole block on Rue Gomis, is the driving force behind much of the artistic and cultural endeavours in Dakar. It produces a regular guide to upcoming events and has a performance arena on site that hosts regular live events and films. The American Cultural Centre (☎ 823 11 85) is on Rue Abdoulaye Fadiga, near the main post office, while the British Council (☎ 822 20 15), Blvd de la République, and the British-Senegalese Institute, Rue 18 Juin, near Place de Soweto, both have libraries. The German Goethe Institut (☎ 823 04 07) is on Av Albert Sarraut.

Medical Services

For emergencies, the main government-run hospitals are Hôpital Principal (☎ 839 50 50) at the far southern end of Av Léopold Senghor, and Hôpital le Dantec (☎ 822 24 20) on Av Pasteur, where you'd probably be taken in a real emergency, such as after a road accident.

For illnesses and minor injuries, go to a private clinic (where expenses are covered by your travel insurance). Normally, your embassy will have a list of doctors used to dealing with nonresidents, particularly those speaking your language.

SENEGAL

If all this fails, places to get help include Clinique du Cap (☎ 821 36 27), just south of Hôpital le Dantec, and Clinique Pasteur (☎ 822 13 13) at 50 Rue Carnot, west of Place de l'Indépendance, which is the best place to go if you're after a malaria slide.

Dakar has many pharmacies. Those with 24-hour service include Pharmacie de la Nation (☎ 823 40 01) on Av du President Lamine Guéye, and Pharmacie Mandela (☎ 821 21 72) on Av Nelson Mandela near the Hôpital Principal.

Dangers & Annoyances

Dakar has a bad reputation for muggings, scams and petty theft, frequently in broad daylight. Less worrying, but very annoying, are street traders and hustlers. To enjoy Dakar you have to be prepared to handle these characters. For some initial ideas, see Precautions under Dangers & Annoyances in the Regional Facts for the Visitor chapter.

Notorious mugging hotspots are the beaches around Dakar, in and around the markets, Av Pompidou and Place de l'Indépendance (especially outside the banks). Pickpockets operate wherever wealthy tourists can be surrounded by crowds, such as at the train station and on the Île de Gorée ferry.

Thieves often work in groups. One guy will touch your back, causing you to stop. A second tries to grab your wallet, while a third acts as a decoy. Watch out for 'traders' with only one item to sell. Beware, too, of people offering small gifts 'for friendship' – nothin' comes for nothin'.

Genuine street traders, of course, are not thieves. Some, however, may work with thieves to slow down potential targets. Either way, unless you genuinely want something, ignore them or try a firm but civil *non merci* (no thank you).

Despite these warnings it's important to remember that only a tiny percentage of visitors are robbed, and a tourist being physically harmed is almost unheard of. None of the places mentioned here are 'no-go' zones, just places where you should be particularly vigilant. Aggression is not a typical Senegalese trait. Most Senegalese are genuinely hospitable and wouldn't dream of hassling guests in their country.

THINGS TO SEE

The **IFAN Museum** *(Institut Fondamental d'Afrique Noir; Place de Soweto; admission CFA2200; open 8am-12.30pm & 2pm-6.30pm daily)* is one of the best museums in West Africa and is a testimony to former President Senghor's interest in promoting African art and culture. Lively, imaginative displays show masks and traditional dress from the whole region (including Mali, Guinea-Bissau, Benin and Nigeria) and provide an excellent overview of styles, without bombarding you with so much that you can't take it all in. You can also see beautiful fabrics and carvings, drums, musical instruments and agricultural tools, though there are no English explanations and, sadly, not much from Senegal itself.

Also on Place de Soweto is the **Assemblée Nationale** (National Assembly or Parliament), where you should again be able to mix with the politicians once renovations to the bar and restaurant are complete.

The handsome white **Palais Présidentiel** (Presidential Palace) is surrounded by sumptuous gardens and guards in colonial-style uniforms. It was originally built in 1907 for the governor at the time, General Roume, who used to lend his title to the street outside, although it's now renamed Av Léopold Senghor.

The **cathedral** on Blvd de la République was built in the 1920s, although it's nothing special architecturally. More interesting are the colonial buildings – the **Govournance** and **Chambre de Commerce**, both on Place de l'Indépendance; the fine old **hôtel de ville** (town hall), nearby; and the church-like train station, a short distance further north.

The impressive **Espace Cultural VEMA** *(☎ 821 70 26; open 9am-1pm & 3pm-7pm when there is an exhibition)*, in an old warehouse near the Île de Gorée ferry jetty, has monthly exhibitions. When there is an exhibition the *café-bar* (with inside and outside seating) opens for business.

Out from the city centre is the **Grande Mosquée** (built in 1964) with its landmark

CENTRAL DAKAR

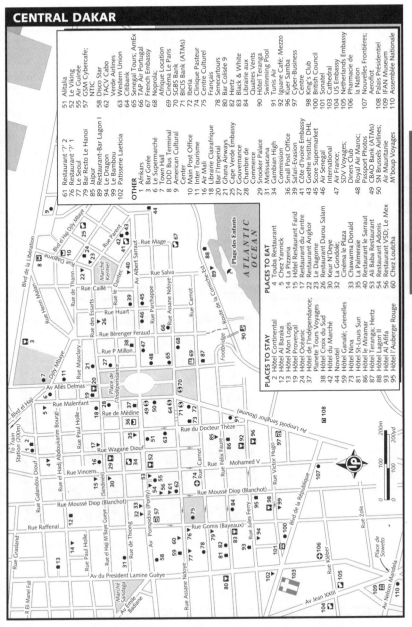

SENEGAL

51 Alitalia
52 Le Viking
55 Air Guinée
57 GSM Cybercafe;
    NTIC
58 Disco Star
62 TACV Cabo
    Verde Airlines
63 Western Union
64 Citibank
65 Senegal Tours; AmEx
66 TAP Air Portugal
67 French Embassy
68 Noprola;
    Afrique Location
69 Cinéma Le Paris
70 SGBS Bank
71 BICIS Bank (ATMs)
72 Iberia
74 Clinique Pasteur
75 Centre Culturel
    Français
78 Senecartours
80 Bar Colisée 9
82 Hertz
83 Black & White
84 Librairie aux
    Quatres Vents
90 Hôtel Teranga
    Swimming Pool
91 Tunis Air
92 Iguane Café; Mezzo
96 Kuer Samba
97 Cyber-Business
    Centre
98 King's Club
100 British Council
101 Cathedral
103 Sonatel
104 US Embassy
105 Netherlands Embassy
106 Pharmacie de
    la Nation
107 Nouvelles Frontières;
    Aeroflot
108 Palais Présidentiel
109 IFAN Museum
110 Assemblée Nationale

OTHER

1 Afrikars
3 Bar Gorée
6 Le Supermarché
7 Town Hall
8 DDD Bus Terminal
9 American Cultural
    Center
10 Main Post Office
11 Inter Tourisme
16 Air Mali
18 Librairie Clairafrique
20 Bar l'Imperial
21 Ghana Airways
25 Cape Verde Embassy
27 Gouvernance
28 Chambre de
    Commerce
31 Metissacana
34 Gambian High
    Commission
36 Small Post Office
39 Safari-Evasion
41 Côte d'Ivoire Embassy
43 Goethe Institut; DHL
45 Score Supermarket
46 Air Senegal
47 Air France;
    International
    SDV Voyages;
    Diners Club
48 Royal Air Maroc;
    Passport Photos
49 CBAO Bank (ATMs)
50 SN Brussels Airlines;
    Air Mauritanie
    M'boup Voyages

61 Restaurant '?' 2
76 Restaurant '?' 1
77 Le Seoul
79 Bar Resto Le Hanoi
85 Jaipur
89 Restaurant-Bar Lagon I
94 Le Dragon
99 Le Bambou
102 Patisserie Laeticia

PLACES TO EAT

4 Touba Restaurant
5 Chez Yannick
14 La Pizzeria
15 Hôtel Restaurant Farid
17 Restaurant du Centre
22 Restaurant Angkor
23 Le Dagorne
26 Restaurant Darou Salam
30 Keur N'Deye
32 La Gondole;
    Cinéma le Plaza
33 Chawarma Donald
35 La Palmeraie
40 Restaurant le Sarraut
53 Ali Baba Restaurant
54 Restaurant Adonis
56 Restaurant VSD; Le Mex
60 Chez Loutcha

PLACES TO STAY

2 Hôtel Continental
12 Hôtel Al Baraka
13 Hôtel Mon Logis
19 Hôtel Provençal
24 Hôtel Océanic
37 Hôtel de l'Indépendance;
    Planete Tours Voyages
38 Hôtel Croix du Sud
42 Hôtel du Marché
44 Novotel
59 Hôtel Ganalé; Grenelles
73 Hôtel Nina
81 Hôtel St-Louis Sun
86 Hôtel le Miramar
87 Hôtel Teranga; Hertz
88 Hôtel Lagon II
93 Hôtel Al Afifa
95 Hôtel l'Auberge Rouge

ATLANTIC OCEAN

Plage des Enfants

minaret, floodlit at night. The mosque is closed to the public, but it's worth coming here anyway because the surrounding area, called **La Médina**, while not picturesque, is a lively bustling place contrasting sharply with the high-rise city centre. Few tourists come here, so there's little hassle from traders.

The **Parc Forestier de Hann** is a peaceful area of woodland about 5km north of the city centre, with paths, benches and a couple of snack bars. It's popular with families and couples at weekends. The attached **Parc de Hann Zoo** is not worth a visit.

West of the centre, and well worth the trip, is the fishing beach and market of **Soumbédioune**, originally a village but now a suburb engulfed by the city. It's best in the late afternoon when the fishing boats are returning with their catch. This is also a major centre of pirogue building, and behind the fish market you'll see carpenters turning planks and tree trunks into large ocean-going canoes. The **Village Artisanal** nearby is full of craft stalls and large groups of tourists.

BEACHES

Dakar has several *plages* (beaches) within easy reach of the city centre. These include the Plage des Enfants, near the Hôtel Lagon II, and the Plage de l'Anse Bernard, near the Hôtel Le Savana. There are also two small sandy beaches off Route de la Corniche-Ouest, about 1.5km northwest of the centre, near an ugly sculpture of a sitting man. These are popular with locals, but keep a close eye on your gear, and be careful of the currents.

Other options include the beaches of **Pointe de Bel-Air**, about 3km northeast of the city centre (CFA1000 by taxi). Here you will find two private beaches, open to the public with fences on the landward side, so personal safety is not a problem. The water here is clean without being crystal clear, but

---

Soumbédioune

The people of Soumbédioune are nearly all Lebu, a small and most fiercely independent ethnic group who live here almost exlusively, as well as in the town of Yoff, north of Dakar.

Fishing

During the week, the beach at Soumbédioune is a hive of activity. Fishermen go out to sea at dawn in large pirogues about 10 to 15m long. They return in the late afternoon with their catch, which is dispatched to the women who sort, prepare and sell the fish at the beach market. Large trucks stand by and the best-quality fish is taken away for export, mainly to Europe and Asia. The best of

Pirogue racing is a serious event in Soumbedieoune, bringing out a competitive edge in the Lebu people

the rest is sold to Senegalese restaurateurs, and the remainder ends up on the market stalls. A huge variety of fish can be seen including barracuda, sea carp, capitaine, prawns, crabs and tuna.

the beach is not exactly photogenic (there's a military base on one side and huge oil tanks on the other). **Plage Monaco** *(formerly Plage Tahiti;* ☎ *832 22 60; admission CFA650),* is the locals' favourite, while the neighbouring **Plage Voile d'Or** *(*☎ *832 86 48, admission CFA650)* seems to be most favoured by Europeans, although the clientele at both beaches is mixed. There are bars, restaurants and cabins (up to six people) at each.

The best beaches near Dakar are at N'Gor and Yoff – see the Cap Vert Peninsula chapter for more details.

ACTIVITIES
Swimming

Most top-end hotels have **swimming pools** that are open to nonguests. The Hôtel Teranga has a pool overlooking the ocean, which is free if you eat at the adjoining restaurant, otherwise it will cost you CFA4500 (CFA7000 on Sunday). The Hôtel de l'Indépendance charges CFA3000 for its roof-top pool with a great view of Dakar (free if you have a meal). At the time of publication an Olympic-sized pool in a huge swimming centre was due to open in the middle of Point E's big *oeuf* (a huge egg-shaped area known to taxi drivers as the oeuf) and will be open to the public for a fraction of the cost of the hotel pools.

Wrestling

Dakar's main arena *(arène)* for traditional wrestling is in Le Médina, near the large Stadium Iba Mar Diop on Av Blaise Diagne (see the boxed text 'Traditional Wrestling' in the Regional Facts for the Visitor chapter for details). For really big-name wrestlers, the fights may be held in the stadium itself. Most matches are announced only on the radio, so it can be a problem finding out when they are held. Saturday and/or Sunday

---

Soumbédioune

The fishermen complain that it used to be possible to get good catches about 5km out to sea. Now they have to go about 25km out. The shortage is blamed on the influx of commercial fishing boats, mainly from countries in East Asia, and they are accused of regularly overfishing.

Pirogue Construction

Behind Soumbédioune beach is an area where the Lebu's fishing pirogues are made. The base of the pirogue is usually made from the hollowed out trunk of a silk-cotton tree (known locally as a *fromager*). This light spongy wood is left outside to absorb water during the rainy season for up to eight months, after which it can be beaten perfectly straight to form the floor of the boat. The sides are then built up around it using long planks of a harder wood such as kola, and finally the bottom half, inside, is coated with tar. When treated like this, the fromager base lasts for years; when the pirogue finally reaches the end of its life, the base may be reused several times in new boats.

Smaller boats usually belong to the Lebu. Large pirogues take months to build, and sell for around CFA12 million (about US$17,000). This is beyond the reach of most fishermen, so many large boats are owned by local business people. They may lease their boat to a team of fishermen, or simply employ them. Either way, they take up to 60% of the profits from each catch.

The Pirogue Race

The Lebu of Soumbédioune used to have an annual regatta with a much-anticipated pirogue race as the main event. Each fishing village along the coast would send a 25-person crew in a specially built racing pirogue to Dakar. Competition was intense, so intense that in 1996 and '97 the race was cancelled following all-out warfare between the crews before they even reached Dakar. At the time of writing the race remained just a memory, but if peace breaks out among the fishermen expect the race to be held on Independence Day (4 April).

One of the highlights of a trip to Senegal is the colourful traditional wrestling matches

are the usual days, starting around 4.30pm or 5pm.

Diving & Kayaking

Scuba diving *(plongée sous-marine)* sites include the rocky reefs and islets around the Pointe des Almadies, and the islands of Gorée and N'Gor. The French-run **L'Océanium** *(☎ 822 24 41,* **e** *oceanium@arc.sn; open Mon-Sat)*, on the Route de la Corniche-Est, arranges a wide range of trips. A half-day dive down to 25m costs CFA13,500, beyond 25m is CFA17,500, while a complete beginners' introductory dive is CFA15,000. All equipment is included. It also rents kayaks for CFA3000 an hour, or CFA5000 for half a day.

Fishing

You can arrange deep-sea fishing at **West Africa Sport Fishing** *(☎ 823 28 58, fax 823 48 37)*, next to the Île de Gorée ferry port. During the fishing high season (May to October) a day out costs a mere CFA280,000.

Restaurant-Bar Lagon I *(☎ 821 53 22, Route de la Corniche-Est)* also has a fishing centre from where you can arrange deep-sea fishing trips. It boasts several world-record catches.

Jogging & Exercise

The favourite joggers' route is along the Route de la Corniche-Ouest from Pointe de Fann, north as far as Mermoz. On Plage de Fann, on the north side of Pointe de Fann, as marked on the Greater Dakar map, is a public fitness course with exercise stations, where people work out and sports teams train. Most large hotels have gymnasiums that nonguests can use. There's also a small gym at Restaurant-Bar Lagon I, where any calories you lose on the exercise bike can be immediately replaced by the seafood on the menu.

Tennis & Squash

Most major hotels have tennis courts that nonguests can pay to use. Private clubs include the **Cercle de l'Union** *(☎ 821 41 69)* on Route de la Corniche-Est, which has tennis and squash courts for CFA2000 an hour; and the **Olympic Club** at the northern end of Route de la Corniche-Ouest in Mermoz.

PLACES TO STAY

Dakar has a very wide range of accommodation from filthy dosshouses to palatial hotels – although, compared to other African capitals, everything is expensive. Despite the choice, demand outstrips supply and it can sometimes be difficult to find a room, especially in the middle and lower price range. Dakar is no place to be searching the streets with a rucksack on your back, especially after dark, so if you find a room anywhere near your budget, take it for one night, and look for something cheaper the next day.

Only hotels in central Dakar are listed here. There are several more hotels in nearby places such as Île de Gorée (a short boat ride from the city), N'Gor (near the better beaches), Yoff (near the airport), Malika and Rufisque (also suitable for people with tents or overland vehicles). All these are listed in the Cap Vert Peninsula chapter.

ALIMENTATION GENERALE
DIALO

Food is generally prepared and cooked in the open, and often sold outside at markets and roadside stalls. Local food is usually safer than Western-style food because it's cooked much longer (sometimes all day) and the ingredients are generally fresh.

The procuring and cooking of food is invariably women's business, as shown by this Bedik woman making a local brew in Bassari country (bottom right) and the women selling fruit and vegetables at market (top & bottom left). Fishing, however, is usually left to the men.

PLACES TO STAY – BUDGET

News from the cheap end of town is that a particularly aggressive breed of bed bugs have taken up strategic positions in the city's budget hotels. When asked if he had any rooms without bugs one hotel manager explained with a shrug, 'I'm sorry, they are all the same.' Hopefully by the time you arrive they'll have moved on to Mali, or anywhere else! The price of all the places in this range includes tax.

Hôtel Mon Logis *(821 85 25)* Rooms CFA6000. Down an alley off Av du President Lamine Guéye, upstairs and unmarked, this is the cheapest place in town and would better be described as a brothel. The walls are wafer thin and the language of lust can be tough to sleep through. Absolutely the last resort.

Hôtel du Marché *(☎ 821 57 71, 3 Rue Parent)* Singles/doubles CFA8600/11,600. Near the Marché Kermel, this place has big, basic fan rooms surrounding a peaceful, shady courtyard. It's not a bad option.

Hôtel l'Auberge Rouge *(☎ 823 86 61, Rue Moussé Diop)* Doubles CFA9500. This old place is well located, but it gets mixed reviews. Some travellers describe it as peaceful; others complain of noisy comings and goings at night.

Hôtel Provençal *(☎/fax 822 10 69, 17 Rue Malenfant)* Singles/doubles/triples from CFA9400/11,800/14,200. This is a popular place near Place de l'Indépendance. As with all cheapies, it is also a part-time brothel, but it's fairly low key. Rooms upstairs are quiet and airy with fan and shared bathrooms (cleaned daily). Downstairs is a cheap snack bar where you can meet other travellers.

Hôtel Continental *(☎ 822 10 83, 10 Rue Galandou Diouf)* Singles/doubles CFA13,000/15,000. Probably the best choice in this bracket, this is a decent, well-organised hotel with friendly staff. The rooms are big and all are air-conditioned (some even have balconies). They each have a shower, though the toilet is outside. There's also a small bar downstairs with a very relaxed feel.

PLACES TO STAY – MID-RANGE

All hotels in this range have rooms with private bathroom. Prices do not include tax (CFA600 per person). Most places accept credit and charge cards.

Hôtel Océanic *(☎ 822 20 44, e hotel-oceanic@sentoo.sn, 9 Rue de Thann)* Singles/doubles with air-con CFA21,600/25,800, apartments CFA33,000/36,800. North of Marché Kermel, this is a pleasant old-style place with spotless air-con rooms and larger apartments – fair value for Dakar. Breakfast is CFA2000. There's a good bar-restaurant with meals from CFA2000 to CFA2500 and a *menu du jour* (meal of the day) for CFA4800.

Hôtel Al Baraka *(☎ 822 55 32, fax 821 75 41, 35 Rue el Hadj Abdoukarim Bourgi)* Singles/doubles CFA25,600/31,200. Spotless modern rooms with air-con, TV, fridge and phone make the Baraka worth the money.

Hôtel Al Afifa *(☎ 823 87 37, fax 823 88 39, e gmbafifa@telecomplus.sn, 46 Rue Jules Ferry)* Singles/doubles CFA35,000/39,600. This place is ageing a little, but it retains some of its lustre. With a bar, restaurant and nightclub downstairs, you won't need to go too far for a drink.

Hôtel St-Louis Sun *(☎ 822 25 70, fax 822 46 51, Rue Félix Faure)* Singles/doubles/triples CFA22,000/28,000/34,000. This older hotel has pleasant air-con rooms around a green courtyard and arranges safe parking for cars.

Hôtel le Miramar *(☎ 849 29 29, fax 823 35 05, 25 Rue Félix Faure)* Singles/doubles CFA25,600/31,200. At the other end of the street from Hôtel St-Louis Sun, this busy place has colourful rooms with air-con, hot shower and TV, and rates include breakfast. Ask for a 6th-floor room.

Hôtel Nina *(☎ 821 22 30, fax 821 41 81, 43 Rue du Docteur Thèze)* Singles/doubles CFA24,600/30,200. Calmer than Hôtel Le Miramar, this nearby place has small air-con rooms with TV and includes breakfast.

Hôtel Ganalé *(☎ 821 55 70, fax 822 34 30, e hganale@sentoo.sn, 38 Rue Assane Ndoye)* Singles/doubles CFA25,000/30,000, apartments CFA32,000/38,000. The swish Ganalé is the best value in this price range. The rooms, bar and restaurant are all pretty classy. Breakfast is CFA3000.

Hôtel Croix du Sud *(☎ 823 29 47, fax 823 26 55, 20 Av Albert Sarraut)* Singles/doubles

CFA31,500/36,000. Right in the middle of town, this '70s-style place was once a good address, but these days the service is as tired as the decor. However, the restaurant gets good reviews.

PLACES TO STAY – TOP END

All hotels in this range have rooms with private bathrooms, accept major credit/charge cards, and have a tour desk where you can arrange excursions, car hire etc. All the prices quoted are standard rates, but if you book through a travel agent, either locally or in your own country, discounts are normally available. Prices do not include tax (CFA600 per person).

Hôtel de l'Indépendance (☎ 823 10 19, fax 822 11 17, e hotelhi@sentoo.sn, Place de l'Indépendance) Singles/doubles CFA50,000/55,000. This rather dreary place is the most central of the top-end hotels and has great views, but they aren't really worth the money. The pool on the roof is the hotel's major plus.

Hôtel Teranga (☎ 823 10 44, fax 823 50 01, Place de l'Indépendance) Rooms CFA95,000-120,000. This is Sofitel's recently renovated tour-group favourite. Facilities include a large swimming pool, tennis courts, sauna, shops and nightclub. It's really very nice – the rooms are beautiful – but is a sea view worth CFA120,000 a night? Plenty think so. Breakfast is CFA10,000.

Novotel (☎ 849 61 61, fax 823 89 29, e novotel@metissacana.sn) Singles/doubles CFA72,000/78,000. Just off the eastern end of Av Albert Sarraut, this is a modern and uninspiring place. Breakfast is CFA8000. Facilities include a swimming pool and tennis courts.

Hôtel Lagon II (☎ 889 25 25, fax 823 77 27, e lagon@tpsnet.sn, Route de la Corniche-Est) Singles/doubles CFA72,000/ 80,000, suite CFA120,000. This place is so '70s you fully expect the Bee Gees to appear at the bar in sequined jump suits. But the rooms, perched on stilts at the edge of the ocean, have grand views.

· *Hôtel le Savana* (☎ 849 42 42, fax 849 42 43, w www.hotelsavana.com, Route de la Corniche-Est) Singles/doubles CFA74,000/ 80,000, up to CFA140,000. If you want to be part of the Dakar 'in' set, head to this 100-room hotel in a beautiful setting overlooking the ocean. Facilities include swimming pool, business centre, fishing deck, private jetty, tennis courts, nightclub, sauna, gym and sailboards for hire.

PLACES TO EAT

Sick of rice and peanut sauce? Can't face another round of *yassa poulet* (grilled, marinated chicken)? Whether you've been in Africa a while or have just arrived you're going to love Dakar's rapidly maturing culinary scene. The French cuisine, a hangover from the colonial past, is a particular highlight, but there's more to Dakar than entrecote and *crème brulée*. Cape Verdean, Indian, Vietnamese, Thai, Lebanese, Italian, Korean and Mexican, plus a remarkable array of seafood eateries are also available, and then there's the Senegalese food...

Most of the eateries listed here are in or near central Dakar, but there are also a couple in the Point E district.

Restaurants

The restaurants listed here are arranged according to the cuisine they serve, although there's a lot of overlap. For example, in some places you might easily find African, French, Lebanese and Vietnamese food on the same menu.

African There are dozens of African restaurants in Dakar, these ones are particularly good.

Keur N'Deye (☎ 821 49 73, 68 Rue Vincens) Dishes from CFA1500. Highly recommended, this place offers well-prepared Senegalese specialities and a good range of vegetarian dishes. Most nights there will be a griot playing the kora, and this is a great place to watch a performance at close quarters.

Chez Loutcha (☎ 821 03 02, 101 Rue Moussé Diop) Dishes CFA2500-3500. Open noon-3pm & 7pm-11pm Mon-Sat. Ignore the air-conditioned front room and head out back to the fan-conditioned garden, where the fountains embellish an aquatic theme. The Cape Verdean and 'Euro-Africaine' cuisine is excellent and comes in enormous serves, and there's often a griot playing the kora here as well. One well-travelled reader described Loutcha as 'among the best places I've eaten anywhere in the world'. That's a big call, but for the money, this should be your first stop.

Restaurant VSD *(Chez Georges;* ☎ *821 0980, 91 Rue Moussé Diop)* Mains CFA3500. Open 7am-midnight daily. There's not much jazz at this intimate place any more, but the West African and international dishes are still good value.

Les Gourmandises Africaines *(*☎ *824 87 05, Rue 3, Point E)* Mains CFA3000. Open noon-3pm & 7pm-11pm daily. Hidden away in the backstreets of Point E this place is well worth seeking out. The *thiouf* (rice and fish; CFA3000) is done to perfection, as are several other Senegalese specialities.

European Senegal's cultural heritage means Dakar has a wide choice of bars, bistros, cafés and restaurants doing French food.

Restaurant le Sarraut *(*☎ *822 5523, Av Albert Sarraut)* Menu du jour Mon-Fri CFA6500. Open 8am-midnight Mon-Sat. The adjoining bar gives Sarraut a vague air of rural France, and the food has been recommended.

Chez Yannick *(*☎ *823 2197, Rue Malenfant)* Mains CFA5000. Open lunch & dinner daily. French food and a few miscellaneous international dishes are served in an airy outdoor setting, especially popular for lunch.

Le Dagorne *(*☎ *822 20 80)* Dishes CFA5000-10,000. Open 7am-2.30pm & 7.30pm-10.30pm Mon-Sat. Near Marché Kermel, this is one of the better French eateries. It has a bustling, energetic atmosphere inside, courtyard seating and a superb menu with many tempting choices.

Le Bambou *(*☎ *822 06 45, 19 Rue Victor Hugo)* Mains CFA6000-10,000. Open lunch & dinner Mon-Fri, 8pm-midnight Sat. If money is not a concern, then Le Bambou, east of the cathedral, gets top marks for its food and service – the *chateaubriand flambé* (flaming steak; CFA7900), prepared at the table, is worth considering.

La Pizzeria *(*☎ *821 0926, 47 Rue el Hadj Abdoukarim Bourgi)* Pizza & pasta CFA3500. Open 7pm-1am daily. La Pizzeria has excellent pizza and pasta, and a smooth fish soup for CFA2500.

Seafood With so many fish being landed in Dakar every day, it's little wonder the city does such good seafood. (See also Pointe des Almadies in the Cap Vert Peninsula chapter for more seafood restaurants.)

Hôtel Croix du Sud *(*☎ *823 29 47, fax 823 26 55, 20 Av Albert Sarraut)* The hotel might be tired, but the restaurant is often recommended. Meals will cost you around CFA5000.

Restaurant-Bar Lagon I *(*☎ *821 5322, Route de la Corniche-Est)* Mains from CFA7000. Open noon-3pm & 7.30pm-11pm daily. Done out like an old-style cruise liner, complete with sails, rails and lifeboats, this place is classy and very expensive. The nautical image is continued if you eat the excellent seafood on the deck – which stands on stilts in the ocean.

Le Niwa *(*☎ *822 20 29, Île de Gorée ferry wharf)* Dishes CFA3000-6000. Open 8am-9pm daily. Right above the Gorée ferry 'departure lounge', this place has indoor and outdoor dining and is popular for lunch.

Asian Dakar's exposure to the Orient has expanded to give it, we'd venture to suggest, the best range of Asian food for thousands of kilometres.

Restaurant Angkor *(*☎ *637 57 78, 12 Rue Dagorne)* Dishes CFA2500-CFA4000. Open lunch & dinner Mon-Sat. Despite the name and (incredibly) one of the giant, gaudy paintings of Angkor Wat that Cambodia has become infamous for, this place near Marché Kermel is, in fact, a cheap Chinese restaurant. The food fills a space.

Bar Resto le Hanoi *(*☎ *821 32 69)* Mains CFA3500. On the corner of Rue Carnot and Rue Gomis, this place is renowned for its good-value Vietnamese food and lively bar.

Le Dragon *(*☎ *821 66 76, 35 Rue Jules Ferry)* Mains CFA3000-5000. Open 6pm-11pm Mon-Sat. More expensive than the Hanoi, the Vietnamese food here is pretty good.

SENEGAL

Le Seoul (☎ 822 90 00, 75 Rue Assane Ndoye) Dishes CFA5000-8000. Open noon-3pm & 7.30pm-11pm daily. The Korean food here is as pleasant as the Korean courtyard surrounds. The *sam ae tang* (chicken and ginseng soup; CFA8000) and the *yook gae jang* (spicy beef and vegetable soup; CFA5000) were both subtly prepared and very tasty.

Jaipur (☎ 823 36 46, Rue Félix Faure) Dishes CFA4000. Open 7pm-11pm Mon-Sat. You'll see advertisements for this Indian restaurant as far away as Mbour, but after all the anticipation come mixed reviews – enough positive ones to make the curries and vegetarian baltis worth a try.

Le Jardin Thailandaise (☎ 825 58 33, 10 Blvd du Sud) Meals about CFA8000. Open lunch & dinner Mon-Sat. In a pleasant garden setting in the upmarket Point E district, this place was all the rage with the expat community when we visited. The food is the best Thai you'll find, but then there's little in West Africa to compare it with. Prices are a bit steep.

Miscellaneous Some of the nonaligned restaurants include:

Hôtel-Restaurant Farid (51 Rue Vincens) Dishes CFA2500-4000. Open Thur-Tues. This restaurant offers traditional Lebanese fare. A local favourite for years, it doesn't look flash, but the food is.

Mezzo (☎ 822 58 88) Meals CFA8000. Just back from Rue Jules Ferry, near the Iguane Café, Mezzo is a marked contrast to the Farid – stylishly designed and serving a range of unorthodox international dishes and excellent salads. Fondant is not on the menu, but is worth asking for. Mezzo is renowned as having the best ice cream in the country; the *corossol* is a Senegalese specialty.

Le Mex (☎ 823 67 17, 91 Rue Moussé Diop) Mains CFA3500. Open noon-2am daily. It's not quite El Paso, but the tapas (CFA5000), *paninis* (filled breads; CFA1600) and other meals are a pleasant change. After 11pm the lights dim and the dancing begins.

Cafés & Patisseries

Dakar has some excellent French-style *patisseries* (pastry shops) and *salons du thé*

(tea shops), good for a hot drink and cake, and to escape for a while from the heat and hustle of the city. All these places also sell ice cream, crepes, sandwiches and snacks, and some also sell beer.

Busy places along Av Pompidou include *La Palmeraie (☎ 821 1594)* opposite Alitalia, which serves an array of breakfasts that is talked about across the country; and *La Gondole (☎ 821 8858)*, near the Cinéma le Plaza, which is famous for its ice cream.

Patisserie Laeticia (☎ 821 7548, Blvd de la République), opposite the cathedral, is calmer but service can make you feel invisible. Most patisseries open for breakfast and close around 7.30pm, although some on Av Pompidou sell beer and stay open until late.

Street Food & Cheap Eats

All over Dakar booths sell coffee with bread and butter for around CFA350. For something more substantial, along Rue Assane Ndoye you'll find women cooking food in big pots and serving hot, filling meals such as rice and sauce for around CFA500, although most close by mid-afternoon.

Chawarmas are sold throughout the city for around CFA800. Favourites on Av Pompidou include *Chawarma Donald*, where city workers queue three deep as Donald slices away in furnace-like heat; *Ali Baba Restaurant (☎ 822 52 97)*, which offers classier surroundings and a bigger range of Lebanese dishes; and *Restaurant Adonis (☎ 822 40 86)*. Ali Baba and Adonis are open from 8am to 2am, while Donald's is more a daytime business.

The next four places are particularly good examples of a fairly common genre: the Senegalese restaurant serving large portions of good food for not much money.

Touba Restaurant (☎ 823 76 46, 20 Rue Wagane Diouf) Dishes CFA600-1000. North of Av Pompidou, this place serves filling meals fast, and the *mafé* (thick groundnut sauce) is top notch.

Restaurant du Centre (☎ 822 01 72, 7 Rue el Haji M'Baye Guéye) Dishes CFA1500-2000. Open 8am-midnight daily. Around the corner from Touba, this is a step up and there's far more available on the menu. There's also a rather more upmarket version upstairs.

Restaurant Darou Salam *(Rue des Essarts)* Dishes CFA800-1000. Open 8am-6pm Mon-Fri. On the other side of the centre, this place serves filling African meals and is a popular lunch stop.

Restaurant '?' *(☎ 822 5072, Rue Assane Ndoye)* Dishes CFA1500. Best value in this range are these two places (ask for 'Restaurant Point d'Interrogation') known as 1 and 2 but, perhaps as a result of a two-for-one deal on signs, both have 'Restaurant ? 2' on their neon signs. Not that it matters, both are clean and friendly, open in the evening as well as all day and sell filling and exceptionally flavoursome African dishes.

Self-Catering

For imported items and food, the biggest and best place in Dakar is the **Score Supermarket** *(☎ 821 86 12, 31 Av Albert Sarraut)*. This place also has a good range of women's sanitary products, a few English magazines and plenty of other nonfood items.

Alternatively, *Le Supermarché (Av Allés Delmas)*, three blocks north of Place de l'Indépendance, has slightly cheaper prices for a much smaller range of stock. Fruit and vegetable vendors also sell their produce outside Le Supermarché. Of course, if you're looking only for food you need never enter a supermarket as we know them. Shopping for fruit and vegetables in the Marché Sandage will be far more entertaining (and cheaper), but some people have trouble dealing with the idea of eating unrefrigerated meat that has been hosting countless flies for Allah knows how long.

If you're in Point E, the *Ecomarché (☎ 824 40 95)* at the corner of Av Cheikh Anta Diop and Rocade Fann Bel Air (immediately north of the canal) is your best bet.

ENTERTAINMENT
Bars

All the big hotels have bars. *Hôtel de l'Indépendance* is the most notable with its rooftop bar by the pool. Drinks here are expensive (small beers CFA1000), but worth it for the fantastic views at sunset – although the height of the parapet means you have to sit on the table to enjoy them.

If you stand on tiptoe at Hôtel de l'Indépendance you can look down on a few of the many bars on or near Av Pompidou. These include *Le Viking (Cnr Av Pompidou & Rue Mohamed V)*, open from 10am to 3am, which is a European-style bar with sport on its TV; and *Snooker Palace (☎ 822 9487, 44 Rue Wagane Diouf)*, where the tempo rises late at night.

Much calmer are *Bar l'Imperial (☎ 822 2663)*, at the north end of Place de l'Indépendance, and *Bar Colisée 9 (☎ 821 2217, Cnr Av du President Lamine Guéye & Rue Félix Faure)*, which are both smart places where small draught beers cost around CFA800. There are several other watering holes on Rue Félix Faure.

Underneath the Hôtel Ganalé is *Grenelles*, a classy and imaginatively decorated place popular with expats and Peace Corps volunteers, especially during the 6pm to 8pm happy hours (two pints of Flag for CFA1800).

Down near the Île de Gorée ferry terminal on Blvd de la Libération, *Bar Gorée* is more African and entertaining than the bars around Av Pompidou. It has cheap beer (CFA600), a mysterious *vin rouge* that packs a punch for CFA180, snacks and food. Bands regularly play here and, if not, the DJs soon get things moving. There are likely to be plenty of people here, most of them not too well off, so don't take too many valuables along.

Music Venues, Nightclubs & Discos

Dakar is one of the best cities in West Africa for live music and has several nightclubs where Senegalese bands perform at weekends – especially on Saturday night. Discos are usually held on Thursday, Friday and Sunday. Most places have an admission fee of about CFA1000 to CFA2000 (although women often get in free), up to CFA5000 if a band is playing. Sometimes the admission includes your first 'free' drink; otherwise beers are about CFA700 to CFA1500, depending on how classy the place is. Check papers and listings magazines such as

SENEGAL

SENEGAL

Nightclubbing

It's Friday night, you're all decked out in your gladdest rags and ready for a night on the dance floor, African style. Prepare yourself for a fun night out, but also to witness some African/Western culture clash up close. Like anywhere, nightclubs in Senegal vary from place to place, but most follow the Western model – lots of mirrors, fancy lighting, huge amps and, yes, spinning disco balls. It's in the music and on the floor that you'll notice the difference.

Generally, the DJ will start with an African set, maybe some tried and trusted Youssou N'Dour to get the patrons in the swing. This will be followed by an R&B set, using whatever music he's been able to get from the US, before another African set kicks in, this time perhaps with a Congolese flavour. Western pop is next, then more African beats before a short set of techno, which clears all but the most hardcore off the dance floor. The trend is easy to spot: African sets are far and away the most popular, with smiling faces all around in contrast to the studied concentration on display (or is that just boredom) when the techno cranks up. When it comes to dancing, the Senegalese are as energetic as you'd like when in a group, but lone dancers, be they men or women, have been known to dance in front of mirrors for hours until the right partner pitches up.

Dakar Tam Tam and *L'Avis* to see what's on. And don't expect the music to start before midnight – most people don't arrive until about 11pm.

Club Thiossane (☎ 824 6046, Sicap Rue 10) World music fans should head for this hot and crowded club in La Médina, north of Marché Sandaga. It's owned by the legendary Youssou N'Dour, and when he's not touring the man himself performs here most Friday and Saturday nights. Club Thiossane can be very hard to find, and seeing as you probably won't be heading there until late it's best to take a taxi – it's pronounced Cho-sahn and all the drivers know it. If you are navigating your own way from central Dakar take the Route de la Corniche-Ouest to Soumbédioune, turn right on Blvd de la Gueule-Tapée, and then take the fifth right turn – the taxi is so worth it!

Similarly popular with the Dakarois is *Le Sahel* (☎ 821 2118, Centre Commercial Sahm), which is on the northeast corner of the intersection of Av Blaise Diagne and Blve de la Gueule-Tapée, about 3km northwest of Marché Sandaga.

In central Dakar, fancy clubs and discos include *King's Club* (32 Rue Victor Hugo), the New York–style *Kuer Samba* (☎ 821 2296, Rue Jules Ferry) and the popular *Iguane Café* (☎ 822 6553) opposite. For cheaper fun try *Black & White* (☎ 821 5054, Rue Gomis),

where you will find admission and beer are more reasonably priced.

Metissacana (☎ 822 20 43, Rue de Thiong) This is a sort of bar/cybercafé/music venue all wrapped into one. There is occasional live music (Baaba Maal has played here), with small beers CFA800 and meals around CFA3500.

With an emphasis on local acoustic music, *Planete Culture* (☎ 824 1655, Av Cheikh Anta Diop, Point), a few kilometres north of the centre, is a popular option. It's owned by local band Frères Guissé, who play in the outdoor setting at least once a week. It's open 6pm to 3am Monday to Saturday.

To find out what's happening at any of these places, stroll past during the day and look at the notices outside.

Theatre

There are many cultural events held at *Théâtre Daniel Sorano* (☎ 822 17 15, Blvd de la République), which is in an enormous building that also houses the Canadian embassy. To see what's on, check the posters outside the theatre or at the box office. The Ensemble Instrumental, the Ballet National du Sénégal, the Mudra Dance Group and the Théâtre National du Sénégal perform here on occasion. Also watch for the *semaines culturelles* (cultural weeks) when there are presentations by other African countries. Various shows are also put on at the *cultural centres* (see Information earlier in this chapter).

Cinemas

Dakar has several good cinemas, including *Cinéma le Plaza (☎ 823 8575, Av Pompidou)*, near La Gondole, and *Cinéma le Paris (Rue Carnot)*, opposite the Hôtel Teranga; both show major releases and charge CFA1000 or CFA2000. Films in English are dubbed into French. The *British-Senegalese Institute (☎ 822 4023, Rue 18 Juin)* does occasionally show films in English.

SHOPPING

Dakar's two major markets, *Marché Sandaga* and *Marché Kermel*, are both very lively and a major attraction for visitors. Unfortunately, both are plagued by hustlers offering to be your 'guide' or 'assistant'. If you can't ignore them, complain to a stallholder that the hustlers are putting you off buying. Alternatively, hire one 'guide' to minimise the hassle from others.

The larger Marché Sandaga is very much aimed at locals, and you can buy just about anything here, although don't expect too many souvenir stalls. The sheer choice of fabric stalls is a real draw. Colourful, baggy cotton trousers and shirts are popular, but you can buy any cloth you fancy and have it made by the local tailors into something to your own design. The best way of doing

Clusters of pear-shaped jewellery are typical of the ornamental pieces popular with the Wolof

this is to have them copy something you've already got. Cloth starts at about CFA1000 per metre, and a tailor will charge about CFA2500 to copy a shirt.

If you are after recorded music, check out the stalls in and around Marché Sandaga on Av Emile Badiane. Youths also stroll the sidewalks of Dakar with boxes of cassettes and CDs for sale. Prices depend on the popularity of the musician and the quality of the recording, but tapes go for around CFA1500 and CDs CFA5000. Another option is *Disco Star (☎ 822 27 91, 59 Av Pompidou)*, which sells locally made cassettes for CFA2000, imported cassettes for CFA5,000 to CFA13,000 and imported CDs for CFA13,000 to CFA20,000.

Marché Kermel has more on offer for tourists, with stalls selling carvings, baskets, leatherwork and other souvenirs, plus flower and fruit sellers. The smart new hall you see today was built after the main market hall burnt down in 1993.

Marché de Tilène, at the heart of the Médina, is well worth a visit. It was built in the colonial days when the Médina was created as a 'township' for Africans. This place is crowded with the sights and sounds of a traditional African market, and relatively free of tourists (and thieves), although you may need a guide anyway as the original market hall is hard to find among the modern sprawl of tin-roofed shops and houses.

Another hassle-free market is in the residential suburb of Castors, on the northern side of the city, about halfway between the centre and the airport. Many of the city buses terminate just west of here.

One of the most popular places for buying souvenirs is the government-sponsored *Village Artisanal*, near the fishing beach of Soumbédioune on Route de la Corniche-Ouest. You'll find a tremendous display of wooden carvings, metal work, gold and silver jewellery, ivory, tablecloths, blankets, leather goods and clothing, but a lot of the stuff is churned out very quickly and you have to search hard for good-quality pieces. These guys will almost certainly try to charge you several times the real value of whatever piece you've got your eye on (as you'd expect at a tourist market). If you don't fancy the hard bargaining, you could head to the small souvenir shop beside the ticket office at the Gorée ferry terminal in Dakar. This place has fixed prices for reasonably good carvings and fabrics, so even if you don't buy it's a good place to check out just to get an idea of what you should be paying.

For better-quality African art, head for Rue Mohamed V, between Av Pompidou and Rue Assane Ndoye, where several small shops have lots of high-quality masks, carvings and other objects from all over West and Central Africa. On the same street you will find shops selling Moroccan or Algerian-style carpets, leatherwork, pottery and Maghreb clothing.

For gold and silver, the best place is *La Cour des Mours (69 Av Blaise Diagne)* in a small alley, north of Marché Sandaga. A few of the Mauritanian silversmiths who gave it its name have returned home since being expelled a few years ago, and there are now numerous Senegalese traders. Even if you're not interested in jewellery, a trip to this fascinating old district is highly recommended. You'll also find silversmiths in other parts of Dakar; there's a row of three on Rue Victor Hugo. Silver is often sold by weight, so it's worth checking current prices with a local before you buy.

GETTING THERE & AWAY
Air
The airport is in Yoff and is officially called the Léopold Sédar Senghor International Airport. Details on flights between Dakar and international or regional destinations are given in the regional Getting There & Away and Senegal's Getting There & Away chapters. Flights within Senegal are currently limited to Air Senegal International's service between Dakar and Ziguinchor, Cap Skiring and Tambacounda. See Senegal's Getting Around chapter for further information.

For international flight inquiries, reconfirmations and reservations, airline offices in Dakar include the following:

Aeroflot (☎ 822 48 15) 3 Blvd de la République
Air Algérie (☎ 823 55 48) Place de l'Indépendance
Air France (☎ 829 77 77) 47 Av Albert Sarraut
Air Guinée (☎ 821 44 42) Av Pompidou
Air Mali (☎ 823 24 61) 14 Rue el Haji M'Baye Gueye, near Rue Vincens
Air Mauritanie (☎ 822 81 88) Place de l'Indépendance
Air Senegal International (☎ 823 56 29) 45 Av Albert Sarraut
Alitalia (☎ 823 38 74) 5 Av Pompidou
Ghana Airways (☎ 822 28 20) 21 Rue des Essarts, just off Place de l'Indépendance
Iberia (☎ 823 34 77) Place de l'Indépendance
Royal Air Maroc (☎ 843 47 52) Place de l'Indépendance
SN Brussels Airlines (☎ 823 04 60) Place de l'Indépendance
TACV Cabo Verde Airlines (☎ 821 39 68) 105 Rue Moussé Diop
TAP Air Portugal (☎ 821 00 65) Immeuble Faycal Rue Assane Ndoye, just off Place de l'Indépendance
Tunis Air (☎ 823 14 35) 24 Av Léopold Senghor

Public Transport From Dakar

destination	Peugeot taxi	minibus	Alham
Karang (Gambia)	4500	3500	3000
Kaolack	2600	1500	1250
Mbour	950	750	670
Richard Toll	4950	3880	3440
Rosso	4950	3880	3440
St-Louis	3100	2445	2150
Tambacounda	6800	5100	4400
Thiès	900	700	600
Ziguinchor	6500	5000	4500

Bus & Bush Taxi

Buses and Peugeot taxis for long-distance destinations leave from Gare Routière Pompiers, 3km north of Place de l'Indépendance. To get there from Marché Sandaga, take an 'Alham', *car rapide* or a taxi – from Marché Sandaga or the Place de l'Indépendance a taxi should cost about CFA500 to CFA750. Some sample fares (in CFA) from Dakar are listed here. Prices are the same in both directions.

Journey durations are impossible to quote with certainty, but, for example, Dakar to St-Louis by Peugeot taxi takes about four hours, to Tambacounda about seven hours and to Ziguinchor from nine to 11 hours, depending on your wait at the Gambia River ferry. Buses take about half as long again, while the journey time in a minibus can be double.

If you want a Peugeot taxi, ignore the touts who tell you they've all gone and try to push you into an Alham (see the boxed text 'Touts at the *Gare Routière*' in the Getting Around Senegambia chapter). Walk past the minibuses and Alhams to where the Peugeot taxis are lined up with signs indicating destinations. There are *always* Peugeot taxis, although you can wait a long time for them to fill in the afternoon. Going in the morning is always best.

Another option if you're heading for Tambacounda, Kaolack, Touba or St-Louis is 'express bus'. This is a good, fast, safe, reliable service, and comfortable too if you get a proper seat rather than a stool in the aisle. Fares are about 70% of Peugeot taxi prices – the fare to Tambacounda is CFA4000. Buses leave from a petrol station that doubles as a bus station at an intersection on Av Malik Sy, near the Gare Routière Pompiers; go the day before you travel to reserve a seat and check departure times, or call ☎ 821 85 05.

Some incoming transport may terminate at Gare Routière Kolobane, about 2km further north of Gare Routière Pompiers, on the other side of the autoroute, though this is rare.

Train

The train from Dakar goes to Bamako in Mali via several towns, including Thiès, Diourbel and Tambacounda, but it's quicker and cheaper to go by road and most people do. For details of the train to Bamako, see Senegal's Getting There & Away chapter. Passenger trains from Dakar to Kaolack no longer run, and they go to St-Louis only at holiday times.

Boat

The ferry MS *Joola* is supposed to sail between Dakar and Ziguinchor twice weekly in each direction, via Île de Carabane. For more details see Senegal's Getting Around chapter.

GETTING AROUND
To/From the Airport

Dakar's taxis have meters but they are never used. The official rates from the airport to the centre of Dakar are displayed on screens in the arrivals hall of the airport – CFA3000 during the day and CF3500 from midnight (not before!) to 6am. The drivers will swear to Allah the posted rates no longer apply, so hard bargaining is required. You can change money or draw from an ATM inside the terminal.

A taxi from the airport to Yoff or N'Gor should be CFA1500, but the drivers still try to charge CFA3000 (this is understandable, as after the short ride they give you, they go right to the back of the queue at the airport). If you're not getting anywhere with taxi drivers, and want to save money, it's easy enough to walk out of the airport to the main road and flag down a taxi there. This is

SENEGAL

> ### Airport Taxi Scams
>
> Arriving at Dakar airport, be prepared for touts and hustlerss. A common trick is for the tout to 'find' you a taxi (there are always loads at the rank just outside the terminal building) and then come with you into town. On the way he'll tell you whatever hotel you're heading for is full, and you're welcome to stay at his place for a small fee. This may be a genuine earner or it may be a con. We've also heard of incidents where touts and taxi drivers have colluded to rob passengers. The best way to deal with either case is to find your own taxi.

especially worth doing if you're not heading into the city centre. From the city centre to the airport, the fare should be around CFA2500.

You can also get DDD bus No 8, via Yoff, for CFA200 to or from the city. To get to the bus turn right out of the terminal and walk past the taxis. Buses leave every half-hour, but do not run from around 9pm to 6am.

Bus

The large, clean and blue DDD (Dakar Dem Dikk, formerly Sotrac) buses serve the city centre and places around Dakar. They cost CFA140 for short rides and up to CFA200 for the longer rides. You get on at the back door and buy your ticket from the conductor's booth. For short trips in the city it's usually easier to use a car rapide or Alham, but for longer trips to the towns and villages around Dakar the DDD buses are a good option.

Some useful routes from central Dakar include: No 5 to Guédiawaye; No 6 to Cambérene; No 7 to Ouakam; No 8 to Yoff and the airport; No 9 to Liberté VI; No 15 to Rufisque; and No 16 to Malika. The main bus station for places east of Dakar, such as Rufisque, is on Blvd de la Libération. Other buses run through the centre of town and terminate at the old Palais de Justice, near the tip of Cap Manuel.

It's worth noting that the municipal bus service was closed for almost a year after the newly elected President Wade ordered an audit of state assets. Sotrac was found to be more than US$40 million in debt. DDD have since taken over the routes and route numbers have changed, so it's worthwhile checking before you get on to make sure the bus is going where you want it to.

Alham

Following the same routes as the DDD buses are privately owned buses, usually white 30-seater Mercedes known as Alhams or N'Diaga N'Diaye. Fares are usually CFA50 or CFA100 depending on the length of the trip. Destinations and routes are not marked, so you'll have to ask or listen for the call from the bus boy.

For destinations north of the city centre, including N'Gor and Yoff, Alhams go from

Place Lat Dior, near Av Peytavin, west of Marché Sandaga.

Car Rapide

If you don't see a bus going your way, you can always hop in a car rapide – a dilapidated blue and yellow minibus stuffed with people. Some are genuinely (and frighteningly) rapid; others crawl along. Their prices are about 25% lower than Alhams. They go to most places but their destinations aren't marked, so you'll have to listen carefully to the destinations the young assistants yell out as they fly past. When you want to stop, just tap a coin on the roof or window.

Taxi

Taxis around Dakar are plentiful, but while the cars are fitted with ancient-looking meters, neither locals nor tourists use them. Instead every taxi trip is preceded by a short negotiation process. At first you might pay a bit over the odds, but you'll soon get an idea of how much a trip is worth. Rare indeed is the driver who will let you walk away rather than take a fair price.

For a short ride across the city centre, the fare should be from around CFA300 to CFA400. From the Place de l'Indépendance to the Gare Routière Pompiers, locals pay CFA500, and you'll probably pay CFA750. At night (midnight to 6am) all rates are double. Drivers outside top-end hotels will try and charge you much more than this and many will simply refuse to take you for the usual fee, as they'll lose their place in the queue and may miss out on a big-spender. Wherever you go, remember locals do not tip, although many tourists do.

For a longer hire, taxis should cost about CFA3500 per hour within the city centre, although this depends how much driving you want to do. If you do need a taxi for the day, set aside a half an hour for price negotiations. Unless you know exactly where you're going, don't include petrol in the price as this asks the driver to speculate. Agree to a daily rate for the car only, and pay separately for the petrol that you use. To avoid problems at the end of the day, verify at the beginning that the petrol gauge is operating.

Car

All the major car-rental agencies have similar rates. For the smallest models, they charge between CFA17,000 and CFA20,000 per day, as well as CFA160 to CFA190 per kilometre, around CFA4000 per day for insurance and 20% tax – it soon adds up. The major self-drive car-rental agencies in Dakar are:

Avis (☎ 849 77 57) There are branches at the airport and the Hotel Meridien President

Budget (☎ 822 25 13, fax 822 25 06) There are branches at the corner of Av du President Lamine Guéye and Av Faidherbe, with agents at the airport and the Hotel Meridien President

Europcar (☎ 822 06 91, fax 822 34 77) There are branches at the corner of Blvd de la Libération and Allées Delmas

Hertz (☎ 822 20 16, fax 821 17 21) There are branches at the airport and Hôtel Teranga, and another in Rue Félix Faure in central Dakar

Independent car-hire companies include:

Africars (☎ 823 18 50) 14 Rue Galandou Diouf. Africars has several other bases around the country.

Afrique Location (☎ 823 88 01) 28 Rue Assane Ndoye

Assurcar (☎ 823 72 51, mobile 638 48 55, W www.assurcar.sn) Assurcar, near the Gorée ferry pier, is cheaper than Senecartours. A Peugeot 205 is just CFA11,000 per day (CFA16,500 for a weekend), plus CFA110 per kilometre, and a Suzuki 4WD is CFA20,000 per day plus CFA200 per kilometre.

Noprola (☎ 821 73 11) 29 Rue Assane Ndoye, near Hôtel Taranga

Senecartours (☎ 822 42 86, fax 821 83 06, W www.senecartours.com) 64 Rue Carnot. This company is reliable, with good vehicles and slightly lower prices than the internationals. It also does special weekend and *prix forfeiture* (lump sum) deals; for example, a small car for one week including all tax, insurance and unlimited kilometres is CFA250,000. The same deal for a 4WD is CFA55,000, with 1200km free and CFA350 per kilometre thereafter. It also has an airport branch (☎ 820 17 34).

Although rented vehicles cannot usually be taken across borders, most companies allow their cars to go into Gambia. But if you do this, make sure all paperwork is absolutely in order, as the Gambian police just love checking Senegalese hire cars. For a list of all operators see W www.au-senegal.com/transport_en/location.htm.

Cap Vert Peninsula

The Cap Vert peninsula stretches away beyond downtown Dakar, punctuated by a series of satellite towns and fishing villages that have expanded with the city and now blur into what has become Greater Dakar. But these various suburbs and settlements are far from uniform.

To the east of the city centre, about 3km offshore, is Île de Gorée (Gorée Island), one of the earliest European settlements along this part of the coast, and today a haven of history and peace within easy reach of the frenetic activity of Dakar. To the west are the Îles de la Madeleine, a national park with not a single historic site but plenty to see and a great place to just chill out in the rock pool.

North of the city centre, at the western tip of the Cap Vert peninsula, is Pointe des Almadies – the western extent of the African continent. Along the coast from here are N'Gor and Yoff – the former an untidy mix of fishing village and seaside resort favoured at weekends by escapees from the crowded city, and the latter a compact traditional town with a fascinating cultural heritage and little in the way of tourist facilities.

East of here is the vast sprawling settlement of Dagoudane-Pikine (usually just called Pikine), stretching across the neck of the peninsula and almost connecting the north and south coasts. Pikine is technically a separate entity, but in reality it's a working-class suburb of Dakar that has expanded so rapidly that it now has a larger population than the capital itself.

Beyond Pikine, the Cap Vert peninsula begins to widen and merge with the mainland. Within easy reach of Dakar are several more interesting places to visit, including the beaches at Malika, the monastery of Keur Moussa, and the great pink lagoon of Lac Retba (often called La Rose).

ÎLE DE GORÉE

Only 28 hectares in area, Île de Gorée (Gorée Island) is a wonderfully peaceful place with around 1000 inhabitants, no tar roads and no

Highlights

- Stroll around the historic streets of Île de Gorée, the first European settlement in Senegal and one-time slaving centre

- Escape the city to the small campements of Malika and the vast emptiness of the Atlantic beaches

- Stand on the westernmost point of Africa at Point des Almadies, and enjoy a fantastic fish meal on the beach afterwards

- Float in Lac Retba, the great pink saline lagoon and busy traditional salt-collecting area

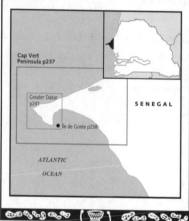

cars (or fumes) or bicycles. The colonial-style houses, wrought-iron balconies, narrow streets and trailing bougainvillea give it a calm Mediterranean feel, and Gorée is a popular place for visitors and locals to escape the crowds of Dakar. The small beach near the ferry jetty is often busy at weekends.

Information & Guides

It is not obligatory or even necessary to take a guide around Île de Gorée, although their knowledge can add considerably to your visit. Freelancers lurk at the ferry jetty, but it's

SENEGAL

CAP VERT PENINSULA

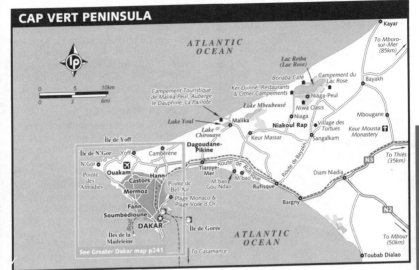

SENEGAL

better to hire official guides at the Syndicat d'Initiative (tourist office; ☎ 822 97 03) open 9am to 1pm and 2.30pm to 6pm Tuesday to Sunday. The fee is CFA2500 per person for a half-day tour.

A very useful book is *Gorée – The Island and the Historical Museum*, produced in English and available for CFA3250 in some Dakar bookshops.

Things to See

There's plenty to see on the island and you could easily spend a day here. The **IFAN Historical Museum** *(admission CFA200; open 10am-1pm, 2.30pm-6pm Tues-Sat)* at Fort d'Estrées on the northern end of the island has pictorial and physical exhibits portraying Senegalese history up to the present-day, but it's all in French. The fort was built by the French is 1850.

Better is the **Musée de la Femme** *(admission CFA300; open 10am-5pm, Tues-Sun)* with displays on the role of Senegalese women that are brought to life by the enthusiastic museum guide (CFA350). There is also the dull **Musée Maritime** and the more famous **Maison des Esclaves** (see the boxed text later in this chapter). These two museums are

open morning and afternoon, except Monday, and charge CFA300.

Le Castel is a rocky plateau giving good views of the island and across to Dakar. It's covered with fortifications dating from different periods, including two massive WWII guns, which sank a British warship in the harbour. The *Tacoma* lies beneath a buoy which the ferry loops around as it

Cannons decorating a corridor at Île de Gorée's Fort d'Estrées

ÎLE DE GORÉE

1 Fort d'Estrées; IFAN
  Historical Museum
2 Post Office
3 Hostellerie du Chevalier
  de Boufflers; Ann Sabran
4 Musée Maritime
5 Town Hall
6 Relais de l'Espadon
7 Navy Hospital

8 Police
9 Auberge Keur Beer
10 Syndicat d'Initiative
11 La Maison des
   Esclaves
12 Musée de la Femme
13 St Charles Church
14 Mosque
15 Chez Madame Siga

To Dakar
(3km)

Tacoma
Shipwreck

Ferry Jetty

Bars &
Restaurants

Tourist
Market

Public
Gardens

Steps

Le Castel

0   50   100m
0   50   100yd

approaches the island. Le Castel is now inhabited by a group of Baye Fall disciples
(for more information on these, see the
boxed text 'Marabouts & Brotherhoods' in
the Facts about Senegal chapter).

There's a little **tourist market** located
just behind the row of bars and restaurants
facing the ferry jetty. It's full of souvenir-
quality crafts and materials, but the bargaining here is far more relaxed than in
Dakar.

Opposite the market is the old colonial
hotel **Relais de l'Espadon** (formerly the
home of the French governor). It was closed

in 1975, and has stood virtually derelict for
many years now. Talk of it being renovated
into a top-quality hotel has so far been just
talk. South is the old **Navy Hospital**, which
is used as housing by many of the island's
residents. North is the old **hôtel de ville**
(town hall).

Places to Stay & Eat

For a room in a *private home*, inquire at
some of the bars and restaurants facing the
ferry jetty. Rates start at CFA7500 per room
for a night.

Syndicat d'Initiative (☎ 822 97 03,
ⓔ s.i.goree@metissacana.sn) Rooms CFA
10,000-15,000. This is the cheapest official
place, with very good rooms for rent.

Auberge Keur Beer (☎/fax 821 38 01,
ⓔ keurbeer@sentoo.sn) Doubles without/
with bathroom CFA23,000/CFA25,000.
Near Syndicat d'Initiative, this stylish place
has friendly, efficient French management.
The shared facilities are pristine and the included breakfast is filling. If the hotel is
full the staff will help you find private
rooms in town.

Hostellerie du Chevalier de Boufflers
(☎ 822 53 64, ⓔ goreebboufflers@ns.arc.sn)
Mains CFA4000-6000. This place is named
after a colonial governor and is best known
as a restaurant. You pay for the historic location, and the shady terrace overlooking
the harbour, as much as for the food. It has
a few rooms in a separate building that cost
CFA18,000 or CFA23,000 each.

Ann Sabran (☎ 826 94 29) Meals
CFA2500. Next door to the hostellerie, the
Ann Sabran has a cosy, portside barrio feel
inside and shaded tables outside. The meals
are decent and you can buy excellent sandwiches for CFA1000.

Most other places to eat are in a rect-
angle facing the ferry jetty, with meals
around CFA2000. Prices are chalked up on
boards outside. For cheaper fare seek out
Chez Madame Siga, a small, sky-blue
house near the top of the ramp up to Le Castel. Locals here are served *tiéboudienne*
(rice baked in a thick sauce of fish and vegetables) for CFA1000 (although this may
have to be ordered in advance).

Maison des Esclaves

Île de Gorée was a busy trading centre during the 18th and 19th centuries, and many merchants built houses in which they would live or work in the upper storey and store their cargoes on the lower floor. La Maison des Esclaves is one of the last remaining 18th-century buildings of this type on Gorée. It was built in 1786 and renovated in 1990 with French assistance. With its famous doorway opening directly from the storeroom onto the sea, this building has enormous spiritual significance for some visitors, particularly black Americans whose ancestors were brought from Africa as slaves.

Walking around the dimly lit dungeons, particularly after a visit to the historical museum, you will begin to imagine the horrors. The Slave House curator will provide further gruesome details, but in reality, despite the name, it's unlikely that La Maison des Esclaves was used to hold many captive slaves, apart from those who 'belonged' to the merchant and maybe a few for trading. In fact, some historians have pointed out that although an important slaving culture existed here, and the island was a vital trading centre and strategic port, Gorée itself was never a major slave-shipment point. The sheer practicalities of little space and a lack of drinking water would have made transferring large numbers of people difficult. Of the 20 million slaves that were taken from Africa, only 300 per year may have gone through Gorée, and even then, the famous doorway would not have been used – a ship could not get near the dangerous rocks and the town had a perfectly good jetty a short distance away. Additionally, records show that the original owners were the mixed-race family of a French navy surgeon called Jean Pepin, not (as it is claimed) Dutch merchants – they were ejected from Gorée by the French in 1677.

The historians who refute Gorée's position are anxious to avoid accusations of revisionism, and emphasise that many millions of slaves were taken from West Africa in the most appalling circumstances, and that the slave trade was undeniably cruel and inhuman. But they see the promotion of Gorée as an historical site of significance to the history of slavery as mere commercialism based on distortion – a cynical attempt to attract tourists who might otherwise go to Gambia's Jufureh or the slave forts of Ghana. It seems to boil down to emotional manipulation by government officials and tour companies of those Americans and others who come here as part of a genuine search for cultural roots.

**Written with assistance from Chris de Wilde (specialist in
19th-century West African history)**

Getting There & Away

A ferry runs regularly from the wharf in Dakar, just north of the Place de l'Indépendance, to Gorée. The trip across takes 20 minutes and costs CFA5000 return for foreigners.

ÎLES DE LA MADELEINE

The Îles de la Madeleine are west of Dakar, about 4km off the mainland, and were declared a national park in 1985. They consist of a main island called Sarpan and two other islets, plus several lumps of volcanic rock that stick out of the water at low tide. Unlike Gorée, the Madeleines are not inhabited – at least, not by humans – but Sarpan is home to some interesting dwarf baobab trees, and the

islands are particularly noted as a good place to watch sea birds. There are breeding colonies of common cormorants, plus northern gannets, bridled terns and red-billed tropic birds – the latter a beautiful specimen with narrow sweptback wings, and long tail streamers in the breeding season. You may also see ospreys. You may also see turtles and dolphins.

Even if you're not interested in birds or small trees, a visit to the islands, combined maybe with some snorkelling, diving or swimming in the beautiful natural pool, and a scramble ashore on Sarpan (the only place a boat can land) makes for a great day out. Go on a weekday and remember to take a hat, as there's virtually no shade, and all the food and water that you'll need. The islands are sometimes known as Îles aux Serpents, a corruption of Sarpan, which is erroneous as there's not a snake to be seen.

If you want to know more about the islands a ranger will accompany you for whatever price you can negotiate.

Getting There & Away

To reach Îles de la Madeleine go to the office of the Eaux et Forêts (water and forestry) department on Route de la Corniche-Ouest, just a few metres north of Casino Terrou-Bi on Pointe de Fann. It's a small building, on the coast side of the road, and is easy to miss. Once here, what used to be a tedious process could now not be simpler. A park ranger will take CFA1000 for your entry fee, and another CFA3000 per person for the 20-minute pirogue ride out there (CFA2000 if you are in a group of four or more). Children under 10 are free. The pirogue runs fairly frequently, taking about 10 people at a time. When you buy your ticket you specify when you want to return and the pirogue will come and pick you up. Easy.

Alternatively L'Océanium (listed under Activities in the Dakar chapter) runs visits to Îles de la Madeleine for CFA5000 per person, although you should phone first to arrange to join a group.

N'GOR & POINTE DES ALMADIES

The Pointe des Almadies is just 13km from central Dakar. Anyone who's been to the Cape of Good Hope, Britain's Land's End or any other continental extremity, might be keen to add this to the list. To do so just scramble over a some of the black rocks sticking out of the surf.

Nearby is a strip of dirty sand, a rubbish-strewn car park, a tatty Village Artisanal and a line of ugly restaurants. In mitigation, most of the restaurants, and especially the shanties on the beach, serve good food, and become popular at weekends and evenings (they look much better at night), but at other times Almadies has a windswept and semi-abandoned air.

East of the point, the sheltered **Plage N'Gor** (N'Gor Beach) at is good for swimming, and has a much better atmosphere, with a couple of increasingly popular 'surf camps' and a collection of shack-like restaurants where you can enjoy cheap seafood and a cold beer. A short boat ride across the bay to **Île de N'Gor** (N'Gor Island), takes you to the best beach of all. The island is rough and rocky on the ocean side, but with two clean and safe beaches facing the mainland. The fare is CFA500 for the round trip, which includes the use of obligatory life jackets.

Places to Stay & Eat

Pointe des Almadies Hidden away behind high walls and yet blindingly obvious is *Club Med*, which dominates much of the point. Most guests book from Europe, but if you want to stay some travel agents in Dakar can make bookings.

It's hard to miss the huge *Hotel Meridien President* (☎ 869 69 69, fax 869 69 99, W *www.lemeridien-dakar.com)*, undeniably the finest hotel in and around Dakar, which has every facility (including its own golf club and heliport) and prices to match – rooms start at CFA86,000 and go much, much higher.

Back at the beach the best-value *local food* is found right on the sand. Several shanty-like structures house an array of crepe-making and fish-barbecuing tools that are well worth investigating.

Nearby are several smarter restaurants, all specialising in seafood. *La Récif des Almadies* (☎ 820 11 60), open lunch and dinner Thursday to Tuesday, also has French and Vietnamese dishes for less than CFA4000 and gets good reviews. *La Pointe des Almadies* (☎ 820 01 40) open Tuesday to Sunday, has mains for about CFA3500 and has been popular for years.

Plage N'Gor Accommodation options in the village's maze of lanes include *Waly's Surf Camp* (☎ 820 27 57) with basic rooms for CFA8000, and the infinitely better *Surf Camp Colé* (☎ 820 29 39) with air-con doubles for CFA10,000, a giant rooftop

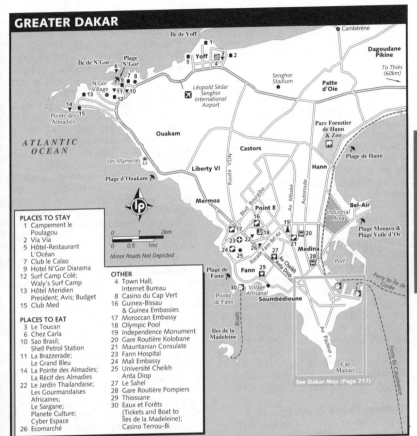

GREATER DAKAR

SENEGAL

PLACES TO STAY
1 Campement le Poulagou
2 Via Via
5 Hôtel-Restaurant L'Océan
7 Club le Calao
9 Hotel N'Gor Diarama
12 Surf Camp Colé; Waly's Surf Camp
13 Hôtel Meridien President; Avis; Budget
15 Club Med

PLACES TO EAT
3 Le Toucan
6 Chez Carla
10 Sao Brasil; Shell Petrol Station
11 La Brazzerade; Le Grand Bleu
14 La Pointe des Almadies; La Récif des Almadies
22 Le Jardin Thailandaise; Les Gourmandaises Africaines; Le Sargane; Planete Culture; Cyber Espace
26 Ecomarché

OTHER
4 Town Hall; Internet Bureau
8 Casino du Cap Vert
16 Guinea-Bissau & Guinea Embassies
17 Moroccan Embassy
18 Olympic Pool
19 Independence Monument
20 Gare Routière Kolobane
21 Mauritanian Consulate
23 Fann Hospital
24 Mali Embassy
25 Université Cheikh Anta Diop
27 Le Sahel
28 Gare Routière Pompiers
29 Thiossane
30 Eaux et Forêts (Tickets and Boat to Îles de la Madeleine); Casino Terrou-Bi

family room for CFA20,000 and the vivacious Mrs Colé running the show. You'll need to ask for directions to find these places, but don't be talked into watching the seemingly daily 'baptism' unless you've got plenty of money to 'donate' to your 'guides'. The same applies to getting a piece of the ancient, sacred baobab near the mosque.

. The monolith on the headland to the east is *Hotel N'Gor Diarama* (☎ 820 10 05, fax 820 27 23), with rooms at CFA40,000. Next door, *Club le Calao* (☎ 820 05 40, fax 820 11 80) is a quasi resort, popular with groups, and has comfortable and reasonably priced

thatched bungalows from CFA12,250 per person for bed and breakfast.

The best part of this beach is the collection of *restaurants*, where you can enjoy seafood and a cold beer overlooking the beach, with views out to Île de N'Gor.

The number and size of the eateries has grown in recent years. *Le Grand Bleu*, at the east end of the beach, has friendly staff, excellent shrimp sandwiches for CFA1000 and grilled prawns for CFA3500. The much smarter *La Brazzerade* (☎ 820 03 64) specialises in charcoal-grilled seafood and has a *menu du jour* (meal of the day) for

CFA7000. There are also a few pleasant but pricey rooms.

Back from the coast, beside the Shell petrol station, is *Sao Brasil* (☎ *820 09 41)*, a bar and restaurant in a garden setting that makes good pizzas and seafood dishes for about CFA4000.

Nearer the airport is *Casino du Cap Vert* (☎ *820 09 74)*, a complex that has blackjack, roulette and game machines, a smart restaurant with an evening menu for CFA8000, a floor show and a disco (open every night).

Île de N'Gor Private weekender *cottages* can sometimes be hired for a few nights when the owners are away, and plenty of other owners seem happy to let out a room for a few nights. For details ask around on the beach.

There are two *restaurants*, with meals in the CFA2500 to CFA5000 range, plus a couple of *huts* where you can buy drinks and cheaper meals such as grilled fish for CFA1000, or a bowl of fish and rice for CFA500. You can also hire simple *cabines* (sun shelters) and water sports equipment. At the west end of the western beach is *Chez Carla* (☎ *820 15 86)*, a restaurant with a reputation for some of the best Italian food in the Dakar area, with dishes about CFA3000. It also has a few overpriced double rooms for CFA15,000, or CFA20,000 with breakfast.

Getting There & Away

To reach Pointe des Almadies or N'Gor, you could take a No 8 bus from central Dakar out towards the airport, and take a taxi from there for about CFA700. Otherwise Alhams run along Av Cheikh Anta Diop all the way to N'Gor for about CFA100. A taxi from central Dakar will cost about CFA2000.

YOFF

A short distance east of N'Gor, but contrasting sharply in feel, is the town of Yoff. On the map it may look like just another suburb, but there's a vital sense of community here that marks it out from other places around Dakar. The people of Yoff are almost exclusively Lebu. Sometimes classified as a branch of the Wolof, they are a fiercely independent group who have inhabited this area for many centuries. Despite, or because of, their relatively small population (they number a few thousand, whereas the Wolof are counted in millions) they have remained culturally intact. The town itself is self-administering, with no government officials, no police force and, apparently, no crime. In fact, it was regarded as a separate state by the French colonial authorities before Senegal itself became independent.

The Lebu of Yoff are nearly all members of the Layen, the smallest of the four Islamic brotherhoods that dominate life in Senegal (for more details see the boxed text 'Marabouts & Brotherhoods' in the Facts about Senegal chapter). The founder of the brotherhood, Saidi Limamou Laye, is believed to be a reincarnation of the Prophet Mohammed, and his large **mausoleum** is highly revered, and a place of pilgrimage for Muslims on Islamic holidays – particularly at the end of Ramadan. The mausoleum is the large white building topped with a green onion-shaped dome, on the beach at the eastern end of town.

At the northern end of town, about 1km from the mausoleum, is the main fishing beach, where large pirogues are launched into the giant rollers and the day's catch is sold straight from the sand. The Lebu fishermen have a healthy respect for the sea, and a belief in the spirit it contains, represented by a large snake. If the waves are too large, the boats stay safely on the beach.

Even if the waves weren't so dangerously large, and even if the beach wasn't covered in the town's rubbish, Yoff beach is no place for swimming or sunbathing: Skimpy clothing is most inappropriate in this staunchly Muslim community. Forget about 'entertainment', too – there are no clubs or bars in Yoff, and even private drunkenness is frowned upon. This is a place to come and just wander around, slowly and respectfully, properly dressed and without a camera, simply taking it all in.

Perhaps because the Lebu wield less power than the Wolof, electricity in Yoff can be very scarce indeed. It's not unusual for there to be a daily outage, sometimes two. When the power is working there are a

Yoff Healers

One of the most interesting aspects of life in Yoff is the traditional *ndeup* ceremonies where people with a mental illness are treated and healed. People come to be cured from all over Senegal and Gambia and even from other neighbouring countries such as Mali and Guinea-Bissau. Despite the town's Islamic heritage, the ceremonies are totally animist, and based on a belief that psychological sickness is the result of possession by spirits. The leaders of the Leyen brotherhood turn a blind eye to the 'pagan' ceremonies and the two beliefs comfortably coexist.

The healing ceremonies usually last one day, but can be longer for serious illnesses, and usually take place about twice a month. The traditional healers sacrifice animals (a chicken or cow depending on the seriousness of the illness) to invoke intervention from guardian spirits, and place the sick people into a trance-like state that allows malevolent spirits to be drawn out. Some observers have noted that the process is similar to voodoo ceremonies that take place in other parts of West Africa. The healers' services are not cheap; families of people who need treatment reportedly pay large sums (the equivalent of many years' salary), and often several sufferers are treated at the same time.

The ceremonies take place in the centre of Yoff and can attract large crowds of local people. Tourists are tolerated, but even watching can be a disturbing experience. It's best to go with a local and keep to the sidelines. Waving a zoom lens around would be the height of insensitivity.

couple of places offering Internet access. The best is at the *mairie* (town hall), on the street that runs parallel to the airport road at the eastern end of town, where an hour on a good terminal is CFA1000.

Places to Stay & Eat

Campement le Poulagou (☎ 820 23 47, mobile 657 41 67) Rooms CFA6000 per person, half board CFA9000. This long-standing place is on the northern side of town, with a fine balcony overlooking the beach where the fishing boats are launched. Accommodation is in basic double or triple rooms and rates include breakfast. If you fly into Dakar and phone the campement the owner will come and pick you up, but make sure you speak to the owner himself. Otherwise a taxi ride to the campement (ask for the campement at the *plage des pêchures*) should cost CFA1500.

Via Via (☎/fax 820 54 75, mobile 656 05 01, ⓔ viavia@sentoo.sn, Route des Cimetières) Singles/doubles CFA9000/16,000, quad rooms CFA7500 per person. At the eastern end of Yoff, this is the nearest Dakar has to a backpackers' lodge, and is a great place to head for comfort and orientation if you're just off the plane. The rooms are clean and brightly decorated, even if the rates are a bit

steep for what you get (bathrooms are shared). But the food is good and the atmosphere is friendly and relaxed. The multilingual management can provide information about Senegal and arrange courses in basic Wolof and traditional *djembe* – where you learn to make and play the drum. Snacks and meals in the bar-restaurant cost from CFA1000 to CFA4000. If you're coming at a busy time, it might be worth reserving a room before you arrive.

Hôtel-Restaurant l'Océan (☎ 820 00 47, ⓔ hotelocean@sentoo.sn, Rue de l'Océan) Singles CFA12,000, doubles CFA14,000-30,000. This more upmarket place overlooks the sea on the western side of Yoff. It has big rooms and a vast restaurant serving French, Lebanese and Senegalese specialities (mains around CFA4500). The swimming pool juts into the sea, and at high tide waves break into the pool.

Le Toucan (☎/fax 820 90 39) Meals CFA3000. Follow the signs from the main road to this rooftop restaurant, where the Senegalese fare takes a while to come but is worth the wait.

Getting There & Away

Yoff is near the airport, and the places to stay listed above are most easily reached from there by taxi – the fare is CFA1500. From Dakar's city centre, a taxi to Yoff should cost around CFA2000. By public transport, take DDD bus No 8. Buses loop through one part of the village, but in order to reach either Hotel-Restaurant l'Océan, Campement le Poulagou or Via Via you have to get off on the main road and then walk down a street towards the beach. All places are signposted.

MALIKA
About 15km east of Yoff, and about 25km from central Dakar, is the village of Malika (also known as Malika-sur-Mer). A short distance outside this village are three places to stay, all rated highly by travellers with their own vehicle, and by anyone else who wants to escape Dakar and spend some time on the huge unspoilt beach. If you want something more energetic, you can walk to Lac Retba (see later in this chaprter) along the beach. It takes about three hours each way. The beach is pounded by some of the best waves on the coast, but if you chose to swim, note that the currents can be very strong and several people have drowned here in recent years.

On rare occasions travellers have reported being hassled while walking along this beach, so it's best not to carry too many valuables around.

Places to Stay & Eat
Campement Touristique de Malika Peul (☎ mobile 658 48 67) Camp sites CFA2000 per tent, huts CFA4000. This place is right on the beach, with basic huts and camping that make it popular with Dakarois wanting a weekend away. There's a small bar-restaurant, with lunch CFA1000, dinner CFA1500 and beers for CFA500, plus shops near the Malika bus station if you want to self-cater. If you want to learn how to drum or play the kora (a stringed instrument), a teacher can be arranged.

East along the beach are two smaller places. *Auberge le Dauphin* (☎ 837 96 73, mobile 643 57 71) has basic rooms for CFA7000 with breakfast and staff so relaxed as to be almost comatose. About 100m away, just above the high water mark, *La Paillote* (☎ mobile 634 7828) is probably a better bet with simple huts for CFA5000, plus CFA3000 per person for half board. The shared bathrooms are clean and there's a super balcony with (if you're standing) views up and down the coast.

Getting There & Away
From Dakar, take bus No 16 to Malika, and opposite the bus station follow a sandy track towards the ocean (look for the small sign to the campements). After about a 15-minute walk, you pass a football field with a wall around it; take the left fork and it's another 15 minutes. Alternatively, a taxi from Dakar is CFA4500.

If you're driving, the most direct route is to turn left off the main road between Dakar and Rufisque at Tiaroye-Mer. It's easier, however, to continue for about 6km beyond Tiaroye-Mer to another left turn on a tar road (a signpost says 'Sedima'), which leads towards Keur Massar. About 3km from the main road you reach a crossroads. Go straight ahead for Keur Massar, Niaga and Lac Retba, or turn left for Malika.

LE VILLAGE DES TORTUES
On the Route de Bayakh, just north of the village of Sangalkam, is the fascinating Village des Tortues *(The Village of Tortoises;* ☎ *658 99 84; open 9am-5.30pm daily; adult/child CFA3000/2000)*. The village is actually a nonprofit reserve that was set up as a haven for injured tortoises and is now home to more than 600. There are several different varieties, but the main attractions are the giant African spurred tortoise *(Geochelone sulcata)*. This species is the largest continental tortoise on earth, and there are scores of them in the village, ranging in size from tiny, newly hatched versions to 'Grand Dad', a 92kg gentle giant (unlike 'Grand Ma', who has a healthy dislike of staff and visitors alike). The expert staff conduct informative tours, explain the intricacies of the tortoise shell and regularly fish small species (even the one that bites) out of murky ponds. All in all, this place is well worth an hour or so.

To get here, take a bus or Alham to Rufisque and then another Alham heading for Kayar; ask to be let off at the village (you'll see the huge sign on your left). Alternatively, a taxi from Rufisque will cost about CFA2000.

LAC RETBA (LAC ROSE)

Lac Retba is usually known as Lac Rose (the Pink Lake), especially by the tour companies in Dakar who bill it as Senegal's answer to the Dead Sea. The lake is also famous because the annual Paris-Dakar motor rally traditionally finishes here. Surrounded by dunes, this large shallow lagoon is 10 times saltier than the ocean and is also renowned for its pink hue when the sun is high. The colour is due to the high concentrations of minerals in the water, and as a result is much more impressive in the dry season, when the water is low. You can swim here, buoyed by the salt.

If pink water and effortless floating aren't enough to entice you, the small-scale, salt-collecting industry on the southern side of the lake may be of more interest (see the boxed text 'Collecting Salt at Lac Retba'). Getting here without your own transport can be a sweat, particularly with a 5km

Collecting Salt at Lac Retba

On the south side of Lac Retba (Lac Rose) is an area called Niaga-Peul, from where local people go out to collect salt from the lake. The lake is shallow, so they wade up to their waists and use digging tools to scrape the salt off the lake bed and load it into flat-bottomed canoes. When the canoe is full, and the water only millimetres below the rim, it is punted back to the shore, and the salt carried onto the bank itself in buckets. Each salt collector builds his own pile of salt – marked by his initials – and members of the family are also involved; the women do most of the carrying work. The good-quality salt is put straight into 25kg sacks, and sold to middlemen from Dakar who come each morning with trucks and pick-ups. The poorer-quality salt gets loaded in bulk, and is taken elsewhere for processing. The workers get paid less than CFA400 for each 25kg sack, less for the low-grade salt.

walk in the heat from Niaga village, and in the middle of the day you may be competing for space around the lake with coach loads of tourists from Dakar. Once they have left, it is a very peaceful place, and if you have the time it is worth a visit.

Places to Stay & Eat

Undoubtedly the best place to stay, and arguably the best place to eat, is *Bonaba Café* (☎ *mobile 638 75 38)*. Hidden away on the far side of the lake, this ultrarelaxed place is run by a friendly British couple and has simple bungalows with half board for CFA9000, and clean outdoor bathrooms. There's a pool, hammocks, beer and delicious food. To get there, walk from the touristy area for 2km over the dunes, with the lake on your right; take a pirogue from the salt village for CFA3000; or drive anticlockwise around the lake until you can't go any further. If you're in doubt, get one of the local boys to show you the way for a small contribution to his new football. Next door to Bonaba is *Chevaux du Lac* (☎ *mobile 630 02 41)*, where you can go horse riding with Frenchwoman Veronique for between two hours (CFA6000) and six days (CFA400,000), although the latter is for experienced riders only.

At the lake, most places to stay and eat cater to tour groups from Dakar, and are much busier at lunch time than in the evening. The most pleasant option is *Ker Djinné* (☎ *826 71 41)* with rustic bungalows for CFA3000 per person and chicken yassa (CFA4000) for lunch every day. Around the lake toward the salt collectors is *Niwa Oasis* (☎ *822 20 29)*, which has rooms with bathroom for CFA10,000 but looked a bit neglected when we passed. Opposite here is where the Paris-Dakar Rally winner collects the trophy.

Further along is *Campement du Lac Rose* (☎ *mobile 638 10 19)*, a more upmarket establishment with air-con rooms and other such luxuries.

The campements all do meals; otherwise you can eat at the *restaurants* near near Ker Djinné, where people also go swimming/floating.

Getting There & Away

There is no direct bus to Lac Retba from Dakar. You have to go to Keur Massar (not to be confused with the monastery at Keur Moussa – see later in this chapter), which can be reached by DDD bus No 11, or by an Alham travelling on the same route. If the DDD bus only goes to Malika, you can find local minibuses onto Keur Massar from there. From Keur Massar local minibuses run to Niaga village (CFA300), from where it's 5km to the lake. Alternatively, you can go to Rufisque and take a minibus to Keur Massar, or you might be lucky and find something going directly from Rufisque to Niaga.

By taxi, a round trip – including an hour or so at the lake – will cost around CFA20,000. You could also consider joining an organised excursion from Dakar – see Organised Tours in Senegal's Getting Around chapter for more details.

If you're driving from Dakar take the main road towards Rufisque and, about 6km beyond Tiaroye-Mer, turn left on a tar road (a signpost says 'Sedima'), which leads over a crossroads and through Keur Massar (5km from the main road). About 3km beyond the village, in an area called Niakoul Rap, take a road on the left (there's no signpost, but the fruit seller on the junction seems resigned to giving directions) to reach Niaga and Lac Retba.

RUFISQUE

Rufisque is a busy transit town about 28km east of central Dakar. It was an important settlement in colonial times, and if you look carefully through the dust and fumes, you'll realise the main street is lined with imposing old French-style buildings. There is little reason to stop here – unless you want to avoid arriving late in Dakar.

Near Rufisque are two campements that are ideal for overlanders. *Hippo Camp* (☎ mobile 646 05 41, e hippo-tours@gmx .de) is run by a German couple who have a reputation for knowing their way around the back roads of the region. Drivers will find this an ideal place to meet other overlanders, arrange spares, change sump oil etc. The beach-front camp is well signposted; camp sites are CFA2500, while single/double rooms are CFA5000/7500. *Campement l'Oasis* (☎ 836 16 48, mobile 643 86 58, e ecm@sentoo.sn, Km 24 route de Rufisque) is on the main road on the western edge of Rufisque and has camp sites for CFA2500 and rooms from CFA10,000.

Getting There & Away

Rufisque is on the main road out of Dakar and there's plenty of transport, including DDD bus No 15, plus frequent Alhams and *cars rapides* (a form of bush taxi, often decrepit; cheaper than an Alham). The road is notoriously congested and slow, so you might consider taking the local commuter train – there are several services each day.

KEUR MOUSSA MONASTERY

For something to do on a quiet Sunday morning, you could visit the Benedictine monastery at Keur Moussa, which is southeast of Lac Retba and about 50km from Dakar on the road towards Kayar. The 10am mass, with a largely local congregation plus several tourists and expats, features unusual music combining African instruments and Gregorian chants. The church itself is unremarkable, but the paintings behind the altar are reminiscent of the ancient Coptic Christian art of Ethiopia. Afterwards the monks sell CDs and cassettes (CFA10,000 and CFA3000 respectively) of their music, prayer books and other items.

Getting There & Away

By bus you have to go to Rufisque and change for a minibus heading to Bayakh or Kayar. Ask the driver to drop you off at a junction 2km after the minibus turns off the main road, from where a dirt track leads east for 1.5km to the monastery – it's signposted and all the drivers know it. Getting a lift back to Dakar shouldn't be difficult as many people will be going that way after the mass.

If you are driving, take the main road from Dakar past Rufisque, towards Thiès and St-Louis. About 21km after Rufisque, turn left towards Bayakh and Kayar.

Continue for 2km and then turn east (left) on a dirt track to the monastery.

KAYAR

North of Keur Moussa the road leads through Mbougane and Bayakh to Kayar, a fishing village where the coastline swings from the east towards the north, marking the start of the Grand Côte. Its picturesque setting and proximity to Dakar make it a popular destination for tour groups (often linked with a trip to Lac Retba) and consequently it is also frequented by 'guides' and souvenir sellers.

There are two places to stay. *Auberge de Cocotiers* (☎ 953 50 41) is easy enough to find as you enter town and infinitely preferable if you're driving. If not, *Auberge de l'Océan Bleu* (☎ 953 50 58) is pretty basic but has nice rooms about a 500m walk north of town on the beach – you cannot drive here. Both auberges have rooms for CFA6000 to CFA10,000.

SENEGAL

Petite Côte & Siné-Saloum Delta

The Petite Côte (Small Coast) runs for about 70km south of Dakar, between Rufisque and Joal-Fadiout. The southern stretch of the Petite Côte provides reliable weather conditions and this, combined with clean sands and the relative proximity to Dakar, makes it Senegal's second-best beach area after Cap Skiring in Casamance, and by far its most popular in terms of visitor numbers.

The main concentration of tourists is at Saly-Portugal, near the town of Mbour, where big hotels cater almost exclusively to package-tour groups, mostly from France. So many tourists fly into Dakar and transit directly to Saly that a new international airport is to be built on the Petite Côte. The government sees this area as the axis around which the future of Senegal's tourist industry will revolve.

Elsewhere along the coast, independent travellers can find small *campements* (see the boxed text 'Village *Campements*' in the Casamance chapter) and guesthouses catering for a range of budgets.

About 60km south of Mbour, the coast is cut by the mouth of the Saloum River. The beach gives way to lagoons and mangrove swamps (although still with a few small stretches of sand), and the labyrinthine creeks of the Siné-Saloum Delta. The landscape is different from the Petite Côte, with shimmering flat lands, dotted with palm groves, lagoons and small, traditional villages.

Highlights

- Meander from one small seaside village to the next along this beautiful stretch of coast
- Walk the wooden bridge to Fatick, the island where everything is made of shells, and Muslims and Christians live in complete harmony
- Discover village life under the big shade trees of Yayeme
- Venture into the maze of mangrove creeks and forested islands that is the vast Siné Saloum Delta

Petite Côte

The Petite Côte proper starts where the main road between Dakar and Mbour turns away from the coast after Rufisque. Smaller roads turn off the main artery and lead down to coastal villages, such as Toubab Dialao, Popenguine and Somone, which have beaches and a couple of low-key accommodation options. For some reason very few

travellers stop here, which makes this area a perfect escape from the madness of Dakar, and a sharp contrast to the package-tourist hell that is Saly-Portugal. Mbour, about 80km south of Dakar, is effectively the capital of the Petite Côte. It's a good jumping-off point for various places along the coast and on the northern side of the Siné-Saloum Delta.

Saly-Portugal is 8km north of Mbour. It has almost 20 hotels, most facing the ocean, and gets packed out with European tourists during winter (especially over the Christmas period) and at Easter. To get the place to yourself, come some time between May and October, when accommodation is much cheaper (although some hotels close completely during the low season). If you want to be alone, you're better off avoiding Saly altogether.

South from Mbour, there are more hotels at Nianing and Joal-Fadiout. Further south, near the northern part of the Siné-Saloum Delta, the villages of Palmarin and Djifer, between the ocean and the delta, have some good accommodation options.

The places in this section are arranged north to south down the coast.

TOUBAB DIALAO

The hoteliers here seem to want to turn this fishing village into a work of art. The interest in art was started by a Frenchman named Gerard, who owns the very highly rated **Sobo-Bade** (☎/fax 836 03 56, sobobade@ sentoo.sn). This place is built on a small cliff, is surrounded by beautiful gardens and overlooks the beach and ocean. There is a range of rooms and prices, from simple four-bed rooms for CFA5000 per person, to

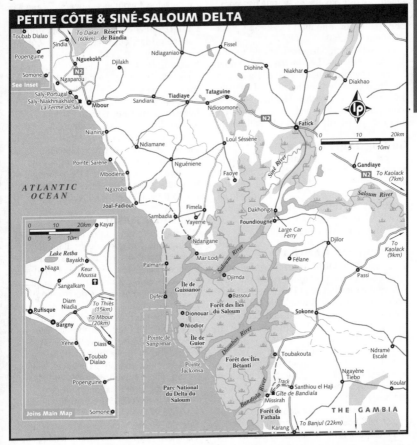

PETITE CÔTE & SINÉ-SALOUM DELTA

SENEGAL

double bungalows with bathroom and sea view for CFA17,000. Meals cost from CFA2500, with vegetarian choices and a *menu du jour* (meal of the day) for CFA5500. Sobo Badé is constantly evolving and has been described as Tolkienesque. The artistic theme is complemented by excellent workshops in dance, writing, percussion and sculpture.

La Source Ndiambalane (☎ 836 17 03, e boulang@telecomplus.sn), next door, has a similar shell-art theme, similar rooms and similar prices. Just across the way is *Auberge La Mimosa* (☎/fax 826 73 26), which doesn't have a view, but has comfortable rooms and self-catering facilities at CFA10,000 for a double. Pizzas and pasta are about CFA2500.

For something different speak to the woman who runs *Le Rocher*, the simple eatery on the beach north of Soba Bade. She can organise a very civilised meal of fish, meat and African dishes at a dining table (complete with cloth and wine glasses) on the sand. Six people will pay CFA2000 each.

Getting There & Away

To get here from Dakar, take anything headed for Mbour and get off at Diam Niadia, where there's a big junction and the roads to Thiés and Kaolack divide; local minibuses run from here to Toubab Dialao for CFA250. Alternatively, in Bargny, you may find something direct.

RÉSERVE DE BANDIA

This small wildlife reserve *(admission CFA7000; open 8am-6pm)* is on the east side of the road between Dakar and Mbour, about 5km south of Sindia. You can't miss the large entrance gates and sign flanked by two giraffes. Privately funded and well managed, this reserve is worth a visit. Unfortunately, however, walking is not allowed – you need a car or you can join a tour organised at one of the large hotels at Saly-Portugal (which is how most visitors get here).

The reserve features rhinos, monkeys, giraffes, buffaloes, jackals, ostriches, a variety of antelope and lots of birds. There are also some interesting Serere burial mounds and a baobab tree where griots were once interred.

A map and information sheet is available at the main gate.

POPENGUINE

Twenty years ago Popenguine was *the* place for wealthy Dakarois to come. Then it stopped being trendy and became a really cool and unpretentious place to chill for a couple of days. One street back from the beach at the south end of town, *Ker Cupaam* (☎/fax 956 49 51) is the pick of the accommodation options. It's a campement run by a local women's cooperative and has comfortable bungalows with bathroom for CFA10,000 including breakfast. Food is available here, but a better bet is *L'écho-Côtier* (☎ 637 87 72), a restaurant on the beach that has a large and varied menu and a *plat du jour* for CFA5000. For a cheaper meal, or an after-lunch drink, wander north past the headland to another stretch of beach and the *Chez Ginette* (☎ 957 71 10), a rustic little bar, open Wednesday to Monday, where you can drink cheap beer while the waves lap at your feet. Ginette also has some very basic rooms for rent.

From Dakar, head for Mbour and get off at Sindia, from where infrequent bush taxis run to Popenguine for CFA200.

SALY-PORTUGAL

It's easy to forget you're in Africa in **Saly-Portugal**. It's the sort of coastal holiday destination found all over the world: palm-lined beaches, package tourists aplenty and more than a dozen big hotels grouped together in a *domaine touristique* (tourist zone) with restaurants, banks, shops and a casino. The strip of beach that borders this zone is reserved for the European tourists who pack the domaine during winter, so the only Senegalese you're likely to see will be working in the service industry. However, Saly can be fun. There's lively nightlife and plenty of restaurants, both local and European.

BICIS and SGBS have branches near King Karaoke, both with ATMs. There are also two Internet centres: the extortionately priced Planet.Saly in the Centre Commercial; and an unnamed place in the village centre that's better in every way. It's worth picking up the free cartoon-style map of Saly-Portugal.

A small selection of hotels is listed here, although most cater for groups and do not even have rates for individuals. If you phone before arrival, discounts may be available, but this is more easily done through a tour agency in Dakar, many of which offer special rates.

Les Cocotiers (☎ *957 14 91, fax 957 30 39,* w *www.hotel-cocotiers.com*) Singles/doubles CFA22,500/27,000. This hotel is less fancy than most in Saly, but it is right on the beach. Sadly, while the value here is good, the hotel has blighted its view with a monstrous concrete pavilion and walkway out over the water – be sure to tell them how ugly it looks.

Hôtel Village Club des Filao (☎ *957 11 80,* e *nffilaos@sentoo.sn*) Half board CFA33,360 per person. This enormous 110-room complex is pretty uninspiring, but it does come complete with *animateurs* to rev up the guests and make sure no-one gets bored.

Savana Saly (☎ *939 58 00, fax 957 10 45,* e *savana@telecomplus.sn*) Singles/doubles with half board CFA45,000/55,000. This is a top-end place, but the fun looks just a little too contrived.

Getting There & Away

The hotels of Saly-Portugal are 3km off the main road, about 5km north of Mbour. There is no public transport. Taxis charge CFA1000.

SALY-NIAKHNIAKHALE

For a little bit of Senegal just south of the big hotels, visit this village, which begins about where Les Cocotiers hotel is and stretches south from there. The small and highly rated ***Auberge Khady*** (☎/*fax 957 25 18)*, with Belgian-Senegalese management, is a very vibrant place about 200m back from the sea. Simple but comfortable singles/doubles with bathroom and breakfast cost CFA14,400/21,600, bungalows are CFA21,600/27,300. Rates are about 25% lower in the low season. Khady also has an excellent restaurant; fish lovers will be salivating over the grilled dorade (CFA3500). It's positively goluptious.

Make sure you ask about the Friday night 'Senegalese soiree'.

To reach Saly-Niakhniakhale go through the Saly-Portugal *domain touristique*, aiming south, right to the end of the line of big hotels, then down a dirt road and through a gate. The Auberge Khady is well signposted.

About 1km south of here along the dirt road that parallels the beach is the ***Ferme de Saly*** (☎ *957 50 06, mobile 638 47 90,* e *farmsaly@yahoo.fr)*, which is far more in tune with its natural environs than anywhere else in Saly. It's a solar-powered country retreat, which has been run by jovial travelling Frenchman Jean-Paul for 30 years. His photos of Saly in the '70s are amazing – there is not a hotel in sight. Huts with half board and bathroom cost CFA15,000 per person. This drops to CFA12,000 from June to November, whilst singles/doubles with breakfast are CFA8000/14,000 all year round. Food is available (much of it home grown) and is eaten in the rustic bar on the beach. Perfect!

For something cheap and Senegalese, try the ***Dibieterie Black & White*** (☎ *551 29 97)*, open 10am to midnight, on the dirt road leading to the Ferme.

Both the Auberge Khady and the Ferme de Saly arrange excursions and fishing trips, and some of the resorts at Saly-Portugal offer water sports for nonguests. A taxi from Mbour to anywhere in Saly should cost about is CFA1500.

MBOUR

About 80km south of Dakar, and 5km south of Saly, Mbour is a major fishing centre; the 200m-long market on the beach, plus all the surrounding marine-related commerce, is a site to behold. The market is a favourite for tour groups from Saly and thus attracts a motley crew of hustlers, though they're less persistent than their brethren in Dakar. As a major transport junction Mbour makes a good jumping-off point for places along the coast.

The *gare routière* (bus station) is at the north end of town on a street leading down to the fish market. Most of the action is south of here: a BICIS bank; the Cyber Espace

SENEGAL

(☎ 956 47 87), open 9am to midnight and charging CFA1500 an hour; and the Cinema Hollywood, which screens French movies at 9pm every night for a whopping CFA250.

Places to Stay

There are a few places to stay scattered around town, all of them south of the fishing market.

Le Citronniers (☎ 957 24 57) Singles CFA20,000, bed in a 4-bed room CFA12,000. In the heart of town, on the square in front of the church, this hotel has friendly management but the simple rooms are a little bit overpriced. Rates include breakfast.

Centre Touristique Coco Beach (☎ 957 10 04, fax 957 10 77) Rooms CFA15,000. On the beach near Le Citronniers is Mbour's biggest hotel. It looks like it hasn't seen a lot of care in the past two or three decades, but all the rooms have bathroom and air-con and are excellent value. There are all manner of facilities, but the pool (CFA2000 for nonguests) is the one you'll like most.

Le Bounty (☎/fax 957 29 51, e bounty@ sentoo.sn) Singles/doubles CFA15,000/ 20,000. A few blocks south of Coco Beach, along the sandy street that runs nearest to the ocean, this small and colourful place has a convivial atmosphere and a lively bar. Air-con is an extra CFA2000. It organises tours to the Siné-Saloum delta.

In this area are several places where local people have opened rooms to travellers. **Chez Charley** is one of these and has a few basic doubles in a family compound for CFA10,000 with breakfast, or bungalows with kitchen and bathroom for CFA15,000. Ask a local boy for directions.

Hôtel Club Safari (☎ 957 19 91, fax 957 38 38) Singles/doubles/triples CFA14,000/ 28,000/36,000. Five blocks south of Le Bounty this place has comfortable air-con rooms set around a pool and attracts plenty of French groups. Breakfast is included.

Places to Eat & Drink

In the centre of town near the market **Café Rest Luxembourg** (☎ mobile 636 88 39) is a reliable option with meals for CFA2000 to CFA4000. The multilingual manager is a great source of local information, and a beer (CFA700) with him is a pleasure. Around the corner is a **snack bar** with chawarmas for CFA700.

Away from the coast, off Av Demba Diop (the main drag) near the Total petrol station, is **Kalom's Jakbah**, a popular local place with chawarma, *dibi* (grilled goat or mutton), *mafé* (a thick brown groundnut sauce) and other meals for CFA500 to 2000. Good European fare can be found on the beach behind Le Bounty at **Le Kassoumaye** (☎ 957 35 24), open 9am to 11pm Thursday to Tuesday. Huge dishes cost about CFA3000 and there is an impressive range of desserts. There are a couple of comfortable, good-value rooms upstairs costing CFA15,000 and CFA20,000.

About 700m north of town, on the road to Dakar, **Le Massai** (☎ 664 92 9), is open 9am to 10pm, and the menu changes regularly. We enjoyed chicken curry (CFA2000), *calamar morocaine* (Moroccan calamari; CFA1800) and *crepes au chocolat* (CFA1500). A further 300m along, *l'Escale* (957 16 46), open 8am to midnight, is an old favourite and with good reason. French-style meals are CFA3000 to CFA4000 and pasta is CFA1500.

For dancing, the main spot is **Le Djembe** in the centre of town, where the number of men selling bread, meat and eggs outside is testament to its popularity. Don't even think about arriving before 1am.

Getting There & Away

Between Mbour and Dakar is CFA950 in a Peugeot taxi, CFA770 in a minibus and CFA670 in an Alham. If you're travelling south down the Petite Côte, or into the Siné-Saloum Delta, minibuses cost CFA400 to/from Joal-Fadiout.

NIANING

Nianing is 10km south of Mbour. It has a line of hotels along the main street, most fronting onto the beach, but these are smaller and more pleasant than the Saly strip and the village itself is much quieter than Mbour.

Among the mid-range places in the village centre is **Les Bourgain Villees** (☎ 957 52 41), a small, no-frills family-run place about 50m back from the beach. Doubles/quads cost about CFA10,000/15,000 and breakfast is CFA1500.

Other places in town include *Hôtel Campement Le Ben' Tenier* (☎ 957 14 20, e *bentenier@telecomplus.sn*), a clean and friendly place with English-speaking management and bungalows in a quiet garden. Singles/doubles cost CFA10,600/16,000. Breakfast is CFA2000 and excellent French meals are available for around CFA5000. Similar in style, but more expensive, is *Auberge des Coquillages* (☎/fax 957 14 28, e *tidiane@telecomplus.sn*), with singles/doubles for CFA26,000/28,100. There's a small pool (CFA1000 for nonguests) and a private beach. Good local food can be found at *Chez Annick* on the main road, where about a dozen varieties of grilled fish can be had for CFA1500 each.

South of here, the top-end *Club Aldiana* and *Domaine de Nianing* cater almost totally for pre-arranged groups.

Getting There & Away
Nianing is on the main road between Mbour and Joal and all public transport stops here.

MBODIENE
The small village of Mbodiène is on the coast about halfway between Nianing and Joal. It has a mix of traditional buildings and weekend cottages for well-off Dakarois. The *Gîte de Fasna* is about 2km off the main road, with thatched huts in lovely gardens. It's aimed mainly at visiting French anglers, but anyone is welcome. The huts are a bargain at CFA7500 a double and CFA10,000 for triples. They have a shower inside, but the toilets are separate. Breakfast is CFA1500 and other meals are CFA4500.

As you head south turn right down a dirt road just before you get to Mbodiene village.

JOAL-FADIOUT
The twin villages of Joal and Fadiout are about 110km south of Dakar at the end of the tar road that runs along the coast. Joal (the birthplace of former president Léopold Senghor) is on the mainland, while Fadiout is on a small island reached by a long wooden bridge. It is an easy day trip from Dakar, and all the tour companies run excursions here.

The island of Fadiout is composed entirely of oyster and clam shells that have been deposited over the centuries. The village of Fadiout covers the island and everything is made of shells – they cover the maze of narrow streets and are embedded in the walls of the houses. Parts of the island look squalid, but the centre has a definite charm.

The citizens of Joal and Fadiout are rightly proud of their religious tolerance. Christians and Muslims live in harmony here, with Fadiout's shrines to the Virgin Mary and large church complemented by an equally large mosque. The overall feel is one of harmony, and Fadiout has a very relaxed atmosphere.

A huge, ancient shell mound is reached by another wooden bridge and is home to both a Christian and Muslim cemetery. From here, in the morning and evening you'll see horses and carts crossing the long causeway through the mangroves to fields on firmer ground. Nearby is a group of curious basketlike **granaries** on stilts outside the village. They were built many years ago after the originals were destroyed when a blaze tore through Fadiout. Now even if the village burns down again, at least the food for the rest of the year will be safe.

Places to Stay & Eat
Joal The best cheap place to stay is *Relais 114* (☎ 957 61 78), run by the friendly Mamadou Baldé (a former acrobat who is very proud of his performing pelicans) and his English-speaking son. Basic, clean rooms with fan are CFA7500 and sleep one to three people. Breakfast is CFA1500. Simple meals start from CFA2500, a three-course menu is CFA5000 and beers are CFA600. There's off-street parking for those with their own vehicle.

More upmarket, but lacking the Relais' soul, is *Hôtel le Finio* (☎/fax 957 61 12) near the bridge to Fadiout. Rooms with bathroom and fan are CFA6000 per person, and twice the price with air con. Breakfast is CFA1500 and other meals about CFA2000.

At the end of the bridge to Fadiout is *Le Sénégaulois* (☎/fax 957 62 41), which is mainly a bar but also has a few clean but overpriced rooms at CFA14,000. Owner Olivier can also change money.

Fadiout In the winding streets of the village, *Campement les Paletuviers* (☎/fax 957 62 05) has simple singles/doubles for CFA4800/9000, including breakfast. Other meals are about CFA2500, and beers CFA600. There's a terrace out the back overlooking the creek – pleasant at high tide, but a bit whiffy when it's low. You'll have to ask directions to this place.

Getting There & Away
A minibus to/from Mbour is CFA500. If you're heading on down the coast, from Joal to Palmarin costs CFA800. A Peugeot taxi goes directly to Dakar most mornings (without changing at Mbour) for CFA1500.

PALMARIN
The village of Palmarin (actually four villages in a group) is 20km south of Joal-Fadiout, where the beaches of the Petite Côte merge with the labyrinthine creeks of the Siné-Saloum Delta. The road from Sambadia winds along a series of causeways (some impassable at high tide) and through shimmering flat lands dotted with palm groves, traditional villages, shallow lagoons, mud flats and patches of salt marsh that attract huge flocks of wading birds.

Near the village of Sessene, a part of Palmarin, the *Campement de Palmarin* (☎ 635 87 89) is on a sandy beach under the palms where very basic (no fans) and slightly weather-beaten bungalows cost CFA5000/8500 for singles/doubles. This place is operated by the villagers and all profits go to local projects such as schools or health centres. Behind the campement is a large lagoon – an excellent area to see wading birds. Nearby is the *Gite Touristique l'Eden* (☎ mobile 668 79 68), a resort-style place with full board for CFA15,000 or CFA19,000 per person, depending on the season.

Getting There & Away
Palmarin is most easily reached from Mbour, via Joal-Fadiout and Sambadia

(where you may have to change). The fare from Joal to Sambadia is CFA400 in a *car rapide* (a form of bush taxi, often decrepit; cheaper than an Alham), and from Sambadia to Palmarin it's CFA300.

DJIFER
The fishing village of Djifer (also spelt Djiffer and Djifere) is 15km south of Palmarin on the Sangomar peninsula. The peninsula is a long thin strip of sand separating the Atlantic Ocean from the mouth of the Saloum River – making it a possible jumping-off point for trips into the Siné-Saloum Delta. The peninsula also shelters the river mouth from the worst of the ocean weather, and at the far end of the village is a huge fish market and 'port' where many colourful fishing boats are drawn up on the sand.

Living at the end of a sand bar has its drawbacks. There is no electricity, running water or sewerage in most of the village, and while to some this will make Djifer even more 'African', others have described the village as a 'cesspit'. The truth is that the beaches on both sides of Djifer are strewn with litter and, more disturbingly, human stools, and the locals living here are as concerned about it as you will be.

Shifting Sands

The Sangomar peninsula protects the mouth of the Saloum River from the large Atlantic rollers. In the 1980s a large storm washed away part of the peninsula, turning its southern end into a separate island, although it may be tenuously linked to the mainland at low tide. The French word for this feature – *presqu'île* ('nearly an island') – is most appropriate. More recently, in December 1997, another large storm caused the sea to breach the peninsula between Palmarin and Djifer, washing away the road, flooding the village and making Djifer itself a *presqu'île*. Most people blamed El Niño, but other observers say rising sea levels mean it will happen again. If Djifer has disappeared by the time you read this, don't be completely surprised.

Needless to say, it's wise to take a cautious approach to swimming.

Boat trips to various places in the delta can be arranged at Campement la Mangrove, with prices starting at around CFA25,000 per boat, up to CFA35,000 for a full day. Campement Pointe de Sangomar also runs excursions. A four-hour trip to visit some nearby islands and the fishing village of Dionouar costs CFA15,000 to CFA20,000 per boat.

Places to Stay & Eat

Djifer has two campements. The smarter *Campement Pointe de Sangomar* (☎ 835 61 91) is popular with groups of French hunters, and for facilities is still the best value, with bungalows for CFA6000 per person or doubles with bathroom for CFA13,000. Half board is also available. The quieter *Campement la Mangrove* (☎ 956 42 32) is in a tranquil position 2km north of Djifer. It's a locally run endeavour offering basic huts with shared bathrooms for CFA5000 per person, and camping.

The campements both provide food; otherwise, there are several basic *gargottes* (small eateries) in Djifer; *Café Ponti* and *Che Marco* both do fisherman-sized helpings for CFA600.

Getting There & Away

Djifer can be reached from Mbour, via Joal-Fadiout and Sambadia – see Getting There & Away under Palmarin earlier in this chapter for details. Another option is by pirogue to or from Ndangane or Foundiougne (see Siné-Saloum Delta following).

If you're heading to Gambia, cramped, uncomfortable and notoriously unsafe pirogues go from Djifer to Banjul a few times per week for around CFA3000 per person. The trip takes about five hours, but may involve an overnight stop on a midway island. You have been warned! On arrival in Banjul go to the immigration office at the port and not the one in the city centre.

Around Djifer

Places to visit near Djifer include the islands of **Guior** and **Guissanor**, across the river mouth from the Sangomar peninsula.

These islands are beautiful, tranquil and almost completely devoid of tourist facilities. On Guior, there are the small fishing villages of **Niodior** and **Dionouar**, and an upmarket lodge for anglers.

The campements in Djifer run excursions to the islands, or you can charter a pirogue yourself from a local fisherman to go across to Dionouar. Expect to pay between about CFA10,000 and CFA15,000, depending on waiting time and your powers of bargaining. The public boat, which runs between Djifer and Dionouar for CFA500 per person, is cheaper, but it only goes once a day in each direction, usually leaving Djifer about 1pm.

Siné-Saloum Delta

South of the Petite Côte, between Kaolack and the Gambian border, the 180,000-hectare Siné-Saloum Delta is one of the most beautiful parts of Senegal. Formed where the seasonal Siné and Saloum Rivers meet the tidal waters of the Atlantic Ocean, it's a swampy area with mangroves, lagoons, open forests, dunes and sand islands.

Part of the area is included in the Parc National du Delta du Saloum. You won't see large mammals here, apart from the occasional warthog and perhaps a sea cow in the lagoons, but the area abounds with several monkey species, including the rare red colobus, and the range of habitats makes it particularly good for birding. Even if you're not a wildlife fan, you should visit the delta for the fascinating scenery alone. A trip by pirogue down one of the river branches to see the pelicans, flamingos and other birds, or to visit some of the island fishing villages, is well worth doing.

Along the edges of the delta are several hotels and campements, where tours can be arranged, and which make good bases for exploring by car, on foot or by pirogue. Note that all unsurfaced roads in the area can be difficult in the wet season.

NDANGANE & MAR LODJ

Ndangane (pronounced ndan-garn) is on the northern side of the delta, on a branch of the

Saloum River. It has grown considerably over the last few years from a sleepy backwater into a thriving tourist centre with a wide range of accommodation. Ndangane has two parts: the touristy area, where the tar road from Dakar ends by the boat jetty, and the village proper, a short distance to the west. From either area, you can get boats across the river to the village of Mar Lodj (also spelt Mar Lothie), a peaceful haven cut off from the rest of the country by the delta. Several local-style campements make this a great place to relax for a while.

There's no bank here, but the Business Centre le Sine, about 400m along the Fimela road, has Internet access from 8am to noon, and 4pm to 9pm. Fishing trips and boat rides can be arranged at most of the hotels and campements, with pirogue trips to Mar Lodj and Île de Oiseaux costing about CFA4500 a head, with a minimum of four. Get anywhere near the river and you'll be offered all sorts of trips. There are two English-speaking guides worth seeking out: Jimmy (☎ 936 39 84/5), who is very good and also speaks seven other languages including Spanish, Italian and French; and Lamine Sarr, who can be contacted at Le Baobab restaurant. These guys will organise the pirogue, and all prices are negotiable.

Places to Stay & Eat

Ndangane Most of the accommodation and eating options are located around the end of the road to Fimela, which is also where most boat trips depart from. Nearest to the water is *Chez Mbake* (☎ 936 39 85, mobile 669 35 25), a family-run place with five basic bungalows for CFA5000 per person.

Next stop away from the river is the *Hôtel le Pelican du Saloum* (☎ 949 93 30, e snpel ican@sentoo.sn), a 68-room resort offering half board in plush rooms for CFA27,000 per person. Opposite is *Gite Rural le Cormoran* (☎/fax 949 93 16, W www.chez.com/lecor moran), a smaller, friendlier French-run place with good, clean bungalows in a pleasant setting. Singles/doubles B&B cost CFA12,000/ 18,000, and meals are about CFA3500.

Continuing north to the junction, turn right along a dirt track to get to more accommodation. The *Annacardiers* (☎ 949 93 13) is excellent value with clean rooms with bathroom and fan for CFA7500 per person. A few metres further is *Hôtel Cordons Bleus* (☎ 949 93 12, e cordons.b@ sunumail.sn), which has the full array of facilities. Plush bungalows and singles/doubles with half board are CFA28,600/49,600.

All the hotels do food and there are several restaurants. A good option is *Le Petit Paradis* on the main drag, which serves local dishes (CFA800) or Western dishes (CFA3000), all spiced up with inspiring conversation (in English) from the dignified and erudite owners. Also worth a look is *Le Baobab* (☎ mobile 653 40 73), out past Cordons Bleus, where an English-speaking local couple serve excellent seafood (CFA3000) and pizzas (CFA5000), among other things, in a more traditional, village-style setting.

Mar Lodj The campements here have formed an association and all charge the same: singles/doubles B&B CFA10,600/ 19,200, less in the low season. Note that none have electricity yet.

Mbine Diam (☎ mobile 636 91 99) has double huts in a shady garden; *Le Bazouk* (☎ mobile 690 58 00) is small and relaxed, with pirogues for hire; the larger *Limboko* (☎ mobile 647 41 66) offers fishing and boat excursions from CFA2000 per person. The best value is the appropriately named *Nouvelle Vague* (☎ 936 39 76, mobile 634 07 29), with its ten new bungalows, six of them overlooking the river. Most of the campements will collect you from Ndangane for free if you call ahead. All the campements organise boat trips or walks to the surrounding villages, which are highly recommended.

Further along the river, the upmarket *Campement Mar Setal* and *Campement Hakuna Matata* deal mainly with groups, and reservations are essential.

Entertainment

For a drink the *Bar/Restaurant les Piroguiers* has thatched shelters in a nice position overlooking the river in Ndangane. For late-night action check out the lively *Pothio Nightclub* on the road to Fimela.

Getting There & Away

Take any bus between Kaolack and Mbour, and get off at Ndiosomone, from where bush taxis shuttle back and forth to Ndangane. You can go directly by bush taxi from Dakar to Ndangane for CFA1500. From Mbour you can take bush taxis via Sambadia and Fimela.

To reach Mar Lodj from Ndangane there's an occasional public boat charging CFA250 one way. Otherwise, you have to charter. This should cost CFA4000 for the boat, but if there are more than four tourists the fare is CFA1000 each.

You can charter a pirogue between Ndangane and Djifer for about CFA15,000. To, or from, Foundiougne is about CFA25,000.

YAYEME

About 1.5km down a sandy track from Fimela is the tiny village of Yayeme. At first there seems to be nothing remarkable about Yayeme, but a few directions from helpful locals will see you to *Daan Sa Doole* (☎ mobile 635 52 74, ℮ aloukum@hotmail.com), right in the middle of the village. This ecofriendly campement has been set up by a couple of multilingual young travellers around a giant mango tree. It's the ideal place to experience rural Senegalese life without hassle, and without being confronted by a bus full of tourists. Bungalows with bathrooms are CFA9000 per person and simpler rooms come for cheaper prices – there's something quite liberating about the *au naturel* showers and toilets. Campers are also welcome. Call ahead between June and October.

It's easy enough to get here from Fimela, just walk out along the road to Sambadia and take the left fork after 200m. Alternatively, call from Fimela or Sambadia for directions.

FOUNDIOUGNE

At the northwestern edge of the delta, where a ferry crosses the Saloum River, the one-time French colonial outpost of Foundiougne (pronounced foun-dune) is relaxed and easy to reach, and is a good place to arrange pirogue trips around the delta.

The Campement le Baobab (Chez Ismaila) offers pirogue trips and fishing excursions costing CFA25,000 per half-day and CFA30,000 per day for the boat, although prices are negotiable according to the petrol and time required. A lift to Djifer or Ndangane costs CFA30,000 and to Toubakouta/Missirah it costs CFA30,000/38,000. The Campement le Baobab (Chez Anne-Marie), Auberge les Bolongs and the Indiana all arrange excursions at similar prices.

Alternatively, ask around at the ferry jetty. A pirogue with petrol and captain costs CFA25,000 for a full day or CFA14,000 for a half day, although rates are negotiable and depend on the amount of fuel used.

Places to Stay & Eat

A string of campements runs west from the ferry pier, all of them offering meals.

Saloum Saloum (☎/fax 948 12 69) Rooms with bathroom for 1-3 people CFA15,000. A community-run place with a few comfortable rooms overlooking the river, this place is both friendly and good value.

Next are the two versions of *Campement le Baobab*, bitter enemies after a family feud. The newer camp, also known as *Chez Anne-Marie (☎ 948 12 62)*, is on the riverfront and has good-value rooms (and the baobab tree) for singles/doubles/triples CFA8000/14,000/18/000, with breakfast if you stay longer than one night. Two female readers have written to say this place is ideal for single women travellers. Most of the staff are women and they are very welcoming. Meals are about CFA2000 to CFA3000.

Opposite is *Campement le Baobab No 1 (Chez Ismail; ☎/fax 948 17 08)*, where the original version remains in an old two-storey French building. Clean bungalows with shower, net and half board are CFA10,000.

L'Indiana Club (☎/fax 948 12 13) Rooms CFA8,500 per person with breakfast; CFA12,000 with half board. Next stop is this Swiss-run place where the rooms have shared bathroom. The European and Senegalese food here has a good reputation, with meals costing about CFA4000. This place is also home to the only pool in town.

Auberge les Bolongs (Chez Daniel et Jany; ☎/fax 948 11 10, Ⓦ www.lesbolongs.com)

Bungalows for 1-3 people CFA10,000. This is a big place, close to Campement Indiana, though shade trees are at a premium. The food is good (two courses CFA3500, full menu CFA5000), there's a bar on the beach and picnics can be organised.

Foundiougne Hôtel (☎ 948 12 12, fax 948 12 10) Singles/doubles/triples CFA25,000/38,000/39,000; doubles with half board CFA53,200. This upmarket hotel has a beautiful setting on the river and clean and comfortable air-con bungalows that are a bit overpriced. Breakfast is CFA3500, lunch or dinner is CFA7500. There's a swimming pool, as well as sailing, windsurfing, hunting and fishing.

Beside the ferry pier is **La Cloche**, a charming white Italian restaurant complete with Italian chef. The food here is great value at CFA4000 for three courses. The only drawback is the river doesn't smell too good at low tide. The nearby **Bar Ronier** is the alternative drinking hole and has cheaper beer (CFA700).

Getting There & Away

By road, Foundiougne is reached from Passi, which is on the main road between Kaolack and the Gambian border at Karang. A minibus from Kaolack to Foundiougne is CFA600. If you can't find one going direct, get anything going between Kaolack and Karang, and get off at Passi. The fare from Passi to Foundiougne is CFA375.

You can also reach Foundiougne from Fatick, 150km from Dakar between Mbour and Kaolack. Take a bush taxi to Dakhonga where you can take a ferry across to Foundiougne. Leaving Foundiougne, the first ferry departs at 7.30am and connects with a minibus at Dakhonga, which goes all the way to Dakar for CFA1300.

To reach other parts of the delta by boat, you can take excursions to Ndangane, Djifer, Toubakouta or Missirah, organised through one of the hotels, or directly with a local boatman. Alternatively, ask around for the public pirogue service that goes from Foundiougne to Djifer on Tuesday (and occasionally on other days), via villages along the Saloum River.

The Foundiougne Ferry

The ferry across the Saloum River between Foundiougne and Dakhonga was given to Senegal by the USA (locals told us it was a *cadeaux* in exchange for their help in the Gulf War) and is run with military precision.

The ferry leaves Foundiougne and Dakhonga at the following times, daily except where indicated.

Foundiougne	Dakhonga
7.30am	8.30am
9.30am	10.30am
11.30am	12.30pm
3pm*	3.30pm*
	(*except Wed)
5pm	6.30pm

The ferry fare is CFA100 per passenger, CFA2000 per vehicle. A ride across by pirogue (if the ferry isn't running) is CFA125, or at least CFA1500 for the whole boat.

TOUBAKOUTA

The village of Toubakouta is south of Sokone, just off the main road. Its position, between the road and a major branch of the Saloum River, makes it easy to reach and (along with Missirah) a good base for exploring the waterways on the southern side of the Siné-Saloum Delta. Birding is good in this area. Even if you're not a fan of our feathered friends, you'll enjoy watching flamingos, fish eagles, herons and egrets, especially when they roost at night at the bird reserves, a short boat ride away.

The Hôtel les Palétuviers offers walks in the forest with visits to nearby villages (CFA6500) or trips by 4WD (CFA12,000 to 23,000). The best thing to do is to get out on the water: tours by pirogue range from CFA8000 per person for an evening trip to the nearby Île des Oiseaux, to CFA31,000 for an all-day tour of the delta. A delta trip will include the mouth of the Saloum River at the Atlantic Ocean, where dolphins are sometimes seen. You can also arrange fishing trips or visits to shell mounds.

In the town there is a Dutch-funded cybercafé called CyberLynda (☎ 936 94 41), which charges CFA2250 an hour.

Places to Stay

Hôtel les Palétuviers (☎ 948 77 76, fax 948 77 77, W www.paletuviers.com) Singles/doubles B&B CFA39,000/47,000, half board CFA42,000/55,000. This is one of the best-quality places on the whole delta, with around 50 double cottages in large grounds. All have air-con and private bathrooms and are furnished to a high standard. Other facilities include a bar with terrace, air-con restaurant and large swimming pool, and you can partake of any number of day trips and activities, including fishing. The Belgian management also operates *l'Île des Palétuviers* on the remote Île de Bétanti, west of Toubakouta, and *Plage d'Or* on the Senegalese side of the island of Djinakh, near the Gambian border. Both offer exclusivity in beautiful bush settings.

Hôtel Keur Saloum (☎ 948 77 15, fax 948 77 16, W www.keursaloum.com) Singles/doubles with half board CFA36,000/58,000. Near Hôtel les Palétuviers, this place has bungalows, and a bar overlooking the beach beside the river. It's dedicated to huntin', shootin' and fishin' (as the photos in the bar indicate), and boats are available for hire.

If your wallet is not quite fat enough for the top-end places, try *Keur Youssou (☎ 948 77 28, mobile 634 59 05)* or *Les Coquillages du Niombatto (Chez Laye Loum, ☎ 936 34 41, e layoum@hotmail.com)*, both of which have comfortable double bungalows with bathrooms for CFA12,500 including breakfast, and offer cheaper tours than the big hotels. Any kid in town will show you the way.

Getting There & Away

Toubakouta is just off the main road between Kaolack and Karang (the Gambian border), about 70km from Kaolack. A bush taxi from Kaolack to Barra via Karang is CFA2100, but you won't get any discount for getting off early. It's cheaper to go by Alham; the fare to Toubakouta is around CFA1000.

MISSIRAH

Missirah is a small village south of Toubakouta, and is one of the nearest points to the **Parc National du Delta du Saloum** *(admission CFA2000 per day)*. The vegetation in the park includes tidal mud flats, mangrove swamps and the dry, open woodland of the Forêt de Fathala. Red colobus monkeys are plentiful but shy, so the dry season, when the trees have fewer leaves, is best for seeing them. The village itself is famous for the enormous *Fromager Legendaire* tree on the banks of the river, variously estimated at between 200 and 1000 years old.

You enter the national park just south of Missirah village and proceed 6km to the park headquarters, where you pay the admission. Plans for an office in Missirah itself should have been realised by the time you read this.

About 2km east of Missirah, the *Gîte de Bandiala (☎ 948 77 35, e gitedubandiala@sentoo.sn)* is a peaceful, low-key and good-value place and a great base for exploring this part of the delta. Accommodation is in simple bungalows and is good value at half board/full board CFA13,000/18,500 per person. The friendly management can make suggestions for forest walks, and in the bar-restaurant are some useful bird charts with names in French and English. The gîte also has a water hole where monkeys, warthogs and other animals come to drink. Tours by pirogue on the nearby creeks and lagoons cost CFA20,000 per boat for a half day, and fishing can be arranged.

Getting There & Away

From Kaolack take any vehicle going along the main road towards Karang, get off at Santhiou el Haji (about 80km from Kaolack) and walk 8km west through the forest and tsetse flies. Less strenuous would be to get off at Toubakouta and take a bush taxi for CFA300, or a taxi for CFA4000. If you're leaving Missirah for Karang there is a bush taxi that leaves about 7am every morning (CFA500), but you'll need to organise a place the night before.

Another option is to get a private taxi all the way from Kaolack – this will cost CFA15,000 to CFA20,000.

West-Central Senegal

This chapter covers Senegal east of Dakar and north of Gambia. This area includes the important towns of Thiès, Kaolack, Diourbel and Touba – the heartland of the Muslim brotherhoods – and the villages of the Grande Côte (Great Coast). Places in this chapter are described roughly west to east.

THE GRANDE CÔTE

The Grande Côte is the name given to the whole coastline of Senegal north of Dakar and the Cap Vert peninsula. The coast to the south of Dakar is smaller and hence is called the Petite Côte.

The Grande Côte starts at Kayar and continues all the way to the mouth of the Senegal River near St-Louis. Between these two points, the coast is one long uninterrupted beach and, at low tide, it's possible to drive a car the whole way along it – as competitors sometimes do in the final stage of the Paris-Dakar Rally. But the dry landscape, strong ocean winds and dangerous seas mean the Grand Côte was not settled like the Petite Côte, and it has never been developed for tourism in the same way. Behind the beach is a wide strip of coastal dunes, covered in grass and light bush. In an attempt to prevent erosion of this area, several long, thin re-afforestation zones have been established.

Mboro-sur-Mer

The easiest point to reach on the Grand Côte is Mboro-sur-Mer (shown on some maps as Mboro Ndeundekat), a fishing village about 60km northeast of Dakar. Its nearest neighbour to the south is another fishing village called Kayar, regularly included in local tour itineraries, but Mboro-sur-Mer is off the beaten track and hence is rarely visited by tourists.

Places to Stay The delightful *Gîte de la Licorne* (☎ 955 7788) is right on the beach about 500m south of the village. Comfortable singles/doubles cost CFA11,200/16,400 with breakfast, and there are also a couple of

family-size bungalows where each extra person pays CFA5200. Meals in the open-air bar-restaurant, complete with board games and shelves of books, cost about CFA4000. The Gîte is usually closed from June to October and at any time it's highly recommended that you book ahead. Self-catering is possible as fresh fish is just minutes away. If you luck out at the Gîte, ask around town; locals have been known to offer informal lodgings.

Getting There & Away The easiest way to reach Mboro-sur-Mer by public transport from Dakar is via Thiès – local minibuses run to Mboro for CFA800. You can also get here from Tivaouane. From Mboro to Mboro-sur-Mer is about 5km and you'll probably have to walk. If you're in a hurry, a Dakar taxi will get you here for about CFA20,000.

THIÈS

Just 70km east of Dakar, and with over 260,000 people, Thiès is officially Senegal's second-largest city, although when you arrive you won't believe it. The central area is small enough to cover on foot and, compared with Dakar, life seems to move in slow motion along the dusty streets under the big shade trees. Only when you start heading east do you realise how far this city sprawls. Thiès has one major attraction: a world-famous **tapestry factory** (see the boxed text 'Tapestries of Thiès' later in this chapter). If tapestry is not your bag, check out the nearby **Musée de Thiès** (☎ 951 15 20; open 9am-6pm; admission CFA500). It's located in a building within a fort built as the French garrison in 1864 and once you've found the staff to unlock the museum building, you'll find a fascinating history of Senegal's railways, though it is all in French.

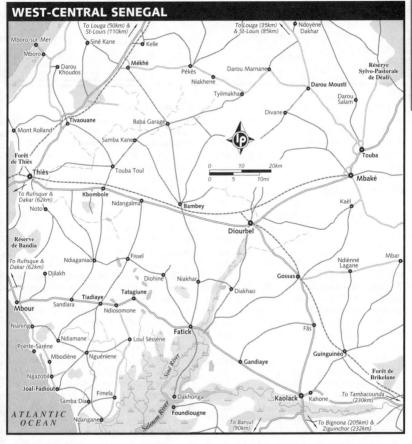

WEST-CENTRAL SENEGAL

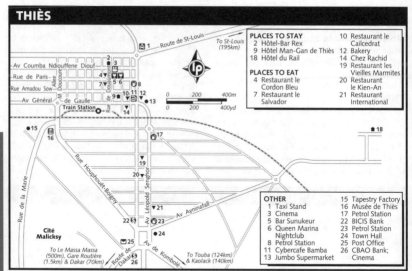

THIÈS

Route de St-Louis

To St-Louis
(195km)

Av Coumba Ndiouffene Diouf
Rue de Paris
Rue Amadou Sow
Av Général de Gaulle
Train Station

Rue de la Marie

Cité Malicksy

To Le Massa Massa
(500m), Gare Routière
(1.5km) & Dakar (70km)

Rue Houphouët-Boigny

Av Léopold Senghor

Av Ayninafall

Av de Kombole

To Touba (124km)
& Kaolack (140km)

0   200   400m
0   200   400yd

PLACES TO STAY
2 Hôtel-Bar Rex
9 Hôtel Man-Gan de Thiès
18 Hôtel du Rail

PLACES TO EAT
4 Restaurant le
   Cordon Bleu
7 Restaurant le
   Salvador
10 Restaurant le
   Cailcedrat
12 Bakery
14 Chez Rachid
19 Restaurant les
   Vieilles Marmites
20 Restaurant
   le Kien-An
21 Restaurant
   International

OTHER
1 Taxi Stand
3 Cinema
5 Bar Sunukeur
6 Queen Marina
   Nightclub
8 Petrol Station
11 Cybercafe Bamba
13 Jumbo Supermarket
15 Tapestry Factory
16 Musée de Thiès
17 Petrol Station
22 BICIS Bank
23 Petrol Station
24 Town Hall
25 Post Office
26 CBAO Bank;
   Cinema

The *gare routière* (bus station) is on the southern outskirts of town, around 3km from the centre. If you come in from Dakar, this is where you'll be dropped, and you'll have to get a taxi for CFA325 or walk into town.

Places to Stay

Hôtel-Bar Rex (☎ 951 1081, fax 951 4889, 197 Rue de Douaumont) Rooms without/with air-con CFA7000/9600. Centrally located three blocks north of Av Général de Gaulle, this hotel has musty but otherwise clean rooms with bathrooms. The staff are friendly and there's safe parking.

Hôtel Man-Gan de Thiès (☎ 951 1526, fax 951 2532, Rue Amadou Sow) Singles/doubles with bathroom CFA13,600/17,200. Not far from the Hôtel-Bar Rex, this place has a pleasant garden courtyard and clean rooms with air-con.

Hôtel du Rail (☎ 951 2313) Singles/doubles CFA8900/9300. This old two-storey place will delight colonial rail fans with its trainspotter memorabilia. It is about 1.5km east of the centre, and has large, tranquil air-con rooms with bathroom. Meals are available in the open-air restaurant.

Places to Eat

Apart from the hotel restaurants, a stroll down Av Léopold Senghor will reveal the cheapie *Restaurant International* (☎ 951 4269), the clean and tidy *Restaurant les Vieilles Marmites* (☎ 951 4440) and the more expensive *Restaurant le Kien-An* (☎ 951 11 96), which has French, Senegalese and Vietnamese specialities from CFA2500. North of the railway tracks is a *bakery* and a *Jumbo supermarket*. *Street food* is available at the train station and, in the evening, outside the cinema.

On Rue de Paris, north of Av Général de Gaulle, is a cluster of eating places, which are very good value. These include the *Restaurant le Salvador* (☎ 951 52 04) and the *Restaurant le Cordon Bleu*, with Senegalese food for about CFA500 and Western dishes from CFA750.

On Av Général de Gaulle, the *Chez Rachid* (☎ 951 1878), open noon to midnight, does good chawarma for CFA850. Opposite and smarter is *Restaurant le Cailcedrat* (☎ 951 1130), open 7am to midnight, which serves beers, coffees, snacks for CFA750, larger meals for CFA1500 to CFA4000 and Lebanese specials, such as

Tapestries of Thiès

The factory of the Manufactures Sénégalaises des Arts Décoratifs (☎/fax 951 11 31) was one of the many artistic endeavours inspired by President Senghor during the 1960s. Today, the factory is run as a cooperative, with designs for the tapestries chosen from paintings submitted by Senegalese artists.

The size of the tapestries varies, but most are around 3m high by 2m wide. Preparing the design is a fascinating and elaborate process, taking many weeks. A large sketch of the painting is produced for the weavers to use as a pattern, but it is a reverse of the original because tapestries are made on the loom upside down.

All the weaving is done on manual looms, and two weavers complete about 1 sq metre per month. Only eight tapestries are made from each design. Most find their way around the world as gifts from the government to foreign dignitaries; there's a huge tapestry hanging in Atlanta airport and another in Buckingham Palace. Others are for sale, but at CFA500,000 per sq metre, most of us will be content to admire them in the exhibition room, which is open from 8am to 12.30pm and 3pm to 6.30pm weekdays, and from 8am to 12.30pm weekends. The entry fee is CFA1000. Individual visitors are not normally shown the workshops where the tapestries are actually made, but if you are genuinely interested, the exhibition supervisor might be able arrange for you to be shown around. If you phone ahead, your chances are better.

kofta for CFA2000 and hummus for CFA1500.

Le Massa Massa (☎ 952 1244) Hidden away about 2km out of town, this French restaurant is a contender for best food, and best value, in Senegal. The fish soup (CFA1800), lasagne (CFA2700), and steak in Roquefort sauce (CFA4200) are all excellent, and the French family who runs the place is charming. To get there, it's easiest to take a taxi (CFA400), though you might still need to give directions: take the road towards Dakar and look for the signs pointing right immediately after the second Shell petrol station. The area is called Cite Malick Sy. Dishes cost about CFA3000 and the restaurant is open for lunch and dinner.

Entertainment

For a cheap drink with the locals, try *Bar Sunukeur*, open 2pm to 4am, next to the cinema. For something more lively, the *Queen Marina Nightclub* (☎ 952 15 15), open from 11pm to 5am, plays a good mix of music for an admission of CFA1000.

Getting There & Away

Bush Taxi & Minibus Bush taxis and minibuses leave from the gare routière on the southern outskirts. A private taxi between the town centre and the gare routière costs CFA325. Fares in a Peugeot taxi include Dakar (CFA900, one hour), Kaolack (CFA1600, two hours, 140km) and St-Louis (CFA2350, four hours, 196km).

Train The train station ticket office is on Av Général de Gaulle. The express trains en route to Bamako (Mali) come through Thiès every Wednesday and Saturday morning. The 1st-class fare from Thiès to Tambacounda is around CFA10,000. The 2nd-class fare from Thiès to Tambacounda, Kayes and Bamako is about CFA6000 less than if you catch the train from Dakar (although 2nd-class tickets on this train are hard to get in Thiès). For more details see Train in Senegal's Getting There & Away chapter.

There is also a commuter train that runs less frequently than it should to Dakar (CFA600) via Rufisque (CFA300) Monday to Saturday.

TIVAOUANE

This town lies just east of the main road between Thiès and St-Louis. It's a centre of the Tijaniya brotherhood (see the boxed text 'Marabouts & Brotherhoods' in the Facts about Senegal chapter). The **mosque** is built in Moroccan style, although it's neither as large as the one at Touba, nor as interesting as the one at Diourbel. Unless you're a fan of early-20th-century Islamic architecture, or your visit coincides with a Muslim festival (especially the Prophet's Birthday – see the boxed text 'Islam' in the Facts about Senegambia chapter), you might as well cruise on by. If you decide to stay, along the main road are hotels, restaurants and shops.

DIOURBEL

Diourbel (pronounced jur-bell) is significant because it was the home of Amadou Bamba, founder of the Mouride Islamic brotherhood, who lived here from 1912 until his death in 1927. His time here was at the insistence of the colonial government, who held him under house arrest and forbade him to enter the holy city of Touba, 48km to the northeast.

The Bamba family still live in the town, in a palatial compound which, according to

---

Bamba

Amadou Bamba was born around 1850 and was Senegal's most famous and influential marabout. He was a charismatic Islamic evangelist and, as a relation of the Wolof leader Lat Dior and member of the wealthy land-owning Mbacke clan, was accorded very high status. By 1887 he had gained a large following and founded the Mouride brotherhood, which emphasised the importance of physical labour (ideally working in Bamba's own plantations) as a path to spiritual salvation. This initially fitted neatly with the French administration's attempts to improve its territory's economic output, but Bamba's anticolonial stance and local power base led eventually to his being exiled.

Bamba returned to Senegal in 1907 and, despite his continued anticolonial rhetoric, became a secret ally of the French; they both had much to gain from keeping peasants working in the groundnut fields.

Even today, Bamba remains an iconic figure, and the convenient alliance between the brotherhoods and the government remains a major feature of modern Senegalese politics.

---

our guide, has walls 313m long (313 is the number of prophets in the Quran and a mystical number for Muslims). Nearby is the town's main mosque, built between 1919 and 1925; it's smaller, neater and, it has to be said, more aesthetically pleasing than the vast structure at Touba.

You are allowed to visit the mosque outside prayer times. Ask someone to find you the *responsable* (who is a sort of caretaker figure) and he'll show you around. A small fee for his trouble is appropriate. Remember to take your shoes off at the gate. Men should wear long trousers and women should wear a skirt and a scarf to cover their head and shoulders.

Diourbel has no hotel, but there are a few cheap eating houses on the main street and around the gares.

Getting There & Away

Plenty of traffic runs through Diourbel on its way to Dakar or Touba. There are two bus stations about a 10-minute walk apart, one serving Thiès and Dakar, the other Touba and Kaolack. Peugeot taxis go to Dakar (CFA1720, three hours, 146km), Thiès (CFA900, 80 minutes, 76km) and Touba (CFA700, one hour, 50km).

TOUBA

Touba is the sacred focus of the Mouride Islamic brotherhood, and its founder Amadou Bamba is buried in the giant mosque that dominates the town and the surrounding plains.

Pilgrims come to Touba at any time, but the high point of the year is a mass pilgrimage called the Grand Magal (48 days after the Islamic New Year), which celebrates Bamba's return from exile in 1907 after being banished for 20 years by the French authorities. At this time, about half a million Mouride followers flock into town from all over Senegal and Gambia. Although it is fascinating to visit during the Magal, note that it is almost impossible to find an empty seat in a vehicle headed for Touba. You also have to be very careful about what you wear, and how you behave. And keep your wits about you: pickpockets

Market Touba

That travelling salesmen, middle men and beggars vie for space at the Touba market should be no surprise – the town's role as a spiritual centre disguises the fact that it has long been one of the biggest cogs in Senegal's political and economic machinery. Though Senegal attained independence in 1960, Touba has unofficially retained its autonomy. Senegalese police are rarely seen, and the Mourides run their own welfare services. They also enjoy extensive trading relations both in Senegal and internationally. In New York police reckon 90 per cent of the street merchants illegally peddling watches, handbags and the like are Mourides, and estimates are that every month more than US$1 million is repatriated from small businesses offshore.

There are no tax collectors in Touba – its revenues come from the donations of followers – and no-one is sure exactly how much is bought, sold or bartered within the city, or how much of Senegal's economy is in fact Touba's 'shadow' economy. What is certain is that Touba's economic contribution is sizable, and its market is the cheapest place in the country to buy just about anything, especially imports – including, if you believe the locals, an AK-47.

As you wander through the streets around the mosque, the most obvious sign of the prosperity of the city is that every space is being used to display goods for sale. And between the shops and stalls move roaming salesmen peddling everything from fruit and fake Rolexes to Bamba icons and skin-whitening cream.

love the crowds in Touba just as much as anywhere else.

No alcohol or cigarettes are allowed in the mosque or anywhere else in the town at any time. Note also that although there's a small restaurant on the main street of Touba, there are no hotels – as they are seen as dens of iniquity. The nearest place to stay is at Mbaké, about 10km to the south.

However, for all its holiness, Touba is also home to possibly the biggest market in Senegal.

Mosque

The construction of the mosque started in 1936 under Bamba's son, who became caliph (brotherhood leader) on his father's death. Subsequent caliphs have added to the mosque to cater for the ever-growing crowds of followers, and expansion continues today.

The mosque is of the Mecca style and it's sheer size is almost overwhelming. The various stages of construction (from vast concrete columns to detailed plaster decorations) add an extra dimension, and an exhibition of photos in the *bibliothèque* (library) shows the many phases of construction. A separate Quranic library is claimed to be the largest on earth.

Non-Muslims can visit the mosque outside prayer hours. Guides are available, and it is inappropriate to enter the mosque without one. Some speak English. Fees are completely negotiable and should be agreed beforehand. About CFA1000 for an hour's tour would be fair.

Getting There & Away

To reach Touba from Dakar costs CFA3000 in a Peugeot taxi and CFA1200 by Alham. A day trip to Touba is possible, but you'd do the place more justice by coming to Mbaké, staying there for two nights and visiting Touba for the day.

MBAKÉ

This unremarkable town makes a good base from which to visit Touba. The ***Campement Touristique le Baol*** (☎ 976 55 05, fax 976 84 79) has spartan rooms (perhaps to put pilgrims in an ascetic mood) in a homely setting. Singles/doubles cost CFA9500/ 12,700. The English-speaking staff can arrange guides to Touba. There are also a few *cases de passage* (basic places to sleep) around the market area, where you'll also find food in a range of *gargottes* (simple eateries) and a *dibitierie* (grilled-meat stall).

There's an SGBS bank past the turn-off to Touba.

KAOLACK

Kaolack (pronounced koh-lack) is a regional capital and is the centre of Senegal's groundnut industry. Midway between Dakar, Diourbel, Tambacounda and Gambia, it is often regarded by travellers as little more than a junction, but it's a lively city well worth visiting for a day or two.

Things to see include the large Moroccan-style **Grande Mosquée**, the pride of the Tijaniya brotherhood, and the second-largest covered **market** in Africa (after Marrakesh). The market is the heart of town and looks as if it hasn't changed for decades. It's surrounded by oriental arches and arcades, a grand entrance, a large central patio and an imposing clock tower. Despite these attractions few tourists come here, so there's very little hassle. It's a great place just to have a wander around and soak up the atmosphere.

Banks include CBAO and SGBS, both of which have ATMs, and you can also change money at the Super-Service supermarket on Av Filiatre. The Cadicom.sn Internet Bureau (☎ 940 00 00, Av Cheikh Ibra Fall), open 9am to midnight, has a good service for CFA1000 an hour. Check out what's happening, regarding cultural pursuits, at the fantastically decorated Alliance Franco-Senegalaise (☎ 941 10 61, Rue Galliene).

Places to Stay

Etoile du Siné *(941 44 58, Av Valdiodio Ndiaye)* Rooms CFA9500. Much better value is this friendly place on the main road to Tambacounda. The spotless rooms come with breakfast, and there is safe parking.

Auberge de Carrefour *(☎ 941 90 00, ℮ auberge.carrefour@caramail.com, Av Valdiodio Ndiaye)* Singles/doubles CFA8500/12,600. This new place has comfortable rooms with bathroom and fan, and enthusiastic management.

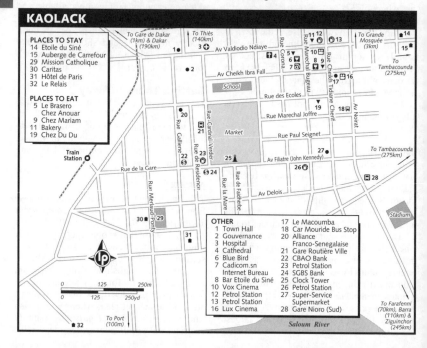

KAOLACK

PLACES TO STAY
14 Etoile du Siné
15 Auberge de Carrefour
29 Mission Catholique
30 Caritas
31 Hôtel de Paris
32 Le Relais

PLACES TO EAT
5 Le Brasero
   Chez Anouar
9 Chez Mariam
11 Bakery
19 Chez Du Du

OTHER
1 Town Hall
2 Gouvernance
3 Hospital
4 Cathedral
6 Blue Bird
7 Cadicom.sn Internet Bureau
8 Bar Etoile du Siné
10 Vox Cinema
12 Petrol Station
13 Petrol Station
16 Lux Cinema
17 Le Macoumba
18 Car Mouride Bus Stop
20 Alliance Franco-Senegalaise
21 Gare Routière Ville
22 CBAO Bank
23 Petrol Station
24 SGBS Bank
25 Clock Tower
26 Petrol Station
27 Super-Service Supermarket
28 Gare Nioro (Sud)

Mission Catholique *(☎ 941 25 26, Rue Merlaud-Ponty)* Dorm beds CFA2000, singles CFA5000. This might be worth a try, but it's often full and the dorms are strictly single-sex affairs.

Caritas *(☎ 941 27 30, Rue Merlaud-Ponty)* Singles/doubles CFA10,000/15,000. Opposite the mission, this two-storey building with a green roof has modern rooms with bathroom and air-con.

Hôtel de Paris *(☎ 941 10 19, fax 941 10 17, Rue Galliene)* Singles/doubles CFA 20,000/25,000. This top-end place has air-con rooms and facilities include a small pool, but it is overpriced when compared with Le Relais. Breakfast is CFA2200 and good meals are CFA4000 to CFA5500.

Le Relais *(☎ 941 10 00, fax 941 10 02, e horizons@sentoo.sn, Plage de Kundam)* Singles/doubles CFA22,200/27,200. Southwest of town and right on the river, this place is the best in Kaolack. It's well managed and has a tempting pool and adjoining bar. Rooms have bathroom, air-con, TV, phone and even an Internet connection.

Places to Eat

For cheap eats there are several ***gargottes*** near the gares routière, and ***street food*** can be found around the market. The food at the ***Hôtel-Restaurant Adama Cire*** is cheap and filling, with big bowls of *mafé* (groundnut sauce) or rice and fish for CFA500, chicken yassa for CFA800 and a whole grilled chicken for CFA5000.

Chez Mariam *(☎ 941 45 85, Rue Cheikh Tidiane Cherif)* Mains around CF2500. Open Mon-Sat. Northeast of the centre, Chez Mariam has chawarmas and burgers for CFA500 to CFA1000 and other meals for a little more.

Chez Du Du *(☎ 941 87 67, Rue des Ecoles)* Mains CFA1500-2000. Open 9am-midnight. Best for quality and atmosphere, this place has chawarmas for around CFA700, pizzas for CFA3000, omelettes from CFA1000 and a huge choice of main meals. Beers are CFA600.

Le Brasero Chez Anouar *(☎ 941 16 08, Av Valdiodio Ndiaye)* Meals about CFA3000. Open 7am-midnight. Good food

and atmosphere make this one of the most popular places in Kaolack, especially for lunch. The mafé (CFA750) and chicken (CFA2800) are particularly good, with pizzas (CFA2500) and draught beer (CFA600) also available. English-speaking Anouar is full of good advice.

Entertainment

There's quite a scene after dark in Kaolack. It centres around ***Blue Bird*** *(☎ 941 5350, Rue Marechal Bugeau)*, open 8am to 3am Monday to Saturday and 6pm to 2am Sunday, where food can be followed by dancing in the adjoining, and very popular, nightclub. Just over the road is the boisterous ***Bar Etoile du Siné*** *(☎ 936 45 930)*, open 9am to 2am, not to be confused with the small hotel of the same name. A block east is the ***Vox Cinema***, an open-air affair with movies at 9pm every night. After the flick you could head to ***Le Macoumba*** *(☎ 941 65 59, Av Cheikh Ibra Fall)*, open 10am to 4am, which is a restaurant that gets steamy later on.

Getting There & Away

The town has three gares routière: Gare de Dakar, on the northwestern side of town, for western and northern destinations; Gare Nioro (Sud), on the southeast side of the city centre, for Ziguinchor, Gambia and Tambacounda; and Gare Routière Ville for local bush taxis.

You can travel to or from Dakar by Peugeot taxi (CFA2600, three hours), minibus CFA1500 (five hours) and Alham CFA1250 (six hours). A Peugeot taxi to the Gambian border at Karang is CFA2000 (two hours); to Thiès is CFA1600.

Another option is the express bus *(car mouride)* – see Tambacounda in the Eastern Senegal chapter for more details. The car mouride leaves from the corner of Av Noirat and Rue Marechal Joffre, though there's nothing there to suggest it's a bus stop.

Getting Around

To reach Gare de Dakar from the city centre in a taxi or horse-drawn carriage *(calesh)* costs CFA400. If you go from Gare Nioro (Sud) to Gare de Dakar it's CFA500.

Northern Senegal

Senegal's long northern border is defined by the Senegal River, flowing in a great arc westwards from the Fouta Djalon highlands in Guinea, through Mali and continuing for some 600km between Senegal and Mauritania. The river, its adjoining creeks and floodplains are a lifeline, but only a short distance away the landscape is dry and vegetation is sparse. North of the river, the deserts of Mauritania mark the southern edge of the Sahara; to the south the Ferlo Plains stretch into central Senegal, almost reaching Kaolack and Tambacounda.

The river region is the homeland of the Tukulor people, although this and the Ferlo area is also inhabited by the Fula people. In recent years the pastoral Fula have found their cattle-grazing areas increasingly restricted as groundnut farmers (mainly Wolof) establish plantations, often inspired by the powerful marabouts, and encroach onto supposedly protected *sylvo-pastorale* (pastoral) reserves. Some areas of the Ferlo are also set aside as wildlife reserves, although these semidesert areas are hard to reach and have no tourist facilities.

Apart from St-Louis and the surrounding area, the northern part of Senegal is rarely reached by travellers, but it provides a useful route between the north and east of the country, especially if you're heading between St-Louis and Tambacounda or the parks of Djoudj and Niokolo-Koba. Overland drivers linking Mauritania and Mali also find this route easy and enjoyable.

St-Louis & Around

The Senegal River flows westwards towards the Atlantic Ocean, but currents and winds have pushed sand across its mouth for thousands of years, changing its course. Now the final section of the river runs south, separated from the ocean by a long narrow peninsula – the Langue de Barbarie. The original city of St-Louis was founded

Highlights

• Wander the streets of historic St-Louis, where colonial architecture, good food and jazz can all be experienced in a relaxed, African atmosphere

• Spot some of the hundreds of varieties of birds in Parc National des Oiseaux du Djoudj

• Watch 200 fishing boats surf onto the long, wide beaches of the Langue de Barbarie

• Find friendly Fula herders in faded French outposts on the slow road along the Senegal River

in the 17th century on a strategic island near the river's mouth, between the mainland and the peninsula, although it has expanded to cover a much larger area today.

St-Louis makes a good base from which to explore northwest Senegal, and several wildlife reserves lie within an easy day's travel – including Parc National de la Langue de Barbarie, at the southern tip of the eponymous peninsula, and Parc National des Oiseaux du Djoudj, the world-famous bird sanctuary.

SENEGAL

ST-LOUIS
pop 147,100

When you consider the enormous impact the French had on this continent it's fascinating to think that the place where it all began has barely changed for more than a century. Founded on a strategically important island in the Senegal River in 1659, St-Louis was the first French settlement in Africa. By the 1790s it had become a busy port and trading centre with a racially diverse population of 10,000. Most notable among the residents of St-Louis at this time were the *signares* – women of mixed race who temporarily 'married' European merchants based in the city, and thereby gained great wealth and privilege. They initiated Les Fanals, the festival of decorated lanterns, which still occurs in St-Louis in the weeks around Christmas and also accompanies the annual St-Louis International Jazz Festival.

In the early 19th century, St-Louis became the capital of France's new African colonies. Dakar became the capital of French West Africa in 1904, but St-Louis remained the capital of Senegal (and Mauritania) until 1958, when everything was moved to Dakar.

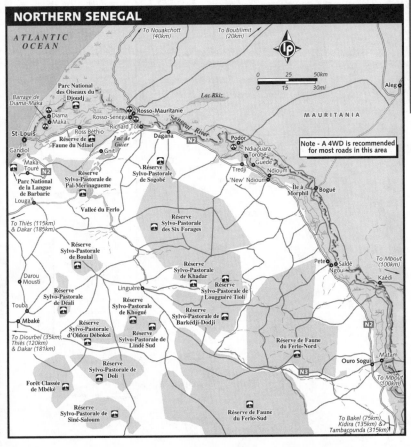

SENEGAL

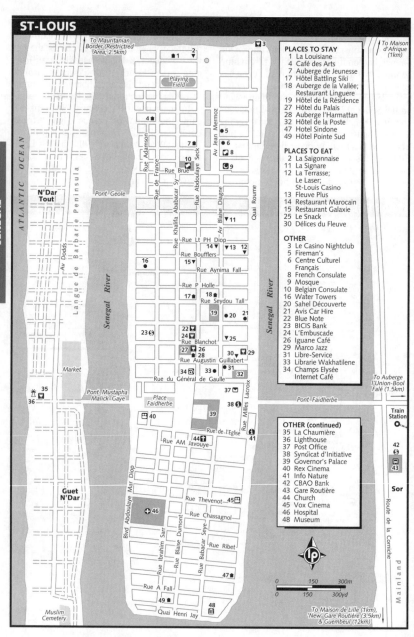

ST-LOUIS

To Mauritanian Border (Restricted Area; 2.5km)

To Maison d'Afrique (1km)

ATLANTIC OCEAN

N'Dar Tout

Langue de Barbarie Peninsula

Senegal River

Market

Guet N'Dar

Muslim Cemetery

Playing Field

Pont Geole

Av Dodds

Rue Adamson

Rue de France

Rue Brue

Rue Khalifa Ababacar Sy

Av Jean Mermoz

Rue Abdoulaye Seck

Blaise Diagne

Quai Roume

Rue Lt PH Diop

Rue Boufflers

Rue Aynima Fall

Rue P Holle

Rue Seydou Tall

Rue Blanchot

Rue Augustin Guillabert

Rue du Général de Gaulle

Senegal River

Pont Mustapha Malick Gaye

Place Faidherbe

Rue de l'Eglise

Rue Milles Lacroix

To Auberge l'Union-Bool Falé (1.5km)

Pont Faidherbe

Train Station

Sor

Rue AM Javouye

Blvd Abdoulaye Mar Diop

Rue Thevenot

Rue Chassagnol

Rue Ribet

Rue Ibrahim Satr

Rue Blaise Dumont

Rue Babacar Seye

Rue A Fall

Quai Henri Jay

Route de la Corniche

Mainland

To Maison de Lille (1km), 'New' Gare Routière (3.5km) & Guembeul (12km)

PLACES TO STAY
1 La Louisiane
4 Café des Arts
7 Auberge de Jeunesse
17 Hôtel Battling Siki
18 Auberge de la Vallée; Restaurant Linguere
19 Hôtel de la Résidence
27 Hôtel du Palais
28 Auberge l'Harmattan
32 Hôtel de la Poste
47 Hotel Sindone
49 Hôtel Pointe Sud

PLACES TO EAT
2 La Saigonnaise
11 La Signare
12 La Terrasse; Le Laser; St-Louis Casino
13 Fleuve Plus
14 Restaurant Marocain
15 Restaurant Galaxie
25 Le Snack
30 Délices du Fleuve

OTHER
3 Le Casino Nightclub
5 Fireman's
6 Centre Culturel Français
8 French Consulate
9 Mosque
10 Belgian Consulate
16 Water Towers
20 Sahel Découverte
21 Avis Car Hire
22 Blue Note
23 BICIS Bank
24 L'Embuscade
26 Iguane Café
29 Marco Jazz
31 Libre-Service
33 Librarie Wakhatilene
34 Champs Elysée Internet Café

OTHER (continued)
35 La Chaumière
36 Lighthouse
37 Post Office
38 Syndicat d'Initiative
39 Governor's Palace
40 Rex Cinema
41 Info Nature
42 CBAO Bank
43 Gare Routière
44 Church
45 Vox Cinema
46 Hospital
48 Museum

0   150   300m
0   150   300yd

St-Louis Jazz

Jazz is a big thing here – and it's not just the shared name with St Louis, Missouri in the USA, where blues and jazz originated. Way back in the 1940s jazz bands from St-Louis (Senegal) were playing in Paris and elsewhere in Europe. Worldwide interest was revived in the early 1990s when the St-Louis Jazz Festival was first held, with mainly local bands performing. Now renamed the St-Louis International Jazz Festival, this annual event is held the second weekend of May, and attracts performers and audiences from all over the world. Obviously the festival is the best time to see jazz in St-Louis, but if you're thinking of avoiding the crowds and the inflated room rates by coming at another time of year then be warned: performances can be very infrequent indeed. More information is available from the Centre Culturel Français (see Cultural Centres later in this chapter). For more background, have a look at *St-Louis Jazz,* a book by Hervé Lenormond (French text, published by Editions Joca Seria, Nantes, France), which outlines the history of jazz in Senegal and has some wonderful photos of musicians from Africa, America and Europe performing in St-Louis.

St-Louis expanded slowly, taking over part of the mainland (called Sor) and the Langue de Barbarie peninsula, but the face of the island itself barely changed throughout the 20th century. This policy of neglect led unwittingly to the conservation of a range of classic architecture and then to the island's classification as a Unesco World Heritage site in 2000. Buildings are now being renovated at an impressive rate, so it's worth visiting this easy-going city soon, in case the air of faded elegance is replaced by that of an all-too-perfect tourist town.

Orientation

The city of St-Louis straddles part of the Langue de Barbarie peninsula, the island and the mainland. From the mainland you reach the island via the 500m long Pont Faidherbe; another two smaller bridges link the island to the peninsula. The island was formerly the European quarter, with many grand old houses, a few of which still retain their gracious wrought-iron balconies, while others have literally fallen down. The peninsula was the African quarter; today it's a thriving fishing community called Guet N'Dar.

Maps

The large *St-Louis et de la Region du Fleuve Senegal*, a cross between a cartoon and an aerial photograph, is available in bookshops and hotels for around CFA3000 and is well worth the money. Most useful is the leaflet,

St-Louis de Senegal – Ville d'Art et d'Histoire, which has a city map showing a suggested walking route taking in various historical features.

Information

The Syndicat d'Initiative (☎ 961 24 55, e sltourisme@sentoo.sn), next to the post office on the island, has a notice board with news of local events and helpful staff who are happy to answer questions without trying to sell you anything. There is a new guide to St-Louis in English and Italian; ask about it here.

St-Louis has a very good website (W www .saintlouisdusenegal.com).

Local hustlers and unofficial guides will offer you tours and souvenirs. Don't be afraid to say no.

Money The BICIS bank on Rue de France changes money and also has an ATM (Visa only). It's open from 7.45am to 12.15pm and 1.40pm to 3.45pm Monday to Thursday and 7.45am to 1pm and 2.40pm to 3.45pm Friday. CBAO has a small branch with an ATM at the *gare routière* (bus station) in Sor. Alternatively, try the reception at any large hotel – although most will only accept French francs.

Post & Communications The Art Deco–style post office is on Rue du Général de Gaulle opposite the Hôtel de la Poste. You can make phone calls from any hotel, but most télécentres (where rates are cheaper) are across the bridge in Sor. The Champs Elysée Internet Café (☎ 961 80 29), on Rue du Général de Gaulle has decent terminals, charges CFA500 per hour and is open from 8am to midnight daily.

Travel Agencies The main company in St-Louis is Sahel Découverte (☎ 961 42 63, fax 962 42 64, W www.saheldecouverte.com) on Av Blaise Diagne. It can arrange air tickets, car hire, hotel reservations, and it also offers a range of tours in and around St-Louis (see Organised Tours later in this chapter).

Bookshops There are two bookshops on Av Blaise Diagne that both sell maps and postcards. The Librairie Wakhatilene (☎ 961 13 25), at the southern end of this street has a few English-language magazines and newspapers, but no books.

Cultural Centres The Centre Culturel Français (☎ 961 15 78, W www.ccfsl.sn), Av Jean Mermoz, is open from 8.30am to 12.30pm and 3pm to 6.30pm weekdays. It has a library and café, publishes a regular guide to events in St-Louis, hosts films, concerts, art exhibitions and is also the centre for the St-Louis International Jazz Festival (see the boxed text 'St-Louis Jazz' earlier in this chapter).

Things to See

Designed by Gustav Eiffel and originally built to cross the Danube, the **Pont Faidherbe**, linking the mainland and island, was transferred to St-Louis in 1897. The bridge is a grand piece of 19th-century engineering – 507m long with a middle section that once rotated to allow ships to steam up the Senegal River. Taxis run across the bridge, but it's worth walking for the view.

Immediately after crossing to the island, to the right you'll see the old **Hôtel de la Poste**. Opposite is the Art Deco–style post office, where, for a small fee, local guides will take you onto the roof, which offers good views of the bridge and surrounding city. Behind the post office is the former **governor's palace**, which was a fort during the 18th century and

is now a government building. Across the road is a **church** that dates from 1828 and, despite its modern appearance, is apparently the oldest operating church in Senegal.

Place Faidherbe, with its statue of the famous French colonial governor, is in front of the governor's palace. North and south of the place are some of the island's 19th-century houses, still essentially intact. Several good examples lie on Quai Henri Jay to the south.

At the southern tip of the island is a **museum** *(admission CFA500; open 9am-noon & 3pm-6pm daily)* containing some fascinating old photos of St-Louis and other exhibits relating to the northern region.

From Place Faidherbe another bridge, Pont Mutapha Malick Gaye, links St-Louis to Guet N'Dar, the fishing part of town on the Langue de Barbarie peninsula. After crossing the bridge, go straight ahead to reach the lighthouse and the beach. Forget sunbathing, though – every morning, some 200 pirogues are launched from here into the sea. They return in the late afternoon – surfing spectacularly on the waves – to unload their fish on the sand. A line of trucks waits to transport the catch to Dakar, from where some of it is shipped to Europe.

At the southern end of Guet N'Dar, on the river side, pirogues are lined up on the beach and fish dry on racks by the side of the road. Women boil up fish in vast drums, and the steam mixes odourously with the early morning sea mist. Further south is the **Muslim cemetery**, where each fisherman's grave is covered with a fishing net.

Further down the Langue de Barbarie peninsula you'll find several hotels and *campements* (inns) as well as some good beach spots. This area is called l'Hydrobase, and was a vital refuelling point for flying boats travelling between Europe and South America in the 1930s. A **monument** to early aviator Jean Mermoz stands next to the road.

You may be stopped by police if you go north from Guet N'Dar, as the border with Mauritania is only 3km away.

Places to Stay – Budget

Mainland On the north side of Sor, *Auberge l'Union-Bool Falé* (☎ 961 38 52)

The people of Senegambia place great importance on personal grooming; this includes dressing in the best clothes possible and regularly having their hair styled. You will see many examples of vibrant street art advertising the local 'saloon', but don't expect a drink with your cut.

ARIADNE VAN ZANDBERGEN

FRANCES LINZEE GORDON

ARIADNE VAN ZANDBERGEN

ANDREW BURKE

Fabric of various styles and designs features strongly in the life of the people of Senegambia. Traditional weaving, as seen here at the Tanji Village Museum (middle right), in western Gambia, is still practised and colourful cloth is sold in the markets throughout the region.

might well be a shoestringers' favourite, but it can be very hard to find. Head for the village artisinal and when you get there start asking. Rooms with fan are CFA4600 per person, singles/doubles with bathroom are CFA8100/13,200, while a mattress on the roof is CFA2500.

Maison de Lille (☎/fax 961 11 35) Singles/doubles CFA5000/10,000. This community hostel, 2km south of the bridge on the mainland, is basic but clean. Rates include breakfast.

Island The long-standing *Hôtel Battling Siki (Rue Abdoulaye Seck)* might be cheap, but several readers have had bad experiences here. Both the rooms and shared bathrooms are grubby. Breakfast is CFA600. Singles/doubles CFA5000/6000.

Both the following *auberges* are clean and friendly, with shared bathrooms and rooms with two, three, six or eight beds, but the price per person remains the same wherever you sleep. This makes it good value if you're in a double, but a bit steep for what is effectively a dorm.

Auberge de Jeunesse (☎ 961 24 09, fax 961 56 73, e pisdiallo@yahoo.fr, Rue Abdoulaye Seck) Beds CFA5500 per person. Much better than Hôtel Battling Siki, this place has simple but spotless rooms, with nets and fans, on an upper floor surrounding a cool courtyard.

Auberge de la Vallée (☎ 961 47 22, Av Blaise Diagne). Beds CFA5000 per person. Rates include breakfast. Tours can be arranged through the *auberge* and they also rent bikes, but some readers have had trouble with the 'unscrupulous' management.

Café des Arts (Rue de France) Dorm beds CFA3500, doubles CFA7000. This small but colourfully decorated place near the north end of the island has a real family feel and it is way off the tourist path. The rooms are basic, with shared bathrooms.

Langue de Barbarie All the hotels and campements along the Langue de Barbarie are very close to the beach, but they're a long walk from town, although most places have bikes for hire or can arrange a taxi for you.

Auberge la Teranga (Around St-Louis map; ☎ 961 50 50) Singles/doubles CFA6400/8400. About 2.5km south of town, this Senegalese-run place is aimed squarely at backpackers. Rooms sleep two to five people and the shared bathrooms are clean. The friendly people running the place assured us the rooftop restaurant could serve anyone any time, though it didn't look like it had served many recently. Meals are CFA1500 to CFA2500.

Camping l'Ocean (Around St-Louis map; ☎ 961 31 18, fax 971 57 84) Camp sites CF1000 per person, singles/doubles with bathroom CFA11,200/15,200. Next along, and probably the best value, this relaxed place, ideal for travellers with vehicles and/or tents. The rooms are clean with fans and bathrooms, air-con is an extra CFA5000. You can hire a tent for CFA1000.

Places to Stay – Mid-Range & Top End

Most top-end places accept credit cards.

Mainland On the north side of Sor, the small and clean hotel *Maison d'Afrique (☎/fax 961 45 00)* is apparently very popular with visiting musicians – there are even pictures of Youssou N'Dour here, though they have turned sepia with age. Singles/doubles are CFA9600/12,600, triples and quads are CFA7600 per person. Breakfast is CFA500, it's an extra CFA2000 if you want your own bathroom and CFA1000 for air-con.

Hôtel Coumba Bang (Around St-Louis map; ☎ 961 18 50) Singles/doubles CFA21,600/26,200. About 7km from the bridge, just off the road towards Dakar, you will find this 50-room hotel, with a tranquil riverside garden and swimming pool. Breakfast is CFA2500. Taxis from town charge from CFA500 to CFA1500 for the trip here.

Island At the far north end of the island, the small and peaceful *La Louisiane (☎ 961 42 21, fax 961 61 15, e louisianne@tpsnet.sn)* offers great value and a stunning location. Singles/doubles with fan and bathroom will cost you CFA13,600/17,200, triples/quads CFA5900. An annexe a couple of doors down has rooms for about CFA2000 less. The friendly owners speak French, English and German and can arrange tours. Even if you don't stay it's worth a visit for the mouth-watering local and European food at very reasonable prices. Highly recommended!

Auberge l'Harmattan (☎ 961 82 53, Rue Augustin Guillabert) Singles/doubles CFA15,000/18,000. What started as a restaurant has expanded into this good-value *auberge*. Rooms in the historic building have bathrooms and air-con, and the patio is a fine place to relax. The food downstairs is not bad either, with meals for about CFA3500.

Hôtel du Palais (Rue Blanchot) Singles/ doubles/triples/quads CFA15,000/17,600/ 21,800/26,000. The Palais has seen better days, but the palatial upstairs rooms with balconies are reasonably good. Breakfast is CFA1400.

Hôtel de la Résidence (☎ 961 12 59, fax 961 12 60, e hotresid@sentoo.sn, Av Blaise Diagne) Singles/doubles/triples CFA27,600/ 33,600/38,600. This place is better than Hôtel du Palais, but the air-con is not always up to cooling the large rooms. All rooms have bathroom. Breakfast is CFA2500. The nautically flavoured bar is the focal point of well-to-do St-Louisian nightlife, and the restaurant serves excellent, if expensive, food. Bikes can be hired, or they're free for guests.

Hôtel de la Poste (☎ 961 11 18, fax 961 22 13, e htlposte@telecomplus.sn, Rue du Général de Gaulle) Singles/doubles/triples CFA27,000/33,500/39,500. Dating from the 1850s, the passengers on the flying boats (and the mailbags presumably) stayed here in the old days, and you're still paying for this slice of history. The hotel's Safari Bar is full of colonial flashbacks, balding animal heads and all, but the rooms will disappoint.

Hotel Sindone (☎ 961 42 45, fax 961 42 86, e sindone@arc.sn, Quai Henri Jay) Singles/doubles from CFA25,600/27,200. This stylish and airy hotel has rooms with air-con, TV, bathroom and phone, and is the best on the island. Half the rooms have stunning views over the river, for which you'll pay about CFA3000 extra. The restaurant is popular with locals, serving mains (CFA5000), crepes (CFA2500) and huge salads (CFA3500).

Hôtel Pointe Sud (☎ 961 58 78, Rue Ibrahim Sarr) Doubles CFA28,000, studios CFA32,500, suites CFA48,500. At the south end of the island this place is also pretty good. Studios and suites have cooking facilities, and the rooftop bar/restaurant is the perfect place for breakfast (CFA2500).

Langue de Barbarie About 1km south of Camping l'Ocean, *Hôtel Mermoz (Around St-Louis map; ☎/fax 961 36 68, w www .hotelmermoz.com)* has comfortable bungalows, a pool and a bar-restaurant. Singles/ doubles without bath are CFA12,000/16,600. Larger rooms with bath and air-con are CFA10,000 more. Breakfast is available for CFA2000, and the *menu de jour* (meal of the day) costs CFA8000. It has bikes for hire, and a jet ski is also available for CFA5000 per 15 minutes. Room prices usually drop by 25% in the low season.

Hôtel l'Oasis (Around St-Louis map; ☎/fax 961 42 32, e nicooasissl@arc.sn) Singles/ doubles CFA11,200/17,000, with bathroom CFA15,700/23,600. Many travellers recommend this place, about 4km south of the centre, and the friendly, multilingual Belgian management. There are simple, good-quality huts (up to CFA33,500 for four people); or high-standard bungalows with bathroom – all with breakfast. Meals are excellent and start at CFA2500, ranging up to CFA4500 for a three-course *menu de jour*.

Hôtel Cap St-Louis (Around St-Louis map; ☎ 961 39 39, fax 961 39 09, w www .hotelcapsaintlouis.com) Singles/doubles without bath CFA10,400/14,800, singles/ doubles/triples with bath CFA19,000/ 28,300/ 32,700. Almost next door to Hôtel l'Oasis is this resort-style place with simple rooms and air-con bungalows. Facilities include a swimming pool, strictly for guests, and a tennis court. Breakfast is CFA2500, other meals are priced from CFA3000 to CFA5000 and the evening menu is CFA7200. Discounts can be had for weekends and multiple night stays.

Résid Hôtel Diamarek (Around St-Louis map; ☎ 951 57 81, fax 961 55 04,

e) hoteldiamarek@sentoo.sn) Doubles from CFA19,500, bungalows CFA31,500. Open Oct-Aug. Last on this strip, and the newest, this French-run place will appeal to families with its two-bedroom, two-bathroom self-catering bungalows. Prices vary according to the season, with bungalows up to CFA50,000 over Christmas.

Places to Eat

More tourists mean more money and, you guessed it, a growing number of cuisines and restaurants. The hotels also do food, and some of it (especially that at La Louisiane) is quite good.

Just north of the bridge, the *Délices du Fleuve (☎ 961 42 51, Quai Roume)* lives up to its reputation for excellent pastries. In the city centre there are a couple of *chawarma joints* on Av Blaise Diagne. North of here, *Restaurant Galaxie (☎ 961 24 68, Rue Abdoulaye Seck)*, *Restaurant Linguere* on the ground floor under Auberge de la Vallée, and *Fleuve Plus* on Rue Lt PH Diop all do good Senegalese food for around CFA1500 to CFA2000. The *Restaurant Marocain (Cnr Av Bloaise Diagne & Rue Lt PH Diop)* is also popular, with good, cheap food in a traditional setting.

Le Snack (Av Blaise Diagne) Pizzas CFA3500. Open lunch & dinner. Locals say this place has the best pizzas, and the ice cream's not bad either.

La Saigonnaise (☎ 961 64 81) Mains CFA3500. Open noon-midnight daily. If you fancy a taste of Asia, this Vietnamese restaurant at the north end of Rue Abdoulaye Seck complements its great location (looking to Mauritania) with traditional and very tasty Saigonnaise fare. Both the owner and the chef are originally from Saigon, and you can even be pedalled around town in a cyclo for CFA3000 an hour.

La Signare (☎ 961 19 32, Av Blaise Diagne) Meals CFA7000. Open lunch & dinner Thur-Tues. Considered one of the top eateries in St-Louis, La Signare offers a truly top-notch *menu du jour* (meal of the day) costing CFA7000.

La Terrasse (☎ 961 53 98, Quai Roume) Meals CFA7000. Locals say the French and international food here is the best in St-Louis. It is part of the casino complex.

Self-caterers will save money and have more fun shopping in the **market** just north of the bridge in Guet N'Dar. For European goods and French wine, head for the **Libre-Service market** on Av Blaise Diagne.

All the places to stay along the Langue de Barbarie serve meals. Additionally, the beach between the Mermoz and Oasis hotels has friendly *shack-like bars* where you can get a drink and, if you order in advance, maybe even a meal.

Entertainment

Bars & Live Music The *Hôtel Battling Siki* (Rue Abdoulaye Seck) is named after Africa's only heavyweight boxing champion, which is appropriate as there's a good chance you'll see fists flying first-hand if you stop in here for a drink. Instead, for a couple of quiet ones with the locals, we recommend *Fireman's*, just north of the Centre Culturel Français, which has the cheapest beer around but, to quote one regular, 'the worst shitter in Senegal'.

Cleaner facilities and more-expensive drinks can be found in several bars just north of the centre. The *Blue Note (Rue Abdoulaye Seck)* is a vaguely subversive scene with a mixed crowd. A couple of doors south, *L'Embuscade (☎ 961 7741)* has tap beer and tapas, while on the next block is *Iguane Café (☎ 961 52 12)*, a Cuban-themed bar. *Marco Jazz (e) benedettoma@yahoo.fr; Quai Roume)*, a little north of the bridge, is an intimate venue and the best place to see live jazz. Email to get an idea who's playing when.

> ### Battling Siki
>
> Battling Siki became the first (and only) African heavyweight boxing champion of the world in 1925. Born in St-Louis, his real name was M'Barick Fall, and he won the fight when he was just 28 years old. His reign was short-lived, however, as he was assassinated the same year in the USA. His nephew now runs the Hôtel Battling Siki.

Nightclubs For a taste of how Senegal's bright young things let their hair down, head to *Le Laser (☎ 961 53 98)*, part of the St-Louis Casino complex on the Quai Roume. There's a CFA2000 cover for tourists, which includes a drink, and it's open Wednesday to Sunday. *Le Casino Nightclub*, on a pontoon at the north end of the island, has nothing to do with the casino, but it does get lively on Friday and Saturday. In Guet N'Dar, *La Chaumière* is a bar and nightclub that's popular with both locals and tourists where you'll see more sweat and less make-up.

Getting There & Away

Bus The gare routière is on the mainland 100m south of Pont Faidherbe (a taxi from here to the city centre on the island costs CFA250). The fare to or from Dakar is CFA2150 by Alkham, CFA2445 by minibus and CFA3100 by Peugeot taxi. A Peugeot taxi to Thiès is CFA2345.

To or from Richard Toll by Peugeot taxi costs CFA1540. A Peugeot taxi to Gandiol, from where boats to the Parc National de la Langue de Barbarie leave, costs CFA250.

Note that a vast new gare routière has been built about 4.5km south of the Pont Faidherbe, but transport workers have so far refused to use it. If this has changed by the time you arrive you can expect a taxi to the island to cost about CFA800.

Train The train station is just north of the gare routière, but despite being World Heritage listed, it's closed and in serious need of repair. Train services between St-Louis and Dakar only run during holiday times and Muslim festivals (when people go to visit their families), though there is talk of services resuming more regularly.

Getting Around

Car Cars can be hired from the Avis agency at CFAO (☎ 961 19 86), Quai Roume, north of the Hôtel de la Poste. Small cars cost CFA30,000 per day, including tax and 100km free. The agency is closed on Sunday.

Bicycle To get around St-Louis and the surrounding area, several hotels and *auberges* hire out steel roadsters for about CFA2500 and mountain bikes ('VTTs' in French) for CFA5000 per day.

Organised Tours The leading tour operator is *Sahel Découverte* (see Travel Agencies earlier in this chapter). Excursions to Parc National de la Langue de Barbarie cost CFA16,000 per person, and Parc National des Oiseaux du Djoudj costs CFA20,000 for a whole day. Lunch costs an extra CFA5000. Other tours include a half-day *broussarde* (tour in the bush) for CFA16,000, a full day to Lac de Guiers (CFA28,000) and a fascinating day trip into Mauritania for CFA40,000. Longer tours into Mauritania, including a desert bivouac, cost about CFA50,000 per day. All prices are based on a minimum of four people, but kids under 10 are half price and individuals can usually join others on the same trip. Remember that guides generally only speak French.

Many hotels in St-Louis offer excursions, but most simply refer you on to Sahel Découverte. *La Louisiane* offers tours to Lac de Guiers for about CFA20,000 per person, depending on numbers. The *Hôtel de la Poste* charges around CFA25,000 per person.

The syndicat d'initiative also arranges tours at similar rates, and it also has two English-speaking guides.

You can organise a tour to Djoudj or Langue de Barbarie with a local guide. Some are members of a professional organisation, others are independent, but they all charge about CFA4000 per person per day. On top of this you must pay for transport (usually a good taxi), which the guide will arrange for CFA20,000 to Djoudj and CFA7500 to Langue de Barbarie; split between the group. In addition each person must pay a park entry fee (CFA2000 at both) and the cost of the boat ride (CFA3000 for Djoudj or CFA2500 for Langue de Barbarie).

If you're a keen bird-watcher, it's worth noting that while the official guides claim to know their birds, most of them are familiar with the common species only and are unlikely to know their English names. The bird-guide setup that exists in Gambia has yet to hatch in Senegal.

Local youths in St-Louis will probably approach you with offers of cheap trips to Djoudj and Langue de Barbarie, charging less than the official guides. This can be a good way to save money, but your chances of disaster are higher, so this may be worth avoiding unless you have a personal recommendation. Before agreeing to anything, clarify who pays for park entrance fees.

To get to Djoudj or Langue de Barbarie under your own steam you could just hire a taxi and not take a guide at all. Daily rates are around CFA20,000 to Djoudj and CFA7500 to Langue de Barbarie. However, entry to Djoudj costs another CFA5000 for the car (official guides have a permit, which means this charge is waived). It's very important to hire a taxi in good mechanical condition, with a driver who knows the way (especially for Djoudj). Also, make it clear beforehand what time you plan to return, never pay the whole fare in advance and be sure the driver has enough fuel to get you there and back – taxis are notorious for running on empty.

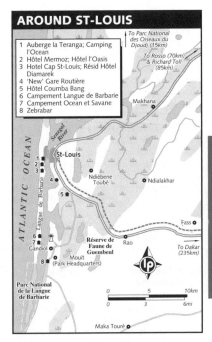

AROUND ST-LOUIS

1 Auberge la Teranga; Camping l'Ocean
2 Hôtel Mermoz; Hôtel l'Oasis
3 Hotel Cap St-Louis; Résid Hôtel Diamarek
4 'New' Gare Routière
5 Hôtel Coumba Bang
6 Campement Langue de Barbarie
7 Campement Ocean et Savane
8 Zebrabar

AROUND ST-LOUIS
Réserve de Faune de Guembeul

This reserve *(admission CFA1000; open 7.30am-6.30pm daily)* is small, accessible and easy to explore on foot. It's about 12km south of St-Louis, just east of the road to Gandiol. Measuring about 700 hectares, the landscape is a mixture of lagoon, mud flat and dry woodland protecting the populations of endangered Sahel animals, which include dama gazelles, patas monkeys and sulcata tortoises. There are also many birds around the lagoon – 190 species have been spotted here – and there are plans to introduce other Sahel mammals into the reserve.

The park is easy to reach by any bush taxi going between St-Louis and Gandiol, or by private taxi or rented bike. Guided walks cost CFA7000 (includes entry fee) for three hours, less if you have more people.

Gandiol & Mouit

Gandiol is a small village on the mainland, about 18km south of St-Louis. During the rainy season large areas of the surrounding flat landscape are covered by shallow

seawater lagoons. In the dry season, the waters recede to leave pans of white mud and salt. The salt is collected by local women and used locally for cooking.

From Gandiol, ferries cross to the two campements on the southern end of the Langue de Barbarie, and this is also the starting point for organised boat tours of the national park. Some tour boats leave from the lighthouse, north of the village. If you want to hire a boat, ask here or at the village.

About 2km south of Gandiol is the smaller village of Mouit, where you will find the national park headquarters. Another 500m further, on the edge of the river, is *Zebrabar* (☎ *mobile 638 18 62,* W *www.regio-team .ch/zebrabar),* a fine campement predominantly aimed at overlanders in vehicles, although anyone who makes it to this secluded spot is made very welcome by the multilingual Swiss managers. Camping is on the grass below palm trees and sites are CFA2000 per person; singles/doubles in simple huts are CFA6000/9000; while more comfortable bungalows are CFA12,000/15,000. Breakfast is an additional CFA1000 and good meals cost from CFA2000. The managers can set up visits to the park, arrange boat hire with local fishermen (CFA2500 per hour), tell you the best place to see birds or lend you a kayak.

Getting There & Away A bush taxi runs a few times each day from St-Louis to Gandiol (CFA300). Sometimes this taxi continues to Mouit, otherwise you'll have to walk the last 2km from Gandiol to Mouit and 2.5km to Zebrabar. A private taxi all the way from St-Louis to Zebrabar is CFA2500.

If you're driving, turn off the tar road where it swings a sharp right (west) just before the village. If you've got a GPS, Zebrabar is at N 15° 51' 900 W 16° 30' 720.

Parc National de la Langue de Barbarie

This park *(admission CFA5000 per person; open 7am-sunset daily)* is 20km south of St-Louis. It includes the far southern tip of the Langue de Barbarie peninsula, the estuary of the Senegal River (which contains two small islands) and a section of the mainland on the other side of the estuary. The park covers a total area of 2000 hectares, and is home to numerous water birds – notably flamingos, pelicans, cormorants, herons, egrets and ducks. From November to April these numbers are swelled by the arrival of migrants from Europe.

Although you can walk on the sandy peninsula of the Langue itself, once across the mouth of the river and on the mainland, the usual (and best) way to experience the park is by boat, which can cruise slowly past the mud flats, inlets and islands where the birds feed, roost and nest.

If you chose to come to the park independently, you must first go to the park office at Mouit to pay your entrance fee. At the river you can hire a pirogue for CFA7500 or, for three or more people, CFA2500 each.

Places to Stay In a wonderful position, at the southern end of the Langue de Barbarie,

about 20km from the city centre, are two campements. They are outside the park, across the river from Gandiol.

Campement Langue de Barbarie Singles/doubles CFA10,600/15,000. Run by Hôtel de la Poste, this smart place is in a wonderful position at the southern end of the peninsula, about 20km from St-Louis centre, and offers cottages for rent. Breakfast is CFA2000 and meals cost CFA6000.

Campement Ocean et Savane Half board CFA18,600, full board CFA20,600. Run by Hôtel de la Résidence, this place is more relaxed and is good value, with accommodation in large Mauritanian-style tents.

Both the above places provide meals, boat transfers and opportunities for fishing and sailboarding. To stay at either place you must first make a reservation through the appropriate hotel in St-Louis.

Getting There & Away The usual approach is by boat from the mainland, normally from Gandiol or Mouit. Another option is to join an organised tour from St-Louis – see Getting Around under St-Louis earlier in this chapter for more details.

Parc National des Oiseaux du Djoudj

This park *(admission CFA2000 per person, plus CFA5000 per car; open 7am-dusk daily)* is 60km north of St-Louis, on a great bend in the Senegal River, incorporating a stretch of the main river, with numerous channels, creeks, lakes, ponds, marshes, reedbeds and mud flats, plus surrounding areas of dry woodland savanna. This, along with the fact that it's one of the first places with permanent water south of the Sahara, means that a great many bird species are attracted here, making it a sanctuary of global significance. It is a Unesco World Heritage site, and the wetlands have been listed as a Ramsar (the international wetland conservation convention) site.

The park is most famous for its vast flocks of pelicans and flamingos, and many people come here on tours from St-Louis purely to see these intriguing birds. Even if you have no interest in ornithology, observing birds at such close quarters is fascinating. Other easily recognisable species include spur-winged geese, purple herons, egrets, spoonbills, jaçanas, cormorants and harriers. From November to April, various migrants from Europe, especially waders, arrive. Keen bird-watchers will recognise many of the European species but the sheer numbers that assemble here are very impressive. Around three million individual birds pass through the park annually, and almost 400 separate species have been recorded here.

There are also a few mammals and reptiles in the park, most notably populations of warthogs and mongooses and a famously large python that lurks by the edge of the lake. Other mammals you might be able to spot here include jackals, hyenas, monkeys and gazelles.

To see the pelican colony you need to take a boat ride; this costs CFA3000 per person for a standard two-hour trip. The park can be visited at any time of year, but it's only officially open from 1 November to 30 April. At other times someone will be there to take your money, but there's little to see and there are no boat rides.

Places to Stay At the park headquarters and main entrance, *Hostellerie du Djoudj* (☎ 963 87 02, fax 963 87 03) has a swimming pool (open to nonguests if you eat at the hotel), nice gardens and comfortable rooms. Singles/doubles are CFA22,600/ 30,000 and it is open 1 November to 31

May. Breakfast costs CFA2000, the *menu de jour* is CFA7000 and snacks and sandwiches about CFA2500. You can arrange boat rides, although to explore beyond the standard pelican colony route will require you to charter a boat – around CFA10,000 per hour. Lifts in the hotel vehicle cost CFA20,000 for three hours, but simple drop-offs and pick-ups can be negotiated. They also have mountain bikes for hire. Bookings can be made direct or at the Club de Calao in Yoff.

Station Biologique Rooms CFA6500 per person. Situated at the park headquarters and main entrance, this low-key camp with clean rooms is mainly for research groups, but is also open to the public. Camping is allowed and decent meals cost CFA3500, or you can eat at the Hostellerie.

Getting There & Away Most visitors reach the park on an organised tour or with a local guide (see Getting Around under St-Louis earlier in this chapter). You can also hire a taxi from St-Louis for about four hours for CFA7000. If you're driving from St-Louis, take the paved highway towards Rosso for about 25km. Near Ross-Béthio you'll see a sign pointing to the park, which is about 25km further along dirt tracks.

Travellers have also reported that it's possible to join a tour from St-Louis, but rather than return with the group stay in the park for a few days and then hitch a ride out with other tourists.

SENEGAL

Birds & Tours

The tours offered by companies, hotels and guides in St-Louis to Parc National des Oiseaux du Djoudj all follow the same pattern, leaving at around 7am to reach the park by 8.30am. First they drive to the jetty for a two-hour boat ride through the creeks, the highlight and sole purpose of which is to view the enormous pelican colony. After lunch you drive to see flamingo flocks on the lake's edge.

Trying to do something 'unusual' will cause all manner of confusion and, notwithstanding Djoudj's status as one of the most important bird reserves on earth, there is no real setup for ornithologists. Keen bird-watchers hoping to see a good range of species on an organised day trip from St-Louis are likely to find the visit quite frustrating. A better option might be to forget the local guides and hire your own taxi, or spend several days exploring the national park alone – either on foot, rented bike, chartered boat, or all three. There's no map, but the park staff will be able to point you in the right direction.

Senegal River Route

The Senegal River marks the country's northern and eastern borders. In the mid-19th century, French colonial forces built a chain of forts – Dagana, Podor, Matam, Bakel, and Kayes (in today's Mali) – to defend their territory against the army of Omar Taal and others opposed to French expansion. Around the forts grew towns and trading centres, which later developed into major settlements, linked by boats plying the river between St-Louis and Kayes.

Today, most traffic uses the main road that runs parallel to the river (yet it is rarely close enough so that you actually see it), although it is still possible to travel along sections of the river by pirogue. Apart from a few small sections, this road is smooth all the way from St-Louis to Tambacounda, though there's not much petrol along some stretches.

This is as near to the desert as you can get in Senegal. The landscape is dry and the vegetation sparse. Sand drifts across the road, and the traditional banco houses would blend almost completely into the background were it not for the local Tukulor custom of decorating the outer walls in bold stripes of red, brown and yellow. To an independent traveller, it could seem a lonely route. But precisely because of the vast open spaces, the welcoming Fula population and the lack of tourists, a slow journey along the Senegal River route could be the most rewarding aspect of your visit.

ROSSO-SENEGAL

The fly-blown frontier town of Rosso-Senegal is around 100km northeast of St-Louis on the Senegal River, where a ferry crosses to Rosso-Mauritania. This ferry is the main route between the two countries (see Senegal's Getting There & Away chapter). The main street is full of hustlers, smugglers, moneychangers and minibus touts, and most travellers entering the country from Mauritania jump straight on the first transport out of town, escaping the melee as soon as possible.

If you get stuck, your only choice of accommodation is *Auberge du Walo* 2km from the ferry. Basic double huts with bathroom are CFA8000. There's no running water and although this place also claims to be a restaurant-bar-patisserie, meals are only prepared on order and there's not a beer or cake in sight.

The journey to Dakar costs CFA4950 by Peugeot taxi, CFA3880 by minibus and CFA3440 by Alham. To St-Louis the fare is CFA1540 by Peugeot taxi and CFA1070 by Alham. A local bush taxi to Richard Toll costs CFA300. For more information on crossing the border see Senegal's Getting There & Away chapter.

RICHARD TOLL

About 20km by road from Rosso is the town of Richard Toll, once a colonial administrative centre and today the headquarters of

Château de Baron Roger

Baron Jacques Roger was the governor of Senegal in the 1830s, and built this château as a weekend retreat on the banks of the Taouey River, a tributary of the Senegal River, some 100km upriver from St-Louis, the colonial capital. The surrounding ornamental park (which now resembles a jungle) was laid out by Claude Richard, who also helped introduce groundnut plantations to the region; hence the name Richard Toll, which means Richard's Garden. Later inhabitants of the château included Roger's successor, Louis Faidherbe. It was also used as a monastery and school, and is now apparently home to a few families.

Sadly, it is in a very bad state of repair but worth visiting for a glimpse into the colonial past, and the views from the rooftop. You should be able to walk around outside at any time, but to get inside come after midday. You might be asked for a small *cadeau* (donation).

Senegal's sugar industry. You'll pass great cane plantations as you come into town from the west. There's little of interest, but if you stay overnight here, an evening stroll to the **Château de Baron Roger** at the eastern end of town, across the bridge, whiles away an hour or two (see the boxed text 'Château de Baron Roger'). You can change money in the CBAO bank on the main street, opposite the gare.

Cheap places to stay seem nonexistent. The ***Hotel la Taouey*** *(☎ 963 34 31)* on the river, north of the main street, has adequate but bare singles/doubles for CFA13,600/16,800. The ***Gîte d'Étape*** *(☎ 963 36 08)*, down a dirt road opposite the gare, occupies one of the most beautiful positions on the whole river, though the rooms are overpriced at CFA22,600/26,500 and have dodgy air-con.

On the main street are several eateries. ***Restaurant la St-Louisiane*** *(☎ 963 9467)* serves *mafé* (thick brown groundnut sauce), fish and rice (both CFA400) and couscous with beef (CFA800), while ***Ker Mimichon*** does chicken meals for CFA1500.

PODOR & ÎLE À MORPHIL

On the Senegal River, at the northernmost point of the country, Podor was an important settlement in the colonial era, but it's off the main road and fairly insignificant these days. There's a large fort, several old military buildings and a lycée – still in use despite its ageing years, but only fans of history and colonial architecture will get excited here.

The place to stay is the ***Gîte de Douwaya*** *(☎ 630 1751)*. Opposite the gare routière, this place is owned by famous musician Baaba Maal, who hails from Podor, and is run by his friendly English-speaking cousin. Clean double rooms are CFA8000 and come with breakfast ... if the cook can be found. The only bar in town is also here and there's music and dancing at weekends. The *hôtel de ville* (town hall) also has a couple of air-con rooms for CFA7500.

To get to Podor turn off the main road about 100km east of Richard Toll at the village of Treji (also spelt Tredji or Taredji). About 10km down this road on your right,

in the village of Wouro Madiyou, there is a mosque and ruined **mausoleum**. About 2km past here the road crosses a bridge, on to a long thin island called **Île à Morphil** (see the boxed text 'Île à Morphil').

An occasional Peugeot taxi travels between Podor and St-Louis (CFA3100, four hours, 262km) sometimes continuing all the way to Dakar (CFA6000). The alternative is to get a local bush taxi to the main road at Treji (CFA375), and then take an Alham to Richard Toll for CFA1500 or St-Louis for CFA2500. If you're heading west, a Peugeot taxi to Ouro Sogui (CFA4000, five hours, 222km) is best; a minibus costs CFA2000 but takes twice as long.

MATAM & OURO SOGUI

Matam is 230km southeast of Podor, and Ouro Sogui is at the junction where the road to Matam tuns off the main road. The road between the two runs 11km along the top of

---

Île à Morphil

Île à Morphil is a long thin island between the main Senegal River and a major channel that runs parallel to it for over 100km. Podor is at the western end of this island. About 2km after the bridge on the road into town, a dirt road turns off right (east), and a signpost indicates distances to a string of villages along Île à Morphil, all the way to Saldé at it's eastern end, where a ferry crosses over to Ngoui on the mainland, from where you can reach Pete, on the main road.

Travellers with wheels and plenty of time have reported that this is an interesting route, and that the traditional villages of Guede and Alwar are particularly scenic. At the village of Ndiom you can cross south onto the mainland to reach a 'new town' (also called Ndiom) not shown on most maps, which boasts petrol stations, a market, new mosque and hospital, and a *campement* (inn) under construction. From Île à Morphil it's also possible to cross into Mauritania at the Bogué ferry, about halfway along the island which – although a roundabout route – avoids the hassle at Rosso.

SENEGAL

a causeway with plains and marshes on either side, which are frequently flooded in the wet season. Over the years Matam has declined, while Ouro Sogui has grown into a lively trading centre and transport hub for the Senegal River route and the Ferlo plains. Ouro Sogui even has two banks, both of which looked like they were having ATMs installed when we passed. In contrast, Matam has been left to decay, a fact that has resulted in rioting on more than one occasion.

Matam's waterfront is a testimony to busy days gone by, with several old warehouses and a large sloping quay topped with bollards where riverboats once moored. But today there's little left of the fort and not even a hotel, although the government lodging at the *préfecture* has been known to take guests.

In Ouro Sogui, the best-value accommodation is the *Auberge Sogui* (☎ 966 11 98) opposite the market, which has just-passable rooms without/with air-con for CFA5000/7500, though the shared bathrooms are grubby. Don't confuse this with the *Hotel Auberge Sogui* (☎ 966 15 36), a huge white monolith with air-con doubles for CFA15,500. Opposite is the *Hotel Oasis* (☎ 966 12 94) with musty singles/doubles for CFA10,500/12,500 and an adjoining Internet bureau. There are several cheap eateries on the same street including *Restaurant Teddoungal* where beef and spaghetti costs CFA1000, and some good *dibieteries* (grilled-meat stall). If you're around at the weekend ask about the soiree at the lycée.

Ouro Sogui's gare routière is on the northern side of town, on the road towards Matam. Battered Peugeot taxis run to Dakar (CFA9250) and Bakel (CFA4000, two hours, 148km); or an Alham costs CFA2600.

If you look at any map of Senegal there is a road leading from Ouro Sogui southwards across the Ferlo plains to the remote town of Linguère. Unfortunately, this road is pretty bad and no sane-minded individual should attempt it without the aid of a 4WD. There is no public transport. If you do get to Linguère a tar road continues to Touba and Diourbel from where Dakar or Kaolack are within easy reach.

BAKEL

Bakel is 150km from Matam, and really in eastern Senegal, although still very much with a feel of the north: hot, dry and sandy. Of all the towns along the river, Bakel is the most interesting, a picturesque place set among a scattering of rocky hills with several colonial buildings. The prefecture in the old fort overlooking the river is still in good condition. Officially, it's closed to the public but not many tourists come here and management seems happy to allow people to wander around. The large octagonal lookout tower at the southern edge of town and the nearby military cemetery are easily reached, but sadly the stairway inside the tower has been stolen and only the bravest soul will be able to reach the top. The abandoned Pavilion René Caillé, on a hill next to two large water tanks, gives great views over the town.

Places to Stay & Eat

The *Hôtel Islam*, about 500m east of the gare routière, has spartan rooms for CFA3000 per person, but add a noisy air-conditioner (which you might well need in Bakel) and the price skyrockets to CFA10,000/20,000. Shoestringers might be able to sleep on the roof. The restaurant serves rice and sauce for CFA400 or *ragout de mouton* (mutton stew) for CFA750.

About 2km from the centre on the riverfront the *Hotel Ma Coumba* (Hotel Boundou, ☎ 983 51 08) is better, but still pretty spartan. All rooms are CFA10,000 with air-con and bathroom.

The street between the main tar road and the Hotel Islam is lined with *restaurants*, *dibieteries* and *food stalls*, and the grass hut near the entrance to the gare routière does excellent coffee as well as egg sandwiches.

On the waterfront is *Bar-Resto Mbodick* (☎ 937 9031, mobile 654 4623), the only watering hole in town that also serves meals to order for CFA1500. The patron, Mamadou Loum, can provide information about boats going up and down the river.

Getting There & Away

If you come from Ouro Sogui on a vehicle bound for Kidira you might be dropped off at the junction 5km south of Bakel, from where local bush taxis shuttle into town. At 4.30am, except on Fridays an express bus *(car mouride)* leaves Bakel from the petrol station at the entrance to town for the border town of Kidira (CFA1000, one hour, 60km), and on to Tambacounda (CFA3000, four hours, 184km). Be there early (yes, by 4am) or you won't get a seat. Other vehicles leave when they're full, which could take a while.

For the adventurous, motorised pirogues go between Matam, Bakel and Kayes, leaving Bakel from the 'port' near the Bar-Resto Mbodick every couple of days. This is also where ferries cross the river to Mauritania, and the police/customs post is here. Some boats also go to Matam and Kidira. There is no set schedule – you just have to ask around.

KIDIRA

The main crossing point between Senegal and Mali is the border town of Kidira, where the main road and the railway between Dakar and Bamako cross the Falene River, marking the frontier between the two countries. Most travellers cross the border by train, but an increasingly popular road option is possible. For more details see Mali in Senegal's Getting There & Away chapter. If you get stuck in Kidira a reader reports that there is a *campement (☎ 983 71 65)* just out of town.

Eastern Senegal

Eastern Senegal is hot and flat, with a savanna landscape covered by bush and baobab trees. In the far southeast the plains give way to the rolling foothills of Fouta Djalon in neighbouring Guinea. For many years, the region's main attraction has been Parc National de Niokolo-Koba – one of the largest parks in West Africa. There's a higher chance of seeing large mammals here than anywhere else in Senegal. The town of Kedougou has also become a popular base from which to explore the rugged hills and picturesque villages of Bassari country, an area that contrasts strikingly with other parts of the country.

TAMBACOUNDA

Tambacounda lies at a major crossroads with routes leading east to Mali, south to Guinea, west to Dakar and Gambia, and southwest to Ziguinchor. 'Tamba' is also the main jumping-off point for visits to Parc National de Niokolo-Koba and the increasingly popular Bassari area in the far southeast of the country. There's not much to see in Tamba itself, but if you're a history or railway fan it's worth wandering around the train station and the three blocks to the north, where once-grand French-era villas share space with expansive but neglected gardens.

The town has two main streets: Blvd Demba Diop runs east-west, parallel with the train tracks; and Av Léopold Senghor (usually shortened to Av Senghor) runs north-south. The latter has shops, an Internet bureau and the SGBS bank, which can exchange money and give cash advances on credit cards.

There are two *garages* (as the bus stations are known in Tambacounda) – one on the eastern side of town for vehicles headed towards Kidira and the Mali border, and a larger one on the southern side (west of Av Senghor) for most other destinations. The latter place swarms with touts, so watch your gear carefully.

Highlights

- Search for wildlife in the varied habitats of Parc National de Niokolo-Koba, Senegal's largest park
- Cool off under a mountain waterfall at Dindefelo in the hills of Bassari country

All taxi trips around town, for example from the train station to the southern garage, cost CFA250.

Places to Stay

Apart from Chez Dessert, these hotels all run tours to Parc National de Niokolo-Koba (see Organised Tours under Parc National de Niokolo-Koba later in this chapter).

Chez Dessert (☎ 981 16 42, Av Senghor) Rooms CFA3000 per person. A shoe-stringers' favourite for many years, this place has changed hands but still offers simple rooms, some very simple, and a small kitchen where you can prepare your own food.

Hôtel Niji (☎ 981 12 59, fax 981 17 44, e nijihotel@sentoo.sn) Singles/doubles CFA11,200/14,000. Just off Av Senghor, this place has fair fan rooms with bathroom; air-con is an extra CFA4000. It also runs *Hôtel*

Niji Annexe, which has thatched round houses in a shady garden compound.

Hôtel Asta Kébé (☎ 981 10 28, fax 981 12 15, e astakebe@metissicana.sn) Singles/doubles with air-con CFA16,000/21,000. This place is the best in town, but that's not saying much. However, it does have a swimming pool that nonguests can use for CFA1500, and fan rooms are a lot cheaper.

Hôtel Keur Khoudia (☎/fax 981 11 02) Singles/doubles CFA11,700/16,000. West of the centre, this establishment offers decent bungalows with bathroom and air-con, as well as extremely lethargic management. Breakfast is CFA1200.

You can often find people waiting at the south garage to offer *private rooms* for rent.

Places to Eat & Drink

There's a wide choice of *gargottes* and other cheap eateries at the main garage. You should be able to find something you like at *Chez Eva*, *Chez Asta* or *Chez Fatima*, all in a row on Blvd Demba Diop just west of the train station. They serve an interesting mix of local meals for CFA500 to CFA2000, and Asta claims she serves beer 24 hours.

The *Bar-Restaurant Chez Francis (☎ 643 12 31)* on Av Senghor is the most popular spot in town, with excellent steak and chips for CFA3000 and cheap, ice-cold beer. *La Hortencia*, near the train station, does the best salads in town, while *Chez Kadeyssa*, just off Av Senghor, does the best sandwiches. Opposite the southern garage is *Chez Nanette* (open from 8am to midnight daily), another favourite, with local dishes plus meals such as spaghetti for about CFA1500.

For drinking, *Le Ninkinanka (☎ 636 00 46)*, on Av Senghor, is small but very friendly and is a great place to sip a beer while watching the world go by. In stark contrast is the outlandishly large *Complex Leggaal Pont (☎ 981 77 56)*, east of the centre on Blvd Demba Diop, which has a restaurant (open 8am to midnight daily), a bar (open 11am to 4am daily) and a very popular nightclub (open 11pm to 4am daily), which gets quite heated at times.

Getting There & Away

Bus & Bush Taxi From the *garage* on the eastern side of town vehicles go to the Mali border at Kidira (CFA4000 by Peugeot taxi, three hours; CFA2700 by minibus or

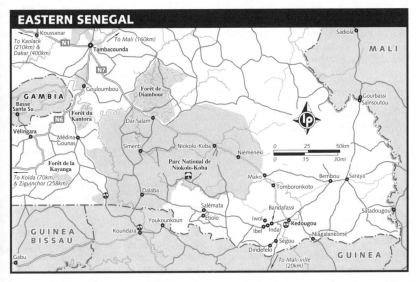

TAMBACOUNDA

PLACES TO STAY
16 Hôtel Niji
17 Hôtel Niji Annexe
18 Hôtel Asta Kébé
22 Chez Dessert

PLACES TO EAT
2 La Hortencia
5 Chez Eva; Chez Asta;
   Chez Fatima
11 Bar-Restaurant Chez Francis

12 Chez Kadeyssa
20 Chez Nanette

OTHER
1 Post Office
3 Petrol Station
4 Petrol Station
6 Police
7 Complex Leggaal Pont
8 Car Mouride Bus Stop
   & Ticket Office
9 SGBS Bank
10 Internet Bureau
13 Petrol Station
14 Garage
15 Pharmacy
19 Bakery
21 Le Ninkinanka

To Hôtel Keur Khoudia (100m) & Dakar (467km)

Public Garden

Market

Blvd Demba Diop

Train Station

To Garage for Buses to Kidira (900m), Parc National de Niokolo-Koba Office (1km) & Kidira (186km)

Av Léopold Senghor

Blvd Kandioura Noba

River (seasonal)

0   200   400m
0   200   400yd
Some Minor Roads not Depicted

To Vélingara (90km) & Kedougou (243km)

get on the bus in the order they bought tickets. The first 40 or so get good seats but latecomers end up on stools in the aisle. The express bus also goes to Kidira (CFA2000, three hours, daily except Friday) and Kedougou (CFA2500, three hours, daily except Wednesday).

For details on transport to/from Guinea, see Senegal's Getting There & Away chapter.

Train The express train between Dakar and Bamako (Mali) passes through Tambacounda four times a week – twice in each direction (see the Getting There & Away chapter). The eastbound train passes through on Wednesday and Saturday evening; the timetable says it departs at 7.05pm, but it's usually nearer 9pm. Officially, a section of seating is reserved for passengers who board at Tamba. In reality, 2nd class is nearly always full, but 1st-class tickets are usually available. The ticket office opens a few hours before the train arrives, but tickets can sometimes be bought the day before. If you get really stuck, look out for touts selling unused tickets on the platform. Fares from Tambacounda are:

destination	1st class (CFA)	2nd class (CFA)
Kayes	8060	10,995
Kita	14,710	10,970
Bamako	19,320	14,165

PARC NATIONAL DE NIOKOLO-KOBA

Niokolo-Koba, a beautiful area of wilderness covering about 900,000 hectares, is Senegal's major national park. The landscape is relatively flat, with plains which become marshy after rain, and is interspersed with small hills – the highest is Mt Assirik in the southeast. The park is transected by the Gambia River, a vital water source for the park's animals, along with two tributaries – the Niokolo-Koba and the Koulountou. Vegetation is spectacularly varied; dry savanna woodland and grassland, gallery forest along the rivers, and patches of bamboo, ponds and marshes. Niokolo-Koba's global importance is recognised by

Alham). Vehicles to most other destinations go from the larger garage on the southern side of town. A minibus to Vélingara is CFA1000, from where you can cross into Gambia. To Dakar by Peugeot taxi is CFA6800, and by Alham CFA4400; and a Peugeot taxi to Kedougou is CFA3500, and to Koalack is CFA3000.

The express bus (car mouride) leaves from outside the Transport Alzhar ticket office daily at 4.30am sharp for Kaolack (CFA2500, five hours) and Dakar (CFA4000, eight hours), but buy a ticket early the day before. Names are called out and passengers its designation as a World Heritage site, as well as an international biosphere reserve.

Some 350 species of birds and about 80 species of mammals inhabit the park. African classics such as lions (about 500) and leopards are here but, apart from the leopards in the enclosure near Simenti, are very rarely seen. Depending on who you believe, by early 2002 the number of elephants in the park was either none or 15. This could change, as 11 elephants were due to be airlifted in from Burkina Faso in May 2002 as part of a project sponsored by USAID aimed at repopulating the park.

You do have a good chance of spotting waterbucks, bushbucks, kobs, duikers, baboons, monkeys (green and patas), warthogs, roan antelopes, giant Derby elands, hartebeests and possibly buffaloes. Chimpanzee troops are occasionally seen in the eastern and southern part of the park. Hippos and three types of crocodiles – the Nile, the slender-snouted and the dwarf – live in the rivers.

The park was neglected until the early 1990s, and poaching has also been a problem, but recent international funding for development as part of the Parc Transfrontalier Niokolo-Badiar transnational ecosystem (which includes areas in neighbouring Guinea) has improved the situation. Several NGOs are also working directly with the surrounding populations to help conserve the resources found in the park, such as ronier palms and bamboo.

A glossy visitor guide is available at the park entrance, with a park map and illustrations of some of the wildlife you could see. However, it's in French and costs CFA6000.

Information
Dar Salam is the main park entrance gate for tourists on the main road between Tambacounda and Kedougou. (The park does have a few other entrance gates, but these are hard to reach and rarely used.) The focus of Niokolo-Koba is Simenti, about

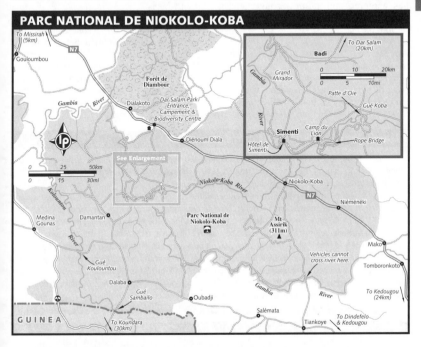

one hour's drive south from Dar Salam. A park office, visitor information centre (which has a rather forlorn exhibition) and the large Hôtel de Simenti are here. Many animals are concentrated around the Simenti area, although a wider selection can be found in the eastern sector of the park.

Details about track conditions and other aspects of the park can be obtained from the park headquarters in Tambacounda (☎ 981 10 97). Plans for a Dar Salam Biodiversity Centre were also being realised at the time of writing.

When to Visit Parc National de Niokolo-Koba is officially open from 15 December to 30 April, though you can visit any time. During the rains, and until late November, most park tracks are impassable without a 4WD. In December and January, conditions are pleasantly cool, but the best viewing time for wildlife is during the hot season (April-May) when the vegetation has withered and animals congregate at water holes. The park gates are open 7am to 6pm daily.

Access You must have a vehicle to enter the park, and walking is not allowed, except near accommodation sites or in the company of a park ranger. Travellers without a car can visit the park using public transport, taxis or an organised tour. All tracks, except those between the park gate and the Simenti area, require a 4WD, even in the dry season.

Fees & Guides The entrance fee is CFA2000 per person and CFA5000 per vehicle for 24 hours. Park-approved guides can be hired at the gate or Simenti for a standard CFA6000 per day. These guys have all completed a training course, but only a couple have any extensive knowledge of birds and animals (though this is now changing).

Places to Stay & Eat

At the main park entrance, *Dar Salam Campement (☎ 981 25 75)* has clean bungalows with bathroom for CFA6600, or camping for CFA3000 per tent. Meals, such as the cross-cultural spaghetti with beef yassa (CFA3500), are also available. Camping is permitted inside the park, but there are no facilities at all; campers must be fully self-sufficient and that means having your own wheels.

Most people choose to stay at *Hôtel de Simenti (☎ 982 36 50)*, a concrete monstrosity that would look more at home in an East London estate than this pristine wilderness. However, it is in a spectacular position overlooking the Gambia River. Ramshackle huts that suit one or two people are CFA7000, singles/ doubles with air-con are CFA15,000/ 20,000, and full board is CFA25,845/41,140.

Dar Salam Biodiversity Centre

For years trying to get information about Niokolo-Koba has been only marginally easier than spotting the park's elusive elephants. But that is set to change with the opening of the Dar Salam Biodiversity Centre at the park entrance in mid-2002.

Funded by the United Nations and developed with the help of the US Peace Corps, the centre is designed to provide information to tourists, and to educate communities in surrounding villages in how best to exploit their proximity to the park while at the same time conserving its biodiversity.

From a visitor's point of view, there will be displays of plants and animals (both alive and dead), guided plant and bird walks and discussions, traditional dance ceremonies and an artisinal boutique where your money can go directly into the community when you buy a souvenir. For their part the villagers will be trained in natural resource management and forest-fire prevention, and students will come from schools far and wide. The centre will need your support to survive so make a point of stopping, or asking your guide to stop, to check it out.

Thanks to Peace Corps Volunteer Jamie Lovett for information on the Biodiversity Centre

You can travel throughout Senegambia on various forms of public transport, including the *car rapide* (middle left) – its slowness belies its name. The best way to explore this wonderful region, especially watery wonderlands such as the Baobalong Wetland Reserve (bottom), is by boat.

Don't miss a chance to ride in a pirogue, whether touring the palm groves in the Casamance River estuary (top), exploring the mangrove-lined banks of a Gambia River *bolong* (creek; middle) or paddling in the shallows just outside Dakar (bottom)

Niokolo-Koba Guides

While the knowledge of the Niokolo-Koba guides is slowly improving, most are still some way short of their counterparts in East and Southern Africa. However, there are a couple of exceptions. One is Ibrahima Kouyate, who has been guiding in the park for 13 years and has amazing knowledge of animals, birds and their habitats, but speaks only French. Another is Sekhou Dabo, the only guide who speaks English, who, while relatively new to guiding, has had several good reports. Both are based at Dar Salam and, as the village has no phones, can be difficult to find. Your best bet is to ask for them in the Dar Salam Biodiversity Centre at the park gate.

Otherwise breakfast is CFA2000, and filling meals are served for CFA5000. The hotel organises half-day drives for CFA6500 per person (minimum of four people), and the nearby visitor centre offers boat rides for CFA3500 per person, or walks in the bush with a ranger for about CFA3000, depending on your powers of negotiation.

You can also walk to a nearby hide overlooking a water hole/grazing area (depending on the season), where you'll almost certainly see as many animals as you would from the back of a vehicle. If your visit is between mid-June and mid-December you'll need to book ahead if you want a room ready when you arrive.

Camp du Lion is a small campement 6km east of Simenti in a beautiful spot in the bush beside the Gambia River. Very simple huts are available for CFA7000 and camp sites are CFA3000. Meals are CFA3500. This place is reachable in an ordinary car and it has a 4WD for excursions at CFA6000 per person for half a day. You can also walk to the nearby Pointe de Vue, where hippo and other animals can be sighted drinking on the opposite bank of the river.

The town of Kedougou can also be used as a base for visiting the park (see Bassari Country later in this chapter).

Organised Tours

Four- or five-day all-inclusive tours from Dakar to Niokolo-Koba range from about CFA150,000 to CFA200,000 per person, with a minimum of four to six people (see Organised Tours in Senegal's Getting Around chapter for more details). However, most visitors choose one of the following options from Tambacounda.

Hotels The Hôtel Niji in Tambacounda will rent you a 4WD for CFA75,000 for one day, CFA125,000 for two days and CFA50,000 for every day thereafter. This includes fuel, driver/guide and admission for the car, while you pay for your park fees, food and accommodation.

Local Taxi You can hire a taxi for one or more days. City taxis are generally old wrecks and unlikely to make it. The Peugeot taxis are more reliable and have higher clearance, which will get you as far as Simenti, Camp du Lion and the main central area (to see more park and animals you will need a 4WD).

Taxi prices will vary enormously. Some drivers quote CFA50,000 per day, but CFA30,000 including fuel is a more reasonable rate. We've heard from other travellers who have haggled longer and harder and paid CFA20,000 per day. Remember to allow for all the other costs involved (eg, admission, guides etc). The driver should pay for his own food and accommodation (the campement doesn't charge drivers).

If you don't want to launch headlong into haggling for taxis, seek out the *chef du garage* (a sort of manager-cum-Mr Fixit). He will find you a driver who you can then negotiate with. Carefully check the taxi's condition, and if the rains have recently finished, it's a good idea to call in at the park headquarters to ensure the track to Simenti is passable by 2WD.

Getting There & Away

To reach the park by public transport, take a Kedougou minibus from Tambacounda and get off at the Dar Salam park entrance. The fare is sometimes CFA1000, but you'll usually have to pay the full Kedougou price (CFA3500). From Dar Salam, you'll have to hitch to Simenti with a tourist or park vehicle, and these can be few and far between. Failing that, from the park gate you can radio Hôtel de Simenti to send their 4WD (CFA15,000 one way). There is also an official transfer available between the Hôtel Keur Khoudia in Tamba and Hôtel de Simenti (same management), which costs CFA60,000 per car return.

Getting Around

Simenti is the best place to base yourself if you don't have a car. The Hôtel de Simenti organises half-day 4WD safaris for CFA6500 per person (minimum of four people), and the nearby visitor centre offers morning or evening boat rides for CFA3500 per person or walks in the bush with a ranger for CFA2500 to CFA3500.

From the visitor centre, a path leads for a few hundred metres to a hide overlooking a water hole/grazing area (depending on the season). You are likely to see as many animals here as from the back of a 4WD.

BASSARI COUNTRY

The far southeast corner of Senegal is often called Bassari country after the local Bassari people, who are particularly noted for their traditional way of life and picturesque villages. The Bassari often feature on tour itineraries, but they are in fact just one of many tribes who inhabit this area. Other groups include Fula, Wolof, Bambara, Malinké and Bedik.

The landscape is hilly. It's actually a northern extension of the Fouta Djalon hills in neighbouring Guinea, and is well vegetated, making it a pleasant contrast to the hot and dusty plains found elsewhere in Senegal. The Fouta Djalon is where the region's major rivers (the Senegal, Gambia and Casamance) rise, and is also the source of West Africa's greatest river – the Niger.

The landscape has made Bassari country a popular destination for hiking, biking and motorcycling. Specialist tour companies in Dakar are arranging trips and ever-growing numbers of adventurous travellers have

started to come this way. The base for finding guides and making arrangements is Kedougou. Only a few years ago, you would have had a hard time trying to explain to a local why you wanted to go walking in the bush to the tops of nearby hills. Now the guides find you.

Kedougou

Kedougou is the largest town in southeast Senegal. It has lost some of its remote feel now that a tar road from Tambacounda links it to the rest of the country. Before this road was built Kedougou seemed to have as much in common with Guinea (the border is only 30km to the south) as it did with the rest of Senegal. But now Dakar is within a long day's journey, and while the dirt roads through the Fouta Djalon still remain some of the worst in West Africa, gradually Kedougou is turning to face Senegal.

The colourful market is famous for its indigo fabrics, many of them from Guinea, which sell for half the price asked in Dakar. Other facilities include a petrol station, several *télécentres* and Internet access for CFA3000 an hour at the Kedougou Multi-Service. There's also the blue-fronted Alimentation de Dioubo (☎ 985 11 90), where English-speaking 'Darryl' has a well-earned reputation for running the best little supermarket in town, and is a mine of information on the local area and how best to get around. All of these places are on or near the main street, which is also home to the *gare routière*.

Places to Stay & Eat These places all arrange tours in the surrounding area or to Parc National de Niokolo-Koba.

Campement Diaw (☎ 985 11 24) Doubles without/with air-con CFA6,000/12,000. This campement is east of the garage and offers accommodation in huts. The shared bathrooms are clean, the atmosphere is tranquil and the food is good value (breakfast CFA1000; meals CFA3000).

Campement Moïse (☎ 985 11 39) About 200m down the street opposite the garage, this small and friendly place has clean rooms at the same price as Diaw. It also has a 4WD and a rare 250cc trail bike for hire.

Relais de Kedougou (☎ 985 10 62, fax 985 11 26) Doubles without/with air-con CFA9,000/16,000. This is a more upmarket, French-run place in a picturesque riverside setting that attracts mostly hunters. Breakfast costs CFA1800 and other meals (CFA5500) can be eaten by the pool.

Hippo Lodge Safari Huts without/with bathroom CFA4000/6000. About 5km east of town, this lodge is owned by the Relais and is on an even more beautiful bend in the river. The huts, bar and restaurant are very tastefully decorated, the only potential drawback here being the distance from town.

All the accommodation places serve food, otherwise there's a good choice of *cheap eateries* around the market and garage – try the bean sandwiches (CFA150). Sunset drinks are often taken on benches outside the Alimentation de Dioubo. Most other drinking is done in the hotel bars, or later at the back of the market in *Bar Africa (☎ 985 13 95)*, *the* nightspot in Kedougou.

Getting There & Away The fare between Tambacounda and Kedougou is CFA2000 in a minibus, CFA2500 in the express bus that leaves at 5am except on Wednesday, and CFA3500 in a Peugeot taxi. The main road (a source of great controversy when it was widened and tarred) passes straight through Parc National de Niokolo-Koba, but park fees are not payable if you are in transit.

If you're travelling towards Mali, there's no regular public transport, but occasional intrepid overland drivers sometimes go this way. Complete all your exit formalities in Kedougou, as the border post on the route to Kéniéba is unreliable.

If you're heading for Guinea, there's an occasional 4WD or 'dump truck' from Kedougou to the town of Mali (called Mali-ville to distinguish it from the country) for CFA6000, from where a Peugeot taxi to Labé is CFA5000. The truck can take several days to fill with passengers, and the journey itself takes at least 24 hours. Trucks leave more frequently straight after the rainy season, and might also leave from Ségou. Alternatively, you could walk or ride a bike – see the boxed text 'Hiking & Biking to Guinea'.

Around Kedougou

Kedougou makes an excellent base for visits to the many traditional villages in the surrounding hills.. They are accessible by foot, bush taxi or a combination of the two. Bikes can also be hired at some of the campements (around CFA1500 per day), but most of these are heavy steel roadsters.

One of the nearest villages is **Bandafassi**, actually the capital of Kedougou district, even though it's smaller than Kedougou town. The inhabitants are mainly Fula and Bassari, and the village is renowned for its basket-makers. There's a shop selling cold drinks where you can refuel before hiking to the top of the hill overlooking the village, which has wonderful views over the surrounding savanna. About 2km further west is the tiny village of **Indar**, a Bedik village where there is a small *campement* beside the road with traditional huts for CFA5000.

Ibel is a predominantly Fula village 7km southwest of Bandafassi. Local people often have huts in their compound which they're happy to let out, usually at less than camp rates. Otherwise head through town to the *Baobab de Ibel*, a sort of village campement with huts for CFA2500 per person. From Ibel it's another 2km uphill to the Bedik village of **Iwol**, dominated by a huge baobab tree the local people regard as sacred.

Continuing west from Ibel, you reach the village of **Salémata**, 83km from Kedougou. While Fulas are the predominant tribe in town, the villages in the spectacular surrounding hill country – at over 400m it's some of the highest ground around – are almost all Bassari. The best day to visit is Tuesday – when the *lumo* (weekly market) is held. Every year (usually in May) there's a major Bassari circumcision ceremony held here. A bush taxi from Kedougou is CFA1200.

Salémata has a small and friendly *campement*, where double huts with private shower are CFA7500 and meals cost around CFA3500. Steep prices, but you pay for the remote location. A good day walk from here takes you to the village of **Etiolo** (15km round trip).

One of the most popular destinations from Kedougou is the village of **Dindefelo**, 38km

SENEGAL

SENEGAL

Hiking & Biking to Guinea

We started from Dindefelo at 7.30am on a Sunday by paying two locals CFA500 for each bike to be carried to the top of the first hill, between Afia and Dande. From here we began biking for about 22km (mostly uphill) through crop fields, a few villages and many creeks. The scenery was beautiful. As we were only going for the night we bypassed the border control at Louga by keeping to the narrow trail – all the Senegalese know the way. The trail is also the shortest route to the village of Chiange, where we arrived after many punctures and gladly left our bikes in the chief's compound.

It was 3.30pm by now and we walked along a trail for about 13km up the mountainous Massif du Tamgué, all the way to Mali-ville. In places it's relatively steep, but from the plateau at the top the views were astounding. In the rainy season they say you can see all the way to the Gambia River and Kedougou. The path is easy to follow and runs across several plateaus and through several villages where there are always people around to help with directions. You can also see the Dame de Mali rock formation to the east of this trail. We eventually arrived at 9pm, having done the last couple of hours by flashlight.

The best day to go is Sunday, when about 50 people take the path for the huge market in Mali-ville. You need to be in good shape. We weren't carrying heavy bags, but we did carry lots of water and we also filtered water from the creeks we passed. If you're walking the whole way it will obviously take longer, but you shouldn't have any problem sleeping in a village along the way.

Vonnie Moler

southwest along a road via Ségou (32km) that is so bad it should only be attempted in 4WD or on some form of bike. There's a lumo held here on Sunday, making the village lively and ensuring there's plenty of transport allowing you to get there and back within a day. Alternatively, you can stay at the Casamance-style *village campement* (☎ mobile 658 87 07), sometimes called Campement de la Cascade, which offers simple cement huts for CFA2500 per person, bucket showers and an attractive thatched *paillote* (thatched hut) where visitors can eat meals (typically chicken and *fonio*, a type of grain) for around CFA2000 (pricey, yes, but the money goes to village projects).

From the campement you can hike 2km along a beautiful trail to a spectacular 100m waterfall with a deep, green pool at the bottom, wonderful for cooling off after your walk. The campement charges CFA500 to visit the falls, which also goes to village fund, and will probably insist you take a guide.

At the entrance to Dindifelo is a restaurant called *Africa Cascade* (☎ 985 13 04), or Chez Camara, where simple meals are CFA1500 and simple rooms cost CFA2000/3000.

From Dindifelo it's possible to hike into Guinea. We heard from two Peace Corps volunteers who combined pedal power and foot slog to do just that.

Casamance

Casamance is the region of Senegal south of Gambia. It differs geographically and culturally from the rest of the country, being a well-watered, relatively fertile area, where the majority of people are Diola (Jola) and non-Muslim.

The central feature, and one of the main attractions of the area, is the Casamance River. It features a labyrinth of picturesque creeks and lagoons and is dotted with small islands, areas of palm grove, forest, mangrove swamp and lush estuary vegetation. It is a perfect place to tour on foot, by bike or by pirogue. During the dry season it's a temporary home to millions of migratory birds. Another attraction is Cap Skiring, on the coast near the border with Guinea-Bissau, which has quite simply the finest beach in the country.

The gateway to the region is Ziguinchor, the small and accessible capital with a laid-back atmosphere, cheap hotels, and wide avenues bordered by flowering trees. From Ziguinchor Casamance divides into three main areas: Basse Casamance (Lower Casamance) is the area west of Ziguinchor and south of the river; Casamance Nord (North Casamance) is the area north of the river; and Haute Casamance (Upper Casamance) is the area east of Ziguinchor. A unique *campements rurals integrés* (CRI) system operates right across Casamance, allowing you to stay in local-style lodges, get an insight into traditional rural life and know that villagers will benefit directly from the money you spend.

If all this sounds too good to be true, well, it is. Casamance has been the subject of an on-again, off-again 20-year secession movement. As you'll read later, it's a war that was still in full swing when we researched this guide, and much of the tourism infrastructure has suffered as a result. Still, from a traveller's point of view, it's not a bad time to go: hotels are rarely full, the beaches are quiet and prices are outrageously low. Tourist numbers have

Highlights

- Swim by day and party by night at Cap Skiring, home to the best beaches in Senegal

- Explore the vast maze of creeks, lagoons and islands of the Casamance River

- Sleep in a converted mission (and drink in the chapel) on remote Île de Carabane

- Learn how to beat the Diola drum at one of Kafountine's lively beachside *campements*

- Live it up in Ziguinchor, the laid-back, great-value capital

been low for several years and some hotels and *campements* (inns) have shut or fallen into disrepair, while others have remained impressively spick-and-span. Some of the campements we have listed in this chapter were closed at the time of research, but are likely to reopen as things pick up. Staff at the hotels in Ziguinchor may be able to tell you which campements are open, otherwise ask at the CRI office there (see Ziguinchor later in this chapter for further information).

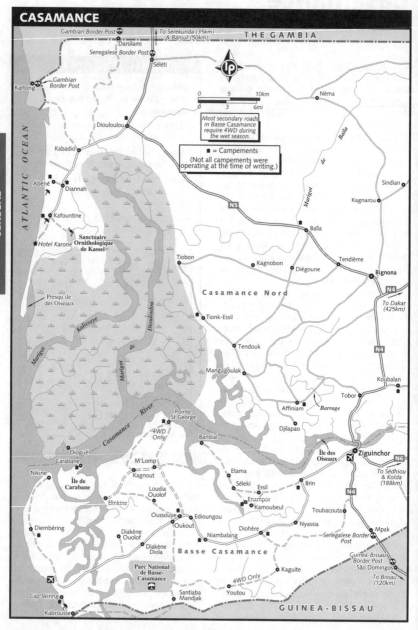

HISTORY

The Diola people of Casamance have a long history of resisting the rule of outsiders. It's a sentiment that underlined their outright rejection of slavery (both European and African), their refusal to accept France's colonial administration and the bloody war being waged by those seeking secession from Senegal.

In the 19th and early 20th centuries, the French colonial authorities controlled their territory through local chiefs. In Casamance, however, the Diola people do not have a hierarchical society and thus had no recognised leaders. The French, therefore, installed Mandinka chiefs to administer the Diola, but they were resented as much as the Europeans, and Diola resistance against foreign interference remained extremely strong well into the 1930s.

In 1943, the last Diola rebellion against the French was led by a traditional priestess called Aline Sitoe Diatta, from Kabrousse. The rebellion was put down and Aline Sitoe was imprisoned at the remote outpost of Timbuktu in neighbouring Mali, where she eventually died. She has been called the Casamance Joan of Arc, and for many years the Diola people of Kabrousse believed she would return and lead them to freedom.

The conflict that has plagued the region for the last 20 years originated from a pro-independence demonstration held in Ziguinchor in 1982, after which the leaders of the Mouvement des Forces Démocratique de la Casamance (MFDC) were arrested and jailed. Over the next few years the army clamped down with increasing severity, but this only galvanised the local people's anti-Dakar feelings and spurred the movement into taking more action.

In 1990, the MFDC went on the offensive and attacked military posts. The army responded by attacking MFDC bases in southern Casamance and over the border in Guinea-Bissau, which had been giving covert support to the rebels following a coastal territorial dispute with Senegal. As always, it was local civilians who came off the worst, with both the Senegalese army and the MFDC accused of committing atrocities against people who were thought to be sympathetic to the opposite side.

As the '90s wore on, cease-fire agreements were signed and broken as periods of peace repeatedly ended in violence. In 1995, four French people touring Casamance disappeared. The Senegalese government blamed the MFDC, while Father Diamacoune Senghor, the MFDC's leader, accused the army of trying to turn international opinion against the rebels.

Peace talks continued but, following the government's refusal to consider independence for Casamance, a group of hardliners broke away from the MFDC and resumed fighting.

Meanwhile, Father Diamacoune urged his supporters to continue the search for reconciliation with the government. A new cease-fire was agreed in late 1997 but it did little to slow the mounting death toll, and during the following three years about 500 people were reported killed. His authority fading, Father Diamacoune unexpectedly signed a peace deal in March 2001. While the agreement provided for the release of prisoners, the return of refugees and the clearance of landmines, it fell short of the full autonomy many rebels sought. Divisions within the MFDC deepened; a bloody battle was fought between two opposing factions and many in Casamance had begun referring to some of the rebels as bandits, or common thieves. The power struggle at the top of the movement had still not been resolved in April 2002.

Any agreement on autonomy, and thus peace, seems as far away as ever, and the people of Casamance will have to live with this long-running, low-level conflict for some time yet.

INFORMATION

Casamance is fortunate to have an excellent website for prospective visitors: [W] www .casamance.net. Run by Philip Chiche of Hôtel le Flamboyant in Ziguinchor, it lists almost every hotel and restaurant in the region, and regularly updates prices and other details. Many of the lodgings listed in this chapter have sites hosted by this website, which is in French and English.

SENEGAL

To Go or Not to Go?

It's the nature of news that you hear more about killing than about living, and in the case of Casamance good news is hard to find. This means the vast majority of Senegalese have little idea what is going on in Casamance, and so you shouldn't rely on their judgment when deciding whether to go to Casamance.

So how do you know whether it's safe or not? The simple answer is that absolute safety cannot be guaranteed. But you can take some comfort from the fact that as of early 2002 the rebels were sticking to their policy of not targeting tourists. This doesn't mean civilians are not suffering; they are. But for most the suffering is greater for the lack of tourists and our dollars than any direct confrontation with separatist fighters.

While researching this book I was in a bush taxi that was stopped by rebels just after crossing the Gambian border at Darsilami. Three armed men in tattered fatigues welcomed me to 'Casamance' and said: 'Enjoy your visit, this is a wonderful place.' Whether these were the same men who three weeks earlier had murdered a priest and two bush-taxi drivers at a similar checkpoint, I will never know.

During the following two weeks although I saw plenty of government soldiers I encountered no trouble whatsoever. Before each trip into rural Casamance I was sure to check on the latest security situation. In Ziguinchor you can ask at your hotel or the CRI office, but a more grass-roots picture may be gleaned by talking to bush-taxi drivers: if they are reluctant to go, you should be too. Another sensible tactic is to make sure you are not the first on the road in the morning or the last in the evening, and never drive at night. In Gambia, the bush-taxi drivers in Serekunda and Brikama usually have the latest information.

As a result of the unrest, some campements have closed or fallen into disrepair, but others remain defiantly clean and open. If the situation improves, more places are likely to reopen as tourists return. As in most guerilla wars there are no front lines in Casamance, but this is no reason to avoid it entirely. Most areas have seen action at some point, but in most villages they haven't seen a man with a gun in years. The only real permanent no-go zone is the Parc National de Basse-Casamance, which has been closed for years because of land mines. Rest assured that unless you just wander off on your own accord, people will simply not allow you to get too close to trouble.

Andrew Burke

GETTING THERE & AWAY

There are airports at Ziguinchor and Cap Skiring. Air Senegal International flies every day between Ziguinchor and Dakar for CFA44,000 one way, with flights continuing to Cap Skiring twice a week. However, it's easier to get to Cap Skiring or Banjul by road from Ziguinchor. See also Getting There & Away under Ziguinchor later in this chapter.

GETTING AROUND

Casamance can be toured by car, public transport, by bicycle or on foot. You can hire a car through the hotels and campements in Ziguinchor (see Getting Around under Ziguinchor for more details) or Cap Skiring. Another option is to hire a taxi for the day (see Getting Around in Ziguinchor later in this chapter).

If you want go on foot, the walking is not difficult along the banks of the estuaries, although occasionally you will encounter marshy areas. At most tributaries you'll find someone with a pirogue who will take you across for a small fee.

For cycling, the smaller *pistes* (tracks) are often too sandy, even for fat-tyred mountain bikes, but there are several good dirt roads in the area which are rideable. The main tar roads are also OK on a bike, although you need to keep your eyes and ears open, because what little traffic there is tends to go quite fast, and there's little room for error. If you want to avoid the long stretches of tar, or if you just get tired, you can always load your bike onto a bush taxi.

Wherever you go, it's worth resting during the hottest part of the day, which is usually around midday. At any time, wear a hat and take lots of water to drink. For specialised hiking and biking tours, contact Casamance VTT in Oussouye (☎/fax 993 10 04, e casavtt@yahoo.fr).

Local Guides

If you want to leave the roads and main tracks, to explore quieter areas on foot or by bike or pirogue, a local guide is recommended. As well as showing you the way (a maze of paths and trails crosses the region, with very few signposts, and there's not always somebody on the spot to give directions), guides can also introduce you to aspects of Casamance life that you might otherwise miss. With a guide, you'll feel less of a stranger and probably be greeted more easily by local people. Trips are often punctuated by informal visits to friends and relatives in distant villages, which is a great way to meet the locals.

The best way to find a guide is by asking around at your hotel, or the places which rent bikes. A personal recommendation from other travellers is always worth seeking. The Hôtel Relais de Santhiaba and Hôtel le Flamboyant in Ziguinchor are both able to recommend reliable, enthusiastic and knowledgeable guides. Rates start at about CFA5,000 per day.

Ziguinchor

pop 206,000

Ziguinchor (pronounced zig-an-shor) is the largest town in southern Senegal, as well as the main access point for travel in the Casamance region. Situated on the southern bank of the serpentine Casamance River estuary, Ziguinchor was originally established at a point where ferries could easily cross from one side to the other, although now there is a large bridge over the river. On the northern side of the river are some typically charming villages that can be visited on day trips from Ziguinchor.

Ziguinchor is the sort of place that grows on you. As you come into town, the quiet and dusty streets don't look too promising, but there's a pleasant, laid-back atmosphere, very little hassle, and the best-value places to stay and eat (for all budgets) in the whole country.

ORIENTATION

Ziguinchor's suburbs sprawl into the surrounding bush, but the central area is quite compact and can easily be covered on foot.

The focal point of the town is the Rond-Point Jean-Paul II (a traffic circle named after the Pope) from which many streets radiate. Leading east is Av Carvalho (formerly Blvd Foch), linking the centre to the *gare routière* (bus station). From near the gare, main roads head north to Dakar and also east to Tambacounda. A rather optimistically wide boulevard leads south towards Guinea-Bissau, but beyond the town it soon becomes a narrow, potholed strip winding through the bush.

From Rond-Point Jean-Paul II, Rue Javelier leads north through the town centre, past shops, restaurants and a bank before reaching Rue du Commerce, which runs along the southern bank of the Casamance River.

The road heading southwest from the rond-point passes the cathedral and becomes Av Lycée Guignabo (or Route de l'Aviation), passing the market and the Centre Artisanal before reaching the airport, which is 3km from the centre.

INFORMATION
Tourist Offices

The closest thing Ziguinchor has to a tourist office is the bureau of the Campements Rurals Integrés (☎ 991 13 75) at the Centre Artisanal. Manager Adama Goudiaby has run the office for years and can provide details on CRI campements or help with general queries.

Veronique and Philip who run Hôtel le Flamboyant on Rue de France are also happy to share their knowledge with anybody stopping by for a drink or meal.

SENEGAL

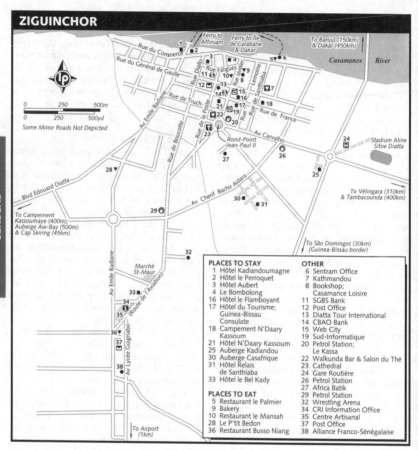

ZIGUINCHOR

Ferry to Affiniam
Ferry to Île de Carabane & Dakar
To Banjul (150km) & Dakar (450km)
Casamance River
Rue du Commerce
Rue du Général de Gaulle
Rue Diallo
Rue Fargues
Rue de Santhiaba
Lemoine
Rue Javelier
Rue de Truch-
Av Emile Badiane
Rue de la Poste
Rue de Boucotte
Casamance
River
Rue de France
Av Carvalho
Rond-Point Jean-Paul II
Stadium Aline Sitoe Diatta
Gare Routière
Some Minor Roads Not Depicted
0   250   500m
0   250   500yd
Blvd Edouard Diatta
Av Chérif Bachir Aïdara
To Vélingara (310km) & Tambacounda (400km)
To Campement Kassoumaye (400m); Auberge Aw-Bay (500m) & Cap Skiring (45km)
To São Domingos (30km) (Guinea-Bissau border)
Av Emile Badiane
Marché St-Maur
Route de l'Aviation
Av Lycée Guignabo
To Airport (1km)

PLACES TO STAY	OTHER
1 Hôtel Kadiandoumagne	6 Sentram Office
2 Hôtel le Perroquet	7 Kathmandou
3 Hôtel Aubert	8 Bookshop;
4 Le Bombolong	Casamance Loisire
16 Hôtel le Flamboyant	11 SGBS Bank
17 Hôtel du Tourisme;	12 Post Office
Guinea-Bissau	13 Diatta Tour International
Consulate	14 CBAO Bank
18 Campement N'Daary	15 Web City
Kassoum	19 Sud-Informatique
21 Hôtel N'Daary Kassoum	20 Petrol Station;
25 Auberge Kadiandou	Le Kassa
30 Auberge Casafrique	22 Walkunda Bar & Salon du Thé
31 Hôtel Relais	23 Cathedral
de Santhiaba	24 Gare Routière
33 Hôtel le Bel Kady	26 Petrol Station
	27 Africa Batik
	29 Petrol Station
PLACES TO EAT	32 Wrestling Arena
5 Restaurant le Palmier	34 CRI Information Office
9 Bakery	35 Centre Artisanal
10 Restaurant le Mansah	37 Post Office
28 Le P'tit Bedon	38 Alliance Franco-Sénégalaise
36 Restaurant Busso Niang	

Veronique speaks English and can help with setting up excursions or hiring local guides.

Money
Money can be changed (very slowly) or you can get an advance against a credit card at the CBAO on Rue de France, or SGBS on Rue du Général de Gaulle. They are each open from 7.45am to noon and 1.15pm to 2.30pm Monday to Thursday, and from 7.45am to 1pm and 2.45pm to 3.45pm on Friday. Around the back of SGBS, on Rue Fargues opposite the Hôtel Aubert, is Ziguinchor's only ATM, taking Visa and MasterCard.

Post
There are post offices on Rue du Général de Gaulle and on Av Emile Badiane (formerly Rue du Dr Olivier) south of the Centre Artisanal. The latter is better for parcels.

Telephone
There are several private *télécentres* along Rue Javelier, and in the surrounding streets.

Email & Internet Access
There are two cybercafés on Rue Javelier, both of which charge CFA1000 per hour. Web City (☎ 991 10 44), open 10am to

midnight, offers a reasonable service, but Sud-Informatique (☎ 991 15 73, W www .sudinfo.sn), open 9am to midnight, has faster machines and better facilities, including Satellite TV tuned to European football.

Travel Agencies

Diatta Tour International (☎ 991 27 81, fax 991 29 81) on Rue du Général de Gaulle can arrange air tickets, tours, hotel and campement reservations, car hire and fishing trips. It's also the DHL agent. Another option is Casamance Loisire (☎ 991 43 62) on Rue Javelier, which is apparently run by the former boss of Air Senegal.

Bookshop

The best bookshop in town is on the northern (river) end of Rue Javelier, with a good selection of titles on Senegal and Casamance (mostly in French), as well as some English-language magazines. You can also buy soft drinks and read your newspaper on the outside terrace.

Cultural Centres

The Alliance Franco-Senegalese (☎ 991 28 23), open 9.15am to noon and 3pm to 7.15pm Monday to Saturday, is at the southern end of Av Lycée Guignabo. There are exhibitions, courses and cultural events, plus a pleasant garden restaurant.

Consulate

The Guinea-Bissau consulate (☎ 991 10 46) is opposite the Hôtel le Flamboyant and is open from 8am to 2pm weekdays. With CFA5000 and a photo, you can get a visa in five minutes.

THINGS TO SEE & DO

The Marché St-Maur (Av Lycée Guignabo), 1km south of the centre towards the airport, sells fresh food and other items, and is well worth a visit. Nearby, vendors at the Centre Artisanal sell a wide variety of crafts from the area, including wooden carvings and fabrics. This is also where the town's hustlers lurk.

Back in town a wander along Rue du Général de Gaulle reveals an impressive range of French architecture, the old post

office being just one example begging to be renovated.

Near the Rond-Point John-Paul II is Africa Batik (☎ 991 2689), which offers batik-making courses at the bargain rate of CFA5000 a day, including materials.

ACTIVITIES

At the Auberge Aw-Bay, 3km out of town on the road to Cap Skiring, you can hire a bike for CFA3000 to CFA5000 or arrange pirogue excursions to Affiniam for CFA10,000 for one person per day, or CFA12,000 with food.

The Hôtel Relais de Santhiaba rents mountain bikes for CFA5000 per day or roadsters for CFA2500. They also arrange tours by bike and/or boat in the surrounding area. A day-trip by pirogue to Djilapao, Affiniam and the Île de Oiseaux costs CFA6250 per person with a minimum of four. Rates are higher for fewer people. See also Around Ziguinchor later in this chapter for more details on possible day trips.

PLACES TO STAY – BUDGET

Auberge Kadiandou (☎ 991 10 71) Rooms without bathroom CFA4000, singles/doubles with bathroom CFA5000/6000. This small place is one of the cheapest in Ziguinchor. It's attached to a local-style bar-restaurant of the same name, near the gare routière, which is handy if you want to get moving early. Rooms are small but very clean.

Hôtel le Bel Kady (☎ 991 11 22) Singles/ doubles/triples/quads CFA3500/4500/5000/ 6000. Near the Marche St-Maur, this rustic place has been popular with backpackers for years, with its cheap prices, friendly management and general good vibes. The rooms are basic but decent, though some travellers have complained of inconsistent cleanliness. If you want a fan and mosquito net add CFA1000. Breakfast is CFA600, and meals with a local or Cape Verdean flavour are CFA800 to CFA1500. Beers are CFA600.

Ziguinchor also has two cheap campements, both 3km west of the centre on the road to Cap Skiring.

Campement Kassoumaye (☎ mobile 630 12 85) Rooms CFA3300 per person. This first one is just north of the highway at the

SENEGAL

landmark radio antenna, but the mosquito nets are broken, bathrooms filthy and not really worth it.

Auberge Aw-Bay (☎/fax 936 80 76) Rooms CFA3500, plus CFA600 tax per person. The ambience and attitude is better at this campement, 100m further along the Cap Skiring road on your right. The clean rooms come with nets and fan and management is friendly and well informed. Breakfast is CFA1500 and other meals CFA2500.

Campement N'Daary Kassoum (☎ 991 1189, Rue de France) Singles/doubles with shower CFA4000/5000, doubles with bathroom CFA6000. Near the centre of town, this place (not to be confused with the much pricier Hôtel N'Daary Kassoum) could do with a lick of paint, but it's clean and functional enough. The rooms are huge – some bathrooms are big enough to sleep four.

Le Bombolong (☎ 938 80 01) Rooms CFA8000, extra bed CFA2100. Situated between the ferry jetty and port, this place has very nice rooms, but their proximity to the hotel's nightclub means disturbed sleep at weekends.

Hôtel Relais de Santhiaba (☎ 991 11 99) Singles/doubles without bathroom CFA4000/7000, with bathroom CFA6500/10,500. Off Av Cherif Bachir Aidara, this place is highly recommended. The cheaper rooms are fairly spartan, but they, like all of the rooms and bathrooms, are very clean. Breakfast is included in the price, but a fan costs an extra CFA1000 and air-con CFA2500. The hotel hires out decent mountain bikes and basic roadsters, and arranges tours by bike and/or boat in the surrounding area.

Auberge Casafrique (☎/fax 991 41 22) Singles/doubles without bathroom CFA5000/7000, with bathroom CFA8,000/10,000. Diagonally opposite the Santhiaba, this place is a bit soulless but has very clean rooms (some with real baths), with air-con an extra CFA2500. The manager speaks English and is proud of the monkey and pelican shackled in the front yard, though the subjects of this pride don't seem quite so pleased.

PLACES TO STAY – MID-RANGE & TOP-END

Hôtel le Perroquet (☎ 991 23 29, Rue du Commerce) Singles/doubles/triples CFA8500/11,500/15,000. Right on the river and beside the pirogue pier, this is a great-value place. All rooms have bathroom and there's a great bar and restaurant with a commanding view of the Casamance River.

Hôtel Kadiandoumagne (☎ 991 11 46, fax 991 16 75, Rue du Commerce) Singles/doubles CFA15,600/19,200. Next door to the Perroquet is this top-quality and tongue-twisting place, pronounced kaj-and-oum-an. All rooms have air-con. Overlooking the river, the bar is ideal for sundowners and for watching birds and boats go up and down. It's also one of the few places in the country that can boast wheelchair access.

Hôtel N'Daary Kassoum (☎ 991 14 72, ⓔ ndaary@hotmail.com, Rue de France) Doubles CFA11,000. The cheapest in this range is this place, which has good-quality but rather austere rooms with air-con and modern bathrooms. Breakfast is CFA1500.

Hôtel Aubert (☎ 938 80 02, Rue Fargues) Once the doyen of Ziguinchor hotels, this place was being renovated when we visited, but should be open by late 2002. Facilities will include a small pool and a restaurant. Rates will not be cheap.

Hôtel le Flamboyant (☎ 991 22 23, fax 991 22 22, ⓔ flamboyant@casamance.net, Rue de France) Singles/doubles CFA13,600/16,200. This classy place is possibly the best value in the country! The spotless rooms come with bathroom, air-con, fridge, phone and TV, and then there's the swimming pool right outside the door! Opposite le Flamboyant, and owned by the same amiable and well-informed French couple, is *Hôtel du Tourisme*. On the ground floor you will find a popular bar and good restaurant. Cheaper rooms are also available (singles/doubles CFA6000/7000).

PLACES TO EAT

A good street for cheap food is Av Lycée Guignabo, around the Marché St-Maur, which has many cafés, bars and *gargottes*. One of the town's most popular cheapies is

Restaurant Busso Niang, 15m down a side alley one block south of the junction of Av Cherif Bachir Aidara and Av Lycée Guignabo, where meals start at CFA400 a plate.

Most of the hotels in Ziguinchor have restaurants, including these two:

Hôtel Relais de Santhiaba Meals CFA2400-CFA3000, pizzas from CFA1800. Gerard, the French owner here, prepares good meals at reasonable prices, with meat and fish dishes available as well as delicious pizzas.

Hôtel du Tourisme Mains CFA3000. Open noon-2.30pm, 7pm-10pm daily. It doesn't look like much during the day but after dark the subtle lighting gives this place a vaguely colonial feel. Not so the menu, with the restaurant offering pizzas from CFA1500 and a range of other main courses for around CFA3000.

Other restaurants worth trying include the following:

Restaurant le Palmier (☎ 936 81 81, Rue du Commerce) Dishes from CFA1000. Open 24 hours. Near the port, this dimly lit place serves Senegalese, Guinean and Casamance specialties and other meals, such as fish and chips, for CFA1500.

Restaurant le Mansah (☎ 936 81 46, Rue Javelier) Dishes around CFA2000. Open 8am-midnight. This place is recommended, with meals such as grilled chicken, *tiébou-dienne* (rice baked in a thick sauce of fish and vegetables) and prawn brochettes in *sauce piquant* (prawns grilled on a skewer with hot sauce), all with chips and all at bargain prices.

Le P'tit Bedon (☎ 991 26 53, Av Emile Badiane) Mains CFA4000. Open lunch & dinner Tues-Sun. One of the best places to eat in Ziguinchor, this place has a big selection of European dishes, of which the beef stroganoff (CFA4500) and the *poisson veracruz* (fish in a spicy Mexican salsa on a bed of rice; CFA4000) are especially good.

For fresh bread there's a *bakery* opposite Restaurant le Mansah on Rue Javelier selling baguettes and the odd pastry 24 hours. Some of the following bars also provide food.

ENTERTAINMENT
Bars & Nightclubs
Most of the hotels listed in Places to Stay earlier have bars. Among them, the *Hôtel Kadiandoumagne* and *Hôtel le Perroquet* are both super spots for sundowners. Otherwise the rond-point is a good place to start.

Le Kassa (☎ 936 83 00) Open 8am-2am daily. This is a popular local haunt and is surprisingly good considering it's attached to a petrol station. Early in the evening it's an eatery, with local and European dishes from CFA1500, but the CFA600 beers get things swinging after 11pm.

Walkunda Bar & Salon du Thé (☎ 991 18 45) Open 9am-1am. Also on the rond-point is this classier place (silver service, wine glasses), where both the beer and the French food come refreshingly cheap: beer CFA600 and most meals CFA2000 to 3000.

If dancing is more your thing stick around at Le Kassa, or try the smart nightclub at *Le Bombolong*, or the more downmarket scene at *Kathmandou (Rue du Général de Gaulle)*, with less gadgetry and cheaper drinks.

SPECTATOR SPORTS
Wrestling matches usually take place during the dry season (November to May) on Sundays starting at around 4pm, at the 'arena' (which is really a dusty field) east of Av Lycée Guignabo.

GETTING THERE & AWAY
Air
Air Senegal has an office (☎ 991 10 81) at the airport. See Getting There & Away at the beginning of this chapter for details of flights to and from Ziguinchor.

Bush Taxi, Minibus & Bus
The gare routière is 1km east of the centre. Most transport to Dakar leaves between 7am and noon, and goes via the Trans-Gambian Highway, crossing the Gambia River on a ferry between Soma and Farafenni. You can also travel to Dakar on one of the buses that leave Ziguinchor around midnight, or early hours of the morning, from the gare routière. These buses arrive at the Gambian border

SENEGAL

before it opens, reaching the river in time for the first ferry across, and arriving in Dakar at about noon to 2pm. You can get on the bus any time during the evening or night and sleep there until departure. Some sample fares (in CFA) are:

destination	Peugeot taxi	minibus	Alham
Bissau	4500	-	-
Cap Skiring	1250	900	-
Dakar	6500	5000	4500
Elinkine	1250	750	-
Kafountine	2000	1500	1500
Kaolack	5000	3500	2500
Kolda	2850	2500	-
Oussouye	1000	750	-
Séléti	2000	-	-
Soma	2500	2000	-
Tambacounda	6500	4500	-

Boat

The MS *Joola* is supposed to run twice weekly between Dakar and Ziguinchor via Île de Carabane, but was out of service for most of 2001. If it is operating, visit or call the Sentram office (☎ 991 22 01) at the port to check that departure times have not changed.

GETTING AROUND
Taxi

The official rate for a taxi between Ziguinchor centre and the gare routière (1km) is CFA300. It's supposed to be the same price between the centre and the airport (4km), and even between the gare routière and Auberge Aw-Bay on the west side of town (3km), but for these longer rides you'll probably have to pay from CFA500 to CFA750. The main taxi rank is at Rond-Point Jean-Paul II.

Car

The setup for hiring cars in Ziguinchor is quite informal, but Diatta Tours International (see Information earlier in this chapter) and most hotels will be able to help. Minor details such as insurance are sometimes a little hazy, but cars usually come with a driver, which cuts the hassle

---

Taxi Drivers from Hell

It's impossible to tell on a short trip across town just what sort of character your taxi driver might be. Even the most mild mannered of men might morph into a maniac when let loose on the open road.

And so it was that, having missed the pirogue, I hired a taxi and set off for Affiniam. The first part of the trip was fine, but once we turned onto the dirt road the driver, Boubacar, revealed a certain leadenness of foot. At first I thought maybe we were sliding all over the place to minimise the risk of ambush. But I hadn't heard of any rebels around this area, and after he found the techno tape I realised he was just having fun on the unfamiliar dirt roads.

We reached Affiniam in what must have been record time, but it wasn't until we started heading back that I realised Boubacar had just been warming up on the outward trip. When we ran over a goat at high speed I was forced to have a few not-so-quiet words with him. But when we flew through a village where children played beside the road, and then side-swiped a nervous calf, enough was enough. It's all well and good to enjoy your driving, but this was just silly, not to mention life threatening to all involved.

Fortunately I'd paid nothing up front and when I carefully explained to Boubacar that his fee would not be forthcoming should he maim any more living creatures, he finally slowed down.

Andrew Burke

---

with paperwork or deposits. Expect to pay around CFA25,000 per day plus fuel. Another option is to hire a taxi; if you pay for fuel, the daily rate should be around CFA20,000. It's best to get going early, especially if you're taking a long trip – you don't want to be on the roads after dark, and neither does your driver if he has to get back to Ziguinchor.

Bicycle

For getting around town, you can't beat a bike. These can be hired from several places, including the Hôtel Relais de Santhiaba and the Auberge Aw-Bay.

Bicycles for hire vary considerably: you might find a decent mountain bike (*vélo tous terrains* or VTT), but mostly your choice is limited to old steel roadsters. These are OK if you take your time and don't race around. Mountain bikes cost about CFA5000 a day (roadsters are about half this), although you should be able to negotiate good deals if you want to hire one for a week or so.

AROUND ZIGUINCHOR
Djilapao

A popular day trip is a pirogue ride to the villages of Djilapao and Affiniam (see Casamance Nord later in this chapter), on the northern bank of the Casamance River. At Djilapao you can visit some **traditional mud-brick buildings** called *cases étages*, unusual because they have two storeys, and the house of a local artist, which is decorated with relief murals of various designs (some rather risqué).

Most trips also go to **Île des Oiseaux** (Island of the Birds), which is fascinating, even if you're not greatly into birds. With very little effort you can see pelicans, flamingos, kingfishers, storks, sunbirds and many more.

Getting There & Away Most hotels in Ziguinchor offer excursions to Affiniam and Djilapao, including Hôtel Relais de Santhiaba and the Hôtel le Flamboyant – see Activities under Ziguinchor earlier for more details.

The Restaurant le Mansah can also put you in touch with a reliable pirogue man, though rates are higher than those offered by the Relais Santhiaba. For day trips to Affiniam, Djilapao and Île des Oiseaux, the

---

Village *Campements*

Among Casamance's attractions are its *campements rurals integrés* (CRIs), often simply termed *campement du village* (village campement). They are humble lodgings built by villagers with government loans and run as cooperatives. Profits are reinvested to build schools, maternity clinics and health centres.

There are 10 CRIs in Casamance, but the ongoing violence and the resulting prolonged downturn in tourism meant only four were open at the time of research. The closed campements are in Diohère, Elinkine, Oussouye, Tionk Essil, Koubalan and Baïla. However, if peace is restored and tourism picks up, the campements will swiftly be knocked back into shape. In the meantime, rest assured that if you turn up and the campement is closed, accommodation will soon be found. Those that remain open are in the villages of Affiniam, Enampor, Pointe St George and Kafountine.

When you arrive you'll probably find a campement built in the local style, with lighting by oil lamp, although unlike many village homes most showers and toilets in campements have running water.

Prices (per person in CFA) at all CRIs are standardised:

bed (with mosquito net)	3000
breakfast	1800
three-course lunch or dinner	2500
half board	7300
full board	9800
beer	750
soft drink	400
mineral water	1000

The CRI office is at the Centre Artisanal in Ziguinchor, but its reservation system only works with at least a month's notice. As well as the CRIs, there are many privately owned campements with similar facilities and prices, although the profits go to the owner rather than to the village as a whole.

SENEGAL

charge is CFA15,000 per person for two passengers, or CFA13,000 per person for six, including a meal at Affiniam. Alternatively, you can just hire the whole pirogue for CFA50,000 per day.

It's also possible to arrange things with local boatmen who loiter at the jetty near the Hotel Kadiandoumagne. Prices start at around CFA25,000 for two people on an all-day trip to Affiniam and the Île des Oiseaux, including lunch. These rates are negotiable, especially if you don't want to eat, or want to go somewhere else as well. If you're a bird-watcher, this trip can be very enjoyable, but don't believe any young boatman who claims to be an *expert ornithologique*.

Rates are cheaper if you go for a shorter time, but this way you'll spend most of your trip crossing the river and miss the banks or mangrove creeks where the birds are more interesting. Remember not to hand over the full payment until you get back.

A final option to consider is the public ferry to Affiniam – for more details see Affiniam under Casamance Nord later in this chapter.

Basse Casamance

Protracted wanderings through the bush might not be recommended if men are still running around with guns, but if things settle down Basse Casamance is an excellent place for hiking and biking.

One circuit worth considering involves a combination of hiking and public transport and can be done in seven to 12 days. Go from Ziguinchor by bush taxi to Brin; hike to Enampor, then either hike direct (or take a bush taxi via Brin) to Diohère, Niambalang or Oussouye. From Oussouye, hike or take a bush taxi to Elinkine; take the boat to Île de Carabane; return to Elinkine and either go via Oussouye or directly by pirogue to Diakène Ouolof. Get a boat or bush taxi to Cap Skiring; head north to Diembéring, then return to Ziguinchor by bush taxi.

A possible tour by bike takes you from Ziguinchor to Brin or Enampor, then to Oussouye and on to Elinkine via M'Lomp

on what's left of the tar road. Go over to Carabane by boat, return to Elinkine and then go on to Oussouye on the old road via Loudia Ouolof, before continuing to Cap Skiring and/or Diembéring.

BRIN

Brin is a small village on the main road between Ziguinchor and Cap Skiring, where the dirt road to Enampor branches off. At the heart of the village is *Campement le Filao*, with bungalows set in a lush tropical garden and rates slightly lower than CRI prices. The simple rooms can get a bit warm, but then you can do as the locals do and cool off with a few CFA450 Flags. Brin is often overlooked, but it's in a nice area. You can walk in the surrounding forest or fields, or take pirogue rides on the nearby Casamance River.

ENAMPOR

Enampor is 23km directly southwest of Ziguinchor. The *village campement* is a huge, round mud house, called a *case à impluvium*, which is worth a visit even if

Cases à Impluvium

Across Casamance there has traditionally been at least one *case à impluvium* in most Diola villages. The impluvium is in effect a huge, round mud house. They are made using beams of ronier palm and mangrove wood, both of them impervious to termites, with thatched grass on the roof.

Historically, during wartime villagers would shut themselves inside the impluvium for safety. Rainwater would be funnelled into a large tank in the centre of the house through a hole in the roof (which also admits a wonderful diffuse light). The largest impluviums could hold 40 villagers and their cattle.

With the mud and thatch useless against modern weapons there are few impluviums left. Two of the better examples are the village campements in Enampor and Affiniam, while the fanciest of all is the Alliance Franco-Senegalese in Ziguinchor.

you're not staying here. There are other such houses in Casamance, but this is a good example. To sleep and eat here you pay the standard CRI prices. It's best to bring your own sheet. If you just want to visit, the manager will show you around for CFA100.

There are two minibuses per day from Ziguinchor to Enampor and nearby Séleki (CFA400). Another option is to get a bush taxi to Brin and walk the 13km to Enampor through palm groves, fields and villages, taking the left (southerly) fork at Essil, the halfway point. Moving on from Enampor it's possible to go by pirogue to Oussouye – or just about anywhere else in Casamance – ask around in the village.

DIOHÈRE & NIAMBALANG

Diohère and Niambalang are small villages on the main road between Brin and Oussouye. The *village campement* at Diohère and the private *Chez Theodor Balouse* in Niambalang were both closed when we visited. If you need to stay here, just speak to the village chief and a bed will be found.

OUSSOUYE

Roughly halfway between Ziguinchor and Cap Skiring, Oussouye (pronounced oo-sou-yeh) is the main town in the Basse Casamance area. It's a sleepy place, although the market can get lively some mornings, and it makes a good base for tours in the surrounding area.

Oussouye is home to Casamance VTT (☎/fax 993 10 04, e casavtt@yahoo.fr, W casavtt.free.fr), a really inspirational little company that specialises in tours of the area. Benjamin, the English-speaking French owner, rents mountain bikes for CFA4000 a half-day and CFA7500 for a full day, and organises guided cycling, hiking and pirogue tours from CFA9500 per day, or CFA12,500 with meals. Longer tours can also be arranged at similar per-day rates. During the wet season bikes can only be rented by the day. Benjamin also organises the Trophée Kabekel bike race. To find Casamance VTT ask at the campements for Chez Benjamin.

Also worth visiting is **Galerie Bahisen**, run by a French-Senegalese partnership on

---

Trophée Kabekel Bike Race

Every two years, Oussouye is the unlikely home to 'the most convivial bike race in Senegal', the Trophée Kabekel. Organised by Benjamin of Casamance VTT, the race is designed to showcase this beautiful but neglected piece of Senegal and is one of the few organised community events in a region where there's not often cause for communal celebration. The Trophée is open to all comers and the 2001 event attracted cyclists from as far as Austria and the US, as well as dozens of locals on a wide assortment of bikes (one guy's conveyance was more like a huge ghetto blaster on wheels). There are categories for men (local bike or mountain bike over a 36km course) and women, who cycle their 23km course on 30 VTTs (mountain bikes) provided free by Benjamin. There's also a 3km wheelchair race. The next Trophée Kabekel will be held on 5 April 2003, with races expected to follow annually or every two years. For details of the course or to register for the race (spots are limited) go to W kabekel.free.fr, or call Casamance VTT (☎ 933 10 04).

---

the road towards Cap Skiring. Local artists make beautiful, well-finished works in wood, terracotta and other traditional materials in contemporary designs. Much of the stuff is exported to Europe, but prices for items bought locally are very reasonable. You can also buy traditional medicines, with instructions in several languages.

Places to Stay

The *village campement* was closed when we visited, which was a pity as it's a beautiful example of local, mud architecture. However, two other places are open, both on the same dirt road leading north toward Elinkine from the *rond pointe*.

Auberge du Routard (☎ 993 10 25) Rooms CFA3000, half board CFA5500. This is a jovial place where the ladies of the case can be found making batiks in the centre of a small impluvium, an art they will teach you for a small fee. Basic, clean rooms have shared bathrooms. Breakfast is CFA1500.

SENEGAL

Campement Emanaye Oussouye (☎ *933 10 04,* e *emanaye@yahoo.fr,* w *emanaye .free.fr)* Singles/doubles CFA4500/6000, half board CFA7500 per person. About 300m from Auberge du Routard, but with better-quality rooms all with bathroom, is this new place run by a former Casamance VTT guide. *Emanaye* means rice in Diola, and the campement is in traditional mud dwellings beside the local rice fields.

Campement des Bolongs (☎ *993 10 41, fax 936 90 10)* Singles/doubles CFA7000/ 10,000. This place is east of town, about 1km down a very sandy track near the village of Edioungou, is an ambitiously large place in a beautiful, tranquil setting overlooking a *bolong* (small river). The clean and comfortable rooms have bathroom; breakfast is CFA2000 and other meals are about CFA4000.

Places to Eat & Drink
On the main street, *Restaurant 2000*, *Restaurant Sud* and *Chez Rachel* all serve local meals for about CFA700, the latter living up to its 'service rapide' slogan. The *Télécentre et Buvette du Rond-Point* is an ideal place for a quiet drink and any urgent phone calls you may need to make.

Pots

Edioungou, a small village just east of Oussouye, has been a centre of pottery-making for many years. Until recently, customers were local people from other parts of Casamance, but the women who make the pots have been assisted by a development organisation to sell their wares to tourists.

Items range from spherical bowls and jugs, which have a pleasing purity of design and organic simplicity, to more elaborate cups and candle holders. The work is distinctive because the potters add a mixture of soil and crushed shells to their clay and when fired the pots take on the look of burnished leather. You can buy the pots in Edioungou, Oussouye and at stalls and markets elsewhere in Casamance.

The nightlife is impressive for such a small place, with two entertaining venues at the east end of town; *Chez Rene* is good for a quiet drink under the paillote, while the *Bolong Nightclub* is more lively.

Getting There & Away
All bush taxis between Ziguinchor and Cap Skiring pass through Oussouye, so getting here is easy. See the fare table under Ziguinchor earlier in this chapter.

M'LOMP
On what is allegedly a tar road between Oussouye and Elinkine you'll pass through the village of M'Lomp, which has several two-storey **mud-brick houses** *(cases étages),* and some other houses with brightly decorated walls and pillars, all unique to this part of West Africa. The old lady who lives in the largest *case étage* near the main road will give you a tour for a small fee. The tour will undoubtedly include the enormous fromager tree, at least 400 years old and sacred in the village, that towers above the first case étage.

Decent food can be found at *Le Pionier*, open 8am to 11pm daily, just east of the junction, with local and European meals for CFA500 to CFA1000, and big smiles for free.

POINTE ST GEORGE
Pointe St George lies to the north of M'Lomp and Oussouye on a large bend in the Casamance River. The old Hôtel Pointe St George remains closed, but a new *village campement* is operating. You'll need a 4WD to get here by road, or a pirogue from Ziguinchor will cost about CFA15,000.

ELINKINE
Elinkine is a busy fishing village that is the jumping off point for Île de Carabane. Hundreds of fishermen and their families have moved to Elinkine from all over West Africa in recent years and the results are less than inspiring. The beach that was described by some as a 'paradise' a few years ago is now filthy. All three campements here have closed, though there is suggestion one (which was burnt down) might reopen.

Shark's Fin Soup

Three words go a long way toward explaining the fall from grace of Elinkine: shark's fin soup. It is the prevalence of sharks in the waters near Elinkine, and the willingness of Asians to pay stacks of money for the privilege of eating their tasteless cartilage, that has drawn many of the fishermen. Shark fishing is carried out almost exclusively by Ghanaians, because while the local Diola people understand the value of the fins, Muslims will not eat shark and apparently the local non-Muslims find the meat less than appetising. But while the Ghanaians sell thousands of fins a year, they seem to have little idea of their end use. One fisherman asked: 'What do they do with the shark fins?' When told they were eaten in soup he replied in amazement: 'What, they don't even make anything out of them? Just soup?'

There are normally several Alhams each day from Ziguinchor to Elinkine, via Oussouye for CFA750. The timetable for transport from Elinkine is less predictable. Occasional Peugeot taxis also cover this route, and the fare is CFA1000.

ÎLE DE CARABANE

Île de Carabane (sometimes spelt Karabane) is a really cool place to just hang out and not do too much. A beautifully peaceful island near the mouth of the Casamance River, it was an important settlement and trading station in early colonial times. The French legacy is now largely ruins, but you can still see the Breton-style church and the remains of a school, and along the beach is a cemetery with the graves of settlers and sailors, including a Capitaine Aristide Protet, who apparently died when he was hit with a poison arrow during a Diola uprising in 1836 and was buried with his dog. The beach is good for swimming (you may see dolphins in the distance) and the island is also an excellent bird-watching site.

There are no landline phones on Carabane and mobiles only work in one spot, so when telephoning any of the following

establishments you will have to leave a message and someone will call back.

Places to Stay & Eat

The following places are listed from east to west. All serve food.

Campement Barracuda (☎ mobile 659 60 01, fax 936 90 10) Rooms CFA7500 with half board. Catering mainly for anglers, this place has a lively bar. Fishing excursions cost CFA20,000 to CFA35,000 per boat. Shorter trips for birding or visiting local villages cost around CFA8000.

Hôtel Carabane (☎ mobile 633 17 82) Singles/doubles CFA11,000/16,000. This delightful and well-maintained hotel is set in a lush and shady tropical garden on the beach between the campements. Formerly a Catholic mission – the chapel is now the bar! – the colonial-era buildings were converted into a hotel in the early 1990s. The price of the classy rooms includes breakfast, and the excellent three-course menu du jour (meal of the day) is CFA4500. Reservations can be made through Diatta Tour International in Ziguinchor (see Information under Ziguinchor earlier in this chapter).

Chez Helena (☎ mobile 654 17 72, fax 821 73 05) Rooms/half/full board CFA4000/6000/8000. Yes, you read right, this place is truly a bargain. It's run by friendly, English-speaking Helena and the rooms are more than comfortable.

Campement Badji Kunda Bed only CFA2500, full board CFA12,000. About 500m further along the beach, this place has a decidedly carefree and arty ambience. The owner, Malang Badji, is a sculptor and painter; his works (and those of other local artists) are on display and for sale here. If you're staying for a few days and you don't mind paying for materials, you can try your hand at local glass painting or pottery. Breakfast is CFA1500 and other meals about CFA3000.

Apart from the hotels, there are a couple of low-key places just above the waterfront. **Le Kaati** (Chez Babs), open 6am to midnight, is a couple of tables where seafood and other dishes cost CFA2500, and beer is CFA800. Larger is **Le Calypso**, open 9am to midnight, with more expensive meals but cheaper beer, though the 'video club' seems out of place on such a peaceful island.

Getting There & Away

Île de Carabane is reached by motorised pirogue from Elinkine. There's usually a boat at 3pm, returning at 9am the following morning, but this is not guaranteed. Otherwise, you need to hang around on the waterfront until you see a boat leaving. The fare is CFA750 and the ride takes 30 minutes. Alternatively, you can charter a boat for about CFA8000 each way.

If you've got a group, or money, Helena can organise a boat to take you just about anywhere. Destinations and prices include Diembéring (CFA17,400); Cap Skiring (CFA19,200); Ziguinchor (CFA50,000); and Kafountine (CFA54,000). You can also get to Île de Carabane on the MS *Joola* – when it's running. (See Senegal's Getting Around chapter for details.)

CAP SKIRING

The beaches of Cap Skiring are some of the finest in West Africa, and it's no coincidence there are several resort-style hotels here. Like Saly and the Atlantic coast in Gambia, Cap Skiring attracts plenty of European package tours, but there's more to it than that. The village is a lively place and there are plenty of cheaper campements appealing to independent travellers. If you want a few easy days of sun and sand, with the option of a bit of partying after hours, this is the place.

Orientation

The village of Cap Skiring is 1km north of the junction where the main road from Ziguinchor joins the northsouth coast road. It has shops, restaurants, bars and nightclubs, a market and a gare routière, but no Internet café when we visited. Just outside the village you can't miss the high walls of the Club Med complex, or the *prison touristique* as it's known locally. Most other hotels and campements are south of Cap Skiring village, along the coast road towards Kabrousse, 5km away.

Places to Stay

You'll find accommodation for all budgets in Cap Skiring, most of it overlooking the beach and offering all the associated facilities and activities you'd expect, though with greatly differing quality and price. Half- and full-board deals are available everywhere, and in some of the bigger hotels are all that's available. Tours and day trips can be arranged at most hotels.

Places to Stay – Budget

Just south of the junction is a sandy track leading towards the beach and the first three campements listed here.

Le Mussuwam (☎/fax 993 51 84) Rooms without/with bathroom CFA3000/6000. This is a big place with lots of clean but uninspiring rooms. Rooms with air-con and hot water are CFA13,000 (CFA10,000 without hot water), and full board is an extra CFA5000 each.

Auberge de la Paix (☎ 993 51 45) Rooms without/with bathroom CFA3000/6000 per person. This is a friendly place with a family feel (and family rooms sleeping up to six are available). The renovated rooms with bathroom are best – check out the traditional Diola ceilings. Breakfast is CFA1500.

Campement Chez M'Ballo (☎ 936 91 02) Rooms without/with bathroom CFA4000/7500. Possibly the pick of the cheap places on this strip, M'Ballo is a good-value option with a relaxed and friendly atmosphere.

Campement le Bakine (☎ mobile 641 51 24) Rooms/half board CFA3000/7000 per person. On the Ziguinchor road, near the junction, this campement is a favourite with French artistes and has a creative feel. African music performances are promised for Wednesday and Saturday, and lessons are available in drumming, dancing, painting and sculpting. The rooms are simple but adequate.

Campement les Paletuviers (☎/fax 993 52 10) Rooms/half board CFA8000/CFA12,000. This is essentially a disco in the village with a campement out the back. The comfortable rooms surround the new pool, which may or may not be open all hours. This is not one for light sleepers.

Places to Stay – Mid-Range & Top End

These places are listed north to south, and many take credit cards.

Hôtel Résidence Kacissa (☎ 993 52 58, fax 993 52 59) Rooms/half board CFA12,000/ CFA20,000, villas CFA200,000 per week. On a quiet stretch of beach north of Cap Skiring, this place was almost finished when we visited and is almost as big as its management's plans. The double rooms and villas are comfortable and good value. There are a range of prices, depending on the season, but most are fair. The self-catering villas house a family of four.

Auberge le Palmier (☎ 993 51 09) Doubles with bathroom CFA10,000. In Cap Skiring village, the rooms here are reasonable, but it's the bar-restaurant, its excellent *plat du jour* (dish of the day; CF3500) and colourful clientele that seem most popular with visiting Frenchmen. Air-con is an extra CFA2000.

Hôtel la Paillote (☎ 993 51 51, fax 993 51 17, ✉ paillote@sentoo.sn) Half board from CFA30,000 per person. Opposite the junction where the road comes in from Ziguinchor, this hotel is in a prime position and has bungalows set in lush tropical gardens. It's renowned for superb French food and a refined ambience, and a drink on the terrace is the perfect way to watch the dramatic Atlantic sunset.

Villa des Pêcheurs Aline Sitoe (☎ 993 52 53, fax 993 51 80, ✉ sitoe@arc.sn, 🌐 www .villadespecheurs.com) On the same beach-front strip as the campements, this is a wonderful place with six comfortable rooms (all with bathroom) overlooking a tranquil stretch of beach. Excellent meals are taken outside on the terrace and there is a small bar. The managers speak some English and will go out of their way to ensure a smooth and enjoyable stay. Fishing is their specialty, and boat trips can be arranged. For more information, including prices, contact the Hôtel le Flamboyant in Ziguinchor.

Hôtel les Hibiscus (☎ 993 51 36, fax 993 51 12, ✉ hibiscus@sentoo.sn) Rooms CFA26,000 per person. Right on the border of Guinea-Bissau near Kabrousse is this small and tasteful hotel in lush gardens on the beach, where cool bungalows are decorated with stunning murals and local fabrics, and include breakfast.

Also near Kabrousse are *Le Royal Cap* (☎ 993 51 19, fax 993 51 27) and *Le Kabrousse* (☎ 993 51 26), while 2km north of Cap Skiring is *Le Savana Cap* (☎ 993 51 52, 993 51 92). These three ageing deluxe hotel resorts are part of the Senegal Hotels group and all three were closed for renovation when we visited. When open they are popular with package tourists; however, if you arrive alone half board will cost you from CFA40,000 to CFA60,000.

Places to Eat

All the hotels offer food, and Cap Skiring village has several cheap eateries, with Senegalese dishes in the CFA500 to CFA1000 range. One local favourite is *Mamans*, a few metres back from the main street, with large plates of Senegalese fare for CFA500, while next door is *Chez Lena Gourmandis* (☎ 936 91 16), with similar food, but higher prices to cover luxuries like tablecloths.

Also on the main street is *Chez Delphine* (☎ 993 52 76), open 8am to 2pm and 5pm to midnight, the best pizza joint in town, with all local ingredients and an interesting array of local varieties: try either the Africa or Feeling (both CFA3900). Delphine opens at 5pm and once the last pizza is consumed, she'll be found on the dance floor at Case Bambou.

Up a grade is *Restaurant la Pirogue* (☎ 993 51 76), opposite the Hôtel la Paillote, which has a good three-course menu for CFA6000.

Self-caterers will find there are plenty of local shops and a small *fruit market* in the village, or head to the *Mini-Marché Chez Gnima*, open 7am to 1pm and 4pm to 8pm daily, just south of the junction.

Bars & Nightclubs

The hotels and campements all have bars, most with incredible ocean views. For something more lively head into the village, where several bars line the main street. The *Black & White Bar*, open 10am to 3am, is a small place playing reggae music in a mellow atmosphere. Beers are CFA800. Next door is *Le Bambou Bar*, open 6pm to 3am, another intimate place but with cheaper beer (CFA600). Opposite here is the big, gaudy *Case Bambou* (☎ 993 51 78), open 10.30pm to 4am, the hottest nightspot in town where hideously expensive drinks are popular with well-to-do locals and Club Med staff.

Getting There & Away
See Getting There & Away early in this chapter for details of Air Senegal International flights to Dakar. Bush taxis (CFA1250) and minibuses (CFA900) run regularly throughout the day between Ziguinchor and Cap Skiring, although there's more traffic in the morning. Alternatively, you can go by pirogue through the creeks between Cap Skiring and Île de Carabane for about CFA20,000. You cannot cross the border to Guinea Bissau at Kabrousse.

Getting Around
Most hotels and campements have bicycles for hire and can arrange car hire or pirogue trips on the creeks inland from the coast. Day trips start at around CFA15,000 for the boat. You can arrange to be dropped off at Elinkine or Carabane rather than returning to Cap Skiring.

Auto Cap4 (☎ 993 52 65, mobile 637 48 28) has an eclectic mix of 4WDs for hire starting at CFA25,000 a day, and falling to CFA20,000 a day for weekly rentals.

DIEMBÉRING
To escape the hustle and bustle of Cap Skiring, head for Diembéring (pronounced jembay-ring), nearby to the north, where the authentic African feel is in marked contrast to its neighbour's touristy vibe. The quiet and hassle-free beach is about 1km from the village.

The place to stay is *Campement Asseb* (☎ 993 31 06), a spacious and peaceful place near the big fromager tree at the entrance to town. The rooms are a bit rough around the edges, but fair for the CRI rates. Unfortunately, *Campement Aten-Elou*, on a hill overlooking the village, is closed. For food, head to the *Restaurant le Diola* at the entrance to town and give Anna plenty of warning. Local dishes are about CFA1200, sandwiches CFA400 and beer CFA500.

Diembéring can be reached by bicycle, although the road is sandy and hard work in the heat. A private taxi to/from Cap Skiring costs CFA5000 each way, or you can get the daily minibus from Ziguinchor, which passes through Cap Skiring around 5pm and returns early next morning.

PARC NATIONAL DE BASSE-CASAMANCE
This national park has been closed for several years now and, with no-one quite sure whether land mines have been laid in the area or what fauna remains, looks certain to remain closed for the foreseeable future.

The park measures about 7km by 5km and there are several vegetation zones: tropical forest and dense undergrowth give way to open grassland, tidal mud flats and mangrove swamps. Before it was closed there were quite a few animals, especially red colobus monkeys and duikers, as well as a herd of forest buffaloes and populations of bushbucks, porcupines, mongooses, crocodiles and leopards. The park had a good network of trails, plus several *miradors* (lookouts) for viewing birds and animals.

If and when the park reopens, the best option is to stay in Oussouye and visit the park for the day by bike or taxi. Make sure you ask about the latest security situation before setting off.

Getting There & Away
From Oussouye go 2km west on the main road towards Cap Skiring, and turn left (south) at the signpost for the park. The park entrance is 8km down the sandy road towards Santiaba Mandjak. Once you enter the park, keep heading south for half a kilometre, then take the first right to reach the park headquarters.

Casamance Nord

If and when things settle down, there are some good areas for cycling in Casamance

Nord. The tracks are green and shady, although there are a few difficult patches of deep sand. A local guide who knows all the interesting short cuts and turnings can save a lot of time. A suggested route from Ziguinchor involves catching the public ferry across to Affiniam, and riding to Tionk-Essil (a good base for two days or more) then on to Baïla, returning to Ziguinchor via Bignona to Koubalan. However, this route could not be recommended at the time of writing.

AFFINIAM

A few kilometres north of the river, Affiniam is very easy to reach from Ziguinchor by boat, and is a popular day-trip destination. The main feature at Affiniam is the **impluvium** (see the boxed text 'Cases à Impluvium' earlier in this chapter), which is also the CRI campement. The traditional thatched roof of this *impluvium* has been replaced with unsightly corrugated iron, which is a pity for tourists and photographers, but far more practical for those living there. It's worth staying longer than a day and exploring the surrounding area, where visitors rarely venture.

The *village campement* has rooms and meals at standard CRI prices. Few people actually stay the night here, which is a pity because this is a genuine Casamance experience and Donatine, the manager, is an absolute scream. The rooms are very basic, but the bathrooms are clean.

Getting There & Away

There is a public ferry from Ziguinchor every Monday, Wednesday and Friday morning, as well as other days if there's sufficient demand. It stops at 'le port d'Affiniam' (about 1km from the campement) for one hour then returns. The fare is CFA500.

Alternatively, you can reach Affiniam by bike (if you're fit) or car: turn off the main road from Ziguinchor about 2km south of Bignona and cross the barrage to the northeast of Affiniam.

Many of the hotels in Ziguinchor offer excursions that include a visit to Affiniam, or you can arrange your own trip – see Activities under Ziguinchor and Around Ziguinchor earlier in this chapter.

TIONK ESSIL

The village of Tionk Essil (also spelt Thionck-Essyl, and various other ways) is about 20km northwest of Affiniam, in the transition zone between the mangrove swamps and the sandy forests, making its campement one of the most remote in Casamance. But getting here is well worth the effort – the surrounding area is peaceful and beautiful, and there's a good community spirit among the villagers. Many young people who've lived in Dakar have chosen to return home to Tionk Essil because the quality of life here is better. In 1997, 40,000 trees were planted by local youngsters to help regenerate the mangroves. To get here from Ziguinchor, catch one of the occasional bush taxis or hire a bike, car or private taxi.

The *village campement* has been variously occupied by the military or just plain closed for quite a while now. But if you arrive the villagers will find lodgings for you – probably in the local mayor's house.

BIGNONA

Bignona is a crossroads town, where the main route to/from Banjul joins the Trans-Gambia Hwy 30km north of Ziguinchor. It's a sleepy place full of crumbling colonial buildings and old men on mopeds.

The depressing **Hôtel le Kellumack** (☎ 994 10 11) has singles/doubles at CFA4000/5000. It's on the north side of town, near the police station. If you're coming into town from Diouloulou, turn left just after the bridge. Nearby and much better is the old colonial-style **Hôtel le Palmier** (☎ 994 12 58), with rooms for CFA5000, or CFA7000 with hot water, and breakfast for CFA800.

KOUBALAN & BAÏLA

Koubalan is a few kilometres to the east of the main road between Ziguinchor and Bignona, and is reached by bush taxi from Ziguinchor (CFA500) or, if the tide is right, by pirogue. Baïla is just off the main road between Bignona and Diouloulou. The *village campements* in both have been closed for some time, but locals promise to reopen them once tourism picks up

SENEGAL

DIOULOULOU

This village is some 20km south of the Gambian border, where the road to Kafountine branches off the main route between Serekunda (in Gambia) and Ziguinchor.

If you get stuck here, **Relais Myriam** (☎ 936 95 91) has very simple bungalows with/without bathroom for CFA4000/2000 per person, though the bathroom might disappoint as it's just a bucket shower. There is electricity from 7pm to 7am and a promise from the manager that 'soon it will be all day'.

Kafountine & Abéné

Kafountine and Abéné are the hip face of tourism in Senegal. The two villages on the coast just south of Gambia have spawned more than 20 guesthouses, often the sort of place where the staff seem happy to drum the day away and everything is 'cool, mon'. The villages are separated from the rest of Casamance Nord by a large branch of the River Casamance called Marigot Dioloulou (*marigot* means creek).

This isolation has meant the area has largely avoided the conflict of the separatist movement, although there was a brief clash here in April 2002. It also means the area looks more to the north than to the south: there's a relatively large proportion of Muslim Mandinka and Wolof mixed in with the Diola population, and people go to Brikama in Gambia for their shopping more often than they go to Ziguinchor.

The area around Kafountine and Abéné has attracted several Senegalese and European artists, and many of the campements arrange courses in drumming, dance and batik-making, and have exhibitions and performances. This is a very good place to slow down for a few days and explore the local culture. On most weekends there's a performance somewhere; you just need to ask around. There's even the small annual **Abéné Festivalo** celebrating music, dancing and theatre. It's usually held for 10 days from December 24 and attracts artists from across West Africa and Europe. For details see the website W www.alnaniking.co.uk/festival.

The creeks and lagoons around Kafountine are wonderful areas for watching birds, especially waders and shore birds. The most accessible place is the small pool near the Campement Sitokoto. A bit further away are several *bolongs* (rivers) and *marigots* (creeks) that are also rewarding. Certainly the most enjoyable viewing platform is the bar at Esperanto, where you can watch over the lake while imbibing a soothing sunset drink.

The Sanctuaire Ornithologique de la Pointe de Kalissaye is a group of sandy islands at the mouth of the Marigot Kalissaye, but they are usually covered in water. Most bird-watchers now head for the highly rated Sanctuaire Ornithologique de Kassel, which is about 5km southeast of Kafountine.

Another place is the Presqu'ile des Oiseaux, a narrow spit of land between the ocean and a creek, noted for its huge populations of Caspian terns. It lies south of the Hotel Karone; the hotel's management can arrange trips by 4WD vehicle, and are happy to provide keen bird-watchers with more information.

KAFOUNTINE

Kafountine is a spread-out village, about 2km from the ocean, near the end of the road from Dioloulou. On the coast itself is a large fish market and beach from where the boats are launched. This is a busy place, almost like a separate settlement, with several shacks and huts, a petrol station (for the boat engines) and even a *télécentre*. Trucks from Ziguinchor and Dakar come to load up with fish when the boats come in. Fishing times depend on the tide, but it's well worth going to see the boats being launched or, more spectacular still, when they come back after a long day at sea, surfing in on the rollers.

North of the fishing area, a huge empty beach leads northwards up the coast, past Abéné and almost to the Gambian border. Kafountine itself has the same disposition as most of the guesthouses – time is something these people are not short of. If you're arriving from Serekunda in Gambia you'll

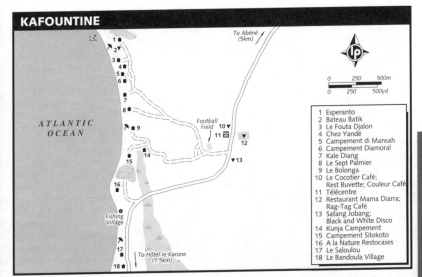

KAFOUNTINE

To Abéné (5km)

ATLANTIC OCEAN

Football Field

To Hôtel le Karone (1.5km)

Fishing Village

1 Esperanto
2 Bateau Batik
3 Le Fouta Djalon
4 Chez Yandé
5 Campement di Mansah
6 Campement Diamoral
7 Kale Diang
8 Le Sept Palmier
9 Le Bolonga
10 Le Cocotier Café;
   Rest Buvette; Couleur Café
11 Télécentre
12 Restaurant Mama Diarra;
   Rag-Tag Café
13 Satang Jobang;
   Black and White Disco
14 Kunja Campement
15 Campement Sitokoto
16 A la Nature Restocases
17 Le Saloulou
18 Le Bandoula Village

SENEGAL

probably feel like you just shifted from fifth gear down to neutral. Not a bad thing.

There are several *télécentres* in town but no Internet access or bank.

Places to Stay

Accommodation at Kafountine is spread along several kilometres of coast, and falls loosely into two areas: the northern strip, reached by turning right on the sandy road as it leads west from the village; and the southern strip that stretches along the main road south of Kafountine village. The following places are listed north to south, though this is not a complete list. Note that most of the phone and fax numbers are for *télécentres* in the village, so you'll have to leave a message.

Northern Strip These places are listed from north to south.

Esperanto (Chez Eric & Antonella, ☎/fax 936 95 19, e *antoeric@hotmail.com)* Bungalows/half board CFA7500/12,500. Esperanto is in a wonderful location between the sea and a bird-filled *bolong*. The attractively decorated and very comfortable rooms fan out from an open-sided bar. Breakfast is CFA1500. Call ahead in September.

Le Fouta Djalon (☎ 936 94 94) Rooms/half board CFA9,000/15,000. This place has red-brick bungalows in extensive gardens. The French management offers bike hire, birding and fishing trips as well.

Chez Yandé (☎/fax 936 95 19, e *kam erer_Gmbh@t-online.de)* Doubles CFA6000. This is a friendly campement where the price includes breakfast, and English-speaking Yandé is a wealth of information. The rooms are pretty simple and the pool was empty when we visited, but with a few people around this place could be a lot of fun.

Campement Diamoral (Chez Espagnol) Rooms/full board CFA2500/6000. This Catalan/Senegalese enterprise is about as cheap and uncomfortable as you get here, but it's family atmosphere and optimistic, carefree attitude make up for the total lack of luxuries. The food is an interesting mix of Spanish and African and is reported to be pretty good. Next door is the similar *Campement di Mansah*, also a work-in-progress, but it has an emphasis on drumming lessons for CFA2500 an hour.

Kale Diang (☎/fax 936 95 19, e *kaledi ang@hotmail.com)* Rooms CFA3200 per person. On very well-forested land once considered sacred by the local community, this Dutch-run establishment by the beach has comfortable rooms with clean bucket showers and an emphasis on traditional living – a genuine example of ecotourism (yes, without the generator). Food here is excellent: breakfast is CFA1200, lunch CFA1800 and dinner by lantern-light CFA3200. Highly recommended! Ask about pirogue excursions with Fela the Rasta griot.

Le Sept Palmier Bed CFA1500. As the name suggests, this place has seven palms along the beachfront. Rooms here are basic but sleeping is less important than drumming and smoking. All meals are CFA1000, drumming lessons CFA4000 an hour.

The next three places are reached by taking the left fork of the dirt road just after the football pitch – there are plenty of signs.

Kunja Campement Rooms CFA2500 per person. A little tired-looking, this is another simple place with bungalows in a large shady garden. Breakfast is CFA1000 and other meals are CFA1500 to CFA3000. Drum and dance lessons are available.

Le Bolonga (☎ 994 85 15) Rooms/half board CFA5000/10,000. Another good-quality place, this one has spotless rooms and fully functioning bathrooms. The food is very good it has quite simply the best fish (baked) and chips (hot and crisp) in Casamance. There's a calming ease about the English-speaking management.

Campement Sitokoto (☎ 994 85 12) Just south of Bolonga this village-run place has rooms and meals at standard CRI prices. Rooms are basic but clean and the shared bathrooms have running water.

Southern Strip At the heart of the fishing village and just above the high-water line, *A la Nature Restocases* (☎ 994 85 24, e alana ture@metissicana.sn) is an elaborate, two-storey, beachfront venture with a rasta feel, lush garden, hammocks, drummers, basic bungalows and a solar-powered Internet connection. B&B is CFA4500, half board is CFA7500.

South of the fishing centre on the narrow spit of sand are neighbouring places that are both quite good.

Le Saloulou (☎/fax 994 85 14, w www .saloulou.com) Rooms/half board CFA8000/ 14,000 per person. This place, well organised and seconds from the surf, offers fishing trips in the sea or *bolongs*. Breakfast is CFA2000 and all rooms have a bathroom.

Le Bandoula Village (☎ 994 85 11) Rooms CFA12,000. This Senegalese-Swedish operation offers good, clean rooms for one to three people, making them great value for threesomes. Breakfast is CFA2500 and all rooms have bathroom.

Hôtel le Karone (☎/fax 994 85 25, e karone@telecomplus.sn) Half board CFA22,500 per person. About 2km further south is this upmarket hotel in extensive gardens. There's a pool about 50m from the beach, and the thatched bungalows have air-con and hot showers. There's a vehicle for hire for trips to nearby bird reserves, and jet skis, bikes and kayaks can also be rented.

Places to Eat

At the south end of town, just north of the Black and White disco, is *Satang Jobang*, a school for women aged from 16 to 32. The women learn to cook and to make clothes and batiks. They also produce a wonderful marmalade and sell their wares in the boutique. Otherwise you can sample their cooking by ordering lunch before 9am – they're open to all sorts of suggestions, even that regional rarity 'vegetarian food'.

Near Le Fouta Djalon campement (and directly inland from a wrecked ship) is *Bateau Batik* (☎ 936 95 20, e bateaubatik@ hotmail.com), a café and batik workshop run by the friendly German-Senegalese team of Ingrid and Sobroco. You can come just for a coffee or soft drink, or you can look at the batiks on exhibition, maybe buy one, or learn to make your own. Lessons cost CFA3000 per hour for 4 to 6 hours and get good reports.

In Kafountine village there are a few cheap eateries in the market, most offering similar fresh local fare at cheap prices. These include the *Restaurant Mama Diarra* and the neighbouring *Rag-Tag Café*. Just north of the market on the opposite side of the road are *Le Cocotier Café Rest Buvette*, open 8am to midnight, and the *Couleur Café*

(☎ 936 95 20), open 8am to midnight, which is as much bar as restaurant. The *plat du jour* (usually an African dish) costs CFA500 to 1000. A few metres further north is the ***Restaurant/Bar Le Baobab***, open 7am to midnight, which is darker and popular with French expats. Meals are about CFA2000 and beers CFA500.

Almost all of the hotels and campements serve food, but most require a fair bit of warning. Among the better ones are *Kale Diang*, *La Bolonga* and *Chez Yandé*. Chez Yandé offers good food, including Indian and vegetarian specialities (such as chicken in ginger, and okra madras).

Getting There & Away

From Ziguinchor, bush taxis run directly to Kafountine (CFA2000 in a Peugeot taxi), or take any vehicle to Diouloulou, from where local bush taxis run to Kafountine for CFA500.

You can also get bush taxis from Serekunda or Brikama in Gambia, although direct traffic usually goes via the back roads and the sleepy Darsilami border rather than the main crossing at Séléti, so you won't get your passport stamped on the Senegal side (see the boxed text 'The Darsilami Border'). Brikama to Kafountine is CFA1200

The Darsilami Border

Bush taxis from Brikama to Kafountine often go via the remote Darsilami border. The taxi (usually a minibus or Alham) will stop at Darsilami so you can be stamped out of Gambia. However, the area on the Senegal side has long been controlled by antigovernment groups so while armed men may look at your passport, there won't be any stamp. If you arrive in Abéné or Kafountine without a stamp, don't panic. The usual procedure is to head up to Séléti the following day, chat with the border police, perhaps offer them a cigarette, and get the stamp. A simpler alternative is to get your hotel to do this for you. In Abéné, the guys from the Campement la Belle Danielle will do it for about CFA2000, no sweat.

(D30). Another option is to cross the border just south of Kartong.

Getting Around

All bush taxis stop in Kafountine village centre. If you continue walking southwards down the dirt road, you'll find a couple of local taxis shuttling up and down between here and the fishing beach.

Alternatively, bikes can be hired from a shop in the market, and from some of the campements. Rates are standardised at CFA2500 per day, but may be negotiable depending on the quality of the bike.

ABÉNÉ

Abéné is 6km north of Kafountine. There's a selection of places to stay, either in the village itself or a couple of kilometres away on the beach. It's much quieter than Kafountine, although harder to reach by local transport.

From the village it's 2km along a sandy track to the beach, past a small craft village near the junction where a track goes off to the upmarket Village-Hôtel Kalissai.

At the Campement la Belle Danielle in the village centre, bikes can be hired for CFA2000 per day, and car hire can be arranged at CFA35,000 per day with petrol and driver. Excursions *à la nature* to see monkeys in the bush, or by pirogue on the sea or in the creeks inland, can also be arranged, and you can buy souvenirs and postcards here.

If you want something a bit different, there's a place called **Oasis**, off the track leading to the beach from the village, which offers yoga, meditation and massage.

Places to Stay

Campement la Belle Danielle (☎ 936 95 42) Rooms/half board CFA2500/6000. Open Nov-June. This relaxed but well-organised place is in the heart of the village. Excursions are available and one of the friendly Konta brothers speaks good English. If you're coming from Kartong in Gambia, call ahead and the camp will send a Land Rover to collect you, and for a small fee will take your passport to Séléti to have it stamped.

The next three campements are all at the end of the road leading from the village to the beach. *Maison Sunjata* (☎/fax 994 86 10, e nfo@senegambia.de) Rooms/half board CFA7500/ 13,000 per person. Call ahead July to October. This small German-run place has clean, comfortable rooms. *Campement le Kossey* (☎ 994 86 09) Rooms CFA5000 per person. Along the beach is this more up-market Italian-run place, where you'll find comfortable bungalows. Half board is CFA10,000. *O'Dunbaye Land Ecole de Danse* (☎ 936 95 14) Rooms with half board CFA6000. Next door to Campement le Kossey, this relaxed place, known as Chez Thomas, offers high quality drum and dance lessons for CFA8500 per session.

Le Kalissai (☎ 994 86 00, fax 994 86 01, e kalissai@sentoo.sn) Singles/doubles CFA26,000/30,000. Take a right as you head towards the beach and 3km north is the vast, classy Le Kalissai, which has plush air-con bungalows in a pleasant shady palm grove.

Places to Eat
There are cheap eateries around the market, plus a couple of places along the road to the beach. Near the beach, and the campements, is *Restaurant Chez Vero* (☎ 936 95 14), which has decent meals for about CFA2000.

Getting There & Away
You can get to Abéné by any transport heading to Kafountine, although the village is 2km off the main road, and the beach is a further 2km, which you'll have to walk. All public transport to Kafountine stops at the turn-off to Abéné, near a village called Diannah. However, most drivers will take the slight detour to drop you at Abéné. The road to the Hôtel Kalissai is signposted about 3km before the road to the village.

Haute Casamance

SÉDHIOU
Some 100km east of Ziguinchor, on the northern bank of the Casamance River, Sédhiou is on your way to/from Tambacounda, or can form part of a loop through this little-visited part of Casamance. From Tanaf, on the road between Ziguinchor and Kolda, local bush taxis go to Sandinièr, from where a ferry crosses to Sédhiou. There are also bush taxis between Sédhiou and Bounkiling on the Trans-Gambia Hwy.

The *Hôtel la Palmeraie* (☎ 995 11 02, e philippe.bertrand@apicus.net) caters to hunters, and has comfortable air-con bungalows in a garden by the river for CFA12,500/ 20,000.

KOLDA
Kolda is a larger place with an easy atmosphere. Combine this with the cheapest beer in the country and all of a sudden it doesn't matter that Kolda is devoid of sights.

Life in Kolda centres on the three blocks opposite the post office in the centre of town, where you'll probably be dropped if you're coming from Ziguinchor. As you cross the bridge the first left is Rue Elhadji Demba Koita, where you'll find the drab *Hôtel Moya* (☎ 996 11 75), where doubles without/with air-con are overpriced at CFA10,800/ 13,800. Opposite here is the *Bamboo Bar*, open 8am to 4am, an earthy but popular drinking hole. A block back from the river is the *Hôtel Hobbe* (☎ 996 11 70, e diahobbe@sentoo.sn), with much better rooms (complete with TV and beds that would make an '80s porn star blush) without/with air-con for CFA11,000/16,250. There is also an Internet bureau.

There's good *street food* near the market, and a couple of blocks back from the post office is the *Darou Salam Restaurant*, open noon to 10.30pm. As one Peace Corps Volunteer put it, this place 'doesn't look much from the outside, but the food tastes good on the inside'. You can choose between two local dishes of the day at CFA350 each. South across the bridge and left is the stylishly decorated *Badaala* (☎ 996 10 12), open 8am to 4am, a little taste of Dakar where you can sit on the upstairs terrace and watch the stars come up before heading downstairs to party at just CFA400 a beer.

Bush taxis leave from a gare routière about 2km outside town on the road to Sedhiou. A Peugeot taxi will cost CFA2500 to Tambacounda, and CFA2850 to Ziguinchor.

Language

Colonial Languages

The sheer number of indigenous tongues spoken in Gambia and Senegal means that a common language is essential. Whereas Swahili developed in East Africa as a way for all the tribes to communicate, in West Africa the languages of the former colonial powers – French in Senegal and English in Gambia – have become each country's common language (or lingua franca).

We assume most readers of this book have a comfortable grasp of English, but some pointers for survival in French are provided here. Note that the French of France often differs from the French of Africa: for starters the French of Africa is pronounced with an accent which makes it easier to understand for English ears. Conversely the French you speak with an *accent terrible* is more likely to be understood in *les marchés de Dakar* than on *les boulevards de Paris*.

FRENCH

Though we have used the polite verb form 'vous' in the following phraselist, the informal form 'tu' is used much more commonly in West Africa; you'll hear *s'il te plaît* more than *s'il vous plaît*, which may be considered impolite in France unless spoken between good friends. If in doubt in Africa (when dealing with border officials or any older people) it's always safer to use the polite 'vous' form.

Useful Words & Phrases

The following words and phrases should help you communicate on a basic level in French. Masculine and feminine forms of words are indicated by m and f repsectively.

Pronouns

I	*je*
you (sg)	*tu/vous* (informal/polite)
he/she	*il/elle* (m/f)
we	*nous*
you (pl)	
they	*ils/elle*

Greetings & Civilities

Hello/Good day.	*Bonjour.*
Goodbye.	*Au revoir/Salut.*
Good evening.	*Bonsoir.*
(Have a) good evening.	*Bonne soirée.*
Good night.	*Bonne nuit.*
How are you?	*Comment allez-vous/Ça va?*
Fine, thanks.	*Bien, merci.*

Basics

Yes.	*Oui.*
No.	*Non.*
No, thank you.	*Non, merci.*
Please.	*S'il vous plaît.*
Thank you.	*Merci.*
You're welcome.	*De rien/Je vous en prie.*
Excuse me.	*Excusez-moi/Pardon.*

Small Talk

What's your name?	*Comment vous appelez-vous?*
My name is ...	*Je m'appelle ...*
How old are you?	*Quel âge avez-vous?*
I'm 25.	*J'ai vingt-cinq ans.*
Where are you from?	*D'où êtes-vous?*
I'm from ...	*Je viens ...*
Australia	*de l'Australie*
Canada	*du Canada*
Europe	*de l'Europe*
Japan	*du Japon*
USA	*des Etats Unis*

Language Difficulties

Do you speak English?	*Parlez-vous anglais?*
I understand.	*Je comprends.*
I don't understand.	*Je ne comprends pas.*

Getting Around

I want to go to ...	*Je veux aller à ...*
What is the fare to ...?	*Combien coûte le billet pour ...?*
When does the ... leave/arrive?	*À quelle heure part/arrive ...?*
bus	*l'autobus*
bus (intercity)	*le car*
train	*le train*
boat	*le bateau*
ferry	*le bac*
Where is (the) ...?	*Où est ...?*
airport	*l'aéroport*
bus station	*la gare routière*
bus stop	*l'arrêt d'autobus*
port	*le port*
ticket office	*la billeterie/ le guichet*
train station	*la gare*
Which bus goes to ...?	*Quel autobus/car part pour ...?*
Does this bus go to ...?	*Ce car-là va-t-il à ...?*
Please tell me when we arrive in ...	*Dîtes-moi quand on arrive à ... s'il vous plaît.*
Stop here, please.	*Arrêtez ici, s'il vous plaît.*
Please wait for me.	*Attendez-moi ici, s'il vous plaît.*
May I sit here?	*Puis-je m'asseoir ici?*
Where can I rent a ...?	*Où est-ce que je peux louer une ...?*
bicycle	*bicyclette*
car	*voiture*
address	*adresse*
daily	*chaque jour*
early	*tôt*
late	*tard*
number	*numéro*
on time	*à l'heure*
ticket	*billet*

Directions

How far is ...?	*À combien de kilomètres est ...?*
Which?	*Quel/Quelle? (m/f)*
Where?	*Où?*

left	*gauche*
right	*droite*
here	*ici*
there	*là*
next to	*à côté de*
opposite	*en face*
behind	*derrière*
north	*nord*
south	*sud*
east	*est*
west	*ouest*

Around Town

Where is the ...?	*Où est ...?*
bank	*la banque*
beach	*la plage*
embassy	*l'ambassade*
market	*le marché*
museum	*le musée*
pharmacy	*la pharmacie*
police station	*la police*
post office	*la poste*
I want to change ...	*Je voudrais changer ...*
money	*de l'argent*
travellers cheques	*des chèques de voyage*

Accommodation

Where is the hotel?	*Où est l'hôtel?*
May I see the room?	*Puis-je voir la chambre?*
How much is this room per night?	*Combien coûte cette chambre par nuit?*
Do you have any cheaper rooms?	*Avez-vous des chambres moins chères?*
That's too expensive.	*C'est trop cher.*
This is fine.	*Ça va bien.*
air-conditioning	*climatisation*
bed	*lit*
blanket	*couverture*
camp site	*camping*
full	*complet*
hot water	*eau chaude*
key	*clef or clé*
room	*chambre*
sheet	*drap*
shower	*douche*
toilet	*les toilettes*

washbasin	*lavabo*
youth hostel	*auberge de jeunesse*

Shopping

Where can I buy ...?	*Où est-ce que je peux acheter ...?*
Is/Are there ...?	*(Est-ce qu')il y a ...?*
How much is it?	*Ça coûte combien?*
That's too much.	*C'est trop.*
big/small	*grand/petit*
more/less	*plus/moins*
open/closed	*ouvert/fermé*

Time, Days & Numbers

What's the time?	*Quelle heure est-il?*
At what time?	*À quelle heure?*
When?	*Quand?*
now	*maintenant*
after	*après*
today	*aujourd'hui*
tomorrow	*demain*
yesterday	*hier*
morning	*matin*
afternoon	*après-midi*
evening	*soir*
day	*jour*
night	*nuit*
week	*semaine*
month	*mois*
year	*an*
Monday	*lundi*
Tuesday	*mardi*
Wednesday	*mercredi*
Thursday	*jeudi*
Friday	*vendredi*
Saturday	*samedi*
Sunday	*dimanche*
January	*janvier*
February	*février*
March	*mars*
April	*avril*
May	*mai*
June	*juin*
July	*juillet*
August	*août*
September	*septembre*
October	*octobre*
November	*novembre*
December	*décembre*

Emergencies – French

Help!	*Au secours!*
Call the police!	*Appelez la police!*
Call a doctor!	*Appelez un médecin!*
Thief!	*(Au) voleur!*
I've been robbed.	*On m'a volé.*
Leave me alone!	*Fichez-moi la paix!*
I'm lost.	*Je me suis égaré/ée.*

0	*zéro*
1	*un*
2	*deux*
3	*trois*
4	*quatre*
5	*cinq*
6	*six*
7	*sept*
8	*huit*
9	*neuf*
10	*dix*
11	*onze*
12	*douze*
13	*treize*
14	*quatorze*
15	*quinze*
16	*seize*
17	*dix-sept*
18	*dix-huit*
19	*dix-neuf*
20	*vingt*
21	*vingt-et-un*
22	*vingt-deux*
30	*trente*
40	*quarante*
50	*cinquante*
60	*soixante*
70	*soixante-dix*
80	*quatre-vingts*
90	*quatre-vingt-dix*
100	*cent*
101	*cent un*
1000	*mille*
one million	*un million*
first	*premier*
second	*deuxième*
third	*troisième*
fourth	*quatrième*
fifth	*cinquième*

African Languages

The diverse tribes and ethnic groups of Gambia and Senegal are spread across the national boundaries, and each has their own language or dialect. According to the Summer Institute of Linguistics 1996 Ethnologue there are up to 50 distinct languages spoken in the region, at least 15 of which have over 15,000 speakers. Some of the native tongues spoken as a first language by a significant proportion of people are listed here (although many people speak at least two indigenous languages). Note that the phrases reflect pronunciation and not correct spelling.

DIOLA

The Diola people inhabit the Casamance region of Senegal, and also south-western Gambia, where their name is spelt Jola. Their language is Diola or Jola, not to be confused with the Dioula or Dyola spoken in Burkina Faso and Côte d'Ivoire. Diola society is segmented and very flexible, so several dialects have developed which may not be mutually intelligible between groups even though the area inhabited by the Diola is relatively small.

Hello/Welcome.	kah-sou-mai-kep
Greetings. (reply)	kah-sou-mai-kep
Goodbye.	ou-kah-to-rrah

FULA (FULFULDE/PULAAR)

The Fula people are found across West Africa, from northern Senegal to as far east as Sudan and as far south as Ghana and Nigeria. The Fula are known as Peul in Senegal, and are also called Fulani and Fulbe. There are two main languages in the Fulani group:

- Fulfulde/Pulaar, spoken mainly in northern and southern Senegal, includes the Tukulor and Fulakunda dialects.
- Futa Fula, also known as Fuuta Jalon, one of the main indigenous languages of Guinea, also spoken in eastern Senegal.

These far-flung languages have many regional dialects and variations, and are not always mutually intelligible between different groups.

The following phrases in Pulaar should be understood through most parts of Senegal. Note that **ng** is pronounced as one sound (like the 'ng' in 'sing'); practise isolating this sound and using it at the beginning of a word. The letter **ñ** represents the 'ni' sound in 'onion'.

Hello.	no ngoolu daa (sg)
	no ngoolu dong (pl)
Goodbye.	ñalleen e jamm
	(lit. 'Have a good day.')
	mbaaleen e jamm
	('Have a good night.')
Please.	njaafodaa
Thank you.	a jaaraama (sg)
	on jaaraama (pl)
You're welcome.	enen ndendidum
Sorry/Pardon.	yaafo or
	achanam hakke
Yes.	eey
No.	alaa
How are you?	no mbaddaa?
I'm fine.	mbe de sellee
Can you help me please?	ada waawi wallude mi, njaafodaa?
Do you speak English/French?	ada faama engale/ faranse?
I speak only English.	ko engale tan kaala mi
I speak a little French.	mi nani faranse seeda
I understand.	mi faami
I don't understand.	mi faamaani
What's your name?	no mbiyeteedaa?
My name is ...	ko ... mbiyetee mi
Where are you from?	to njeyedaa?
I'm from ...	ko ... njeyaa mi
Where is ...?	hoto woni?
Is it far?	no woddi?
straight ahead	ko yeesu
left	nano bang-ge
right	nano ñaamo
How much is this?	dum no foti jarata?
That's too much.	e ne tiidi no feewu
Leave me alone!	accam! or
	oppam mi deeja!

1	*go-o*
2	*didi*
3	*tati*
4	*nayi*
5	*joyi*
6	*jeego*
7	*jeedidi*
8	*jeetati*
9	*jeenayi*
10	*sappo*
11	*sappoygoo*
12	*sappoydidi*
20	*noogaas*
30	*chappantati*
100	*temedere*
1000	*wujenere*

one million   *miliyong goo*

MALINKÉ

Malinké is spoken in Senegal's east. With speakers numbering over 250,000 it is recognised as one of the country's six national languages. While it is similar in some respects to Mandinka, the two are classed as separate languages.

Good morning.	*nee-soh-mah*
Good evening.	*nee-woo-lah*
How are you?	*tan-ahs-teh?*
Thank you.	*nee-kay*
Goodbye.	*m-bah-ra-wa*

MANDINKA

Mandinka, a national language of Senegal, is the language of the Mandinka people found largely in central and northern Gambia, and in parts of southern Senegal. The people and their language are also called Mandingo and they're closely related to other Manding-speaking groups such as the Bambara of Mali, where they originate.

Greetings

In common with many other predominantly Muslim groups, the Wolof and Mandinka use the traditional Arabic Islamic greetings: 'Greetings', *salaam aleikum* (lit. 'peace be with you'), 'Greetings to you too', *aleikum asalaam* (lit. 'and peace be with you').

In this guide, **ng** should be pronounced as the 'ng' in 'sing' and ñ represents the 'ni' sound in 'onion'.

Hello.	*i/al be ñaading* (sg/pl)
Good bye.	*fo tuma doo*
Please.	*dukare*
Thank you.	*i/al ning bara* (sg/pl)
You're welcome.	*mbee le dentaala/ wo teng fengti* (lit. 'It's nothing.')
Sorry/Pardon.	*hakko tuñe*
Yes.	*haa*
No.	*hani*
How are you?	*i/al be kayrato?* (sg/pl)
I'm fine.	*tana tenna* (lit. 'I am out of trouble') *kayra dorong* (lit. 'Peace only')
What's your name?	*i too dung?*
My name is ...	*ntoo mu ... leti*
Where are you from?	*i/al bota munto?* (sg/pl)
I'm from ...	*mbota ...*
Can you help me please?	*i/al seng maakoy noo, dukare?* (sg/pl)
Do you speak English/French?	*ye angkale/faranse kango moyle?*
I speak only English.	*nga angkale kango damma le moy*
I speak a little French.	*nga faranse kango domonding le moy*
I understand.	*ngaa kalamuta le/ngaa fahaam le*
I don't understand.	*mmaa kalamuta/ mmaa fahaam*
Where is ...?	*... be munto ?*
Is it far?	*faa jamfata?*
Go straight ahead.	*sila tiling jan kilingo*
left	*maraa*
right	*bulu baa*
How much is this?	*ñing mu jelu leti?*
That's too much.	*a daa koleyaata baake*
Leave me alone!	*mbula!*

1	*kiling*
2	*fula*
3	*saba*
4	*naani*
5	*luulu*
6	*wooro*

7	*woorowula*
8	*sey*
9	*kononto*
10	*tang*
11	*tang ning kiling*
12	*tang ning fula*
20	*muwaa*
30	*tang saba*
100	*keme*
1000	*wili kiling*

one million   *milyong kiling*

WOLOF

Wolof (spelt Ouolof in French) is the language of the Wolof people, who are found in Senegal, particularly in the central area north and east of Dakar, along the coast, and in the western regions of Gambia. The Wolof spoken in Gambia is slightly different to the Wolof spoken in Senegal; the Gambian Wolof people living on the north bank of the Gambia River speak the Senegalese variety. Wolof is used as a common language in many parts of Senegal and Gambia, often instead of either French or English, and some smaller groups complain about the increasing 'Wolofisation' of their culture.

In this guide, **ng** should be pronounced as the 'ng' in 'sing' and **ñ** represents the 'ni' sound in 'onion'.

Hello.	*na nga def* (sg)
	na ngeen def (pl)
Good morning.	*jaam nga fanane*
Good afternoon.	*jaam nga yendoo*
Goodnight.	*fanaanal jaam*
Goodbye.	*ba beneen*
Please.	*su la nexee*
Thank you.	*jai-rruh-jef*
You're welcome.	*agsil/agsileen ak*
	jaam (sg/pl)
Sorry/Pardon.	*baal ma*
Yes.	*wau*
No.	*deh-det*
How are you?	*jaam nga am?*
	(lit. 'Have you peace?')
I'm fine.	*jaam rek*
And you?	*yow nag?*
What's your	*naka-nga sant?*
(first) name?	
My name is ...	*maa ngi tudd ...*
Where do you live?	*fan nga dahk?*

Where are you from?	*fan nga joghe?* (sg)/
	fan ngeen joghe? (pl)
I'm from ...	*maa ngi joghe ...*
Do you speak English/French?	*deg nga angale/ faranse?*
I speak only English.	*angale rekk laa degg*
I speak a little French.	*degg naa tuuti faranse*
I don't speak Wolof/French.	*mahn deggumah wolof/ faranse*
I understand.	*degg naa*
I don't undestand.	*degguma*
I'd like ...	*dama bahggoon ..*
Where is ...?	*fahn la ...?*
Is it far?	*soreh na?*
straight ahead	*cha kanam*
left	*chammooñ*
right	*ndeyjoor*
Get in!	*dugghal waay!*
How much is this?	*lii ñaata?*
It's too much.	*seer na torob*
Leave me alone!	*may ma jaam!*

Monday	
Tuesday	
Wednesday	*allarba*
Thursday	*al*
Friday	
Saturday	
Sunday	

0	*tus*
1	*benn*
2	*ñaar*
3	*ñett*
4	*ñeent*
5	*juroom*
6	*juroom-benn*
7	*juroom- ñaar*
8	*juroom- ñett*
9	*juroom- ñeent*
10	*fuk*
11	*fuk-ak-benn*
12	*fuk-ak- ñaar*
20	*ñaar-fuk*
30	*fanweer*
100	*teemeer*
1000	*junneh*

Glossary

Items marked G or S are used only in Gambia or Senegal respectively.

afra – grilled meat, or grilled meat stall (G)

Alham – white Mercedes bus, also called N'Diaga N'Diaye in Dakar

auberge – in France it's a hostel, but in West Africa it's used (occasionally) to mean any small hotel

benechin – rice baked in a thick sauce of fish and vegetables (G)

beignet – simple deep-fried donut (S)

bisap – a purple drink made from water and hibiscus leaves

bolong – literally 'river' in Mandinka; when used in an English context it means creek or small river (G)

boubou – the common name for the elaborate robe-like outfit worn by men and women (also called grand boubou)

brochette – cubes of meat or fish grilled on a stick (S)

cadeau – gift, tip, bribe or a hand-out (S)

calesh – horse-drawn taxi usually seating about three people behind the driver

campement – could be loosely translated as 'hostel', 'inn' or 'lodge', or even 'motel'; it is not a camping ground (S)

car rapide – minibus, usually used in cities; often decrepit, may be fast or very slow (S)

carte – menu (S)

case – hut (S)

case à impluvium – large round traditional house, with roof constructed to collect rain water in central tank or bowl (S)

cases étages – two-storey mud houses (S)

case de passage – very basic place to sleep, often near bus stations; with a bed or mat on the floor and little else, and nearly always doubling as a brothel (also called *chambres de passage* or *maison de passage*) (S)

chacori – yogurt mixed with pounded millet and sugar

chawarma – snack of grilled lamb slices and salad in pita bread sandwich similar to a donor kebab

cheri – pounded millet

cheri bassi – black-eyed beans, millet and groundnuts pounded together

chop – meal, usually local-style (G)

chop-shop – basic local-style eating house or restaurant (G)

climatisée – air-conditioned (often shortened to clim)

commissariat – police station (S)

compteurs – meters (usually in taxis and *télécentres*) (S)

dash – bribe (noun); also used as a verb 'You dash me something ...' (G)

demi-pension – half board (dinner, bed and breakfast) (S)

deplacement – private hire (of a taxi) (S)

dibieterie – grilled-meat stall (S)

domodah – *groundnut* sauce with meat or vegetables mixed in

Ecowas – Economic Community of West African States

essence – petrol (gas) for car (S)

factory – fortified slaving station

fanals – large lanterns; also the processions during which the lanterns are carried through the streets

fête –festival (S)

fufu – mashed cassava (G)

garage – bus and bush-taxi station (G)

gare routière – bus and bush-taxi station, (also called autogare and gare voiture) (S)

gargotte – simple, basic, eating house or stall (S)

gasoil – diesel fuel

gendarmerie – police station/post (S)

gîte – in France, this means a small hotel or holiday cottage with self-catering facilities. In West Africa it is occasionally used interchangeably with *auberge* and *campement* (S)

griot – traditional musician or minstrel who also acts as historian for a village, clan or tribe
groundnuts – peanuts
grigri – a charm or amulet worn to ward off evil (pronounced gree-gree; also written grisgris or grisgri)

harmattan – the light winds from the north which carry tiny particles of sand from the desert, causing skies to become hazy from December to February
hôtel de ville – town hall (S)

IMF – International Monetary Fund
in sha' Allah – God willing, ie, hopefully (Arabic, but used by Muslims in Africa)

latcheri – pounded millet
lumo – weekly market, usually in border areas

mafé – thick brown *groundnut* sauce
mairie – town hall; mayor's office (S)
maison de passage see *case de passage*
marabout – Muslim holy man
marigot – creek (S)
MFDC – Mouvement des Forces Démocratique de la Casamance
menu de jour – fixed-price meal
mobylette – moped

ndeup – ceremonies where people with a mental illness are treated and healed (S)

occasion – lift (noun), or place in a car or bus (often shortened to occas) (S)

palava – meeting place
paletuviers – mangroves (S)
pagne – a length of colourful cloth worn around the waist as a skirt (S)
paillote – thatched sun shelter (usually on beach or around open-air bar/restaurant) (S)
patron – owner, boss (S)
pension – simple hotel or hostel, or 'board' (S)
pension complète – full board (lunch dinner bed and breakfast) (S)
pension simple – bed and breakfast (S)
pétrole – kerosene (S)
Peugeot taxi – usually a Peugeot 504 or 505, with seven seats (also called a *sept-place* in Senegal)

pirogue – traditional wooden canoe, either a small dugout or large narrow sea-going fishing boat
plasas – meat cooked with vegetable leaves in palm oil (G)
préfecture – police headquarters (S)
pression – draught beer (S)

Quran – Islamic holy book (also called Koran)
quatre-quatre – four-wheel-drive car (4WD or 4x4)

Ramsar – an international convention primarily concerned with the conservation of wetland habitats and associated wildlife
riz yollof – vegetables and/or meat cooked in a sauce of oil and tomatoes

salon du thé – tea shop (S)
Senegambia – the region of Senegal and Gambia
Sentram – Senegal's maritime transport organisation (S)
sept-place see *Peugeot taxi*
serviette – towel (in bathroom) (S)
serviette de table – table napkin, serviette (S)
serviette hygiénique – sanitary pad, feminine pad or feminine towel (see *tampon hygiénique*) (S)
snack – a place where you can get light meals and sandwiches. It's not the food itself (S)
Sonatel – Senegal's phone company (S)
syndicate d'initiative – tourist office (S)

tampon – stamp (eg, in passport) (S)
tampon hygiénique – tampon (also tampon periodique and *serviette hygiénique*) (S)
taxi-brousse – bush taxi (S)
taxi-course – shared taxi (in cities) (S)
telecentre (G) or **télécentre** (S) – privately owned telephone bureau
tiéboudienne – Senegal's national dish, rice baked in a thick sauce of fish and vegetables (S)
toubab – white person

ventilé – room with a fan (S)
yassa poulet – grilled chicken marinated in an onion-and-lemon sauce (S)

LONELY PLANET

You already know that Lonely Planet produces more than this one guidebook, but you might not be aware of the other products we have on this region. Here is a selection of titles that you may want to check out as well:

Africa on a shoestring
ISBN 01 86442 663 1
US$29.99 • UK£17.99

Healthy Travel Africa
ISBN 1 86450 050 6
US$5.95 • UK£3.99

French phrasebook
ISBN 0 86442 450 7
US$5.95 • UK£3.99

Read This First Africa
ISBN 1 86450 066 2
US$14.99 • UK£8.99

Travel Photography
ISBN 1 86450 207 X
US$12.95 • UK£7.99

West Africa
ISBN 1 74059 249 2
US$29.99 • UK£18.99

Available wherever books are sold

Lonely Planet Guides by Region

onely Planet is known worldwide for publishing practical, reliable and no-nonsense travel information in our guides and on our Web site. The Lonely Planet list covers just about every accessible part of the world. Currently there are 16 series: Travel guides, Shoestring guides, Condensed guides, Phrasebooks, Read This First, Healthy Travel, Walking guides, Cycling guides, Watching Wildlife guides, Pisces Diving & Snorkeling guides, City Maps, Road Atlases, Out to Eat, World Food, Journeys travel literature and Pictorials.

AFRICA Africa on a shoestring • Botswana • Cairo • Cairo City Map • Cape Town • Cape Town City Map • East Africa • Egypt • Egyptian Arabic phrasebook • Ethiopia, Eritrea & Djibouti • Ethiopian Amharic phrasebook • The Gambia & Senegal • Healthy Travel Africa • Kenya • Malawi • Morocco • Moroccan Arabic phrasebook • Mozambique • Namibia • Read This First: Africa • South Africa, Lesotho & Swaziland • Southern Africa • Southern Africa Road Atlas • Swahili phrasebook • Tanzania, Zanzibar & Pemba • Trekking in East Africa • Tunisia • Watching Wildlife East Africa • Watching Wildlife Southern Africa • West Africa • World Food Morocco • Zambia • Zimbabwe, Botswana & Namibia
Travel Literature: Mali Blues: Traveling to an African Beat • The Rainbird: A Central African Journey • Songs to an African Sunset: A Zimbabwean Story

AUSTRALIA & THE PACIFIC Aboriginal Australia & the Torres Strait Islands •Auckland • Australia • Australian phrasebook • Australia Road Atlas • Cycling Australia • Cycling New Zealand • Fiji • Fijian phrasebook • Healthy Travel Australia, NZ & the Pacific • Islands of Australia's Great Barrier Reef • Melbourne • Melbourne City Map • Micronesia • New Caledonia • New South Wales • New Zealand • Northern Territory • Outback Australia • Out to Eat – Melbourne • Out to Eat – Sydney • Papua New Guinea • Pidgin phrasebook • Queensland • Rarotonga & the Cook Islands • Samoa • Solomon Islands • South Australia • South Pacific • South Pacific phrasebook • Sydney • Sydney City Map • Sydney Condensed • Tahiti & French Polynesia • Tasmania • Tonga • Tramping in New Zealand • Vanuatu • Victoria • Walking in Australia • Watching Wildlife Australia • Western Australia
Travel Literature: Islands in the Clouds: Travels in the Highlands of New Guinea • Kiwi Tracks: A New Zealand Journey • Sean & David's Long Drive

CENTRAL AMERICA & THE CARIBBEAN Bahamas, Turks & Caicos • Baja California • Belize, Guatemala & Yucatán • Bermuda • Central America on a shoestring • Costa Rica • Costa Rica Spanish phrasebook • Cuba • Cycling Cuba • Dominican Republic & Haiti • Eastern Caribbean • Guatemala • Havana • Healthy Travel Central & South America • Jamaica • Mexico • Mexico City • Panama • Puerto Rico • Read This First: Central & South America • Virgin Islands • World Food Caribbean • World Food Mexico • Yucatán
Travel Literature: Green Dreams: Travels in Central America

EUROPE Amsterdam • Amsterdam City Map • Amsterdam Condensed • Andalucía • Athens • Austria • Baltic States phrasebook • Barcelona • Barcelona City Map • Belgium & Luxembourg • Berlin • Berlin City Map • Britain • British phrasebook • Brussels • Brussels, Bruges & Antwerp • Brussels City Map • Budapest • Budapest City Map • Canary Islands • Catalunya & the Costa Brava • Central Europe • Central Europe phrasebook • Copenhagen • Corfu & the Ionians • Corsica • Crete • Crete Condensed • Croatia • Cycling Britain • Cycling France • Cyprus • Czech & Slovak Republics • Czech phrasebook • Denmark • Dublin • Dublin City Map • Dublin Condensed • Eastern Europe • Eastern Europe phrasebook • Edinburgh • Edinburgh City Map • England • Estonia, Latvia & Lithuania • Europe on a shoestring • Europe phrasebook • Finland • Florence • Florence City Map • France • Frankfurt City Map • Frankfurt Condensed • French phrasebook • Georgia, Armenia & Azerbaijan • Germany • German phrasebook • Greece • Greek Islands • Greek phrasebook • Hungary • Iceland, Greenland & the Faroe Islands • Ireland • Italian phrasebook • Italy • Kraków • Lisbon • The Loire • London • London City Map • London Condensed • Madrid • Madrid City Map • Malta • Mediterranean Europe • Milan, Turin & Genoa • Moscow • Munich • Netherlands • Normandy • Norway • Out to Eat – London • Out to Eat – Paris • Paris • Paris City Map • Paris Condensed • Poland • Polish phrasebook • Portugal • Portuguese phrasebook • Prague • Prague City Map • Provence & the Côte d'Azur • Read This First: Europe • Rhodes & the Dodecanese • Romania & Moldova • Rome • Rome City Map • Rome Condensed • Russia, Ukraine & Belarus • Russian phrasebook • Scandinavia & Baltic Europe • Scandinavian phrasebook • Scotland • Sicily • Slovenia • South-West France • Spain • Spanish phrasebook • Stockholm • St Petersburg • St Petersburg City Map • Sweden • Switzerland • Tuscany • Ukrainian phrasebook • Venice • Vienna • Wales • Walking in Britain • Walking in France • Walking in Ireland • Walking in Italy • Walking in Scotland • Walking in Spain • Walking in Switzerland • Western Europe • World Food France • World Food Greece • World Food Ireland • World Food Italy • World Food Spain **Travel Literature:** After Yugoslavia • Love and War in the Apennines • The Olive Grove: Travels in Greece • On the Shores of the Mediterranean • Round Ireland in Low Gear • A Small Place in Italy

Lonely Planet Mail Order

Lonely Planet products are distributed worldwide. They are also available by mail order from Lonely Planet, so if you have difficulty finding a title please write to us. North and South American residents should write to 150 Linden St, Oakland, CA 94607, USA; European and African residents should write to 10a Spring Place, London NW5 3BH, UK; and residents of other countries to Locked Bag 1, Footscray, Victoria 3011, Australia.

INDIAN SUBCONTINENT & THE INDIAN OCEAN Bangladesh • Bengali phrasebook • Bhutan • Delhi • Goa • Healthy Travel Asia & India • Hindi & Urdu phrasebook • India • India & Bangladesh City Map • Indian Himalaya • Karakoram Highway • Kathmandu City Map • Kerala • Madagascar • Maldives • Mauritius, Réunion & Seychelles • Mumbai (Bombay) • Nepal • Nepali phrasebook • North India • Pakistan • Rajasthan • Read This First: Asia & India • South India • Sri Lanka • Sri Lanka phrasebook • Tibet • Tibetan phrasebook • Trekking in the Indian Himalaya • Trekking in the Karakoram & Hindukush • Trekking in the Nepal Himalaya • World Food India **Travel Literature:** The Age of Kali: Indian Travels and Encounters • Hello Goodnight: A Life of Goa • In Rajasthan • Maverick in Madagascar • A Season in Heaven: True Tales from the Road to Kathmandu • Shopping for Buddhas • A Short Walk in the Hindu Kush • Slowly Down the Ganges

MIDDLE EAST & CENTRAL ASIA Bahrain, Kuwait & Qatar • Central Asia • Central Asia phrasebook • Dubai • Farsi (Persian) phrasebook • Hebrew phrasebook • Iran • Israel & the Palestinian Territories • Istanbul • Istanbul City Map • Istanbul to Cairo • Istanbul to Kathmandu • Jerusalem • Jerusalem City Map • Jordan • Lebanon • Middle East • Oman & the United Arab Emirates • Syria • Turkey • Turkish phrasebook • World Food Turkey • Yemen **Travel Literature:** Black on Black: Iran Revisited • Breaking Ranks: Turbulent Travels in the Promised Land • The Gates of Damascus • Kingdom of the Film Stars: Journey into Jordan

NORTH AMERICA Alaska • Boston • Boston City Map • Boston Condensed • British Columbia • California & Nevada • California Condensed • Canada • Chicago • Chicago City Map • Chicago Condensed • Florida • Georgia & the Carolinas • Great Lakes • Hawaii • Hiking in Alaska • Hiking in the USA • Honolulu & Oahu City Map • Las Vegas • Los Angeles • Los Angeles City Map • Louisiana & the Deep South • Miami • Miami City Map • Montreal • New England • New Orleans • New Orleans City Map • New York City • New York City City Map • New York City Condensed • New York, New Jersey & Pennsylvania • Oahu • Out to Eat – San Francisco • Pacific Northwest • Rocky Mountains • San Diego & Tijuana • San Francisco • San Francisco City Map • Seattle • Seattle City Map • Southwest • Texas • Toronto • USA • USA phrasebook • Vancouver • Vancouver City Map • Virginia & the Capital Region • Washington, DC • Washington, DC City Map • World Food New Orleans **Travel Literature**: Caught Inside: A Surfer's Year on the California Coast • Drive Thru America

NORTH-EAST ASIA Beijing • Beijing City Map • Cantonese phrasebook • China • Hiking in Japan • Hong Kong & Macau • Hong Kong City Map • Hong Kong Condensed • Japan • Japanese phrasebook • Korea • Korean phrasebook • Kyoto • Mandarin phrasebook • Mongolia • Mongolian phrasebook • Seoul • Shanghai • South-West China • Taiwan • Tokyo • Tokyo Condensed • World Food Hong Kong • World Food Japan **Travel Literature:** In Xanadu: A Quest • Lost Japan

SOUTH AMERICA Argentina, Uruguay & Paraguay • Bolivia • Brazil • Brazilian phrasebook • Buenos Aires • Buenos Aires City Map • Chile & Easter Island • Colombia • Ecuador & the Galapagos Islands • Healthy Travel Central & South America • Latin American Spanish phrasebook • Peru • Quechua phrasebook • Read This First: Central & South America • Rio de Janeiro • Rio de Janeiro City Map • Santiago de Chile • South America on a shoestring • Trekking in the Patagonian Andes • Venezuela **Travel Literature**: Full Circle: A South American Journey

SOUTH-EAST ASIA Bali & Lombok • Bangkok • Bangkok City Map • Burmese phrasebook • Cambodia • Cycling Vietnam, Laos & Cambodia • East Timor phrasebook • Hanoi • Healthy Travel Asia & India • Hill Tribes phrasebook • Ho Chi Minh City (Saigon) • Indonesia • Indonesian phrasebook • Indonesia's Eastern Islands • Java • Lao phrasebook • Laos • Malay phrasebook • Malaysia, Singapore & Brunei • Myanmar (Burma) • Philippines • Pilipino (Tagalog) phrasebook • Read This First: Asia & India • Singapore • Singapore City Map • South-East Asia on a shoestring • South-East Asia phrasebook • Thailand • Thailand's Islands & Beaches • Thailand, Vietnam, Laos & Cambodia Road Atlas • Thai phrasebook • Vietnam • Vietnamese phrasebook • World Food Indonesia • World Food Thailand • World Food Vietnam

ALSO AVAILABLE: Antarctica • The Arctic • The Blue Man: Tales of Travel, Love and Coffee • Brief Encounters: Stories of Love, Sex & Travel • Buddhist Stupas in Asia: The Shape of Perfection • Chasing Rickshaws • The Last Grain Race • Lonely Planet ... On the Edge: Adventurous Escapades from Around the World • Lonely Planet Unpacked • Lonely Planet Unpacked Again • Not the Only Planet: Science Fiction Travel Stories • Ports of Call: A Journey by Sea • Sacred India • Travel Photography: A Guide to Taking Better Pictures • Travel with Children • Tuvalu: Portrait of an Island Nation

Index

Abbreviations

G – The Gambia   S – Senegal

Text

Bold indicates maps.

Boxed Text

MAP LEGEND

CITY ROUTES

Freeway	Freeway
Highway	Primary Road
Road	Secondary Road
Street	Street
Lane	Lane
	Unsealed Road
	One-Way Street
	Pedestrian Street
	Tunnel
	Footbridge

REGIONAL ROUTES

	Tollway, Freeway
	Primary Road
	Secondary Road
	Minor Road

BOUNDARIES

	International
	State
	Disputed
	Fortified Wall

HYDROGRAPHY

	River; Creek
	Canal
	Lake
	Dry Lake; Salt Lake
	Spring; Rapids
	Waterfalls

TRANSPORT ROUTES & STATIONS

	Train
	Tramway
	Cable Car, Chairlift
	Ferry
	Walking Trail
	Walking Tour
	Path
	Pier or Jetty

AREA FEATURES

	Building
	Park; Gardens
	Market
	Sports Ground
	Beach
	Cemetery
	Campus
	Plaza

POPULATION SYMBOLS

✪ CAPITAL	National Capital	● CITY	City
◉ CAPITAL	State Capital	● Town	Town
		• Village	Village
			Urban Area

MAP SYMBOLS

▪	Place to Stay	▼	Place to Eat
		●	Point of Interest

✈ ✕	Airfield; Airport	✝	Church	🏛	Museum
⊖	Bank	⊞	Cinema		National Park
⌇	Bird Sanctuary		Embassy/Consulate	⊙	Petrol Station
✪	Border Crossing	♀	Golf Course	✚	Police Station
🚌	Bus Stop/Station	✚	Hospital/Pharmacy	✉	Post Office
⛺	Camping Area		Internet Café		Pub or Bar
🚐	Caravan Park	※ ※	Lookout		Ruins
⌂	Cave	⚑	Monument		Shopping Centre
					Stately Home
					Swimming Pool
					Taxi Rank
					Telephone
					Tourist Information
					Transport
					Winery
					Wildlife Reserve/Zoo

Note: not all symbols displayed above appear in this book

LONELY PLANET OFFICES

Australia
Locked Bag 1, Footscray, Victoria 3011
☎ 03 8379 8000 fax 03 8379 8111
email: talk2us@lonelyplanet.com.au

UK
10a Spring Place, London NW5 3BH
☎ 020 7428 4800 fax 020 7428 4828
email: go@lonelyplanet.co.uk

USA
150 Linden St, Oakland, CA 94607
☎ 510 893 8555 TOLL FREE: 800 275 8555
fax 510 893 8572
email: info@lonelyplanet.com

France
1 rue du Dahomey, 75011 Paris
☎ 01 55 25 33 00 fax 01 55 25 33 01
email: bip@lonelyplanet.fr
www.lonelyplanet.fr

World Wide Web: www.lonelyplanet.com *or* AOL keyword: lp
Lonely Planet Images: lpi@lonelyplanet.com.au